From Liberal to Labour with Women's Suffrage

Frontispiece
Catherine E. Marshall, c. 1910–14 (F. Marshall papers)

From Liberal to Labour with Women's Suffrage

The Story of Catherine Marshall

JO VELLACOTT

McGill-Queen's University Press
Montreal & Kingston • London • Buffalo

© McGill-Queen's University Press 1993
ISBN 0-7735-0958-5

Legal deposit second quarter 1993
Bibliothèque nationale du Québec

∞

Printed in the United States on acid-free paper

This book has been published with the help of a grant from the Social Science Federation of Canada, using funds provided by the Social Sciences and Humanities Research Council of Canada.

Canadian Cataloguing in Publication Data

Vellacott, Jo
    From Liberal to Labour with women's suffrage
    the story of Catherine Marshall
    Includes bibliographical references and index.
    ISBN 0-7735-0958-5
    1. Marshall, Catherine, 1880–1961. 2. Suffragettes – Great Britain –
Biography. 3. Women – Suffrage – Great Britain – History. II. Title.

HQ1455.M37V45 1993   324.6'23'092   C92-090719-9

This book was typeset by Typo Litho composition inc.
in 10/12 Baskerville.

For the next but one generation, with love: to Sarah, Dylan, Vanessa, Daniel, and Kurt

Contents

Preface

Reputable historians perhaps do not fantasize, and I have been scrupulous in building my picture of Catherine Marshall and my account of the events in which she played a part on solid evidence, documentary and occasionally oral. But I have a persistent fantasy, capable of documentation to only a limited extent, but so germane to the story that I offer it here by way of introduction.

In 1956, over forty years after the date at which the part of Catherine's story told here concludes, she returned for the last time to Hawse End, the house in which so much of her early and middle life had been spent. That much is known; she left, as usual, a paper trail, although in this case only a small one, a mere handful of letters she had received while she was in the Lake District. She does not seem to have stayed at Hawse End itself, but at Swinside, a neighbouring guest house. She and her brother, Hal, had decided to sell the house, perhaps had already sold it, and she came north to see it once more, and to clear out the last of her belongings.

Saying goodbye to Hawse End and its surroundings of lakes and mountains was hard. But they would endure for others. Something else had to be done, and she had a decision to make. Walking heavily and with a stick, as she always did now, she went up to the house, knowing what she would find. Back in the days before and during the first of the two wars she had lived through, she had known she and her friends were making history.[1] At first she had kept the paperwork because she might need it again, and because it was always difficult for her to throw papers away. As the years passed, she was less and less often at Hawse End. During the months she spent there in 1939–40, when she made it a home for refugees from Nazi-occupied Czechoslovakia, she was too busy to do much sorting, so the piles grew, rather than diminishing.

Reason to keep them grew too. A number of books by militant suffragettes had come out before the war, and even a few by Catherine's nonmilitant colleagues in the National Union of Women's Suffrage Societies (NUWSS). The statesmen she had influenced had written memoirs, as well. There was only one of all of them that she had been able to read without pain and anger, though she no longer shared such thoughts with others. The suffragettes claimed all the credit for women's achievement of the vote. The politicians, at best, barely mentioned women's suffrage, and never described their own gradual conversion, in which her energetic, gracious, and persistent work had played a part; if there was any mention, it was of militancy, which they had agreed at the time was overplayed, and which was now – with their help – totally eclipsing the history of the nonmilitants. Millicent Fawcett, long-time president of the NUWSS, and Ray Strachey, who had succeeded Catherine as parliamentary secretary, were the historians of the NUWSS. They told the nonmilitant side of the story, and on the whole more accurately; but their accounts may have been the hardest of all for Catherine to read. In their retrospect they had reordered the priorities of those days, and, consciously or unconsciously, the bitterness of wartime disagreements had led simply to the virtual omission of almost the whole group of dynamic young leaders who had taken the NUWSS to the position it enjoyed in 1914. And Mary Stocks, in her biography of Eleanor Rathbone, had ascribed all the "Parliamentary goodwill" built up before 1919 to the young Ray Strachey, with no mention of Catherine. Only her friend Helena Swanwick, in her autobiography, *I Have Been Young*, told a story that Catherine recognized, and it was necessarily incomplete.[2]

Catherine was not one to live in the past; she never even talked to her two young nephews about the challenging days of the women's suffrage campaign. But she had a keen sense of history, and of the stuff of which it is made. She may have known that even the NUWSS's own archives, in the Fawcett collection, had somehow been culled, and that her surely copious correspondence with the London office had disappeared. The minutes of meetings still existed, and a run of the *Common Cause* (the NUWSS weekly journal), so the skeleton was available, but to put flesh on the bones there might well be no collection comparable to her own. Surely, she thought, as she looked at the mass of files and loose papers, someone would want to tell the true story soon, and to get it right. She had never attempted it herself, and would not do so now; perhaps she knew the tale could not be told without a great deal of credit accruing to herself, and seeming to boast was a sort of schoolboy anathema that she may have carried with her since her childhood in (but not of) Harrow School. Besides, she was still busy, living in the present.

So she stood leaning on her stick, looking at the papers, picking one up here and there, feeling a momentary excitement as some event came vividly back to her, putting it down again. Should she try to interest some library in making room for them? But no; the papers were not quite old enough, she was no longer well known, and above all, there was no academic interest in women's history, and archival imagination might find it hard to make the leap needed to suppose there ever would be.[3] Should she just have them pulled outside, and set fire to them, sending up in smoke long chapters of her eventful life? But it was not just a part of her own life that would go up in smoke; it was a part of the history of women. The gaining of the vote *had* been important, even if some expected results had not followed yet, and even if interest was at a low ebb in the mid-1950s. More, Catherine had always thought means as significant as ends, and her papers held a very different story of the methods used to gain the vote from any that had been published so far. Perhaps there was nothing further she could do to ensure the preservation of the evidence, but she would not be the direct agent of its destruction. She had arranged for the help of a strong young man from a local farm to come and help her; now she asked him to pile all the files and loose papers into hampers, and to lug them out to an old shed in the grounds, where they would not be in any one's way. Having seen that done, she left.

If there was anything further that Catherine hoped to do, it was never done. The papers stayed in the hampers, the hampers stayed in the shed. As the shed became more and more decrepit, the rain came in in a few places; the only visitors were sheep, birds which flew in and out (not without leaving traces of their passing), and a few curious and ignorant people who tore off a few stamps or ripped out an autograph.

Hawse End was now the property of the county education authorities, who used and still use it as a centre for outdoor adventure training, a use which I am sure delighted Catherine, who had had her own adventure training there. In 1962, the shed was becoming a dangerous nuisance, so they decided to pull it down. Fortunately, like Catherine six years before, they decided against a bonfire, and instead invited the newly appointed county archivist, Bruce Jones, to come and see what he could make of the mess they had found.[4] He knew, and could find out, nothing of Catherine Marshall, who had in fact died in London the previous year, but he recognized that he was looking at something of great value. He piled the papers into at least forty large boxes, consigned only the empty hampers to the flames, and took the collection back to the Record Office in Carlisle.

In 1969, I went to England for the summer, courtesy of a grant from the Canada Council, to do research on Bertrand Russell's activities during the First World War. I harboured a secret dream that I might be the first person to find the archives of the No-Conscription Fellowship; but, if these exist, they are still hidden. However, someone – perhaps Edward Milligan, then librarian at Friends House, Euston Road – mentioned that there was a collection of Catherine Marshall's papers, of unknown size and condition, in the Cumberland Record Office. I knew her by name by this time, as someone who had worked with Russell in the NCF, so I went there to see what there was. Manuscript by Bertrand Russell leaped to my eye in almost every box I opened (and may have helped to clinch Bruce Jones's decision to keep the papers), but the RO had no staff or money to have the collection sorted, and the papers were unusable as they were. I hung around for a few days and finally asked whether Bruce Jones would allow me to sort them. He agreed, and I spent the rest of that summer, and later all the time and help for several years that I could squeeze out of another Canada Council grant, and other fellowships tenable in Britain, in doing the preliminary sorting into chronological order. Since then, they have been re-sorted according to modern archival principles, and have been used by a number of scholars.

As I worked, I found I had indeed the greatest single source for the NCF. At least as exciting to me was what was being revealed about the other activities of the unknown Catherine Marshall. I soon knew I had to write her biography; fortunately, I did not know how long it would be before I could be free enough to complete even this first instalment.

The project was first conceived as a biography of a remarkable woman who had been omitted from history. One important theme clearly would be the nonmilitant women's suffrage movement, about which little indeed had been written when I first came on Catherine Marshall's papers. As my research deepened and widened, myths went down like ninepins, and I saw more of the real significance and effectiveness of the movement. It became apparent that Catherine Marshall's work was essential to an understanding of feminist history of the period, and also that it could not be understood or fully valued outside the context of "mainstream" British political history of the early twentieth century. Finally, I reached the further conclusion that the obverse was also true; here was material which could illuminate British political history, and bring new understanding to the controversial prewar era.

Meanwhile, there has been an immense amount of research and writing on the period leading up to the First World War. The best books to come out on the women's suffrage movement are Sandra Holton's analytical *Feminism and Democracy*, which makes good use of the Marshall collection, and Leslie Parker Hume's *The National Union of Women's Suffrage Societies*, a much-needed straightforward history of the organization. I have found both of these valuable in providing the framework for Catherine's work. Among mainstream historians of Britain, the political history of the early twentieth century has been the subject of intense study and controversy, with a particular focus on electoral politics and the relations of Liberalism and Labour, and my indebtedness to writers in this field also will become apparent. But the two streams, feminist history and traditional political history, have tended increasingly to compartmentalize, to the extent that at times to read the work of "malestream" and feminist historians together is to be left with a bewildering sense of looking down two separate tunnels, with little or nothing in the way of connecting passages.[5] Both fields are impoverished by the bifurcation.

Catherine Marshall's experience in the women's suffrage campaign helps to break down the artificial separation. A study of her work is not only a vital part of women's history, but locates the policies and activity of the nonmilitant organization squarely where they belong, in the political history of the time, and has light to shed on the ongoing historical exploration of Liberalism and Labour.

The book ends, suddenly, as so many things did, at 4 August 1914. The twelve months that began in August 1913 were a strange period for anyone interested in politics to live through, with tension building around the Irish Home Rule controversy against a kaleidoscope of preparations (lacking consistent direction in every one of the three parties) for the general election that must come in late 1914 or in 1915 at the latest. For the historian, it is perhaps an even stranger period, since it was not the general election that came, but war. We are left with a handful of broken threads, causes whose effects never came to pass, questions which would have been answered on the hustings and at the polls, but can be answered now only by speculation. This is one, though not the most important, of the reasons why the striking work done by Catherine Marshall and her associates has been allowed to pass into oblivion, and the whole women's suffrage story trivialized and distorted. To recapture that work is to open the door to a better understanding of the struggle, not only from the crucial point of view of the women who were suffragists, but as it affected male politicians of all parties. However much men might wish it otherwise, the role accorded to women in the long term, and the resolution of the franchise issue in the immediate future, were problems or opportunities that would not go away, and with which the ideologies and practices of Liberal, Conservative, and Labour alike had to deal. The war, of course, clouded the view; indeed, it facilitated the manufacture of a convenient facesaving smokescreen behind which women could be given the vote with many of the real questions left unresolved. But our task now is to put ourselves back into the climate of prewar Britain, as if we knew no more than Catherine of the jolt that would change the world's direction in August 1914.

St. Leonard's School, St. Andrews

Acknowledgments

Many people have given of their time and expertise to help during the long gestation of this work. Above all, my thanks go to Margaret Kamester, who has been tirelessly generous in putting at my service her research and editing skills, advice, sheer hard work, and sense of humour; and to Richard Rempel, who has constantly given me the benefit of his knowledge of the period, and who has read and reread the manuscript at several stages.

My warm appreciation also goes to my son Doug Newberry, who guided my reluctant feet (and hands) gently and generously into the paths of appropriate technology; to Mary Newberry, who was there at the beginning, and came back again at the end; to Soo Newberry, who helped sort the papers, shared her studio, and was a source of support and joy in so many ways; to John Isaac, who also helped with the sorting; to Susan Shea, whose exceptional research skills saved many hours of my time; and to Eleanor Segel, who turned up just in time to act as midwife to the book; to Isobel Bliss; Stella Gaon; Laurel Hood; Victorya Monkman; and Janet Wiegand; and to Margaret Atack, who assisted with the index.

It is a particular pleasure to express my appreciation to Frank and George Marshall, the nephews of Catherine Marshall, and the absolute model of what a biographer could hope for in the family of her subject – interested, helpful, and open about research material, but never seeming anxious about what would be written; I hope that they will enjoy the aunt I give them here, who, I gather, differs from the one they knew. Other members of the Marshall family were also helpful and hospitable, particularly Tom and Nadine Marshall, who invited me to their house to talk with them and to meet Horace and Rachel Marshall. Brian Harrison generously gave me a copy of his notes on an interview he had with T.H. Marshall, and a part transcription. Special thanks are also due to the following, who provided me with information, agreed to be interviewed, or helped with research in various ways: the late Lord Brockway; Aylwin Clark; James Duffield; Tom Faber; Queenie Fulker; Agnes Fyfe; Tom Graves; Mark Greenstock; Isobel McCallum Clark; Lord Rochdale; Catriona Stewart.

Others who have shared ideas, information, and enthusiasms include Naomi Black; Blanche Wiesen Cook; Sheila Fletcher; Sandra Holton; Tom Kennedy; F.M. Leventhal; Jill Liddington; David Mitchell; Sybil Oldfield; W.G. Rimmer; Barbara Roberts; David Rubinstein; my colleagues and students at the Simone de Beauvoir Institute, Concordia University; my colleagues on the advisory committee of the women's studies program at St Lawrence College, Kingston. Much-needed encouragement and practical help have come from Beverley Darville; Irene England; Arpi Hamalian; Evelyn Reid; Anne Rempel; Mair Verthuy; Gus Sinclair.

I have been sustained at various times by funding or facilities provided by the following, and am deeply grateful: the Canada Council; the Social Sciences and Humanities Research Council of Canada; the Institute for Advanced Studies in the Humanities of Edinburgh University; the Calouste Gulbenkian Foundation, from which I held a Fellowship at Lucy Cavendish College, Cambridge; and that exceptional college itself; Woodbrooke Friends Study Centre; Queen's University; Concordia University with particular thanks to Wendy Knatchell of Inter-Library Loan Services; the Scottish National Library.

I acknowledge with pleasure the use of the following collections, where the staff or private owners have been helpful in every way: the Cumbria Record Office, with thanks to Bruce Jones and David Bowcock; the NUWSS papers, autograph letter collection, and periodical collection in the Fawcett Library at the City of London Polytechnic, with the special thanks that all researchers in this area owe to the work and encouragement of David Doughan; the Bertrand Russell Archives, with special thanks, as ever, to Ken Blackwell; the Barbara Strachey Papers, seen by the great courtesy of Barbara Halpern Strachey; the Manchester Public Libraries; the Labour Party Archives; the Swarthmore College Peace Collection; the British Library of Political and Economic Science; Girton College Archives; Lloyd George Papers (by correspondence); St Leonards School Archives (by correspondence); the Suffrage Collection at the Museum of London; private papers in the possession of Frank Marshall; the Schwimmer Lloyd Collection, Rare Books and Manuscripts Division, New York Public Library, from which I obtained material through the help of Edith Wynner, who also kindly did the research and translation.

I am grateful to the following people and institutions who have kindly given permission to reproduce material originally published or owned by them. Every effort has been made to trace the copyright holders of material quoted; I much regret if any have been missed: Frank and George Marshall and the Cumbria Record Office for all quotations by Catherine Marshall and from her papers; Helen Blackstone for quotations from Maude Royden's letters to Catherine Marshall; Dr B.L. Rathbone for material by Eleanor Rathbone; Barbara Halpern Strachey for quotations from Ray Costelloe Strachey.

Finally, I appreciate the friendly and skilled help and support I have had from my editor, Judy Williams, and the staff of McGill-Queen's University Press, especially Joan McGilvray and Philip Cercone.

Newlands House, Harrow School (Drawing by E.M. Greenstock)

Abbreviations

BRA	Bertrand Russell Archives
CC	*Common Cause*
CEM	Catherine E. Marshall
CEMP	Catherine E. Marshall Papers
CM	Caroline Marshall
CRO	Cumbria Record Office
CUWFA	Conservative and Unionist Women's Franchise Association
DNB	*Dictionary of National Biography*
EFF	Election Fighting Fund for Women's Suffrage
ELFS	East London Federation of Suffragettes
FEM	Frank E. Marshall
FMP	Frank Marshall Papers
HEGB	Hawse End Guest Book
HGM	Henry George Marshall (Hal)
HMS	Helena M. Swanwick
HNB	Henry Noel Brailsford
IAV	International Archive for Women, Amsterdam
ILP	Independent Labour Party
IWSA	International Women's Suffrage Alliance
KDC	Kathleen D. Courtney
KWSA	Keswick Women's Suffrage Association
LG	David Lloyd George
LL	*Labour Leader*
LRC	Labour Representation Committee
LSWS	London Society for Women's Suffrage

LWSU	Liberal Women's Suffrage Union
MFGB	Miners' Federation of Great Britain
MG	*Manchester Guardian*
MGF	Millicent Garrett Fawcett
MLWS	Men's League for Women's Suffrage
MPL	Manchester Public Library
NAC	National Administrative Council (of the ILP)
NAWSA	National American Woman Suffrage Association
NEC	National Executive Committee (of the Labour party)
NLOWS	National League for Opposing Women's Suffrage
NU, NUWSS	National Union of Women's Suffrage Societies
NWF	North-West Federation
P/date	found with envelope postmarked with this date
PLP	Parliamentary Labour Party
PSF	People's Suffrage Federation
SCPC	Swarthmore College Peace Collection
SLC	Schwimmer-Lloyd Collection (New York Public Library)
TPL/WS	Toronto Public Library Women's Suffrage files
TU	Trade Union
TUC	Trade Union Congress
WCG	Women's Cooperative Guild
W's F	*Women's Franchise*
WFL	Women's Freedom League
WILPF	Women's International League for Peace and Freedom
WLA	Women's Liberal Association
WLF	Women's Liberal Federation
WLL	Women's Labour League
WNASL	Women's National Anti-Suffrage League
WS	Women's Suffrage
WSPU	Women's Social and Political Union
WSS	Women's Suffrage Society

Catherine and Hal Marshall, c. 1884 (F. Marshall papers)

Left: Caroline Marshall, retirement portrait, 1904 (F. Marshall papers)

Below: Catherine, Caroline, Frank, and Hal Marshall, c. 1893 (F. Marshall papers)

Our International Guests Outside the House of Lords.

Reading from left to right are : Mr. Goldstone, M.P., Mr. Henderson, M.P., Miss Crookenden, Mr. L. Richardson, M.P., Mr. L. E. Harvey, M.P., Miss Bergman, Mr. J. Parker, M.P., Frau Lindermann, Frau Schwimmer, Mrs. Chapman Catt, Mr. F. D. Acland, M.P., Miss Furuhjelm, Mrs. McCormick, Mme. Brigode, Mr. Dickinson, M.P., Miss Courtney, Mr. Ramsay MacDonald, M.P., Miss Marshall, Lord R. Cecil, Mr. Walter Rea, Miss Sheepshanks, Miss P. Strachey.

IWSA and British politicians outside Parliament, July 1914, *Common Cause*, 1 August 1914; the photo is by the London News Agency and also appeared in *Jus Suffragii*. (International Archief Vrouwenbeweging, Amsterdam)

[MISS STRACHEY, MISS MARSHALL, MRS. RACKHAM, MRS. HARLEY, MRS. FAWCETT, MISS COURTNEY, MRS. AUERBACH, MISS ROBERTSON.]

Above: NUWSS deputation to Asquith, August 1913 (Catherine E. Marshall Collection, Cumbria Record Office)

Above right: Postcard produced by the Artists' Suffrage League. Women in New Zealand had gained the vote in 1893.

Right: The Keswick municipal women's suffrage banner, c. 1912, found with Catherine Marshall's papers and now held in the Cumbria Record Office.

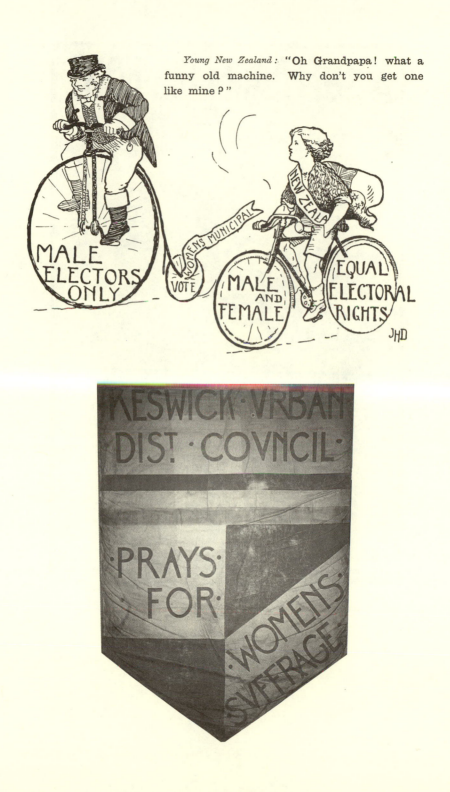

Young New Zealand: "Oh Grandpapa! what a funny old machine. Why don't you get one like mine?"

"A Suffragette's Home," postcard produced by the NLOWS, c. 1909

From Liberal to Labour with Women's Suffrage

1 Late Victorian Liberal Youth, 1880–1907

On 28 April 1880, Caroline Marshall, experiencing the onset of labour, went upstairs to give birth to her first child, Catherine. "That most wonderful moment," she wrote many years later to her daughter, "that few speak of ... with enough wonder. Was it to be death or new life that awaited one? A total change in any case. You certainly did that – life has never been the same since! What would the new life be? I thank God a good one, that I love and am thankful to have had a hand in however faulty an one."[1]

Catherine was not an easy child. She was eager and boisterous, she dominated her younger brother, Hal, she was an original, she was somehow larger than life, and yet her health was poor. She never fitted well into the mould of a Victorian young lady, and she was fortunate that her parents, an enlightened and progressive couple, tried to obtain procrustean conformity in only a few matters.

In 1869, shortly after graduating from Trinity College, Cambridge, Frank Marshall, Catherine's father, then aged twenty-two, had been appointed to a mastership in mathematics at Harrow.[2] In August 1876,[3] when he was twenty-nine, Frank married Caroline Colbeck, the sister of a colleague. Caroline was twenty-three years old, and taught at a small school for girls (and young boys) together with another sister, Margaret, three years her senior, and a sister-in-law, Florence Colbeck. Despite some ill health, Caroline went on teaching after marriage, but apparently resigned as soon as she found herself pregnant with Catherine in August 1879.[4] Several months after Catherine's birth, a relative still wrote anxiously of

Caroline's health: "you do not seem to be any better than you ought."[5] The second and last child, Hal, was born in June 1883. Whether Caroline ever went back to work in "the little school" is uncertain; her interest in teaching certainly continued and her involvement with educational classes for girls and small boys is mentioned in the *Women's Who's Who* of 1913.[6] Her life must have become enormously more fully occupied in 1889, when Frank "built and opened" the first purpose-built Harrow School house, calling it "Newlands"[7] after the much-loved valley in the Lake District to which the Marshalls would later retire.

From the age of nine, then, Catherine's childhood was spent in the privileged masculine atmosphere of a British public school house over which her father presided as housemaster and where her mother exercised domestic dominion. Both parents cared warmly for their charges, although scraps of evidence suggest that Caroline was less enamoured of and less well suited to her role, which came not by choice but as a consequence of marriage. Frank's career was to him assuredly a chosen vocation, and it was one in which he won affection as well as respect. When he first went to Harrow, he may have been admired for his traditional male achievements; a pupil later listed some of these, recalling him as a "Scholar of Trinity, Cambridge, a high Wrangler, winner of the Colquhoun Sculls, a notable cragsman and skater in his own Lake country, and a bold climber in the Alps."[8]

But Frank Marshall lacked conceit and was remembered in the long run for more enduring qualities. A former pupil, A.C. Pigou, recalled his first impression: "Friendliness, I think, and openness and sympathy – anything but the clouded terrors of authority. You knew that he really cared about what you did and thought, and about the House and your place in it. Later on that first impression widened and deepened. ... He had a very definite idea of what he wanted his house to be – not a forcing ground for scholars or for athletes, but a place of comradeship and growth." Pigou described Frank Marshall's gift of genuine interest in all around him, his devotion to the concept of as much self-governance as possible among the boys of the house, his ability to take good-humoured mockery. Even more strikingly, Pigou wrote, "When real disaster came to us we saw him more nearly. A boy died in the holidays: he spoke to us of that as though he had lost a son. A boy died in term by drowning. He could not trust himself to read prayers to the House that evening – as head of the House I had ... to read them. ... He saw clearly and felt deeply and did not hide his heart."[9]

Catherine was inevitably greatly affected by this environment. Directly, she developed what the boys were supposed to imbibe: intellectual interests, honesty, a love of sports, a commitment to fair play, an ambition to succeed, even a stiff upper lip. In all these she was encouraged by her parents, yet at the same time she was confronted by an ambivalence: except for her mother, her role models at home were men and boys, and the attributes she was developing were not highly regarded as feminine characteristics by the world at large; nor was it possible that her destiny could be the same as that of a Harrow boy.

Not all Catherine's time was spent in her home. From early childhood she and her brother were sent on extended visits to relatives or to the seaside – sometimes because of illness at home, or so that her parents could enjoy a holiday together. Even before her fourth birthday, Catherine's parents printed their letters to her in block capitals, which suggests that she was beginning to read. One letter written to her at the seaside admonishes her a little anxiously to take great care of Hal, to teach him to talk, to be a good little sister to him, to read him the letter, and to give him twice three kisses and then two more. For herself she is praised for her bravery in sea bathing – evidently it had not come easily – and urged to learn to swim by the time she is five.[10] Kindness to Hal was frequently urged on Catherine at this time; he was not only younger but probably by nature gentler than she, and may have suffered under her imperiousness. Despite a lack of parental sexism remarkable for the period, both children, too, are likely to have had to put up with comparisons from other relatives and acquaintances which neither found it easy to fulfil. While Catherine was certainly not "ladylike," Hal may well have been seen as not "manly" enough.

The busyness of Frank and Caroline did not prevent an affectionate closeness, and it was not unknown for Caroline and Catherine to take a holiday alone together. When Catherine was nine years old, she and her mother went to Margate, although Caroline does not seem to have had high expectations of this popular southern resort. She wrote to Frank: "C[atherine] is perfectly happy except that she is longing to bathe. We went to the sands this morning and for a charming drive this afternoon. The air is certainly beautiful and the cornfields clover poppies and wide sky lent a charm to the country I had not remembered that it could *possess*. But on the people! I never did see such. We come home by boat on Monday if you please. C[atherine] is wild with delight at the thought. Mine is tempered because I have done it before."[11]

Catherine's formal education began at the small private school run by her aunts, where Caroline Marshall had taught. The school seems to have been a happy place, giving an intelligent, academically sound education to the children of professional people, many of them themselves educationalists; the moral tone was high but the atmosphere not repressive. Catherine was also provided with a German governess and with instruction in music. In early adulthood, she recalled an aspect of her own mental development, ascribing the unusual exercise she outlined to a time when she had been often alone. One of her "favourite amusements" as a child, she claimed, had been what she had named a "thought-fight":

I would take some seeming paradox, and, having ranged the conflicting facts in opposite camps, I would "think" first on one side, then on the other, and try to achieve some definite result. Sometimes one side would rout the other, sometimes they would come to terms, sometimes both would have to retreat baffled and exhausted, leaving the issue undecided; it was in fact a kind of mental game of chess in which the same player moves all the pieces black and white alike. ... [I would] try to get at the underlying truth which I felt even then would reconcile and explain the apparently conflicting facts ... my very ignorance was in one way an advantage, affording as it did an outlook unclouded by prejudice, a[n] independence of attitude unfettered by conventionalities.

Catherine claimed that this had been her way of dealing with "the perplexing problems of life" which present themselves, as she said, "to the crude imagination of childhood."[12] It was certainly a remarkable way of training her mind for future political exercise.

Music was important to both Marshalls and Colbecks. Harrow School had been blessed from 1864 to 1885 with the presence of the colourful John Farmer,[13] a music teacher and composer of unconventional background and an immense capacity for inspiring enthusiasm, who preached and practised the doctrine "that music is a great instrument for the education and salvation of all mankind, and that the way to its enjoyment must be kept open for the simple and lowly and not be monopolized by the privileged few, whether the privilege be one of wealth or of special gifts."[14] Letters of the Marshalls refer frequently to concerts and to music participation of various kinds, and with this encouragement, it is not surprising that by the time Catherine was thirteen years old she was earning enthusiastic comments from her piano teacher. But there is one ominous note. "Don't play when you have a headache," he writes, and whether coincidentally or not, this is the last entry in her practice register.[15]

When the children were in their teens, the Marshall family went regularly for the long school holidays to their house near Keswick, in Cumberland. Frank Marshall's family had been flax-spinners in

Leeds who had prospered substantially in the nineteenth century, and had bought property in the Lake District.[16] John Marshall had been something of a trend-setter with his purchase of Derwent Island in 1832, even before the railway made the area more accessible. On the island is a fine eighteenth-century house, where Frank, after his birth in London in 1847, spent much of his youth; but the property of course passed through the elder line, and was now in the possession of Frank's nephew, John. Frank had built a solid stone house, Hawse End, in beautiful wooded lands on the edge of Derwentwater, facing the island and looking beyond it to the height of Skiddaw. There could hardly have been a more lovely place for children to grow up in. Catherine was not compelled to behave like a decorous young lady, and, though Queen Victoria still reigned, she rejoiced in a tomboyish vigorous outdoor life, scrambling over the hills, playing tennis, going for long walks, canoeing, swimming and diving in the lake. A cousin, Tom Marshall, remembered her rushing whooping along the springboard below the house, folding her long legs up to grasp them in a "honeypot" and plunging into the cold lake with a resounding splash. The visiting cousins "had to follow," indeed she organized their activities "very powerfully." While Tom enjoyed this, he remembered her as "a very managing type ... no doubt about that." His elder brother Howard, closer to Catherine's age and more reserved than Tom, "didn't like her very outgoing manner and her noisiness." Eighty years later Howard Marshall's main recollection was of her "bossiness," under which he had obviously smarted. Tom said frankly that Howard had "detested" Catherine, and despite his own more friendly memories, he dismissed any notion of her having influenced him intellectually.[17]

That there were tensions is clear. The source and the symptoms are not easily distinguished from each other, but by the age of thirteen, Catherine was subject to severe headaches, was notoriously accident-prone, and chewed her fingernails. Understanding and advanced as her parents were, much blame for all these misfortunes, and even for what was considered to be her excessive height, was laid on Catherine herself. A gloomy aunt undertook to help her fight her besetting sin, so Catherine dutifully (and I am sure with meticulous truthfulness) sent progress reports listing the number of times she had bitten her nails, striving always towards a new deadline for giving up the despised habit. Aunt Rosa replied:

Your last list gives two yes's in 8 days. This ought to be encouraging, inasmuch as it would seem that the habit is less constantly indulged in. But on asking Mother how the nails were looking she tells me that they are no better in appearance, at all. How can this be, I wonder. I am afraid that when you do worry them, you damage them so much that it is one step forward and two back! keeping them far off recovery. Is it so? I am so very sorry about it. But I will try to keep hope uppermost, darling – if you will try on, and on, better. Now holidays are coming – I wonder if this will be better or worse! Midsummer is past, Christmas is past, how about Easter?[18]

The accidents were more jocularly regarded. Even before her thirteenth birthday, Catherine (temporarily nicknamed "Banana" for some unknown reason) could get a letter asking: "How are you and how many accidents have you had since I last saw your face? I'm pretty certain that they are uncountable."[19] She accepted the characterization, and banged, scraped, twisted, broke, and bruised her limbs throughout her teens, and indeed during most of her life. Was she just clumsy and overdaring? It seems more probable that in youth at least the accidents and the nail-biting were both, at least in part, the product of stress.

In the phrase of the time, she was probably thought to be outgrowing her strength. Poor Catherine can hardly have failed to be self-conscious on the subject of her height; when she was sixteen her brother wrote to his parents that a foreign school-friend of his who had met her "always remembers Catherine as a 'Very tall thing', and … looks up and points to the ceiling." The letter was forwarded to Catherine, now away at school. The teasing of a brother is one thing, though not necessarily painless, but from her parents too the first response to the news that she had measles was to hope that she had not grown ("They sometimes do with measles").[20] Catherine must have felt almost as guilty as she did over the nail-biting.

Too much should not be made of Catherine's childhood and adolescent traumas, which were so much less than those of many girls of her time or indeed of any time; but then people, and especially women, have suffered a great deal from excessive guilt feelings and from a low self-esteem, and these human limitations originate in such juvenile experiences, even in an enlightened and loving home. As an adult, despite apparent self-confidence, Catherine sometimes cringed inwardly in self-accusation, while finding it hard – like many overcriticized people – to accept even just and well-meant censure. But if this pattern was set in early life, so too were traits of humour, outspokenness, and the ability to live life to the full. Tom Marshall remembered her, above all, as "good fun," recalling "that familiar rippling giggle" which lit up her whole face and was to remain with her all her life. He spoke also of her "zest for … life", her "spirit of adventure" and her initiative.[21]

In 1896 Catherine went to boarding school. At sixteen, she was a couple of years older than the usual age. Perhaps the delay was caused by unspecified anxiety about her health, evidence on which is confusing. Certainly there were already the headaches, and Catherine herself later referred, in an undated essay (which may even have been fictional) to having been much alone as a child and having been "for a considerable time ... debarred on grounds of health from reading."[22] Yet when she caught measles, her mother's letters speak of such illness as a new experience for her.

Catherine was sent to St Leonards School, at St Andrews in Scotland, a top-ranking, progressive girls' boarding school. She arrived for her first term with an extremely heavy cold and a bad cough, and "deeply scored ... on the brow" by some kind of pin worn by a cousin she had affectionately embraced when saying goodbye. Shortly afterwards she injured her foot and developed measles. No wonder she dreamt of home every night during her first weeks away. It was probably this series of misfortunes which prompted one of her friends to write that she thought Catherine "must have a very original character" and to ask when she meant "to finish her excentricities [sic]."[23]

The warmth and closeness of the Marshall family emerge clearly from letters to Catherine at St Leonards. Aunt Florence Colbeck wrote about how she would be missed in the Harrow school, and sent her a fruit knife "as you are such a vegetarian"; her brother wrote with obvious admiration from his preparatory school and sent her word puzzles; a number of cousins kept in touch. Her father and mother wrote regularly, although term time was busy for them too, and although they sometimes had to admonish her to write, even if it were only a postcard. Her father painted a pathetic word picture of the effect of her casualness about writing: "Two pitiful parents sit like two young sparrows on the gravel waiting for the dutiful daughter to put a fly in their mouth ... and she does not do it!" On another occasion Frank sent a telegram when no letter came, explaining, in a following letter, "that Mother, and I in a less degree, get anxious when we don't hear from you. And it matters very much that Mother should not worry herself over anything just now."[24] Frank showed considerable concern over Caroline's health during these years.

Catherine's parents were not afraid to show affection. In response to her homesickness, Caroline wrote, "If you dream of home every night, do you never see me in St. Andrews? I fancy that some part of me comes pretty often."[25] She told Catherine, too, of her old governess's ability to know without being told of her ex-charge's illness, and her letters were always full of small items of news, ranging from the activities of Harrow "Old Boys" to accounts of intrepid cycling trips taken by both parents – who ventured out on a tandem bicycle as early as 1885. A particularly delightful letter speaks of a "grease slide" made by some convalescent boys on the top landing: "I had a lovely turn on it without being caught by 'Franky' [Frank Marshall's nickname], but watched with much amusement by one of the boys."[26] Caroline sent Catherine flowers from Hawse End and forwarded things forgotten or specially requested, with a touch of weary humour: "I am sending off your requisitions, may their shadow be less – and hope you will get them all tomorrow."[27]

Both parents offered occasional political comments, siding, for example, with the Greeks in the Balkan troubles, but hostile to the miners' cause in the 1897 strike, where, Frank said, "the real issue is whether unions may forbid the masters use of the best machinery the showers question was rather an after-thought [sic]."[28]

From her father Catherine received careful and lucid answers to every question she asked about her studies, and much gently offered advice, rarely condescending or belittling. He relished contact with her expanding intelligence, and enjoyed explaining an astronomical or mathematical theory to her, or discussing music he had heard and the book he was reading; at other times he would exchange limericks, spoonerisms, or other schoolboy jokes with her. His first letter after she went to St Leonards was long and serious, full of advice he had been prevented from giving her because "I never got the chance to say 'good bye'"; the letter is worth quoting at some length:

Mother has written me delightful accounts of the place, and of Miss Grant. ... I do think it must be a nice place, and that you have plenty of older friends [friends and relatives who taught at St Leonards or lived nearby] – if you find, as I expect, some very nice girls you will be uncommonly happy.

I don't believe that you will ever get better lessons than Aunt Florence's go where you will. But she has taught you what real thorough thoughtful work is, and you can always practice it for any teacher. When you have got used to the new ways and the new drill wh. is needed in large classes you will soon get along with your new teachers. Do not be discouraged to find that you know less than your neighbours in mathematics. You have I expect *thought* more about it than most of them and you will find the knowledge come very quickly when you give more time to it. I know that you will do very well in them in the end.

I feel sure too that you will choose nice friends, and behave nicely to the Blunts, Burnetts or Butlers when you go to see them.

I hope you will really get into punctual ways quickly, for if not you will get into trouble.

There are just two things, my dear child, that I want particularly to say, though you know how much we both feel about them.

Be very careful not to make excuses, even though you have really something to say. You are not quite ready enough to own to yourself that you have made a mistake or been wrong. One ought to judge oneself *more* severely than anyone else can. Kind and sensible people will always make allowances for one. Not one excuse in a thousand really holds water. One must get over one's difficulties not make excuses of them.

The other thing is, – now that you are making such a new start it is a good time to cure little habits, – especially that tiresome one with the nails. One makes one's will and resolution strong for big things by practising them on little.

You know how pleased we shall be when you win finally and fully in those little struggles. Tell me if I can help you.

This is a very serious letter, but the next shall be a merrier one.

I miss you very much. ...[29]

Her parents' love and expectations, and her own failures, surely lay heavy on Catherine at times.

Founded in 1877 on the initiative of the Ladies' Educational Association, and with the financial backing of substantial professional men, St Leonards was a school which had been developed with courage and farsightedness to excel, rather than simply to provide for girls an imitation of the education available to boys at the British public schools. Nevertheless, it owed much to the public school tradition, and to the felt need to prove that young women could handle and enjoy the same education as young men of the upper class.[30] In common with most of the new girls' schools, St Leonards placed a great emphasis on competitiveness; Catherine entered into it all with great fervour, and even five years after she left school was still following interhouse competition in sports with avidity.

Catherine's teachers were women, most of whom had pioneered in female academic work, now visibly achieving and respected for their achievements; the school was well run by women for women, the first school of any standing in Scotland to be headed by a woman. Julia Grant, who succeeded Miss Dove as headmistress in 1896, was a powerful formative influence on Catherine, who could have echoed words Grant had used in describing the school as she saw it as a pupil: "We had so much that it was new for girls to have. We had freedom, we had trust, we had stimulating teachers, healthy physical exercise; we had sympathy, understanding, encouragement, the excitement of competition with keen kindred spirits, the interest of being pioneers in a small way; we had Miss Lumsden and we had Miss Dove."[31] In Catherine's account, Miss Grant's own name would have taken the place of her forebears of twenty years previous. And in 1898, complaining of a lack of top-quality candidates for the prestigious headmastership of Harrow, Frank Marshall wrote to Catherine that it was a pity Miss Grant was debarred by her sex from applying.[32] Although it is unlikely that Julia Grant would have accepted such an honour – her mission was not to young men, but to their sisters – it was high praise and offered sincerely.

Catherine continued to work at her music, probably beginning serious singing lessons at this time, though her father expressed anxiety lest her young voice or her "weak hands" be overworked. In sports, mainly cricket in summer and field hockey and lacrosse in winter, Catherine revelled and would probably have done well had she not continued to be plagued by her unfortunate propensity for injuring herself. ("You unlucky person, why go and hit your own self when there are plenty of others to do it?" asked her mother, and begged her not to be "too ferocious at cricket.")[33] As was appropriate in St Andrews, Catherine also took up golf, but the more exhilarating sports undoubtedly pleased her more.

Debating was a new interest. Formal debating was an exercise encouraged in forward-looking women's educational establishments (including women's university colleges), presumably as a conscious step towards overcoming generations of indoctrination against women holding and publicly expressing opinions. Catherine was elected chair of the school debating society; Frank Marshall, as ever taking her activities with great seriousness, wrote to advise her to "insist on a degree of ceremony that seems almost comic. It really keeps debate from degenerating into chatter. ... When you pull someone up for breaking rules do it a bit pompously."[34] School journalism also attracted Catherine; she edited a house paper, but narrowly missed being made chief editor of the school magazine. A minimum of rules and a large measure of student self-government were matters of policy at St Leonards, and Catherine became a monitor in her second year; "Up goes your hair of course!"[35] wrote her mother. Later she became acting head of both the house and the school, still finding time to take part in a performance of Gilbert and Sullivan's *HMS Pinafore*.

During Catherine's second year at school, at about the same time as her parents had to break to her the news of the death of her aunt Florence, to whom she owed her early education and much encouragement, love, and wise thinking, Catherine was faced with making a decision about whether to be confirmed in the Church of England. As for many young people, and perhaps particularly when she was made vulnerable by her grief, it was a time of searching for Catherine. But the handful of letters relating to it – which have only come to light when this book was nearly complete – are also important for another reason. In all the paper Catherine left behind her, religion is seldom mentioned, yet the more I knew of her, the less likely it seemed that she lacked interest and religious convictions. Later in life, she found some spiritual nurture in an unorthodox group, practising a form of sacred dancing, and she and her mother shared an interest in theosophy. The early exchange of letters shows something of her own seeking, and also of the caring climate in the Marshalls' home.

Over confirmation, not surprisingly, Catherine had difficulty making up her mind, feeling that she needed to know more, and having specific difficulties with some of her own notions which she feared were unacceptable. She turned to her parents for help, writing to Caroline, "Of course there is a great deal of good in the English Church, but yet there are some things I feel as if I should never believe. ... but then it is hard to tell where Christianity ends and the Church begins. ... I do feel [the preparation] would do me a great deal of good, but I do not want to do anything insincerely." She felt her knowledge was very inadequate, and said she would be happy to do whatever her parents thought best. She outlined what seemed to her "the chief obstacles," which included her inability to believe in a personal God, and consequently in the forgiveness of sin and eternal punishment. The biggest stumbling block, however, was her firm belief in reincarnation, a belief shared by her mother, though not by her father. Her long letter ended wistfully, "I wish I could talk to you instead of writing."[36]

Caroline replied promptly and practically, making it plain that Catherine should feel free to begin the preparation, and to withdraw later if she thought right; or, if she would rather, to wait another year, doing some studying meanwhile. And she explained that while, indeed, there were clergy who would find Catherine's views inappropriate, there were others who would not. Caroline affirmed her own belief in a "Higher Being," but not in quite the usually accepted sense. She elaborated usefully on something Catherine had said about God not being a separate being: "I believe the personal God of most people *is* their Higher Self." Caroline added, "I am conscious that I am not the best person to advise you on Church matters for I have never concealed from you that I am an outsider. At the same time I should be greatly distressed at being a stumbling block and have no sort of feeling against it, if you find you desire to become a full member. But I cannot choose for you, I can only earnestly desire that you may choose the best for your spiritual progress and usefulness to others."[37]

Caroline's position as "an outsider" may well have been why Catherine addressed her plea for guidance to her first rather than to Frank, who was a member of the Church, and who, as housemaster, took part regularly in the preparation of boys for confirmation. But he too responded with understanding to her letter, making it clear that he claimed no knowledge of dogma, and that he saw few certainties, holding that, "In religion as much as in any other subject it is most necessary that the opinions you hold should be your very own, – that matters more to my mind than exactly what they are." He said that "people who think they have 'a definite creed' ... are as a rule people who have not thought much, or will not let themselves think. And that I trust will never be your position." He addressed Catherine's stumbling blocks one by one; for him they were "partly a matter of wording, and not really fundamental, though they may still matter enough to keep you from joining the church. ... I shall be content with whatever you do."[38]

Catherine had not found anyone at school who could really help her. "Mr Owen" (presumably the minister charged with preparation for confirmation) "would only be shocked," and the usually helpful Miss Grant, reflecting the big religious controversy of the period, had said that if Catherine's views "were at all Unitarian, she did not think I ought to be confirmed." Catherine thought they probably were, in that "I never think of Christ as a supernatural or miraculous manifestation of God, any more than any one of us in whom God dwells is a miraculous manifestation of Him." Catherine decided to wait until she had had the opportunity to talk the whole thing out with her parents, and Frank wrote reaffirming that he thought her decision had been a good one, and was comfortable with what he had learned of her seeking.[39]

When Catherine first wrote home about confirmation, she had expressed a willingness to be guided in her decision by her parents; by the end of the exchange she had made up her own mind, even if only to give herself more time to talk with them. Even her first letter had shown how important it was to Catherine to think things through, and Caroline's and Frank's responses had struck the right note to help her with this, never belittling her concern, discussing, in a nonprescriptive way, everything that was troubling her, and affirming her right and her competence to think independently of her parents as well as of the school and church authorities.

Academically, Catherine's grounding at her Harrow school and at home stood her in good stead. She had lapses from grace: shortly after she went to St Leonards, her father wrote, with more asperity than he usually showed: "Mother has just read me your letter with the account of the French mistress and the examination. So you are at your old game of doing examinations without preparation."[40] But he had seldom occasion to reprove her for "such wickedness" and Catherine enjoyed most of her school work. She had an aptitude for languages; and she came top of her class in Euclidean geometry, finding the riders of the third book "scrumptious."[41] Although Frank Marshall preened himself at one time on being "the proud father of a future scholar,"[42] far more concern was expressed lest his daughter should work too hard than that she should not work hard enough. After Catherine's recovery from measles her mother wrote, "It is just as well to begin lessons quietly after all this long absence: your brain might be addled,"[43] but the joking reference covered a growing fear that the girl's health would not stand up to the strain of prolonged study. A year later Catherine's load had to be lightened; Caroline wrote: "I am so glad that you have been let off some work. Miss G[rant] did it before my letter arrived, which speaks v. well for her! ... So please darling, take things as quietly as you can. The rest on and off your back will be a great help I am sure."[44]

Miss Grant had assured Caroline that Catherine was "safe for the certificate without push or worry." The "certificate" Catherine was studying for at this time was in music, and her mother wrote a month later: "I am glad you trilled well in your examination and hope it will soften the heart of the examiner. ... Try and take things calmly. It is wear and tear of good material to be very nervous and does no one and nothing anything but harm. I hope you will do well in sports and not do yourself some deadly injury!"[45]

Since no specific illness seems to have been diagnosed, it might be possible that all these anxieties reflect the gloomy prognostications of some contemporaries regarding the unfitness of the female brain for sustained intellectual endeavour, were it not so out of character with the advanced ideas of Caroline and Frank Marshall, and with the whole tone of the school they had chosen for their daughter. I am inclined to accept rather that Catherine did indeed exhibit worrying symptoms of overstrain – including her proneness to injury, headaches, possibly some back trouble, occasionally earache and deafness (exacerbated, characteristically, by being hit on the head by a cricket ball).[46] There was also some recognition of what was to be a long-enduring trait, that she did not herself know when to slow down and would push herself beyond the bounds of common sense in any cause which interested her. In any event, while lecturing poor Hal (who was already painfully apt to compare himself unfavourably with his sister and with a brilliant Colbeck cousin, his contemporary at Marlborough) on his "laziness,"[47] the Marshalls repeatedly urged Catherine not to work too hard, to drop some of her studies, to "keep calm I beg," to "take care of yourself and come home whole," to "take things quietly." As we have seen, Julia Grant concurred. The question of Catherine's proceeding to university never seems to have been seriously mooted, though several of her friends went on to Oxford or Cambridge. But meanwhile she continued to throw herself into her work and her play. She did well in the music examination, winning an award.

Catherine left school with the beginnings of a good liberal education; music, classics (including Greek), mathematics, English, history, a little science, and some grounding in several modern languages. More important, she had been in touch with a practical approach to advancement for women of her class, and could see, though dimly, the opening of breathtaking new vistas for all women.

Catherine had to leave St Leonards, it seems, a little earlier than she might have chosen, although she was nineteen years old. Her mother was still unwell and Catherine was needed at home. Careers for women lagged behind even the provision for improved education, and among St Leonards women "the great majority left school to return to their own homes, to play their part in social life and to undertake voluntary work for the community."[48] And, one might add, to await marriage. Catherine's life prospects, far from being poor, promised considerably more interest than the average. Her parents intended her education to continue, in a very liberal sense. Immediately after leaving school in March 1899 she joined them for a European holiday – Bayreuth, the Rhine, the Bavarian Alps. At some time she and Hal went on a cycling tour together in Germany; and several visits were exchanged with German students of their own age. Catherine corresponded throughout 1899–1901 with a number of German friends, particularly with a young man called "Julius," nicknamed "Little One." During the next few years she had other holidays abroad, in Switzerland, Italy, and elsewhere, and made innumerable visits within Britain to relatives and old school friends, meeting many interesting people; there were also cycle tours with other young women in Wales and the Lake District.

Few of Catherine's own letters survive from these travels, although there is some evidence that she was a good correspondent by this time. But occasional passages in letters to her light up the turn-of-the-century experience. In January 1904 she was evidently delighted by the electric trams she saw in Munich. An elderly correspondent, Emily Bowles, replied from Southampton: "I am so pleased with your appreciation of the electric trams. There is no other public conveyance here – and I am never tired of seeing the swift bright clean creatures – without cruelty to beasts – gliding and *feeding*. They are dangerous without great outlooking – and I have more than once been snatched from the jaws of death by a kindly arm when one was gliding noiselessly into my pocket."[49]

Catherine's music lessons continued; she studied history with a tutor; she kept up her languages; she joined something called the "Scribblers' Club" and practised prose and poetry writing. Her most successful adventure in the latter genre may have been a piece entitled "To ——", a long and carefully developed love poem which turns out in a surprise denouement to be written to the poet's bicycle. Interestingly, a prose piece shows her trying to work out her thoughts on "Humility and Self-Respect."[50]

Catherine took her continuing studies seriously, and during the most propitious periods at Harrow aimed to spend as much as seven hours a day at them. But she had "taken over all the household accounts and Mother's writing work";[51] these had to take precedence over her own work, and many interruptions were caused by visitors in the House. No doubt, and with some reason, her parents considered the help Catherine was able to give as a valuable part of her training as well as of use to themselves. As far as the "writing work" (presumably letters to parents, orders for supplies, and so on) was concerned, it may indeed have proved so. As for the accounting, I wish I knew how Catherine viewed this chore: neither this obligation nor the provision of Catherine with a personal clothing and spending allowance were the least bit effective in fostering in her an orderly approach to finance. Perhaps there was too much interference, perhaps she had insufficient real responsibility, perhaps her parents nagged, perhaps on the other hand they gave her insufficient instruction, or possibly the ability to handle money was simply left out of Catherine's makeup. Whatever the reason, money matters were a blind spot for the whole of her life. But clothing was something Catherine enjoyed, and she must have appreciated having her own allowance, by no means a universal privilege among well-to-do young women at that time. The amount allowed her in 1900 was £3–3–4 a month, probably a not ungenerous sum.[52] Good clothes were not yet generally mass-produced, and those that were did not always come in unusual sizes; when Catherine ordered six pairs of black openwork stockings, extra large in length and foot, she was warned that they would cost extra as they would have to be specially made for her.[53]

Evidence suggests that an unrealistic amount was expected of Catherine during these last Harrow years, whether by her parents or by herself. At times she struggled with poor health and low spirits. Her school friend "Hirstlet" (Margaret Hirst) wrote in October 1901 that she was more sorry than she could say that Catherine had had "all this worry." "I did hope," she added, "that you were really all right again." Catherine had evidently admitted to overworking, and Hirstlet agreed with the diagnosis, saying that certainly she had seen it that way when they had been together in March. She urged Catherine to be sensible, adding a blunt warning: "You must know that every time you get tired and knocked up you are putting yourself a little further on the road towards operations and voicelessness and invalidism (I know I am being brutal)." Catherine, she said, should get away from Harrow for visits although "I know you want to be of use at home."[54] Catherine responded cheerfully, perhaps defensively, claiming that although her days were full she was enjoying her work tremendously, especially her history lessons, which she found "delightful, although rather formidable."[55]

Whatever Catherine's health problem was, she was plagued by it for at least a year, and at times she was going from Harrow to London every day for treatment by what she referred to as "my rubbers," presumably for massage, under the care of Neil Arnott, an osteopath. Yet when she was well – and she seems to have been healthy enough for much of the time – she had abundant physical and psychical vigour.

Harrow was not without its concerts and other recreations, but the holidays in the Lake District provided an altogether different sort of life. From the back of Hawse End, Catherine could walk straight up on to Catbells, a small mountain yielding spectacular views. Just across the valley beyond Catbells, perhaps twenty minutes' walk from Hawse End, begins the ascent of Causey Pike (just over two thousand feet), a satisfying craggy peak whose top could be reached by the energetic Marshalls within an hour or two. Hawse End still stands in woodland which includes numerous rhododendrons probably planted by the Marshalls, with a long frontage on Derwentwater. Guests were sometimes met at the Keswick railway station and rowed across the lake, the shortest way to Hawse End, and surely the quickest way to a sense of having left city cares behind. Every season had its delights. One February, probably about 1901, Catherine, just back from the Christmas break, sat down to write to a cousin somewhere in a warmer climate:

It is hard to imagine you basking in summer weather, as I suppose you are by this time, while we are kept shivering with wind and snowstorms. We had horrid weather up at Keswick, but enjoyed ourselves immensely in spite of it. The neighbourhood has become very gay the last few years. One week we had 3 dances (one at Carlisle) in 4 days – not bad for the country, is it? We also have great hockey matches in the Christmas and Easter holidays, and cricket and regattas in the Summer; so altogether we have very gay times up there, even if we have not a house-party of our own. You would hardly recognize the house if you saw it now. We have added on two small new wings since you were last there, and several windows. We are building a gardener's cottage, stable, cow-byre, etc at present. We have been going through a good deal of anxiety about the land between us and Brandelhow lately, as the owner wanted to cut down all the wood, and sell it to a man whose ambition is to build bungalows along the shore of the lake! We heard the first tree being felled one morning as we were sitting at breakfast. Father dropped his knife and fork and rushed to the scene of action in time to stop any more damage from being done. He subsequently bought up the part next to our land, and the National Trust Society has just succeeded in raising subscriptions to preserve the rest. So it is safe now.[56]

Privilege, it seems, did something to save Britain's heritage.

The year 1903 was a hard one for the Marshalls. Caroline's brother George had lived much of the time abroad for some years, as manager of the Bank of Egypt in Cairo; his health was poor, and he seems to have found the English climate trying. In May, 1903, he was in Florence on his way home to visit the family and became seriously ill, so ill that Caroline went off to be with him, and he died on 5 June. As soon as she had left England, however, her other brother, Charles, now also a Harrow housemaster, became acutely ill with appendicitis, and on 11 June he too died.[57] One of Frank's brothers, Stephen, died the following year. Marshalls and Colbecks were a warm, close family and the shock of these deaths overshadowed Frank's and Caroline's remaining time at Harrow. The end of his career and the business of handing over the reins must have been difficult to handle at this time. In December 1904, when it was over, Catherine and her parents went on vacation in Italy and Switzerland for five months, joined by Hal during his Easter vacation from Cambridge, and then made the final move to the Lake District, already so much a home to them.

The alterations at Hawse End had been in the interest of turning the house from a holiday refuge into a full-time residence. The Marshalls had long felt themselves at home among the local people. Their frequent holiday visits ensured that they kept in touch with the other gentry families round about, a remarkable number of whom were relatives, whether summer visitors or permanent residents, and in the first years of the twentieth century there was a lively social life in the Lake District. At Hawse End there were visitors, and sometimes house parties. Catherine and Hal claimed they could walk for two weeks in the area, staying every night in a different place and always with family.[58] As for the cousins on the Island, plans for activities with them were made by standing on the shore and bellowing through a megaphone.[59]

Probably only the most socially conscious visitors recognized the other reality of Cumberland; the nineteenth century had seen the county's rise as a significant industrial area, exploiting the fortuitous combination of coal, iron ore, water power, and a good port, Whitehaven. By the first decade of the twentieth century, water power was of less importance, and industry was increasingly concentrated in the West Cumberland coastal towns where the iron, coal, and ship-building industries flourished. Some of the mines scattered through the valleys closed, others remained open. While the fashionable tourist industry dominated Ambleside and Windermere, towns such as Penrith and Keswick still catered to many miners.

The Marshalls themselves are not to be numbered among the summer visitors and well-to-do residents who neither knew nor cared how their neighbours lived. They enjoyed an extraordinarily privileged life; but at least they were aware of this, and they believed that privilege carries responsibility. Further, they were deeply imbued with a belief in the progress of humanity (such an obvious premise to most well-off people, and all liberals, at the beginning of the twentieth century) and they did not back away from social change in the service of progress. Frank Marshall had spent his life teaching the elite; after retirement he worked towards making secondary education available to all, including girls as well as boys.[60] It was said of him that "to be a good citizen and a good neighbour was a passion with him,"[61] and he demonstrated this in many ways, with real love and concern and an unfeigned interest in everything around him. In later years, according to Tom Marshall, despite his earlier athletic prowess, and a continuing delight in walking in the hills, "his face was slightly twisted and he had a gammy leg ... but he was full of kindness and we all loved him. ... He was very gentle." He remained intellectually rigorous, looking always for the "sound principle behind any solution."[62] The principles, practice, and politics of life were surely vigorously discussed daily at Hawse End, enriched by a stream of interesting and distinguished visitors.[63]

Even the Marshalls' pastimes have something to say about the character of their family life. They had developed their own version of a Lake District sport called "Manhunt," a version altogether less elitist than the original form, which was strictly a young man's game, invented and played almost exclusively by Cambridge undergraduates, taking more than one day of strenuous chasing over the mountains, and followed by a great beer-drinking session in a village inn.[64] The game played from Hawse End was athletically only a shadow of the original, but provided an afternoon's enjoyment for a great many people of both sexes and a wide age-range. The territory was restricted to a bare hill called Swinside (now reforested) and the rules were carefully drawn up to ensure that men and women took part together without the latter being seriously disadvantaged by physique or their more restrictive clothing. Two "hares" (Hal was usually one of them) were released at different places and had to find and reach each other without being caught. They were hunted by two packs of "hounds" (accident-prone Catherine generally risked life and limb to lead one pack): the hounds ran in pairs, a man and a woman together. When a hound caught a hare, the capture was not effective until he (or she) was joined by her (or his) partner, and for this twenty seconds were allowed. Local farmers, local gentry, and the Marshalls' house guests took part, the turnout sometimes numbering as many as forty people. Tea was served at Hawse End afterwards. Catherine was probably largely responsible for devising this social version of Manhunt, and certainly did the organizing most of the years when the game was played, as it was every September except one from 1901 to 1908.[65] After that Catherine was using her organizing ability in a wider field, though it seems the game was revived in 1913.

Among the young people who joined in the Manhunt from time to time were Josie Low and Jermyn Moorsom. Jermyn's family lived at Fieldside, a big house on the other side of Keswick; his father was one James Moorsom, KC. Josie was a lively, very modern young woman from Berwickshire, a friend of Jermyn's and devoted to both Catherine and her mother, who had apparently rescued her from some unpleasant scrape she had got into on an earlier visit to Fieldside. She was evidently thought to be a bad influence on Jermyn and was not welcome there from that time on. Hawse End, by contrast, was for her "the cheerful windowseated merry house to which I so yearned in the days of my haunted visit at Fieldside," and Caroline was "just a darling!"[66] Josie corresponded alternately flippantly and earnestly with Catherine, whom she clearly looked up to. Jermyn was not Josie's only admirer; indeed she and he and a young man called Malcolm, together with a fourth generally referred to as "the Platonist," made up a lively group of young people enjoying, as they hoped, new approaches to life and friendship. Even Jermyn sometimes thought Josie went too far with her smoking, motoring, and particularly the wearing of short skirts. The last were probably four inches off the ground at most, in spite of Josie's bold response: "If people can't love one with our skirts 'kilted up tae the knee' they must just not!"[67] But in August 1908 such determination to defy convention put Josie and Jermyn in hot water again. Josie came to the Lake District for a walking tour with a woman friend named Louis [sic] Walker. They stayed together at the Scawfell Inn, but Jermyn (now known as Jerry) and his friend Malcolm drove over daily to visit them. Jerry "dared not confess," but Malcolm and Josie felt the Moorsoms should know. The result was everything that might have been expected and more. Mr Moorsom "grew purple": "When pressed for a reason, he said that I had polluted Jermyn's mind, encouraging him to batten on vile literature – ("Shakespeare for instance?" enquired Malcolm)" and added that Josie was intriguing to marry his son. "The scene ended like a play. 'I wish to God you would marry her *yourself* sir,' shot out Jermyn's father, and left the room." Malcolm, Josie added lightheartedly, was planning to do just that, and they would all live together.[68]

Catherine's letters to Josie and to Jermyn have not been preserved, but she clearly responded with a great deal of openness and understanding, and perhaps underneath it, a tinge of envy of the kind of friendship they had developed. Catherine hinted to Josie that she herself was resolved not to marry and Josie replied in an unusually serious (and idealistic) vein: "[M]y mind, knowing nothing of the matter – cannot help rebelling at any such idea. ... If you don't the better for many helpless people whom you will help: but if you do, the better for one man, for the country, and the future. Is this very obscure? I have a kind of prejudice against the ordinary more or less material marriage; but of the higher union, which knits body and soul and spirit all together for eternity – one can't help seeing that earth holds very little better than that."[69]

Josie, it is not hard to guess, was contemplating marriage: but not to Jermyn; instead, she followed the Moorsoms' suggestion by marrying Malcolm. Jermyn was much criticized for continuing his friendship with Josie during the engagement and Josie more harshly for not breaking it off for his good: Catherine vigorously defended the "relationship" when she overheard the criticism. Jermyn regarded the attack as "the most damned impertinence." Catherine had told him that Jermyn and Josie's friendship had taught her that she had made a big mistake in her own life, but he replied that she did not know quite everything about it although "you've taken so much pains to understand."[70] Unfortunately we have been unable to find out to what mistake Catherine was referring, and this remains the only suggestion of an early love interest.

One other feature of life at Hawse End has to be mentioned. All such "gentlemen's houses" depended on servants to make life comfortable, in those days before labour-saving devices. The end of this kind of life was coming – war or no war – and the writing on the wall can be seen in the extent to which servant problems loom in all female correspondence. Caroline Marshall brought with her the difficulties she had experienced in Harrow, where, on one occasion, she had been so "run down ... chiefly by endless servant worries" that her health had only been restored by a month's holiday by herself in Switzerland after the school term ended.[71] In the Lake District, good help was even harder to come by. I do not know what made Caroline Marshall hard to work for; if she was tactless and overbearing with servants, she may also have been so at times with Catherine, although so much of affection and support for her daughter come through in her letters. Relations, however, recall her as somewhat formidable and not as approachable as Frank. Tom Marshall said, "I always thought that she was a bit severe, ... we were a little frightened of her."[72]

Whatever part Caroline played in her misfortunes, Hawse End was two miles by little-frequented road and path from the small town of Keswick, though directly accessible by ferry (I believe) at certain times of the year. There was probably not much to attract resident servants used to more populous areas: they came, but they did not stay. On one occasion, Caroline wrote to Catherine: "The new cook will not stay: wants a whole K[itchen] M[aid]. She fully agreed to what I could give and she has given the place no trial at all – wants to go at once and has cost me £2.10 with journey, fee and b[oard?] wage and going to [illegible] in a bus instead of getting into the p[ony] cart. Now of course I have lost Chorley's cook and another." So desperate was Caroline that the quality of cooking seems to have been her least concern; she continues: "She is a v. bad cook ex[cept] the porridge which is delicious, but I should have struggled through. Life is earnest and very tiresome. No wonder one wants to get away from a house."[73] Local help was sometimes more reliable, but was in need of training, and, by current standards, of basic socialization. Catherine, breathing the prevailing class-ridden domestic air, wrote a character sketch of a young girl from a nearby farm, emphasizing her sterling reliability and cheerfulness, but suggesting that her acceptance into the household as a lowly "between-maid" was the fulfilment of her highest ambition, and more than she could have expected.[74]

Except for Caroline's recurring servant problems, I doubt if Catherine's parents ever regretted their choice of the Newlands valley for their retirement. For Catherine, too, there was much to enjoy in life at Hawse End. She gave singing lessons to local children, had schoolfriends to visit, and travelled constantly among friends, writing in July 1907, "I have paid 42 visits in the last year and a half."[75]

Her education continued, and is hard to evaluate by any conventional yardstick. The emphasis on singing must not mislead us into thinking she was being pointed in the direction of Victorian female "accomplishments." Frank valued amateur music as a source of enrichment for men as well as for women, and not as a privilege which should be restricted to the wealthy. He took John Farmer's philosophy with him to the Lake District, organizing concerts, playing his cello, and encouraging Catherine to sing and to teach singing.

Little of Catherine's academic education took place in formal institutions, and may have been to some extent undisciplined, though I do not think it lacked depth. How much she read haphazardly and how much of her reading was pursued systematically is hard to document. During the few years immediately after she left school, when she was trying to help out in the running of the Harrow house, and was herself also often seriously unwell or undergoing time-consuming treatment, she probably did not follow through on the reading she hoped to do, or make full use of the expertise available to her from her father's friends on the Harrow staff. The amount of travelling and visiting she did in the next few years, educational as it was in itself, may also have made serious reading difficult, although I am not sure of this; days could be relatively long and uncluttered where you did not have to cook or clean or even take responsibility for those who did. And at times her studies were the major focus of her life; for instance, when she went to London at the beginning of 1907, it was to study. She attended many public lectures and some courses, and she joined Chelsea Public Library, writing to her cousin Lord Monteagle to ask him to sponsor her for membership. (He replied that he would be proud to do so, adding rather patronizingly: "How learned you must be growing.")[76] Catherine's pursuit of knowledge often arose from a felt need; and when she wanted to work in a certain field, prime resources were open to her. In 1906, she became interested in the problems of poor relief and unemployment, and almost at once economics became part of her self-set curriculum. She studied under the guidance of two of the most distinguished economists of her day, a privilege which young men went to Cambridge to enjoy.

One of these two economists was himself still a young man, Arthur Cecil Pigou, only three years older than Catherine herself, and later the author of the deeply affectionate memorial to Frank Marshall. He had known Catherine and her parents since his early teens when he had gone to Harrow "a shy and timid boy" (but with an entrance scholarship) and had been greatly influenced by Frank Marshall, his housemaster.[77] Pigou had gone on to be head of the House and head of the school, gaining honours in sports as well as academically. At King's College, Cambridge he took a first in history and then took the moral sciences tripos, which finally led to his specialization in economics. Since 1901 he had been giving an important course on advanced economics, and since 1902 had held a fellowship at King's. He had published his first book in 1905.[78] His mentor at Cambridge was Alfred Marshall, professor of political economy and elder statesman of the discipline, whose economic theory was to dominate British economics until the rise of Maynard Keynes. Alfred Marshall was no relation to Catherine's family, but seems to have taken an interest in her studies and – probably through the medium of Pigou – provided her with reading lists, as did Pigou himself. Ironically – and with seeming inconsistency, since he had done much for women's education at Newnham – Alfred Marshall did not favour the admission of women to degrees, and his influential opposition during the controversy of 1896 helped to set the cause back for many years.[79]

Pigou's interest at this time was in the development of a theoretical understanding of the tensions between the satisfactions (the "welfare") of the individual and of the society, and of the means by which they might best be balanced and maximized.[80] He was often at Hawse End. As well as the affection in which he clearly held the Marshalls, he was, like Frank and many other university men of the nineteenth and early twentieth centuries, a great lover of the mountains, walking and climbing in the Lake District and the Alps. He later had his own cottage at Buttermere, within ten miles of Hawse End.

The ultimate proof of the soundness of Catherine's education will emerge in the story of her life; she was to converse with statesmen, politicans, and economists with confidence and even with authority, an assurance that for her can only have been born of solid knowledge and much previous discussion. What is hard to determine is where all this preparation was perceived to be leading. No evidence remains to tell us whether Catherine would have liked to pursue a career, whether this was ever considered, and if so why no steps towards it were ever taken.

Despite the seeming fullness of her life at Hawse End, Catherine sometimes looked back wistfully to her school years, visiting St Leonards when she could, taking an interest in the doings of younger cousins and acquaintances who had followed her there, and "longing very much" to see Miss Grant again. "I realize ever more and more," she wrote in 1903, "how valuable your help was from the frequency with which I long for it again. It was not so much anything you said or did – I do not think I ever actually told you any of my difficulties, though you always seemed to understand things without being told – but it was your whole point of view which was so helpful."[81] Here Catherine put down her pen, possibly in tears, and, probably thinking she was revealing far too much of herself, she did not finish the letter. There is no reference here to the independence which had been encouraged at St Leonards, but Catherine may sometimes have longed for, and felt ungrateful for longing for, an end to her dependent position, light as were the hands that held the reins and purse-strings. She may have contrasted her position with that of Hal, still a gentle and unassuming young man with less than her drive and ambition, and probably less ability (though presumably with better health), who had done reasonably well at Marlborough, but had left Cambridge without completing a degree, and was now working in a junior management position on the railway in Yorkshire.

For his part, although his letters show an increase in self-confidence at this time, Hal was finding his new life somewhat lonely. The towns on the Carlisle-Leeds Midland line where he served were busier then than now, with many active textile mills still in operation, but they did not provide the kind of company he was used to, and at this time he did not (and was not expected to) have the ability to communicate across class barriers soon to be developed by his sister. Catherine visited often at weekends in 1906 and 1907; they would sometimes take off together for one of the smaller villages, such as Clapham, where there were "ripping walks and gorgeous views," and where they stayed in "the little inn by the station" at a cost of only a few shillings.[82]

Catherine could not travel and make visits all the time and forever, and at Hawse End she tried to make a fulfilling life out of what had been a glorious way to spend holidays. She worked hard on her singing teaching, she organized and took part in concerts, she tried to improve the general behaviour and health of her pupils, not only cautioning them against wildness on the way to and from lessons, but also advising the boys not to smoke as youngsters and the girls to avoid tight clothing. The choir she coached sang at Newlands Church and consisted of about twenty young people, mostly those who had left school already; they practised at Hawse End.[83] She enrolled in a dairy class, which her father described in a letter to Hal: "I dropped down to the Newlands School and tried on my way back to [order] 20 quarts of cream daily for the next week! for Catherine and Talbot are attending a dairy class at Stair, and that much extra supply will be wanted! I spent 3 hours in the afternoon looking on at them, and we are eating the butter they made today. Excellent butter as far as the making goes, but a little tasteless. There is an active class of ten, and a first rate teacher."[84]

Catherine never despised domestic work, impressing her friends in Germany with her willingness to roll up her sleeves and dry dishes,[85] and did not mind sewing and mending. Responsibility for housekeeping was another matter. In late 1905 she took over much of her mother's work (Caroline was still frequently unwell). In reply to a letter in which Catherine had evidently protested herself happy, but with some reservations, a former governess wrote: "You will get used to the housekeeping in time, and it is nice for you to feel you are able to save your dear Mother from having to do it. I was amused at your planning meal[s] 3 weeks ahead! Don't you laugh at me any more!!"[86]

But the housekeeping was not a success. When Catherine left in January 1906 to spend two months in London, she left chaos behind her. Caroline was angry, and wrote complaining about "another Harrods bill ... if paid where is the receipt, and if not, why not? ... if you could only know how annoying and irritating these undone little things are, you would not do it. It takes far more time and makes double and treble work. Daddy and I have spent time each day hunting up receipts. ... You spoil good work and make work by this fatal lack of doing what should be done then and there."[87]

Was Catherine's inefficiency a defence against doing what she disliked? Against getting trapped permanently in a situation she did not suit? There had been a terribly final ring to the governess's well-meant "You will get used to the housekeeping in time." If it was resistance on Catherine's part, it was certainly unconscious; she went on trying to fit herself into the appropriate form and to find ways of being of service, and surely felt inept and guilty at her failures. Perhaps the climax of triviality was reached in 1907, when she was earnestly setting herself to judge the laundering skills of aspiring local girls. A friend wrote to give her serious advice on the matter: "A well-ironed handkerchief should have a certain amount of gloss and stiffness (without starch) just enough to make it look of some importance in the world."[88]

But Catherine, that able, headstrong young woman, would not find her salvation or her way to serve through the gospel of the well-ironed handkerchief (or even the promptly paid bill). Already by this time, a door was opening into politics and the burgeoning women's suffrage movement.

Newlands Schoolroom and Church, Newlands Valley, Keswick

2 Bringing the Women's Suffrage Cause to the Lake District, 1907–9

Like most human beings, the Marshalls lacked total consistency. On the one hand, there are their advanced political and social views, the excellent education they ensured for Catherine, the sharing of causes between mother and daughter, the lack of condescension in exchanges between father and daughter, the wholehearted support of her political activities by both parents. On the other hand, a perhaps understandable concern for her health led to overprotectiveness and was expressed in outright orders as to where she might stay and what kind of clothing she should wear; marginally acceptable for a sixteen-year-old, but inappropriate for a twenty-year-old and downright absurd when directed to a twenty-six-year-old. When Catherine was on her way to spend some time in London at the beginning of 1906, her mother wrote: "if the Kenyons can really give you a *warm and a dry bed* and room you can stay – but can Aunt M[argaret] ensure *this*? I mistrust servants especially Mrs. K's and I do not want you to start London with a cold. And you must take a wrap in any case for the return also a change of boots and stockings: it may be pelting with rain and you will tire yourself to pieces."[1]

Above all, there is the anomaly of the acceptance by all the family – as far as we know including Catherine – that she would never need, perhaps never be permitted, to earn her own living. Others of her contemporaries accepted this as a parental decision in their own cases, and a matter requiring considerable courage even to raise;[2] in Catherine's case it seems more likely that it was raised, discussed, and decided – but, regrettably, without leaving a trace in writing.

Possibly it was not so much the matter of a career that was ruled out, as of a paid job; later, for Catherine to have a career in politics came to seem an option to be welcomed and pursued.[3]

Catherine's close family at least does not seem to have estimated her value in terms of her marriageability, a common criterion of the period. She was accustomed to easy and comfortable conversation with men of all ages, experience which was to be of inestimable political use to her, and she had a number of good friends among men as well as women. But she cannot have been completely independent of cultural dictates; even the feminism of the period strongly emphasized woman's role as wife and mother.[4] By the age of twenty-six some part of her probably felt that she had failed in what was expected.

The Marshalls can only be understood in terms of prewar Liberalism; Catherine was born and bred a liberal – small "l" and large "L." Liberalism of course was no monolith, although individual Liberals tended to make the assumption that whatever they meant by Liberalism was what was meant by all, including politicians; how disastrous this assumption could be was suggested by the test case of suffragism and shown up sharply by the advent of war in 1914. "Liberal idealism" best describes the school of thought which permeated Catherine's upbringing; a compound of beliefs in anti-imperialism, progress, opportunity for all, education, human rights, maximum freedom without exploitation, improvement of material conditions, internationalism.

The so-called "New Liberals" were even then attempting to add to this list the lacking element of an economic class analysis. Pigou undoubtedly discussed his theories on his visits to Hawse End; he held the opinion that a more equal distribution of income would increase overall economic welfare. It was said of him that "He was a passionate believer in justice. ... To him it was just and proper to treat all men as equals and to treat the poor as if they were equal in value and capacity to the rich."[5] Probably the Marshalls were also familiar with the work of the better-known and more radical J.A. Hobson, whose *Imperialism* appeared in 1902. Although stopping short of any condemnation of capitalism in itself, Hobson's theory of the economic and political evil resulting from very uneven distribution of wealth (resulting, in his view, in "under-consumption" and "over-saving") went much farther than Pigou, although even the views of the latter were controversial, and threatening to classic laissez-faire liberal theory.[6]

Later Catherine described her political development at school and at home to an audience of Liberal men: "Ever since I was old enough to think about politics at all I have been a Liberal. When I was still almost a child I read Mill's *Liberalism* and *Representative Government* and *Subjection of Women* (most boys, I find, read the first two and leave out the third). I was profoundly impressed by them. The first speech I ever made in my life as a schoolgirl was in defense of a free press. My first political speech I ever made, soon after leaving school, was in the cause of free trade."[7]

Catherine and Caroline were actively involved with the Liberal party before leaving Harrow. Politically astute suffrage women were ready to make use of the weapon handed them by the Corrupt and Illegal Practices Prevention Act of 1883, which had reduced the amount of money that could be spent in election campaigns and had correspondingly increased the role of the women's party organizations; conditions might be attached to help given now that it was so much needed. Catherine's account of the experience at Harrow, where Caroline was the first president and she the first secretary of the local Women's Liberal Association (WLA), provides an interesting example of the influence of women in politics before suffrage, and of the way in which Liberal suffragist women saw their interests wrapped up with those of an enlightened Liberal party. "We formed a W.L.A. at Harrow because the men w[d]. do nothing. It was a very Conservative Constituency, had only twice been contested by a Lib. candidate at all. The men all said it was hopeless and did nothing. We set to work in 1904 and did all the registration canvassing of our polling district – it had been neglected for years – and held 5 large public meetings and weekly smaller ones and stirred up the Men's Lib. Club. In the general election of 1906 a Liberal was returned for the Division, for the 1st time, and he did not hesitate to say that he owed his election 'very largely to the splendid work of the Liberal women.' He was a staunch suffragist, or we should not have worked for him."[8] Keswick also had its WLA, which Caroline and Catherine joined when they moved to Hawse End.

Although the renewal of suffrage activity has often been credited almost solely to the actions of the Women's Social and Political Union (WSPU), which was founded in 1903 and began its militancy (mildly, at first) in 1905, the nonmilitant National Union of Women's Suffrage Societies (NUWSS, NU) was far from moribund. For British suffragism probably the most significant development, though local in scope, was the campaign of the women textile workers, in Lancashire and Cheshire, who had not only presented giant petitions in 1901 and 1902, but continued to work actively for trade union support.[9] In 1903, too, the NU, now that the Boer War was over and rumours of a general election were in the air, sponsored a national convention in defence of the civil rights of women, in London.[10] Further, a groundswell throughout the Western world was evidenced by the founding of the International Women's Suffrage Alliance (IWSA) in 1904, and by this time there had already been some successes.

When the Liberal party gained a massive parliamentary majority at the beginning of 1906, some Liberal women suffragists expected the milennium. Hopefulness – and frustration – engendered an escalation in suffrage activity throughout the country, and the early attention-getting activities of the WSPU helped to swell the ranks and coffers of the nonmilitant societies as well as its own.

Catherine worked vigorously in the election campaign of January 1906 for the causes – still inseparable to her – of suffrage and Liberalism. She was beginning to gain some reputation among her acquaintances as a political activist. Some of her friends took such interest and activity for granted; Margaret Hirst wrote her congratulations on the favourable results at Harrow and in Cumberland and Westmorland, commenting in the same letter that at Whitby "we are heartbroken" at the loss of Noel Buxton.[11] For other friends, Catherine's venture into public life seemed so exotic as to be out of reach; one wrote wistfully of her own situation and admiringly of Catherine's, saying: "I hope very much to do something if my family will only let me." She went on to say that she would like to go abroad to work and to learn a language, and added that she was sorry to hear that Catherine's political career was ended; she had hoped some day to hear her friend address a mass meeting.[12]

Oddly enough, all the evidence is that indeed Catherine's political career, if not ended, was temporarily at a standstill. Throughout 1906, once the election was over, her active participation ceased. In this, her twenty-seventh year, she made a round of visits, listed twenty-two species of birds as "Nesting Visitors" in the Hawse End guest book (together with ten whose songs were heard but whose nests were not found), struggled unavailingly with the household accounts, went for a six-day cycle tour through the Lake District with her friend Margaret McKerrow (strenuous indeed, given the cycles, the clothes, and the roads of those days – and they covered an impressive itinerary),[13] organized the annual "Manhunt," and in general appears to have settled back into a bucolic indifference to politics. But Catherine and Caroline may merely have been waiting to see what the new government would do.

The suffrage societies were not inactive; a major deputation met with the prime minister, Sir Henry Campbell-Bannerman, on

19 May 1906. Disappointed with the results, but still optimistic, the NUWSS stepped up pressure on the Liberal party, announcing that it would conduct special campaigns in the constituencies of prominent Liberal opponents of the suffrage. Most Liberal suffragist women, however, had not ceased to believe in the good faith and long-term reasonableness of Liberal government and Liberal statesmen. Only one, Margaret Ashton, until now a noted Manchester Liberal, turned sharply around immediately after the deputation to Campbell-Bannerman and threw in her lot with the Labour party as more likely to take the women seriously.[14] In October the WSPU made headlines with the arrest of eleven of its members, and in December the NU, in one of its first and last acts of support for the militants, gave a banquet for the suffragettes on their release from jail.[15] Among Catherine's papers is a pamphlet describing the May deputation, and other major suffrage events were surely fully discussed by the family and their guests at Hawse End.

Catherine was becoming known as a person with political and social knowledge and concerns; in late 1906 an acquaintance urged her to stand for office as a Poor Law guardian in the local election to be held the following March, writing: "Some more reforming ladies are very badly wanted; and I should be *so* glad to have you to help me. If you can make up your mind to be continually snubbed and disappointed and to have your schemes continually delayed, it is very interesting work; and sometimes there are successes and encouragements which make up for all the rest!"[16] Catherine would be qualified to stand as one of five guardians for Keswick by virtue of having resided there for twelve months. She is unlikely to have been deterred by the realistic rather than rosy description of the work, but she did not pursue the suggestion.

Throughout 1907 the story is much the same. While the NUWSS revised its constitution, Catherine enjoyed the skating offered by a long cold spell; in London for some weeks of study in January, she joined an Eton skating club (carefully concealing her Harrow connections). While the famous "Mud March" of the National Union gathered in Hyde Park on 9 February, Catherine visited her cousins on Derwent Island. She was in London again when W. H. Dickinson's private bill for a limited measure of women's suffrage was talked out on 8 March; if she attended the debate, no evidence remains. While the NU held its annual council meeting in Newcastle (July), Catherine studied how to judge competency in ironing; while the Men's League for Women's Suffrage (MLWS) held its first public meeting at the Queen's Hall in London (December), Catherine was preparing for "a very gay Christmas" with many dances, a house party, and (in January 1908) a concert at the small school in the Newlands Valley, at which she and her father were, as often, among the star attractions.[17]

The Marshall family may have been spending a bit more time on political work than here appears. At some time during 1907, Catherine canvassed a small sampling of local opinion on the women's suffrage question; a scrappy list in her handwriting of fifty-three local women who "signed Women's Suffrage Declaration 1907" interestingly includes the occupations of a number of them. Two were grocers, three kept boardinghouses, two were "servants" (in addition to one housemaid and one cook), others (one each) were a milliner, a confectioner, a baker, a photographer's assistant, a postmistress, a farm worker (or farmer's wife), and a schoolmistress. The list is interesting both for the variety of occupations and for the number of working women prepared to commit themselves. A few women were listed who evidently had not signed but were "known to be in favour" or "known to be opposed to Women's Suffrage," the latter including Mrs Moorsom, the mother of Catherine's friend, Jermyn.[18]

Meanwhile, the militant and nonmilitant societies were rapidly increasing their activity, and the intervention of the NUWSS in by-elections – especially the Wimbledon by-election in May 1907, when Bertrand Russell stood as a suffrage candidate – was somewhat restoring the balance of attention, if only because of the unpleasant but newsworthy behaviour of the antisuffragists, who threw eggs and let mice loose at a Wimbledon meeting.

The year 1908 was a year of important suffrage events, and began on a hopeful note for the NU, with the prospect of a meeting with H.H. Asquith, then the chancellor of the Exchequer, on 30 January. By this time, Campbell-Bannerman was ill, and it already seemed probable that Asquith would be his successor. For this reason, and despite the fact that (as Asquith was at pains to point out) franchise questions were no part of the mandate of the chancellor of the Exchequer, the NU was encouraged by his agreeing to meet with them, and momentarily by his assertion that he was not "a case-hardened or fanatical opponent to the claims of women." But he made it clear there was no chance of the government taking the initiative "in this Parliament ... even if we were, which I frankly tell you we are not, unanimous in our views as to the expediency of the change itself." He put the onus back on them, saying: "I do not think you will bring this change about until you have satisfied the country that the majority of women are in favour of it, and until you have made greater way than you have at present in convincing the male electorate that it is expedient not only in the interests of women, but in the still larger and wider interests of society as a whole. That is the great task which those of you who are engaged in this work have before you."[19] If Asquith thought or hoped that the women would be discouraged by so distant a goal, he miscalculated the effect of his words, which the women took as a challenge.

The meeting with Asquith had coincided with the opening of the session, and a month later, Henry Yorke Stanger's private women's suffrage bill passed second reading in the House of Commons with a majority of 179. Further progress was blocked, but at least it provided confirmation of a respectable number of supporters in the House, and seemed to justify some expectation that Asquith might indeed come round, since there was known to be considerable potential for support among ministers. In April, Asquith replaced the dying Campbell-Bannerman as prime minister, and a deputation from the NU to Winston Churchill, who became president of the Board of Trade in the ensuing cabinet shuffle, came away believing that Churchill would and could influence the cabinet favourably.[20]

The stated aim adopted by all the suffrage societies at this time (and so promoted by Catherine when she began to speak publicly) was to obtain the vote for women on the same terms "as it is or may be granted to men," an aim maintained for its hoped-for consistency with a nonparty stance, its lack of comment on any other possible franchise reform, its relative simplicity, and its feminist logic. Catherine apparently found it well-received at the grassroots level, perhaps because it could mean different things to different people. Much has been made – and was made at the time – of the argument (commonly used by Liberal antisuffragists) that to give the vote to women on the terms that it was then held by men, which included a property component, would upset the political balance in favour of the Conservatives.[21] This may or may not have been true, but it is a mistake to believe that the suffragists clung to the formula "as is or may be" simply on abstract feminist principle. The alternative offered by the government was never true adult suffrage, which many (not, of course, all) suffragists would have accepted readily, and which would in no way have conflicted with the formula. Not even in 1917 was this to be offered. In May 1908, the most that Asquith would suggest was a government bill for a broader male suffrage, which might conceivably be amended to include some or all women. The occasion of this offer, if that is not too firm a word for it, came when, as prime minister, he again received a deputation, this time of Liberal suffragist MPs. The kernel of his statement was that "he would not oppose an amendment including women to the

measure of electoral reform that was part of the Government programme, and admitted that two-thirds of the Cabinet were in favour
of this reform. But such an amendment must ... be of a democratic
character and backed by the overwhelming support of the men and
women of the country."[22]

Interpretations of this statement differed startlingly. No wonder
Helena Swanwick called it an obscure pronouncement.[23] On the one
hand, Bertrand Russell, then a member of the NU executive, declared: "Mr. Asquith's promise to the deputation of Suffragist members is the most important event which has yet occurred in the
history of the movement. The effect of his promise is that, provided
we can maintain our majority in the House of Commons, Women's
Suffrage will – barring unforeseen accidents – become incorporated
in a Government Bill. It is therefore to all intents and purposes as
good as if the Government had directly taken up the enfranchisement of women."[24] But Millicent Garrett Fawcett, president of the
NU, with a far longer experience behind her of the manoeuvring of
politicians, quickly dissociated the executive from this rosy view. Her
own opinion, she wrote, was that "Mr. Asquith ... was keeping up his
character as an opponent of Women's Suffrage by trying to run our
barque on the rocks of Adult Suffrage. ... In offering this "concession" it appears to me that he contrived to do as much harm as possible to the Women's Suffrage Movement, and refrained completely
from identifying his party with it."

Mrs Fawcett thought, with some justification, that her view was
confirmed by what had happened the previous Tuesday in the
House of Commons, a few days after the deputation: "On being
questioned ... whether, if a Women's Suffrage Amendment were
carried on a Government Reform Bill, Women's Suffrage would
then become part of the programme of the Liberal party,
Mr. Asquith replied: 'My hon. friend has asked me a contingent
question in regard to a remote and speculative future.'"[25] Asquith's
flippant answer does indeed suggest that Russell had been mistaken
in concluding that the prime minister's remarks to the deputation
justified the conclusion that "there is every likelihood that women
will acquire votes before the next General Election."[26] However, despite Fawcett's response and an equally critical one – also public –
from his brother, Lord Russell,[27] Bertrand Russell declared himself
unrepentant "tho' I think that the suffragists, by minimizing
Asquith's concession, may succeed in persuading him into taking
their view of his meaning. Mrs. Fawcett regards his remarks as deliberately intended to postpone w.s. by raising the Adult Suffrage
bogy, and this view is held by almost the whole of our Executive. I

am in disgrace all round."[28] The question of adult suffrage as an ally or a threat to the women's cause continued to be of political concern in the NU executive and in Parliament.[29]

The WSPU had much less interest, and faith, in the Liberals, and had lost patience with the new government within a few months.[30] Nevertheless, the overreaction of the politicians and the police to what were at first the mildest of disruptive tactics galvanized support for the women's suffrage cause even while it alienated some. In the early days the NU admired and appreciated the dramatic impact on public opinion made by women who were not only breaking out of the drawing-room image, but were willing to go to prison. While the leaders had no plans to change their own methods, they were aware that the whole movement was benefiting by the publicity.[31] NU membership surged in 1907, and continued to rise rapidly; funds increased gratifyingly; and the number of affiliated societies more than doubled (from 29 to 64) between October 1907 and January 1909.[32] Holton uses the term "symbiotic" for the relationship between the two wings;[33] this may not be too strong down to 1907 and possibly into 1908, but once the WSPU had turned to window-breaking and to harrassment of speakers at Liberal meetings, the NU found their work constantly hampered by the activites of their suffragette sisters, making it harder for them to get any share of press attention, turning off some supporters, and giving an excuse to the lukewarm to reject the cause.

The terms "militant" and "nonmilitant" are clearly misnomers, with their suggestion of passivity on the constitutionalist side,[34] and have probably contributed something to the undue proportion of credit for the suffrage agitation which has gone to the WSPU. The NU rode the wave of interest not by adopting the WSPU's tactics, but by making itself into a remarkable pressure group, using a wide variety of methods, from deputations to large demonstrations, to bear on public opinion, parliamentary opinion, party political opinion, the trade unions and the women's movement. If militancy connotes forceful activism, the NUWSS was militant from 1907. However, for clarity's sake, we may leave the names "militant" and "suffragette" to those who have held them for so long, but I shall (as Holton does) use the terms "constitutionalist" and "women's suffragist" rather than "nonmilitant" for the other wing.

The first steps to internal reform of the NU had been taken before Catherine took up the cause in earnest. The changes made in the NU constitution in January 1907 had made it a more effective and democratic working body, with an elected executive, responsible to a council of representatives from the local bodies, meeting quarterly and having responsibility for the formulation of policy. Soon afterwards the NU had opened an office, with a full-time staff.[35] At this time the main suffrage groups, in effect, shared a weekly newspaper, *Women's Franchise*, each with a few pages appearing under its own imprint; the NU had a regular section.[36] All in all, two-way communication between the branches and the centre had been greatly facilitated, and from this time on the left hand of the NU knew, and expected to know, what the right hand was doing. Not incidentally, this never took place in the WSPU; although a constitution was adopted by a general meeting in October 1907, it was never put into effect.[37]

Even those able to take some encouragement from Asquith's statement in May 1908 saw it as reinforcing the need to rouse and demonstrate support for the cause, and, whether at Catherine's initiative or her mother's, the Marshalls decided that the time was ripe to bring the women's suffrage issue to the Lake District. In September, Catherine wrote a report of the events of summer 1908, so the story can be told in her own words:

Our Association came into being on May 18th., when a few ladies known to be in favour of Women's Suffrage met at Hawse End, by invitation of Mrs. Frank Marshall, and decided to form a branch of the National Union of Women's Suffrage Societies in Keswick. A committee was formed, rules drawn up, and active propaganda work started at once. It was unanimously decided that our object should be votes for women on the same terms as for men, and that the Association should be a strictly *non-party* organization; we also pledged ourselves to *peaceful and constitutional methods only*. Our work was to consist of spreading the principles of Women's Suffrage by means of meetings, of letters to the press, of distributing literature on the subject, and of "promoting intelligent interest and a sense of responsibility among women with regard to political questions". In furtherance of this policy meetings have been held at Braithwaite, Portinscale, Grange, Stair, Bassenthwaite and Brigham. Miss R. Spedding, Miss M. Broatch and Miss C. Marshall volunteered to hold a series of outdoor meetings in the neighbouring villages, and they were fortunate in enlisting the help of various suffragists who were staying in the districts. The audience at these meetings averaged between 50 and 100 in numbers; in every instance a resolution in favour of votes for women on the same terms as for men was enthusiastically carried. Questions and objections are always asked for, and the discussion raised has always been conducted seriously and in a friendly spirit.[38]

Men usually outnumbered women at these meetings. The open-air meetings mentioned so briefly in the report became an important part of Catherine's contribution. Initially, they took enormous courage. While she had been schooled in debating and encouraged to speak up (and so had a big advantage over many suffragists), there was still a world of difference between addressing a group of one's fellow-students and launching into a controversial issue with an unknown audience made up more of the curious than of the committed, and generally including at least one argumentative or hostile questioner. Catherine later admitted that she had walked through the woods to her first outdoor speaking engagement with a feeling of terror.[39] But she was a good speaker and related well to her very varied audiences, who would usually include miners, ironworkers, working women, some tourists, and casual passersby.

Enough of Catherine's rough notes remain to enable us to reconstruct a characteristic speech, in this case one given probably in the spring of 1908, and give us the rare opportunity to listen in on one of the frequent occasions that made up the women's suffrage campaign at the grassroots. Catherine's approach was eclectic; she clearly thought there was every reason in the world for women to have the vote, and so, with no inconsistency or insincerity, she selected those arguments which would most appeal to the audience in front of her, and used them skilfully to carry her hearers with her.

Catherine's major theme for this audience was women's need of the franchise,[40] but first she clarified exactly what it was that women were asking for, and tried to dispel some of the rumours that were in circulation. Suffragists, she said, were not asking to sit in Parliament, and they were not even asking for votes for all women. They were not demanding any change in the franchise, simply: "That a woman who possesses the qualifications which would enable her to vote for a representative in Parliament were she a man, shall not be debarred by law ... simply because she is a woman." She anticipated the question "Why not go for Adult Suffrage?" and gave a simplified answer, directly in line with NU official policy, declaring that the suffrage business was to get the vote for women, and that adult suffrage was a separate and distinct question. For the more limited goal, she pointed out, members of all parties worked with the NU. She went on: "What we want, then, is votes for women on the same terms as men. We hold that women need the power of voting for a representative in Parliament just as much and for exactly the same reasons as men need it. I have never yet heard an argument for giving votes to men which does not apply [equally to women]."

Catherine looked then at reasons why men had the vote and what the franchise did for them, stressing the power which the vote bestowed, not on individuals but on groups of people with common interests. "Popular government" was an empty and hypocritical phrase while half the population were denied the vote. Women, said Catherine, sometimes queried their own need for the vote: "Don't the men do what we want in the end if we will only have patience?" Here Catherine would tell one of two old stories to make her point (and to provide light relief). One was the fable of the old woman whose pig would not get over the stile, and whose dog refused to give it a nip to set it on its way. The old woman finally achieved her end by a whole series of threats and bribes involving a cat, a mouse, a rope, a butcher, a cow, water, fire, a stick, and the dog. Women, said Catherine, think it would have been simpler if the old woman could have got hold of the stick and done her own beating.[41]

The other apt story much used by Catherine concerned a farmer and his wife, living so far from town that he only went in twice a year, leaving his wife at home. She sent her "butter money" with him, telling him what to buy for her. But the farmer brought her what he thought suitable, not what she wanted – dancing slippers in place of strong shoes, a bright silk dress instead of a practical dark linen, and finally a glass vase instead of a saucepan. At last, "the Farmer's wife lost all patience and scolded the Farmer well. The Farmer felt very injured and said, 'I took a great deal of trouble about buying that vase, I thought you would like it better than a saucepan.' To which the Farmer's wife replied 'Do not buy what *you think I would like,* but bring me what I *ask for*; and next time you go to town, *take me in the cart too,* John.'"[42]

Catherine mentioned existing laws which did not meet women's needs, listing laws restricting women's right to work and conditions of work, and the marriage laws. She stressed that the big problem was that without votes, women could not get attention paid to their needs. One of a number of examples was the women's suffrage movement itself, where year after year many signatures had been collected in support, but nothing had been done, and now: "At this moment, with a majority of 179 in the House of Commons on Mr. Stanger's second reading, and 420 members pledged, [with a] majority in Cabinet too, the Government 'cannot find time' for a third reading, though there is to be a special autumn session." She also cited, as "Absurdities overlooked" by male legislators, the fact that married women could serve on county councils, but could not vote in parliamentary elections, and the legal anomaly, often having serious consequences, that the law did not recognize the mother as a parent.

If woman's place was in the home – and Catherine, in common with most women's suffragists, would not have questioned that much of a woman's time and attention was centred there – this did not provide an escape from politics: "In fact the mother of a family is perhaps more concerned with politics than any one else." The price and quality of food, the health and education of the children, housing, even the relations of husband and wife, were all dealt with by modern politics. All of these concerned women as much as men, yet they were not consulted.

Summing up, Catherine said that she had tried to show why women want "and *ought* to want" the vote, and that by standing aside and saying "Politics is not my business" women were neglecting their duty to their homes and their children as well as to themselves, their less fortunate sisters and their country. In a fervent peroration, she claimed the right of women to honour their inheritance and not to refuse to care for justice and liberty just because "we happen to have been born women." Her final appeal was to the men "to come forward and help us … [to] recognize us as fellow human-beings, fellow citizens, neither the slaves nor the enemies of man, but his natural helpers in all that concerns the welfare of the human race." But Catherine would not let her audience leave with a rosy glow and no concrete plans, so she concluded with an admonition that those who were not helping were holding the cause back; every elector convinced of the injustice of refusing women the vote must use every means in his power to change the situation. Those electors who had no time to give should at least circulate literature and join a women's suffrage society. She underlined the value of this gesture to prove publicly that they wanted women's suffrage, and to make opponents reconsider; as electors themselves, their voices counted.

In this talk, Catherine includes something for everyone, and carefully avoids any mention of party politics. The official nonparty stance of the NU laid constraints on its speakers, but there were also ways in which it was liberating. Here, at the very periphery of the political sytem, education directly focused on the topic of women's rights and women's disabilities was taking place in a way which would not have been possible had party machinery and party reflexes been called into play.[43]

In June 1908, Catherine travelled to London with her cousin's wife (Mrs John Marshall of Derwent Island) and two other members of the KWSA for a grand procession and demonstration organized by the London Society for Women's Suffrage (LSWS), the NU, and the Women's Freedom League (WFL). Over ten thousand women took part, including not only members of suffrage societies "brought by special trains to London from all parts of England," but "Colonial women with some International representatives. … medical women

and University women in cap and gown, teachers, women in business, office women, writers, artists, actresses, musicians, nurses in
uniform, gymnastic teachers, gardeners, farmers, home makers,
etc., followed by a large contingent of working women mainly organised by the Women's Co-operative Guild." The occasion was made
colourful by "distinctive banners of very remarkable beauty, specially designed for the occasion by the Artists' League for Women's
Suffrage." The effect of the demonstration, which was followed by a
meeting in the Albert Hall, "surpassed the expectations of the pro-
moters. The streets throughout the long line of march were
crowded with spectators, and the press notices showed that the procession had been singularly impressive in respect of its numbers, its
representative character, its spectacular effect, and the reception it
met with on its march."[44]

A personal account of the impact of the event came from Josie
Low, who wrote: "I was much interested to see the effect of these
two affairs [the demonstration and the procession] upon my father.
Being a very just man, he has never attempted to deny that our
claims were just; but for political reasons he hoped that they would
be long in being granted. Well, when he had read the account of the
Procession, quoth he – "They'll have to get it now! I'm very sorry,
but I don't see how it can be withheld much longer!'"[45] However,
Asquith was less impressed than Judge Low, and the suffrage societies had no doubt of the need to keep up the pressure.

From this time on, women's suffrage began to take over Catherine's
life. She returned from London inspired, and found plenty to do. In
July the suffrage caravan organized and staffed by Newnham students came through Cumberland and Westmoreland. Catherine,
more than any one else along the caravan's route, made elaborate
preparations to ensure that full advantage was taken of the visit. She
made their coming known through a notice in the *English Lakes Visitor* and *Keswick Guardian* which gave their whole route, asked for
local contacts, and explained the philosophy of the National Union,
"the body that pursues peaceful and constitutional methods," and
she planned a splendid reception for them in Keswick itself, clearly
seeing it as just the boost needed for the new and enthusiastic KWSA.
So exceptional were the preparations that Ray Costelloe, one of the
six young caravanners, confessed as they approached Keswick, "We
are terrified ... these meetings have been tremendously advertised!!
However it's rather exciting," and again, "We are terribly afraid of
getting to Keswick, because of all their preparations for us but it's
exciting too."[46]

Ray Costelloe's next letter home came from Hawse End, and she reported that they had reached Keswick in time for the planned midday meeting: "When we got there swarms of suffragists came rushing up to meet us, and we were overwhelmed with offers of lunch and tea and bed etc." Two to three hundred[47] turned up for this first meeting, held in the market place, and Ray voted it a "great success. Lots of reporters, large collection and hearty support." Unfortunately, a mid-afternoon meeting which was to have been held "on the lake (the audience to be in boats)" had to be cancelled because of rain and "a wild wind." Instead, Ray reported: "they rowed us over to the island on which Mrs [John] Marshall lives. It is a *heavenly* place – the whole island a garden, with the house in the middle, and a perfectly exquisite garden it is."

After their visit to the island, some of the caravanners walked three miles to Hawse End for tea, a short rest and a swim, and then were driven back to Keswick for an 8 p.m. meeting in the market. Ray reported: "Though it rained quite hard at times we had a crowd of over 600 all eagerly listening, and a very good majority voted for our final resolution. We all spoke well and [were] inspired by the very good hearing we got: and we collected £3 and met with immense support from men and women. We are awfully encouraged, and the local Society is very pleased with us I think! Ellie and I drove back here, where Miss Marshall is putting us up most luxuriously. ... Its all the greatest fun, though horribly hard work."[48] Catherine wrote of this meeting that "a resolution was passed ... with only 2 dissentients – who refused an invitation to address the meeting and state their views!" Next day (22 July) the weather cleared and the meeting on the lake was held before the caravanners set off again. The support of the KWSA went with them: "Besides the meetings actually organized in Keswick the Hon. Sec. [Catherine] and Miss Spedding corresponded with a large number of persons along the caravan route – in Maryport, Workington, Cockermouth, Grasmere, Ambleside, Windermere, Kirkby Lonsdale, Carnforth, and as far afield as Skipton in Yorkshire – enlisting support, getting letters put in the local papers, and preparing a good reception for the Caravan."[49]

The caravan venture of the Newnham students was based on the popular socialist Clarion vans, and reached a wide audience of rural people together with those in scattered industries and some in the larger towns. In the main, speakers were well received, although there were exceptions. Outside London, at the very least, the mythology of the NUWSS as no more than a bourgeois drawing-room movement bears no relation to reality. This kind of imagination and daring, supported by Catherine's enthusiasm and effective organizing, was like new blood pumping through the veins of the old NU. The KWSA report continues: "The tour was so successful that the Nat. Union decided to start another one officially, through Northumberland and Yorkshire and N.E. Cumberland. Miss Marshall was again applied to for help, and people were written to wherever possible. Excellent meetings were held at Penrith and Carlisle."[50]

Another new suffrage enterprise, this one initiated by Catherine, was quickly picked up and used elsewhere. Even before the KWSA had been formed, Catherine had "kept a small stock of Suffrage Literature which she has lent to anyone inclined to be interested in the question. It has proved a most successful means of propaganda, and it was decided last month to open a stall in Keswick market on Saturday mornings for the sale of Suffrage Literature ... letters have been received from all parts of the country asking for help in starting similar stalls. Some of our Committee went to Cockermouth last week to start one there, and Penrith opened one with very great success this week."[51]

The women and men who gathered at Derwent Hill on 11 September 1908 for a celebratory at-home, and to hear the report on the KWSA's first quarter, had reason to congratulate themselves on the phenomenal amount which had been done. There was no chance of their being allowed to rest on their laurels. Plans were made "to hold more meetings in the winter and to continue in our present methods with re-doubled zeal," and members were reminded that "Our chief want is more workers. At present the work falls too heavily on a few shoulders. If everyone would undertake a small share we might achieve great things." To make sure that all felt able to take part, Catherine, as honorary secretary, spelled out "some of the ways in which help can be given by those who have not much time or money to spare," and suggestions were invited "as to new and more effective ways of working."[52]

In contrast to the slow pace of 1907, Catherine was now so fully occupied that it is almost a relief to find that she had managed to take a week off just before the KWSA at-home, for the usual Hawse End house party and week of activities, including the Manhunt, a tennis tournament, and a gymkhana – not exactly a restful week, but at least a change. Not that Catherine is likely to have forgotten the suffrage cause, even for that one week. A little time must surely have been spent on good-humoured instruction for the lighthearted Josie, whose admiration for Catherine's activities had prompted her to become involved, but had not motivated her to much serious study of the movement; she had written cheerfully a few weeks earlier: "I find I have joined two leagues, quite incompatible in tactics; the Freedom League, and the Social Union (I think). If the election comes I shall have to spend the morning breaking Mr. Asquith's windows, and the afternoon in declaring that our methods are entirely peaceful. We are going to have a meeting here, you know; at least I hope so, if father doesn't object."[53] Mercifully, the Marshalls had a good sense of humour, but surely Frank Marshall was off target when he decided that Josie lacked "frankness"; Josie carries conviction when she describes it as her "greatest weakness."[54]

Before her short September break, Catherine was already busy with the arrangements for a suffrage speaking tour of the region made in mid-October by no less a person than Millicent Garrett Fawcett. Catherine had represented the KWSA at the quarterly council of the NU on 14 July 1908 in Edinburgh, rushing off there immediately after the visit of the Newnham students. The autumn meeting was held at Leicester on 9 October, and KWSA was represented this time by Caroline Marshall and Minnie Broatch, another active member. Mrs Fawcett presumably came straight on from Leicester to Cumberland; she spoke at Kendal and Ambleside on 12 and 13 October, and then stayed with the Marshalls at Hawse End from 14–20 October, addressing meetings at Keswick, Workington, Maryport, and Cockermouth before going on to speak at York on 21 October. Catherine urged members "to come and hear her, and to make the meeting as widely known as possible."[55] The Keswick association had established unusually good relations with the local press, and Catherine made sure that the most was made of Fawcett's visit: "Mrs. Fawcett's speeches were fully reported in all the local papers, and in several of them (notably at Kendal) a spirited correspondence was opened on the Women's Suffrage question."[56]

Inspired by all this, three women made their way to Manchester in time to represent Keswick in the great women's suffrage demonstration there (23–24 October), where they "carried our banner, and the private one kindly lent by Mrs. John Marshall, in the Procession."[57] Meanwhile, the tour was followed up, in the Keswick area, by a canvass for new members, carried out by Catherine and a Mrs Knight. Kendal and Ambleside started their own societies. Catherine had made a conscious effort to encourage the formation of local committees to make arrangements for visiting speakers, such as the caravanners and Mrs Fawcett, rather than parachuting speakers in with outside support, because of her hope that local societies would emerge from these committees.[58] The Keswick group, however, was often able to provide experienced chairpersons and speakers when needed. Everything possible was also done to support the Penrith society, which was "the result of the energetic work of four local Suffragists ... who have shown a splendid example of zeal and perseverance in the face of much greater difficulties than we have had to contend against here." The Penrith group had also had "a very good friend in the Editor of the *Mid-Cumberland Herald*." Where such rapid advance could not be managed, at least a start was made, and Catherine reported that by early 1909 there were suffrage correspondents in all towns and most villages within twenty miles or so of Keswick, who were "organizing quietly and steadily with a view to the General Election."[59]

The reports of the KWSA's first year of operation express warm thanks to the men who have assisted in the work; when they are named, Frank Marshall's name is always among the leaders. By the end of a year, the organization had 250 members, of whom as many as 50 were men. The men seem to have been genuinely supportive and unassuming, making no attempt to hold office or dominate the women's organization, but ready to help in any way needed.[60]

The number of meetings held in one relatively lightly populated area may make one wonder not only at the industry of the suffrage workers but at the toleration of the audiences. In fact, the attendance at repeated suffrage meetings has to be ascribed in part to the lack of alternative amusement; and Catherine and her fellows were good at providing variety. Early in January 1909 they offered an entertaining evening of suffrage plays, performed by an informal group of women led by Isabella Ford, a long-time suffragist and labour organizer from Leeds, and an old friend of the Marshall family; the audience filled the largest hall in Keswick. The performers stayed at Hawse End, signing the guest book with names such as "Lady Bounder" and "Mrs. Fairly."[61]

The literature stall initiative continued to attract attention and emulation; Catherine was invited to give an account of the enterprise to a meeting of the London Women's Suffrage Association (LWSA) in November, and "it was also described in *Women's Franchise* and the *Queen* by an unknown correspondent." The idea was taken up widely, and won commendation in the annual report, at the annual NUWSS meeting of 27 January 1909. Indeed, the intense activity of the KWSA could not go unnoticed. Catherine's "Report on the lst nine months," submitted for inclusion in the NU annual report, was printed in full, and was the longest from any of the branches, not because of wordiness but because so much had been done.[62]

3 Broadening Support for Women's Suffrage in the North-West, January to November 1909

If the advance of the cause in Keswick was becoming known in suffrage circles, Keswick's reputation as a hotbed may also have attracted attention among those who were on the opposite side. The Women's National Anti-Suffrage League (WNASL) had held its inaugural meeting in London on 21 July 1908, and was now enjoying its most active period of recruitment and public meetings.[1] On 13 January 1909, less than a week after the successful evening of suffrage plays, the antisuffragists held a meeting in Keswick, featuring Mrs Somervell, one of the WNASL's leading speakers.[2] Catherine was present, and "listened with interest to the speeches." The next morning she composed a lengthy response, which was published in full in the *Mid-Cumberland Herald* on 16 January. In it, Catherine addresses the arguments of the speakers point by point rather than developing the positive suffrage position as she did in her speeches, but it is of considerable interest since it encapsulates some of the much-repeated arguments for and against enfranchising women.

The man who chaired the meeting had apparently made much of the fact that women were in a majority, and could therefore outvote men. Catherine countered this on principle and on practical grounds of its irrelevance: "Would he consider it justifiable in any other circumstances, I wonder, for the minority to say to the majority, 'You out-number us, therefore you must have no voice, or we might not be able to get our own way?' And do men really think that from the moment women get votes they will all be of one mind and vote the same way? Why, we are not even all agreed about wanting to have votes!" Where the chair had argued that the benefit of the community must take precedence over mere "justice," Catherine turned this upside down, maintaining that previous extensions had taken place on grounds of justice "and have re-acted for the benefit of the country as a whole, as any act of justice is bound to do."

Of more interest is Catherine's response to the argument "that the concession of the vote to women would necessarily carry with it the right to sit in Parliament." Officially, the NU at this period was careful to limit its demand quite strictly to the vote, and Catherine often began speeches by pointing out that suffragists were not asking for any further privileges. So she first addressed this point by citing the example of Norwegian women, who had gained the vote in 1907 without the right to sit in Parliament. Further, she said, even if a woman were admissible to Parliament, she would only gain entry if a (mixed) constituency wanted her to be their representative. For her own part, however, Catherine thought "that the admission of women to Parliament would come in time, simply because the men would demand their help in the ever-increasing domestic side of legislation, so that they themselves might be free to devote more of their time and attention to those larger Imperial affairs which we are told are peculiarly their province."[3]

Do we detect a note of irony in Catherine's concession to the separation of spheres? Later, certainly, she was to protest the exclusion of women from decisions of peace, war, and empire; at this stage she may not have thought through the implications. Or she may have decided there was no need to alarm the men. Whether this was a conscious strategy or not, the women's suffrage cause benefited from the women's own perception that they did not want to change their role, only to exercise it in the public sphere. How much of that sphere should still be left as men's undisputed territory was not under discussion, except when the issue was deliberately raised by antis such as Mrs Humphry Ward, who pointed out that the work of Parliament necessarily included the serious matters of foreign policy and defence, "where," she held, "men's experience alone provides the materials for judgment," as well as those considered appropriate to women.[4] Meanwhile, good use could be made of the absurdities of men legislating in matters where *they* had no claim to be the experts. "What more incongruous spectacle could you have than that of 600 men, sent to Parliament to safeguard the 'security of the Empire,' sitting in solemn debate over the various clauses of the Children's Bill, deciding what cribs babies should sleep in, and what kind of fender would best prevent children from falling into the fire?" asked Catherine, and continued, "It seems to me the men were distinctly trespassing on that 'woman's sphere' of which we hear so much when we ask to have a voice in these and similar matters. The antisuffragists entirely approve, they say, of women serving on local governing bodies which deal with internal affairs. But the laws relating to these internal affairs are only ADMINISTERED by the local bodies; they are MADE by Parliament. In the election of the law-MAKERS the women have no voice."

A common antisuffrage argument was that women could not spare the time to vote. Under the leadership of Mrs Humphry Ward, herself combining strenuous opposition to suffrage with local government work, the WNASL nevertheless encouraged women to take part in municipal affairs, seeing these as an appropriate extension of the domestic role. Somervell had made both these points, and Catherine jumped on the illogicality, and threw in a barb directed at the speaker, declaring, " local government work ... would make infinitely greater demands on their time than the duty of voting once every four or five years. ... Voting is not a profession, taking up several hours a day. It does not take most people nearly so long to vote as it took Mrs. Somervell to make her speech, yet a good many women had time to listen to her last night."[5]

While Catherine accepted that women had special qualities, worth preserving, these were not for her the attributes sentimentally wished on them by men. She continued caustically: "Our old friends, the 'pedestal,' 'shrine,' and 'bloom of womanhood' arguments made their appearance in one form or another in the course of the evening. We were warned that we should lose our most valuable qualities if we 'entered the field of politics.'" As she pointed out, "Women have been told, at different stages of their progress, that being educated, and earning their own living, and riding bicycles, would have this disastrous effect, yet there are women who do all these things without sacrificing any valuable womanly quality. Besides, are not local government matters politics? And what about the Primrose League and the Women's Liberal Federation, and the demand for women canvassers at election time? ... It is a little late in the day to talk about women 'entering into' politics."

As for Somervell's statement that "Upon the joint work of men and women the destiny of the country depends," Catherine declared herself prepared to take this for the motto of the women's suffrage movement, which was calling for complementarity in politics as elsewhere. Somervell also claimed that those demanding equality were confusing the women's movement with the women's suffrage movement. Catherine maintained that "the latter is but the logical outcome of the former." Improvements in education and job opportunities and the demand for their political support had all made it impossible to turn back the clock and now deny them the vote.

A Miss Hilton responded to Catherine's letter, and Catherine wrote again. A considerable part of the letter was taken up with the effect to be expected from women's numerical preponderance – in retrospect an absurd question, but one which much occupied the antisuffragists; Catherine was right to take it seriously. While she went to great lengths to demonstrate mathematically how small was the threat, her summary remark went to the kernel: "The antisuffragists' assumption that a majority of women would be disastrous means that they think men's wishes ought always to prevail over the wishes of women, whereas we hold that the only sure basis of just and good government is the consent of THE MAJORITY OF THOSE GOVERNED, irrespective of sex."

Catherine dealt more briefly with Hilton's other points, mostly just spelling out yet more clearly what she had said in her first letter. In particular, she denied the validity of any supposed "consultation" of women, for example by their appointment to Royal Commissions, since those appointed were "ONLY THOSE WOMEN WHOM THE MEN CHOOSE TO CONSULT," and concluded: "Besides, if this were a satisfactory way of being represented why not let it suffice for men as well, and do away with all the cumbersome and costly machinery of a House of Commons? If the Parliamentary vote does anything for those who possess it, then women are handicapped by not possessing it; if it does nothing for those who possess it, then there is a most unwarrantable waste of time and work and money at every election, and our whole system of government is based upon a sham."[6]

In this correspondence Catherine naturally makes use of the standard arguments used by suffragists. Nevertheless, there is a blend here of herself and her organization, and an intriguing blend too of liberal feminism and social feminism. Her arguments range comfortably from equal rights and justice to practical matters of how the law will mind the baby. She shows no sense of having to choose between arguments based on equal rights and arguments based on women's role as primary nurturer.[7]

Before January was out, Catherine had helped facilitate another important development in the Lake District, the formation of a local branch of the Men's League for Women's Suffrage. The umbrella organization had been in existence for nearly two years, offering support to all the women's suffrage societies, and attempting to raise voters' consciousness. Catherine, with Minnie Broatch, sent out a circular on 18 January to those they thought might be interested, inviting them to a special meeting convened by the KWSA, with an all-male platform of speakers. Frank Marshall chaired the meeting, which was well attended. Although some antisuffragists also turned up, supporters came in sufficient numbers to enable the inauguration of a Cumberland and Westmorland branch.[8]

At the end of January 1909, after one day of skating on Bassenthwaite Lake,[9] and even before she had finished dealing with the aftermath of the Keswick antisuffrage meeting, Catherine travelled to London to spend about two months on educational, recreational, and suffrage pursuits. She and her mother were members of the Sesame Club, a women's club which mounted an impressive series of lectures and debates annually on a range of subjects, including (in 1909) Socialism, Cosmic Consciousness, Taste and Morals, Ireland and Home Rule, Luxury and Happiness, Woman as Lawmaker.[10] An added attraction was that the Sesame Club was a gathering place for theosophists; Caroline appears to have had a long-standing connection with theosophy, and Catherine was also attracted. Annie Besant had been a guest at Hawse End in 1900.[11]

Catherine also went to dances and concerts; for the first week or two her parents were with her in London, and together they took advantage of everything that was on in the way of music.[12] But Catherine was not now likely to forget the suffrage movement, and kept in touch with what was going on both in London and in Cumberland. Although there are few details available of how she spent her time in London during this visit, it is probable that she became better acquainted with some of the leading suffragists of the NU, who had already taken notice of her strikingly effective work in the Keswick area. She and Caroline were also known to some as members of the London Society for Women's Suffrage (LSWS),[13] whose meetings she may have attended when she was in London.

Suffrage activity in London was intensifying, and here, too, the antisuffragists were trying to muster support. The WNASL held a big rally at the Queen's Hall on 26 March 1909. Catherine asked Jermyn Moorsom, then in London, to go with her, and they planned to dine together first. As it turned out, Jermyn fell ill and had to cancel the engagement, making new plans to meet her for dinner at a later date, and talk "an hour of suffrage at least, besides quite different things. I see so few people – thro' my own fault I know – that when you who are in the middle of everything, come to see me, I feel like a backwater which has remained stagnant and sullen by itself, suddenly stirred into life by an outlet from the main stream."[14] Jermyn or no Jermyn, Catherine, along with many fellow-suffragists, apparently attended the rally. Unfortunately, she left no account, but it was probably there that she picked up an impressive collection of antisuffrage pamphlets, which remain among her papers.

As the strength of the WNASL grew, more women were persuaded to speak publicly against women's involvement in public life, and antisuffrage meetings became a commonplace all over the country.[15] The suffragists claimed that they were not much worried: Edith How-Martyn wrote in 1909, "If they only come out to say they don't want a vote, still they have come out, and their further progress is only a question of time."[16] Catherine expressed relief rather than alarm, writing: "Whilst we are thanking those who have rendered good service to the cause, we must not forget to mention our friend the enemy – the Anti-Suffragists. Their meetings no less than ours, have helped to educate public opinion on this question, and have brought us in many new members."[17]

At the beginning of April, just before leaving London, Catherine attended Mrs Fawcett's at-home, given for Mrs Chapman Catt,[18] the United States suffrage leader, who was in London for a meeting of the IWSA later in the month. Before going back to Hawse End, she took a short holiday, first visiting Birmingham to help her friend Margaret Hirst with the proofreading of her first book.[19] During her brief two-day visit she also walked around Bournville (the Cadburys' new model village outside the city), and fitted in a visit to the cathedral "to see Burne Jones windows (lovely colour) and Art Gallery (not much)," before lunching with Emily Gardner, secretary of the Birmingham and Midlands Women's Suffrage Society,[20] probably to share thoughts on NU regional organization which would bear fruit later.

Catherine went from Birmingham to York to spend a pleasant few days with her brother, sightseeing and walking in the surrounding countryside during the day, often making music together or with friends in the evening, and on one occasion attending a dance. Exceptionally, Catherine kept a diary from time to time during this year (or, rather, made notes in her date book), and short as the entries are, they give something of the flavour of her enjoyment, particularly of the countryside. On 9 April, for example, they "Took lunch to Rivaulx Abbey, then up valley to Old Byland, and across moor to Hambledon and Sutton Bank, getting lovely view over edge westward. Home by Rivaulx: abt. 20 miles. Lovely – but very footsore."[21] They were blessed with good weather almost every day; but it was, after all, April. When the showers came they were undeterred, and on one wet morning, even "ran with [the hounds] for 1 ½ hours through Duncombe Park," afterwards eating "wet sandwiches in [a] cottage porch," and later driving back by pony-cart in a "gorgeous sunset".[22]

For several days of the holiday they were joined by Jermyn Moorsom. Catherine and he were good friends during this time; as we have seen, he sometimes accompanied her to concerts, meetings, and lectures[23] when she was in London, and they corresponded with some regularity, recommending books to each other and commenting on those they had read, sometimes disagreeing. Among the books they discussed that year was George Gissing's *The Odd Women*, for which Jermyn was unable to share Catherine's enthusiasm; his first reaction was that "It preaches the gospel it has to preach quite adequately but I confess I found the sermon rather long." Later he wrote again, commenting, with a prejudice and elitism of which he was clearly unconscious: "I expect you liked it because of the contribution it makes towards the cause, also because you have enough sympathy to spare for the strange half-diseased one-sided people it describes, who only depress me by their poverty."[24] Urged on by both Catherine and Caroline, Jermyn read E.M. Forster's *A Room with a View* (published the previous year) not once but twice, and on second reading agreed that "I must say I do think it amazingly good this time." Catherine had also sent him Charlotte Perkins Gilman's *Women and Economics*, on which we do not have his comments.[25]

If not as active in the suffrage movement as Catherine might have wished, Jermyn at least took it seriously, and they clearly found many topics of common interest. In part, perhaps she was bent on educating him – after all, his parents were among the most noted antisuffragists in the Keswick area – but by now she surely found him an enjoyable and even a stimulating companion, and even the education was two-way, as he was determined to have her share his devotion to the works of Turgenev.[26] During his few days with them on this holiday, her diary records evenings spent in talk as well as in music, and when she and he walked for a whole day alone together, they took time out in the middle of the day to sit about and talk.[27]

For his part, Jermyn undoubtedly needed Catherine's friendship. Although he and Josie had never been engaged, he was deeply fond of her, probably more close to being in love with her than she had been with him, and the Marshalls had long been in his confidence.[28] Malcolm had gone out to India, where Josie had followed him; they were now engaged and planned to be married in July. "They have been extraordinarily happy and miserable by turns," wrote Jermyn. "... It is very strange to see so closely into 2 other people's lives: rather overpowering."[29] Since it had always been understood (at least by Josie) that she and Jermyn would not marry,[30] no one saw this as breaking up the friendship, and indeed Jermyn continued to spend some time with his friends during the weeks leading up to the wedding;[31] it may have been harder for him than the exuberant Josie was equipped to understand.

On 15 April, it was time for Catherine to catch the afternoon train back to Keswick, travelling on another "gorgeous day," with "beautiful views all across [the] moors."[32] She came home refreshed and full of good spirits, to take up what had now become a very full and purposeful life. She seems to have been well in body at this time, delighting in the long walks of her holiday and of her daily life in the Newlands valley.

Despite her increasing involvement in the suffrage movement, as long as Catherine remained based at Hawse End, she kept up her other activities in the neighbourhood. Teaching singing at the little Newlands School and now at Braithwaite School as well was a serious commitment. As soon as she came home she was much occupied with preparation for and participation in a music festival, helping at both valley schools with their final practices, and even going to Keswick one evening "to help Mr. Burnett's choir in last rehearsal," and coming back to Hawse End across the lake at 10 p.m., when it was very dark, and the boat "ran aground 3 times in Lingholme woods!"[33]

As spring turned into early summer, social occasions multiplied, with tennis parties and many visitors at Hawse End. The wedding of Josie and Malcolm was planned for mid-July, although it does not seem that Catherine was expecting to travel to Josie's home at Berwick for it. But sad news came from Jermyn. Tragically, the unnamed fourth friend "in our quartet with Josie and Malcolm," about whom we know much less and who never seems to have been well known to Catherine, committed suicide a few days before the wedding, even though he had been with the others "every day in London and was coming to the wedding."[34]

Catherine's social life becomes increasingly difficult to separate from her suffrage life; the names of family and old friends take turns (or blend) in her date book and in the Hawse End guest book with the names of known suffrage activists, both local and national.[35] Much activity was planned for the summer. Meanwhile, at the end of April 1909, Lloyd George had introduced his famous budget, which was to start the chain of events leading to reform of the House of Lords, and presenting both difficulties and opportunities for the women's suffragists, and we can be sure this too was much discussed.

Led by Catherine, the KWSA, once established, committed itself to outreach throughout the whole region, far beyond Keswick and the immediate vicinity. On 2 June 1909, for instance, Catherine spoke at a meeting of about forty at Carlisle, which was shortly followed by the formation of a local women's suffrage society, affiliated to the NU.[36] On this occasion, speaking presumably to an audience of the converted, Catherine laid out many of the same arguments she used with her outdoor audiences, but her notes (although bearing every sign of having been written, as they often were, at top speed) show a particularly careful and systematic organization which may have been designed in part to make the material useful to other beginning speakers, and probably also reflects her own developing sophistication as a speaker. Her main headings were "What we want," "Why we want it," and "How we are trying to get it." The subheadings under "Why we want it" provide a splendid example of the harmonious blending of pragmatic feminism, equal-rights feminism, and social feminism; Catherine stressed equally, with examples, "Women's *need* of the vote," "Women's *right* to vote" (coupling this with "*fitness* to vote"), and "Women's *duty* to vote."[37]

Catherine corresponded regularly with supporters in a number of communities, including the industrial towns and ports of West Cumberland, and tried to keep closely in touch with the other vigorous young societies now active in Cumberland and Westmorland; Ambleside and Penrith rivalled Keswick in their level of activity. Always on the lookout for ways of providing varied fare and continuing stimulation for suffragists and potential converts in the area, Catherine wrote to the *Common Cause* in June appealing to any "keen Suffragists" who might be planning a visit to Cumberland to "combine a pleasant holiday with a useful piece of work for the cause," by volunteering to help collect information or to speak at village meetings, where they were promised varied audiences, made up of ironworkers, colliers, farmers, or summer visitors.[38] At the KWSA quarterly general committee meeting on 24 June, Catherine, as honorary organizing secretary, announced a wide range of coming events, extending through the summer and into the autumn.[39]

The most immediate of these, following shortly after the meeting, was a Cumberland women's suffrage "Special Effort," focusing particularly on Whitehaven, Workington, and Maryport, for which the main speakers were Isabella Ford and the same Ray Costelloe who had been such a success with the caravan the previous summer.[40] They must have formed an interesting and delightful pair. Ray Costelloe was twenty-two, definitely middle-class, but from a far from typical background. Her mother was American, now married to the art critic, Bernhard Berenson. When not at Oxford, Ray called Florence home, and she had also travelled in the western United States, and had spoken on women's suffrage in women's colleges in the eastern United States. She had taken the maths tripos at Newnham, and had also spent time at Bryn Mawr. She had published a novel called *The World at Eighteen,* and had attended the International Women's Suffrage Congress in Amsterdam in 1907. In response to Catherine's request for autobiographical notes, she provided all this information, adding, perhaps a little disingenuously, "I'm afraid there really isn't anything very spicey[sic] to tell you. I haven't been married secretly or otherwise, and I haven't had any thrilling adventures."[41] Isabella Ford, although much in demand as a speaker, also kept no formal autobiographical notes handy, and responded to Catherine's request as spontaneously as did Ray. She did not specify her age (which was fifty-four), but said "I don't know *when* I first began on w.s. ... many years [ago], and before it was in fashion." She was "and always [had] been" a parish councillor, and was a life member of the Leeds Trade Council. She had been in France, Germany, Italy, Switzerland, and Belgium examining the wages of women textile workers and speaking. She had written pamphlets on work, wages, and suffrage, and had been continually active in union concerns in the Leeds area. "The strikes I've been in had better be ignored!! ... Say anything probable! for there's nothing to say – Only I'm quite a delightful person??!"[42] Although herself from a middle-class background, Isabella Ford had been active in labour struggles since 1891, when she supported a mill girls' strike in Bradford.[43] Great as might be the differences of age and background between these two, they had a good deal in common. But while years of working together would only strengthen the warmth and respect between Catherine and Isabella, Catherine and Ray were later to have serious differences.

The outdoor campaign in the rather rough areas of the Whitehaven and Cockermouth constituencies was not expected to be any summer picnic, particularly in light of the antagonism currently being roused by the militants. Catherine prepared the ground with her usual thoroughness. She wrote to Miss Catharine Pattinson in Whitehaven, asking her to take on the task of divisional secretary for the NU, and requesting a lot of local details which would be of use in the coming campaign. Catherine's letter has not been preserved, but Pattinson's reply has, and is a sharp reminder of some of the difficulties suffragists laboured under, as well as of the extraordinary amount of detailed work that went into making a success of this kind of drive. She agrees to take on the job of divisional secretary, as long as it "can be done chiefly by writing." She regrets that she "cannot be present even at the Whitehaven meetings." She will be "tied ... for the next half-year," since both her sisters will be away, and "my mother and I will be alone until November. As she is not strong, you will understand that I cannot undertake anything that will necessitate my leaving home."

Catharine Pattinson followed her regrets with ten pages of invaluable information on the best times and places to hold open-air meetings, rooms that might be available for indoor meetings, suitable accommodation for the speaking party, market days, early closing afternoons, location of the two coal mines which form the main industry, a warning that the miners work shifts round the clock and do not leave the mines for "the dinner hour" (but those on night work might be attracted, as they "spend a good deal of their time standing at the street corners"), names and locations of the other industries (tanning, a mill, and a timber yard). There are, she says, no factories where women work, so the time of day will make little difference to them, but meetings should not go on too late at night. The market place is a good location in that it is close to the miners' cottages, but it is also near the docks, so "very likely ... there will be some very rowdy characters." Her brother, John Pattinson, owns the mill, and might permit a meeting in the yard there, though she does not believe he will agree to chair one, as "I don't think he is sufficiently worked up to the point, yet. I hope he may later." Miss Pattinson also warned Catherine that Whitehaven was a difficult place in which to keep anything going for more than a short time.[44]

Clearly, there was no strong core in Whitehaven of the already converted, who could be counted on for support and assistance. Catherine's preparations included sending notices to all the local papers, spending two days in the area the week before, and, on the day of the first meeting, personally "distributing handbills (the only form of advertisement we could afford) and getting into talk with the groups of men and women who usually congregate at street corners during the dinner-hour."[45] Her notice to the papers had been accompanied by a letter "explaining the aims and methods of the National Union,"[46] and taking great care to emphasize its respectable history and adherence to constitutional methods, and to dissociate it from "recent disturbances at Westminster, ... the breaking of Ministers' windows, [and] the interruption of Public Meetings."[47]

Catherine sent notices of the coming meetings to influential people whose help she hoped to enlist, or whose opposition she at least hoped to disarm by making sure they were forewarned. The mayor

of Whitehaven expected to be away at the time of the meetings, and
wrote, "I sincerely hope they may not give rise to disturbance or
breach of the peace. The extraordinary and unlawful antics of the
militant suffragettes whose procedure I am glad to observe you dis-
own, have brought the cause of 'Votes for Women' into contempt
and derision and there is always a risk of disorder, out of pure mischief, when meetings in support of the movement are being held."
For himself, he added, he favoured women's suffrage, which he
thought would come in when there was a Unionist government.[48] A
factory owner in Seascale named Herbert Walker notified Catherine
that he had sent the circulars out in his works, adding that he
thought the meeting would be crowded, and hoped it would be
quiet, "as you have chosen a stand dangerously near the docks. I am
glad that your society is proceeding along constitutional lines, there
is no doubt as to the equity of your cause."[49]

Overall, the campaign was declared "a triumphant success." Catherine wrote a full account for the *Common Cause*, which documents
the success, but in passing also shows that such successes were not
lightly won. Catherine describes the first meeting, timed for 7:30,
down by the docks:

At seven o'clock Miss Ford and Miss Costelloe, who were motoring from
Leeds, had not arrived, so I hired a lorry and walked through the town,
carrying the Keswick banner, a forlorn little procession of one, accompanied
by a rabble of small boys and a shower of banana skins and other unpleasant
but harmless missiles (why do small boys always seem to have an inexhaust-
ible supply of such ammunition in their pockets?). Miss Bendelack, who had
come over from Keswick by a later train, met me at the scene of action, and
together we mounted the lorry at 7:30. The street was packed with a dense
crowd of people. I spoke for an hour to a delightfully attentive and responsive audience, then I had to close the meeting, as my voice gave out, and the
motor had not appeared. For the next twenty minutes the lorry was be-
sieged by eager purchasers of literature and badges, and we sold out our
whole stock. The small boys who had begun by throwing banana skins made
honourable amends now by helping us to sell the literature and offering to
carry our banner. One boy, John Clifford by name, had befriended us from
the first, before we became popular, and had held our banner for us gal-
lantly all through the meeting. So we appointed him our standard-bearer,
and he turned up to perform that office at all our subsequent meetings in
Whitehaven. Miss Ford and Miss Costelloe arrived about ten o'clock, wet
through and hungry, having had various misadventures by the way.

During the next three days they held a further ten meetings;
Catherine's account shows the variety of settings and the mixed au-

diences to be expected. After a mid-day meeting in the Whitehaven Market place, they held another meeting at the other end of the town later in the afternoon, to catch the workers at the mills and coal-pits, who changed shifts at two o'clock. "We again had a large and interested audience, with a fringe of private carriages," Catherine reported. "Several people stayed to talk and ask questions afterwards, including the Conservative candidate for the division. In the evening we motored to Maryport, where we addressed a big crowd down on the quay-side. We arrived late, but the moment our motor appeared people came hurrying from all directions, like minnows after a bit of bread, and we were able to start our meeting at once. We had decorated the motor (Miss Costelloe's car, which she drives herself) with red and white ribbons, and hung a blackboard on at the back with the time and place of the next meeting chalked upon it. We found it an excellent advertisement; we were soon known by sight in all the neighbouring villages."

The following day took them to Workington; their mid-day meeting was not large ("about 100, perhaps") because one of the ironworks was closed and the other not fully operational – also, it rained. Caroline Marshall and another KWSA member joined them for the afternoon gathering, held "in the heart of the town. We were told afterwards that the pick of the working-men of the town had been there. They were keenly interested, and stood about in groups afterwards discussing the speeches." The interest raised led to word being passed around, and a far bigger audience than anticipated turned up for the evening meeting. Since the weather was so bad, they had taken the only room available, although it was one of the largest halls in the town, and they did not expect to be able to fill it. In fact, it was packed and they were told "that several hundred people had had to go away disappointed." Ray and Catherine spoke briefly, and Isabella Ford "made a stirring and impassioned speech, dealing with all the most serious aspects of the question. The audience was deeply moved, and listened for fifty minutes in breathless silence, except for the outbursts of applause that followed the speaker's most telling points." Catherine too was moved, declaring, "I shall never forget the look of those earnest faces, many of them showing signs of want and suffering, for times are bad in Workington, and many a worthy citizen has lost his vote through having to go on the rates to get food for his starving children. We moved a resolution to send up a petition to Parliament to grant Women's Suffrage; it was seconded by a man in the audience and carried, with only three dissentients. I think everyone in that large audience voted." After a question period, at which "a number of sympathetic and intelligent questions were handed in," the meeting broke up at about 9:30, but "the audience begged us to take the room again the following night, with the partition removed to allow more room, and undertook to fill it. We returned home in a very happy frame of mind." Four meetings were held the following day, including the return visit to Whitehaven, which was again packed (as promised). Everywhere the speakers found the crowd sympathetic and almost unanimous in support of the women's suffrage resolution.[50]

The factory owner, Herbert Walker, however, wrote again in August, in response to a request for funds, but this time with a sour note, which may have had something to do with the reception given to Isabella Ford, who was after all a noted socialist and trade unionist as well as a suffragist. He wrote nastily of "your lack of the precious metal which is unfortunately for you mostly to be found in masculine keeping. Speaking for myself I am not disposed to help you in this way because, while nobody can say there is not equity in your cause, still you want more than I think you ought to have and I should rather you have nothing than get what you want." The suffragists could not expect to please everybody, and even Walker congratulated Catherine "on your own great success when left alone by your fellow workers. I ... have heard golden accounts."[51]

Not only did visiting speakers provide variety and make it possible to meet the special needs of certain areas, but working alongside other suffrage women gave Catherine a wonderful opportunity to widen her own understanding. Never a slow learner, she had doubtless learnt a great deal about the suffrage issue during Millicent Fawcett's visit the previous fall, and she could have had no better tutor than Isabella Ford in the process of developing the links between labour and suffrage.

The suffrage struggle was taking place against a tense political background, giving rise to complex cross-currents. The women's cause had a very low priority for Asquith, and yet his remarks in May 1908, as we have seen, had reinforced the need for a big campaign which would draw in support from both men and women. Indeed, much of the activity of the women's suffrage movement, from at least mid-1908, can be seen as a conscious response to Asquith's demand for proof of widespread support.[52] Further, his promise of a move towards reform of the male franchise had persuaded some suffragists that the best hope lay in working for adult suffrage, while convincing many others the biggest threat was manhood suffrage. The government's continuing official indifference to women's suffrage, despite the favourable parliamentary majority, posed serious questions as to whether women's suffragists should now regard the

Liberal party, from which so much had been hoped, as the prime enemy, or merely as a temporarily delinquent friend and still the best
hope there was. Relations with the Liberal party were further complicated by the constitutional problems which were rapidly escalating to crisis level as the Conservative House of Lords rejected one
after another of the Liberal government's reform measures.

All these elements in the situation elicited responses from the
women's suffrage organizations, and defined the landscape in which
the struggle would take place. Catherine's work can be seen as an integral part of those responses. Her campaign in Cumberland was
not simply an attempt to get more supporters but to develop the relationship between women's suffrage and fundamental social issues.
Further, she was keeping very closely in touch with NU policies.

If the goals of the NU were to build membership, multiply
branches, bring the suffrage issue before the public, deepen constituency work, make use of by-elections, and begin preparation for the
next general election, Catherine's activities could, and in some instances did, serve as a model of ways to work towards these goals.
Late in May 1909, the *Common Cause* began a series of articles under
the general heading "The Compleat Organizer" on such topics as
"Getting up a meeting," "Open Air Meetings," "The Young Society,"
the functions of officers in a branch, and so on. On nearly every subject, Catherine had already had considerable experience by the middle of 1909, and was herself frequently consulted, especially after
the triumphant first annual report of the KWSA. At about this time,
too, in a move which surely met with Catherine's approval, the NU
provided notebooks to divisional secretaries, in which detailed information was to be recorded on everything that could be of use to electoral organizers – including names and views of local worthies as
well as of MPs and previously unsuccessful candidates, attitudes of
the clergy, strength of political clubs, suitable accommodation, transport facilities, the nature of occupations in the area, major and
minor industries, factory shifts and public house hours, suitable
halls and outdoor sites, possible locations for campaign offices,
names of local newspapers, editors and their suffrage views, and
much more.[53]

Catherine's Cumberland campaign also bears looking at in relation to the adult suffrage question. Sandra Holton's illuminating
work [54] shows that the issue was indeed a crucial one, but that there
was more than one possible approach to it. Briefly, women's suffrage
could possibly be attained through adult suffrage, but at the risk
(variously estimated) of a final stop at manhood suffrage: or adult
suffrage could be brought nearer through a thoroughly broad-

based campaign for women's suffrage. As Mrs Fawcett was fond of pointing out, no general popular agitation was going on for the extension of the franchise to the many men still without the vote, and there was no logical reason for the women to hold back until this developed, still less to merge (or submerge) their cause in the wider claim, and take the time and energy from their own campaign for this work.[55]

Even Margaret Llewelyn Davies, moving spirit of the People's Suffrage Federation (PSF), admitted that it would be a long process to create a visible widespread demand for universal suffrage. However, PSF leaders saw adult suffrage as the principled route to a democratic franchise, and because of the fear among Liberals, including some of the most influential, that the "as is or may be" formula would work to Unionist party advantage, they thought it the soundest strategy. Adultists tended to view women's suffragists as selfish proponents of a propertied vote. Some may have been – indeed some few of the more conservative certainly had no mind for a truly democratic franchise. Bertrand Russell commented caustically (in a private letter) that "Women who merely want to be among the oppressors rather than among the oppressed don't seem to me to be worthy of much sympathy." He wrote this in 1907, when he was still on the NU executive, and while he still held that "it seems plain that Adult Suffrage can only be got after a tremendous agitation, extending over many years." If there was any truth in his description of the NU at that time as "largely undemocratic,"[56] it was to prove itself within a few years capable of remarkable change and great effectiveness, by which time Russell had left the NU for the new People's Suffrage Federation. The changes would be carried forward by exactly the kind of work that Catherine was now initiating.

When Catherine in her speeches dismissed adult suffrage as a separate question from that of the women's vote, she was following the line officially blessed by the NU, but the whole direction of her work in Cumberland shows that, from the start, she was not interested in a suffrage campaign that would take place only in drawing rooms, and benefit only well-to-do women. When the KWSA was formed, it was indeed initiated by "a few ladies,"[57] meeting at Hawse End. Undoubtedly there were branches which not only began but continued in this way, but Catherine's energetic and innovative work was directed towards bringing the women's suffrage issue before all sections of the population, and those she soon had working for the cause throughout the surrounding area included many working women, as well as addressing both male and female workers.

Even if the women free to give most time to the KWSA were still middle class, the appeal, and the ground of that appeal, were moving into a much wider sphere. Holton has shown the significance of the emergence of "democratic suffragism" as an educative force which would eventually make possible the essential link between the struggles for the removal of disfranchisement on the grounds of lack of property and on the grounds of failure to be born male. Holton has taken her examples primarily from Edinburgh, Manchester, and Newcastle, all places where there was a more developed labour consciousness and Labour party activity.[58] Catherine's work in Cumberland at this early period was more diffuse, and without a specific political Labour orientation; in any event, she was not yet ready to pull up her own roots in the Liberal party. The official non-party stance of the NUWSS also helped postpone the resolution of any personal doubts which may have arisen. But what she was doing was important, moving both herself and her constituents towards linking the women's cause with that of the workers.

In the long run, democratic suffragism was to prove the way around both the simplistic overconfidence in principled Liberalism shown by such as Bertrand Russell and the excessive rigidity of Millicent Fawcett, who, excusably but unconstructively, may have continued too long to regard any suggestion of a wider franchise as part of a sinister plot to sabotage the women's claim (as indeed, it was on occasion). However, she too came to embrace a democratic franchise within a few years, if with some reservations.[59]

As for the attitude to be taken towards the Liberal party, this was a knotty question for the NU, whose nonparty stance had never effectively concealed the fact that the majority of its members were devoted Liberals, like the Marshalls. Liberal connections were particularly predominant among the leadership and in the south.[60] The WSPU leadership was perhaps more genuinely free from party interest (and therefore, some would say, more able to be single-minded on the suffrage issue) than the NU. The Pankhursts and their organization had come from socialist beginnings, but had now dropped the connection and had indeed alienated much (not all) of their working-class and Labour support.[61] They had identified the government in power as the villain, and took the view that all Liberal MPs must be held responsible, no matter what their personal opinions or their voting records. Accordingly, the WSPU by-election policy was to oppose all Liberal candidates, who "must be made to suffer for the sins of the government they support."[62] They did not question candidates of any party as to their views on suffrage, and

would support an antisuffragist against a suffragist, just as long as
the latter stood for the Liberal party. They claimed that this was consistent with a nonparty stance because, were the Liberal government
to be replaced by a Unionist government with an equally unsatisfactory record and approach, it would receive the same treatment.[63]
This policy did not necessitate any long-term involvement in constituencies, and WSPU headquarters often parachuted their most aggressive speakers and hecklers into a by-election at short notice, not
always to the satisfaction of the local affiliate, which may have had a
less simple approach.[64]

Helena Swanwick held that "work at by-elections, and the organizing of constituencies in view of elections should take precedence of
all other work undertaken by the N.U.,"[65] and indeed the NU took
constituency work increasingly seriously, seeing by-elections as a
forum for educating the public, challenging party positions, bringing pressure to bear on the government, and sustaining a committed
majority for suffrage in the House of Commons. Behind this, too,
was the knowledge that the next general election, whenever it
should come, might be critical.

Formulation of a policy to pursue was more complex. The weight
of Liberal members in the NU surely played a part in a certain le-
nience towards any Liberal candidate or MP who showed even a
small measure of sympathy for the suffrage cause, but it may be unfair to regard this as solely partisan; the attitude of encouragement
rather than confrontation is consistent with an overall commitment
to win the way by argument and reason, combined with the use of
sanctioned forms of political pressure. The NU policy had far more
riders and provisions for contingencies than the simple WSPU policy
outlined above, and whenever a by-election was called, a decision
had to be made on the action to be taken. In addition, every council
meeting saw challenges and modifications to policy in response to
the political situation. In October 1908, the NU defined its policy, in
a leaflet which also set out that of the WSPU for comparison. The NU's
guiding principles were defined as follows: *"Broadly speaking,* it takes
one of three courses: – (a) It either runs a Women's Suffrage Candidate of its own; or (b) It supports the Candidate who declares himself the best friend to the cause of Women's Suffrage; or (c) Where
all the Candidates are equally favourable or unfavourable, it takes
no side; but does propaganda work in the constituency throughout
the bye-election." The leaflet spells out the details: support for a candidate will depend on satisfactory answers to questions, a commitment to women's suffrage in his election address, and his record.
Prominent antis may be opposed even if other candidates are not en-

tirely satisfactory; established friends may be supported even against others whose answers are satisfactory, except where both are proven friends of women's suffrage.[66]

These policy decisions provided the background to Catherine's work for suffrage. As she gained in experience, she also began to think of ways in which the NU's operation could be made more efficient; she had a flair for comprehending the larger setting, however busy she might be with the details of day-to-day organization. Although the new constitution of 1907 had given the NU a democratic structure, the immense expansion of the succeeding two years had brought problems of its own. Much vital work was taking place at the periphery. New societies like the KWSA did not look to the London headquarters to help them do their day-to-day organizing – and the London office would have had to disappoint them if they had. There are hints, too, that despite infusions of fresh blood – notably Helena Swanwick and Kathleen Courtney – the old guard on the executive was perceived as finding it difficult to keep up to the pace of change, and as possibly being too much dominated by the people and the drawing-room methods of the LSWS. Blaming Mrs Fawcett – perhaps unjustly – Margaret Llewelyn Davies commented on what she saw as her "teap[arty] view," although conceding that it might be "useful as a reassuring element to the backward."[67]

The 1907 constitution was effective in enabling the NU to define a uniform policy and to present a united and consistent front, but was of less use on the organizational side. A multiplicity of small and expanding societies all running campaigns around the same time with no structure for coordinating their efforts was inevitably inefficient in some respects. This had come home sharply to Catherine when she discovered that "a well-known speaker" had been booked by one society for July, by another, "not thirty miles away," for October, and that a third society "within 20 miles of both of them wanted the same speaker also, but could not fit in with either of the dates chosen."[68] Before the quarterly meeting of the KWSA general committee on 24 June 1909, Catherine drew up a resolution to be sent in for inclusion on the agenda of the NU council meeting to be held at Nottingham in July, reading: "That local branches of the Nat. Union be encouraged to form groups according to Counties, or other convenient geographical boundaries, for the purpose of cooperating in the organization of public meetings, so that full advantage may be taken of the visit of any well-known speaker in the neighbourhood."[69] Moving the resolution at Nottingham, Catherine's two main lines of argument were "economy of *money within societies*, and what is even more important still, economy of the *time and*

strength of speakers. "She said that there need be no elaborate multipli-
cation of machinery, and suggested a simple way of operating. She
spoke "from the Organizer's point of view," and the resolution was
seconded by Isabella Ford, "from the point of view of the speaker."[70]

The Keswick resolution, which was carried, was the first step in a
move towards decentralization in the NU. The Birmingham society
had also brought a resolution to Nottingham, suggesting that
thought should be given to the institution of divisional councils.[71]
Although Catherine had urged the merits of her scheme on grounds
of its simplicity, as against the "serious constitutional and legislative
changes" involved in the Birmingham scheme, she may privately
have seen it, without dismay, as opening the door to a further move
in that direction. When those changes came the following year, she
and Emily Gardner of Birmingham seem to have been in agreement. Meanwhile, after further discussion at the next quarterly in
October, a committee representative of the executive and of all regions was to be set up to study the Birmingham scheme.[72]

The energetic campaign in Cumberland continued unabated after
the Nottingham success and the visit of Isabella Ford and Ray
Costelloe. Catherine had a number of enthusiastic women helping
her by this time, but there can be little doubt that the driving force
came from her. August was a relatively quiet month, with Catherine
taking her turn a couple of times at the suffrage stall in Keswick
market, and spending a good deal of time with house guests at
Hawse End, while making and remaking arrangements for September, which was another month full of suffrage events. When the illness of an expected speaker forced a postponement of a planned
campaign in the Egremont division, Catherine and other speakers,
mostly local, rapidly substituted a local mini-campaign, with the aid
of a Liverpool suffragist who had responded[73] to an offer of a bun-
galow "in private grounds," with "beautiful views of the surrounding
mountains," and board and attendance at a moderate cost, which
was offered to any "party of Suffragists who would help us out" by
speaking.[74] The main focus for the month was a series of open-air
"village meetings," including two or three in small hamlets in the
Newlands Valley itself, where there really were no villages (except
for Braithwaite at the entrance to the valley), and ranging over the
neighbouring valleys of Borrowdale and Patterdale. Accounts of
these meetings indicate the usual careful preparation, with attention
paid to the nature of the particular audience, and each speaker
agreeing to put the emphasis on a particular angle, to avoid duplica-
tion. The KWSA had been making its presence felt for just over a

year, yet good audiences still turned up – helped perhaps by the presence at most meetings of a small but vocal opposition.[75]

Hearing, at rather short notice, that a revision court was to meet in Keswick to hear claims for inclusion on the parliamentary register, the KWSA seized the opportunity to make their point in another way. Fourteen KWSA members, women householders, sent in claims "to have their names placed in the Parliamentary register," and the number "would have been much larger if there had been more time to organise." When the revision court was held on 22 September, Catherine appeared as "Agent" for the women claimants. "The Revising Barrister," the *Common Cause* reported, "courteously allowed her to state the grounds on which the claim was made," and gave at her request, and at length, "the legal grounds on which the exclusion of duly qualified women is justified. The question was treated seriously throughout. The claimants were given seats on the magistrates' bench, and Miss Marshall was invited to take her place between the Conservative and Liberal agents – beautifully typical of our non-party attitude! The Revising Barrister complimented the claimants on the 'dignity and ability' with which the claim had been preferred and supported. The local papers have all commented favourably on the proceedings, and most of them ... have reported the speeches of Miss Marshall and the Revising Barrister verbatim."[76]

Suffrage meetings of various kinds continued throughout the early part of October; Catherine noted in her date book those which she attended, including one addressed by her father at Carlisle on 7 October, and others at Penrith, Keswick, and Rochdale during the next few days, but we have few details. She does not seem to have gone to the NU quarterly held in Cardiff at the beginning of the month. The regular winter season activities were starting again in the Newlands Valley, and she was giving singing classes at two schools. She appears also to have been going to extension lectures, but where or on what subject we do not know. For exercise (besides all the walking around the valley that her various commitments must have entailed), she hoped to play hockey every Saturday.[77]

An imaginative suffrage venture was a discussion or speakers' group, which got off to a challenging start on 2 November, when Catherine and her mother and two other women went as "Antis," role playing the attitudes they found typical among suffrage opponents. "Mrs. Noble" took the view that women had "much higher duties than voting"; "Mrs. Earnest" held that women's suffrage would increase divorce and other evils; "Mrs. Gushington," played by Caroline, was "flighty and inconsequent," bothered by the way men said they would "miss our influence dreadfully," refusing to keep to the point and declaring herself "quite unshaken by logic, because her opinion is based on a 'deep feeling.'" Catherine's own role must have been a show-stopper; she went as "Miss Blandish," claiming that influence was a much higher ideal than conversion, and that the "Helplessness of women appeals to men, and calls out their chivalry," that it was good for women to be helpless, as this obliges them to cultivate tact, and so on. The presentation was sprung on the rest of the class without warning, and it was their task to try to convert the determined "antis" who confronted them.[78]

Catherine thought she herself could still do with practice. As the new season got under way she was "overwhelmed ... with demands to go and speak," but rather surprisingly, she wrote: "I do wish we had a really good speaker up here. I am improving, but it is a great effort to me and costs me dear in nerves. However apparently that does not show, as I find people are convinced I enjoy it!"[79]

The winter of 1909–10 was to prove strenuous for the suffragists, even more so than they could have foreseen. Meanwhile, Catherine spent a pleasant few days at Cambridge in early November with her father, visiting at Trinity College, where the master of Trinity was H. Montagu Butler, who had been headmaster of Harrow when Frank first went to teach there, and whose family had been close personal friends of the Marshalls ever since. Catherine had often stayed there, and the Butlers visited Hawse End from time to time, and had been there for a few days the previous summer.[80] Frank went straight home from Cambridge, and Catherine went on to London, where she visited with relatives, watched the Lord Mayor's Show, went to art galleries and lectures, and met with Jermyn – who felt it would be a waste to go to the theatre with her "when we might be talking." In spite of all this social activity, much of Catherine's brief time in London was taken up with suffrage contacts; she met several times with Emily Leaf (a Newnham graduate and a keen young suffragist), visited the offices of the NU and of the LSWS, and lunched with a Mr Brooke who had devoted much of his short holiday in the Lake District in September to speaking for the KWSA.[81]

Catherine doubtless followed the news with great interest during this time, and made use of the opportunity to discuss events with London suffragists. Lloyd George's reform budget had been passed in the House of Commons on 4 November 1909, a direct challenge to the House of Lords, where it was in fact rejected on 30 November. The constitutional crisis raised all kinds of issues for suffragists, which we shall look at in the next chapter.

4 General Election; NUWSS Restructuring, November 1909 to May 1910

The rejection of the budget by the House of Lords at the end of November 1909 led immediately to the dissolution of Parliament and the calling of a general election, with polling to take place spread out over nearly four weeks (as was the practice at that time), from 14 January to 9 February 1910. Here was an opportunity that the women's suffragists could not miss. Yet the constitutional crisis severely complicated the issues, particularly for Liberal suffragists. Not only did most support the government on principle in its challenge to the Lords' veto, but that same veto was one of the stumbling blocks in the path of franchise reform.

Catherine's party loyalty still lay with the Liberals. Liberal suffragists had been greatly disappointed by the government's failure to take up the cause, but most were not yet totally disillusioned. As Leslie Parker Hume writes, "the assumption that the Liberal party was the natural champion of the suffrage movement" died hard.[1] Catherine's "burning ... zeal for the great principles of liberalism"[2] had not left her, and these, she believed, must inevitably lead Liberal politicians to move in the right direction. In June she had been struck by an editorial in the *Common Cause* which had first answered the arguments commonly put forth to support the view that the issue of the women's vote was damaging to the Liberal party, and had then strongly made the point that, in any event, there was no validity in balancing the interests of the Liberal party against those of the suffragists, that justice to the women was integral to liberal principles, and that accordingly any who claimed to be "a Liberal first and a suffragist second," and who would support the bringing in of a reform bill which left the women out, had not understood "the meaning of the great tradition under which they profess to serve." It was up to Liberal men to make it clear to their leaders that the matter was to be taken seriously.[3] Catherine wrote to the editor praising the article, and ordered a dozen copies to lend.[4]

On 18 November 1909, after her return from London to Keswick, and while the outcome of the budget crisis was not yet decided, Catherine had a chance to give some Liberals (men and women) a push, or perhaps a helping hand, in that direction; she was invited to take part in a public debate arranged by the Keswick Liberal Club, giving us the opportunity to see Catherine stepping out of the non-party role usually imposed on her by her position.

Beginning with a half-joking reference to her own "amazing courage"[5] in standing up before them (the ordeal was doubtless exacerbated by the presence in the chair of Mr James Moorsom, Jermyn's irascible and antisuffragist father),[6] Catherine made it clear that this would be very different from the speeches she now made all the time on behalf of the NU. "Generally I have to keep my own political opinions in the background because I am an official of a nonparty organization," she began. "But tonight there is no taint of the secretary about me; I come before you frankly as a Liberal, speaking to Liberals on women's suffrage from the Liberal point of view. I want to make it quite clear that I speak on this occasion for myself alone, not on behalf of any suffrage society."

Catherine outlined her own education in Liberalism, and lost no time before making her central connection between Liberal ideals and the suffrage cause: "Tonight I want to ask the Liberal men of Keswick to come forward and help us in the great battle that is being fought for the political freedom of women. I want to try and make you realize, if I can, that we are not merely a handful of clamourous [sic] women, tiresomely trying to divert attention from the great political issues before the country, but that the principles we are fighting for are the great fundamental principles of Liberalism and that the foe we are fighting is that old spirit of Privilege, of Monopoly, which has always barred the way to progress, the opposition of those who possess power to those who demand Liberty."

Then followed a brief account of the existing situation in the suffrage movement. There were, Catherine claimed, fourteen national organizations working for women's suffrage, all except one demanding simply equality under whatever franchise laws should exist. The one society with a different demand was the new People's Suffrage Federation (PSF), going for adult suffrage and available to those who felt this was the only thing they could work for. With a light touch, she threw in a rationalization for the "as is or may be" policy: "With proper womanly humility we do not presume to dictate what these qualifications shall be; we are content to accept the conditions which men in their wisdom have made for themselves." At the same time she addressed the Liberal fear of a big increase in the propertied vote, claiming that it had been estimated that 82 per cent of those enfranchised under the present requirements would be women earning their own living.[7]

Catherine spoke briefly about the militant suffragettes, mainly to stress that the NU, "by far the largest suffrage organization in the country," worked only by peaceful and constitutional methods, condemning "any appeals to violence and disorder in political propaganda," not only because of the harm the NU believed was being done to the cause but because it was wrong to use this kind of tactic to bring pressure to bear. Responsible statesmen, however, were also to blame because of their inaction. "Mr. A[squith] refuses to receive deputations not only from the Militants but from the Const[itutional] Suff[ragist]s who have committed no offence against the law," she said, "and pretends to be unable to distinguish between our policy and theirs, and puts off Mrs. Fawcett with the taunt that it will be time enough for him to receive deputations when we have agreed among ourselves as to what we really want, though he knows perfectly well that Const[itutionalists] and Mil[itant]s are asking for exactly the same thing. He first demanded evidence that women want the vote, and then refuses to allow the evidence to be put before him. Can you wonder that such an attitude creates a spirit of bitterness and rebellion among the less patient workers?"

After this, Catherine dealt briefly with women's right to vote, inquiring succinctly: "As we are only asking for the vote for duly qualified women we should rather ask by what right is the vote withheld from women?" As for women's fitness to vote, she pointed out that there was no test of fitness for men, and if there were she thought as high a proportion of women as men would qualify; meanwhile, the parties eagerly made use of women to canvass at elections. She elaborated, as she did in her more general speeches, on women's need of the vote, "and the nation's need of the women's point of view in politics," but she put more stress, for this audience, on underlying principles, saying: "Women need the vote for precisely the same reasons as men need it – because the only basis of just government is the consent of the governed, and women have to obey the laws as well as men; because those who have to pay taxes should have some control over those who have the spending of them and women have to pay taxes just the same as men; because voteless sections of the community ... have no direct constitutional way of bringing pressure to bear to get grievances remedied, and women are liable to have grievances just as much as men; because in short the vote is the constitutional means of protection against misgovernment and of obtaining immediate reforms."

Catherine gave concrete examples of how women suffered directly through lack of the vote, and used again her favourite story of the old woman and the pig. Then she turned to the country's need of the women's help in solving "the grave social problems that confront politicans today." Women could not accept "protection" from knowledge of the "ugly things in the world," and trying to combat them without votes "was like trying to dig a plot of ground with a child's spade." She went on: "Besides all you do for women by legislation, all philanthropic work, pauperizes them unless you give them the power to help themselves."

The whole tone of the speech had concentrated on the positive case for suffrage, but Catherine expressed her hope that some of the points most commonly made by the antis would be raised in the course of the debate. Moving towards a conclusion, she stressed the role the men had to play, telling them, "I want to try and rouse your sense of responsibility. You tell us to be constitutional. Do you realize the resp[onsibility] you take on yourselves when you say that? The only const[itutional] way of getting a reform is by pressure on the gov't through the electorate. You are the electorate, you men have this great power of the vote."

As before, she spelled out ways in which the voters could and must help, declaring that whether the vote was won with help or "in the teeth of opposition from the men" would in the long run determine whether or not women would "come into their heritage at last with their hearts full of the bitterness and antagonism which always results from justice denied and freedom withheld – a spirit which should never exist between men and women, but which alas! has been springing up within the last few years and unless the cause is removed will soon grow, I fear, to such proportions that it may take generations to dispel it."

In her peroration, Catherine declaimed:

I appeal to *you* – do not let it go down in history that the Liberal men of England did not lift a finger to help their countrywomen to win political freedom, that you could sympathize with Young Turks and Kaffirs and Indians who demanded rep[resentative] gov't and could trust [your] late foe in Africa, but would not trust your own fellow countrywomen. We are not an alien race; we are your own sisters and daughters and wives and mothers, descended from [the] same forefathers as you, inheriting [the] same traditions of justice and love of freedom; we are Englishwomen and are asking for what Englishmen have taught us to value – justice, liberty, the power to help effect[ive]ly. ... If you really believe in the great principle of representative government what can possibly be more important than the representation or non-representation of half the country? If it is true that the only basis of just government is the consent of those governed, how dare you go on governing them without ever asking them for their consent? Do you expect a party false to its first great principle with regard to half the nation it governs can prosper, can inspire respect or loyalty? We appeal to you to have faith in the great principles you profess. Make your voice heard in the land – let Liberalism once more stand forth as it has so often done in the past on the side of right and justice and the defence of the oppressed and down trodden.

Catherine then put the motion: "That this meeting of the Keswick Liberal Club urges the government to include the enfranchisement of women on the same terms as men in their promised Reform Bill." The unfortunate Mr Norman Robinson whose task it was to oppose the motion had a hard act to follow, and his speech, briefly reported in the *Common Cause*, suggests that he was unable to find many arguments that Catherine had not already answered, except in the emphasis that he chose to lay on the dangers posed "in international matters involving the supremacy of the country," where "men and women might come into collision and prevent that supremacy being maintained." Anthony Wilson, as respondent to Robinson, replied with some generalized praise of women's patriotism. All the others who joined in the debate spoke in favour of the motion, which "was carried with two dissentients, the members of the club only being allowed to vote." A gratifying rider was added "that copies should be sent to Mr. Asquith, to the Chief Liberal Whip, and to the Liberal agent for the North Western Division of the Liberal Federation."[8]

As far as we know, Catherine's speech at the Liberal Club made no mention of the general election that all knew must shortly be announced; curious as this may seem, it may have been a wise move to avoid the risk of introducing too many complicating factors.

Catherine spent only two weeks at home at this time, weeks filled with her accustomed mixture of singing and suffrage. The most significant suffrage event was the inaugural meeting at Penrith on 27 November of an informally constituted North-West Federation (NWF) of the NU, the follow-up to the resolution carried by KWSA at the national level in October, and the forerunner to more formal changes being planned in accordance with the Birmingham resolution. At this meeting "the Federation scheme drawn up by Miss Marshall ... was discussed and adopted. A co-operative plan of campaign for the coming general election was agreed upon, and Miss Gardner's Re-organisation Scheme was discussed."9

Important meetings called Catherine south again on 4 December. The NU was much exercised, once more, over what should be its election policy, and Catherine represented the KWSA at a special council, called as soon as the election was announced, to meet at the Caxton Hall in London on 6 December. Her second commitment was to a meeting of the committee to consider Miss Gardner's scheme, to which she had been elected in a formal postal ballot held in November.10

The December special council took as its starting-point two resolutions passed at the quarterly of the previous October. One mandated "strong efforts ... to get Voters' Petitions in every Constituency," to be organized by local societies. The second urged all NU societies "to obtain without delay promises from their local Parliamentary candidates to include the enfranchisement of women in their election addresses," and to give wide publicity to the candidates' answers. To avoid a clash with the election, the decision was easily made to defer the annual council, which should have been held in January, to March.

In addition the executive had prepared a resolution "That the General Election policy of the Affiliated Societies be propaganda work, except in the case of noted opponents or noted supporters," and spelling out two questions to test the candidate's position. A lengthy discussion followed, and several amendments were moved. A great many women spoke, probably some with a degree of heat not reflected in the dry minutes of the meeting. Catherine, still a learner in the national council, remained silent. At first glance few of the issues appear to be substantive, but considerable differences, political and methodological, underlay disagreements on such matters as whether "'propaganda work only' was an unnecessary giving away of what arms they had," the extent to which they should try to accommodate supporters of all parties, whether it mattered to have "other Women's Societies pulling in different directions," whether it was not "useless to ask [candidates] questions if they could only do propaganda work" (this from Emily Gardner), whether provision should be made for wholesale support of a party's candidates in the (unlikely) event that any party should make women's suffrage one of the planks in its platform, and if so, whether this should apply only to the "two chief" parties or to the Labour party as well. The policy discussion became so entangled in amendments and amendments to amendments that it seems to have been broken off. An uncontroversial resolution to ask the prime minister and the leaders of the opposition parties to receive a deputation, which would ask them to declare their intentions regarding women's suffrage, was passed; and the delegates went to lunch.

In a better mood (or a more docile one) following the lunch break, the council passed the original resolution almost unchanged. The main work of the afternoon centred on a resolution introduced by Helena Swanwick, which would have opened the door to special campaigns specifically supporting "a selected number of prominent men" from all parties, but which lost out – again after prolonged discussion – to a resolution authorizing the running of "special campaigns in the constituencies of the Members of the present Cabinet and in the constituencies of prominent men from the Unionist and Labour parties, with a special view to securing large Voters' Petitions."[11]

As far as it is possible to generalize about this meeting, the newer members of the executive, together with some up-and-coming council delegates, can be seen as advocating new departures and a more adventurous approach, and as showing interest in the Labour party's potential, while the old-timers had a more cautious attitude, or, as they might have said, a more realistic grasp of the possible, of the extent to which the NU's resources could be stretched in the nation-wide challenge of a general election. But while the differences are striking (and some of the more go-ahead probably left frustrated), equally striking is the sense of a real forum developing for discussion and the airing of divergent views.

A major factor underlying the tension in the council was undoubtedly the anxiety of many, especially among Liberal suffragists, to do nothing to weaken the government's capacity to solve the constitutional problem. Frank Marshall was so alarmed by a manifesto by Mrs Fawcett which appeared in the *Times* shortly after the council, and which he interpreted as making "women's suffrage predominant over all other questions," that he wrote to her to explain that such a policy "would be quite fatal" in Keswick's Liberal constituency. The KWSA, he suggested, would "have to choose between ceasing to exist, and publicly dissociating ourselves from the Union."[12] He wrote as if on behalf of Caroline and Catherine as well, or on behalf of the KWSA, but one wonders whether Catherine (who had after all been at the council) was in agreement with his objections, although it is safe to assume that she shared his concern about the constitutional issue. In any event, Mrs Fawcett seems to have been able to put his mind at rest with a single careful letter, in which she also expressed her appreciation of "the splendid work you have done up in Cumberland and Westmorland."[13]

The eleven members of the committee to consider "Miss Gardner's scheme for reorganization" met the day after the special council.[14] It was Catherine's first experience of working on a committee with some of the leading members of the national organization, though she was by now well known to many of them, and was certainly in her element in discussion of this type of reform, and able to bring in the positive experience of the nascent North-West Federation. Proposals were prepared for the coming annual council meeting in March.

Before leaving London on 9 December, Catherine went to yet more meetings, and fitted in some time with Jermyn, who had made a painful decison that he must give up his best friends;[15] if the friends referred to were the now married Malcolm and Josie, we have to conclude, sadly, that the modern idealistic relationship Josie had hoped for had proved unworkable.

Back at Hawse End, Catherine plunged into a round of seasonal activities, concerts, singing classes, and a KWSA social, meanwhile starting work on the Cumberland election campaign.[16] By 13 December (presumably with help from her suffrage colleagues) she had ready for printing a long manifesto, setting forth the objects pursued by the NU (as passed at the Cardiff council), explaining its commitment to "peaceful and lawful methods only," outlining the work already done in the region, setting forth the intention to concentrate on the divisions of Carlisle, Whitehaven, and Cockermouth, and calling for help with every facet of the campaign. A tear-off sheet invited volunteers to send in their names to Catherine with offers of everything from funds or the loan of a car, carriage, or cart, to speaking, canvassing for signatures to the electors' petition, accommodation for out-of-town workers, help in committee rooms, or service as a steward at a meeting.[17]

By 15 December Catherine was ill, and had to cancel appointments for that day not only to speak at Penrith at 4:30 p.m.(Caroline took her place), but to follow this by catching a train to Carlisle to take part in a debate at the YMCA there in the evening.[18] However, if absent in body from the meeting of the Carlisle suffrage society, Catherine was there in spirit – and had made sure that also present were copies of her very concrete "Appeal for Help" with the Cumberland election suffrage campaign, which formed the topic of discussion and planning.

She was determined to be fully fit for the election itself, and, uncharacteristically, she seems to have stayed at home most of the next
few weeks, although undoubtedly much occupied with correspondence and arrangements for the coming effort. The NU supplied
printed copies of the planned electors' petition, together with a
leaflet of "Instructions to Workers,"[19] to be sent out to those who volunteered to collect signatures. As organizing secretary of the KWSA,
Catherine wrote a letter on 5 January to all the local papers, which
was also printed up for circulation as a leaflet. In it, she explained
the voters' petition, linking this with the adherence of the NU to lawful means, and their consequent dependence on the support of
those who already had the vote. She named the candidates in the
Whitehaven and Cockermouth divisions, all of whom were said to
support women's suffrage, and all except one of whom had promised to mention it in their election addresses. She gave the addresses
of the NU committee rooms which would be open for a week before
polling day in all three constituencies, and made it plain that help of
all kinds (in money or person) would be welcome. Frequent indoor
and outdoor meetings would be held, and Mrs Fawcett herself was to
make a three-day visit, speaking in each constituency.[20]

The Marshalls' own constituency of Mid-Cumberland, which included the flourishing suffrage societies of Penrith and Keswick, was
the constituency of James Lowther, the Speaker of the House of
Commons, and so was exempt from contest, no doubt a disappointment to Catherine, who had put in so much work there. The suffragists collected signatures for the petition, but could do no more in
the constituency. There was no women's suffrage society in either
Whitehaven or Cockermouth, so the Keswick suffragists took on the
task of working these districts (with Miss Pattinson's help in
Whitehaven), while the Carlisle society (still rather new and not yet
very strong) undertook to work its own area, with help from Penrith.
Making use of their new "federated" organization, the Cumberland
societies agreed to raise a joint fund, and appealed for £100 from
the county. The whole Cumberland election exercise is a splendid
example of the kind of cooperative operation made possible by the
federation scheme, though Catherine's individual contribution by
way of advance planning and "inspiring leadership"[21] also played a
disproportionate role.

The account of election week can be given in Catherine's own
words: "We could not afford more than a week's campaign, but into
that week we put the very concentrated essence of hard work. Miss
Rathbone and Miss Pattinson and I paid preliminary visits to the
scene of action, and Miss Dover took up her quarters at Maryport

(making this her Xmas holiday) a fortnight before Polling day, and did useful work engaging Com[tee] Rooms, etc." With the help of these and four other women, committee rooms "in good positions" were opened in Whitehaven, Maryport, Workington, and Cockermouth by 12 January.[22] On 11 January they were joined by a Mr Theodor Gugenheim, of the MLWS, who "generously devoted 10 days of his annual holiday to helping us."[23] Catherine and he "held several meetings every day, mostly out-of-doors – 22 altogether in 7 days."

In her election speeches Catherine laid stress again on the responsibility of the voters to right the wrongs of the nonvoters, who have no other redress; and she picked up on the election's central issue – that of the much-touted need to break the monopoly of the House of Lords: "We women too are fighting against a monopoly," declared Catherine, " – the greatest monopoly in [the] hist[ory] of the world, only men's eyes are so blinded by custom and long acquiescence in the injustice of it that most of them do not see it – the monopoly of all legis[lative] power not by one *class*, at expense of another, but by one sex over the other – and what is more by the minority of the people over the majority."[24]

Together Catherine and her colleague from the Men's League must have made an entertaining and challenging pair. They were certainly energetic; Catherine's report sheds a rare light on the experience of an election:

We had large and interested audiences, in spite of the horrible weather. Mr.Gugenheim's eloquent speaking made a great impression, and his help in every way has been invaluable. On the 15th Mrs. Fawcett joined us, and spoke at two meetings in the Whitehaven Town Hall; on the 17th she spoke at Maryport and Workington, bringing our week's work to a fitting climax. Whitehaven polled on the 18th; and the Cockermouth Division on the 19th.

We were reinforced by helpers from Keswick for the two polling days, but even so we were terribly understaffed at Whitehaven. Signatures were coming in fast, notwithstanding, but when it began to get dark out workers were advised to withdraw from the Polling-booths, as it was expected that there would be rough times in the evening. The population of Whitehaven (a coal-mining town and seaport) is rather a turbulent one; feeling ran high between the supporters of the three rival candidates, and the result of the poll was to be declared that night. So very reluctantly we called in our outposts and closed our Committee Room.

We have learned since from the police that we could have kept on safely till 8 o'clock, and that we missed hundreds of signatures; the voters were asking for us everywhere, and were eager to sign. We should probably have got at least 2000 names they say (out of an electorate of 3050); as it was we only got about 700.

The following day we had to man the polling booths at Maryport, Workington and Cockermouth. Mrs. Frank Marshall had joined us on the 17th and took over the polling day organization at Maryport, where she and Miss Dover were helped by a most efficient and zealous staff of local sympathizers enlisted after Mrs. Fawcett's meeting there. Mr. Gugenheim took charge of the Workington arrangements, where we had some excellent local helpers, and a gallant army of recruits from Keswick who arrived early and stayed till the last train back at night. The Cockermouth arrangements were organized by Mr. Bolton of the local Conservative Club, who has been a good friend to us in more ways than one. He fitted up a small wooden shed, in which our Petitioners sat in comparative warmth and shelter, at the exit from the polling station.

It was a hard day's work, and the weather was horrible. It blew a gale all day and was bitterly cold, but it did not rain which was a great thing. We met with the utmost kindness and courtesy everywhere. At some of the Polling stations our workers were invited inside to sit by a fire, and one Presiding officer sent out a copy of the Daily Mail for the beguiling of any chance spare moments.

The spirit in which the voters signed did one's heart good. "Ay, that A will, and pleased to do't" was the frequent reply to our request, and those who had signed went and fetched others, and if need be argued hotly with them on our behalf. "It's nobbut justice they're asking for." "They should a had it fifty years since". "A'll sign it; A had a Mother." The police helped us; the Party agents helped us (all three parties in both Divisions had collected signatures to our Petition in their Committee Rooms); even the small boys helped us. During the last two hours of the day, when voters thronged and we wanted at least six hands apiece, the boys were invaluable. They volunteered to hold extra Petition blocks, and proved most capable exponents of our case. "They're Soofferagists not Soofferagettes", "they're not wanting to git into Parlyment"; "It's for women as pays rates and taxes same as the men". They collected a number of signatures for us.

When the Polling booths closed we found we had got about 1700 signatures in Workington alone. The returns are not all in yet, but our total number in the County is about 3000. A total number of voters in the district we covered is something over 6000; we were not able to work more than the three chief towns in the Division.[25]

Others might describe the work of collecting signatures as "painful and harassing and tedious,"[26] and in some places it undoubtedly was; hostile police were even known to have warned some suffragists that if they asked voters for signatures, they might be taken up for solicitation (as prostitutes).[27] But without doubt Catherine had had a good time, and it is not hard to guess that those who worked along-side her had enjoyed themselves too, as well as knowing they had made a real contribution. Catherine's friend and colleague, Louis Walker of the Westmoreland Women's Suffrage Association, had had a more difficult experience in Carlisle, where she felt the local members had taken less than their share of the load, and had been extravagant with the finely stretched funds of the federation; and she probably lacked Catherine's experience, and consequent confidence, in dealing with overexuberant children – Catherine's boys' singing classes must have been of great help here. Walker had turned faint: "the tiresome fainting ... was partly the gasfire – and partly the difficulty of working with the children as soon as school hours were over – shouting screaming – kicking the door without ceasing."[28]

The total number of signatures collected by the NU, in the 250 constituencies where the work was carried on, was estimated at just under three hundred thousand, and others besides Catherine were able to report a remarkably friendly reception. Alys Russell, for example, found that "a large majority ... have been willing to sign; working men have volunteered to take the petition to their pals and get them to sign." Most of the petitions were presented to Parliament soon after it met.[29] The other major women's suffrage societies had also been active during the election, in the main refraining from acts of aggressive militancy, but doing their best to oppose government candidates everywhere, generally by the means of public meetings.[30]

While there can be no doubt that suffrage was brought to the public consciousness at this election as never before, only the most blinkered disciple could claim that it had come anywhere near centre stage in competition with the constitutional issue concerning the power of the House of Lords, or with the issue of free trade versus protection and the recurrent problem of Irish Home Rule. It had been an election generating "immense interest," wrote Bertrand Russell, "I don't think the country has ever been so excited"[31]; and at least the suffragists had made their cause visible.

Russell himself had been among those who had decided that the nonparty stance of the NU would hamper him too much at this time; he had resigned from the NU executive because he "wanted a free hand to support Liberals" at the election (where in fact he worked for Philip Morrell).[32] He had long been restless and dissatisfied with what he saw as a lack of vision in the NU leadership,[33] and after the election he planned to take up work for the PSF instead. Margaret Llewelyn Davies had completed the conversion she had been working on. Helena Swanwick saw Russell's secession as "one of the worst blows we shall ever have," and wrote to him in something close to agony: "I can't bear to tell you how I feel about your resignation. There's no sense in handing on merely painful emotions and my own arise from a misconception of how you felt about women's position. To me the indignity and injustice of women's position is a shame that scorches me and the conviction that no man apparently in all the world can feel it like a woman is one that is at last being hammered into me. I have for so long tried to believe it is not so and to refrain from bitterness towards the many because I believed in the few. But now I am beginning to feel there are indeed none and bitterness is flooding me." She added a postscript: "But for what you have done and doubtless will still do for women, thanks all the same."[34]

Politically, the outcome of the election was something of a stand-off. The Liberals had lost their overall majority; the Unionists came a close second, although the attack on the budget and the constitution had probably cost them seats. The Liberals could form a government, but could not pass legislation without support from among the minority parties, Labour and the Irish Nationalists.[35]

The election safely over, Catherine was able to take a breather. Unfortunately, as she was so apt to do, she had pushed herself too hard, and was laid up for a few weeks after the campaign. Annie Dover, one of Catherine's co-workers, was not surprised to hear that she was unwell, and felt they had all worked too hard, but she still declared herself "ready for another campaign, if need be, for the same object."[36] Catherine was not too ill to write and receive extensive letters during this time, following up on the good work of the campaign, and straightening out the accounts. In light of what we know of her past and future inefficiencies (to put it mildly) in handling money, it is unnerving to find her responsible at this time for the federation's funds; but on the whole she seems to have managed well, though one cheque made out to her, but presumably for the funds, remains uncashed among her papers.[37]

By early March 1910, Catherine was in Cambridge, taking part in a series of suffrage plays and meetings at Newnham and Girton,[38] at least a change of pace. By this time, however, she was gearing up for the climax of the work of Emily Gardner's committee. The delayed annual council took place on 19 March, and it was here that the new major revisions to the constitution were presented.

When Catherine had made her proposals the previous year for a measure of regional cooperation, she had probably had in mind, as she said at the time, not much more than an increase in efficiency. The NU had grown so rapidly in the past two years that indeed it could not effectively be run from the London office, and some measure of decentralization was essential. Her experience on Gardner's committee, at council meetings, and (doubtless) in a number of private conversations with others taking leadership roles in the provincial societies, particularly in the north, had shown her that there was another major objective to the planned reforms, one she fully endorsed. It was, as Holton has said, "an attempt by the more influential provincial societies to wrest back some authority from the central executive."[39]

Although the 1907 constitution had opened the way for some new blood to enter the executive, Bertrand Russell's view of it as dominated by a rather conservative element, of limited vision, was shared by a number of others. Like Russell, some members left to join other organizations,[40] but in the main the active suffrage leaders refused to adopt what was essentially a pessimistic view, and instead of abandoning the NU set to work to change it to meet their needs. Evidence that Catherine had been actively engaged in promoting change, with others of the more radical NU members, is given later that year in a letter from a London friend, who wrote: "I have often wondered whether you survived those rampageous days of meetings and 'soirees', and if you succeeded in upheaving the London Committee, and infusing new blood into its ranks!"[41]

Gardner's committee of eleven was by no means made up only of those who wanted to see major change, nor had they found it easy to reach agreement, but they had produced what they hoped was a workable and might possibly acceptable proposal. However, the council meeting took place against a background of tension. Some had trouble understanding the purport of the changes, which were necessarily complicated, the difficulty centring (as in all federal systems) on striking a balance between the new federations and their powers and the control of the national executive. Resistance to the increased sharing of decision-making came especially from the executive "old guard," and some leading members of the LSWS. And some undoubtedly saw it as a vote of no confidence in the old leadership, and even as a personal attack on Mrs Fawcett, who was rightly seen as having played a unique role in keeping the cause alive through many barren years, and as still more effective than another leader would have been likely to be. But there are built-in hazards in being a leader of anything for forty years, and she had not completely escaped either a tendency on her own part to autocracy or the inclination of some followers to think she could do no wrong and to jump to her defence. She knew there was discontent; there had been an incident at the October council,[42] and only a few days before this March meeting Walter McLaren (a member of the NU executive) had passed her a letter he had received from Dr Ethel Bentham (a leading member of the Newcastle society, and active in the Women's Labour League), full of stinging criticism of the way the executive had handled the appointment of a new secretary and other officers. Although, in her reply to McLaren, Fawcett brushed the criticism aside, the underlying stress was there.[43]

The new organization of the NU that emerged at the end of a long and difficult discussion left the local societies as they were, each with its own committee, and mandated them to set up regional federations, "groups of Local Societies federated together for purposes of co-operation," each with a committee elected by its constituent societies, and differing only from Catherine's original concept in that the committee must include at least one member of the national executive. The general council, which was now to meet twice yearly (once in London and once in some other large town), closely resembled the old quarterly councils, consisting of delegates from every separate society in the NU, together with the whole of the executive. The national executive and officers were to be elected by the general council at its February meeting. Finally, there was a brand-new provincial council, consisting of two annually elected representatives (to whom was later added one officer) from each federation, to meet twice yearly, between the general council meetings, together with the whole national executive. Policy could only be decided by the general council, but any action consistent with approved policy could be undertaken by the provincial council,[44] which also clearly provided a forum for the development of new initiatives which could be brought to the general council.

The crucial new provincial council seems to have been largely Catherine's brainchild, though she had worked it over with others, and discussed it in the KWSA, whose approval she had for taking it to Gardner's committee. Despite support from Emily Gardner and from the North of England Society, she had been unable to gain a majority in the committee in its favour.[45] Yet without some arrangement of this kind, the new federations would be no more than instruments of administrative convenience, and would do little to alter the balance of power between the centre and the provinces, which was really what the whole thing was about. Fortunately, Catherine and her scheme had had a second chance.

Even the carefully unemotional official report of the council meeting cannot conceal that a great deal of frustration surfaced. The

constitutional issue took up the entire day, other important business
– the perennial issue of election policy – having to be dealt with in an
unplanned evening session lasting until 10 p.m. By late afternoon
feelings were running high, and an impasse had been reached. At
this juncture Catherine courageously introduced a slightly modified
provincial council scheme as an amendment, and was immediately
followed by two members (both men, as it happened) whose patience
had worn out and who moved to end discussion and get on with
other business, a motion described indignantly by another member
as "the most undemocratic motion brought before the meeting." In
the outcome, time was allowed to hear support from Maude Royden
and Louis Walker, before the two men got their way and were able
to move the closure, at which point Catherine's amendment was put
and carried.[46]

Maude Royden, who felt that the executive had shown itself at the
meeting as "appallingly out of touch with the Council," wrote to
Catherine a few days later: "I dare say the N.U. will never realize
what a debt it owes to you for your amendment – or only some few
of the rarer sort will! ... having talked it over with you, I was duly impressed with its importance. I cannot conceive how you managed to
look so calm and collected, and to think so clearly, as you did. You
had the worst moment of the whole of that awful day, in which to induce people to hear reason – *Oh*, how awful it was."[47]

Catherine, for her part, gave much of the credit to Royden's own
"eloquence at the critical moment." Between them, they had convinced the council, although the passage of the amendment took
place, as Catherine admitted, "to our delighted surprise."[48] Emily
Gardner thought that few indeed had had much idea of what had
been achieved; she too wrote to Catherine: "What did you think of
Sat. and how do you think our scheme emerged from the melting
pot? My firm conviction is that you and I alone of the whole assembly have any idea of what the object of the scheme is and how it will
work out!" But she still had serious concerns, continuing, "My reason for writing is that I am afraid that unless we bestir ourselves
nothing will be done to carry it out. The Keswick amendment was
carried, wasn't it? But Miss Mason said at the end 'We meet again in
six months'. I am quite sure that they have no idea of what your
amendment means and how it is to be carried out. It is a horrible
thought that a plan of organisation, which really could do so much,
is left to be carried out by people who either do not like it, or do not
know what it means. ... Seriously, I do think that the actual
organisation ought to be done by you or me."

Although Catherine did not "offer to take it off the hands of the office,"[49] as Gardner went on to suggest, a significant role in carrying out the reorganization was played by those who most wanted to see it happen. Catherine, and not the national office, drew up an admirably simple one-page leaflet outlining the new structures, how they were to be elected, what were their functions, and when they would meet,[50] had it printed in Keswick, and distributed it from Hawse End for "2d a dozen, post free."[51] As editor of the *Common Cause*, Swanwick gave space to explanatory articles, and (despite Gardner's forebodings) there is no evidence of a lack of cooperation on the part of the office or of the executive. Indeed, Edith Dimock was ready with what seem like well-informed advice and help on the details of drawing up constitutions for the new federations.[52]

Catherine's North-West Federation had of course been informally constituted in the previous November (1909), and held its formal inauguration, at Penrith, on 28 May 1910; Catherine had been "able in the Com^tee to quote ours as already existing and working well." She was not exaggerating when she claimed that "we in the North are largely responsible for the institution both of the Federations and of the Provincial Council."[53]

Remarkably, it was just two years since a small gathering at Hawse End had marked the beginning of the KWSA. Catherine was re-elected as honorary organizing secretary of the KWSA at its second annual meeting on 31 May, and was elected as chair of the NWF and as one of its two provincial councillors; in all, a heavy load to take on. Louis Walker became the honorary secretary and the second councillor, and Maude Royden was chosen to represent the national executive on the federation committee.[54] The state of parliamentary politics gave every reason to expect that there would be plenty of work to do, both in the NWF and at the centre. And a new initiative was already under way, and would determine the direction of the NU's work for the coming months.

5 Conciliation Attempted, and Another General Election, June to December 1910

The closeness of the general election result of January 1910 and the continuing failure to find a solution to the problem of the Lords' veto made a new election before too long seem probable. Meanwhile, with many members of all parties pledged and supposedly committed to the cause (the NU estimate was 323),[1] yet with no prospect of a satisfactory government-sponsored franchise bill, the even balance of parties in the House of Commons suggested a new strategy, which took shape as the Conciliation Committee, and private members' bills known as the first and second Conciliation Bills. The import of this phase of the suffrage campaign has been discussed elsewhere;[2] we shall focus on its impact on Catherine's work, and how it formed part of the forces drawing her into closer involvement with the central political work of the NU.

Henry Noel Brailsford was an author of some distinction, and a member of the ILP, but better known and remembered as a radical journalist. He was a founding member of the MLWS and (at this time) primarily a supporter of the WSPU, in which his wife was active. In January 1910 he wrote to Mrs Fawcett proposing the formation of a committee of suffragist MPs from all parties, together with women from the suffrage societies, to work out a bill that would be acceptable to the women and to the government and could gain the goodwill of suffragists in all parties.[3] The idea of including the women on the committee was soon dropped, mainly because of reservations expressed by both the NU and the WSPU, but both societies gave support to the concept. Brailsford prevailed upon Lord Lytton (brother of the militant Lady Constance Lytton, and himself known as an idealistic Unionist) to preside over the committee, now called the Conciliation Committee; nearly all the members were MPs (Brailsford himself was not), and they quickly, and probably appropriately, decided that they did not want more outsiders or any women to join them, since much of their work involved private negotiation among the parties and the leaders.[4]

Within a few weeks, the text of a proposed "Conciliation Bill" was ready. The committee had agreed on a formula close to that of the women's municipal franchise, based on occupation rather than on ownership.[5] Brailsford was clearly a little nervous that he might not be able to gain support from the NU, since the departure from the old formula of "the same as is or may be" made some Liberal suffragists uneasy.[6] He need not have worried; Mrs Fawcett declared herself delighted, saying that *she* "would accept any Women's Suffrage bill that had a reasonable chance of passing,"[7] and the NU, on Brailsford's suggestion, announced publicly: "That the National Union while maintaining its demand for the vote for women on the same terms as it is or may be granted to men would welcome any removal of the sex disability as an instalment of justice."[8]

Two or three months of euphoria followed. Support in and out of Parliament seemed widespread;[9] David Shackleton, a Labour MP, introduced the bill on 14 June; it was given second reading with two days of debate on 11–12 July, and was passed by a majority of 110. Despite this result, the time of optimism was over; by a slightly larger majority, the bill was referred to a committee of the Whole House, which made it dependent on government goodwill for the granting of further facilities;[10] and the extraordinarily hostile speeches made in the second-reading debate by Lloyd George and Churchill, as well as by Asquith himself, did not augur well for such dependence. Brailsford, after the care he had taken in the formation of the Committee, must have found particularly intolerable Lloyd George's ill-informed reference to the Conciliation Committee "whoever they may be – a committee of women meeting outside," coming to the House and dictating to them, "a position no self-respecting Legislature can possibly accept!"[11]

Meanwhile, the rising star of the Conciliation Bill provided a new focus for the suffrage campaign. Catherine soon became an expert exponent and defender of the bill to Cumberland audiences, although she spent less time in the Lake District and more time in London on suffrage business than she had in previous summers, and no active speaking campaign was planned to begin before the late summer. The influence of the KWSA, however, can be seen in the publication of a leader on women's suffrage in the *West Cumberland Times* on the day before the Conciliation Bill was introduced, which divided credit for the strength of local support between Catherine's "zeal and organizing ability" and the fact that "the suffragettes are not now on the rampage."[12] Later in June, too, an all-male nonparty public meeting was held in Keswick to express support for the bill; Frank Marshall was among those on the platform.[13]

More important still, perhaps, and a new departure, was the use of the new federation to bring pressure to bear on members of Parliament. On 6 June, the officers of the NWF sent letters to those Cumberland and Westmoreland MPs who were known to be favourable to women's suffrage, and to the leaders of all four parliamentary parties. The MPs, urged to do all in their power to support the Conciliation Bill, were told: "We welcome the bill most heartily because although it does not establish complete equality between men and women with regard to the franchise laws, it abandons once for all the old contention that womanhood is in itself a disqualification for the vote."

After spelling out the ways in which it was thought that the new bill met the objections of members of all parties, the letter went on to speak of the support found among voters in the region – that is, in the constituencies of these MPs – declaring that "there is a strong and growing feeling in this part of the country that the continued refusal to listen to the claims of these women is neither just nor expedient," and going on to detail the number of meetings that had been held, both public and by political clubs, the near unanimity of the support at these meetings for suffrage resolutions, and the number of signatures gained for the petition (giving the round number of "over 6,000" for the three constituencies together, and the specific figure for that particular MP's constituency). "The feeling of the electors," declared the letter, "... was universally friendly and sympathetic when they understood that we did not adopt or approve of militant methods." While there had been some difference of opinion as to the terms on which the franchise should be granted, the work of the Conciliation Committee had "found a solution of this question which should allay the fears of all Parties."[14] One of the MPs, Sir John Randles, who was a member of the Conciliation Committee, got a special letter of appreciation.

The letters to the party leaders made substantially the same general points, interwoven with skilfully selected particularities, reflecting Catherine's political knowledge and acumen. For A.J. Balfour, leader of the Unionist party and a long-time supporter of women's suffrage, there was a special pat on the back, and emphasis on the moderation of the bill, which "we feel sure ... will commend it to our friends in the Unionist Party." For John Redmond, there was a reference to the earlier support given by his party, the Irish Nationalists, to the Stanger bill, and to the suffrage work done "during the past year in the coal-mining and iron-working towns of Cumberland, where there is a large Irish population, and we have met with most encouraging sympathy and support." For George Barnes, then chair of the Parliamentary Labour party (PLP), the emphasis was similar, with the stress laid on the remarkable enthusiasm met with from working-class men, who had more than once begged them to hold more meetings nearby, or in a large hall. For Asquith the tone was much more challenging – indeed, absolutely direct and uncompromising; the letter is worth quoting at length:

We write ... to ask you most urgently to grant facilities for the Bill about to be introduced ... by the Conciliation Com^{tee} for Women's Suffrage. We will not repeat any of the reasons why women are asking for the Parliamentary vote. We recognise that you are opposed to the demand and are not likely to change your opinion. But we would respectfully remind you of the following facts: –

1) That a majority of each of the 4 Parties in the House of Commons is in favour of the principle of Women's Suffrage.
2) That this Bill has been drafted by a joint Committee representative of all the Parties on lines which have been accepted by all.
3) That a majority in the Cabinet itself is in favour of Women's Suffrage.
4) That you said yourself in speaking in the Albert Hall on Dec.10th, 1909: "The Government has no disposition or desire to burke this question; it is clearly an issue on which the new H. of C. might be given an opportunity to express its views."

A refusal in face of these facts to give facilities for a Second Reading of the Bill would be equivalent to a declaration that so long as a Liberal Government is in power there is no hope for a Women's Suffrage Bill; it would be a justification of the Militants, and would bring despair to large numbers of Liberal women who have tried to work for Women's Suffrage without deserting the Liberal party.[15]

The replies to these letters were unremarkable; from supporters Catherine received responses of guarded optimism, from Asquith and Balfour no more than an acknowledgment through a secretary.[16]

Catherine planned to be in London by the middle of June, but was delayed by illness, missing some of the excitement and activity surrounding the build-up to the introduction of the Conciliation Bill, but arriving in time for much of the increased pressure from then until the second reading. The major women's suffrage societies had all agreed to support the bill, the WSPU had declared a truce, and even the PSF was giving lukewarm approval. Much to Brailsford's distress, attempts to arrange a joint demonstration between the NU and the WSPU had fallen through, foundering mainly on a lack of trust on the part of the NU, when the WSPU would not give an absolute commitment to refrain from a return to violent methods before or during the affair;[17] so each group held its own meetings and public events throughout a busy month. By now, most NU activists, in common with Catherine, smarted constantly under the hostility they faced as a result of WSPU action, resulting in anything from physical attack in the streets or at meetings to the defection of hardwon converts, the necessity of continually reassuring other needed supporters, and the frustrating difficulty of attracting media attention to the reasoned argument. The NU decision to keep its distance was probably wise as well as inevitable.[18]

Catherine's primary purpose for being in London is not clear, and she left no helpful diary for this period. Suffrage was certainly one focus, even though, for at least part of the time, she was furthering her study of singing, and she seems to have taken time out to go to the Varsity cricket match at Lords, to the Eton and Harrow match, and perhaps to a rose show. She probably made use of the opportunity to do some shopping, in particular for the remarkable hats which were in vogue at the time. Her father indeed hoped that she was enjoying "a blessed lull" in suffrage activity, except for going to Bristol[19] as a KWSA representative at the NU council meeting there, the first since her amendment had pulled order – and some might say, victory – out of the disaster of the March meeting. She does not seem to have played a very active part at Bristol; it was perhaps one of her virtues not to speak unless she had something to say, but her tall figure must have been well known to many by now. Her annotated agenda indicates that she supported a resolution to admit the press – her own experience had been positive and she thought that at least the provincial papers would be sympathetic. (Royden, however, opposed admitting the press, saying trenchantly, "The moments when you want to banish the press are the least foreseen. You don't [know] what may raise a storm – you can't say kindly leave the room while we fly at each other's throats. We may sacrifice having controversial matters thrashed out for the sake of keeping up appearances.")[20]

Back in London, Catherine followed up the earlier letters of the NWF by a further round of missives to the "favourable local MPs," drawing their attention to the date set for the division, urging them to vote against referring the bill to a Committee of the Whole House and to make sure they paired with an antisuffragist if they were unable to be in the House for the vote.[21] A strong contingent from the northwest, including Catherine and her brother, Hal, attended the NU demonstration on 9 July, and Catherine may have been in Trafalgar Square again a week later when the antisuffragists put on a show, purportedly much enjoyed by the suffragists, who claimed that they kept meeting only each other, and that the questions of the day were "Have you seen *any* Anti-Suffragists?" and "*Are* there any Anti-Suffragists here?"[22].

The word "conciliation" in the title of the new bill caused some confusion. At the outset, it is true, Brailsford had entertained a short-lived hope of achieving a position which would be acceptable to the government, but the composition and stated object of the Conciliation Committee even in its earliest published statements,[23] and the whole direction of its work, should have made it clear that (in the face of an intransigent prime minister) this had been modifed almost at once to an attempt to reach a compromise between suffragists in the different parties. There was never the slightest attempt to pretend otherwise. Nevertheless, some antisuffragists took the view that it was they who were supposed to be conciliated, a view that is not made less bizarre by the credence given to it by a respected modern historian, who apparently concurs with the notion that there was something dishonest about "attracting support on contradictory grounds from politicians whose philosophies diverged."[24]

Catherine tackled the question in a letter to the press on 25 July, under the heading "WHO IS CONCILIATED BY THE CONCILIATION BILL FOR WOMEN'S SUFFRAGE?"[25] In part, the letter reads:

There seems to be some confusion in many people's minds as to whom the Conciliation Bill for Women's Suffrage (now before Parliament) is designed to conciliate. Will you allow me to explain ... what is perhaps a natural misunderstanding?

The Conciliation Bill, which was formed by a committee of members of the House of Commons, drawn from the four political parties, was not designed to conciliate the anti-suffragists. That would, of course, be impossible, since they are opposed to the whole principle of Women's Suffrage. Neither was it designed to conciliate the militant ("Suffragette") and non-

militant ("Suffragist") section of the Women's Suffrage movement. That
would have been unnecessary, because, though we differ fundamentally in
our methods of working to attain our object, there has never been the slightest divergence of opinion between us as to what this object is. ... we are all
agreed on the one point – that the fact of being a woman should not of itself
be a disqualification. ... Whom then does the Conciliation Committee's Bill
conciliate? It was framed to meet an objection of those Members of Parliament who supported the principle of Women's Suffrage, but would not support the extension of the franchise to women on the same terms as to men,
either because they were afraid of "a leap in the dark" or because they
feared that their party might be the loser by the proposed change. It was curious to note that the Liberals opposed the change because they said women
would all vote Conservative, and the Conservatives opposed it because they
said women would all vote Liberal! If both parties were so secure in the consciousness of having "always done the best for the women," as they would
have us believe, one wonders why they were each so much afraid that the
women would all vote against them.

After this dig, Catherine explained the details of the bill, and how
she saw it as a minimal measure, but one which would meet the objections of every political group (except those irrevocably opposed),
and as enfranchising "only those women whose claim to enfranchisement is most urgent if least disputed – the women who are heads of
households."

Between the writing of this letter and its publication in a weekly
paper, Asquith dealt a further blow to the bill. Catherine sent in a
postscript, which was published with the letter. "Since I wrote this
letter," she explained, "the Prime Minister has announced that he
does not intend to give facilities for the further stages of the Bill in
the House of Commons." But the NU was not ready to give up: "We
hope, however," Catherine continued, "that we shall be able to show
reasons for granting facilities which will out-weigh his reasons for
refusing them. We cannot think that his refusal is final and irrevocable. The Government would be in an extremely awkward position if
they had to appeal to the country at the next election 'to ensure that
the will of the people, as expressed by their elected representative[s]
in the House of Commons, shall prevail,'[26] if they themselves have
deliberately frustrated that same will of the people, as expressed by
a larger majority in the House of Commons than they were able to
obtain for their 1909 Budget, or their Veto Resolutions."

It was well argued, but Catherine may have had trouble convincing herself that there was still a future for this particular bill. However, other bills of the same kind might follow. Meanwhile,

technically the bill was not dead, and so still had some usefulness as a focal point, and indeed the NU made the bill the centre issue of its summer campaign. Frank Marshall was among those who claimed that the kind of party truce that obtained while the constitutional conference was sitting provided an opportunity to deal with the women's suffrage question and finally get it out of the way.[27] But in reality the chances of its effective revival in the autumn were slim indeed.[28] The plight of the women might move Liberal MPs to sympathy, and many sincerely wanted to see the wrong redressed. But it was not a wrong under which they themselves suffered, and since the party's leaders declined to take up the question, most were content to let it rest, feeling they had done their bit by casting a vote for the second reading of the Conciliation Bill; it did not seem to them to be worth the risk of embarrassing the party.

Catherine was aware that the attention of MPs (and much public indignation) was focused on the injustice from which they themselves smarted, the power of the House of Lords, and her speech notes show her making capital of this. After beginning an open-air speech boldly by declaring, "I am a revolting woman!", she would say: "I with a very great [number] of other women am in revolt against a big monopoly – the biggest monopoly the world has ever known – I can only suppose it is because it is so very big and so close to our daily lives that you men seem unable to see it, just as the country man said he had not been able to see London because of the houses. We heard a great deal of talk at the Election about the monopoly of power by the H. of Lords, about the monopoly of wealth, about the monopoly of land. If you are going to fight monopolies go for the biggest one first – the entire monopoly of all say in the laws under which we live ... by one sex over the whole of the other sex."[29]

The NWF was well supplied with visiting speakers and NU organizers during the late summer and autumn campaign months of 1910. Helga Gill, a Norwegian suffragist now working as an organizer for the NU (which employed at least ten full-time organizers by this time), spent almost the whole of August in the Cumberland-Westmoreland region.[30] Late September saw a short campaign, in which Selina Cooper was the chief speaker, with her dynamic appeal to working men and women, and her long experience of trade union and suffrage work.[31] In October, Keswick appropriately had the honour of hosting the first meeting of the newly constituted NU provincial council, and full use was made, in the weeks before and after, of the distinguished suffragists which this brought to the area, many of whom also stayed at Hawse End. The wealth of visitors gave Catherine a great deal of work to do in making arrangements, and did not free her from a considerable amount of speaking herself. Although she may often have been a supporting rather than the main speaker, she took a leading role on occasion. On 4 August, for instance, she gave "an excellent and able speech" on the Concilation Bill to five or six hundred people at an open-air meeting in Keswick market place.[32]

The Keswick provincial council meant an immense amount of work for the perfectionist Catherine, but was something of a personal triumph. Initially she had been disappointed at indifference to the new structure on the part of the LSWS,[33] but those who came – and London was at least well represented by members of the national executive – had an interesting and enjoyable time. The *Common Cause* reported that even the "Clerk of the Weather, who has previously shown decided Anti-Suffrage sympathies, has apparently been converted at last, and has smiled upon our Council meeting," which included invitations to Derwent Island and Lingholm, as well as many indoor and outdoor meetings. The business sessions heard reports from the NWF and from three of the new federations from southern England, and discussed ongoing issues such as when and where women's suffrage candidates might be run, and the value of collecting signatures for a women householders' petition.[34]

After the recent stormy national council meetings, the Keswick council had a different feel to it. There was no sense of a "takeover" by the more radical elements, perhaps rather a move to reconciliation and balance between north and south, old-timers and newer activists, traditional Liberals and Conservatives and those from farther left. Helena Swanwick found the spirit new and forward-looking, writing to Millicent Fawcett, "I hope you feel cheered by the Council. I thought there was such a jolly note of confidence in it all."[35]

The NWF moved a resolution at the provincial council "That it be part of the duty of each Federation to keep in touch with all the local newspapers in its area." This was Catherine's chance to enlarge on a side of suffrage work at which she had become expert. From the early days of the KWSA, she had firmly and gently saturated the local press – of which there was much more in those days – with information, reports, correspondence, response to antisuffrage events or news items, and notices of meetings, and she thought that the federations could do even more. She described the work "most admirably" and roused great interest.[36] Helena Swanwick, in her capacity of editor of the *Common Cause*, followed up by asking Catherine to write an article on "The Work of Press Secretaries," which appeared barely two weeks later. As so often, I am struck with the thoroughness of the approach (and with how much more recent groups might learn, *mutatis mutandis*), the more so in that Catherine saw little that was original in her suggestions, only advocating that the federations make use of their network to make the work throughout the country more systematic and effective. She outlined the practical steps to implementing the resolution, urging the appointment of press representatives who would study newspapers, get to know the editors, organize letter-writing, note the presence or omission of women's suffrage in any political speeches, and report on inaccuracies or misrepresentations found in accounts of suffrage activity. She was able to claim enviable results from her own press work.

It does mean a great deal of work. ... I have been doing it myself, though with nothing like thoroughness, in connection with twenty local papers, and it has made very great demands on my time. But the results have more than repaid the cost. Of these twenty papers not one is now hostile; not one ever misrepresents us (that alone is an immense gain); most of them give excellent – almost verbatim – reports of all our meetings, and several support us actively in their editorial columns, and reprint Women's Suffrage articles of their own accord from the "Manchester Guardian" and other sources. Some of the editors needed educating, but one of our chief tasks is to educate public opinion, and the local papers have an important influence on public opinion in country districts. Educate their editors, and you are educating public opinion at its fountain-head. The difference which a favourable local press makes to the success of our propaganda work is simply incalculable. ...

Catherine ended with a list of practical hints and principles, ranging from the tabulation of information on the various papers, through the need to tailor copy to the politics and style of each paper, to a general admonition. "If at first you don't succeed, don't stop trying till you do."[37]

Despite this almost hectic activity, Catherine's music teaching in local schools continued: a curious fragment of correspondence indicates that a school inspector thought very highly of Catherine's work, describing her as "a lady of exceptional talents" and "unlimited enthusiasm," with a "scientific" and "rational" approach. However, Catherine apparently received the report second-hand; defensive as she had a tendency to be, she took in only what little had been said in the way of criticism, and wrote off to "pick a bone" with the inspector. His Majesty's inspector responded with wit and good humour, enclosing a copy of his report (unfortunately not still extant), and explaining what he had meant by the offending comments, as well as drawing attention to the praise he had given. After quoting the phrases given above, he wrote:

What more can I add from my poor stock-in-trade of laudatory expressions? My fund was almost exhausted.

"They *appear* to be somewhat reduced in nervous vitality" means, in plain English, that the children gazed at me with fishy eyes and emitted sounds which, whilst they were not inharmonious, were wanting in vital force. But this was, doubtless, my fault. I did my best to obscure my hideous presence but I quite admit that the atmosphere that surrounds the Inspector is, like CO_2, devitalising not to say vicious in its effects.

The report culminates in a reference to "excellent discipline". Discipline (perhaps I should have written it with a big D) is not to be confused with order. It is the mental and physical condition which is produced by intelligence, interest and attention not the mechanical attitude produced by a familiar word of command. ...

In view of all this eulogy what becomes of the bone – and the meat? ... Seriously, I do think the advantage which the school has gained all round from your visits is incalculable and the managers must be very shortsighted indeed if they do not recognise it. Two years ago Braithwaite School was in a pretty bad state. Its improvement of late has been marked and I am pretty sure that the enlarged opportunities created by the music lesson are responsible for the change.[38]

It was a generous letter, and one hopes that Catherine was able to accept the honest appreciation of the author. The letter helps to give perspective to Catherine's music teaching; paid or unpaid (almost certainly the latter), her work in the village schools was serious professional work, though she was able to give it less time as the suffrage movement became ever more demanding.

Within a year or two, Catherine would be one of the NU's main advocates of a closer liaison with the Labour party, and would herself increasingly identify with Labour goals, but in 1910, as we have seen, her mission was to the Liberal party. She was involved in two closely related projects in the late summer and fall, one directed to Liberal MPs and the other to Liberal women. H.N. Brailsford wrote on 12 August, thanking her for a practical suggestion she had made about the need to set up a system for keeping records of the supportive letters and other details of the campaign for the Conciliation Bill, in order to be able to quote chapter and verse when the measure should be brought forward again. He went on: "It so happens that you have in your area two of the Liberal members who are really most mischievous to us – Mr. Geoffrey Howard [MP for Eskdale] and Mr. Denman [MP for Carlisle]. They are the leaders in the movement to put an adult suffrage Bill in competition with ours. They will probably pose before you as good friends, but in the lobbies no one has been more hurtful to us. Your society could do a great deal to help us if you can so handle them as to convince them that any manœuvres designed to split our ranks and to substitute an extreme party bill for a moderate non-party bill, will be carefully watched and deeply resented by the women of their constituencies."39

Not surprisingly, Catherine wrote at once asking for more detail, and suggesting possible strategy.40 Brailsford did not hold out much hope of winning over Howard, who "will vote for any Suffrage Bill, but ... more than balances that by underground opposition," and who, with his Liberal Suffrage Group, "was pledged to work only on party lines. ... His whole strategy was to drive the Unionists into opposition, and make woman suffrage an ordinary party question." Of Denman, Brailsford said he knew less, but thought he was "a satellite of Mr. Howard and ... probably inspired by him." He commented on Catherine's suggestions and questions; interestingly, the focus had now shifted to the best means of tackling the *Liberal* women, rather than women in general. Brailsford's letter also contains a clear exposition of his view that it was essential to stay with a limited nonparty measure, and refuse subversion by any adult suffrage scheme appealing to the support of only the Liberal party, but still presented as a private member's bill:

Your plan of a deputation seems to me the best. I would take the two separately. Also I think the main point is to stir up the Liberal women in Mr.Denman's constituency to give him a very plain warning. We will do anything that can be suggested to eliminate any trace of plural or faggot voting41 that may remain in our Bill. But Mr. Denman's pure party bill is a disaster, and he ought to be told in the frankest language that such a manœuvre is mere wrecking and will be resented by women as a trick really more dangerous than bold opposition. It would only succeed in losing us our 88 Conservative supporters, while of the Liberals (60) who voted against us not 20 are nominal suffragists. A party Bill cannot get a majority. Even if the Unionists were neutral, it would get so small a majority that no reasonable man could expect the Lords to pass it. We shall never get a suffrage Bill through the Lords without Mr. Balfour's aid, and he will not go further than our Bill.

The best thing to hope for would be that the Liberal women might be stirred up to intimate that they will not again work for Mr. Denman if he persists in his wrecking tactics. In any case in view of Mr. George's arguments for delay he cannot honestly believe that his Bill (which would depend wholly on Mr. George for backing) would be likely to get facilities next year.

P.S. I think it would be a good plan to hold a demonstration for the whole of your area if you could get the friendly M.Ps to attend and speak. It is quite as important to make them feel that they have done a popular thing as to oppose the others.[42]

The stance of the Liberal women was indeed crucial. As we have seen, the Corrupt Practices Act of 1883 had made the voluntary labour of women at elections suddenly indispensable.[43] Within a few years women's party organizations took on new meaning, and women basked in the praise that attended their election work. But there was tension between the strength of the suffrage argument and the habit of deferential and unconditional support which they developed, and which the male politicians took for granted. As early as 1892, the Women's Liberal Federation (WLF) had split on the issue, the prosuffrage group retaining the WLF name, and the more docile body forming the Women's National Liberal Association.[44] The Countess of Carlisle, who became president of the WLF in 1894, had greatly built it up, but despite her apparent personal commitment to suffrage[45] the attitude of even the WLF soon lapsed into ambivalence,[46] particularly after the constitutional question made party loyalty into a priority for many. Many of the most energetic women had left the party organizations to give their full attention to suffrage, either through party-connected societies (for example, the Conservative and Unionist Women's Franchise Association or, within the WLF, the Forward Suffrage Union), or through regular suffrage societies. But enough remained to keep the politicians smug, as well as comfortably assured of free workers at elections.

Catherine was aware that a large proportion of the members of the NWF were Liberals, as she and Caroline were, and she hoped to make use of this to follow up on Brailsford's suggestion, with one characteristic modification; as she described it, "We hoped to *persuade* them to drop a project which was damaging the chances of the Bill; Mr. Brailsford wanted us to *threaten* them with what we should do if they would not."[47] She took Brailsford's letters to the NWF executive, where she gained approval for a special conference,[48] which she hoped would lead to a delegation, as Brailsford had suggested.

In a letter inviting Lady Carlisle to attend, Catherine explained the nature of the planned meeting:

A large proportion of the members of the North Western Federation of Women's Suffrage Societies are Liberals and they are anxious to take some action, as Liberals, apart from the general activity of the Federation, to thank the two Liberal M.P.s for Cumberland for their support of the Conciliation Bill and to urge them to do all in their power to obtain facilities from the Gov't for the further stages of the Bill during the coming autumn Session.

With a view to deciding on the best course of action it is proposed to hold a conference of Liberal members of our Federation on Oct. 29th, probably at Penrith. A circular has been sent out inviting each of the W.L.A.s in Mr. Howard's and Mr. Denman's constituencies to send a representative to it. ... Whether we should be able to agree to any joint action or not we feel that a conference would be extremely useful at this juncture.[49]

Catherine was overextended at this time, and may have been unwise to take on so delicate an issue on top of all she was doing. She had probably had to wait until the NWF committee meeting of 1 October for approval, just before the provincial council met in Keswick, overwhelming Catherine with work. When she wrote to Lady Carlisle, barely two weeks before the planned meeting, the venue was not even settled – in the event it took place in Carlisle, not in Penrith – and many arrangements still had to be made. Although Louis Walker and perhaps others agreed to share the work, it did not go smoothly and a great deal of confusion and some bad feeling arose. Catherine was responsible for the agenda but was unable to get all the information she needed until a day or two before the conference:

When the Sunday of that week came and I was still in ignorance on these points I chromographed cards to go out to the Secretaries of all the W.L.A.s and W.S.S. telling them that the Agenda would reach them on Thursday morning, so that the W.L.A.s could summon their Committees for Thursday or Friday to instruct their delegates, and I made special arrangements with the printer who kindly kept his works open on Wednesday, which is early closing day, in order to print the Agenda for us the moment the necessary information arrived. I went into Keswick myself on Wednesday, corrected the proof as soon as it was ready, and sat waiting pen in hand to add the place of meeting (which was finally settled by telegram whilst the Agenda were printing) and get them all off by the 6 o'clock post. I did the best I could under the circumstances; I was very much upset by not being able to issue the Agenda earlier.[50]

Poor Catherine! The story illustrates not only her own dedication and ability to solve problems, but something of her unreal expectation that others – including even the reluctant WLAs – would be equally prepared to put themselves out for a concern which they may well have seen as primarily hers, and which she found in some cases even conflicted with their sense of what was proper.

The WLAs responded late to the preliminary invitation, and without enthusiasm, a number of them declining altogether. Gilsland WLA, for example, was divided on the women's suffrage question, would not be able to send a delegate, and "think our *M.P* is quite in earnest to grant us the franchise as soon as parliament see there [sic] way clear therefore we are content to wait their time that is what we will have to do."[51] The NU branches, particularly the Carlisle society, were also confused and offended by an error of Louis Walker's, which had led to their being invited to send "delegates," while it had been clear to Catherine – and very important – that the societies "were to be asked to send in names of such of their members as were Liberals and suitable, and willing to attend (as Lib. members of the Federation not as delegates representing their Societies)."[52] More serious still was that Walker had not realized that knowledge of Brailsford's letters should have been kept within the NWF executive, and had mentioned them in her first letter to the women's suffrage societies, but seemingly not in the letters to the WLAs, which in the outcome increased their suspicions that there was a hidden agenda, that they were being manipulated.

Considering how much had gone wrong before the conference convened on 29 October, it is not surprising that the day proved difficult. Catherine's original plan had been to have the same number of women from the WLAs and from the WSS, but this had failed because so few of the WLAs had sent delegates, and a rather artificial procedure was adopted, allowing the WLA delegates each to speak twice and have two votes in an attempt to restore the balance. Notes exist for a speech Catherine planned to make, whose themes and arguments resembled the one she had given to the all-male Keswick Liberals in 1909, but which focused them on the question of the moment, "Is it reasonable and consistent with loyalty to Liberalism to demand that the question shall be dealt with now?"[53] But probably she had to renounce her role of strong advocacy, since she was obliged to chair the meeting, which had not been in her original plan, and the speech may never have been given; perhaps Catherine would have been wasting her breath if she had made it. However, the women's suffragists were able to pull some chestnuts out of the fire, and resolutions were passed acknowledging the Conciliation Bill as the best possible solution given present difficulties, and approving the idea of a delegation.[54] WLA representation on such a delegation would of course depend on the reception given to the idea by branches.

Catherine had driven herself too hard, and had driven Louis Walker almost to distraction. Just before the conference, a letter from Louis indicated that Catherine's instructions had been unclear to her, and concluded: "I *know* I'm doing all this terribly badly but I have simply been unable to give the time owing to this cruel anxiety about my sister Lily. No, she is no better – worse. There are some illnesses one cannot speak about. I really have tried to write more letters on the conference but when I have got home in the evenings I've been really so worn out that I could *not*."[55]

Catherine's own stress can be surmised from the lack of consideration she showed for Louis, although there may be an attempt at restraint in her letter of 14 November 1910:

When can I come and see you? Things have been going badly wrong with the Federation – the Carlisle Society nearly broken up and all sorts of complications – but I have not had time to write to you. ... I knocked up last week with rheumatism and overwork combined, which did not improve matters. The root of all the mischief is your original letter to Carlisle in wh. by some unfortunate misunderstanding, you refer to Mr. Brailsford's letters which I read to the Fed. Com[tee] and meant to be in strict confidence and go no further. I can't possibly explain it all by letter; I spent 2 days in Carlisle trying to clear things up, but I am afraid the harm that has been done with the C[arlisle] and N[orth] C[umberland] Lib[eral] women can never be completely undone. We had nearly won them over to the Deputation – in fact they would have worked with us quite amicably I believe it had not been for those unfortunate letters. I think now I was wrong to read them even to the Com[tee] but I took such care, as I thought, that our consideration of them was strictly confidential.

However, we must meet and talk it all over.

Catherine, perceptive as ever about structures, and still learning – although sometimes too impatient to work strictly within their limitations – recognized that even the cherished federation concept might have its problems: her letter to Louis continued: "The Socie-

ties also resent being *instructed* by the Federation instead of *consulted*
– quite rightly, as I think, with my Liberal prejudices! A federation
of independent units needs v. careful handling."[56]

To the Carlisle wss she wrote a full explanation of what she understood had happened, adding a little sadly: "Our Federation
started so harmoniously and gave such good promise of usefulness
to the Cause and helpful cooperation among the Societies. This has
been a deplorable misunderstanding with your Society, and I am extremely sorry for all the trouble it has caused you and your Committee. I think you showed great loyalty and forbearance by not
seceding from the Federation when you found many of your members were threatening to resign. Fortunately you all knew Miss
Walker, and knew things *couldn't* be as bad as they looked!"[57]

What Catherine seems to have been reluctant to admit was that
not all the fault lay in bungled arrangements, much less with Louis.
Either she herself had seriously misjudged the mood of the wLAs,
their touchiness in face of feminist pressure, and above all their
habit of deference towards their mps, or she overestimated her ability to bring them around. Beatrice Morton, who had attended the
conference as a delegate from a wLA in the Carlisle area, and who
was also a member of the nu, found on going back to her wLA that
"they were very strong against joining the deputation to G. Howard and Mr Denman, so you see I shall not be there after all. ...
[T]hey ... will very likely write a letter explaining that their declining
to join the deputation was not owing to want of keeness [sic] for the
vote but to faith in their, G.H. and D's, good judgment, which is of
course founded on a greater 'know' of all the facts of the case than
is possible for outsiders to glean from the papers." Denman and
Howard, she said, were "keen suffragists ... specialist[s] ... on the
suffrage question," and it would be "presumptuous" to urge them to
go against their own judgment.[58]

In the outcome there was talk of a separate delegation from those
of the wLAs who would not join with the one planned at the conference, to express rather generally their interest in the suffrage question.[59] Catherine's visit to Carlisle may have helped mend bridges; a
long letter she wrote to Beatrice Morton was probably intended to
have the same effect – and she was careful not to impugn the integrity of Denman and Howard – but she had been astonished at the ignorance among the wLAs of the exact position taken by their
members, and she said so. She recognized that the wLAs could not be
experts on all topics before Parliament, but pointed out that some
others, in and out of Parliament, who had made a study of the suf-

frage question, judged the attempts of Denman and Howard to widen the bill as disastrous.[60]

Catherine carried on an extensive correspondence with Denman following the conference, trying to set up the deputation (which was expected to go forward with NU Liberal women and what representatives from the WLAs could be persuaded to take part), and also trying to get from him further explanation of why he had declared that the bill had been killed by the debate and the vote in the House of Commons. Denman was willing to meet with the deputation, but after some unavoidable changes of date, the scheme was overtaken by events when another general election was called. When Catherine finally expressed willingness to put the deputation off, Denman wrote wearily, and a little sarcastically, "I much appreciate your letter and the consideration you are good enough to show for the other work that I have to do, besides representing the women of Carlisle in the House!"[61]

The election was again occasioned by the constitutional crisis which still dominated British politics. While the budget had gone through the Lords without difficulty following the general election of January 1910, the issue of constitutional change to deal with the Lords' veto was unresolved. The one means of coercion up the sleeve of the ministry was to have the King make enough new peers to swamp the House of Lords; or at least to threaten to do so. For the government, a further complication had been introduced by the unexpected death of Edward VII on 6 May; no one was willing to force an answer from George V as soon as he succeeded to the throne. In a last attempt to find a compromise solution, a small constitutional conference was set up with four participants from the government and four members – from Lords and Commons – of the opposition. As long as this was meeting, from 17 June 1910, the crisis was, in effect, held in abeyance, but when it had to declare failure on 10 November, dissolution inevitably followed (on 28 November). So serious an issue had to be taken again to the country, and in any event, the King had committed himself to the making of peers only after the election.[62]

So the suffragists, too, had another election on their hands, with all its opportunities and all its frustrations. Although the suffrage campaign continued unabated, the heavy disappointment over the Conciliation Bill had taken its toll; in April it had been possible for suffragists to write of being "possibly within sight of an immediate realization of part of their demand,"[63] and now in November the

prospect seemed as remote as ever. There was a ray of hope in a
vaguely worded promise made by Asquith on 22 November[64] to give
facilities for a bill some time during the ensuing parliament, should
the Liberals be reelected. But this was more than offset by the renewal of militancy on 18 November, the terrible "Black Friday" of
suffrage history, when the suffragette march on Parliament turned
into a pitched battle lasting several hours, and some police were as
guilty of violence towards the women as they clearly permitted the
worst elements of the crowd to be. Other demonstrations followed.

Brailsford was distraught, on the one hand collecting depositions
from the women who had suffered injury or sexual molestation
from the police on Black Friday, and on the other furious that the
wspu action had "wrecked his diplomacy with Asquith."[65] Indeed,
both he and Lytton believed they had been on the verge of obtaining
a commitment from Asquith and Balfour, as leaders of the two main
parties, to give facilities during the first session of the new Parliament, before the militant action spoiled the chance of this. Whatever
may justly be said (and has been said)[66] about the deep significance
to women of the drama and symbolism of militancy, most suffragists
had as their goal exactly what they said — that is, to induce a male
parliament to give them the vote — and by this time, the actions of
the militants were counterproductive, at every political level. Even in
August, when the truce still stood, Helga Gill had understood that
it would be "a fatal mistake" to hold an outdoor meeting in
Workington, because "Miss Pankhurst had one, and according to ...
Miss Davies and other natives that alienated all support, and it was
only when you had the indoor meeting in Duke Street that 'respectable people' dare consider the question at all."[67] Now, hearing of the
new "Outbreak of the Suffragettes," Louis Walker and Catherine
jointly drafted a letter to the local papers on behalf of the NWF, to
"express our indignant condemnation of the outrages offered to
Mr. Asquith and other members of the Cabinet by members of the
Women's Social and Political Union," and to dissociate the NU from
such activities.[68]

Nevertheless, what Asquith had said, however vague, was better
than nothing, and was made more useful to the movement by The
Times declaring that his statement had made women's suffrage an
election issue.[69] If the first Conciliation Bill had done nothing else,
it had gained considerable press attention, especially, of course, in
papers with more claim to be called liberal than the pontifical Times;
the columns of the Nation, for example, had given prominence to
the bill's progress throughout its career.[70]

The decision to run women's suffrage candidates in the general election produced on the whole disappointing results; only two were run and they collected barely a handful of votes each,[71] although some forum for propaganda was provided. By far the most effective use of the policy occurred in the South Salford constituency – although finally no designated suffrage candidate was run there – and Catherine was much involved. Hilaire Belloc, the incumbent Liberal member (and the deplorable son of a nineteenth-century feminist, Bessie Rayner Parkes), had drawn attention to himself by his antisuffrage position, and especially, it seems, by calling the women's suffrage movement "immoral" and "unsavoury."[72] We have the story of his downfall in Catherine's own words, taken in part from a handwritten draft of a letter to the press, and in part (since the draft is damaged and not all legible) from unsigned reports in the *Common Cause*.

Pressure had begun as early as March 1910, when no election was immediately in sight. As reported in the *Common Cause*: "Last March the South Salford Liberal Association was informed by the North of England Society that unless Mr. Hilaire Belloc was withdrawn, he would be opposed at the next election by a Suffrage candidate, but that if they would adopt a Liberal favourable to the Suffrage we would leave them alone. The Liberals said they could not entertain the offer. Accordingly an Association was started and clubrooms taken, local work was prosecuted with vigour under the able organization of Miss Darlington, and Mr. Clayton consented to be the candidate. The King's death caused delays and changes, and though work was steadily continued ... it was necessary to find another candidate."[73]

Catherine's manuscript picks up the story:

On Nov. 1st as ... so long a period had elapsed ... , the Suffragists again approached the South Salford Liberal Ass[n], renewing their former offer, and suggesting the name of a candidate who would meet their views.

No reply was received from the Committee of the South Salford Liberal Ass[n].

On Nov. 21st it was announced that Mr. H.N. Brailsford, Hon. Sec. of the Committee which framed the Conciliation Bill, would stand as Independent Womens' Suffrage and Progressive Candidate.

On Nov. 22nd it was announced that Mr. Belloc's candidature was withdrawn.

It was expected that the Suffragists would then withdraw Mr. Brailsford, but the Suffragists felt that if the Liberals now wished to reconsider their original offer it was for the Liberals to approach the Suffragists this time. Preparations therefore continued unchecked; Mr. Brailsford's election address was issued and an election agent was telegraphed for from Scotland. When he arrived he found that "everything he had thought of in the train" had already been done. The Suffragists had secured the best Com*tee* rooms and the best halls in the constituency; their canvassing books were all ready, and their Candidate was the only one whose address was already issued.

On Nov. 23rd, the new Liberal Candidate, the Hon. Charles Russell, asked for an interview with the Womens' [sic] Suffrage Com*tee* in order that he might lay his views before them. The Suffragists received him and expressed their willingness to hear his views. He explained that he was a strong believer in Women's Suffrage and expressed the hope that the Suffragists would withdraw their Candidate. When asked if he would declare his support of Women's Suffrage in his Election address he expressed regret that that was impossible, as his address was already in the hands of the printers. The Suffragists said that they could not even consider his proposal that they should withdraw their candidate unless Mr. R[ussell]'s views on w.s. were declared in his election address. Mr. Russell then offered to write a letter to go out to all the electors with his Election Address, pledging himself to ... support the Conciliation Bill or any other Bill giving votes to women on equal terms with men, and [stating that he] would press for facilities in the 1st session of the new Parliament.

The Women's Suffrage Com*tee* after consultation with Mr. Brailsford decided to accede to Mr. Russell's request and withdraw from the field, having gained the object with which they entered on the campaign.

In his speech at his first meeting last night Mr. Russell gave first place to the question of Women's Suffrage; the rest of the speech was devoted to the House of Lords issue. The Liberal Association is negotiating with the Suffragists for taking over their Committee rooms and the halls they had booked for their meetings. The South Salford w.s.a. is going to support the candidature of Mr.Russell.[74]

As for Mr Belloc, the *Common Cause* said: "Let [him] say what he likes now. He has entered into private life. His coarseness and misrepresentations are no longer a blot on South Salford: the men and women of the constituency need no longer blush to hear him speak for them. ... We have ... shown ourselves *formidable* ."[75]

Such fortuitous combinations of circumstances were rare – and even in this instance, Belloc "loudly protest[ed] that the Suffragists had nothing to do with his retirement."[76] Whether there was truth in this or not, the suffragist women and their committed male allies were showing a new degree of political toughness, and had handled this situation as if it were they who were in the driver's seat. The

exact part played by Catherine is not clear; the NU had other experienced organizers in the field, but the NWF had long followed the
saga, and Catherine was certainly in South Salford with Helena
Swanwick, and active in the most critical days.[77]

The election call had come so suddenly that the whole South Salford episode had taken place before the NU's special council could
meet on 26 November 1910, to work on election policy and the fate
of the Conciliation Bill. Catherine went there fresh from the triumph in South Salford. The council passed urgency resolutions welcoming Asquith's statement, but regretting its vagueness, thanking
the Conciliation Committee and Brailsford, and instructing societies
to urge suffragist MPs to ballot for a private member's bill.[78] The
main theme, of course, was election policy, which emerged at the
end of the day generally broadened and strengthened, with a resolution urging societies not only to support women's suffrage candidates where they were being run, but actively to support those who
gave satisfactory assurances, and to do all they could to oppose the
return of MPs who had voted against the Conciliation Bill. The hottest issue was whether to target Liberal candidates, regardless of
their personal view, in closely contested areas, as a protest against
the treatment of the Conciliation Bill. Catherine shared the majority
view that this was unwise policy at a general election. "By-elections
are the time to punish for past offences," she said.[79]

The KWSA had formulated two specific questions which would
have made candidates' "assurances" more concrete, but Catherine
found the Keswick amendment had been reworded by the executive
in a way which "entirely altered" its effect; the specific questions
were gone, so was all reference to a precise commitment to the Conciliation Bill should it be reintroduced, and the amendment now
urged support in very general terms for candidates who declared
themselves in their election addresses and speeches "to be in favour
of Women's Suffrage." Disgusted, Catherine withdrew the Keswick
amendment, planning to protest in writing to the executive. A certain amount of tension between the centre and the periphery is still
evident, though on the whole the tone of the meeting seems to have
been better than at some of the earlier councils.[80]

Exactly one week after the special council, polling in the general
election began.[81] Back at Hawse End, there was no let-up for Catherine, and perhaps her single-mindedness and the speed of developments had led her to neglect the nurture of her local support group;
there had been some murmuring at the October KWSA executive
committee meeting about the tendency of the executive to take too

much upon themselves (they "ask the Gen. Com^tee fast enough when its a rummage sale" said one member).[82] Or perhaps the toll of two elections in one year was being felt; and funds too were low. For whatever reason, when Catherine decided to devote herself to the Egremont division, she had to go it alone. As soon as the election was over she sent a report to the *Common Cause:*

I have been working single-handed in this division for ten days. It is the only Cumberland constituency in which we did not work at the last election, and it is significant that it is the only one whose member voted against the Conciliation Bill. Both candidates in this election were unsatisfactory. The Conservative, who has been re-elected, dislikes to see women taking part in politics, except when "helping" men (i.e., canvassing). The Liberal professed great friendship to our cause, but knew nothing about the Conciliation Bill and would not promise to vote for it. I have been doing propaganda work in the industrial part of the constituency, holding open-air meetings immediately preceding the candidates' meetings, and getting electors to go and question the candidates on Women's Suffrage. It has been hard work covering the ground alone, and without a motor or carriage; but the pioneer work done by Miss Helga Gill in the same district last August has made it easier than it would have been otherwise. I was told that the people of those mining towns and villages were very rough, and that I should not get a hearing, especially in the midst of a very keenly contested election. But we know that we can always count on fair play and a good hearing from the men of Cumberland. So I disregarded the pessimists. I have had large and perfectly orderly crowds ... and have met with sympathy and good-will everywhere. The resolution (urging the candidates, if elected, to support the Bill) was carried at every meeting ... and copies were taken to the candidates by some of their principal supporters. The men are keenly interested and eager to help. ... They will hardly believe that their member opposes it. "Voted *agin* it, did he? But it's simple joostice." One unrepentant heckler was set upon by the whole of the rest of the audience after our meeting. I heard them arguing with him hotly as I came away. I think we can safely count on pressure being brought to bear on Mr.Grant when the Bill comes up again. The local papers have given good reports ... in spite of the unusual demand made on their space at election time.

As well as all this, Catherine fitted in an indoor meeting (surely a relief in a northern November?) in the neighbouring constituency of Whitehaven, and got a branch of the NU launched there. The incumbent Conservative, who was prosuffrage, was defeated, but the new Labour member "has given absolutely satisfactory answers to all our questions, so our cause will not suffer by the change."[83] On the last polling day, Catherine did her Christmas shopping by mail; the Army and Navy Cooperative Society's book department received a small order for books to go to family and friends.[84]

The work of a very full year was over. Catherine had become known throughout the NU, and in this, the year in which she turned thirty, her latent qualities had bloomed. Her political astuteness, organizing skill, courage, and flair for communication (despite an occasional lapse) showed as they had never shown before. The things she did for the cause cannot be separated from what the cause did for her. Less obvious, but not hard to read between the lines, was the direction of her political education. Although she would continue to try to drag the Liberal party along the road she thought it should go, her identification with Liberalism was weakening. Although her upper-middle-class background would always be with her, she communicated freely and with mutual trust and respect with workers. At the end of 1910, she had perhaps more sympathy with the women and men of Whitehaven than with the cousin who wrote of herself and her sister (a couple probably representative of many who missed the chance to break the mould): "I wish we had got heads like yours, to do something useful, but our brains are like two lumps of jelly, and we should die of terror if we ever had even to *sit* on a Platform as ornaments. ... Some day when Sheila and I live together, as 2 old 'decayed gentlewomen', in a villa, with a cat and a canary, we shall feel grateful to you for getting us the vote, and giving us a little position in the world."[85]

6 Organizing Press Work and Experiencing International Suffrage Sisterhood: January to August 1911

Catherine commonly went to London for at least several weeks near the beginning of the year, and now, in 1911, the intensity of the suffrage campaign left no doubt as to how her time there would be spent.[1] Increasingly, Catherine undertook responsibilities at the NU headquarters, and for the national body in different geographical areas, but without completely giving up her local and regional involvement in the northwest. In this, her career reflects the nation-wide development of the NU, the contribution of the provincial societies, the insistence of the north on being heard, the sometimes painful adaptation necessitated by rapid growth and constantly changing conditions. Her political development over the next two years, as well, was closely to parallel that of the NU as a whole, marked by a last attempt to bring official Liberalism on side, followed by final disillusionment both in the Liberal party and in private members' bills, which would always depend on a measure of government goodwill. For strategic reasons, the NU would look to the Left for support; for Catherine, this was to be a move for which she was ready philosophically.

The December 1910 election had made very little change in the composition of the House of Commons. Liberals and Conservatives were evenly balanced, but the Liberals were still in power, with the help of the Irish Nationalists and of the small Labour party.[2] Brailsford supplied the NU executive with a count of the suffrage supporters: 408 members were said to be in favour of some form of women's suffrage; of these, 246 were thought to be reliable, 120 less so, and 42 were adultists. That left 65 MPs said to be "neutral," and 193 decided antisuffragists.[3] Suffragists had reason to congratulate themselves on the recognition of the issue implied by these figures, which at its best could be interpreted as the "mandate" they had sought; but the mood was made sober by bitter experience and by knowledge of the other factors in the current political picture. Asquith was still intransigent, and would not make women's enfranchisement a part of any government measure. There were not enough determined Liberal suffragists to carry a wide measure through the House, unless it had been initiated by the government.[4] An interparty private member's bill would lose Conservative support if it were too broad, and would arouse opposition from the ministry if it were seen as too narrow. The Conciliation Bill had been designed to meet as many as possible of these difficulties, but it was greatly disliked by influential cabinet members. Amendments to the government's promised Reform Bill, since they again would not be government-sponsored, would be subject to the same knife-edge risks as the private members' bills had faced, and continued to face. All in all, the women's suffragists were still caught between a rock and a hard place. In this dilemma, the NU decided to go with the Conciliation Bill once more; at the least it provided them with a focus for the continuing campaign.

All-absorbing as the suffrage struggle was to those engaged in it, to many politicians and much of the public it continued to be merely a bit of business taking place at the side of the stage, at the most a subplot to the major drama of the confrontation with the House of Lords. The mandate given to the new House of Commons to proceed with women's suffrage was at best shaky, but the government's mandate to tackle the problem of the House of Lords was now firm; all that had been required was for the Liberals to be again able to form a ministry. The bill to limit the Lords' power was introduced on 21 February 1911, passed second reading by a majority of 125 on 1 March, and was through the third stage by 15 May. In the Upper House the committee stage lasted until 6 July, with many amendments being passed, all of which were rejected on the Bill's return to the Commons on 24 July. The second week in August saw the final debate in the House of Lords, a cliffhanger to the end; the bill was finally passed on 10 August (without the threatened mass creation of peers) by a majority of 131–114.

Irritating as it may have been to witness the amount of attention paid to the abolition of the Lords' monopoly of power as against the men's monopoly of power (to use Catherine's analogy), most suffragists recognized from early 1911 that the taming of the Upper House, inevitable before the end of the year, would remove one barrier to the enactment of a women's franchise bill, and they did their best to keep their foothold on the corner of the stage.

The Conciliation Committee had made changes in their bill, to remove all traces of plural voting, or the possibility that it would result in the creation of faggot votes.[5] Several MPs had pledged to bring in the bill if they were successful in the ballot. None of them were, but Sir George Kemp, a Liberal (former Unionist) member for Manchester, agreed to take it up. The Manchester wss played an important part in persuading Sir George.[6] He was also, as it happened, the Marshalls' nearest neighbour on Derwentwater (the Kemps' property, Lingholm, is adjacent to Hawse End), and the husband of Lady Beatrice Kemp, who was active in the KWSA; so there may have been private as well as public pressures on him to get him to agree to step into the breach. The first reading of the new Conciliation Bill was on 9 February 1911, its second on 5 May.

Behind the scenes, the NU still struggled with the aftermath of the structural changes of 1910, in which Catherine had played so large a part. At the annual council, held in Kensington on 26 January 1911, the ballot for officers and positions on the executive assumed a prominence it had never before had. Bertha Mason lost her position as honorary parliamentary secretary to Edith Palliser; Kathleen Courtney replaced Edith Dimock as honorary secretary in a three-cornered contest with Frances Sterling as the other aspirant.[7] This was a radical infusion of new blood, and not painless. Mason had served the NU loyally for years, and had now been overtaken by time and change; she was deeply hurt. Indeed, her displacement was more complete than anyone had intended; unlike other candidates, she had not stood for election to the executive as well as to her position (which carried an *ex officio* seat), and so was suddenly without any place at all in the counsels of the NU. At its second meeting after the council, the executive tried to make amends, passing an urgency resolution to coopt Mason to the executive; they may also have been genuinely anxious not to lose the benefit of her long experience. She refused, giving as her reason a reluctance to override what she saw as the council's decision, but clearly speaking out of great personal pain, which she did not try to disguise.[8]

If Mason was hurt, others were angry. Dr Ethel Bentham also resigned from the executive following the January council, although she had herself been highly critical of the work of both Mason and Dimock; her emphasis on what she saw as the ill effects of the setting up of the federations suggests that she had a clear perception of the struggle as one between the old guard, London-centred, and the sharing of power with relative newcomers from the provinces. Mrs Broadley-Reid resigned not only from the executive, but from the National Union itself,[9] setting up a technical dilemma by declaring herself still a member of the LSWS, which automatically brought NU membership with it, as Edith Palliser told her during a heated exchange at a London suffrage conference, recorded with interest by Catherine.[10] Some letters from branches followed the resignations, but the executive refused to be drawn into further discussion, resolving (on a motion of Margaret Ashton and Maude Royden, both northern members) to "take no action in the matter."[11]

The NU's commitment to internal parliamentary democracy had been tested, and had come through. The election of new members to the executive, full of fresh ideas, brought changes and a certain amount of tension, but it is a mistake to see the committee as continuing divided between two factions, the old guard and the new. Evidently, the advent of new faces and fresh ideas was welcomed by some of those who had carried the burden for a long time, and by none more readily than by Millicent Fawcett, now sixty-four years old and determined to see the cause through.

Catherine was by now definitely part of the group which was moving into positions of influence. Maude Royden was already a close friend and mentor, Helena Swanwick increasingly so, and January marked an important step in what was to be a very long and important working association with Kathleen Courtney; they formally granted each other permission to use first names.[12] Catherine left no account of the January council meeting, but except for one disappointment, and regret that feelings had been hurt, she was probably pleased with the outcome.

Although she stood for no ongoing office, Catherine was a candidate for election as one of the NU's delegates to the conference of the International Woman Suffrage Alliance (IWSA) to be held in Stockholm from 12 to 17 June; but she was not among the twelve chosen.[13] This may have been a big disappointment at the time but, as it turned out, not a long-lasting one; by 2 March, the executive found that the NU was entitled to send twelve alternates as well as twelve delegates, and Catherine's name was back on the list.[14] It was also from the time of the January council that Catherine was among those to whom the minutes of the executive were circulated (other than the committee members). The practice was to have a list of those who were to receive the minutes of any particular meeting, and to rely on them to mail them on from one to another when they had read them. Convenient as it may be for Catherine's biographer, it is almost embarrassing to find that they never (or seldom) got past the first two names on the list – those of Caroline and Catherine – and so are still to be found among Catherine's papers, a testimony to her increasing importance in the NU, but also an example of one of her curious lapses in efficiency. In any event, at about this time, arrangements were made to have the minutes printed and made available to societies for a small charge.[15]

One of the major discussions at the council was on a resolution to adopt a "General Post" election policy, by which suffragists would become more actively engaged at elections, supporting prosuffrage candidates and working against antisuffrage candidates. They were to be enabled to do this without being in conflict with the party of their choice by having each person working in whatever was the nearest constituency where their party's candidate was the better suffragist. Catherine had energetically promoted the scheme before the last election, but had not succeeded in having it passed by the national council, although the NWF had adopted it and had sent out fliers with a tear-off sheet for suffragists to fill in and return, outlining their availability and preference. Catherine indeed saw it as one of the benefits resulting from the federations, which could become "a sort of political labour exchange."[16] To have the policy accepted in January 1911, as it was, might seem rather an insubstantial victory, since it was primarily a general election strategy, and after the two elections of 1910, most people were devoutly hoping that there would be no more in the immediate future. However, the policy was controversial, some seeing it as an abandonment of the NU's non-party stance – which it was not – and others seeing it as a way of recognizing a reality, and so breaking the deadlock of "propaganda only" elections. Catherine and her friends hoped the scheme would increase suffrage visibility at by-elections as well as general elections, and enable more effective use to be made of funds and of the NU's paid organizers, as well as serving its primary purpose of enabling all suffragists to throw their whole energy and enthusiasm into every campaign. Catherine had prepared the ground with her usual thoroughness, by means of a letter to the *Common Cause* just before the council meeting.[17] After the council, she followed up with a full explanation for the general readership, giving practical suggestions on the exchange of accommodation, funding, use of motor cars, and so on, and again reinforcing her view of the value of the scheme: "It is useless to ignore the fact that party feeling is the most potent force in the political arena during an election. We should act on the principle of Ju-Jitsu, which teaches how the weaker combatant may prevail by using the strength of his adversary and turning it to account for his own ends. If we can devise a way of bringing the forces which inspire party feeling and the forces which inspire the suffrage movement into line, so that they reinforce instead of neutralizing one another, we shall gain enormously in driving power."[18]

Catherine's report to the October provincial council on working with the press, and her article in the *Common Cause*, attracted attention and sparked action. At its first meeting on 2 February 1911, the new executive followed up by the appointment of a press committee, consisting of Margaret Heitland, a leading Cambridge suffragist (doubtless well known to Catherine, who visited Cambridge regularly, and worked and acted with suffragists there), Helena Swanwick and Ivory Cripps, to whom were added by cooption Marion Chadwick, Ida O'Malley, and Catherine.[19] Within a month Catherine was appointed honorary secretary and commissioned to set up what was now to be a "department" rather than a committee, as part of a general departmentalizing of head office, implying more continuity, better record-keeping, and more full-time staff service. A regular bi-weekly meeting time was set, and at Catherine's request, Emily Leaf was coopted. Catherine evidently undertook to set the press department going during her London stay. She saw it as having a wide mandate. Efforts were made to get more women's suffrage news into the papers. As usual Catherine had plenty of ideas on how to overcome difficulties; amateur reporters should send in their own reports of meetings which the press had not covered; and, if such reporters were hard to find, societies should organize classes to train them.[20] The London papers were targeted, with a special record being compiled of all references to women's suffrage – and omissions. The editor of the *Daily Graphic* instituted a regular women's suffrage feature; Catherine urged women to repay him by buying the *Graphic* and also the *Manchester Guardian*, which had a good record of taking the women's issue seriously. Plans were made to make sure that the papers did not lack for news of suffrage activities taking place in London, in the provinces, and abroad.[21]

Catherine continued "her wonderful work" until April, by which time she had the department rolling, and was able to hand the task of honorary press secretary over to Emily Leaf before she went back to Keswick. At this time, too, on the recommendation of the press committee, a part-time paid press secretary was appointed to help with the work, and another member coopted to this busy committee to replace Catherine.[22] Her final report was made at the April provincial council meeting, held in Haslemere, and stressed the role of the federation correspondents, and the importance of making full use of the local press.[23]

The women's suffrage organizations were determined to back the second Conciliation Bill with every possible effort, hoping that if they could turn the promised support within the House into a resounding majority, the government, however reluctant, could be persuaded to grant time for further facilities. On 20 February 1911, shortly after the first reading, the MLWS mounted an impressive demonstration; Catherine wrote a full report which appeared, unsigned, in the *Common Cause*.[24] The chair was taken by H.W. Nevinson, the journalist. Well-known speakers included Sir Joseph Walton (Liberal), who moved the resolution of support for the bill; Lord Lytton, who received a great ovation for his work as chair of the Conciliation Committee;[25] and George Lansbury (Labour), who made a hard-hitting speech, firmly laying it on Liberal women "not to do a stroke of work for their Party until this measure had become law," and urging Labour men to vote against any government bill that did not include women. Catherine's new colleague on the press committee, the Rev. J. Ivory Cripps, was one of the minor speakers; he pointed out that the government had only themselves to blame if the Conciliation Bill was not democratic enough to please them, since lack of ministerial support had made the bill dependent on Conservative backing. Madame Marie Brema, of the Actresses' Franchise League, sang dramatic and uplifting songs.

Altogether it was an inspirational occasion, with an enthusiastic audience of women and men, and only one brave antisuffragist prevented the resolution from being passed unanimously. Curiously, public events of this kind, though probably valuable at the time, have worn less well than the down-to-earth (and sometimes acrimonious) working meetings of the NU, where many of us would find ourselves quite at home, once we had become accustomed to the conscious formality of proceedings. The speakers made sensible points, but the atmosphere and some of the rhetoric seem almost as archaic as Marie Brema's emotionally charged songs.[26]

Throughout the spring of 1911, hopes for the Conciliation Bill rose. The militants had resumed their truce, a measure of cordiality between the WSPU and the NU, indeed between all the women's suffrage societies, was reestablished, and a joint consultative board was set up to coordinate the efforts of all groups with an interest in the cause.[27] The NU had been often enough burnt by reaction to WSPU activities to maintain some reserve in its attitude. For example, when Brailsford published the quite shocking results of his inquiry into the action taken by the police against suffrage demonstrators on Black Friday,[28] the executive decided that it would be a "tactical mistake" for the NU to become involved.[29] Despite this, plans were again on foot for a joint demonstration to take place in the summer, despite strong disapproval expressed by the LSWS, although they agreed to cooperate on certain conditions.[30]

Meanwhile, Liberal and other parliamentary supporters and the indifferent or wavering had to be endlessly nurtured, to bring them to the pitch where they would not only vote for the second reading but would press for further facilities. As we have seen, Catherine had made the MPs of the northwest region her particular charge, and had come to know several of them personally. In London, she kept up her contacts, and extended them. She followed the fortunes of Howard, the Eskdale MP, with interest, reported that he had been impressed by suffrage arguments, and learnt that Helena Swanwick saw him as a "nice, kind, not very forcible creature," and entirely in the (adultist) hands of Margaret Llewelyn Davies.[31] Even confirmed antisuffragists were given attention; Catherine drafted a memorial (probably for use by the NWF) to J.A. Grant, the MP for Cockermouth, asking him, if he could not vote for the bill, at least not to oppose it against the wishes of a large number of his constituents.[32]

Threats to the Conciliation Bill came in various forms. Should the bill pass and a new register of voters have to be brought in, normal procedure would have required the immediate dissolution of Parliament, an event seen as likely to be cataclysmic in the already overheated political climate, with the proponents of Home Rule joining those looking for reform of the Lords in their determination not to have the government at risk before these major measures were carried through.[33] Catherine attended the opening of the International Women's Franchise Club (IWFC) on 23 February, where this issue was raised, and there is some evidence that she was present at at least one behind-the-scenes discussion with politicians.[34] In the event, the suffragists made it clear that they would be content to wait until the next general election occurred in the normal course of events, and would not press for a dissolution.

Another disturbing scheme, discussed on the same occasion, was the move to subject the women's franchise to a referendum.[35] A resurgent National League for Opposing Women's Suffrage (NLOWS) had seized on the idea with relish, and promoted it with the public and among MPs, claiming, on rather specious grounds, that not even the women municipal voters wanted the parliamentary franchise. Women's suffragists feared the outcome of a referendum, an awkward position to justify, since they were claiming ever more and more popular support among the voters, to whom the referendum would probably be limited. Legitimately, too, the women did not see why they should be made the subject of an experiment. The idea continued to simmer for some time, and remained as a serious block to cooperation with Unionist suffragists.[36]

The NU was well aware that the second reading was only a necessary preliminary to the real struggle. While an immense amount of organization and effort went into making sure that nothing went wrong at this stage, the campaign was planned to carry on throughout the summer, throughout the year if necessary. When the bill passed second reading on 5 May 1911 by a majority of 167 (although in a half-empty House), the women's suffragists nevertheless were delighted, feeling that they had the fuel they needed for the more difficult task of persuading the government to grant facilities for the further stages. The virulent attack on the bill from the government front bench which had been so major a feature of the 1910 debate was not repeated, if only because of an agreement between the Unionist and Liberal leaders that neither front bench would take part in the debate, supposedly in the interest of saving time.[37] Hope also rested on the fact that, unlike the 1910 bill, no move was made to refer this one to Grand Committee.

Catherine was still in the south during April 1911, attending the provincial council meeting in Surrey on 7 April, and making final arrangements to hand over the press department. She was absent from the KWSA executive meeting as late as 27 April, so may well have stayed in London until the excitement of the second reading was over, and perhaps was in the ladies' gallery for the debate, before heading home to organize regional pressure for the granting of further facilities, and to prepare for the IWSA congress in Stockholm.

During her time in London, Catherine, though still not a member of the NU executive, had been part of subtle but very far-reaching growth within the organization. The federation scheme, in whose acceptance she had played such a major role, had not only freed regional groups to develop the strategies most suited to their areas, but had made the up and coming provincial suffrage leaders much more visible nationally, providing them with a forum – the provincial councils – where they would be both seen and heard, could become acquainted and indeed could reinforce each other. This in turn had led to the election of a significant number of new women to the national executive, where they quickly made their mark and brought in other like-minded women. Not only was Catherine coopted into the new press department, but her successor, Emily Leaf, herself a Londoner, but closely in sympathy with the new wave of leaders, was coopted on to the executive itself, together with Ida

O'Malley.[38] By the middle of the year, Helena Swanwick found her work as editor of the *Common Cause*, and with the head office, so demanding that she resigned her long-held position as honorary secretary of the Manchester society and moved to London.[39] Catherine's vision of the press work, locally and nationally, as one network, was characteristic of the new development of the NU as a nationally integrated pressure group, where the relation between the periphery and the centre would be a two-way street, with information and suggestions passing freely in either direction, and use being made of every means of propaganda and persuasion directed at public and politicians, individuals and parties, government and opposition.

While the work of the regions was facilitated, the work in London was also moving into a new stage. Almost imperceptibly, the emphasis was shifting from formal delegations and impersonal presentations towards a more intimate personal contact with individual politicians in all parties. Brailsford and his Conciliation Committee had done much to initiate this trend, and it was work in which Catherine was to prove particularly gifted; she had already practised it with the politicians of the northwest region. The benefits of the approach included access to information, a better feel for the mood of the House, and, not least, the exposure of a significant number of parliamentarians to individual women who were clearly responsible and who did not fit the stereotypes of the suffragist campaigners endlessly presented by the newspapers.

Despite these developments, with which Catherine had reason to be well pleased, she had not spent every moment of her time in London on suffrage work. Probably one of the things she went to London for was to pursue her studies in singing, although for this year I have no direct evidence of this. But music was never far from her mind, and just before she went back to Keswick she ordered material from Augeners, the big London music publishers, and made inquiries about the prices of some children's singing games.[40]

In addition, other public matters caught Catherine's attention. Suffrage studies understandably seldom have much to say about other legislation introduced by the Liberals during this time, and indeed the nonparty stance of the major suffrage societies tended to keep discussion of controversial issues in their journals on a low key, but it is in the nature of things that women campaigning for the vote should take a lively interest in public affairs, and there was plenty going on at this time. Not only was the major issue of the Parliament bill current, but so was important social legislation, some of it quite radical in nature, and of immense interest to Catherine, with her background of study in economics. At some time during these months she attended a series of lectures on the topic of "Thrift," which formed part of the discussion around Lloyd George's national insurance scheme. Following on the state-financed scheme of old age pensions introduced by Asquith in 1908, the new act set up a compulsory contributory health insurance plan for low-income workers, together with unemployment insurance for certain trades.[41] Catherine heard arguments for and against the scheme, and evaluations of a variety of different schemes. Without (unfortunately) adding comments of her own, she made rather full notes on a speech by a Mr Miller, who attacked the whole scheme with an eclectic mixture of arguments, some of which have still a familiar ring, and which reflect a decided resistance to the position being adopted by the New Liberals.[42] The scheme, although initially well received in Parliament, was original enough to generate a great deal of controversy; on a variety of grounds, opposition came from the Friendly (Insurance) Societies, the British Medical Association, and some Labour representatives.

The northwest had not been out of Catherine's mind during her stay in London. Before the NWF committee met on 1 April, she made extensive notes for Miss Knight and Miss Highton, who would be representing the KWSA. Some items on her list are routine stuff (the raising of money, distribution of literature, and so on) that one might suppose could have been left to the KWSA officers to manage without a reminder from Catherine, but in the main the list provides an example of the kind of networking the NU needed, where her knowledge of the London situation was translated into appropriate action at the periphery. Support for the Conciliation Bill (then still a month off its second reading) was to be raised by meetings, resolutions, letters to MPs in every constituency, and letters to the papers explaining the bill (Catherine enclosed a copy of an article in the *Manchester Guardian* to help with this). Brailsford was collecting statistics of the women municipal voters who would be enfranchised by the new Conciliation Bill, and help was needed to compile this information locally. The same group – the women ratepayers – were to be invited to put pressure on the borough councils to petition the government to grant facilities for the further progress of the bill. Judging by the NWF report published in the *Common Cause* on 11 May, the federation followed through well, carrying out all the suggested actions in support of the bill.[43]

Catherine took a particular interest in the approach to the borough councils, which was still ongoing when she came back to the Lake District early in May. The project had been adopted by the NU, and had already met with success in over fifty boroughs. Catherine had friends and sympathizers in Whitehaven, where the small group who had worked in the 1910 elections had coalesced into a suffrage society,[44] and now presumably helped with the collection of signatures from women ratepayers for the petition which was sent to the town clerk. Catherine made notes describing how she orchestrated the moves, paying careful attention to timing:

Meanwhile I wrote on behalf of the Federation to all the members of the Council giving them notice that this matter would be brought up (my letter reached them the day before the Council met) as we did not want them to feel it had been sprung upon them; saying this Federation wished to support the petition of the women ratepayers; enclosing a copy of the Conciliation Memorandum and a ... leaflet; calling attention to the fact that it is a *non-Party* Bill; that a large no. of the towns in the United Kingdom had already done what they were being asked to do; explaining why we appeal to them. ... I saw the Mayor and the Town Clerk at the beginning ..., went and asked Mover and Seconder myself and saw several of the other Councillors, *esp. those reported likely to oppose.*[45]

The copy of the petition on which Catherine wrote these notes is marked "Please return to C.E.M."; the notes were probably made at the request of someone embarking on a similar attempt. Catherine's flair for handling this kind of move was becoming known, and even she herself must have begun to recognize that she had a real talent for the work, and as with the press work, she wanted to share it. For example, the reports she had sent to the *Common Cause*, describing her election work in vivid detail, were not written (or accepted by the editor) solely to put the events on record, or to boast, or even to be inspirational in a general sense, but to give concrete examples of what had to be done and how to set about it.

In Whitehaven, Catherine's skilful and nonconfrontational approach paid off, and on 10 May, the borough council unanimously agreed to petition the government for further time for the Conciliation Bill. For suffragists, the idea of working through the borough councils had a nice logic to it, which Catherine took the opportunity to point out in a letter to the *Whitehaven News*. The council, she said, had paid attention because the request had come from women ratepayers, enfranchised in the borough. When women taxpayers had votes nationally they would similarly have a claim on the time and attention of Parliament which they did not now possess. Lacking it, they had to go through the local councils simply because this was the one place where they did have representation. Catherine expressed the suffragists' gratitude to the borough council for its unanimous decision, a decision which did not necessarily express support for the bill, "but merely a desire to see the women's case honestly dealt with."[46] The NU persuaded over a hundred boroughs to forward petitions; Cockermouth and Keswick were also among the number. There remains to this day, along with Catherine's papers in the Cumbria Record Office, a banner inscribed "KESWICK • VRBAN • DIS[T] • COVNCIL • PRAYS • FOR • WOMENS • SVFFRAGE," presumably used with pride in later demonstrations. The NU hoped to follow up with a deputation to the prime minister from the dignitaries of the towns involved, but Asquith refused to receive them. Catherine drafted a letter for use in the local press: "Suffragists are used to being [denied the] opportunity of stating their case, but [illegible] feel that a deputation of such weight and importance as this would have been should have received greater consideration, especially from a Prime Minister who has asked for evidence that there is a real demand for this Bill in the country."[47]

May was a busy month in the calendar of the NWF and its constituent societies. As honorary organizing secretary, Catherine had a great deal to report to the KWSA's third annual meeting on 17 May, on the political progress of the cause, on the various meetings of the NU councils and the NWF that she had attended during the year, and on the suffrage campaigns that had been undertaken. Not surprisingly, for her "the great work of the year," as far as the NU itself was concerned, had been the reorganization and decentralization, the launching of the provincial councils, and changes at head office (including the initiating of the press department), for all of which the KWSA could take some credit.[48] An election of officers left the slate unchanged, with Caroline as president and Catherine as honorary organizing secretary.

A couple of days later Catherine was off to Carlisle for the annual meeting of the NWF. Maude Royden, as the representative of the NU national executive, was spending a week on suffrage work in the area, and was one of the principal speakers. Catherine was the other, giving an address on "The Conciliatory Spirit," which was so well received that she was at once invited to speak to the executive committee of the Carlisle Liberal Club.[49]

Only very brief and rough notes survive for the speech Catherine made to the NWF, but they are significant. War and anger might be necessary, she said, but they were purely destructive: "If you want to get things done you must start with [the] desire to make a friend." Wickedness was not what made people into antisuffragists, rather it was timidity and prejudice — things "best met by gentleness." She urged her hearers to *"Deal gently with people's prejudices.* We all love our prejudices and can [rise?] fiercely to [their] defence." Stressing the importance of personally taking trouble, she gave the town councils as an example of where approval was more effective than abuse; whatever their past misdeeds had been, it was better to make friends.[50] Certainly Catherine was describing what she saw as the best way of getting results, but she was also articulating a profound principle of nonviolence – the refusal to dehumanize and distance the opponent.

Many other matters of importance were discussed at this, the first annual meeting of the NWF since its official inauguration. The tensions which had arisen the previous October (over the attempt to gain more support from the Women's Liberal Associations) seem to have disappeared, and the impression now is of a vigorous organization, responsive to the improved communication between the region and the national office. In addition to the usual business items – including the reelection of Catherine to the chair and of Louis Walker (highly praised by Catherine in her opening remarks) as honorary secretary – time was set aside for discussion of issues current in the NU, the major ones being "election policy, Tax Resistance, and various problems connected with the maintenance of a non-party attitude on political questions."[51]

Taking place as it did just two weeks after the triumphant second reading of the Conciliation Bill in June 1911, and before the government had announced its intentions, the NWF gathering in Carlisle, together with organizations and special meetings all over the country, passed an urgency resolution calling for facilities for the further stages, and sent forward a petition which was presented to the House of Commons by R.D. Denman, the MP for Carlisle.[52] Indeed, Catherine was concerned during her short spring stay in Cumberland to practise what she had been preaching, and local MPs were not allowed to forget the Conciliation Bill. She wrote to thank George Kemp for taking on the bill, and kept in touch with Denman and Wilfred Lawson.[53] But it was hard to read the signs for success or failure.

A deputation from the Conciliation Committee tried to arrange a meeting with Asquith, but, as Catherine wrote, "he put them off first from May 22nd to May 24th, and then from the 24th to the 29th, and then finally said he did not think it was necessary for him to see them at all."[54] This was followed by a government announcement that, if yet another such bill was passed with a good majority in the next session, a full week would be set aside for its consideration. Like so many of the government's pronouncements on this issue, the wording used by Lloyd George in the House was ambiguous as to exactly what was being promised, and the suffragists' initial reaction was of anger at the new delay. But statements by Sir Edward Grey in the next two weeks persuaded the suffragists, and even the WSPU, of the ministry's sincerity, and a victory early in 1912 seemed probable.[55] The suffragists began to gear up for what they once more hoped would be one last effort, beginning in the autumn. Until then, Catherine felt that there was little that had to be done, and in place of the usual outdoor summer campaign, she suggested: "in conclusion … that it would be well, for the sake of the cause, that all of us who have been working almost without intermission for these last three years should take a good holiday this summer – a complete rest – in preparation" for the autumn and winter campaign.[56]

In this climate of expectancy, the joint demonstration planned by the NU and the WSPU, together with other suffrage organizations, went ahead; forty thousand women marched from the Embankment to the Albert Hall on 17 June.[57] The date, oddly enough, had been set in conflict with the long-planned meeting of the International Women's Suffrage Alliance (IWSA). Catherine and her mother missed the London demonstration to be in Stockholm (Hal Marshall represented Keswick – and the Marshall family – in the parade). Mrs Fawcett, however, had decided that it was so important for her to be present at this display of unity that she must pass up the Stockholm conference. Her decision may have been a wise one in light of the delicate relations between the militants and the constitutionalists, but it dismayed Carrie Chapman Catt, president of the IWSA, and some of the Swedish organizers, who had looked forward to her presence as someone well known and firmly associated with constitutional methods. Catt wrote from Sweden, a month before the conference, saying she had found a "very bitter feeling against Millitant [sic] methods here"; places promised for meetings had been withdrawn and some subscriptions cancelled following news of the last militant demonstration.[58] But Sweden made the IWSA welcome, even putting out commemorative stamps; the ones Catherine bought are still with her papers.[59]

By the time she set off for Stockholm, Catherine had come a long way from being the rather marginal representative or alternate she had seemed likely to be at the time of the NU council meeting in February. Not only was she now a full delegate, but she had been appointed by Carrie Chapman Catt, on Fawcett's recommendation, to chair the resolutions committee,[60] and was to be the opening speaker at the first discussion session of the conference. Caroline

Marshall was also now among the delegates, and Frank may have been at some of the sessions, since the Marshalls planned to take a holiday together in Scandinavia after the gathering was over.

Attendance at a conference of the IWSA was a sure way to place the wearing day-to-day political struggle in an encouraging context of advance for women (in the Western liberal democracies) that was inexorable, if slow and hard-won. The international story may still serve as an antidote to too parochial a view of the campaign in any one country; those historians, for instance, who do not look beyond the manœuvring of British politicians and parties have not seen the whole picture, a myopia which also, more excusably, afflicted many of those engaged in the struggle.

The IWSA had first been projected at the annual meeting of the National American Woman Suffrage Association (NAWSA) in Washington in 1902, when Carrie Chapman Catt had been president of that body, and had been formally inaugurated in Berlin in 1904, with affiliates in nine countries. Now, in 1911, organizations in twenty-four countries were in membership, and more were on the point of joining. In addition to the tiny (and largely dependent) Isle of Man, where women had been able to vote since 1881, women already had the franchise in New Zealand and in Australia before the IWSA was fully established; since its inauguration women in Norway and Finland had gained the vote, as had the women of five of the United States. During the same period, great advances had been made in a number of countries in gaining the vote in local government.

In her presidential address at Stockholm, Carrie Chapman Catt reflected on these achievements.[61] The women in front of her scarcely needed her encouragement to carry on with their efforts, but were eager to learn from each other's experiences; much of the conference agenda was taken up with short reports from various countries and organizations, which also served to introduce the members to each other. Generally, the language used was English, but delegates might speak in French or German. Some interpretation was provided, but Catherine's fluency in both these languages undoubtedly enriched the time for her, in and out of formal sessions.

The real meat of the business sessions was in the times set aside for discussion of issues, and it was the first of these that Catherine introduced with a ten-minute speech on the Tuesday morning on the role of the enfranchised countries in assisting the international suffrage movement with propaganda, and in countering false reports. Catherine began by commenting on "the sense of International comradeship in a great cause which a congress of this kind gives us," which she wanted to see made "more widespread, more continuous" than would be done simply by reporting back to suffragists at home. She developed her intention in more depth:

Can we not reach a wider public? ... Our chief foes today are ignorance, prejudice, timidity, above all lack of imagination. The chief hindrance to the progress of our movement is not the opposition of bad men, but the lack of imagination of good men – and women – to see what that opposition means, and what our movement stands for; not the opposition of those who possess to those who demand liberty, but the strange inability of those who love liberty themselves, who have often made great sacrifices for the sake of liberty themselves, to see that the spirit which inspires the Women's Suffrage movement is the same spirit which has inspired every other great struggle for liberty since the world began. In England today some of the very men who enfranchised the working men of England in 1884 and gave political freedom to our late enemy in S. Africa turn on their fellow-countrywomen with mocks [sic] and sneers when they too ask for representation and political freedom.

How can we rouse the imagination of these people? How are we to dispel their ignorance, overcome their prejudices, supply their lack of courage?

By spreading the Truth, by showing what have been the results of trusting women and admitting them as fellow-citizens in other countries. Ignorance and prejudice must be met with knowledge, fears will vanish in the light of experience. Imagination must be roused to see all that is at present undone, or ill done, because it can only be well done by men and women working together. People must be made to realize that for a nation to refuse to avail itself of the women's as well as the men's point of view in politics is to deliberately maim its political vision; it is as if a man were to go about the world with only one eye open on the plea that he could see as much as he wanted to without opening the other.

Predictably (in light of her current interest) Catherine explained that in her view the best way of spreading knowledge was through the press. She recognized the difficulty of persuading editors to give space to suffrage news and suggested the formation in every country of a women's press agency. She spoke of what she had learnt from organizing the NU press department: "Women need their own representatives in the Press as much as elsewhere. A great thinking women's public is growing up and men do not realize it. What they think women want is shown by the 'Women's Page' of a men's newspaper of which the Times Women's Supplement was the crowning insult. The question of the circulation of news is largely – chiefly –

a question of demand and supply. If we want Suffrage news to be circulated we must first create the demand and then organize the supply." Catherine elaborated on this theme, illustrating her argument with diagrams. As she had done before in the British context, she urged the suffrage societies to make it their business to supply news to the public press and to demand that news of importance to women be well covered. She also hoped to see a regular interchange of international news and particularly asked that the enfranchised countries make it their business to supply information on the benefits following the vote.[62]

Catherine took copious notes on the conference proceedings, and also collected together the notes made by some of the other British delegates. The wording of the official report is at times close enough to her notes to suggest that she had a hand in its preparation.[63] Throughout, there was much talk of problems and opportunities connected with the press; other major discussions centred on the effects of women's attainment of the municipal vote, and on the relation of women to existing political parties. Catherine played an active role, bringing her experience to bear here, intervening with her flair for the wording of an amendment there. Caroline Marshall also had a part to play, leading a discussion on the best methods of work, and adding a comment on another occasion on the educative value of the campaign to get the support of the municipalities for women's suffrage.

Unfortunately, we have no record of Catherine's reflections on what she felt she gained from the conference, but it came at a time when her horizon, never very narrow, was broadening to include a vision of a greatly changed world. She may have brought away more than she knew. At Stockholm she met many of the leading women of Europe and the United States, some of whom shared and augmented her vision. Dr Aletta Jacobs of the Netherlands, later one of the prime movers behind the Hague Congress of 1915, was a member of Catherine's resolutions committee; Rosika Schwimmer of Hungary was much in evidence, Lida Gustava Heymann and Dr Anita Augspurg of Germany were active. Catherine found the latter in particular a "powerful and eloquent" speaker; and we are reminded of the benefit of Catherine's command of languages. She would meet many of these women again after 1914 in the antiwar movement.[64]

There was, of course, considerable diversity of opinion among the delegates – about everything except the franchise, and since that was naturally the major topic of public discussion, we need to read between the lines for some of the other things that Catherine might observe. Carrie Chapman Catt was a great organizer and leader, whose skills would pilot franchise reform through the maze of United States constitutional amendment; her philosophy was solid, middle-of-the-road, equal-rights feminism. In her presidential address to the IWSA, she stressed women's great need of the vote to help them right the wrongs and inequalities to which they were subject – poor wages, sexual exploitation, personal violence, inadequate educational and career opportunities. All these were things understood by suffragists the world over. A more radical view was scarcely articulated, but can be sensed here and there in the discussions and speeches. Many of the feminists later to be found in the international peace movement were attracted to the IWSA because they saw it as a vehicle for a philosophy which went beyond the gaining of the vote, and even beyond the attainment of a better economic and political position for women, important as these things were. For them, the IWSA's international character was not merely a means to an end, but of value in itself. Equality was essential, but they were moving towards a vision of women entering politics to change the whole nature of society, and a part of that would be a new approach to relations between nations. Only a small part of the program, and that almost incidentally, bore directly on questions of peace and war (for example, a motion initiated by Dr Anna Shaw and amended by Catherine advocating the use of arbitration as a means of settling international disputes was approved), but there was an underlying assumption that women's influence would be towards peace. Catherine's speech reflected a belief in the complementarity of the sexes that was fairly common in the international community of suffragists. Selma Lagerlöf of Sweden, winner of the Nobel Prize for literature in 1909, built her argument on the home as women's gift to humanity, but also as having been something created by women and men together. There were, she claimed, many ideal homes, but there were no ideal states, and would not be until women and men worked together to create them.

We need to be examine carefully what was being said here. Feminists may be sceptical about "ideal homes" in an unequal world, and will recognize the danger of stressing women's traditional roles as wives, mothers, and nurturers; yet the claim that women were to bring something new into public life, and in effect to change its terms of reference, is far more radical than the alternative assumption that women would be just the same as men when they freely entered public life.[65]

The NU was the only British suffrage organization in full membership of the IWSA, though other British women and men were there representing what were called "fraternal" organizations, such as the Women's Tax Resistance League, the MLWS and the Women's Freedom League (WFL). On a motion of Rosika Schwimmer, the IWSA Congress sent greetings to Fawcett, Mrs Despard (of the WFL), and Emmeline Pankhurst on the occasion of the big London demonstration. There was minimal public discussion of militancy, and apparently little approval. The representative of the WFL took the opportunity to describe the methods of that group, focusing especially on the long-term picketing maintained outside Parliament (a classic nonviolent protest, in effect).

The escalation of WSPU methods from peaceful protest to violence, including threats and some incidents of personal violence, and the component of threat and confrontation rather than dialogue which informed most of their activity, have tended to cloud the distinctions familiar to most modern civil rights and antiwar activists between different types of protest, and, I think, clouded them at the time. The NU were righteously "law-abiding" (but struggled with the tax resistance question); the WSPU were neither law-abiding nor nonviolent, although they caused no deaths or serious injuries outside their own ranks. The WFL came nearest to developing an integrated nonviolent civil disobedience, since they were prepared to break the law, but not to risk causing injury; however, perhaps in part because of the experience many WFL members had already had in the WSPU, they had difficulty in defining the limits of confrontation, or developing the positive aspects of nonviolence. "Nonviolence" has to be defined in terms of the spirit in which protest — whether legal or illegal — is carried out, not merely in terms of whether or not anyone gets hurt; essential components are openness and a willingness to dialogue and seek agreement, rather than to threaten the opponent. Catherine's introductory speech, like her description of negotiations with borough councils, showed that she clearly understood that "law-abiding" was not "nonviolent" in spirit if the people on the other side were disparaged and degraded, and as we have seen, she was increasingly concerned to work on those standing in the way of women's suffrage as misguided and capable of conversion, rather than as evil and only to be won over by threats. At Stockholm, indirectly, the groundwork was being laid for the application of this philosophy to international relations as well as to political dealings.

Catherine's understanding of the many faces of socialism may also have increased during the Stockholm congress. One of the most stimulating public discussions took place on the subject of the relation of women and of women's suffragists to political parties, and though the purpose was to deal with strategies rather than assessing the merits of one party against those of another, much could be learnt from the varied experience of women in different countries. Catherine will have found considerable support among socialist women for principles dear to her – notably the expectation of a radically new order to which women and men would contribute side by side, and the emphasis on internationalism. Overall, food for thought was abundant at the IWSA congress, and Catherine took from it those nutrients which she needed in her slow journey towards the Left.

After the Stockholm congress, Catherine left for a much-needed vacation with her parents. Caroline, who suffered from seasickness, may well have decided that, once she had crossed the North Sea on suffrage business, she might as well have a good holiday before returning. Frank and Caroline travelled in Scandinavia for about a month, but Catherine felt she had to be back in Britain in time for the NU council held in Edinburgh on 7 and 8 July.[66] This was not, in the outcome, one of the more memorable councils; the focus was on keeping the momentum going to follow through on the good second reading vote of the spring. Catherine moved that the federations and local societies try to get all the men's political groups in their areas, now making up their fall programs, to set time aside for the calling of a special meeting whenever the women's franchise issue should again be before Parliament.[67]

Catherine was free to enjoy a short visit to friends in Scotland after the council meeting. Back in Keswick in August, and resting up with an attack of rheumatism, she heard the welcome news that the government had won its long struggle with the Lords and had passed the Parliament Act into law. Summer 1911 was also something of a "long hot summer," marked by exceptional heat (it was the hottest summer since 1868)[68] and by serious labour unrest.

On 15 August, Catherine had the rare experience of attending a women's suffrage meeting in Keswick at which, far from being speaker, chair, or even a supporter, her role was that of an open-minded member of the audience. The militants' truce was still on, and Emmeline Pankhurst could spare time to come to Keswick as part of a summer tour to holiday resorts. The reserved cordiality that still existed between the militants and constitutionalists did not extend to the sponsorship of one another's meetings, and Mrs Pankhurst was without benefit of any local branch.

Catherine went to listen without hostility, and on the whole was probably pleasantly surprised; she found Emmeline Pankhurst's logic "clear, forcible [and] convincing." Indeed, much of what Mrs Pankhurst had to say was routine stuff, the kind of thing Catherine herself used in speeches, giving the reasons why women needed the vote, explaining why the Conciliation Bill was the best that could be achieved at the present, drawing attention to the achievements of women in the enfranchised countries, arguing that women would be better homemakers with the vote than without. She commented wittily on contemporary news, such as the newly introduced payment of MPs ("If men like to pay their representatives, let them, but in common decency let them pay themselves, and not expect the women to help").[69] Women antis who wanted to tell the men how to vote (presumably on the suffrage issue) were beyond her understanding; male antis, however, were simply making a confession of inferiority, admitting the need to handicap women because of their greater ability. But there was no great hostility to men shown in the speech; rather, Emmeline Pankhurst spoke of the work of the sexes as complementary.

When the speaker turned to methods, Catherine found her arguments unacceptable. We have already seen Catherine rejecting confrontation for conversion, and basing this not just on strategy but on a refusal to believe her opponents to be wicked. Undoubtedly, Mrs Pankhurst's speech was milder than it would have been during a militant period; she devoted less time to justifying militant methods, instead paying a good deal of attention to explaining the truce, which she described as a businesslike response to the promise of the prime minister to grant facilities for the Conciliation Bill. However, she claimed that the prevalent strikes, and the violence accompanying them, along with the violent language used in the House of Commons, were "an endorsement of our policy." If men with votes armed themselves with guns and stones, still more might "voteless women" do so. More sweepingly, she maintained that "if you are a practical politician you must be prepared to be militant." Catherine commented in a note that "Her argument told against the usefulness of the vote. We believe that the vote is a great power, and we build our hopes on getting the men with that power to use it on our behalf, to win justice for us."[70]

A gulf divided Catherine and others of her way of thinking from the militants. Sandra Holton has claimed that "By and large the suffrage movement was ideologically homogeneous," yet her own analysis of the methods employed and of attitudes to these methods[71] supports my belief that one cannot divorce method from ideology. The rationale of militancy had a lot in common with the curious but oft-repeated argument of the antisuffragists that since physical force was the basis of the state, and women did not fight, therefore they should not vote. Catherine saw legitimate government as government with the consent of the governed, and power as resting in the hands of the voters.

At the end of her talk, Emmeline Pankhurst fielded questions adroitly and, on the whole, with moderation. Catherine seems to have advised a companion against "enter[ing] into any criticism of what she has said so far in favour of militantism," since, as she shrewdly observed, "the audience was not with her." The finishing touch was put when someone (presumably an anti) asked, "Are not militants looked down upon and discouraged, and nonmilitants ignored? Is not [the] movement dying a natural death?"[72] The wave of good humour and unifying laughter which followed provided the answer; no matter their internal differences, the women's suffragists were not about to leave the political scene until victory was theirs.

IS THIS RIGHT ?

THE OPEN MARKET

WOMAN   WHY CAN'T I HAVE AN UMBRELLA TOO ?
VOTER   YOU CAN'T, YOU OUGHT TO STOP AT HOME.
WOMAN   STOP AT HOME INDEED ! I HAVE MY
         LIVING TO EARN.

Postcard produced by the Artists' Suffrage League, c. 1910 (Catherine E. Marshall collection, Cumbria Record Office, Carlisle)

7 The Conciliation Cliff-hanger September 1911 to March 1912

A mood of cautious optimism lasted through the autumn of 1911, and with it the cordiality between the women's suffrage groups. Asquith had reaffirmed his promise to grant facilities for the Conciliation Bill in a letter to *The Times* on 15 June, and again in a letter to Lytton on 17 August.[1] All the suffragists had to do, it seemed, was to keep up the steady pressure, although Lytton warned of the need to keep the bill unchanged to be sure of keeping the support of suffragists from all parties.[2] Most of the active women knew from experience that it was too soon to relax. And Lytton's warning could not be taken lightly; the terms of the bill had gone to the limits of compromise, and the delicate balance between the desires of suffragists of different parties could easily be upset.

Catherine made plans for an active October, and meanwhile did some networking, meeting with local suffragists, and enjoying a ten-day visit from Ida O'Malley in September.[3] The autumn campaign in the northwest got off to a good start, with a number of meetings in September, and three new branches formed that month (eleven by the end of October), though the NWF executive meeting on 30 September was poorly attended; while Catherine was planning the agenda she received quite a little flood of apologies and excuses from members unable to come. All conscientiously sent in their reports or recommendations.[4] Those of Maude Royden (the representative of the national executive) were characteristically forthright; she made a number of specific suggestions for lines of action to be followed, and issued a warning and an exhortation:

"Everybody is saying that the Cause is won. It isn't, and it won't be, unless we nearly kill ourselves in the next six months. But speaking to some of the best and keenest workers in England, as I am, by proxy, now, I would say (a) don't let us kill anybody too soon (b) don't let us spare anything short of that."[5]

The suffrage campaign followed much the same pattern as in previous years, but it was never routine, and the stress was laid on the perceived needs of the time. Maude Royden had urged Liberal women to make sure that Asquith's promise of facilities was known and understood, writing, "Please – Liberal women – rub it into your fellow-Liberals for all it is worth; and it is worth a great deal."[6] Catherine had already arranged to do just that; she began October with a speech to the Carlisle Liberal Club and ended the month attending a meeting of the Keswick Women's Liberal Association, though not as a speaker.[7]

The major concern tempering the NU's optimism at this time was a fear that Liberals, whether misguided suffragists or cynical anti-suffragists, might still insist on introducing widening amendments which would wreck the Conciliation Bill. Lloyd George was known to be convinced that the bill would favour the Conservatives, and while the NU continued to negotiate with him, they found him hard to trust,[8] but knew that he commanded support in the cabinet. Catherine's speech to the Carlisle Liberals had some similarity to the one she had given two years before to Keswick Liberals, and she again stepped out of her nonparty role and identified herself as a Liberal; but the underlying purpose now was to make sure that the need for a narrow bill was understood.[9] R.A. Denman was present, to speak in favour of the Insurance Bill. Catherine wrote next day to thank him for declaring that "when the Women's Suffrage question comes up again next session you will take the course which you think most likely to get a Women's Suffrage Bill placed on the Statute Book," and did not miss the opportunity to ask him to apply to suffrage the argument he had used to urge support for the Insurance Bill, even though, in his words, "It does not purport to be a perfect Bill, only a beginning." Denman sent a short but cordial reply the following day, indicating that he had been conscious of the applicability of his remark to a women's suffrage bill, and expressing satisfaction at the growth of support. Denman was felt to be showing a "satisfactory advance" in his position.[10]

Much attention centred at this time on those women who had the vote in local elections, since it was largely the same group who would receive the national vote under the terms of the Conciliation Bill. They were counted and recounted by suffragists and antis, asked their opinions, and had their socioeconomic status analysed as never before. Before leaving Carlisle, Catherine spoke to the Carlisle Municipal Women, urging them to think of political involvement not as a right, but as a duty to be exercised on behalf of the less fortunate, and to consider not so much women's need of the vote as the country's need of women's influence in politics; rather than bringing politics into the home, what was needed was to make the home count for more in politics.[11]

Keeping the women's cause alive and visible to the public during the waiting time of autumn 1911 was of fundamental importance. Catherine's organization of the press work may have been the biggest single factor in the NU's success in doing this. Emily Leaf was now so fully occupied in carrying on the work of the department that she could not spare time to come to the provincial council meeting in Scarborough on 6 October, and Catherine took her place, giving Leaf's report on progress and chairing a meeting of the federation press secretaries. The value of the work was now well recognized, many societies had structured press contacts, and societies and regions had available to them a wealth of suggestions and guidelines to help them, including a pamphlet Catherine had written on the press work of the NWF.[12]

If a major NU task at this time was to keep the suffragist Liberals sweet, it was also important to pay attention to MPs, including Conservatives, who opposed suffrage. Of the eleven MPs in the NWF area, eight supported the Conciliation Bill, one was the Speaker of the House of Commons, and two were against it. There was not much hope that these last could be converted to active support, but the NWF hoped that they might be persuaded to abstain.[13] The usual intensive autumn campaign, focused as it was on the coming bill, paid particular attention to the constituency of J.A. Grant, one of the recalcitrant MPs. The NWF employed Marguerite Norma-Smith, one of the NU's full-time professional organizers, and she and Catherine held a series of meetings in the Egremont and Whitehaven districts, putting pressure on Grant by resolutions asking him to reconsider his opposition in light of public opinion in his constituency. At every meeting the mover of the resolution was one of Grant's "chief local supporters"; and on every occasion it was passed unanimously, except once, when a single dissentient (a woman) voted against it.[14] In addition, Catherine claimed, "We have won over his Agent completely. He has promised to do all he can to get Mr. Grant to withdraw his opposition. I have great hopes he may *refrain from opposing*, but do not think he would *support* any women's suffrage measure."[15]

Another challenge for Catherine arose from this campaign, giving her a chance to use her skills with a hostile press. As we have seen, Catherine's steady work had brought most of the Cumberland local papers round to giving full, and in most cases favourable, coverage to suffrage events. But Robert Foster, the editor of the *Whitehaven News*, who may have been one of Grant's supporters, remained firmly opposed to women's suffrage. When Norma-Smith and Catherine came into his territory, he took the opportunity to expound his views at some length.[16] They were not startlingly original. In his initial sally, he emphasized the difference between men and women, and gave preeminence to the much-used argument from physical force: laws had to be backed "by fighting if necessary, among ourselves, and as against foreign nations by war." A "truly womanly policy of peace at any price" would result in an ill-defended nation, and "when the women get into difficulties it is the men who have to do the fighting and get them out of trouble."[17]

Unfortunately we do not have Catherine's reply to this, but we do have her answer to his editorial comments on her reply. Foster has to be respected for his willingness to give space (in Catherine's case, a *lot* of space) to the views of those with whom he disagreed – though he always exercised his editorial privilege of setting his readers right in his own columns. Evidently, on this occasion, he had based his arguments on biblical references to the subjection of women. Catherine replied at length:

You quote St. Paul and the marriage service in support of your opposition to women's suffrage. May I remind you that St. Paul, who told wives to be in subjection to their husbands, also told slaves to obey their masters? Would you have opposed the anti-slavery agitation on that account? Some people did at the time. If you turn to a higher authority than St. Paul you will not find this doctrine of the subjection of women in His teaching. ...

You refer to the wife's promise in the marriage service to obey her husband. The husband also makes a promise. He says, "With all my worldly goods I thee endow." Until all men do this I think the less they base their arguments on the marriage service the better. Before the passing of the Married Women's Property Acts it would have been a truer statement of the case if the man had said: "With all thy worldly goods I me endow." ...

I quite agree with most of what you say about the "law of grace" and the "law of force," but I think it is very desirable that men (who at present have all the "force" on their side) should show a little more "grace" to women in this question of the suffrage. Instead of saying "thou shalt not" have any voice in these matters we want them to say "thou shalt" have every possible opportunity for using the special gifts God has given to women for the benefit of humanity, and not be restricted by man-made laws to employing them in certain directions only.

I am sorry to put too low an interpretation on your view of women's influence. You say this influence consists in "faith, hope, and charity," and "it is by virtue of her superior capacity for this grace that woman ... is fitted to be the better half of man." Could we not well do with a little more faith, hope, and charity (especially charity) in our politics, and is it not a pity to leave this important field of human activity entirely in the hands of the "worse half" of mankind?

I take your own estimate for the sake of argument. I do not myself think there can be any question of better or worse as between men and women. The world has equal need of both. As Mrs. Fawcett once said, "You might as well ask which was the better half of a pair of scissors"!

... You say that, "speaking generally, there is no woman who has no man to represent her." Who represents the threequarter-million [sic] widows whom the Conciliation Bill would enfranchise, or the other quarter-million women who are "heads of households which have no male representative?" Take the case of a father with three unmarried daughters, all earning their own living in industries affected by legislation, all of them with strong political opinions, one Liberal, one Conservative, and one a Socialist. How is the father to represent his three daughters by his one vote? You will probably say that the daughters ought not to have opinions, but if you educate people you cannot prevent them from having opinions, and men have passed a Compulsory Education Act which applies to girls as well as boys.

You mistake me if you think I do not give men credit for good intentions when legislating for women. ... But good intentions are not enough. Knowledge and experience are needed besides, and with the best will in the world men cannot have the same knowledge and experience of women's needs that women have, for the simple reason, so often used as an antisuffrage argument, that "Men are men, and women are women." ... The best men are urging the women to press their claim for enfranchisement, because they say the women's vote will strengthen their hands to obtain many urgently-needed reforms. This is not a question of women against men, but of men and women working together for the best interests of the race as a whole.

The editor responded, in a passage headed "Miss Marshall's Crusade," by claiming nastily that Catherine had shown ignorance ("A little knowledge is a dangerous thing," he wrote) in supposing his reference to have been to St Paul, when it had in fact been to the "third chapter of Genesis, which contains the first lesson on the subject of the relations of man and woman," and where she would find: "The Tempter addressed himself to sweet Eve, the weaker vessel, and she was beguiled; and it was 'because thou hast harkened unto the voice of thy wife' that all our woes commenced. The sentence of woman was that 'thy desire shall be to thy husband and he shall rule over thee.'" There Foster rested his argument, except for a brief passage pointing to the availability to men of all the information about women that they might need in legislating; in particular, he mentioned the Home Office's "lady inspectors" of factories, and concluded, "To be informed by women is one thing. To be ruled by women is quite another."[18]

As a rather Freudian footnote to the dispute, we have to add that the advertisement Catherine had taken out in the *Whitehaven News* of 19 October to publicize the coming meetings was still not paid for eighteen months later.[19]

All the steady build-up towards the Conciliation Bill was thrown into confusion on 7 November 1911, when Asquith announced to a delegation from the adultist People's Suffrage Federation that he would introduce a government bill for manhood suffrage, open to amendment to include women. In part, what lay behind this was a series of negotiations between Lloyd George, Brailsford, the Conciliation Committee, and the NU, mediated by C.P. Scott, editor of the *Manchester Guardian*.[20] In effect, Lloyd George was suggesting a trade-off; in return for the NU's support for the introduction of the government bill, he spoke of offering his support and that of Grey, as a leading cabinet member known to favour women's suffrage, for a women's franchise amendment, and should that fail, for the Conciliation Bill. However, when Asquith made his announcement, no concrete agreement had been reached between the NU and Lloyd George, and in any event Lloyd George could not speak for Asquith. Only a handful of the NU executive seems to have known what was going on – indeed secrecy was still felt to be imperative – and Brailsford had well-grounded fears of the reaction to be expected from the WSPU, which had not been brought into the negotiations.

Up in Cumberland, Catherine was not initially among the few NU leaders who knew of the behind-the-scenes activity. Later she gave a vivid description of the effect that the announcement of the proposed Reform Bill had had on active suffragists who had spent the last eighteen months working for the Conciliation Bill, the success of which had seemed at last assured. Asquith's statement had come like a "bombshell" – the "answer to our demand for votes for women [was] votes for more men," an outright insult. No wonder, she said, that women were angry; it looked as if the government meant once more to force a choice between votes for all women or for none – knowing that there was no evidence that the country was ready for all women to have the vote. Indeed, there was a much greater number of people prepared for the enfranchisement of some women than there was for the enfranchisement of all men. It had been difficult not to suspect that the government hoped to sow discord by introducing the whole question of franchise qualification, and by making it a party measure while withholding government support: "[It was] impossible not to suspect a trick. Would they induce us to relinquish [their] pledge for [the] C[onciliation] Bill on assurance that the amendm[en]t would pass, and then either drop [the] amendm[en]t if [the] Lords opposed [it], or merely pass academic 2nd R[eading] of [the] Ref[orm] Bill and then drop it? Until we had a definite assurance from the P.M. on these points we were bound to be suspicious."[21]

The NU executive, struggling to control its initial rage, worked quickly to get a handle on the new situation, calling a special meeting of the executive for 9 November. Kathleen Courtney reported that Brailsford had already come to the office to confer, and the executive decided to issue a manifesto expressing the NU's indignation at the exclusion of women from the proposed bill (which Asquith had said would give the vote to "a man who is a citizen of full age and competent understanding"), to press for inclusion, and failing an unlikely success in this, to work for amendment.[22]

The WSPU, on the same day, announced that the truce was at an end, but delayed the actual resumption of militancy until after a meeting with Asquith, which had been arranged by the NU for 17 November, and at which, in the event, they were joined by many other suffrage organizations, though without any possibility of a commonly agreed approach. The WSPU used the occasion to declare war, refusing to consider the new bill as anything other than a trick. Throwing over the Conciliation Bill as well, they said that only a government women's suffrage bill would now satisfy them.

The NU, on the other hand, in Catherine's words, "did not waste time or energy being angry," or at least in making a public display of their anger. Before the meeting with Asquith, they took steps to clarify the role of Lloyd George. Kathleen Courtney and Helena Swanwick met with him and C.P. Scott on 15 November as part of the attempt to get his commitment firmed up and given public expression.[23] The other urgent need was to determine the exact nature of the proposed Reform Bill, and what specific assurances Asquith would give. The NU deputation came to the meeting with the prime minister with four carefully prepared questions, worth quoting in full as an example of the NU's grasp of significant issues:

1. Is it the intention of the Government that the Reform Bill shall go through all its stages in 1912?

2. Will the Bill be drafted in such a way as to admit of any amendments introducing women on other terms than men?
3. Will the Government undertake not to oppose such amendments?
4. Will the Government regard any amendment enfranchising women which is carried as an integral part of the Bill in all its stages?[24]

Asquith's answers to all four of these questions were entirely satisfactory, and he also stated that his pledge to allow time for the Conciliation Bill still stood. The NU did extraordinarily well to bring anything so concrete away from what must have been a difficult meeting (the *Common Cause* commented drily that "It was not the brilliant idea of the National Union to ask for such an omnibus deputation").[25] Things seemed to be going well after all, with many suffragists, including Catherine, hoping to gain a wider measure than they would have had under the Conciliation Bill.

There were still problem areas. Work would be needed to keep the Conservative suffragists on side; the more enthusiasm there seemed to be from the Liberal front benches, and the wider the measure, the more dubious Conservatives might become. On the other hand, there was some hope that Conservatives, faced with manhood suffrage, might welcome the admission of some women to the franchise as a counterbalance. But Brailsford warned: "While urging Liberals to the maximum, Tories I think must be carefully nursed to stick to the minimum. Their present mind is to run away from suffrage altogether and it will require prodigies of diplomacy to keep them right on our Bill. I think it would be fatal to mention 'on the same terms' to them. They must be asked simply to adhere to our Bill as it stands, and alternatively to vote for an amendment to the Reform Bill on the lines of our Bill."[26]

More serious still was the resumption of militancy; on 21 November, 220 people were arrested at a big demonstration staged by the WSPU in Parliament Square. Still more damaging was the decision of the WSPU to make it impossible for Liberal ministers to speak in public, the more so if they were supporters of the proposed women's suffrage amendment. On 24 November, unmercifully heckled during a speech to the National Liberal Federation at Bath, Lloyd George played into the hands of militants and antisuffragists alike when he declared with relish that the Reform Bill had "torpedoed" the Conciliation Bill. According to Helena Swanwick, he had agreed to omit this offensive phrase from the speech, and only came out with it in the heat of the exchange.[27] Although the NU officers knew that Lloyd George almost obsessively feared the effect of the Conciliation Bill, he was after all presenting himself at this time as the friend of the women, and had privately agreed, in a meeting with Lytton, Scott, Courtney, and Brailsford less than a week before, to support the offending bill as a fallback position should all the women's suffrage amendments to the Reform Bill fail.[28]

Lloyd George's lapse (and the WSPU action that led to it) might well have jeopardized the frail structure of support. The NU officers, who still had ahead of them the task of selling the switch in policy to the membership, in fact held firm despite their indignation, and perhaps even helped Scott to calm down Brailsford, who was beside himself with rage at what he saw as a "total repudiation of our bargain," threatening to denounce Lloyd George's "treachery" publicly unless he made an open declaration of his support within four days.[29] Brailsford feared that he had been too trusting, and let his views be known in letters to Lloyd George and to Millicent Fawcett, and especially in a series of explosive telegrams to C.P. Scott, in which he threatened to "do some torpedoing myself."

When the worst was over, Scott wrote to Courtney (who had been at the Bath meeting), enclosing Brailsford's four telegrams. "It may amuse you to see the enclosed bundle of telegrams from Brailsford," he wrote, "It was touch and go whether there would be a complete bust-up." Scott thought that his own intervention had helped bring Lloyd George back to the need to stand by his commitment, and to let his position be known. He voiced the caveat felt by all the women's suffragists who had to work with Lloyd George when he said: "But he's an impetuous and variable person – some people might apply harsher epithets – and you need to be on your guard in commerce with him."[30] However, the agreement with the NU was of importance to Lloyd George, and he made what restitution he could, in the form of a public statement of support and a message for publication in the *Common Cause*, as well as in private correspondence.[31] The whole incident brings home the centrality of the role now being played by the NU.

Lloyd George was only one of a large number of MPs adversely affected by the resumption of militancy, and the NU caught a good deal of the fallout. Trapped between loss of support, public disapprobation, the WSPU's own renewed hostility to the NU, and a tendency on the part of their friends to hold them responsible – Lloyd George asked Mrs Fawcett what she could suggest – the NU issued a manifesto on 30 November strongly condemning militancy, and once more dissociating itself from the actions of the sister organization.[32] More poignant is the comment, probably made shortly after

this, of a women's suffrage worker in the NWF, who told Catherine
that a Conservative member had reported "that feeling against us is
running very high in his constituency because of the militants," and
added, "It is heartbreaking work rolling these stones of members
uphill and the militants send them crashing down."[33] When the NU
was attacked by WSPU supporters as denouncing "brave fellow-
workers in the great cause of women's enfranchisement," Catherine
responded. She denied that there was any wish or intention of denouncing the members of the WSPU, especially on a personal level,
and said the NU "would gladly remain silent, but that the cause suffers when they do." More important was her description of the situation in the country: "if the opinion in the country is to be brought
to bear effectively on the H. of C. it must be organized. To this work
the N.U.W.S.S. has been devoting itself with unremitting zeal and energy for years, all over the country, in countless places to which the
W.S.P.U. has never penetrated. (There are now very few districts – in
fact v. few constituencies – without their local W.S. Societies, linked
together in Federations and in close touch with the headquarters in
London.) The results of all this patient work are apparent whenever
it is necessary to bring pressure to bear on Members of Parliament,
because they can now be approached at short notice and in the most
effective way, through their constituents."

Catherine had made this exactly true for at least her own federation. "But," she wrote, "all this good work is thrown back every time
there is a fresh outbreak of militancy." She went on to give a vivid
description of the effect of the WSPU's London window-breaking on
the northwest: "A month ago," she claimed, "there were five new Societies in process of formation in my own district. Since the action of
the W.S.P.U. on Nov. 21 promised support has been withdrawn, and
people have refused to come forward and serve on Committees. It
will be necessary to visit the district again, and hold another series of
meetings to explain that we do not uphold militant action, before we
can regain the position we occupied a month ago. It is no exaggeration to say that an afternoon's destructive attack on the windows of
Whitehall has to be paid for by a month's reconstructive work all
over the country, with all the waste of time and energy and money
which that involves."[34]

Catherine's exact whereabouts during the eventful second half of
November 1911 are not known. She may have been on the scene in
London during at least part of this time,[35] but she was also actively
engaged in NWF concerns. A letter to Louis Walker on 22 November
dealt with the difficulty of finding a new president for the federa-

tion, and enclosed full notes on coming work in the federation, with a run-down on what could be expected of every MP in the region. She had decided to wait before writing up a statement on the Reform Bill and the new situation, to be signed and issued by the federation officers, but meanwhile circulated copies of articles published in the *Manchester Guardian* on 18 and 22 November. Louis had expressed the difficulty all the NU's workers were feeling in making "the ordinary person understand our position *now*."[36]

In any event, by the beginning of December Catherine was in Cambridge, staying first at Newnham College and then with the Butlers at Trinity Lodge, and she probably remained in the south long enough to attend the special council in London on 8 December, called by the NU to bring the membership into the discussion of strategy in the changed situation.[37]

By the time the council met, and even more so by the time it concluded its day's deliberations, things were falling into place, and the NU was clear on the next stage of its work. Final details of the amendments to be proposed to the government bill would have to wait until the exact form of the bill was known, but there was no lack of precision in how the NU planned to proceed. Support for the Conciliation Bill would continue, with the prime minister's pledge of facilities still seen as "of the utmost importance." At the same time work would commence on obtaining an amendment to the Reform Bill to bring in the women's franchise on the widest terms for which it was possible to obtain a majority in the House of Commons. Three amendments were envisaged, to be presented in descending order of width: the first would give votes to women on the same terms as men; the second (which was often called the "Norway" amendment because of its resemblance to the franchise won by women there) would enfranchise women householders and the wives of householders – the definition of "householder" was now legally held to include rent-paying occupiers; the third would be on the lines of the 1911 Conciliation Bill. Brailsford was invited to speak at the afternoon session of the council – by which time it had already resolved to continue support for the Conciliation Bill; he spoke on an optimistic note, pointing out a number of advantages which the Reform Bill amendments would have over the Conciliation Bill, particularly in light of Asquith's promise to accept a women's suffrage amendment, once passed, as an integral part of the bill. Brailsford thought the Norway amendment likely to be successful, since this was known to be the measure favoured by Lloyd George and Grey, and he was

convinced that enough Unionists could be persuaded to vote for it to
outweigh any Liberal antisuffragists who were not brought round by
the leadership of the suffragist cabinet members.[38]

The position the NU now found itself in reflected a new closeness
with leading politicians, and the policy to be followed was dependent
on this closeness continuing, in a way that had not previously been
so. The NU had moved almost imperceptibly from working on an *ad
hoc* basis with individual members who would be willing to move,
and to vote for, a private bill, through a somewhat arms-length cooperation with the Conciliation Committee, mediated by Brailsford,
to a direct relationship with Lloyd George and Sir Edward Grey as
well as with the old faithfuls of the Conciliation Committee, including the now sometimes anxious Lord Lytton. The new relationship
coexisted with the need to keep up the pressure and reassurance on
all the individual MPs who had declared themselves in favour of
women's suffrage. Six questions were drawn up "to be put to Members of Parliament in every constituency in order to ascertain what
form of Women's Suffrage will command the largest support in the
House of Commons in the coming session of 1912," asking not only
which of the proposed amendments they would accept but also
whether they would vote against the Reform Bill if no amendment
had passed; whether they would vote for the third reading of the
Reform Bill if women were included; and whether they would support the Conciliation Bill in all its stages, should no women's suffrage amendment to the Reform Bill be carried.[39]

All this was very well, and the women's suffragists were further
cheered by strengthening Labour support, but the year did not end
without its darker moments. On the same day as the joint meeting of
suffragists at the House, Asquith received a deputation from the National League for Opposing Women's Suffrage (NLOWS), led by
Lord Curzon. He treated them with great friendliness, almost as allies, and was reported as saying that the grant of the franchise to
women "would be a political mistake of the most disastrous kind";
the antisuffrage peers felt that they were being encouraged to use
the power still vested in the Upper House to delay the Conciliation
Bill, should it pass the Commons.[40] Meanwhile, Churchill was lobbying for the imposition of a referendum before women's suffrage
should pass into law, a strategy welcomed by all who opposed the
measure. Churchill maintained that the referendum could be as well
applied to amendment to the Reform Bill as to the Conciliation Bill,
and was doing his best to persuade Grey and the volatile Lloyd
George to go along with his idea.[41]

Catherine was back at Hawse End for Christmas. Women's suffrage pervaded even the holiday season; Catherine gave blotters and writing pads in the NU colours as Christmas gifts, and the seasonal house party included Emily Leaf.[42]

January was, as usual, packed with suffrage activity in the northwest. The NWF had managed to raise the funds to pay Marguerite Norma-Smith to work in the region full-time throughout the winter; the NU had by this time a corps of trained organizers who could help out wherever they were needed, on a short- or long-term basis, in by-elections or for routine suffrage campaigns (if these were ever routine) in return for an undertaking by the local societies to pay at least part of the cost of salaries and expenses. Norma-Smith, who was particularly well liked in the NWF, spoke all over the region throughout the first three months of the year, staying with the Marshalls at Hawse End off and on meanwhile. Much of her work this time was to attempt the kind of "damage control" that Catherine had seen would be needed in light of the resumption of militancy. Ethel Snowden also conducted a short speaking tour in the Barrow area early in February.

Catherine accompanied Norma-Smith much less than she had done previously, putting her energies instead into the local women's suffrage society, and on one occasion speaking, together with her father, at a meeting of the Women's Liberal Association in Appleby. Here she lambasted the Liberal women for the opportunity they had lost of inducing the party "to make the enfranchisement of women a plank in their platform. ... Ever since the 80s the WLF has been re-iterating that the Lib[eral] women would be 'hewers of wood and drawers of water' no longer, but every time when an election came they were content to put their own just claims on one side and work at the bidding of their party as before." She also provided the Liberal women with an excellent breakdown of the possible amendments to the Reform Bill, and the quarters from which support for each amendment was to be expected, and characteristically concluded by naming concrete ways in which individuals and the group as a whole could help, from letting Liberal members know their patience was at an end, to joining the NU.[43]

Catherine's last task in the northwest before travelling south to take up her new work was to go with Marguerite Norma-Smith and other suffrage representatives on two deputations. The first and more important was to Thomas Richardson, the Labour member for Whitehaven, to whom Catherine, following through on the decisions of the December council, put the six questions agreed on there, and a seventh on the referendum; Richardson's replies were "entirely satisfactory." The other deputation was to a Mr Moulsdale, who had just been chosen as Liberal candidate for West Cumberland. Similar deputations were taking place all over the country, and Catherine had mimeographed the questions and drawn up instructions for deputations in the NWF area; a copy was sent to the NU executive for more widespread use.[44]

By the middle of the month, Catherine had even more important suffrage responsibilities. The NU's honorary parliamentary secretary, Edith Palliser, was ill, and would be abroad for some time. Catherine agreed to help out when she could come to London, which would be at the end of January. The executive appointed her temporarily as honorary assistant parliamentary secretary and invited her to attend the meetings of the executive.[45] However, she was not sufficiently well known in the NU yet; and when the KWSA nominated her for the same (assistant) position, hers was not the name accepted by vote of the council of 24 February 1912, nor did she win a place on the executive, although she was appointed to two subcommittees.[46] But meanwhile she at last got her feet wet in the job for which she had such outstanding talent, although the lack of clarity in her status was to prove something of an embarrassment.

The threat of a referendum had continued to exercise the NU executive throughout January, and a great deal of effort had been put into dissuading Lloyd George from supporting the idea. Although Catherine was not on the scene at the time, the problem was discussed at Hawse End, and Frank was among the *Common Cause* correspondents firmly putting the case against the idea. With the aid of Scott and Brailsford, the NU had succeeded by the end of the month in persuading Lloyd George not to give in to Churchill. Scott wrote in relief to Courtney, "I think as you say there is very little life left in the Referendum scheme."[47]

If the referendum was one danger receding by the time Catherine came to London, there was no lack of other critical work. Since Asquith's announcement in November, the NU's parliamentary experts and their advisers had been devoting much of their attention to the amendments to be proposed for the government Reform Bill, working on the wording most likely to gain support and seeking out the best people willing to move them.[48] Now, suddenly, within a week of Catherine's arrival, the flexibility of the NU had once more to be exercised when the government announced the postponement of the Reform Bill, with the unfortunate consequence that the Conciliation Bill would precede it. In hindsight, it is debatable whether the women's suffragists were wise to proceed with the Conciliation Bill under these conditions (the WSPU would now have nothing to do with it), but they were caught in yet another Catch-22 situation. The government's promise of facilities still held; many Liberals disliked the bill, but Conservative suffragists might doubt their sincerity if they dropped the narrower bill now. So the major focus of Catherine's term as stand-in for Edith Palliser was to be the rather desperate attempt to put support for the Conciliation Bill together again.

The proposed Reform Bill had changed the map of prosuffrage alliances, and already there was some movement towards forming a new loose coalition of women's suffragists across the party political spectrum and among the various women's organizations. On 14 December Kathleen Courtney and Edith Palliser had represented the NU at a joint conference of suffragists held at the House of Commons to bring together MPs and supporters from a variety of groups.[49] The NU planned to build something permanent out of the nonparliamentary side of this, and Courtney had followed up with approaches to some of the other societies.

As Palliser ran into difficulty with her health, Courtney had presumably had to take over more of the political work, and at the beginning of February the latter apparently handed Catherine a number of files of recent material on the current situation, pertinent to the topics it would be Catherine's responsibility to pursue;[50] foremost among these was the nurture of the new (or revived) joint board, whose formation Catherine was able to report at her first executive meeting on 15 February. Its declared aim was modest – the board was "for the prevention of overlapping in lobbying" and to avoid "needless irritation ... caused to friendly M.P.s thereby"[51] – but clearly the objective was also to move towards openness and as much agreement as possible as to goals. Kathleen Courtney had already approached the Women's Freedom League, which had been happy to join.

Catherine drew up a letter and sent it out to a wide list of those groups which might be expected to have an interest. The WSPU had already made it plain to Brailsford that they wanted no part of any joint lobbying effort. Those replies to Catherine's letter which are still extant indicate that the MLWS welcomed the idea; the Conservative and Unionist Women's Franchise Association (CUWFA) was also glad to join, saying, as expected, that they could only lobby Conservative MPs; the Scottish WLF felt that it was too late to be worth their joining (presumably in light of the closeness of the Conciliation Bill's second reading debate), but claimed to be doing what they could to give support; the ILP said they found it wiser not to join any group not specifically a labour group, but spelled out that this was not "in any spirit of opposition or bigotry"; the Fabian Women's Group joined gladly and reported that they were already working at lobbying Fabian Labour and Liberal MPs on behalf of the Conciliation Bill; the Irishwomen's Suffrage Society also joined.

The Women's Liberal Federation, although its officers entered into correspondence with Catherine lasting over the next few weeks, seems to have had a poor understanding of the purpose of the board, and finally decided not to join; in so doing, as Catherine firmly informed them, they cut themselves off from access to information exchanged within the board.[52] But the WLF was too important to be ignored, particularly in light of news from the NU network that the antis were hard at work in local Liberal party organizations, and had the cooperation of the party agents in some places, so Catherine kept in touch with WLF progress through correspondence and personal contact with her friend Eleanor Acland, active in the WLF, a keen suffragist if perhaps an even keener Liberal, and the wife of Francis Acland, probably the most committed suffragist in the cabinet, although only a junior minister. By the end of February, Eleanor Acland was doing her best to get every WLA executive to pass a resolution in favour of the Conciliation Bill before the second reading (then set for 22 March 1912 but later altered to 28 March). The WLF, and especially its central office, seemed indeed to be advancing to a firmer position (Catherine reported that they were doing effective work), helped perhaps by the new respectability of some open cabinet support; but now, Acland said, reassurance was needed for some Liberals "who think that Ll. George will take a vote for 2nd.R. as a sign that they don't want anything wider."[53]

Although the ILP did not feel free to join the joint board, the response of both sections of the Parliamentary Labour party (PLP) to the proposed Manhood Suffrage Bill was extremely positive. Indeed, Labour had long been supportive also of the women's franchise, but until now this support had been tempered by reservations concerning a narrow women's franchise. The proposed bill, as Jill Liddington has pointed out, went far to breaking down the barriers between the women's suffragists and the adultists.[54] The PLP and the parliamentary ILP had been quick to respond to the changed situation; on 17 and 22 November respectively they had passed resolutions calling on the government to include women in the proposed bill. The national ILP organized a three-month campaign for the beginning of the year, with leaflets calling for "Political Equality," "Adult Suffrage This Year," and the withdrawal of the proposal for manhood suffrage and its replacement by a government measure of full adult suffrage.[55] The national Labour party, at its annual conference, held in Birmingham on 27 January, passed a resolution stating its opinion that "the franchise of all adult men and women should be included in the Reform Bill" and requesting "the Labour party in Parliament to make it clear that no Bill can be acceptable to the Labour and socialist Movement which does not include women."

As far as I know, little has been written, and less was said at the time, about the possible effect this enthusiastic Labour response may have had on Unionist and, more important, on government and backbench Liberal opinion. Liberals who feared the Conciliation Bill as favouring the Conservatives had at least as much reason to fear adult suffrage as possibly boosting the Labour party. The Liberal party agents were aware of the problem, and had made an assessment of the likely effects in various parts of the country;[56] but, while Conservative Unionists could and did argue honestly and openly against manhood suffrage[57] (let alone adult suffrage), it was hard to find good Liberal rhetoric to employ on behalf of a narrow franchise. But the Liberal government undeniably was in no hurry to implement the Reform Bill that Asquith had been promising ever since 1908. Meanwhile, an unintended effect of the promise was to smooth the way towards increased cordiality between the NU and the Labour party. In the long run, this would have far-reaching consequences. In a letter to Mrs Fawcett, however, Ramsay MacDonald, chair of the PLP, hedged his support by explaining that if it were to be further militant activity that led to the omission of women from the Reform Bill, he might not consider himself any longer bound to vote against the final reading. Arthur Henderson, Labour party secretary, seems to have taken a similar position.[58]

Neither the revived Conciliation Bill nor the now more distant Reform Bill amendments did anything to release the NU from the chronic dilemma of keeping Unionist, Liberal, and Labour support all at the same time. As acting parliamentary secretary, Catherine did all she could to help and encourage local societies to keep their MPs up to the mark, and herself was engaged in much bridge-building with important leaders at Westminster, and others who might influence them. Her activities ranged from trying to ensure that Lord Lytton would foster support in the House of Lords to making suggestions to James Mylles, the ILP organizer, on how to make the "Political Equality" campaign more effective.[59] She kept in close touch with Lloyd George, sending him a list of Unionist MPs who had promised to vote for the amendment he favoured (this was the one on "Norway" lines, including married women), and keeping him informed of the NU's campaign of deputations and private meetings with MPS. She also wanted to make sure that he understood the extent of support for suffrage in the north, and especially in the industrial areas. Later, Lloyd George promised Fawcett and Courtney that he would work on the Irish Nationalist vote, which was a matter of concern; the Irish were anxious in case the passage of the bill should lead to a dissolution before the Home Rule Bill was passed. Brailsford also passed Catherine a copy of a letter he had written to reassure Mrs Metge (of the Irishwomen's Franchise League); he was not optimistic about the bill's chances of getting through the Lords without delay, but in any event, the Conciliation Committee had agreed to have the date at which the bill would take effect postponed to 1915. Catherine was also corresponding with Lord Haldane and Walter Runciman about the difficulty surrounding the Irish vote.[60]

Throughout February, the Albert Hall rang with the suffrage debate. On the thirteenth of the month, the ILP, the Labour party, and the Fabian Society jointly sponsored a demonstration in favour of adult suffrage; on the 28th, the antisuffragists had their turn, and in between – on the 23rd – the NU held a big rally, with Lloyd George as the main speaker. Plans had been made for this at least as long ago as the previous November. The purpose of featuring George was clearly twofold, to make his commitment again a matter of public record, and to make support from within the Liberal cabinet yet more visible to the doubting Thomases, especially among the Liberals. In retrospect, perhaps one of the most interesting features of the gathering was the NU's experiment with a new way of maintaining order. Although the NU's official position was that no disruption was expected, they in fact knew well that the WSPU was unlikely to pass up the opportunity to interfere with Lloyd George's speech. However, the NU did not ask for any signed pledge from ticket-holders (a device which may have proved ineffective previously), but instead issued instructions to the sell-out audience, on their arrival, to ignore any disruption that might occur, not to turn around, and above all not to make any verbal response. Lloyd George's speech was indeed interrupted, but the lack of reaction kept the disruption to a minimum, and no one was even ejected. The officers were elated at the success of the new tactic, and Fawcett expressed her appreciation of the cooperation shown, in the next issue of the *Common Cause*. Another cause for congratulation was the remarkable sum raised at the meeting, over £7,000.[61]

Dealing with the escalation of WSPU violence on a wider scale was not so simple. After extensive window-smashing in the first week of March, there were many reports of defections and of difficulties in holding any kind of suffrage meeting in some areas. Even Norma-

Smith wrote from Appleby, "The last militant outbreak is making work here terribly difficult. It really *is* sad!"[62] Although Fawcett may well have been right when she claimed that the militants were a relatively small and decreasing group, they were commanding attention, providing an excuse for those who had any reason to waver in their support, and making it difficult indeed to bring the undecided on side.

Ironically, dislike of the WSPU's methods was bringing some convinced suffrage support over – in money and membership – from the WSPU to the NU; but this was not something that would translate into the needed parliamentary votes.[63] In March, Catherine tried a new and interesting departure, a series of suffrage dinner parties. At first glance, "suffrage dinner parties" sounds like nothing more than confirmation of the myth that the NU never transcended its image as a middle-class "drawing-room" organization, but – whatever the role of "At Homes" and receptions at other times – this was now in reality an initiative very specifically pointed at the immediate need. At the imminent second reading, every vote in the House of Commons would count, and victory here would make the House of Lords the next hurdle, but news was coming in all the time of defections and waverers. If MPs were claiming, as they were, that the actions of the militants had turned them against suffrage, what better than to show the most respectable face of the movement, to demonstrate the strength and stability of the NU, to give the doubtful a chance to meet informally with the convinced and to be exposed to the voice of sweet reason.

The NU had no lack of wealthy and well-known women to call upon to host the parties, and the idea was met with enthusiasm. In hindsight it seems a pity that they began only on 8 March, barely three weeks before the second reading. The targeted guests, members of the House of Commons and the House of Lords, were invited to dine with leading women of the NU. Dinner would be followed by a larger at-home, at which a prominent suffragist spoke – for instance, Mrs Fawcett – and to which a wider range of supporters could be invited. The possibilities of the plan are brought out by a letter from Eleanor Rathbone, leading Liverpool suffragist, to Catherine, in which she suggests the names of two influential men to be invited, Lord Balcarres, the chief Conservative whip, and Mr W.W. Ashley, the junior Conservative whip. "Both," said Rathbone "have Anti leanings, but are considered by no means inconvertible." Although they had been subjected to pressure in their constituencies, something more was needed: "I think [they] genuinely need arguing with and might be inflenced by it." She added the name of another Conservative MP, the Hon. Arthur Stanley, writing, "He has wobbled a good deal; is an 'honest doubter'; usually abstains, but paired *for* last July." Others, too, warmly supported the idea, mentioning particularly the need to counter the effect of militancy, and the need to do propaganda work "among the upper-ten" (an expression meaning much the same as "upper crust") at this critical time.[64]

As the date of the second reading drew near, the NU redoubled its campaign to keep support together. Kathleen Courtney was active alongside Catherine in the political work, and by 7 March Edith Palliser was back in her post as honorary parliamentary secretary. Emily Leaf's press committee, to which Catherine was reappointed in early March, worked hard to counter negative images and to whip up interest. Ida O'Malley's literature committee, revitalized (in part by consultations with Catherine), had prepared a whole new series of leaflets, probably in time for the Albert Hall rally, together with an impressively long list of books, pamphlets and leaflets (some published by the WFL) available from the NU.[65] Interestingly, all these most visible and innovative figures (and Helena Swanwick belongs here, as editor of the *Common Cause*) were among the ranks of the new, mostly younger, women whose activity at NU headquarters had only begun within the past year or two, and who shared a more radical viewpoint with such provincial activists as Isabella Ford and Maude Royden, who were also now on the national executive. Thanks to the continuity of Mrs Fawcett's leadership, and the reassurance provided by the effective democratic structure, very little support had been lost, and the NU executive enjoyed good cooperation in this campaign from branches and London members. Fawcett herself was tireless, making public appearances, and corresponding with leading women of organizational or familial influence to make sure that pressure on MPs came from all possible angles.[66]

Catherine orchestrated nonstop efforts to ensure that every confirmed suffragist MP was reconfirmed, every doubtful one encouraged and shored up, every opponent who showed any openness of mind encouraged to reconsider. To this end she made use of the federations, and of the new joint board; if the federation secretaries reported that there were any MPs from their region whom they had not been able for some reason to approach, Catherine passed the names on to the appropriate women's party organization.[67] She also kept in touch with what was going on in her own federation, hearing from Louis Walker, and getting frequent reports regarding Grant, the unrepentant anti MP from Whitehaven; the final word was that what little hope there had been of converting him had faded in the wake of the last wave of militancy. Another Cumberland MP, Lancelot Sanderson, previously thought to be firm for suffrage, was said to have become evasive on the subject. Reports from other sources echoed this uncomfortable news; at the executive committee meeting of 21 March, Edith Palliser "presented a list of M.P.s who had withdrawn their support." Active as the antisuffragists were at this time – it was thought that Sanderson might have been influenced by an antis' postcard campaign in his area – the militants were overwhelmingly regarded as the source of danger to the cause.[68]

Publicly, the NU, like a political party in an election campaign, kept up an optimistic front down to the day of the second reading. Privately, with their finger now right on the pulse of parliamentary opinion, they knew it was going to be a close vote, although it was not unrealistic to hope that the bill might still squeak by. But there must have been few of the leaders who slept well on the night before the debate, and few who woke without a sinking feeling. If *The Times* was among Catherine's morning reading, that at least probably helped to get the adrenalin flowing: on the morning of the debate the paper published an infamous letter from Sir Almroth Wright, a distinguished physician who had decided to step far outside his own field – bacteriology – and become an authority on the physiology and psychology of women, and he had nothing good to say of these. Women were subject to "periodically recurring phases of hypersensitiveness, unreasonableness, and loss of the sense of proportion," suffered "a complete alteration of character" during pregnancy, had a "tendency to morally warp when nervously ill," and could expect "serious and long-continued mental disorders" at the menopause. (This leaves little of our lives during which we can hope to be sane.) The suffragists were all surplus women, who should go overseas and find themselves husbands. While Wright's diatribe was mainly directed against the militants, this was little comfort to the NU; he condescendingly mentioned "that section of woman suffragists – one is almost inclined to doubt whether it any longer exists – which is opposed to all violent measures," but dismissed them with his own version of the physical force argument, claiming that they hardly knew what they were asking for, which was, in effect, the right to commission the hangman. Few women of any persuasion could stomach Wright's letter, and its circulation by the NLOWS was set in train (apparently by men in the organization) without authorization from Mrs Humphry Ward, although she was chair of the literature committee; she disapproved strongly of the "odious letter ... and of our action in regard to it."[69]

On the afternoon of the debate, many suffragists, Catherine surely among them, made their way to Parliament Square. No

formal demonstration or public meeting would be held, since this
had been made illegal within a mile of the House while Parliament
was in session, but the NU had agreed with the WFL to encourage
their members to gather in the square, wearing their suffrage colours. A room had been reserved at a restaurant on Victoria Street,
where tea and light refreshments were available during the hours of
the debate, from 4 to 11 p.m.[70] The WSPU was not in evidence, since
they had decided to ignore the Conciliation Bill altogether. It was
doubtless a sober and anxious gathering, though some could not believe that the majority they had had the year before could have van-
ished. But this was the case. When the news of the results of the
division finally came down, the Third Conciliation Bill had been defeated at second reading by a majority of fourteen.

8 New Strategy: The NUWSS Looks Left, March to June 1912

The NU executive had arranged to meet in a special session on the afternoon of 29 March 1912, the day after the second reading of the Conciliation Bill. So Catherine, and many others who had stumbled wearily home late on Thursday night when the bad news came down, turned out again the next afternoon to conduct a post mortem, and to begin to work out their next moves. There was a good attendance of executive members, nineteen in all, and H.N. Brailsford came by invitation to part of the meeting.[1]

The executive understood why the bill had gone down to defeat; all the contributing factors were those very dangers they had been trying so hard to circumvent during the previous few weeks. In 1911, the Irish Nationalist party had supported the bill; this year they had voted against it. Less predictably – indeed, by a bit of gratuitous bad luck – the Labour party, which could be regularly counted on for support, was greatly reduced in the House, since thirteen of its members, from mining areas, were off in their constituencies for a crucial ballot on the continuance of the coal strike, one of the series of bitter labour disputes which marked the years from 1910 to the outbreak of war in 1914.[2] Although the miners were the wing of labour least committed to women's suffrage at this time, the NU believed the mining MPs would have voted with the rest of the Parliamentary Labour party for the bill.[3]

Then there were the sixteen Liberals and ten Conservatives who had pledged to vote for the bill, but who voted against it, although many of them had supported the identical 1911 bill. According to a prominent supporter, for most of these the handiest excuse was provided by the recent activities of the militants; the excuse was doubly welcome to those who, recognizing that "the suffrage was becoming unpopular ... grew reluctant to endanger their other political interests by continuing to advocate it," and so "have been for some weeks looking for an excuse to break their pledge."[4] Spineless as this response to militancy might be, the blame was still generally felt by the NU to lie squarely with the WSPU, both for the direct effect of their actions on MPs and for the perceptible falling-off of support in the constituencies. Where the NU had previously had some success in persuading doubting MPs that their constituents would not like them to vote against women's enfranchisement, those same waverers were now getting the opposite message. The WSPU was seen to have contributed even to the defection of the Home Rulers, who had also been the target of recent militant attacks.

Kathleen Courtney came to the meeting with a statement, which served as the basis for discussion and emerged with some modifications as a manifesto for use by members and by press departments. This began by stating firmly that the executive "do not regard the defeat of the Conciliation Bill by the narrow majority of 14 as a sign of hostility to the political enfranchisement of women," and followed with an analysis of the factors responsible, avoiding pejorative terminology but not dodging the issues. Typically, it concluded in a forward-looking mood, urging support for the women's suffrage amendments to the coming Reform Bill.[5]

The executive resolved not to hold any demonstration in London, but encouraged local societies to organize public protests in the constituencies of MPs who had broken pledges, wherever it was felt that these might be useful. Since work towards amendment of the Reform Bill had been agreed upon at the previous November council, the executive thought it unnecessary to call a special council at this time, a decision which was soon to be reversed.

Even behind the closed doors of the executive committee meeting room, as far as we can learn from the minutes, there was no giving way to despair; if enfranchisement was going to take a little longer, well, it was going to take a little longer. The NU was a large solid organization that was not going to go away until the day was won. The minutes convey this without directly articulating it; while most of the time was spent on formulating strategy directly in response to the previous day's disappointment, the names of two new organizers were accepted, a new assistant secretary was appointed, "a new typewriter and Cabinet was decided upon," and alterations to the office were approved.[6] But something more of feeling, if also of humour, can be seen in Catherine's later categorization of MPs; besides the accustomed designations of "Supporters" and "Antis," there are now "Wobblers" and "Rats."[7]

Shortly after the special executive, Catherine left London and went home to Keswick. The confusion surrounding her status on the NU executive throughout her time in London had become worse confounded with the return of Edith Palliser, and had only been resolved after something of a showdown at the executive meeting of 21 March, when Catherine's status was called in question, possibly not for the first time, by Chrystal Macmillan.[8] Macmillan had studied law, and her argument was legalistic and impersonal – indeed, the minutes do not record her as so much as mentioning Catherine by name; but it is hard to believe that there was no animosity in her determination to force the issue. Unfortunately, we do not know the basis of Macmillan's hostility, although she does appear to have been one of those not entirely comfortable with the influx of new members to the executive, perhaps with initiatives being taken there, and certainly with what she seems to have perceived as a tendency of the officers to be too independent of the executive. At any rate, on 21 March, she insisted on putting on record her protest against the decision to make the honorary assistant parliamentary secretary (that is, Catherine) an honorary officer, with a seat and a vote on the executive. This, she claimed, it was beyond the power of the executive to do; her reading of the resolution of the annual council was that it authorized the executive to appoint the assistant on the same basis as the honorary secretaries of the literature and press committees, who were not full members of the executive, but with the proviso that Catherine could be coopted to the executive "should a vacancy occur." Macmillan's protest was duly minuted, and was followed at once by Helena Swanwick's motion, seconded by Kathleen Courtney, that Catherine be appointed honorary assistant parliamentary secretary, with a seat on the executive; this was carried, and the matter was settled.

Later in the meeting Macmillan, who seems to have been having a difficult day, angrily attacked the officers for agreeing to the change of date for the Conciliation Bill second reading (from 22 March to 29 March); Royden responded with a motion to endorse the officers' action. If the vote shows that a residual divide could still appear in the executive, it must also show that the new wing now had a controlling interest; only two voted with Macmillan, twelve against, and the officers abstained. The vote on Catherine's appointment was not recorded in detail, nor do we have any knowledge of what the meeting had been like for her; later in the same meeting, as we have seen, she gave a full account, with apparent composure, of the parliamentary work being done in preparation for the second reading.[9]

Catherine took April, her birthday month, as a holiday, with time to enjoy the advent of spring in the Lake District. Maude Royden felt the break was much needed, writing, "I hope you took more than two days' rest? Oh I hope you did."[10] As far as we know, Catherine was free of formal suffrage engagements in April, although she was at once in touch with leaders of some of the local societies, bringing them up to date on recent developments at headquarters.[11]

In returning to Keswick in April, Catherine followed what had become her practice over the past few years, but this time her stay at Hawse End was to be relatively brief; she planned to be in London again in June, and to stay for the two summer months. Although an extra few months in London may not seem of great moment, her involvement in the suffrage movement was once more making major changes in Catherine's life. When she went to London in June 1912, she was, apparently for the first time, planning to rent rooms on her own, rather than staying with friends. Shortly after she left London in April, Catherine wrote to Mrs Fawcett asking her to allow her to give her name as a reference; Fawcett of course agreed, and said how very glad she was that Catherine would be in London.[12]

The attempt to understand the significance of these developments in Catherine's personal life, and in more general terms in the lives of middle-class women earlier in this century, takes us into surprisingly complex cross-currents. Catherine's private life is less consistently visible to us than her public life, and the all-important relation between the two has to be deduced. Few personal letters remain for this period, for instance. We know her parents were still working together with her in the suffrage cause, indeed were now carrying a good deal of the Keswick work, and they visited her not infrequently when she was in London (one or both were at the one suffrage dinner party of which we have some record), and we have mentioned her continuing closeness with her brother, Hal. She kept in touch with Jermyn; they wrote to each other about books they read, but he was no longer in London and she seldom saw him. Music was still her chosen recreation, even her profession in the Lake District; and a London friend rhapsodized about the treat it had been to go to a concert with "one who can enjoy so splendidly."[13]

We know something, too, of the friendships Catherine was forming within the suffrage movement; she was now (at last) on a first-name basis with Louis Walker, and suffragists from north and south were often to be found among the guests visiting Hawse End when she was there, and sometimes when she was not. And we have seen Catherine throwing herself into work for which she had an astonishing talent, developing self-confidence and earning the respect and affection of her fellow-workers. At just this time, Maude Royden wrote to Catherine (in connection with a report Catherine was to make to the council) of the need to recognize the professionalism of the leading suffragists: "I hope you will give them some idea of the utter devotion of people like Miss Courtney, Miss Palliser, Mrs. Auerback [sic], Miss Leaf, and Miss O'Malley (can't mention yourself, unluckily!) who toil all day and every day and often half the night, without pay and at the cost of their health very often, exactly as if it were a highly-paid profession in which they would earn fortune and fame! People realize a little what the speakers are doing, but *not at all* what the officers do, I think."[14]

A difficulty here, of course, is that full-time unpaid work can only be done by those with private means. By this time there were paid jobs in suffrage organization, and the NU in particular had a team of trained salaried professionals, many of whom came from the industrial women's suffrage societies. A number of speakers, endorsed by the NU, made themselves available to speak to public and private meetings; some of them charged a fee (ranging from five shillings to one guinea, and occasionally as high as two guineas) in addition to the cost of transport to the meeting.[15] Work in the suffrage movement, then, besides providing a vocation and a living for some working women, opened the door a crack towards at least partial independence for some others; from the perspective of the late twentieth century, surely better to earn pocket money than nothing. Yet among middle-class women it was customary to deplore the need to charge a fee. For example, an extremely able and well-educated suffrage speaker, an Oxford graduate who had taken first class honours in English, wrote as if only an unearned income represented true independence – "Oh! for a legacy to make one independent."[16]

Given the financial situation of most middle-class women, there must have been many, married and unmarried, who were altogether prevented from taking part in the suffrage campaign, regardless of their own inclination, or whose activity was held in check. Living at home had indirect effects as well. Mabel Barton, president of the Carnforth and District WSS, wrote movingly to Catherine of her elderly father, a supporter of the local Unionist MP, who was at best unreliable on the suffrage question. The old man had indeed, at her urging, written to the MP in favour of a very limited measure of women's suffrage, but he had "a great horror of much publicity ...

and while he lives, I will not openly thwart him or disregard his wishes, therefore I cannot personally head any deputation that it may be necessary to send to London." Her own sense of tension over the issue is reflected in her offer to resign her position on this account.[17] Unquestionably, Catherine was fortunate in having parents who were supportive. Yet this came far short of independence. We do not know if, at a conscious level, Catherine readily accepted her father's generosity, conforming to the prevailing mores on this issue, or what questions it raised for her.

Two particularly instructive examples from the nineteenth century of the meaning of financial dependence among middle-class women, and of parental attitudes, at widely separated points on the spectrum of liberality, are the cases of Sophia Jex-Blake, whose father did not object to her appointment as a junior lecturer in mathematics at Queen's College until he found that the post was salaried, when he forbade her to take any pay, insisting that "if she must teach she should do so in a voluntary capacity"; and of Barbara Leigh-Smith Bodichon, whose father settled on her a permanent allowance, renouncing altogether his power to control her through the purse.[18] Perhaps surprisingly, Frank Marshall's place on the spectrum is closer to the paternalistic end. And inevitably, control through the purse was accompanied by other forms of tutelage. In effect, Catherine always had to get her father's permission to spend time in London, although he consistently gave the warmest moral support to her suffrage work.[19]

Catherine's personal financial irresponsibility may well have contributed to the difficulty her father had in letting go of the reins; and conversely, resentment, perhaps unconscious, may have done much to feed that irresponsibility. We cannot listen in to the family discussions; and there may have been some serious talking even during Catherine's April vacation in 1912, since she had arrived from London with handfuls of unpaid bills. There is considerable documentation, though inevitably incomplete, of Catherine's personal finances; and whenever Catherine hit London, these became a disaster. She loved clothes, and Carlisle, let alone Keswick, was hardly a fashionable shopping area. Her exceptional height made clothes more expensive and harder to find. She may also have rationalized the added spending on the valid grounds of her public visibility; she had to dress well for her daily encounters with politicians, not to mention such special occasions as a suffrage dinner party at Lady Farrer's (she bought not one but three veils – presumably hat-trimming – two days before this event). Like many others, too, she may have boosted her self-confidence with a new hat or a new blouse; and London streets perhaps were hard on the feet, since she seems to have bought a number of pairs of "boots."[20] There were also direct expenses connected with her suffrage work; it is rather startling to find the NU proposing to pay the train fares of the executive, apparently for the first time, in 1913.[21]

All of this leaves unanswered questions; we do not know whether Catherine's allowance was quite inadequate or whether she simply did not get around to paying bills. In fairness, it must be said that the total owing was never enormous, and most of the items bought were individually small; the size of the bills is not remarkable, just the fact of their being consistently left unpaid. The pattern suggests that she was indeed always overspent, but that her lifelong inability to think about money played a major part in creating the problem – and sometimes there were even suffrage debts that went unpaid; at the end of 1912 at least one Keswick printer was still trying to collect payment for work done as far back as April 1910, and Julia Bendelack had to write three times to remind Catherine that she had not settled an account for some suffrage literature she had taken.[22] That she really was short of money is suggested by a note to the NU treasurer on 1 October, with a cheque for £5; she wrote, "I could not send a donation before because I had been spending twice as much as I could really afford on Suffrage already, and I had to wait to see if I could get through the summer without a new dress!" Sadly, the letter and the cheque remained unsent, and were found with a batch of bills which included a firmly worded request, dated 2 October, from the NU literature secretary to settle her outstanding account. It seems that this time donations were overtaken by debts.[23]

Throughout 1912 bills came in, the same bills again and again, some of them dating from the previous November, from department stores such as D.H. Evans, Harvey Nichols, and Gorringe, from the London Shoe Company, from a corset-makers in Cambridge, and (this a substantial one) from a glovers and hosiers.[24] Catherine seemingly did not have her own bank account until the next year, but was expected to send bills – to a reasonable amount – to her father for payment. Frank was on the whole a just and generous man, well off but without an unlimited amount of available cash. We have to surmise that Catherine did not let him know as the bills piled up; had he known, there is little doubt that his sense of what was right would have required that the bills be paid at once, whatever he might subsequently have said to her. In February 1913, in fact, this is what seems to have happened; Catherine's mounting bills – none of them large, but all long overdue and accompanied by ever more strongly worded requests for payment – came at length to the attention of her parents, and Caroline sent cheques to Catherine, made out to her creditors, to pay them off. And this is where Catherine's behaviour comes near to being perverse; she did not in fact send the cheques out, did not, apparently, even open the envelope containing them, and they remain uncashed among her papers.[25] Did all this amount to a secret embarrassment that kept the seemingly poised and confident Catherine awake at night? Or was she able to push it away at the back of her mind, almost all the time? All we can say, at this distance, is that all her life Catherine, with her genius for organization, never learnt to manage money.

May was the month of the big annual events of the suffrage movement in Keswick and the NWF, and Catherine gave them her attention for the first two weeks of the month; her role had become that of the person with first-hand information from London, and knowledge that would help in its interpretation, rather than of a participant in local organization, though she kept in touch by correspondence and still seems to have given a certain amount of direction.[26] Whatever her personal joys in the Keswick spring, her private anxieties over money, or her wish to touch base with northwest suffragists, too much of interest was taking place at the NU's London office for Catherine to be willing to stay long away.

The executive's first public reaction to the defeat of the Conciliation Bill, as we have seen, had been to treat it as just another hiccup in the long campaign, and to urge women's suffragists to work for the Reform Bill amendments. Clearly, the private member's bill was no route forward. The most devoted of the Liberal suffragist women, while recognizing this, still hoped that the Liberal party could yet be the party to take up the cause, if the NU only declared itself for a wide enough measure, and would put in more years of patient work. In an interesting letter to Catherine, Eleanor Acland conducted her own post mortem on the Conciliation Bill. She felt that the whole conciliation enterprise had been in some way dishonest, because it attempted to rally support from different people for different reasons; but the defeat had been a big setback:

I am rather afraid that I think we are five or ten years from success. ... But I am more and more convinced that our movement has got to be linked on to democracy rather than pure feminism. People are *bored* with feminism, and the militants have given it a bad name. Of course it seems ridiculous to suggest in the face of an adverse majority of 14 that we should chuck the 65 Tory votes. But all the same, with work, we could afford to do so, and we should get much more keen-ness [sic] if one party really liked the Bill. ... We can discount 44 Irish votes (I am really supposing now that the next great struggle will be after Home Rule has passed the Commons), we can add at least 15 Labour votes, and about ten adultists could be transferred, counting 20 on the division. That does not make a complete majority but it gets near enough to give us a working chance. Because I do not believe the Tories would all vote against – I mean the faithful 65. ... Do let us plump for the Liberal party – we aren't there yet, but we could get a big enough majority if we would only be honest.[27]

The NU's officers, however, including Mrs Fawcett, while they might agree with Acland's premise that sponsorship of the women's franchise by a party, which would carry the cause as part of its platform at elections, was essential, were experiencing by now almost total disillusionment with the Liberal party, and were not prepared to put their fortunes in its hands. For the small group of officers most concerned with the NU's parliamentary work the defeat had clinched the need for a climactic change in policy, and within a very few days they had directed their attention towards this change.

Courtney talked the situation over with Brailsford, discussing the unsatisfactory role of Lloyd George, who, in Brailsford's view, "didn't do one single thing he said he would do in connection with the Second Reading,"[28] and the major problem of the defection of the Irish Nationalists in the recent vote.[29] But Brailsford's most important proposal, independently already present in the minds of the NU leaders, was to move towards an agreement of some kind with the Labour party,[30] which had come out with increasingly supportive resolutions in favour of women's suffrage. The major strategic purpose of the proposal was understood. There was no prospect of the Labour party forming a government in the foreseeable future, but the Liberal party was more vulnerable in the House and in the constituencies than it would have been had it had an absolute parliamentary majority, and was especially threatened by three-cornered contests in any place where its majority was narrow.

Again, the apparent unity of thought is striking between Millicent Fawcett and the go-ahead women (not all of them young) now forming the core of the executive – in Holton's terminology, the "democratic suffragists." In her message to the NU in the first issue of the Common Cause following the defeat of the Conciliation Bill, Fawcett had given high praise to the stance of the Labour party and its commitment to the women's cause, and had gone farther than that, writing, "It may well be a subject for careful thought and discussion at our next Council meeting whether, under these circumstances, we should not modify our existing election policy and support Labour candidates whenever they are in the field at a contested election, unless the candidates selected by the other parties have given proof of their sincere advocacy of Women's Suffrage."[31]

Also striking is the sense of the officers' being closely in touch with a network of women of different interests, more radical orientation, and a closer knowledge of the industrial north than the predominantly Liberal, southern, middle-class group who had carried the burden of the cause in the NU so long. Courtney told Fawcett she had had "a letter from Dr. Ethel Williams of Newcastle full of despair at the line the N.U. is taking and suggesting much the same thing with regard to the Labour party."[32] The Newcastle society had long had close ties with local labour bodies, and had suggested policies as early as 1907 to open the door to the kind of thing now being proposed.[33] As late as 1909 Fawcett and others on the national executive had not been ready for such a radical step.[34] Now they were. Spurred on also by "a good many other letters ... urging us to *do* something," Courtney felt that "the question arises as to whether the psychological moment has come for us to enter into provisional arrangements with the Labour party and then lay a proper scheme before a meeting of the General Council." Even before writing to Fawcett she had asked Philip Snowden "quite informally what he thought were the possibilities of any such arrangement."[35]

From this point things moved forward rapidly. The NU executive acted on an initiative from the Newcastle society which coincided with the direction in which the officers were already moving, and called a special council for 14 and 15 May 1912. The executive, again on a resolution brought forward by Newcastle, authorized Courtney to open correspondence with the Labour party; but the need for confidentiality at this stage was felt to be so great that this decision was omitted from the minutes as circulated. Courtney wrote next day to Arthur Henderson, the party secretary, requesting a meeting.[36]

The steps that followed were not simple. The first meeting between the NU officers and Labour party leaders took place only after a very full and careful correspondence had paved the way.[37] Well-prepared with a list of suggested questions to discuss, Millicent Fawcett, Kathleen Courtney, Helena Auerbach, and Edith Palliser met on 30 April with Henderson, James Ramsay MacDonald, chairman of the Parliamentary Labour party (PLP), and Keir Hardie.[38] Negotiations went well enough that the NU officers came away believing they had something concrete to lay before the council.[39] However, there was another cliff-hanger during the intervening two weeks, when some Labour party leaders, notably, it seems, Mac-Donald, got cold feet and asked the NU to water down the proposal, omitting any specific reference to Labour.[40] Some reasons for Mac-Donald's coolness to the initiative will be examined later. Meanwhile, however, the NU replied politely but firmly that the new and important element in the proposal was the specific stated intention to support Labour candidates, and that if this was not included, "it simply represents our present policy, and as such would have no fresh driving power for the purpose of raising money, nor indeed did it need discussion." The only sting is in the tail of this letter, where the writer (probably Kathleen Courtney) adds that she does not know "whether, in view of your attitude, the Executive will wish to press the matter."[41] Brailsford, who had heard of the development from Courtney, wrote to Henderson conveying the same message, but barely concealing the depth of his anger, and emphasizing the possible cost to the Labour party.[42]

For whatever reason, whether Courtney's icy civility, Brailsford's indignant contempt, or a recognition that Labour had a good deal to lose if they backed out now, MacDonald agreed to a last-minute meeting with Millicent Fawcett and Kathleen Courtney, the very day before the council, at which cordiality was restored, along with the all-important reference to Labour candidates in the resolution to be presented to the council the next day. MacDonald took the opportunity to argue his case against any formal public commitment on the Reform Bill at present, saying that he believed that it might encourage the government simply to refrain from introducing the bill at all. The last-minute contretemps may have been of value in clarifying the freedom of the NU to make what statement it would of its own position, together with the inability of the Labour party to make any final commitment until at least the meeting of its executive scheduled for 2 July.[43]

All the exciting events of April and the first days of May 1912 Catherine missed while she took her holiday and attended to regional suffrage business, but she was back in London for at least a few days early in May to attend the special council. If there was anything that she had not been kept up to date with by letter or by the minutes of the executive, she was in the thick of it as soon as she was back in London, and there were others who were as glad to have her as she was to be there. The new policy into which the NU was moving with great rapidity was going to involve a heavy extra load, and the over-extended officers clearly saw Catherine's coming as a godsend, with the flair she had already shown for political work. She had already familiarized herself with the main issue, and had discussed it with the KWSA general committee.[44]

The new policy was not to be expected to pass without opposition. The Cardiff society was so upset when the announcement of the special council arrived that it tried to have the meeting cancelled, and circularized all the NU societies condemning the proposal in such strong terms that the executive reluctantly sent out a further statement correcting what it felt were inaccuracies in the Cardiff letter.[45] Among the members of the executive, the strongest opposition came from Eleanor Rathbone, who wrote to Fawcett of her fears that the plan might alienate loyal Liberal support.[46]

The resolutions to implement the new policy were moved at the council by Millicent Fawcett and seconded by Helena Auerbach. Catherine was among those who spoke in favour, as were Frances Sterling, Kathleen Courtney, Isabella Ford, and Helena Swanwick. Eleanor Rathbone, Margery Corbett Ashby, and E[mily] Davies[47] spoke against it. The officers had little difficulty in obtaining the majority they needed; the policy was passed without significant modification. Fawcett later summarized the decisions:

(1) When deciding whom to support in an electoral contest to take account not only of individual opinions of candidates, but also of the position of their respective parties on Women's Suffrage.

(2) To support individual Labour Candidates especially in constituencies now represented by Liberals whose record on suffrage is unsatisfactory. The candidates will be Labour party candidates, not National Union candidates. The National Union will in no case oppose either Liberal or Conservative who has proved himself a trustworthy friend of Women's enfranchisement.

(3) A fund was opened for the effective carrying out of this policy, and more than 1000*l* [sic] was subscribed by the council in a few minutes. A Committee has since been formed by the National Union Executive, whose duty it will be to augment and control this fund. The Executive Committee will invite Suffragists to serve on this Committeee who need not necessarily be members of the National Union.[48]

Perceptions of the council naturally varied. While Rathbone felt that "extreme tenderness" had been shown "to the consciences and feelings of the Labour party," some others, according to Fawcett, were " disappointed and dismayed by what was considered the tone of ungenerous and carping criticism applied to the Labour party in our discussions."[49] But although Rathbone saw the council as having been hustled into its decision, she went on to make it plain that she was not implying that there had been any deliberate attempt to deny the opposition a hearing, and accepted some responsibility for not herself having asked for more time to be allowed for a full development of the arguments against the new policy. And although she felt unable to subscribe to the new fund, she underlined her continuing loyalty with a very substantial donation to the NU's general funds.[50]

That there was some opposition to the new departure may seem less surprising than the extent of support which it so rapidly commanded. This support cannot be explained only in terms of parliamentary events, but has to be looked at in the light of the whole internal growth and direction of the NU, and developments in its constituency, over the previous two or three years.[51] In the first place, the demand for the franchise "as is or may be given to men," while it was still the official policy of the NU (and surely the only possible long-term objective for feminists), had ceased, with the introduction of the concept of the Conciliation Bill, to be any kind of immutable touchstone. While the franchise proposed under these bills might indeed have been even narrower, what endorsement of them really meant to the majority of women's suffragists, including, by this time (though not necessarily much earlier), Mrs Fawcett, was not a fear of a wider franchise, but a commitment to any franchise women could get, since the enfranchisement of any number of women would break forever the exclusion of women on grounds of sex. When the government's proposal of a Reform Bill opened up the possibility of a much broader franchise, the NU was ready to support even the widest measure of enfranchisement, as it had been to support the narrower; always with the proviso that women must get their toe in, whether the door be open wide or only a crack, and whether all the remaining men walked through it or only a few.

Even more important in acceptance of the new policy were the profound changes which had taken place in the NU itself since 1909. We have seen how Catherine's move towards a position of influence in the national organization of the NU was part of a substantial shift which had taken place over several years, bringing into prominence an able group of suffragists, largely from the provinces, and in particular from the north and the Midlands. While a large part of Catherine's home territory was rural and semirural, the population of the whole NWF region included a considerable industrial component, and we have seen her addressing herself more and more to this numerically significant section of the population. Catherine had probably made speeches to more miners than ever she had women or upper-class men, at any rate in Cumberland. Others of Catherine's colleagues, now influential as officers or on the executive, were from large northern industrial cities, and much of their suffrage activity had been among working women and men there. Further, ever since the WSPU had moved its headquarters to London and had taken up an ever more aggressive militancy, the bulk of Midland working women's support and affiliation was with the NU.[52]

Not only, then, were there women available to serve the NU in leadership roles, with the needed skills and energy to spare, and with the courage for innovation, but they had their base in a broad constituency. As for party sympathies, the executive now included women who were long-time Labour supporters, such as Isabella Ford, some converts to Labour, such as Margaret Ashton, and – Catherine's category – Liberals so disaffected as to be almost ripe for change, as well as a few still-committed Liberals and Unionists. Meanwhile, the NU's paid and trained organizers now ranged eclectically from university graduates, such as Margaret Robertson, to former textile workers, such as Selina Cooper; useful as each might be in her own social environment, by this time it was notable that the best of the organizers spoke to all kinds of groups and were responsible for a great deal of cross-fertilization of knowledge and ideas between women of differing backgrounds.[53]

Short of actually switching party allegiance, many Liberal women in the NU were so angry at the constant blocking of suffrage measures, culminating in the recent defeat of the Conciliation Bill, that they were prepared to welcome a scheme that appeared to offer the chance for positive action, no matter if this could only be done by threatening the interests of their own party. Even Eleanor Rathbone, perhaps the most articulate opponent of the scheme, found herself almost uncomfortably able to see both sides of the question. In the same letter in which she expressed her discomfort with the tone which had developed, she explained to Helena Auerbach something of the ambivalence she felt on the first day of the special council: "Although the balance of argument appeared to me to be against the new plan and I therefore felt bound to oppose it by vote and speech, its acceptance by a large majority was to me personally a considerable relief. If it had been rejected, it would have been impossible to convince others and perhaps even to feel certain oneself that one had not helped to reject a scheme which might have wrought great good to the cause. I was therefore on Tuesday night by no means disposed to shed tears much less to feel resentment over the defeat of my side."[54]

Nevertheless, Rathbone's reservations were not to grow less, and Cardiff WSS continued to be hostile, fearing the effect on local Liberal support. Other societies in the South Wales federation soon expressed concern, and Scarborough wss also protested.[55] But the opponents of the new policy were uncomfortably aware that there were few good options open. Cardiff expressed a firm desire to remain within the union, and at present merely sought assurance that the NU head office would not use the fund in its area without consultation with the local society.[56] Rathbone's approach was rational and conciliatory; she redoubled her efforts to organize Liberal women, in particular through a scheme by which Liberal women would pledge not to work for unsatisfactory candidates. Her objection was to a too-aggressive exploitation of the new policy as much as to the policy itself. But Catherine was unable to persuade her to stay on the NU parliamentary committee,[57] which would have provided a legitimate forum for her moderating influence, as well as exposing her to closer contact with the realities of Liberal attitudes.

Although it was not spelled out, it was undoubtedly in part as a step to blunting the edge of possible resistance to the new policy in the NU that there had been a revival of interest in Catherine's "general post" scheme. In April Maude Royden had written to Catherine urging her, "Do, Oh *do* make people see the *enormous* value of your 'scheme'. I am getting perfectly possessed by it," and at about the same time both she and Kathleen Courtney again promoted it in the columns of the *Common Cause*.[58] The NU executive considered it important enough to be put on the agenda at the special council, and sent forward a resolution calling on societies to "make determined efforts to organise party people in their constituencies in preparation for carrying out Miss Marshall's scheme of transferring workers to suitable constituencies." The KWSA had forwarded a similar resolution to the council from its general committee meeting on 6 May. There is little evidence as to how many suffragists made use of the plan, but we do know of one who had: Catherine's father set a good example, and was able to say, "In Dec[ember] 1910 I left Sir Wilfrid Lawson's constituency where I had gladly worked in January, because his opponent, Sir John Randles had served on the conciliation com[ee] in the interval, and found in S. Westmorland a Liberal and good suffragist Mr. Somervell opposed by a conservative anti-suffragist Captain Bagot."[59]

With the mandate of the Council in hand, the NU executive lost no time before setting up the machinery for the new election fund. Donations were already pouring in to add to the sum raised at the council meeting itself; the impression is of a sense of relief among women's suffragists at finding something concrete to support; by the end of June over £2,000 had come in – this before canvassing for funds had really begun. By the end of July the fund topped £4,000, a substantial sum in terms of election expenses of the day.[60] Catherine was present at the special executive called for the day following the council. It was decided that the officers would serve on the new committee *ex officio*, and three members of the executive, Isabella Ford, Margaret Ashton, and Mrs Stanbury (a London member), were elected by ballot. A rather long list of people to be invited to join was approved, with Catherine's name at the head, suggesting that she had narrowly missed election, and that there were those who saw her as having a special role to fill.[61]

The new committee did not meet formally until over two weeks later, allowing time to make contact with its outside members; besides, all at headquarters had been working so hard in the negotiations with the Labour party and the lead-up to the special council that it is likely that a brief slowdown or break was sanctioned around Whitsuntide. Catherine went north again, to take part in the NWF's annual meeting in Carlisle on 18 May, and in the KWSA annual meeting on 22 May,[62] coming back to London at the beginning of June, as originally planned. At this time she moved into a room at 1 Barton Street, the home of Mary Sheepshanks, where service and meals were provided – and Mary Sheepshanks always had a good cook. Many women of importance in British and international feminism stayed there at one time or another. Mary was already well known to Catherine, and they were to be lifelong friends, with many shared interests and common ideals, though Mary's life had been much harsher than Catherine's. Barton Street is a quiet Westminster street of narrow eighteenth-century houses, unpretentious but graceful, just round the corner from the NU offices on Great Smith Street, and less than five minutes' walk from the Houses of Parliament, an ideal location for one who was to become a constant lobbyist. But it was Catherine's mother who paid the rent, direct to Mary Sheepshanks.[63]

After Catherine's return to London, she attended the regular fortnightly executive on 6 June 1912. As well as further work on the new policy and the composition of the special committee, there was other business to be seen to. A constantly recurring topic at this time was that of the WSPU. After the outbreak of window-breaking at the beginning of March, Emmeline Pankhurst and the Pethick-Lawrences had been charged with conspiracy; Christabel Pankhurst had fled to Paris on 6 March, and now led the militant campaign from there. The conspiracy trial had taken place, as it happened, on the same day as the NU's special council, and resulted in sentences of nine months for each of the defendants, to be served in the Second

Division, where they were soon hunger striking, which in turn led to the horrors of forcible feeding.[64]

The NU was under constant pressure to join the ensuing campaign to have the prisoners transferred to the First Division as political prisoners, and not surprisingly, found themselves much exercised on the question, torn between a residual sense of sisterhood and outrage at the treatment to which the women were subjected on the one hand, and their own conviction, on the other, that the militants had done more to undo the NU's careful work than any antisuffragists could have done, and that they would be further exposing themselves to an undeserved share of public condemnation if they showed any support.

Millicent Fawcett had not joined a recent deputation to Reginald McKenna, the home secretary, but had been reported in the press as having done so (thus surely getting the worst of both sides of the question). At the 6 June executive, Isabella Ford proposed a motion, seconded by Catherine, to send a memorial to McKenna urging that "the Suffrage Prisoners in the recent Conspiracy Trial be given first-class treatment in prison." Not surprisingly, "much discussion" followed. Although the resolution finally passed, as did one to send the memorial to the press, the group which was now working together so comfortably on many topics was divided on this question; Edith Palliser, Frances Sterling, and Helena Swanwick were the dissentients. Swanwick, in particular, had long felt that the NU weakened its cause by not coming out in forthright condemnation of the militants. In July 1912, provoked beyond endurance by a letter from Ramsay MacDonald accusing the NU of trying "to run with the hare and hunt with the hounds," that is, to benefit from militancy while keeping its own nose clean, she resigned from the editorship of the *Common Cause* because she felt the attitude of the executive prevented her from speaking as forcefully against the WSPU as she thought right and necessary.[65]

9 Election Fighting Fund and Reform Bill, June 1912 to January 1913

While public, political, and press attention swirled around the new outbreak of militancy, the far more important development of the NU's agreement with the Labour party passed almost unnoticed, except within the NU itself. The new committee met for the first time on 14 June 1912, and took the name of Election Fighting Fund for Women's Suffrage (EFF). Mrs Fawcett accepted the chair; and Catherine was made honorary secretary, with primary responsibility for launching the new initiative.[1] She was to be the leading headquarters figure of the EFF campaign down to the outbreak of the First World War, her contribution matched only by that of Margaret Robertson, working as head organizer in the field.[2]

Even before the committee met, the new policy had been given a trial run at a by-election at Holmfirth, in which the NU's participation had been handled by special executive meetings, attended mainly by the NU members who had been appointed to the new committee. There was obviously a keen desire to put the policy into effect, especially as it would be a three-cornered contest, with an unsatisfactory Liberal candidate. The executive decided to support Mr Lunn, the Labour candidate, who was a firm suffragist, and allocated money for the campaign to be advanced from NU funds and reimbursed when the EFF was operational. Kathleen Courtney and Catherine went to see Arthur Henderson to discuss how best to manage the details of the cooperation. Together they agreed that a sum (£100) would be paid direct to the local Labour organization running the candidate, and that the help of NU workers would be welcome. Any speakers and canvassers provided by the NU would have to be in sympathy with the Labour party's political position, but there would also be plenty that could be done by any willing suffragists, whatever their political views, in such things as tracing removals, and in clerical work. They agreed that it would be better not to share committee rooms. In addition to the direct help offered to the Labour candidate, the NU set aside money to fund its own work, and provided a total of six paid workers.[3]

As a test case and a first run, the Holmfirth campaign proved promising. The by-election took place on 20 June 1912. The NU and the nascent EFF gave a splendid demonstration of how quickly and efficiently they could go into action, making use of some of the NU's best organizers as the EFF did not have its own staff yet. The previous Labour vote was doubled, though Lunn still came third. The Liberal held the seat, but with a greatly reduced majority. Catherine reported that "The sensational increase of the Labour vote was attributed by the Labour party themselves largely to our effective help."[4] The national press took note of the new departure, and a beginning had been made.

Now that Catherine's position was official, she set to work with a will. Another by-election had been called, at Ilkeston, in the East Midlands, which was to land the EFF in a much less happy situation. Ilkeston was the seat of Colonel John Seely, a Liberal minister, whose appointment to a senior cabinet position as secretary of state for war necessitated his resignation and reelection (under an act repealed in 1926). Seely was an uncompromising antisuffragist who had voted against every women's suffrage measure, and so seemed an ideal target for the new policy, especially as the local Labour party was keen to run an acceptable candidate.

Unfortunately the Labour party's leaders had reasons for not wishing to contest Ilkeston, among them a reluctance to oppose a minister in the present parliamentary situation. EFF members initially knew nothing of this reluctance, and Mrs Cowmeadow, the NU organizer in the area, wrote to the Labour candidate, J. Thomas White, offering the substantial sum of £500 for his campaign, on condition he gained the party's approval, and committed himself to women's suffrage. Cowmeadow's letter was premature. Labour party consent was denied. White seems to have understood the conditions of the offer, and expressed his appreciation for it nevertheless. Meanwhile, unfortunately, the press got hold of the story and reported it on 17 June as if there had been a firm and unconditional offer. Catherine, realizing at once that this could be "very harmful to our relations with the Labour party," went with Courtney to see

Henderson, and characteristically to Ilkeston the next day to investigate at first hand, stopping only long enough to dictate a letter to go to members of the EFF. Cowmeadow's hopes revived again, along with White's, when the ILP considered supporting his candidature, but the EFF and the NU cabled a decision not to offer anything from the EFF, but only the support (at a cost of £50 from general funds) customarily given in any election to the candidate judged best in terms of his suffrage opinions. In the end, Labour party official policy prevailed, and Seely was opposed only by a Unionist (also an antisuffragist).[5]

The incident makes irritating reading, in part because the Labour party, in the person of Arthur Henderson, took a self-righteous and admonitory tone, and assumed that the EFF would take its direction. Even Hume refers to what had occurred as if it had been an attempt at "a circumvention of authority"[6] by the NU (which it may have been on the part of the local ILP). Yet at this point not only had the party made no commitment on its side, but its leaders had, throughout the negotiations with the NU, worked always for the looser rather than the closer association; and they continued to stress that money should be offered to the candidates, never to the central party. However, in the longer view, the care that Catherine took to mollify Henderson was effort well invested in the interest of gaining the confidence of the Labour party leaders, and saving the promising new policy. Catherine's final letter to him about Ilkeston was received relatively graciously (if somewhat condescendingly) as "a clear indication that your Committee desires to do nothing but what is in harmony with our position."[7] Interestingly, Catherine's own view was that "the anticipation of the advent of a Labour candidate with Suffragist support decided the Conservatives to put a candidate in the field in order to take advantage of the split in the progressive vote. Otherwise the seat would probably not have been contested, and the Government would have avoided the damaging blow to its prestige occasioned by the big drop in the majority of a newly-appointed Cabinet Minister. Had a Labour candidate stood, Colonel Seely's seat might well have been seriously imperilled, in spite of his previous large majority."[8]

Catherine told the NU council that she thought the Labour party, as well as the EFF, had "regretted their decision," adding "They and we are preparing for a determined attack on Colonel Seely's seat next time (this is private at present)."[9] Her opinion was probably based on unofficial and local Labour party opinion, rather than on any word from the top party officials. The EFF had still a great deal to learn. Catherine indeed quickly recognized the need to under-

stand the complicated structure and internal dissensions of the Labour party, which differed in important ways from the other parties.
Besides being still a young organization at this time, the Labour
party's constitution gave it some of the characteristics of a coalition
rather than a monolithic body; above all, there were continuing unresolved tensions between the socialist and trade union wings of the
party. Catherine could not alter the structures, but at least she could
and did set out to learn about them. By early July she had prepared
an organization chart of the Labour party national executive for distribution to the NU executive as well as the EFF, and had made notes
on the relationship of the party to the several socialist societies and
to the trade unions. Her diagram is still helpful and is reproduced
here (p. 176).[10]

Ramsay MacDonald, as chair of the PLP, was engaged in a juggling
act, in which he tried to balance socialist ideology and the movement's desire for political independence against the realpolitik of
numerically significant representation in Parliament, tried to keep
the disparate components of the party from flying apart, tried to
weigh present gain against future advantage. Holton describes as "a
major hindrance" to the EFF "the rudimentary nature of Labour
party election machinery,"[11] but true as this was, a far more significant factor was a partially hidden agenda followed by the party leadership. The delicate position the executive in general and Ramsay
MacDonald in particular were in, in relation to three-cornered contests, goes far to explain the continuing difficulty that the EFF experienced in its dealings with the Labour party when it came to
identifying constituencies to be contested.

What neither the EFF nor the ILP branches knew (although some
might speculate) was that there had been a secret agreement between MacDonald and Herbert Gladstone (then the chief Liberal
whip) as far back as 1903, for each party to stay out of certain areas,
and to share certain other two-member constituencies. The pact,
though informal, unofficial, and not rigidly adhered to, had played
a large part in making Labour representation numerically significant in the House of Commons, and had held through the 1910 elections.[12] But the mere suspicion of the existence of some kind of
agreement, and its practical effects, were a recurring source of tension between the Labour party executive and local party bodies, especially those on the socialist left wing. Whether it should still
operate in the next election was a subject of indecision for Mac-
Donald at just this time, making the constant prodding of the EFF
seem like a most unwelcome demand that he declare himself before
he was ready. The potential of the EFF, too, encouraged restlessness

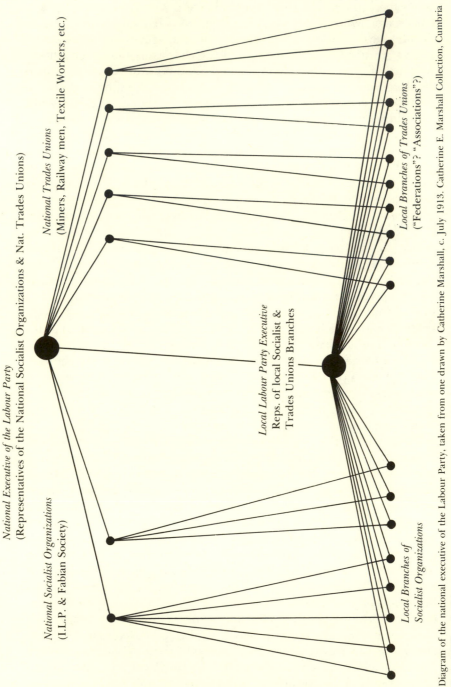

National Executive of the Labour Party
(Representatives of the National Socialist Organizations & Nat. Trades Unions)

National Trades Unions
(Miners, Railway men, Textile Workers, etc.)

National Socialist Organizations
(I.L.P. & Fabian Society)

Local Labour Party Executive
Reps. of local Socialist &
Trades Unions Branches

Local Branches of Trades Unions
("Federations"? "Associations"?)

Local Branches of
Socialist Organizations

Diagram of the national executive of the Labour Party, taken from one drawn by Catherine Marshall, c. July 1913. Catherine E. Marshall Collection, Cumbria Record Office, Carlisle.

in local organizations, and among the many members of the Labour party who disliked the cosiness with the Liberal party. MacDonald was under pressure from the left wing of his own party to move towards more independence, and from some senior members of the Liberal party to move towards a closer relationship – indeed, on 24 June 1912, at exactly the same time as the Ilkeston controversy, he was privately invited by the chief Liberal whip, the Master of Elibank, to join the cabinet, not the first time the idea of a coalition had been mooted.[13] Although he refused the offer, he was reluctant to abandon the electoral arrangement that had given the Labour party its foothold in the Commons. MacDonald also had a number of good friends on the Liberal front benches, significantly including some of the more notorious antisuffragists, one of those closest to him being Seely, the cabinet Minister contesting the Ilkeston riding.[14]

More by-elections followed before the summer was over. Details will be omitted here; an election at Hanley in mid-July was disappointing (as a result, it was thought, of "special local conditions which told unfavourably against the Labour candidate"),[15] but at both Crewe and Midlothian the Liberal lost to the Unionist candidate – indicative of a general trend between the December 1910 election and the coming of the war. Both were previously Liberal seats, and although Labour did not win in either constituency, the Labour vote was substantially increased. The work and the impact of the EFF as they appeared to Catherine can be summed up in her own words:

A candid observer cannot fail to recognise the powerful part that Women's Suffrage had played in these contests. It has been one of the most popular planks in the platform of the Labour speakers; it has never failed to arouse the interest and sympathy of the audience; our own speakers have attracted and held large crowds, often to the detriment of the competing Liberal and Conservative orators. On the eve of the poll in Midlothian the Labour organisers asked for *all* our speakers as well as those who have Labour sympathies. This is notable evidence that Women's Suffrage was popular with the electors. The Labour party has freely acknowledged the help which the well-trained Suffrage workers have been able to give. ... Until a Women's Suffrage amendment has been passed by the House of Commons and thereafter adopted by the Government, in accordance with the Prime Minister's pledge, as an integral part of the Reform Bill, the National Union will pursue its present policy with unremitting energy. It has at its command money, strength, enthusiasm, and an organisation which no party can now ignore. These resources are increasing daily; every by-election adds to its knowledge how to use them in the most effective way, strengthens the belief of its members that its fighting policy in the constituencies is wise and fruitful and justifies its immovable confidence in constitutional methods of bringing pressure to bear on the political machine.[16]

Hyperbolic as Catherine's words may sound, the EFF's view of the value of its own role was shared to a great degree by Labour party candidates, and by some political observers at the time. An interesting development was that the EFF, now so well funded, not only made grants to candidates, supplied help, and paid its own expenses, but offered to lend very substantial sums to fund the Labour candidates at Hanley and Crewe, repayable over the next six months.[17] However, details of EFF funding of candidates were kept confidential at the request of the Labour party.

The main thrust of Catherine's work was to make cooperation with the Labour party an active reality. Being Catherine, and with the backing of the executive and the EFF committee, she interpreted the mandate widely. The success of the EFF must be grounded in sustaining and increasing grassroots Labour support, and in building a solid base of trust and cooperation with the leadership of the Labour party and the PLP. Planning ahead was important, and in particular, work towards the next general election must be begun. Closer to home was the need to keep the NU's own members on side.

The NU had already stepped up its efforts to build connections with Labour at every level. The leaders knew that the success of the scheme depended to a great extent on its acceptance in the Labour movement, and if the experience of other NU speakers was similar to Catherine's, there was reason to hope for sympathy from working men. Already, at the same executive meeting at which the decision had been made to approach the Labour party, plans had been set on foot to have a significant NU presence, with strong speakers, in Merthyr Tydfil, Keir Hardie's seat in the Welsh coal-mining area, at the time of the ILP's Whitsun conference there. An open-air meeting was organized on the Sunday by the NU executive, specifically directed towards ILP delegates, at which the new policy was explained, and an indoor one was held on Whit Monday, in conjunction with the Merthyr WSS. Both meetings were "very successful," and it was reported that the Sunday meeting "had definitely influenced the voting at the I.L.P. Conference," where a resolution favourable to women's suffrage had been passed. A protest from the South Wales federation was met with the explanation that "there had been no intention of keeping the Federation in the dark in the matter; that the meetings were carefully arranged so as to be quite distinct from one another in order that the local society should not be involved in an action of which it did not approve. That the Sunday meeting was regarded as being of national importance."[18]

The NU's determination to make a specific response to the defeat of the Conciliation Bill, in the constituencies where pledged suffragist MP's had defaulted, was not forgotten, and the response, in the event, dovetailed to a striking degree with developing EFF policy. In part it was doubtless shaped by the promotion of the new strategy; in part the neat fit simply reflects the leftward direction of the NU in parts of the country at this time. A joint board, it will be remembered, had been initiated when Catherine was assistant parliamentary secretary just before the second reading, whose primary purpose was to form a liaison between suffragist MPs and extraparliamentary bodies working for women's suffrage. By mid-1912, references occur to a "Joint Campaign Committee," and to a "Women's Suffrage Campaign" (WSC), significantly subtitled "Joint Committee for Securing the Enfranchisement of Women on Broad and Democratic Lines." The list of member organizations confirms that a transition to cooperation with bodies working for adult suffrage had been painlessly achieved, aided by the ministry's promised Reform Bill.[19]

The joint committee's plan of action was to run intensive propaganda campaigns in a number of areas, and exploratory letters were sent out to organizations where the sitting MPs were seen to be unreliable on the suffrage issue. The new departure was that these letters went not only to local WS societies but to branches of the Labour party and the ILP, and to trades councils and other union groups, with the intention of holding public meetings sponsored jointly by suffrage societies and labour bodies, so underlining the potential of cooperation and the threat posed to intransigent antisuffrage Liberals (although the immediate campaign was not directed to the running of election candidates). Replies came in well, some favourable or even enthusiastic, some less so, and by late summer meetings had been organized wherever they were thought likely to be productive.[20] The initiative was both a part of the building of mutual knowledge and confidence between the nonmilitant women's suffrage groups and Labour, and an experiment in working together at the local level.

Catherine was right at home in encouraging a groundswell of working-class support for women's suffrage – an upbeat aspect of her new work in any event, since it seemed to be going steadily forward. More difficult was the task of making sure of the commitment of the Labour party leaders and the PLP. What the NU had hoped for from the outset of the EFF proposal was a firm statement that the party would vote in unison against any franchise bill which did not include votes for at least some women; specifically, what this meant was to vote against the coming government Reform Bill if the women's suffrage amendments were rejected in the House of Commons. Despite favourable resolutions passed at Labour party and ILP conferences, the leaders were reluctant to move, in part because of their wish to avoid a clear breach with the Liberal party. They also seem to have feared a backlash from the membership, and particularly perhaps from the miners' unions if it should come to the vote. They may have been justified; although there had been no big campaign among the men who were still voteless, it would have been, to say the least, a sacrifice unmatched in history for a large body of men to throw away their own advantage – in this case, the chance of enfranchisement – in order to support women's claim. Although many individual Labour candidates, MPs, and Labour bodies had pledged this degree of support,[21] there were others who made it plain that they found it unacceptable; and once more the WSPU helped provide an excuse by renewed militancy in which the Labour party became a specific target. Politically, however, as the NU knew, the case for a firm declaration of intent was that it might be the best means of ensuring that a favourable amendment would be accepted.

Nevertheless, the fact was that as soon as the EFF policy was launched, the Labour party provided something which it was not in its power – or certainly not in the power of its executive – to retract: a base for a completely new propaganda drive, together with a logical and potentially effective political threat to the Liberal party. All that was needed was minimum cooperation from Labour party headquarters, in the provision of a list of constituencies to be contested and the names of the candidates, and the willing acceptance of substantial assistance by those candidates. This last was never in question, despite the work of antisuffragists and the negative effect of militancy. Even without an immediate Reform Bill pledge, the benefits to the NU were tangible enough to make it worthwhile to exercise prolonged diplomacy in relations with the party headquarters; further, the longer the policy was pursued on an assumption of good faith on the part of the party, the less likely it was that that faith could be betrayed. Yet as long as there was no public pledge, an element of risk remained, and those members of the NU who had doubts about the new policy saw the lack of wholehearted open commitment from the Labour party leaders as confirming their fears that the union was giving much – abandoning its friends, and perhaps even its principles – in return for little or nothing. The Labour party's long-awaited executive meeting in July came and went with no public statement being made.

Catherine kept in close touch with Labour party headquarters, communicating almost daily with Henderson on matters concerning by-elections, discussing parliamentary activities and their bearing on the suffrage issue, giving praise where she felt praise was due, making her own suggestions ("I have reason to know that the Irish are particularly accessible to pressure from your party just now. Can't you make use of this fact on behalf of Women's Suffrage?"), urging that Ramsay MacDonald make "a strong speech" on the second reading of the Reform Bill, trying to get Henderson to press for a rewording of an unsatisfactory resolution coming up at the Trade Union Congress, constantly reminding him of the benefits already resulting from the policy of cooperation, setting up an appointment to discuss the extension of the EFF policy, and lauding a hint that the party decision was to initiate more three-cornered contests.[22] Much of what Catherine was doing was simply an exercise in building trust, and promoting closeness by assuming that it existed. Not too often, she would tactfully press the NU's need to have a firmer answer on the Reform Bill question, or would mention items in the press which were damaging to the new policy in one way or another.

No one knew when there might be a general election, except that it had to be by 1915. The fact that in the event the war was to interrupt the normal procedure, delaying the election until 1918, meant that the only elections in which the EFF actually took part were prewar by-elections. But Catherine and the other EFF enthusiasts were in no doubt that by-elections were only a warm-up and a message to the Liberal party "that they stand in danger of losing seats at the next election if no measure of Women's Suffrage is passed this session."[23] Meanwhile, preparation for the general election provided an invaluable way for the EFF to serve the needs of the NU and at the same time to go far towards grappling if not the soul then at least the body of the Labour party to it.

Under the prevailing registration regulations, it was vital to begin preparation for an election well in advance, since it was largely the party agents who encouraged likely qualified supporters to make sure that they got on to the register. Partly because the agitation for completion of the male franchise was so insignificant before it became linked to women's suffrage, it is possible even now (though not excusable) for a women's suffrage historian to assume that after 1884 "virtual universal manhood suffrage prevailed,"[24] whereas Neal Blewett's important research has shown that fewer than 60 per cent of adult males were qualified to vote at any given election, in large part because of the complexities and delays of the registration system.[25] The EFF's growing staff of trained and paid organizers had had years of experience with the NU and were expert on what went into success at elections. Catherine was not modest about what they had to offer, or about the need for it, and there was some (justified) implied criticism of Labour party organization in her planning: "Above all, we must concentrate on preparing the ground beforehand for Labour candidates in chosen constituencies. The great handicap of the Labour party in Holmforth[sic] and Hanley and Crewe was lack of organisation. This lack we can supply. We have the workers, we have the knowledge of what is needed, and 'we have the money too.'"[26]

Pressure from the EFF was not the only factor pushing the Labour party towards embarking on more three-cornered contests, even while MacDonald struggled with his own indecision. Helped by the approach of the general election and even more by the serious labour troubles of the period, Labour was at odds with the Liberal party on a number of occasions. To make matters worse, the Liberal party could not always fulfil its part of the bargain regarding three-cornered contests, since the nomination of a candidate rested in the hands of the local Liberal association. Hanley for instance was perceived as a Labour seat, and when a Liberal candidate entered the field in the by-election of July 1912, Labour MPs withdrew for a time not merely their support but their very selves from the House of Commons. There were dangers to the suffrage cause in such an extreme action; Catherine feared that the government might see it as an ideal opportunity to "hurry on the Com[tee] stage of the Reform Bill whilst they are absent."[27] Yet there was always the hope of getting the Labour party to make women's suffrage one of the grounds for any quarrel with the government "or at any rate one of the conditions for making peace."[28] In the event, no dramatic split occurred, but at the very least the EFF had had the good fortune to come on the scene at a time when some Labour party supporters increasingly wanted to see elections contested.

Catherine's dealings with Labour party headquarters were a model of diplomacy and decorum; in her letters she is careful to defer to the party's right to control the selection of candidates and the constituencies to contest, although in seeking information she also is often subtly suggesting a course of action, and putting a little pressure on to encourage contests in the constituencies of particular interest to the EFF. For example, at a very early stage, Henderson had readily complied with a request from Palliser to furnish a list of some constituencies where Labour candidates would be run in the event of an election, and the names of the approved candidates. But the list had only six names on it and it proved hard to get further names and places. In July, Catherine took a different approach, sending Henderson the EFF's own list of a dozen constituencies in which it was prepared to start work at once, and asking Henderson which of these would definitely be contested by Labour.[29] And the limits of her deference were precisely defined; just over the line, in NU territory, she spoke with authority rather than with deference. She did not ask the party's permission to extend the type of help given by the EFF, rather she simply informed Henderson just what kind of help the NU had agreed upon, what preparatory work would be done in areas selected for contest, how and when the EFF would be setting up in the area. This was the kind of approach favoured by Brailsford, and approved at his initiative by the EFF committee.[30]

MacDonald was more difficult to deal with than Henderson, despite his connection with the ILP, from which came such dedicated suffrage proponents as Keir Hardie and Philip Snowden, and which was considered to be more advanced than the Labour party's trade union wing. As we have seen, he had told Mrs Fawcett in January 1912 that he did not think the Labour party's Birmingham resolution of that month imposed any irrevocable obligation on Labour MPs to vote for the third reading.[31] Moreover, as a man with an old-fashioned and sentimental view of women, he may have been genuinely appalled by escalating militancy. Not only did he continue to stonewall on the question of committing the Labour party to a block vote against the third reading of the Reform Bill if women were not included, but he made more than one remark in public which the women's suffragists considered unfortunate. Not surprisingly, Catherine often found it hard to get an appointment with him. But, like other MPs who were Catherine's quarry from time to time, he was to find her hard to dodge, as the following incident shows.

At the end of June, the EFF was upset by a letter of MacDonald's published in the press, slamming militancy and the fuss over forcible feeding, but seeming in addition to accuse the NU of weakness and of having as little concern for the working women as (in his view) did the WSPU. There was no clear central message in the letter, unless it were to open the door again to the ever-ready excuse that militancy made the enactment of women's suffrage impossible in the foreseeable future. Certainly what was not there was any exhortation to all good women's suffragists, let alone all good members of the Labour party, to rally behind the NU or the new EFF policy.[32] The EFF committee asked Catherine to see him to impress on him the harm his

letter had done "and to urge him to undo it by an unequivocal declaration that the Labour party would vote against the Third Reading
of the Reform Bill if women were not included in it."[33] When Catherine could not get an appointment with MacDonald before the next
meeting of the EFF urgency committee, scheduled only four days
later, "she arranged to travel down to Hanley by the same train
and ... interviewed him on the way." MacDonald told her "the time
was not ripe yet for an official declaration of the Labour party's intentions in regard to the Third Reading of the Reform Bill," but,
said Catherine, "he had since made excellent Women's Suffrage
speeches at Hanley and Crewe, and [she] believed that the other
members of his Committee would keep him up to the mark."[34]

Perhaps more remarkable even than Catherine's ingenuity is her
ability to bring something like this off with a net increase in good
feeling rather than the reverse. But she was not averse to turning
such a setback as the offending letter into a stick to beat the Labour
party officials with; rather than pretending it had not happened, she
mentioned it freely, linking it to damage done to fundraising and
the mutual advantage to be gained from an official declaration of
the party's intentions with regard to the Reform Bill.[35]

With the one exception of the Ilkeston election, the by-election
work throughout 1912 and until near the end of 1913 steadily improved the relationship between the Labour party and the EFF. The
ready acceptance the policy met at the grass roots was in part a tribute to the NU's steady work, and to the ability of working men to distinguish more easily between militants and nonmilitants than some
politicians saw fit to do. But practically, too, there was the Osborne
judgment of 1909, which had deprived the party of funding
through a compulsory levy on trade union funds, and fresh and substantial help in contesting any election was most welcome.[36]

Unfortunately, by-elections did not always similarly improve the
relationship between the local NU societies and either the EFF or the
executive. Where the local society was strongly Liberal, as many NU
branches always had been and still were, the idea of having their organization send people in to work for a Labour candidate as part of
a national campaign could be frightening. Although, in the end, no
candidate was supported by the EFF at East Carmarthen in August,
the by-election there touched on a number of the areas of difficulty
concerning the EFF; indeed, the election threatened to turn into
something of a mirror image of the Ilkeston election, justifying the
fears of the timid within the NU as Ilkeston had come near to justifying the fears of the timid in the Labour party. This was the region
in which hostility to the EFF, within the NU, had been most pro-

nounced from the beginning, with the South Wales federation asking "that the E.F.F. should not be put into action in their area without
their wishes being taken into consideration".[37]

The EFF would probably have been content had no by-election occurred in the region to force the issue. As soon as it seemed that
there would be a three-cornered contest, the NU executive asked
Catherine to go there to talk with the federation officers.[38] The NU
officers involved gave a high priority to maintaining unity by giving
time to the less enthusiastic federations to get used to the new policy,
and seem to have been willing to respect the South Wales federation's wishes, if they insisted, giving only the traditional help
through the NU by-elections committee rather than the EFF. Some
EFF members from outside the NU took a harder line, and at the EFF
meeting on 2 August, Brailsford first suggested that the EFF act in
this election in some way apart from the NU, and when told that that
was impossible, he managed to get majority backing for a resolution
(seconded by Laurence Housman, who was quite new on the committee), declaring: "That in view of the political effect which ought
to be at this juncture at its maximum, we strongly recommend that
at all costs E. Carmarthen be fought."[39] Fortunately, perhaps, the
Labour candidature turned into an on-again, off-again affair, with
little interest shown by the Labour party in a contest which they
thought impossible to win.[40] Eventually the ILP fielded a candidate,
but by this time it was seen as too late for the EFF to take part. The
late-entering Labour candidate, however, was the only one completely satisfactory on the suffrage issue (despite the Welsh suffrage
societies' faith in the right-mindedness of local Liberals),[41] and received the support of the NU at the more modest level provided for
where there was no EFF intervention. Catherine's proposed visit was
also an on-again, off-again affair; despite an urgent correspondence
between local NU officials and headquarters, she did not in the end
go to Wales.[42]

Helena Auerbach wrote to Fawcett while she was on holiday in
August, letting her know of Brailsford's impatience with the hand of
the NU executive on the EFF brake. The letter reached Fawcett at her
holiday address "after many journeyings," and she replied promptly.
"I think," she wrote, "we must not let Mr. Brailsford go astray on the
subject of the relation of the EFF com[ee] to the Nat:Union. The E.F.F.
com[ee] cannot add to its numbers except by the consent of the Nat.
com[ee] and it was expressly laid down ... that a majority of the members of the EFF com[ee] must be members of the N.U. ... The E.F.F.
com[ee] is not strictly speaking one of the NU com[ees] – because from
the outset it was intended to included [sic] members who were not

members of the N.U. But it is subordinate to the N.U. com^{ee} which re-
tains the control by stipulating from the outset that it must have a
majority of the members."[43]

Fawcett, who did not have her papers with her, may have been in-
exact about details of the EFF constitution, but she was undoubtedly
right about the principle of overriding control being intended to remain in the hands of the NU executive; even Brailsford may have
quickly come to realize that any other way of operating would turn
the EFF into a loose cannon which might well destroy the NU.
Fawcett's role as chair was vital – no one else could have kept the NU
on side – but much of the burden of interpreting the EFF to the executive and the executive to the EFF, not to mention the task of explaining both to the membership at large, fell on Catherine's
shoulders.

By the end of July, Catherine was not just a familiar sight but an
indispensable presence in all the working situations and counsels of
the NU. In the course of the summer she had accomplished an extraordinary amount. The EFF was well established and extremely active, experienced in the new approach to by-elections, engaged in
broadening the base of working-class support and in strengthening
the connection of trust and cooperation with Labour party headquarters, and looking towards an all-out effort at the next general
election. As for the NU at large, work towards the amendments to the
Reform Bill was central, and other issues demanded ongoing work
and decisions from the executive, where Catherine's status was
finally properly defined in July when she was appointed to fill the vacancy on the executive caused by the death of Walter McLaren. She
was also appointed to the NU's international committee, now beginning to gear up for the next IWSA conference, to be held in Budapest
in the summer of 1913.[44] Extra work, too, arose in connection with
financial difficulties and administrative changes in the *Common
Cause*, which became an NU responsibility in the latter half of 1912.
In addition, more and more, Catherine was sharing the load of
Kathleen Courtney, the NU's honorary secretary, who had long done
more than her share of the parliamentary work, although increasingly burdened by the severe illness of her brother, which was to end
in his death in mid-August.[45]

All this was very well, but Catherine's coach threatened to turn back
into a pumpkin, if not at midnight on 31 July, then shortly after.
Her parents had agreed to her spending the two summer months in
London, but now she had to come home, and not just for a brief holiday. She did not find it easy to leave her work. Committee meetings

on the first two days of August were followed by days of urgent action in connection with the Carmarthenshire by-election before she returned to Cumberland in the middle of the month, bringing much work with her. The evidence is confusing; some of the few in whom she confided seem to have thought it was only a question of how long a holiday her parents would insist on her taking, others had the impression that she was preparing to give up all her London work and pick up again with the NWF. Exactly what went on between Catherine and her parents is not clear. Catherine evidently gave Brailsford two reasons for her inability to come back to London: she was needed in the NWF; and her father insisted on her taking "a complete holiday," and had decided that this should be in the autumn. Meanwhile, apparently, she was to stay at home. Brailsford was appalled, and wrote to Catherine on 5 August:

I have written at once to Mrs. Cunliffe [the president of the NWF]. Indeed I would do anything to avert the disaster of your departure. I simply cannot imagine how either the Fund or the Parliamentary work would fare, if you really had to go. At any cost of being misunderstood you must please desert your Federation.

I am alarmed by your father's fixing of the date for your complete holiday. I am sure you ought to have a clear four weeks. But could it not be managed rather sooner?

You know what I think, and I need not insist on it. I believe if you had been Parl^y. Sec^y. during the past two years, we might have found ourselves in an altogether different position in the House. The available strength of the N.U. has never been focused and mobilised in any effective way, and until you came there was no idea in your department of how to do it.[46]

Millicent Fawcett shared Brailsford's view, and wrote a careful letter to Caroline Marshall, which, like Brailsford's, is worth quoting at length for what it tells us of how Catherine's work was viewed, as well as for the more oblique light it sheds on the position of women of Catherine's class in general and of Catherine in particular:

I hope you have got Catherine at home by now and that she is enjoying a well-earned holiday after all her splendid work for W.S. in London. I feel I must write a few lines to you and Mr. Marshall to tell you *how* splendid she has been: the new development of our policy, adopted at the special Council in May, has been almost entirely in her hands, and its smoothe [sic] working is almost wholly due to her. She has grappled with all the difficulties as they arose, has dealt with the various (not always trustworthy or straightforward) party politicians with the greatest skill and has as I need not tell you who know her so well, been most unsparing of herself in every way. I think the work has been congenial to her and that she has been happy over it and as far as I can judge her health has not suffered. We do feel most grateful to you and Mr. Marshall for sparing her to us: we have got to look upon her as almost indispensable.

I am afraid that you will say that my gratitude has an eye to the future and indeed it has, for I feel the coming autumn session will be of unparalleled importance in the history of w.s., and our work now depends so much on her perception and judgment that we should feel very lost without her.

So I am hoping very much that she will have a good rest and holiday now and will come back to us in the autumn.[47]

Catherine had written quite calmly to Margaret Robertson: "My family insists on my going away for a week or two towards the end of September before I come back to work in October; I want to get everything in train before I go."[48] Yet there must have been sufficient doubt about her return to motivate Brailsford's and Fawcett's letters, and Mary Mackenzie, the NU's staff parliamentary secretary, and now secretary to the EFF as well, had heard a rumour that she might be leaving.[49] There could hardly have been so much alarm over the mere question of whether she should return in the middle or at the end of September, especially as the NU was itself taking a partial summer recess and had no executive or other committee meetings scheduled between 1 August and 19 September, although the EFF was kept busy by a by-election in Midlothian.

Whatever the problem was, the outcome was that Catherine stayed away for only about six weeks. During August she travelled for a while in the Lake District, probably doing some good walking on the hills, but also keeping up with political issues as they affected women's suffrage.[50] Margaret Robertson visited Hawse End for a couple of days in mid-September. Shortly afterwards, Catherine resigned her position as honorary secretary to the NWF, apparently having made up her mind that Brailsford was right that her service was more urgently needed at the national level. The pride of her parents in her work, and their support for it, are not in question; we have the text of a suffrage speech made by Frank Marshall at just about this time in which he, still a Liberal himself, explained the EFF policy to what was probably a predominantly Liberal audience.[51] Catherine returned to London unhindered at the end of September, and almost at once accepted an increased work-load.

At just this time Edith Palliser, the honorary parliamentary secretary, left town for at least two months to look after a sick friend. Catherine sat down, perhaps with Kathleen Courtney, to assess the needs of the NU's EFF and parliamentary work, and to make a decision about the direction she herself should take. She jotted down the possibilities, the pros and cons, the human resources available. Her very rough notes indicate that Kathleen wanted her to take on the parliamentary work. "P"'s departure ("P" is surely Edith Palliser) from the honorary parliamentary secretaryship evidently was not felt to be altogether disastrous, and [we should] "Not press P. to stay on her own merits;" she is seen as being well liked and of a "high character," but as being unable to "grasp things as a whole," and as being shy and having "no initiative." Catherine noted that "KDC has whole resp[onsibility] on her shoulders."[52] Brailsford's August letter to Catherine had also implied shortcomings in Palliser's work, and Catherine herself had offered (quite tactfully, it seems) to help her.[53]

The exercise helped Catherine make up her mind, and her conclusion is scribbled at the top of the second page: "Parl. more important. Take it." Shortly afterwards, the executive appointed her as honorary parliamentary secretary, at first on a temporary basis, but very shortly afterwards as a confirmed appointment with her name and position on the NU letterhead.

For the EFF work Catherine's notes mention Miss Strachey, and praise her organizational skills, but she is dismissed as "Too rigid. Would try to deal with members by *system*."[54] Notes on the type of leader needed for the EFF indicate that she should have skills in conciliation and tact, and be able to work well with the staff. Perhaps Catherine did not know she was describing herself; in the event, the EFF, which was responsible for naming its own honorary secretary, retained her in that position. She now held the two prime political positions in the NU.

After all the excitement of launching the EFF and the flurry of by-elections forcing it into immediate activity, the main focus shifted in the autumn to the campaign to get women included in the coming Reform Bill. Ever since the defeat of the Conciliation Bill, the NU's sights had been set on the promised bill, and Catherine had never been out of touch with what was being done. Now that she had undertaken the parliamentary work as well as the EFF, she was responsible for both prongs of the NU's political work. Probably at her request, a parliamentary subcommittee was organized, to meet weekly and assist with the escalating volume of work.[55]

The Reform Bill had been introduced on 1 June 1912 and received its second reading on 12 July. Asquith made it plain in the debate that his opposition to the inclusion of women had not lessened, and made capital of the defeat of the Conciliation Bill, pouring scorn on the idea "that the House of Commons is likely to stultify it-self by reversing in the same session the considered judgment at which it has already arrived."[56] The NU began once more to urge the branches in every constituency to organize pressure and publicity by means of public meetings and lobbying their MPs. At the centre the joint campaign committee was working with MPs to formulate amendments and coordinate their presentation, and suffragists of all parties were consulted. The NU would not formulate any amendment, but would support any or all, especially whatever had the best chance of gaining a majority in the Commons. A major public meeting at the Albert Hall was planned for 5 November, as a "working class and labour demonstration" and to raise money.[57] Another important effort was directed towards bringing the National Union of Women Workers (NUWW) on side, and having it pass a resolution of firm support for the women's suffrage amendments to the Reform Bill.[58]

The NU strove to keep together the parliamentary support it had had for the Conciliation Bill, and to get back some that it had thought it had before the failure of that bill. Lord Robert Cecil came to the executive of 4 July to advise on the amendments.[59] His continuing help is interesting in view of the EFF policy, which might have been expected to alienate Conservative suffragists, but he and Lord Lytton had privately expressed cautious approval when the policy was first mooted.[60] Both should be given credit for their genuine dedication to women's suffrage, if not to a fully democratic franchise. In any event, the results of the first elections in which the EFF went into effect showed that the Conservative Unionists stood to be the chief beneficiaries, at least in the short term, from the increase in three-party contests. However, Cecil drew the line at public association with the fundraising activity of the EFF, asking questions about this aspect of the coming Albert Hall meeting, although he consented in the end to speak.[61]

Even before Catherine's official appointment as honorary parliamentary secretary, no one in the NU (and, one suspects, very few in the House of Commons) had a better grasp of the intricacies of the anticipated struggle to introduce women's suffrage by means of an amendment to the Reform Bill. A document she had drawn up in July, headed "Points for Parliamentary Interviews," well illustrates this. By now, the amendments to be proposed had been more or less settled, together with the names of those who would move them and speak to them. Details are not needed here; they remained close to the original thinking,[62] ranging from adult suffrage, through the "Norway" amendment which would enfranchise householding women and wives of householders, to the "Conciliation" or "Municipal" amendment, giving the vote only to those women who qualified for the municipal franchise. These would be presented in order. But first an additional complication had to be disposed of; an amendment to omit the word "male" before the word "person" in the introductory section of the act must be passed before any of the others could be effective; Catherine emphasized that voting for this must be the responsibility of every suffragist in the House: "Unless this is done no qualification whatever can be given to women. The omission of 'male' *does not mean Adult Suffrage*. It would not by itself confer any franchise on women. It merely *opens the way* to amendments, which can enfranchise women on any terms."[63]

The need for this preliminary step caused the suffragists anxiety, as it was poorly understood, or wilfully misunderstood, by many politicians as by the public. Catherine distinguished between arguments to be used to influence Liberal and Conservative MPs:

2. *Liberals* should be asked to vote for the Adultist Amendment. Even if it cannot be carried we want a good vote. It would be unwise to press any *Conservatives* to vote for Adult Suffrage.

3. All *Liberals* must be asked to vote for the "Norway" Amendment, which will be the one specially patronised by Liberal Ministers. They should be told that every effort is being made by the N.U.W.S.S., by Lord Lytton, and by Lord Robert Cecil, to get Unionist support for this. Lord Robert Cecil is going to put his own name down as one of the official backers. In return we expect Liberals to pledge themselves that if this effort fails they will vote for the Municipal Amendment. If Liberals won't act as a Party, and cannot control their Irish allies, they have no right to assume an "all or nothing'" attitude.

Conservatives must be told that there will be great difficulty in getting Liberals to vote for the Conciliation Amendment unless Conservatives will in return make some effort to carry the Norway Amendment. It ought not to be repugnant to Conservatives. It gives two votes to the family, and thus makes the settled married couple, who are presumably the stable element in the nation, more influential than the single lad of 21. "The steadying influence of the married woman" and the fact that Householders "have a stake in the country" are arguments that generally appeal to them. Only reliable suffragists among the conservatives should be pressed urgently to vote for the Norway Amendment, but they must all be most strongly urged not to vote *against* it.

4. All Members, *Liberals and Conservatives alike*, must have the utmost possible pressure put upon them to vote for the Municipal, or Conciliation Committee's, amendment. ...

5. All Suffragist Members ... should be asked to act steadily with one of the three groups which have agreed to work in concert – Mr. Henderson's, Mr. Dickenson's, and the Conciliation Committee. Only by co-operation and unity can anything useful emerge for women. Faddish and wrecking proposals from other quarters must be resisted.

6. It ought to be a point of honour with all Members who genuinely desire the passage of *some* measure of Women's Franchise not to vote *against* any of these recognised Suffrage Amendments, even if he cannot quite bring himself to vote *for* it.

7. Every Member ... should be asked to vote against the Reform Bill on Third Reading if no women have been included in it. If they refuse, suggest that at least they may abstain from voting *for* it. (It should be made clear to *Conservatives* that by voting for a Women's Suffrage Amendment they do not commit themselves to voting for the Bill as a whole on Third Reading).[64]

Notably, this document deals only with the way to be taken with Liberal and Conservative suffragists, probably indicating that it was not expected that Labour MPs would be approached individually; their stance was a matter of the agreement between the party and the EFF, not a matter for personal pressure. Meanwhile, efforts continued to try to bring the Labour party to a public commitment.

As the third reading drew nearer, the connection between the Reform Bill and the EFF work became closer, and it was even more urgent to have some assurance from the Labour party. The work already done at by-elections was of use as a lever, as was preparatory work towards the next election. Candidates who had appreciated what the EFF had done for them at by-elections were asked to write to members of the Labour party executive and the PLP, "testifying to the assistance given by the FF at these elections, and urging the Parl^y party to take a strong line."[65] Catherine's communications with Labour party leaders, too, made more and more frequent and pressing reference to the EFF's need for a firm commitment. Nevertheless, the reassurance was still needed at least as much for doubting NU members as it was to make the EFF policy worthwhile. This is borne out by the Midlothian by-election, in which the EFF, at a joint meeting with the NU elections committee, decided to give its support to the Labour candidate, Robert Brown, despite his refusal to give an unconditional promise to vote against the Reform Bill on third reading if women were not included. In this instance, Henderson, at the party office, was actively involved in the negotiations and showed some keenness to have Brown receive EFF endorsement. Margaret Robertson had met with Henderson and reported: "Mr. Henderson said that Lab[our] candidates were not prepared to go further than this, for the promise to oppose the third reading was unpopular with their supporters. He said, however, that Brown meant, by his answer, to imply that he would use his influence with the Party to induce them to decide in favour of taking this course. He advised Miss Robertson to get a definite statement from him to that effect."[66]

Ultimately, Brown committed himself to voting against the third reading of the bill if it did not include women, in every eventuality except "the inconceivable contingency of the Labour party binding all its members not to vote against the third reading."[67] Catherine was absent when the decision to go ahead was made, and had the good fortune, too, to miss the stormy meeting of the executive which followed in September, when a letter of protest from the Scottish federation was discussed. Helena Swanwick proposed and Isabella Ford seconded a motion of approval for the action of the two committees, and a contrary amendment was moved by Chrystal Macmillan, seconded by Eleanor Rathbone, to the effect that "the Election policy of the Union was not correctly interpreted at Midlothian." The amendment was lost by eleven votes to seven, and the resolution passed by twelve votes to six.[68] The EFF clearly was not yet sailing in smooth waters within the NU.

As honorary parliamentary secretary, Catherine reported on the political situation to the NU council at its October meeting in Manchester. She described the state of affairs as full of hope, because the Reform Bill presented the best chance yet for women, but at the same time as one "of the very gravest anxiety, because the forces of opposition are more determined and better organized than ever before." Continuing pressure from every constituency was vital. But there were a number of unknown factors in the present situation. Catherine thought it unlikely that time would be given to "the 3 specific amendments" before Christmas, "because the Govt. wants all its time for Home Rule." However, the first amendment, the one to expunge the word "male," might be brought forward at any time. If it should be carried, Catherine believed the government would then delay further stages of the bill; if it were lost, "the Govt. w[oul]d feel free to drop the Bill – a great relief. They are eagerly looking for an excuse to do this." A bad outbreak of militancy might provide the climate for the rejection of the needed first amendment, and give the government the chance it was looking for.[69] She went on:

And that brings me to the most important thing I want to say. Unless our societies in the constituencies can counteract the effects of militancy, and keep steady the public opinion they have created in favour of w.s. in their district

all the rest of our efforts will be of little avail. ... Militancy is not now an unfortunate accident. It is one of the definite obstacles – and the most formidable one – which we have got to set ourselves to surmount. It is the
strongest weapon in the antis' armoury. The reason why it is dangerous is
not because it changes the opinion of M.P.s but it alienates support in the
country and makes it possible for an M.P. to think he can vote against us
without incurring any very serious displeasure on the part of his constituents. We must see to it that the public opinion we have created is steady
enough, and enlightened enough to be proof against such set-backs. For a
society to say "we can do nothing in our constituency because of militancy"
is a confession of hopeless failure.

The most "vitally important" work that had to be done, in Catherine's view, was to send delegations to MPs, "as evidence of strong feeling in the country" and also "as a means of obtaining information as
to the support and the *absence of opposition* which can be relied on for
the various amendments." The information would be valuable to
supporters in the House of Commons and in the press in determining tactics. Every MP should receive a deputation, though particular
attention should be paid to "wobblers" and "rats" (those who had re-
neged on their previous pledges). Catherine made use of the document she had drawn up in July to give the delegates pointers on how
to approach MPs of the different parties.[70]

Delegates came to NU councils not just to sit docilely and be inspired and instructed, and Catherine made notes of the points
raised at Manchester, including comments on adverse effects of policies in which she had been instrumental. Among more or less routine points to do with the supply of literature, the dubious value of
big meetings, and the importance of having printed rules for
branches, some commented, for example, that the "New policy
makes it v. difficult to form new societies on non-party lines, and difficult to get – and *keep* – Liberal members," and that "New Societies
get discouraged by having to join both N.U. and Fed."[71]

Wearing her other hat, as honorary secretary of the EFF, Catherine seconded an important resolution, moved by Mrs Fawcett, which
"extended the scope of the EFF mandate by making the fund available for campaigns in constituencies held by Labour members," or
for Labour candidates it had previously supported. More remarkably, the council passed a further resolution, proposed by Catherine
and seconded by Margaret Ashton, to the effect that once work on
behalf of a Labour candidate had been undertaken, it should not automatically be given up if the Liberals then put forward a "tried
friend."[72] These resolutions, the fruit of experience during the EFF's

first few months of operation, had been processed with great care, moving from their initiation in the EFF committee to approval by the NU executive, from which they came to council as executive proposals.[73] In addition, arising no doubt from questions raised by Brailsford's tendency to chafe under NU control, the relation of the EFF to the NU was more precisely spelled out. Not only did the resolution introducing the extended uses of the fund stipulate that this was subject to the discretion of the executive, but a separate resolution specifically drew attention to the EFF's subordination to the executive, and hence to the council.[74]

The extended mandate of the EFF was part of its preparation for the next general election, already occupying Catherine. A number of constituencies were already under the care of EFF organizers, and on 17 October, the NU executive endorsed a further list of places recommended by the EFF as suitable for "special organisation," where work would begin at once. Although one was chosen because a by-election was thought to be likely, the rest were part of a larger strategy to defend threatened Labour suffragists, and to attack the seats of notable Liberal antis and "pledge-breakers." Several other constituencies were under consideration, and the EFF carefully obtained authorization from the executive to continue its research into local conditions "in any constituency where it was thought likely that such action would be beneficial."[75] By the end of the year, Catherine was responsible for ten EFF organizers coordinated by Margaret Robertson, who had been released by the Manchester federation, and for an office staff which included a secretary, a bookkeeper, and a junior clerk. Funding continued to be healthy, and the seriousness of the EFF intent was evidenced by the decision to hold £2,000 in reserve "in order to be in a position at a general election to contest 6 Ministerial seats."[76] Among the useful acquaintances developed by Catherine in the course of the by-election work was Arthur Peters, the chief Labour party election agent, who gave it as his view that Rotherham and Accrington at least would probably be contested "largely owing to the work of the E.F.F. C^{ttee}."[77]

If work towards the general election was the focus of much of Catherine's work for the EFF as the autumn wore on, as honorary parliamentary secretary her job was increasingly concentrated on the Reform Bill. The government was, as Catherine had predicted, in no hurry to move to the third reading, and the NU had to settle down again to the difficult task of keeping parliamentary and public support up to the pitch needed for success when the amendments should at last be before the House. Catherine's address to the council had combined urgency with a measure of hope, but the outlook was not good. Even as the council gathered, the *Standard* published a long report from its parliamentary correspondent, suggesting that the leaders of all the groups (including the Labour party) supporting the government in the House of Commons were seriously considering abandoning all thought of a women's suffrage amendment to the Reform Bill, at least for the immediate future; once more, militancy was the excuse.[78] To make things worse, a situation arose which caused temporary bad feeling between the NU and the Labour party.

George Lansbury, MP for Bow and Bromley in the East End of London, and roughly located at the more radical end of the socialist wing of the Labour party, was a deeply sincere man, a convinced suffragist, and a long-time supporter of the WSPU. The WSPU was now demanding that the Labour party oppose all government legislation until women's suffrage be enacted, and Lansbury decided to throw his weight behind this policy. Failing in October to get it adopted by the Labour party, he resigned his seat to stand as an independent candidate strictly on the suffrage issue.[79]

Lansbury was counting on wholehearted support from the WSPU in his campaign, but though that organization applauded his action, it proved incapable of giving the kind of help he needed. There was mutual mistrust between the local labour representation committee (which had continued its support to Lansbury as an independent candidate) and the WSPU's young, inexperienced, middle-class organizer. Sylvia Pankhurst, who knew the East-Enders better, had been deliberately sidelined by orders from Christabel in Paris. By this time, too, there was scant sympathy between the WSPU and Labour. At Bow and Bromley the WSPU grandstanded on the suffrage issue, and, more important, was out of practice in the serious work of election organizing; rather than doing what was needed to get Lansbury elected it competed with him for attention.[80]

The NU had to make a decision. Here was that rare thing, a male suffragist politician committed to the point of self-sacrifice, and so surely deserving of support, especially as he was opposed only by a Unionist antisuffragist. Yet he had two strikes against him: he was at odds with the party being earnestly wooed by the NU; and he was largely identified with the militant camp which was causing the NU so much pain, and from whom they were anxious at all costs to dissociate themselves. Nevertheless, the executive decided with apparent enthusiasm that he had to be given what assistance they could. Obviously it had to be without recourse to the EFF, both because there was no Liberal candidate and because Lansbury was far from being an approved Labour candidate, but the NU put in a sum comparable to what was available in EFF elections. The LSWS sent in Helen Ward, its chief organizer, with a substantial team, which opened committee rooms. The NU cooperated closely with Lansbury in arranging meetings, and sent speakers (though avoiding sharing a platform with WSPU speakers). Catherine did a great deal of preliminary work, and went down several times; she also paid attention to those things which might be of practical use to Lansbury, such as the provision of motor cars on polling day.[81] Never at a loss for a creative idea, she apparently enrolled a cadet corps (perhaps a way of bringing potentially toublesome youngsters on side) and dressed them in the red, white, and green of the NU; they were described as having "made quite a show."[82]

Despite the serious work put in by the NU, the overall impression left of the election is of a shambles of competing interests, doubtless highly entertaining for the local population, but of little service to Lansbury, who was defeated. However, Lansbury wrote a warm letter to the NU, expressing particular appreciation of the support they had given, especially as he knew they were not in agreement with his declared policy.[83] Lansbury's defeat was followed by an escalation of militancy by the WSPU, which now embarked on a campaign of arson and the destruction of mail; at this time, too, the Pethick Lawrences were driven out of the WSPU.

The NU's show of independence in actively supporting the maverick Lansbury "had caused some soreness in the Labour party."[84] Catherine may well have thought that it might do them good, and we can be sure that she made no apologies, though she did help to heal the breach. She went to see Henderson during the next week and reported "that the feeling of annoyance caused by the Bow and Bromley election was subsiding." She added that Henderson "was to take charge of the interests of Women's Suffrage on behalf of the Party, during the committee stage of the Franchise Bill."[85] By 20 December, Henderson had put it in writing "that the action taken by the National Union at Bow and Bromley would not affect the friendly relations between the Labour party and the National Union."[86]

Catherine believed in personal contact, and had no reservations about setting up formal and informal meetings with anyone to whom she wanted to talk; often she and Kathleen Courtney went together. Catherine's fearlessness was a remarkable quality for a woman in that age; almost as remarkable were her openness and her evident freedom from coquettishness. She was now well known to MPs of all parties, and took it for granted that her tall figure would be recognized in Westminster; in an unexplained but intriguing reference to a decision that she was bringing to the executive as early as July, she asked, "May I act on Snowden's advice? Shall I make a point of being seen with him?"[87] In her encounters, she generally left things better than she found them, and her colleagues were often glad to rely on her to deal with politicians or others who were uneasy about some move the NU had made.[88] As the third reading drew nearer, she kept her finger on the parliamentary pulse. For example, at the executive meeting of 17 October, she reported on the state of party opinion in the Commons regarding the proposed amendments to the Reform Bill, and on their prospects of success. She reported on "a number of interviews with representative people in the House, and a number more in process of arrangement. Every day brought fresh evidence of the effectiveness of the new Election Policy. The most satisfactory feature of the situation was the fact that there are now some number of Members of Parliament working actively for Women's Suffrage in the Liberal, Conservative and Labour Parties. They were all alive to the importance of putting pressure on the Nationalists to prevent a repetition of the tactics adopted by that Party with regard to the Conciliation Bill."[89]

The Irish Nationalists indeed remained a source of anxiety. With the continuing furor over the government's attempt to pass a Home Rule Bill (with the details of which we fortunately need not concern ourselves), it was hardly surprising that the Irish were preoccupied. Worse still, there was a "prevalent belief in the Nationalist party that Asquith and other members of the Cabinet would resign if any w.s. measure were carried."[90] Snowden, with NU support, planned to introduce a women's suffrage amendment to the Home Rule Bill. Catherine and Kathleen Courtney, bold as ever, obtained interviews with both Augustine Birrell, the chief secretary for Ireland, and John Redmond, the Irish Nationalist leader, on 1 November, to question them about their views on Snowden's amendment and how they planned to respond to the amendments to the Reform Bill. Birrell firmly opposed Snowden's amendment, but promised his support in quashing the rumour of resignations, which he said "was new to him," adding that "he would consider any attempt on the part of the Irish to oppose w.s. grossly unfair." Redmond, not surprisingly, was completely hostile to Snowden's amendment, since the electorate "was one of the domestic matters which *must be left* to the Irish people." As for the amendments to the Reform Bill, Catherine must have been more than a little discouraged to discover that "he knew nothing of *several* amendments; thought there was only one – Adult Suffrage to be moved by Sir Edward Grey." The NU officers enlightened him, and also did their best to persuade him that his cause was badly served by "invoking the hostility of women," which, in the absence of official Liberal sympathy, might contribute to increasing Unionist representation in the House through the by-election work of the EFF. However, they came away from the interview believing that Redmond saw his best interests to lie in the defeat of the women's suffrage amendments and the withdrawal of the Franchise Bill, and that little could be looked for from him.[91] Catherine and Kathleen continued to talk to nationalist members, trying to persuade them that their fears were groundless and that there was good Liberal support for the amendments.[92]

Catherine was present at the Commons debate on Snowden's amendment to the Irish bill, which was opposed by the government and went down to the expected defeat. But there had been some encouraging aspects. Snowden had written to Mrs Fawcett, saying he thought "the debate and division had certainly improved the prospects of the Women's Suffrage Amendments to the Reform Bill," and Catherine reported to the next executive meeting "that Mr. Ramsay MacDonald's speech had been a valuable and effective contribution to the debate"; it was in fact the first time MacDonald had made a speech in the House in support of women's suffrage. The executive analysed the division list and agreed to send letters of thanks to the Liberal and Labour members who had voted against the government. The use that opponents had made of the argument that there was little demand for women's suffrage in Ireland prompted the NU to initiate a closer supportive relation with the Irishwomen's Suffrage Federation. Catherine and Kathleen Courtney were quick to follow up on this.[93]

The uncompromising support given by the leaders of the PLP and of the Labour party to Snowden's amendment was one among a number of signs that the EFF could hope for more open cordiality. Catherine and Kathleen had met with Labour party officials at the House of Commons and had found them arranging a deputation to Redmond. They had been told that there was no need for any further secrecy over money given to Labour candidates, and they recommended the NU to get pledges from Labour MPs to vote against the third reading of the Reform Bill if women were not included, and to publish the numbers of these pledges, though not the names.[94]

Over the whole political arena, the signs were much less encouraging. Kathleen reported to the the executive on the political situation in early December, telling them, "that since the last meeting of the Executive the Anti-Suffragist rumour that Mr. Asquith would resign should a Women's Suffrage amendment be passed had been circulating with renewed activity, so too had a variety of damaging theories as to the position of the w.s. amendments to the Franchise Bill. With regard to Mr. Asquith's resignation, Mrs. Fawcett and Miss Marshall had seen Lord Haldane, who emphatically denied the possibility of the Prime Minister taking such a step, and gave permission for this statement to be made on 'excellent authority', on condition that his name should not appear in print in connection with it."[95] Other leading politicians had also denied the rumour publicly. Asquith, however, commented privately that he did not "feel called upon to take any notice of the rumours ... which are circulated without my authority,"[96] leaving the impression that he was quite comfortable with the effect that they might be having.

Equally serious were the continuing questions about the effect of the amendment to omit the word "male," and as to whether the women's suffrage amendments could be ruled out of order for any one of several reasons. In order to counter these rumours various authorities had been consulted: Sir Edward Grey did not foresee any difficulty; Henderson had stated that "The Chairman of Committees has already intimated his acceptance of the amendments";[97] Sir John Simon, who had helped draft the bill, expressed absolute confidence. Catherine wrote a clear statement of the position for the *Common Cause*, emphasizing the denials.[98] What the NU was primarily concerned with was laying to rest what they believed to be unfounded rumours being deliberately circulated to damage the cause; but, in light of later events, the care taken to obtain expert opinion, and the unanimity of that opinion, are of interest.

As the Reform Bill drew near, all the well-tried means of keeping the issue before the public eye were utilized again, but with greatly increased thoroughness. Use was made of the first congress of the Men's International Alliance for Women's Suffrage, held in London in late October, to gain a high profile for the coming struggle. The vast fundraising and propaganda meeting held by the NU at the Albert Hall on 5 November was followed by one a month later at the London Opera House, coordinated by the joint campaign committee.[99] Particular efforts were made to encourage men, as members of organizations and trade unions, or simply in their capacity as voters, to speak out for the women's cause, and to make sure their MPs heard their views. All over Britain, branches and individuals did their best to raise and express public support, by "Deputations, Memorials, letters and post-cards to every M.P.; resolutions from public meetings and organised bodies of all kinds, especially Party organisations."[100] The press was carefully monitored, and responses made wherever possible to inaccurate or damaging reports, especially when they occurred in otherwise sympathetic media. When several unfortunate articles appeared in the *Labour Leader*, Catherine and Kathleen first met with the author, and later Catherine "had a very satisfactory interview" with the young editor, probably her first meeting with Fenner Brockway, with whom she would work so closely during the war. At this time, she found him "quite sound in his support of Women's Suffrage and [he] promised to see that no further damaging statements should be inserted."[101] He shortly began to take an active role in the campaign, speaking publicly for the NU, and supporting the cause within the ILP.

The hectic pace of the Reform Bill campaign continued right through Christmas with scarcely a week's break; the third reading could be expected in mid-January, although the exact date was still not available. The extent of the behind-the-scenes parliamentary work done by Catherine and Kathleen Courtney was perhaps the major new feature. With the aid of the parliamentary committee, they worked nonstop, enlisting extra help to cope with the work of interviewing MPs of all parties; there was an extra rush in January, to deal with MPs whose local societies had not managed to see them.[102]

The work of the joint campaign committee, too, was increasingly focused on the bill, and Catherine undertook to gather all the information she could about the way MPs were planning to vote on the different amendments; coordinating this was another major task.[103] A similar demanding task was to bring together evidence from all quarters of the support for women's suffrage.[104] Meanwhile, the EFF work continued, and Catherine found time in December to visit South Wales, Monmouth, and Bristol, where the EFF wanted to assess the local situation with a view to election work.[105] As well, there were committee meetings, and reports to be prepared for them, and commentaries, reports, and exhortations to be written for publication in the *Common Cause*; since Swanwick's recent resignation from the position of editor, the NU's *Common Cause* committee, on which Catherine played a leading role, was taking a great deal of the responsibility for the paper's content.[106] Faced with the prospect of trying to live up to this example, it is hardly surprising that Edith Palliser, who was not strong, resigned her position as honorary parliamentary secretary when she came back to London, finding it "involved too great a strain."[107]

At the executive of 17 January, Catherine was at last able to report that a timetable had been arranged for the women's suffrage amendments, which would be taken over several days, from 24 to

28 January. She gave a rundown on "the state of feeling in the different parties"; the attitude of the Irish remained "extremely doubtful." Catherine was meeting with Irish leaders, and both the Labour party and the Liberal suffragists were doing what they could to influence them. The Labour party was throwing its support behind every amendment and would even put a special whip on for the narrowest, the "Conciliation" amendment, if the others should fail. Other cheering news was that the Liberal suffragist MPs had persuaded Lloyd George to receive a WSPU deputation, and that the WSPU had declared a truce from militancy until after the voting on the amendments.[108]

The women's suffragists needed all the encouragement they could get. The complexity of the various amendments was so great, and the Irish still such an unknown quantity, that no one could be sure of the outcome. What no one did predict, in these last stressful days, was what actually happened.

10 Reform Bill Débâcle: Catherine Takes Over Political Work, January to May 1913

The debate on the Reform Bill began on Thursday, 23 January 1913. The first of the women's suffrage amendments was to be introduced the following day. But the Speaker, James Lowther, in response to a question, indicated that they might be ruled out of order, as changing the nature of the bill. Although he did not make a definite ruling until Monday, suffragists had no doubt as to what was coming. Catherine attended a special meeting of the NU executive on Friday evening, called originally for last-minute consultation on the amendments, but assuming "special importance on account of the tentative ruling given by the Speaker the previous afternoon."[1]

Even had the Speaker not followed through, the women's suffragists knew that the hint he had given was enough to make a mockery once more of the promise of a free vote in the Commons, and a resolution embodying this conviction, already passed that afternoon by the LSWS, was adopted and sent to the press. There was little else they could do, but letters were immediately sent to the suffragist cabinet ministers asking them to receive a deputation "before any public pronouncement should be made." Asquith was asked to meet with a separate deputation, consisting of Millicent Fawcett, Kathleen Courtney, Edith Palliser, Eleanor Rathbone, and Catherine Marshall – the political leadership of the NU executive – "in order that they might hear from him what course he would propose in view of the non-fulfilment of the Government pledges."[2]

When the executive met again at noon on Monday, 27 January, there may have been frustration, but hardly surprise at the failure to have the planned deputations received; Asquith's secretary wrote that the prime minister "was too much occupied," and Lord Haldane wrote "that it was 'undesirable and indeed impossible' to receive a deputation before the Meeting of the Cabinet." No reply had come from Sir Edward Grey. Only Lloyd George had agreed to a meeting; he "had invited Mrs. Fawcett, Miss Courtney and Miss Marshall to tea on Sunday afternoon."[3] Lloyd George was fond of this kind of informal consultation, and if it was the first time Catherine had met with him in just such a way, it was to be far from the last.

Over tea with Lloyd George and his wife, the NU officers made it clear that in their view even the tentative ruling had destroyed the possibility of a free vote, and "that they would expect the Government to withdraw the Bill."[4] According to Charles Hobhouse, Lloyd George and Sir Edward Grey had urged exactly the same thing in the cabinet as soon as the Speaker's possible ruling was made known,[5] but Lloyd George naturally did not reveal this to his visitors. The NU officers went on to declare that "the only thing that could now be an equivalent of the Prime Minister's pledges was a Government measure for Women's Suffrage." Lloyd George manifestly thought there was no hope of this, "but ultimately said that it was his intention to press for some such arrangement in the Cabinet." He expected that the government would offer facilities for a private member's bill, but Fawcett stated plainly that the NU would not regard this as satisfactory.[6] She left with "a *very unfavourable* impression" of the prospect for "a free vote on the merits of Women's Suffrage as long as there is a divided Cabinet."[7]

We do not know whether Lloyd George had a second pot of tea that day, but he did receive Flora Drummond and Annie Kenney of the WSPU immediately after his meeting with the NU officers. Recognizing that the destruction of the Reform Bill had left the NU no choice but to move to the same demand as the WSPU had adopted some time previously – that is, for nothing less than a government measure for women's suffrage – Courtney made an overture to the WSPU, meeting with Drummond and Kenney to ask "whether there was any prospect of the w.s.p.u. abandoning militancy if all the other Societies were united in demanding a Government measure." Not surprisingly, since the event could be read as having so far justified their stand (and, in their own opinion, their methods), the WSPU's spokespersons "refused to consider this proposal."[8]

Catherine had gone from the noon executive meeting to the House of Commons, and was present to listen to the Speaker's confirmation of his tentative ruling, and to hear Asquith announce the government's decision to withdraw the bill "and to offer full facilities for a Private Member's Women's Suffrage Bill next Session and in subsequent Sessions if carried." But the NU executive had had enough of this route, so subject to "risk from the devices of its enemies," although a decision to reject the crumb offered could not be made lightly. Meeting again on the evening of the same day, the executive, with habitual caution, withheld their refusal to accept the alternative offered until they could get Grey's opinion.[9] Fawcett and Courtney met with Grey and Acland on 1 February, but found neither of the men "was able to make any statement which put the offer in a more favourable light." Catherine, meanwhile,

had discussed the situation with representatives of all the Suffrage groups in the House and they all thought the National Union was quite right to concentrate on demanding a Government Measure and in setting small value on the chance offered by Mr. Asquith. At the same time they all felt that Suffragists in the House of Commons were bound to work for *any* chance which offered, and they hoped the National Union would do nothing that would damage the chances of a Private Member's Bill. Questioned as to whether the adoption of an anti Government policy would have this effect, they thought not, so long as the National Union did not work *against* those members of the Liberal Party who had given really valuable support to Women's Suffrage during the last year. They all agreed that any work in the country for a Government measure would help and not hinder the Bill. None of them had any objection to an anti Government policy.[10]

A formal decision must wait for the next Council meeting, but the executive had its own mind made up, and advised affiliated societies not to waste money and effort working for any private bill.[11]

The Speaker's ruling has been the subject of much analysis. Some cabinet suffragists may have suspected collusion by the Speaker with the prime minister, or possibly with the Tory antisuffragists;[12] at best Lowther, a Conservative member for a Cumberland riding, was personally opposed to women's suffrage and less impartial than he believed himself to be. Connected is the controversy as to the correctness of the Speaker's ruling, women's suffrage amendments having been introduced without hindrance to the franchise bills of 1867 and 1884. A third question is whether the government foresaw the dénouement; Holton argues, with good evidence, that "It seems very unlikely ... that the government had not been expecting just such a reversal for its own bill."[13] The Speaker's failure to give any hint of his thinking, even to make up his mind until the last moment, has also been faulted. More damning still, he spent the fateful weekend of the decision at the home of Lord Rothschild, a major financial contributor to the antisuffrage movement; hardly the best place to conserve either the reputation or the substance of his impartiality.[14]

A further point, often ignored, is that this was an unusual bill in having been drawn up in connection with the prime minister's declared anticipation of a certain type of major amendment, so that the introduction of such an amendment must surely have been in the minds of those who drafted the bill from the outset. The possibility of an adverse ruling had certainly been present in the thoughts of suffragists for a long time. Not only had it been discussed throughout 1912, though generally without great anxiety, but Margaret Llewelyn Davies (for example) had been aware of the problem as early as 1908, when Asquith first made mention of a government Reform Bill, commenting privately that "I suppose one can't be sure ... whether the principle of w.s. *can* be introduced as an Amendment."[15] Given this degree of awareness, one might expect that legislative experts of good will could have found a way to make the measure proof against the fate which overtook it at the hands of the Speaker. Sir John Simon, who had just entered the cabinet as attorney-general, had had a hand in drafting the bill. Catherine believed that he had done his best to "t[ake] every precaution," and found him "very much distressed" about what had happened, believing he had accidentally done Asquith, as well as the women, a bad turn in not foreseeing and preventing the débâcle.[16] However, if, as it seems, he was innocent of evil intent, he may have been culpably naive, despite his legal training and political experience; at best, he failed to anticipate and guard against the Speaker's partiality. Simon's active commitment to women's suffrage dates from this time and it is tempting to think that he may have wanted to make amends. One other opportunity to protect the bill had been missed. The NU had tried desperately, but without success, to get a suffragist minister to speak on the second reading of the bill, "and to say that they supported the 2nd Reading *because the Bill was open to amendment to include women in Com[itt]ee stage*." Catherine was told later "that had one of them done this the Speaker's ruling might have been different."[17]

Asquith was quick to turn the ruling to his advantage. Although, as Philip Snowden among others pointed out, the Speaker had said, "The ruling is not to the effect that no Bill extending the male franchise could have woman suffrage grafted upon it, but that this particular Bill was not so drafted as to permit that to be done,"[18] the prime minister chose to put the wider construction on it, rather than going back to the drawing board and having a bill drawn up that would fulfil his pledge. There is also something more than a little disingenuous in Asquith's response; although his official letter to the King expressed only the utmost surprise and dismay at the "totally new view of the matter" taken by the Speaker, his sentiments, if not his actions, are more accurately revealed in a private letter of 27 January 1913 in which he said, "The Speaker's *coup d'état* has bowled over the Women for this session – a great relief."[19] There is little here of the great political embarrassment imputed to Asquith for which he received so much commiseration from his colleagues, and so much sympathy from historians.

Catherine's mood is hard to assess. At least one acquaintance saw her at about this time as an example that would be hard to live up to, writing, "You are so splendid, Miss Marshall. You never get tired and indifferent – you are always so alive and ready. If I lived with you I would be constantly put to shame."[20] Yet there was an inevitable sense of let-down. Once more, all the hard work of preparing for the amendments to the Reform Bill had come to nothing, and there is some inconclusive evidence that even in mid-December, Catherine had struggled to come up with plans for the parliamentary work without her own continuance in a central role. An undated fragment, found with material of 13 December, is made up of what seem to be lists of possible people to take over the parliamentary work; included is an item, "C.E.M. return year after next? H.M.S[wanwick] in the interim? M.R[obertson]. to be Org. Sec. of E.F.F.? (without an 'Honorary')."[21]

For whatever reasons, the brief new year break had again found Catherine wondering whether to give up the London work as soon as the Reform Bill effort was over. She had had some discussion with her parents; Frank wrote to her on 9 January:

I quite mean what I said about the suffrage work in parting on Tuesday.

I am *perfectly certain* that to imagine you are 'coming home' in any practical sense while liable to be called off every now and then to sort over a federation here or there is a delusion.

You could not settle to anything whatever in this region.

The choice is not between being at home, and doing suffrage work. It is between doing suffrage work in that scattered way or sticking to your job in London.

I think both would claim the whole energy of your life for the time being. Now the choice between these two forms of suffrage work seems to me to be partly that of the cause and partly of your own personal interest and profit.

As far as I have gathered from you the Com^ee want you to stick to the Parl^y work. That is the wish of those responsible for the cause.

As regards yourself, irregular and trying as your present life may be, the other line (directing various local efforts by turns) would be much more so in both respects. Also the interest and personal advantage to you in sticking to the parliamentary work is incomparably greater than any reward the other course can offer you.

In fact I rather suspect that one reason of your proposing the change is that you do not want to monopolise a "plum". Examine your mind carefully and see whether that is not at the bottom of it. Now there you ought to be guided by the wishes of those working with you.

I should regret your being tied to this work longer than the life of this parliament at very longest. But until some one else has been introduced into the work by you, and has shown capacity for taking your place in it I can quite understand their insistence on your staying. One condition must be insisted on, that is the certainty of quite adequate holidays, several months of unbroken change from this work in the year.

So far you have stood the strain very well, and I should not dream of your continuing it unless I thought so.

But as you know we think it too much, and are anxious that it should not continue as incessant as it has been. If you say that the responsibility is wearing you, that is another, and a quite final consideration.

You had better show this to Mrs. Fawcett if you are discussing the matter with her.[22]

Despite the lapse into paternalism towards the end of the letter, Frank's comments, at least as far as they related to the work itself, were in the main sensible and probably helped Catherine in making her decisions. He was probably wrong in believing that Catherine wanted to leave the London work because she might be monopolizing a "plum," although the satisfaction which must have come from her sense of doing an outstanding job in an important cause may well have played a somewhat different role in her indecision. Catherine was the victim of an awkward, sometimes irrational, and often divided conscience; her mother had had some earlier ill-health, Catherine had settled down after leaving school as a "dutiful daughter" at home, and here she was, away from home nearly continuously, engaged in a challenging and fulfilling job, which – who can doubt? – she thoroughly enjoyed, despite the overwork and the stress. Liberal education and liberal parents notwithstanding, she was not altogether able to shake off all of the effects of the repressive culture of her time. Frank's letter reflected an ambivalence which was a mirror image of her own; although he wanted her to make her decision partly on grounds of her own personal interest and advantage – using a tone one might employ in speaking of a career choice – he also took it for granted that her place was still at home, and that she should return there, at the latest, at the end of the current parliament, whether or not the franchise was won.

The decision made, Catherine moved again into Mary Sheepshanks's house at 1 Barton Street, now regarding it as a sufficiently permanent arrangement to order her own stationery, and to have a carpenter come in to hang pictures for her.[23]

Probably few of Catherine's colleagues knew of her painful decision-making. Collectively, the NU came up with its usual sturdy response to adversity, producing its own analysis – in which, not surprisingly, the perfidy of the Liberal government and especially of Asquith loomed large, and the sop of a promise of facilities for a private bill was received with scorn.[24] But again, the major emphasis was on looking forward, and at least the speaker's ruling brought some good in its train. In mid-February Millicent Fawcett wrote to Helena Auerbach, who was a personal friend as well as the NU's treasurer, and who had left just after the New Year for an extended trip, bringing her up to date:

You will long ago have heard of the extraordinary ruling of the Speaker and all its consequences. I feel it has caused a great wave of sympathy with us which must tell in our favour, if the militants do not destroy it and turn the sympathy in the other direction. But at present the feeling is that we have been badly treated. The vote of the Labour conference to instruct their Parliamentary Party to oppose any future Reform Bill which does not include women is of very great importance. We owe it in part to Philip Snowden and in part to Margaret Robertson and her fine work in Midlothian and elsewhere: in part also to the sympathy with our movement called forth by the Speaker's ruling. We are recommending to our Council at the end of this month, the adoption practically of the anti-government Election policy. We shall I think concentrate on a group of seats now held by anti-Suff Liberal ministers, for the general election. The rumour now very strongly is that there is to be a general election before the Home Rule Bill becomes law. ... We hope that the passing of the Trades Union Bill will enable a far larger number of Labour men to stand.[25]

The Labour party conference to which Fawcett referred had coincided with the Speaker's ruling, and Philip Snowden's stirring speech had found a ready audience among the rank and file of the party, where the resolution was carried by 870,000 votes to 437,000, despite some earlier fears that the influx of miners into the party would result in an unfavourable majority.[26] The resolution was thought to be particularly significant as Labour party conference di-

rectives had been declared by the conference to be absolutely binding on Labour MPs, although in the outcome this provision proved
incapable of implementation.[27] Catherine described the resolution's
triumphant passage as "largely the fruits of the National Union's
Election Fighting Fund policy and particularly of the excellent work
done by Miss Margaret Robertson."[28]

Catherine herself had also played a part in the EFF's careful preparation of the ground; a special suffrage supplement had been
issued by the *Labour Leader* for the occasion, paid for by the EFF, and
edited by Helena Swanwick, assisted by Catherine, Kathleen Courtney, and H.N. Brailsford. Copies went out with the *Common Cause*,
and were given to all delegates to the Labour conference.[29] The NU
sent a cable of congratulation, saying that the new policy had justified the women's faith in Labour, and had restored their hope.[30]
Pressure on the PLP came from other sections too. The Women's Labour League (WLL) passed a resolution protesting the Speaker's ruling and condemning Asquith's failure to live up to his pledge. WLL
representatives planned to meet with Henderson to discuss what was
to be done.[31] Henderson indeed was fully supportive, and encouraged the NU to send a deputation, together with the WLL and the
Women's Cooperative Guild, to meet with the PLP; the meeting took
place on 11 February.[32]

Mrs Fawcett's letter to Helena Auerbach had accurately foretold
the direction in which the NU would move. In short order the proposed changes in policy were refined by the executive and put into
shape for presentation to the council, which was to meet at the end
of February. Catherine served on the agenda committee for the
coming meeting.[33]

The council's role in the NU was of great importance. However active the officers, and to whatever extent it was they who proposed,
promoted, and implemented new policies, the council's power to
make the decisions was real, and was jealously guarded. Even in the
dismay following on the Speaker's ruling, when the officers were
reacting to the ruling and to Asquith's offer of facilities for a private
bill, complaints came from Eleanor Rathbone, and from the Liverpool WSS, that policy statements were being made in the *Common
Cause* without the council's authorization. In retrospect, it may seem
that they had a case for thinking that the officers already had their
minds made up, in view of what we have seen of their conversation
with Lloyd George and other statements, but a majority of the executive judged the criticisms unwarranted, claiming that "there was
nothing in the passages indicated which would prejudice the decision of the Council as to future policy, but that they merely empha-

sised ... that nothing short of a Government measure would be regarded as an equivalent to what had been promised."[34]

Such complaints often reflected party political divisions (in itself not without value), but equally important is the light they shed on the good democratic health of the NU; present-day organizations and pressure groups may well envy the care with which an immense section of the membership eagerly and carefully studied the documents sent out to it – a habit constantly demonstrated in other ways as well, not least by an incident in late 1912. Presumably in light of the delicacy of some of the NU's political negotiations, and – for instance – the confidentiality of some of the statements made to the executive by politicians, that committee had become uneasy about the freedom with which the minutes circulated, and had passed a resolution forbidding the local societies to pass them from hand to hand; the minutes were to be available at the societies' executive meetings but were not to circulate. Such a storm of protest ensued that the executive had to reverse its decision (although reiterating the need for care in preserving confidentiality); local executive members refused to be deprived of the opportunity to do their homework thoroughly before getting together.[35]

The council which gathered on 27 February 1913 was the largest yet, attended by 596 delegates representing 288 societies. Some business was left unfinished, but solely because of the amount on the agenda; time was not wasted and all important matters were dealt with. An observer commented on the quality of the debate, and the greatly increased sophistication of the delegates as compared with a few years before, adding a small barb for the male politicians by claiming that "the whole discussion presented an agreeable contrast, in matters of brevity, clear thinking, recognition of facts, directness and sincerity, to those recorded in the pages of Hansard."[36]

The resolutions passed at the council were all in the direction of a harder line. No effort would be wasted on promoting a private member's bill, although nothing would be done to impede it, if introduced. The NU called upon the government, as the only way now open to the fulfilment of Asquith's pledge, to introduce a government bill including a measure of women's suffrage. The Labour party was warmly thanked for its efforts on behalf of the amendments to the abortive Reform Bill, and the resolution passed at the Labour conference was welcomed.

The crux of the new developments in policy centred on elections, and "gave rise to keen debate and some very able speeches"; the outcome was a "large and enthusiastic majority" for the direction in which the executive wanted to move. The objectives of the NU in by-elections were spelled out: to shorten the term of office of the present cabinet in its present shape, especially by opposing antisuffragist ministers; and to strengthen any party in the House of Commons which made an official commitment to women's suffrage. In future no government candidate would be supported, although a "tried friend" would not be actively opposed unless he entered a contest after the NU or EFF had already declared its support for a Labour candidate in the riding. At the general election, the seats of antisuffragist Liberals would be attacked, and especially of ministers; to this end support would be given to Labour or Unionist candidates. The seats of Labour MPs "who have taken a strong line in support of Women's Suffrage" would be defended, and other suffragist Labour candidates, new or old, would be assisted. The questions to be asked of candidates were revised. The centrality of the EFF in all this was recognized; not only was its scope extended, but the executive was given discretion to transfer money from general funds to the EFF; any one wanting to make sure that her contribution was not used for EFF work must now specify this, rather than, as before, earmarking sums intended for the EFF.[37]

Naturally, some heat was generated by the decision to support no Liberals, the most strenuous objection coming from Eleanor Rathbone. Taking advantage of a provision for executive members to speak up, at the time of a council, even when they differed on a policy coming to the council by majority decision of the executive, Rathbone had circulated to delegates a mimeo entitled "The Gentle Art of Making Enemies: A Criticism of the proposed Anti-Government Policy of the National Union," in which she described the policy as starting the NU "on a path of what may be called *constitutional coercion*, as opposed to its previous record of constitutional persuasion," and had seriously questioned the long-term effects likely to result.[38] And after the meeting Maude Royden was accused by a correspondent who had been present of "having seemed ... to assume that delegates who had misgivings about the new policy were actuated by party (i.e. Liberal) feeling, rather than by zeal for Women's Suffrage." Royden apologized with characteristic generosity, making it clear that she had not meant to wound; she explained that the change lay in that the government had previously been thought capable of taking a neutral attitude to a non-party bill, but had shown itself to be actively antisuffragist: so the government must be opposed. Catherine, Royden added, had put the central point precisely when she had said that "*you cannot support a Government candidate without also supporting the Government.*"[39] The case was not closed, but a good majority had voted for the new hard line; repeated disillusion-ment was taking its toll, even among the many suffragists whose choice of party would still have been the Liberals. Not incidental, and in a way lending credibility to Rathbone's fears, is a notable change of language which came in with the EFF, detectable (for in-stance) in the way in which Catherine spoke, uncharacteristically, of the new policy as a weapon, and increasingly came to use warlike metaphors for the struggle.[40]

The election of officers which took place at this, the formal annual council meeting, saw Catherine elected to the position of honorary parliamentary secretary, and to the executive. Executive members and officers had to be nominated by societies, and under the prevail-ing rules this almost amounted to a preliminary ballot. A few candi-dates for the executive received over one hundred nominations, and Catherine's work was now sufficiently well known that she was nom-inated by eighty-five societies. The position of honorary parliamen-tary secretary, left vacant by the resignation of Edith Palliser, was not uncontested; while Catherine was nominated by seventy-eight societies, Chrystal Macmillan was a serious contender, supported by fifty-seven societies.[41]

Unfortunately we do not know exactly how the final voting went, except that Catherine triumphed. Nor do we know which were the regions supporting each of the two candidates, which might shed some light on the background to their rivalry, which remains some-thing of a puzzle. Macmillan, progressive in many ways, active, and from the industrial North, might have been expected to have much in common with the new wave of democratic suffragists now domi-nating the executive, but so often seemed to be at odds with them. Certainly, she constituted herself a watchdog for strict observance of procedure – perhaps every such committee needs one – and, like Rathbone, she was protective of Liberal suffragists; some years later, she was to stand unsuccessfully as a Liberal candidate for the House of Commons.[42] But that the difficulty was partly one of personality is confirmed by an assessment made later by Adela Stanton Coit, in a letter to Millicent Fawcett: "I quite agree with your view of Chrystal Macmillan's character. She is absolutely honest, but often so absorbed in her own particular view of a case that nothing will make her see anything else and she will go on spinning her own thread quite unconscious and unimpressed by what another person says and thinks. She is most tenacious in her own schemes and often ab-solutely non-committal when the scheme originates in anothers [sic] brain; see her withholding her vote in C[ommi]ttee when it is not her proposal."[43]

A big reception for the delegates to the council was marked by a personal tribute to Millicent Fawcett, in the form of addresses from the many branches, presented by the representatives. Catherine and Kathleen hosted an at-home for the executive committee, the organizers and the honorary secretaries of the federations, which proved to be "very pleasant and successful. Many who had been merely names to each other were enabled to meet, and a useful interchange of views was carried on all over the room."[44]

Catherine and Kathleen were becoming a most effective working partnership, and were now close personal friends. After all the work of the council was over they left to recuperate for a day or two in the Surrey countryside, staying at a farm near Dorking, in an area probably already well known to Catherine, and later to become very dear to her. The Marshall family counted among their friends, and sometime visitors to Hawse End, Robert and Elizabeth (Bessie) Trevelyan, who had a house (Shiffolds) at Leith Hill.[45] Probably it had been through them that Catherine discovered this unspoilt area, a great place for a breath of fresh air within weekend reach of London. Now she chose to stay at Abinger Bottom, several miles from Leith Hill, where the Trevelyans' retired gardener and housekeeper kept a secluded farm which could be reached in a hired pony trap, and where it was possible to rent rooms with meals and enjoy the countryside with the minimum of social obligations.[46]

Refreshed, the two were back in London in time for the executive on 6 March. The main business was to appoint the subcommittees. The officers, among whom was Catherine as honorary parliamentary secretary, were on every subcommittee *ex officio*. A list of former members to be asked to accept reappointment to the EFF committee was approved, and Catherine's name was again set down to serve as honorary secretary.[47] A few weeks later, Eleanor Rathbone declined to serve on a new parliamentary subcommittee, and even considered resigning from the executive; Catherine wrote her a friendly and conciliatory letter, expressing her appreciation of her influence and hoping she would stay.[48]

A big public meeting was held by the NU on 7 March to announce the new policy. Here Fawcett opened with a hard-hitting speech condemning the prime minister's attitude: "Liberals are fond," she said, "of chanting the praises of Mr. Asquith's high sense of personal honour. All I can say is that his dealings do not illustrate it." She drew attention to his refusal to meet with the NU when he found himself unable to fulfil his pledge, to the several ways in which the reality of a free vote in the House had been undermined, to his wilful failure to scotch the rumours of his possible resignation should the women's suffrage clauses go through. Then followed a straightforward explanation by Helena Swanwick and Lord Lytton of the changes in NU policy. Philip Snowden spoke in defence of the policy of the Labour party, currently much vilified by the WSPU as sustaining the Liberal government in power; against a background of interruptions from WSPU militants who were present, he made a distinction between support for individual measures acceptable to the Labour party and unconditional support for the government, and praised the EFF policy.[49]

In early 1913, then, Catherine and her fellow women's suffragists were facing a year in which there was no realistic prospect of women obtaining the vote, no immediate measure to which to direct their efforts. This was a dramatic change of tempo: as Catherine wrote to Francis Acland a few months later: "There has never been a time when one could afford to slacken and take a rest. We were always working for a promised opportunity just ahead (do you remember Sir E. Grey's "Concentrate on 1911"?), and we felt everything might depend on our leaving no stone unturned in the next few months."[50] Although Catherine would soon find herself only a little less busy than she had long been, the Reform Bill fiasco resulted in a kind of gearing down for a long uphill grind, in place of the rollercoaster of the past few years of general elections and parliamentary bills.

As it had turned out, it was fortunate that there had been no certainty of success in the Reform Bill, and from the very outset one of the perceived advantages of the EFF policy had been that, in the event of failure to win the franchise through the Reform Bill, "we should already have embarked upon a policy which would hold the promise of success in the future."[51] Psychologically, as well as practically, the benefit now deriving from having this policy in full swing, and if anything likely to attract additional support as a result of the Reform Bill fiasco, was inestimable.

Despite the shift to a less immediate goal, Catherine was orchestrating an intense political campaign from the end of February 1913 on, a phase designed to culminate in the expected general election, but which in fact was to come to an end with the outbreak of war in August 1914. The terms of the campaign had been set by the new policy adopted by the NU council, applied by Catherine with characteristic depth, personal attention, and flair. As we shall see, there were several important threads interwoven in the campaign. While the subject had to be kept before the House of Commons by whatever means were available, the EFF was increasingly the main focus of the NU's political work, involving a variety of activities. The application of the EFF policy and the new antigovernment position to by-elections was now of secondary importance to EFF constituency groundwork towards the general election. There was a continuing need to build confidence between the NU, the PLP, and the executive of the Labour party, the last involving grassroots work with the component parts of that heterogeneous body. In particular, Catherine and the EFF staff were putting a great deal of effort into bringing the trade unions – especially the recalcitrant miners' unions – on side, while strengthening connections with the generally willing ILP section of the Labour party. Catherine was also using her skills to keep or develop relationships with other party leaders, not least those of any promise in the delinquent Liberal party, notably Lloyd George, Sir Edward Grey, and (later) Sir John Simon. At the same time she was fostering the pressure in favour of women's suffrage within all three of the parties, in Parliament and at the grassroots. All of these areas of work were interrelated and were promoted both by conscious planning and by spontaneous use of every opportunity that arose.

The House of Commons must not be allowed to heave a sigh of relief and forget all about women's suffrage. Even in the novel situation of 1913 to 1914, when, for the first time for a number of years, there was no women's suffrage measure to be actively supported in the Commons – and when so much attention was turned to Ireland and to the continuing industrial strife – there were enough parliamentary incidents of interest to the NU to give them the opportunity to assure MPs that they were still watchful at the gates.[52] One of the first of these was the government's Plural Voting Bill, introduced in March 1913.[53] The bill contained provisions, originally included in the Reform Bill, to do away with the right of property owners to vote in all the constituencies in which they held property. Of little moment to women in itself, it was understandably felt by the women's suffragists as an affront, and it raised an issue as to the stance of the Labour party.

Catherine, who never found it easy to leave her work behind, took time during her short Easter break, which she spent in France, to write a long letter to the *Daily Citizen* when the Plural Voting Bill came before Parliament. She began by giving high praise to the generous support for the women's cause expressed in the Labour party resolutions, and she stressed the need that working women had for the vote. She freely admitted that the resolution of the Labour party conference had not made mention of any Plural Voting Bill (though a later one, of the ILP, had done so),[54] and she conceded the superficial logic of a speaker who "'could not regard the taking away of half a million votes from men as being an injustice to women'." But she argued that Labour men should recognize that the principle was still involved, in that the bill would increase the value of the remaining male vote. She challenged Labour MPs on the weakness of their response to their own losses in the Reform Bill's failure, asking: "Why should the whole question of registration reform, and the abolition of the property qualification, so vitally important to the interests of Labour, be quietly dropped out of the Government's proposals? Why should the Labour Party and the women alone be made the losers by the fiasco of last January, while the Government secures its own bit of salvage from the wreck?"[55]

Why indeed, we may echo. The lack of widespread reaction to the Reform Bill contretemps on the part of the many still effectively disenfranchised working men provides reinforcement for the wisdom of the women's suffragists in not choosing to ally themselves with this inertia by going the route of a campaign primarily focused on adult suffrage. Rather than going for women's suffrage through adult suffrage, the NU's drive for the women's vote had some spin-off effect in awakening workers to their own need for a wider franchise and one less hedged about with registration obstacles.

Catherine's main objective was contained in the final paragraph of her letter: "If the Labour Party were to determine to oppose this arbitrary selection of plural voting from the other measures of electoral reform for which opportunity has been repeatedly promised, they would have a strong lever in their hands for putting pressure on the Government to fulfil its obligations to both the Labour Party and the women."[56]

The issue for the PLP, however, was at bottom of a different nature. Some ILP members were willing to risk the parliamentary agreement with the Liberals; the Labour party leadership, and MacDonald in particular, were not.

Nevertheless, Catherine felt that Francis Acland, as a suffragist MP, but first and foremost a Liberal, with whom she had a long meeting on 14 April, "was obviously rather nervous" about the possibility of Labour opposition to the Plural Voting Bill, and upset by the NU's inclination to make an issue of it, which he said would "rouse great hostility among Lib[eral] men and women."[57] Catherine greatly appreciated the consistent help shown her by Francis Acland, whose wife Eleanor was a personal friend; nevertheless, Catherine's notes on the interview show her and Francis fencing cordially but carefully with each other in a sophisticated political fashion, both looking for information and measuring the amount they gave in return. In the event, the Plural Voting Bill passed in the Commons, with Labour opposition coming only from a few stalwarts such as the faithful Philip Snowden and Keir Hardie, but it was defeated in the Lords, and never passed into law, its provisions being eventually subsumed into the 1918 Reform Act.[58]

Although it added little to her case, Catherine, in her letter to the *Daily Citizen*, could not refrain from a reference in passing to George Barnes, a leading trade union MP who had recently slammed the suffragist women as "rich dilettantes." Catherine was sensitive on this issue, and was always deeply hurt by any imputation that the class into which she was born rendered her forever unfit to serve and work with women and men from another background. She had been much upset by the way in which Ramsay MacDonald tended to make his attacks on the militants into a condemnation of all middle-class women in the suffrage movement, and had written to him in October 1912 stressing the community of interest felt by many middle-class suffragists with Labour: "If you think I am exaggerating ask Miss I.O. Ford. She can tell you something of what this struggle means to the middle class women for whom you have so little kindly feeling. Why do you hate us so? ... Your accusation of class-feeling on our side, against the working women, wounds – and shows that you have missed much of the significance of the Women's Movement."[59] Catherine believed passionately that sex and class differences could and should be overcome, and was to suffer more disappointment on both scores later in her life.

Despite the NU's decision to mount no campaign for any private member's bill, Catherine kept a close watch behind the scenes on the progress of the bill introduced by W.H. Dickinson, to enfranchise women householders and wives of householders. The bill had the PM's commitment to further facilities if it should pass second reading, a promise on which Catherine's comment had been "What a sickening familiarity there is about those words!"[60] The Dickinson bill was not drawn up as "an agreed Bill," by any interparty group, as had been the Conciliation Bills, but "was framed by a group of Liberal members, on lines satisfactory to the Liberal party but known to be unacceptable to all but a few Unionists."[61] To the great irritation of the NU, the government had decreed that only two cabinet ministers would speak on the bill, one for and one against, which, as Helena Swanwick wrote in a draft letter to Asquith, "even though it may appear superficially to be equal, puts the Suffragists at a decided disadvantage."[62] The NU held, with justification, that "a majority made up of most of the weightiest speakers in the Government" favoured women's suffrage; the agreement silenced them.[63] Whether the ministers cared enough to mind is another matter.

Catherine talked over the prospects for Dickinson's bill in her meeting with Acland, and thought she had somewhat interested him in the idea that a fair redemption of Asquith's failed Reform Bill pledge would be for the government to take up the Dickinson bill officially, should it pass second reading, but without making this intention known ahead of the time, which, she thought, would make a free vote difficult. And Acland gave Catherine a run-down on the hurdles that would face the bill, even should it leap this first one; with the near certainty that the Lords would use all the powers of delay left to them under the 1911 Parliament Act, it would not pass the finish line before a general election sent the whole suffrage issue back to the starting gate.[64] Catherine was confirmed in her view, which was also the NU's official position, that time and money would be wasted in working for a bill which did not have "any chance of becoming law" even if it passed this stage, as she explained in a letter to Dickinson.[65] In the event, the question of its further progress proved to be academic. The bill reached second reading on 5 May, and was defeated the next day by a majority of 47. The NU's regret was minimal, since it had never invested any hope in the bill. Even Eleanor Acland agreed with Catherine that it was as well to have it go down in May as to have it drag out its life for a few more months.[66] Nevertheless, Catherine made a careful analysis of the division list.[67]

Other opportunities for keeping the women's suffrage issue before the House of Commons were provided at intervals throughout 1913 and 1914 by abortive attempts to introduce Scottish and Welsh Home Rule by private members' bills. The agitation to have women's enfranchisement included in these bills was also useful in providing involvement for the branches in Wales and Scotland, which Catherine helped coordinate. While the women's suffragists based their main case on the claim of women to representation in any governing body, they also turned the antis' own arguments against them, and even such men as C.H. Lyell, the Liberal MP for South Edinburgh, and on the executive of the Anti-Suffrage League, conceded that the case against women's suffrage for local parliaments was weaker than that against women having the vote for the imperial Parliament.[68] Another imaginative suggestion for parliamentary activity originated with the Actresses' Franchise League, who proposed pleading the women's cause at the bar of the House of Commons, but this finally had to be dropped.[69]

The EFF work absorbed a great deal of Catherine's time and attention. Margaret Robertson had soon demonstrated her exceptional political ability and her abounding energy, and had a remarkable grasp of the EFF constituency work, but the primary responsibility remained with Catherine, and it was Catherine who reported regularly to the EFF and NU executive committees, and received their decisions, based on her information and sometimes other factors, as to which constituencies should be worked.

The EFF took part in four all-out by-election contests during 1913 and 1914. Some are dealt with more fully below, but a summary will be useful here. At Houghton-le-Spring (March 1913) and North-West Durham (January 1914), at neither of which had the Labour party previously fielded a candidate, the Liberal candidate was returned with a substantially reduced majority, and Labour made a very good showing, coming close to the Unionist candidate, who in his turn was in both cases a great deal nearer to the Liberal than he had been in the December 1910 election. At South Lanark (December 1913), also contested for the first time by Labour, Labour's showing was numerically not so great, but was enough to turn a Liberal majority of over a thousand into a Unionist majority of 251. At Leith Boroughs, which had been contested by Labour before, but not in the most recent general election, the Liberal was also defeated by the Unionist, by the narrow margin of 16, with Labour again coming in third but with a respectable count.[70] These results were gratifying to Catherine and the other NU workers, and although most historians who have studied the Labour party's by-election fortunes in this period make no mention of the financial and organizational support given by the EFF,[71] candidates and party workers at the time were appreciative,[72] and Liberals uneasy. Some Labour workers, according to Catherine, estimated that at least one thousand of the four thousand Labour votes cast at Houghton could be credited to the help of the EFF.[73] A high profile had been given to women's suffrage in all these constituencies, and the ground prepared for further work.

The NU may have learnt as much from the by-elections where the EFF was unable to play a part as from the ones where it actively campaigned. One of the most interesting was that at Leicester in June 1913. Both the ILP, to which the EFF was increasingly drawn, and the NU thought this an excellent constituency to contest. But it was a two-seat riding, and the other seat was MacDonald's own. The Labour party's central office refused to sanction an official candidate, and a nasty fracas developed, involving not only the local bodies but the ILP's National Administrative Council (NAC) at odds with the Labour party national executive.

The simple explanation is that MacDonald's understanding with the Liberal party was that one seat was for a Liberal, and the other for Labour; if Labour contested the second seat in this by-election, not only might it open the way for a Conservative victory against a split radical vote, but it would lead to MacDonald's losing the cooperation of the Liberals in the coming general election, and so might constitute a threat to his reelection.[74] The Liberal candidate was Gordon Hewart (later lord chief justice of England), who had been chief counsel for the prosecution in a 1912 case in which the manager of the National Labour Press (NLP), the press of the ILP, had been convicted of incitement to damage property for statements which had appeared in the *Suffragette*, of which he was the printer[75] – not exactly the NU's cause, but the latter closely watched anything which bordered on restriction of the freedom of speech. True, in July 1912, just after the prosecution, Hewart had declared himself to have been always "a hearty supporter of the enfranchisement of women," and prepared to work for it, but at his adoption meeting for the Leicester by-election he had carefully built himself a fence to sit on, claiming that he was in favour of the principle of adult suffrage, but that "experience showed that great movements of that kind came gradually,"[76] surely the kind of remark to wring a groan from any NU supporter by this time.

In the event, the Labour party executive was able to prevent the entry of an official candidate; the running of one by the British Socialist party (BSP) led to a great uproar and further increased distrust of MacDonald within the ILP, his own party.[77] Later, the tension between centre and periphery of the Labour party would create difficulties for the NU, but at this time the NU naturally if reluctantly stayed with its mandate, kept its nose clean, and did not send in the EFF, doing instead only the routine suffrage propaganda work of the NU. After the election, handily won by Hewart, MacDonald wrote a friendly letter to Mrs Cowmeadow, the NU's organizer, and Catherine replied, thanking him and enclosing an extract from Cowmeadow's report, characteristically using the occasion both to build bridges and to make sure that MacDonald was exposed to the central message of the report, which stressed "the very good feeling towards the Suffrage question on the part of the working class population of Leicester"[78] – MacDonald's constituents.

As for the anticipated general election, the NU may well have given more focused thought during this period to preparation than did its ally, the Labour party, partially debilitated as the latter was by its complex structure and resultant delays in making crucial decisions.

A major advantage for the NU, of course, was that it knew which constituencies it wanted to target, whereas the leaders of the Labour
party still had to make up their minds on what overall strategy would
be pursued, whether to renew some kind of election agreement with
the Liberal party or to go for an all-out attack involving many three-
cornered contests.[79]

The difficulties of the Labour party, of course, bore on the EFF's
work. From mid-1912 on, Catherine had been making lists – not a
hard task – of constituencies the EFF would like to see contested in
the interest of Labour, or more commonly, to the damnation of Liberal antisuffragists. EFF support was available in two types of ridings,
where Labour opposed a prominent Liberal anti and where "any
completely satisfactory Labour Member [was] likely to be attacked at
the next election (e.g. Mr. Snowden and Mr. Henderson)."[80] By
mid-1913, the EFF lists were stabilizing, and now account was taken
not only of who was to be defeated, but also of realities such as the
likelihood of the Labour party national executive approving the
choice, of local party structures or lack of structure, of the past history of the area, of the resources available, and to a limited extent,
of NU opinion in the constituency. However, it was never the EFF way
to accept the status quo, if it seemed unfavourable, and once the
constituencies had been selected, the EFF went in to develop what
was promising and to change what was not.

The EFF did not wait for a blessing from the Labour party's executive before beginning work in particularly desirable constituencies.
In Accrington and Rossendale, for example, the seats of Harold
Baker (a junior antisuffragist minister, financial secretary to the War
Office), and of Lewis Harcourt, a notoriously virulent antifeminist,
the Manchester EFF's work was focused on making visible and
strengthening the Labour presence in order to make it attractive to
the Labour party to enter candidates. Helped by strong support
within the Manchester federation, the EFF made a great deal of progress; by June 1913 it seemed likely that Accrington would indeed
be contested in the next election;[81] in Rossendale it took a little
longer, in part because of evident reluctance on the part of Labour
party central office to make any commitment.[82] By early 1914, both
were on a list, drawn up by the Labour party's national agent, Arthur Peters, of constituencies that might be contested in the general
election, although both were given as "uncertain." The factors which
would probably have decided the issue were financial feasibility and
the all-important but still covert question as to whether the electoral
agreement between the Liberal and Labour parties was renewed.[83]

Although the NU had made it clear that the decisions as to which constituencies would be made the target of EFF campaigns rested with the NU executive, Catherine knew that special difficulty would attend the work in any place where the local or regional NU was against the implementation of the policy, and the divisive effect this could have on the NU was not to be taken lightly. From the outset, South Wales and to a lesser extent Bristol had been areas of concern, especially as the first included the seat of Reginald McKenna (North Monmouth) and the latter the seat of Charles Hobhouse (East Bristol), both notorious antisuffragist cabinet ministers. Catherine had set herself to find a way around the difficulty, and had been able to report in December 1912 that she "had visited Bristol and S. Wales. E. Bristol w.s.s. had decided to adopt the e.f.f. policy in Mr. Hobhouse's constituency. The South Wales Federation Committee were still unanimously opposed to the e.f.f. policy, their chief reason being that the Labour Party in Wales [whence came a number of the miners' representatives] had not shown itself a good friend to Women's Suffrage, but they were anxious to contest Mr. McKenna's seat and suggested that special work be started there to be paid for out of the transferable Fund."[84]

It was a start, but difficulties over the EFF policy in Bristol and South Wales were not at an end, and continued to cause friction. Similar problems arose in other areas where NU branches had a strong basis in Liberalism, notably in Scotland and in Eleanor Rathbone's bailiwick, that of the West Lancashire, West Cheshire, and North Wales federation, where women's suffragists were commendably active but reluctant to follow the NU's new lead.[85]

Regions in which there was an excess of enthusiasm for the Labour party provided a sort of mirror image of those in which there was hostility to the EFF, and also had to be handled carefully. The North-East Federation, in particular, chafed against NU control, and was unwilling to seek the sanction of the central EFF committee for the close relationship it had with the local ILP and trades unions, even making the assumption that money forwarded from NU headquarters was for use at local discretion.[86]

The overt campaign work and dealings with the local Labour bodies in the selected constituencies were largely conducted by the EFF's own organizers, and by the EFF organizers appointed by a number of the federations, involving them in strenuous campaigning on behalf of Labour, taking part in drives, whether these took the form of joint Labour/suffrage publicity weeks, or were nominally directed simply to building Labour support. The EFF's team of full-time paid organizers was in constant demand, and Catherine's correspondence shows that the better-known of them, and especially those with a good reputation as speakers (for example Selina Cooper and Hilda Oldham) were booked months in advance and could not fill all requests.[87]

Good judgment on the part of those who had, after all, been chosen in part for their Labour party sympathies was needed to distinguish between campaigning for a Labour candidate on grounds of the party's position on women's suffrage and advocating support for the Labour party on more general grounds. Margaret Robertson was seen by some as getting carried away at times, and was admonished to base her speeches on facts, not opinions, not to lead the Labour people to believe that most women would vote Labour, and to remember that the NU's reasons for supporting Labour were suffrage only; "but," Catherine added, "you can find plenty of reasons for supporting [the] individual Labour candidate."[88] By mid-1913, too, Robertson was unquestionably more closely in touch with the labour leadership in some areas than Catherine was, and on at least one occasion she warned the latter off in no uncertain terms, making it clear that she thought any interviews with local officials – in a strongly trade union area, where they were "*very* jealous of outside interference" – should be left to herself or Margaret Bondfield of the Women's Labour League and the ILP.[89]

The work for volunteers was on the whole less controversial, and was an invaluable part of the preparation for the general election. At the provincial council of May 1913, Catherine opened a discussion on "Political Work in the Country" by giving some pointers on the effort needed to bring to fruition the declared policy of the NU, "The object of all work being to get a Government Bill from whichever Party is returned to power at the next Election."[90] The annual electoral register was being drawn up, and since deadlines for registration fell during the summer, work in tracing removals was crucial. "This is very important," said Catherine, "as in all probability the next General Election will be fought on the Register which is compiled this summer. The work consists of a house-to-house canvass, ascertaining the political views of the occupants and making a list of men who are entitled to votes, but will not be put on the register unless they send in claims."[91] Volunteers, she went on, "who would help when the General Election comes," should also be sought, and a note made of what kind of work they could best do. Those Liberal women who were (against the WLF tide) "making a strong stand for suffrage" should be supported, and NU members should cooperate with them, particularly in demanding a suffragist candidate. Preparation could also take the form of "Canvassing to alienate the Labour vote from Liberal Anti-Suffragist Members in constituencies where the Labour vote is strong," and trying, if necessary, to create a demand for a Labour candidate. Once candidates were chosen, they should be given the evidence of national support for women's suffrage, and, Catherine added: "It is very important that Members of Parliament, especially Members of the Government, and prospective Parl^y candidates should be questioned about Women's Suffrage at all the political meetings which they address. When possible the question should be put by electors. Members of the I.L.P. can generally be relied on to help in this way." As usual, Catherine did not fail to remind her audience of the need to make full use of the local press, and she put on local bodies the responsibility for keeping NU headquarters informed of every relevant statement or answer made by candidates in their areas.[92]

Arthur Peters found himself working more and more closely with the EFF and at times the NU organizers. As early as April 1913, Catherine told Eleanor Acland that she, Margaret Robertson, and Peters had "spent [an] afternoon hard at work on plans for the next General Election," arranging to work together on registration and canvassing."[93] Trade union funds would not be available until the spring of 1914, but "we can help them start *at once*." While the development may have been unexpected, it cannot have been hard for Peters to get used to; the Labour party provided him with no such flying squad of experienced political workers as existed in the EFF staff, which by mid-1913 included fourteen full-time organizers specifically trained for work with Labour.[94] And the training they had had was systematic, involving a probationary period, a searching and practically oriented written test, and a thorough evaluation. Details of their pay, working conditions, expense allowances and duties were printed up for their guidance. Kathleen Courtney and Catherine both played a part in the process of finding, instructing, and assessing the organizers.[95] The Labour party, on the other hand, had a very small central secretariat, and no full-time travelling organizers at this time; local agents were often scarce and sometimes inexperienced and incompetent. Registration, particularly vital to this of all parties, was often neglected.[96] Indeed, Labour party organization remained embarrassingly and notoriously bad in some regions, so much so that the EFF staff at times found it hard to tolerate trying to work alongside.[97]

At times Peters requested the help of the EFF, at other times he allowed himself to be educated by them, at yet other times he was ready with the information they needed. For example, Ada Nield

Chew took him to Rossendale in late May 1913, showing him that there "political organisation does not exist" but that "industrial organisation is strong"; Peters accordingly recognized the potential for considerable advance, and thought that solid work might render the constituency ready for a Labour candidate in about a year's time. Chew also besought Robertson not to send a woman organizer into this area, which she was convinced would only respond to a man, at least in the immediate future.[98] The EFF, which did not directly hire men as organizers, tried to overcome the difficulty by offering to fund a Labour party organizer there, an offer which was refused by Henderson,[99] who provided a significant example of the difference between the approach of the Labour party and of the NU when he explained that the party did not place an organizer where there was no candidate or sitting MP. Ada Nield Chew was left to work the riding as best she could, which she did to good effect despite her sex.[100] Again, Peters was delighted to hear that the EFF was undertaking registration in Accrington, and by June he also saw hope in developments in North Monmouth, where he had been working alongside another EFF organizer.[101]

Peters may be presumed to have been ignorant of the complexities which might be posed by a renewal of the electoral agreement; his purpose, as he saw it, was simply to assist in the preparation of as many constituencies as possible to enter a strong candidate into the contest. Accordingly, whatever subtle difficulties might exist in the minds of Labour party leaders, he was in a position to appreciate the EFF contribution without reserve, both as it applied to by-elections and to preparation for the general election.

11   Taking the Cause to the Country by EFF and Pilgrimage, June to August 1913

The EFF work became so pressing in the summer of 1913 that Catherine felt unable to take time out for the big international suffrage event of the year. She had been on the NU international committee since its formation nearly a year before, and very active in preparations for the coming IWSA conference to be held in Buda-Pest from 15 to 20 June; and it had been at her suggestion that the NU executive agreed to pay the fares of the delegates.[1] A number of delegates would extend their European trip and take in other conferences set up elsewhere just before and after the IWSA event; Mary Sheepshanks had left some weeks ahead of the conference date on a speaking tour for women's suffrage.[2] Meanwhile, use was made of the visit of Carrie Chapman Catt, president of the National American Woman Suffrage Association (NAWSA) and of the IWSA, who had agreed to spend some time in Britain on her way to Hungary and again on the way back.[3]

Catherine had been appointed in April as a delegate to the conference, and was planning to go until almost the last minute, when the EFF work became too urgent for her to leave, particularly because of important decisions which would be made in East Bristol and South Wales within the next three weeks. Mary Sheepshanks took her place as a delegate. Carrie Chapman Catt had come up with the idea at the last minute of an international women's costume pageant, and Catherine put a good deal of effort into making sure that the components necessary for Britannia's costume arrived at the conference, together with a person prepared to play the part, even if she could not go herself; she had in any event declined to play the role, which she evidently felt was not suited to her.[4]

Two issues of particular interest to Catherine came up at Buda-Pest; the British section favoured establishing a permanent headquarters, and had also prepared a resolution to set up an international press bureau. The first of these proposals was adopted and plans went ahead to set up headquarters, London being chosen as the location, to the satisfaction of the NU. *Jus Suffragii*, the IWSA journal, would be edited and published from there. Mary Sheepshanks was appointed as full-time secretary to the IWSA at the new headquarters and took on the task of editing *Jus Suffragii*.[5] The international women's press bureau project did not fare so well, and was rejected by the congress, which probably did not think it wise to undertake a second major administrative development in one year. However, the considerable effort which Catherine, working with Helena Swanwick, and also consulting with Carrie Chapman Catt, had put into the project was not all wasted, as plans were made to expand the international press work within the existing structure.[6]

Catherine had prepared two short papers for the congress. One was in response to questions asked of all the delegates, and was an assessment of "The prospects of enfranchisement for British Women in the near future," an admirable summary of the complicated British situation and the frustrating events of the previous two years.[7] Catherine's other paper was on the question, "What relation should Suffrage organisations bear towards political parties?"[8] Although she naturally could speak only from the British experience, the exercise of setting down her thoughts for women of other countries had led her to analyse what was involved in the NU's delicate balancing act between a party and a nonparty stance. She focused on two main themes, the attitude of party women, and the impression that could be made on voters not yet committed to any party. For the first, she gave great prominence to the influence which party women who were suffragists must exercise within their parties, praising the British Labour women, but asserting that "the women within the two older parties are generally content to be merely parts of the party machinery." She added, with some bitterness, "The Women's Liberal Federation has just declared its willingness to continue to work for the Liberal government in spite of the Government's breach of faith with the women over the Suffrage question."[9] The reference was to a resolution passed at the WLF annual conference at Tonbridge Wells on 6 May 1913, which (together with the failure of the Dickinson bill) had provoked Eleanor Acland into writing, "Yes we went to sleep saying damn and woke up saying damn" – strong language from the pen of a woman in the early twentieth century – and had, more usefully, impelled her into initiating the Liberal Women's Suffrage Union (LWSU), a new organization of Liberal suffrage women which would be independent of the party.[10] This move Catherine went on to welcome in her paper, citing also the usefulness of the CUWFA, which "has done excellent work in educating Conservative opinion on the question of Women's Suffrage." More important still was the willingness of these bodies "to withhold support – and to organise the withholding of support – from unsatisfactory candidates."

Catherine elaborated on the need also to put pressure on the unaligned voter, exposing him to arguments for women's suffrage that would incline him at elections to vote for the most supportive candidate and party, so increasing both the suffrage presence in Parliament and the chance that one or both of the major parties would adopt the women's cause. This she thought best done by a "National non-party Women's Suffrage organisation, (in close touch with all the party organisations) whose work is to create and organise a body of non-Party Suffrage opinion, putting Women's Suffrage before any other issue, and exercising pressure on the political parties *from without*."[11] Even though Catherine was unable to go to Buda-Pesth, her two papers made her presence felt there.

We can recognize the NU in Catherine's description of the "National non-party Women's Suffrage organisation" which she extolled. But now that the NU was so caught up in the EFF policy, the NU's claim to be nonparty was held by many contemporaries to be tenuous, if not specious. Clearly, the questioners had some justification, in so far as the Labour party was the only party receiving significant election support in 1913 and 1914. However, Catherine's lobbying activities, as we shall see, were far from one-sided.

Attention had to be paid to keeping up political pressure, and in particular to building up the EFF work. With the goal set farther off, beyond the indefinite date of the next general election, the women's suffragist leaders had to maintain interest among members, and to stimulate public support. The WSPU, explicitly not concerned with the second of these objectives, was set on a course of escalating militancy, in which every act had to be followed by one more dramatic or more shocking; from February 1913 on the WSPU conducted a campaign of arson, bombing, and other forms of violence against property.[12] Meanwhile, the government, caught in its own trap, escalated its violence against the women in prison, making extensive use of forced feeding, often brutally administered, and, by the end of April 1913, passing the "Cat and Mouse Act," which enabled it to discharge seriously ill prisoners, rearresting them when they were sufficiently recovered.[13] The NU was once more faced with the task of dissociating itself from the militants' tactics while not exonerating the government for its share of the responsibility, and not condoning forcible feeding. The *Common Cause* leader-writer was in fact consistent in condemning both as forms of violence, but it was not a position easily grasped.[14]

Meanwhile, the government and many others continued to make use of the argument that it would be improper to give in to force. Catherine wrote to the *Daily Citizen*, taking as her starting point a resolution of the National Liberal Club that "it is not in the best interests of the Empire to grant the suffrage to women, while the present disorder prevails":

What would have happened if this argument had been applied in the case of the Reform agitation in 1832, or of the Irish Nationalist movement, or of the recent unrest in India? Would such a course have been applauded by Liberals as a piece of just or wise statesmanship?

To adopt such a position would be to put a premium on methods of violence. All that the opponents of any movement would have to do in future to prevent its success would be to organise the employment of violence in support of it!

The only safe and statesmanlike way to deal with this or any other question is to deal with it on its merits. Methods of violence should not have power to make our legislators grant an unjust demand; neither should they have power to make them refuse a just one.

I think the real reason in the minds of members of Parliament, who say that they will not vote for any women's suffrage measure until militancy ceases is a fear of being supposed to yield to intimidation.

But the fear of being thought afraid is of all fears the most undignified. It is no less weak to give up a course which you believe to be right for fear of what some people may say than to adopt a course which you believe to be wrong for fear of what some other people may do.[15]

There may be some assumptions in this letter that now seem naive: but there are also things worth pondering in the late twentieth century, when terrorism has become a commonplace.

Bertrand Russell expressed a common feeling when he wrote to Margaret Llewelyn Davies in April, "I am in *despair* about w.s. I think the militants are mad, and the country increasingly hostile."[16] In this climate, no matter how promising the EFF work, or how committed the leadership, something upbeat was needed to keep up the interest and renew the spirits of the thousands of women all over the country who had joined the nonmilitant movement in the last few years, to recruit more, and to present an alternative to violence. The public, too, needed to be reminded that there were these many women, determined to have the vote and to get it by peaceful means. One successful initiative already under way was the enrolment of "Friends of Women's Suffrage" (FWS), nonpaying associates of the NU who came out to public meetings and gave a general support without undertaking specific responsibilities. But more was needed.

The peaceful campaign of the nonmilitants was further threatened by a report that police protection was being refused to suffrage meetings, no matter what the sponsoring organization, or whether or not permission for the meeting had been granted. The NU executive, in cooperation with the LSWS, bravely initiated a series of outdoor meetings in Hyde Park throughout the early summer of 1913, explicitly "in order to maintain the right of free speech," and "agreed that should the police refuse protection ... meetings should still be held."[17] Helen Swanwick and Isabella Ford spoke at the first meeting, on 18 May, and Catherine went along to back them up. There was indeed some kind of an incident in which they were at risk from elements in the crowd; however, the police did not in the end refuse protection and the "hooligans" were kept in check. Catherine, who did not think her strength lay in public speaking, and who was keeping a dozen balls in the air at this time, nevertheless could not stay away from such a challenge and went to the park on a number of occasions. When she spoke, she stressed the importance of rejecting force as an argument; "the only sound basis of Gov[ern-men]t," she declaimed, "is the willing consent of the governed."[18]

But the spirits of the movement all over the country needed a major boost, and a plan was already in train. At exactly the same time that Bertrand Russell was sinking into unconstructive despair, Katherine Harley suggested to a meeting of the NU's organization committee that what was needed was a grand march.[19] The idea caught fire at once, not least with Catherine, who soon proposed that it be called "The Women's Suffrage Pilgrimage." A special committee was formed, the blessing of the executive obtained, and Mrs Fawcett wrote a dedication for publication in the *Common Cause*.[20]

Within a very few weeks the general scheme for the pilgrimage had been sketched in, and sent out to branches. A map was published in the *Common Cause*. Women would walk by eight routes to London, starting from the most distant parts in mid-June, gathering strength on the way and all converging on London at the same time,

to hold a mass gathering in Hyde Park on Saturday, 26 July, followed by a service at St Paul's the following day (although some had
doubts about introducing this religious connection, and it remained
a low-key and unofficial part of the enterprise).[21]

Very thorough plans were worked out by the central and local
committees. A special song was written, and was published in the
Common Cause. Arrangements were made for accommodation with
other suffragists along the routes. For good reasons, a great deal of
thought was given to clothing. Women were encouraged to wear the
NU colours, but perhaps more important, they were strongly advised
not to wear coats of green or purple, the WSPU colours (although the
NU colours also included green), which it was thought might add to
the danger of harassment and attack; a young woman who bewailed
the fact that her new coat was purple was probably not alone, but it
was a serious consideration. The length of skirts was earnestly debated: should the women trail the floor-length skirts then considered proper through all the dust and mud of England's unmade
highways and byways, or should the NU take the bold step of advising that skirts be shortened to an unheard-of four inches off the
ground? In the end, the NU played its part in dress reform by recommending the latter.[22] To be recognizable was important, so the
women wore cockades and scarves in red, white, and green, and carried specially made knapsacks of a common pattern. At least one
London department store served its own purposes, and perhaps
those of the suffragists, by advertising (in the *Common Cause*) a line
of suitable clothing in NU colours.[23]

An account of the beginning of the journey from the northwest,
written for the *Common Cause*, probably by Caroline Marshall, gives
some of the flavour. Following a "huge open-air meeting in Carlisle
on June 17th":

The Pilgrimage proper began on Wednesday, June 18th, at 10 a.m., when
a good procession left the Market Cross with banners in front and a baggage
cart, covered with red, white and green, bringing up the rear. A fine contingent from Keswick, including Lady Rochdale, Mrs. Frank Marshall, Mrs.
John Marshall, ... [and others] had come to Carlisle for the start, bringing
the Keswick banner with them. Lord Rochdale's car and Mrs. Marshall's
pony-cart, bravely decorated with flags, also started from Carlisle and accompanied the pilgrims throughout the whole Federation, being of un-
speakable help and value and enabling us to work a much larger area than
would otherwise have been possible in the time.

It would be difficult to give an accurate account of numbers, as pilgrims
by the dozen have joined us in the towns and villages as we went through.

Some of these have been able to do only a short stage, others have gone forward for much longer periods.[24]

Some (including Lady Rochdale) had walked the whole way from Carlisle to Lancaster (the edge of the federation area), others had done some part of the journey; Caroline Marshall "walked a very large part and would have done the rest but for a most unfortunate ankle sprain." Lady Rochdale walked the whole way to London. Another pilgrim from the Lake District, Mrs Duffield, "walked most of the way from Keswick to Lancaster, and hopes to go on to London." Gladys Duffield was a young married woman who had had nothing to do with the suffrage movement before this time, but who was swept off her feet when the pilgrimage came to Keswick and, perhaps aided by the fact that her husband was in India, left her small daughter with her mother-in-law (who conveniently turned out to be a closet suffragist), and set off at short notice to take part. Later she wrote a fine account of the whole pilgrimage.[25]

The pilgrims were accompanied by an experienced speaker, provided by the federation. Caroline Marshall's account continues:

Impromptu speaking was also done by several other members of the Pilgrimage. ... [E]xcellent propaganda work (house to house canvassing, distribution of literature, and impromptu meetings) was done in every hamlet and cluster of cottages, as well as by the wayside. The pleasantest part of this report is now to come, and may be divided into two headings: (1) The untiring devotion and harmony with which the pilgrims worked, and the true missionary spirit in which they went forth into the highways and hedges, and (2) the unfailing friendliness, eagerness, and even enthusiasm with which they and their message were greeted all along the way through the two counties.

Hostility and ridicule had been prophesied, and the Pilgrimage undertaken in no light or careless spirit by the most sanguine members, but the result was no less than a revelation, to those who doubted it, of the almost universal sympathy given to the Non-militant Suffrage Cause once it is understood.

A very happy feature of the North-western march was the Sunday in Keswick, when the pilgrims were welcomed to Crosthwaite Church by the vicar ... who preached a most inspiring Suffrage sermon. ...[26]

Caroline's account may leave rather the impression of a middle-class junket, but this is not borne out by other accounts. Ethel Snowden was aware that "very few could spare the time to march all the way from one end of the country to the other,"[27] but she made it clear that those who were not of the "leisure class"[28] were also a part of the pilgrimage:

It is equally obvious that those who have their living to earn could not give more than a day now and then to this great demonstration. Women came and went, walked for a few hours or a few days, as they were able to do it, and so strengthened and cheered the little band of stalwarts who tramped from end to end. The expressions of longing that the writer heard from from working-girls and women, that work, or having little children to care for, made it necessary for them to abstain from taking any part in the pilgrimage, were very touching, and spoke of a mass of quiet, unspoken support in the country. ...

Women doctors, teachers, University women graduates, nurses, writers, actresses; preachers, rescue-workers, Temperance workers; women holders of public office, town and district councillors, guardians of the poor, members of education committees; women connected with religious denominations, women Trade Unionists, women organisers – women in every branch of social service, women who are doing some useful work in the world; above all, mothers of little children who realise that the women's cause is the cause of the young, joined the procession at one point or another and helped to swell the great final demonstration in Hyde Park.[29]

As well as those who marched, there were those who came to meetings, organized receptions, offered hospitality, and generally cheered them on their way. Noted support came from working men, trade unionists, and ILP branches, but also from town and city officials, representatives of the professions, and the clergy.

Despite the overwhelming endorsement, few travelled the whole distance without encountering hostility. The northeastern pilgrims reported that the antisuffragists were going one day ahead of them all the way (except for one stretch where the antis had followed an out-of-date route map), so that they often had to counter, if not informed opposition, at least the sometimes dangerous disorderliness of expectant rowdies.[30] When the accounts were finally in, everything had been experienced, from drunken sandwich-board men carrying signs (upside down) that read "Women do not want votes," to rumours of organized riots being planned, from "a mounted police escort," to other police who "were totally unprepared for so large a meeting, and neglected to assist the speakers to a safe passage through the crowd, with the result that some of them were rather badly hustled."[31] Dangerous situations arose, but repeatedly enough of the audience wanted to hear the women, or was prepared to tackle their tormenters, for the suffragists to emerge unscathed; a credit also to the courage and ingenuity of the women, who never panicked and never gave up. An experience in Durham was not untypical: "The first part of the meeting was perfectly orderly, but, half-way through, a small band of University students, out for their usual 'rag', attempted to break up the meeting. To their great astonishment, they met with a very determined resistance on the part of an audience largely composed of workingmen. Some of the students proving somewhat persistent in their efforts, two were seized, rushed down to the river, and ducked."[32]

Some incidents were more serious, with "stones and eggs, vegetable refuse and tin cans ... freely thrown," and platforms "'rushed' in very dangerous and ugly fashion by crowds of ignorant youths." Many pilgrims were bruised, and Margaret Ashton was temporarily lamed by a kick.[33] A curious piece of concrete evidence remains of a nasty and dangerous form of harassment; when the KWSA banner was shaken out fifty years later a number of airgun pellets fell out, probably dating from the 1913 pilgrimage.[34]

Most reports published by the NU played down the violence and harassment, stressing rather the way in which elements in the crowd had come to the rescue of the pilgrims. But there had been enough incidents, and serious enough, for the executive to take a deputation to Reginald McKenna, the home secretary, on 30 July, in particular giving him "evidence of cases in which the organised hooliganism at Pilgrimage meetings had been allowed to go unchecked and unpunished, or in which the police force had been inadequate for the maintenance of order," and telling him, as Catherine reported to the NU executive, "that it was the experience of all the Pilgrims that the trouble was not due to hostile crowds, but to small gangs of rowdies, obviously organised, who came with the intention of provoking riots and breaking up the meetings; that this could have been prevented by adequate police force and proper precautions, as was proved in the case of the majority of the meetings held; but that there was evidently an impression in the minds both of the hooligans and of the police in some places that Women's Suffrage meetings were fair game, and that disorder could be permitted there which would not be tolerated elsewhere."

McKenna replied that he greatly regretted the incidents, and asked for more details, undertaking to write to the authorites in the areas where policing had been inadequate, and adding, "If there is any impression that Women's Suffrage meetings are 'fair game for the mob', we will do our utmost to remove that impression, and give you as full protection as any other persons holding peaceful political meetings. ... I shall certainly do my best to insure that there is absolute fair play for both sides. You are just as much entitled to express your views and get a fair hearing from the public as the opponents of Women's Suffrage are entitled to express their views. ... I should like to add that I sincerely admire the courage with which you ladies have carried on your work, and I assure you that you shall have the fullest protection which is the undeniable right of every law-abiding subject."[35]

On the face of it, it was a proper response, perhaps more than could have been hoped for from an avowedly antisuffragist minister – whose seat was one of those the EFF hoped to threaten in the next election – but a veiled reference to the militants' interruption of meetings was contained in his insistence on "fair play for both sides." He also chose to ignore the evidence presented by the NU, of trouble being deliberately instigated in a number of instances by ringleaders who travelled from town to town ahead of the pilgrims, and spoke in the House of Commons as if problems had been isolated and local.[36] On the whole, however, if there was indeed a deliberate attempt by the antisuffragists to intimidate the pilgrims and to turn public opinion against them, it backfired, making audiences more sympathetic and receptive.

We do not know whether Catherine had been caught in any of the frightening episodes of the pilgrimage, but she was no stranger to hostility and the threat of physical attack. A letter that she wrote to Ramsay MacDonald at the beginning of July – while the pilgrimage was in progress – sheds important light on her personal reaction and the development of her thinking about violence. And it illumines the rather wry response of nonmilitant women, accustomed to threats, abuse, and rough handling from groups of men, to the extreme fragility displayed by politicians in the face of a handful of incidents in which they had been subjected to token personal violence by militant women. MacDonald himself, in fact, had suffered no more than verbal confrontation and harassment. He had evidently tried, at a recent meeting with Catherine, to explain to her how deeply offensive this was to a chivalrous man.[37] Catherine wrote:

You said the other day that you did not think a woman could realize what effect militant methods have on men. I am not sure. Any kind of violence always has a brutalizing effect both on those who employ it and on those ag[ain]st whom it is employed. On the few occasions when I have met with personal violence (from hostile groups in a crowd) I have been astounded – and shocked! – at the effect it had on me. It aroused a fierce desire to retaliate by violence – a desire to hit and *hurt* – which I had never felt before, or suspected that I could feel. It also arouses a feeling of dogged obstinacy, a kind of sulky determination to resist whatever it is that the people who use violence may want one to do, quite irrespective of consideration whether it is a good or a bad thing to do.

It seems to me that militancy has very much this effect on men – and it is not an effect which one is proud of in the light of after-reflection.

Catherine, who was doing her best at this time to recruit "some man big enough to come out and *lead* public opinion" (be he Liberal or be he Labour) went on: "I believe if someone took a really strong line at this moment and said publicly and constantly that those who believe in the prin[ciple] of w.s. ought to be ashamed of letting the actions of a small band of fanatics [out?]weigh all the patient hard work being done by the thousands of women who are advocating the reform by reasonable methods – I believe even now that man would find that he quickly had a strong body of public opinion behind him, and the support of all fair-minded people. Those persons who say that nothing can be done till militancy stops are tacitly admitting that force counts for more than reason – the very proposition of the militants themselves."[38]

Despite the rough incidents, and although participants took care in their reports to stress the seriousness of purpose of the marchers, there can be no doubt that most of the pilgrims were having a good time, a time of adventure, laughter, and companionship, a time of renewal and inspiration, and a time to remember and talk about.

Catherine followed the march with eager interest, and was active on the committee organizing the final demonstration, but was too busy to be actually with the marchers for much of the time. She joined those from the northwest when they reached Oxford, and went to the meetings held there on 19 July.[39] Probably she walked with the pilgrims part of the way from Oxford (one report refers to her as having been "on the road"), but she may have had to be back in London for a meeting at the House of Commons on 22 July. On the evening before the London demonstration, Caroline, Catherine, and Hal Marshall took to dinner the tired but triumphant Gladys Duffield, who had achieved her goal, walking the whole distance from Keswick.[40] The next day Catherine was with the pilgrims again for the final stage, when the women came from four assembly points in different parts of London and made their way to Hyde Park, where Catherine took her place on one of the platforms. The *Nation* published Ethel Snowden's report:

Bright banners unfolded, and several bands played lively music as the marchers started on their way. The President, Mrs. Henry Fawcett, LL.D.

marched alone at the head of the Trafalgar Square contingent, her erect, tense, little body, and face full of the light of joy and triumph, giving no sign that it is fifty years since she made her first suffrage speech! Behind her, under the International Banner, walked Mrs. Chapman Catt. ...

On they marched, these women, as they had marched many times before, to show their faith; but there was a difference. Instead of making rude and personal comments, or, at the best, maintaining a cold silence, the welcoming crowd along the streets turned as the procession passed, and walked with it to the Park. The police had no trouble. Sympathy only was in the air. ...

There were nineteen platforms in the Park [one for each of the NU federations]. What other living cause could command from its own ranks a sufficient number of speakers of real eloquence and passion to fill nineteen platforms? ...

The demonstration of 100,000 people was a glorious sight to the weary marchers. Still finer was the way in which the crowds listened. And when the bugle sounded and the resolution was put, at every one of the platforms there shot up a forest of hands, whilst the number of those against was less than twenty in all. ... let politicians and Cabinet Ministers read and be wise in time: "That this meeting demands a *Government* measure for the enfranchisement of women".[41]

Catherine reported that at the platform she had chaired there were about two thousand in the audience, very attentive and quite responsive, thinning out only when they went to hear Mrs Fawcett speak at another platform, and collecting again at the end.[42]

The word "pilgrimage" was well chosen to catch the sense of the 1913 demonstration. The organizers were in little doubt that the main objectives had been achieved. Internally, it had touched the lives of a vast number of the NU's own members (whether as pilgrims or support), had given them the lift needed to carry on the work, and had drawn in many new people. It had provided the sense of adventure which had been so attractive in the WSPU's challenge to authority, but without the violence now inseparably linked to militancy, except in so far as the pilgrims were themselves the targets of "ugly incidents."[43] A sense of comradeship hard to find in committee rooms had been developed on the road. In comparison to these benefits, the fact that over £8,000 had been raised for the cause was little more than icing on the cake, although the NU had so much work on hand that it could use every penny it received.

As for the impact on the general public, there was less fanfare and less flamboyance about the pilgrimage than about previous suffrage marches in London (although some panache was added by the presence of two aviators who played a role in the final demonstrations), but it was clearly a serious and demanding enterprise, and was received with respect. Even the sheer logistics of the plan were impressive. More important, Catherine had told MacDonald early in July that "our pilgrimage throughout the country is doing much to counteract the effects of militancy," and at its conclusion Katherine Harley wrote: "The National Union has in a very practical way dissociated itself from militant methods, and it will be henceforth useless for the antisuffragists to go about the country telling the people that all suffragists are tarred with the same brush."[44] At this juncture, nothing could have been much more valuable than an increase in public awareness of the size and nature of the nonmilitant movement.

The question whether to make direct political use of the pilgrimage had been much discussed by the NU committees and at the provincial council on 23 May, with some expressing the view that it should culminate in deputations and the appearance on the Hyde Park platforms of various party politicians.[45] The leader writer of the *New Statesman* also regretted (a little prematurely, as it turned out) that there was not "a more pointed finale. ... a deputation to the Prime Minister and the Home Secretary."[46] Catherine seems to have been among those who opposed making it into an overtly political event while it was in progress, presumably believing that this might tend to raise issues that were divisive, and that its prime function was to provide a simple affirmation of the will of women and of public support. Whatever the reason for the decision, it proved to be a wise one. Once the pilgrimage had made its impact, political use could be and was made of it, and Catherine began to make arrangements with party leaders a day or two before the pilgrims reached London.[47] Within a couple of weeks of the end of the demonstration, the NU officers had met, not only with McKenna but with the suffragist ministers, with Bonar Law (the Unionist leader in the House of Commons), and with Asquith himself; Redmond (the Irish Nationalist leader), however, refused, and despite the urging of Lord Robert Cecil, so did Lord Lansdowne, a leading Conservative opponent in the Lords.[48]

One can only speculate, but it seems likely that if Asquith had perceived the women as converging on him from all corners of Britain to demand an audience, he would have refused to have anything to do with them; he had not received a women's suffrage deputation at any time since well before the Reform Bill fiasco. As it was, Catherine was able to announce within a few days that a deputation to the prime minister had been arranged,[49] and she went with eleven others to meet with him on 8 August. She arranged the speakers for this deputation, and decided to put Margaret Robertson on first. Margaret was delighted, and wrote back that she was preparing what she would say: "in fact I am much excited about it for I seem to see an opportunity, if *only* I can do what's in my mind, of touching him in a vulnerable part – making him see himself in the eyes of the working man as a secret supporter of anti-democratic lords and dukes – I shall prepare with extreme care and hope it will come off."[50]

Margaret Robertson's was a perceptive reading of Asquith's psychology. At the outset he readily admitted that it was only the pilgrimage, and the fresh evidence of support which it had brought, that had induced him to see them. Margaret reported on her now very extensive experience of meeting with workers throughout the country, and of the extent not only of sympathy for but of real understanding of the cause which she found; she juxtaposed this with a reference to a newspaper report that claimed that Lord Rothschild had secretly donated £3,000 to the NLOWS, and that much of the antis' funding came from similar wealthy sources. "Working men," she claimed, "were inclined to regard the opposition to Women's Suffrage as a Conservative and Liberal Plutocracy against Democracy." The time when working men did not want their wives to have the vote was past, she said, and now the refusal of the franchise was seen by trade unionists as a move of capitalists anxious to keep women's labour cheap. Asquith was clearly impressed, interrupting once or twice to comment or ask a question.[51] He said (and this was surely an advance) that he was "convinced that if a majority of women and of the electors are in favour of any reform, that reform must be granted," but he resisted any concrete suggestions, and showed no signs that his own opinion was changing. He was defensive on the subject of the failed Reform Bill, claiming mendaciously: "no one was more disappointed than I at the Speaker's ruling," and adding rather smugly, "It is, however, now clear that no Franchise Bill for men could be amended so as to include the women," at which Margaret Robertson broke in sharply, "The Speaker did not say that." The NU had studied the question, and a part of the exchange that followed, involving Catherine, is worth quoting as it appeared in the *Common Cause*, which had been unable to resist a small editorial interpolation (in the form of the word "doubtfully"), but may well be otherwise more exact than the official transcript. Catherine, who questioned some parts of the latter, was remarkable for her ability to take notes almost as rapidly and completely as a shorthand writer, while continuing to take part in the discussion:[52] the *Common Cause* version may have been based on her notes of the most memorable passages:

Miss Marshall: Would it not have been all right if the title of the Bill had been (as in 1867 and 1884) "Representation of the People Bill" instead of (as in 1913) "Franchise and Registration Bill"?

Mr. Asquith: How do you suggest that that would affect the difficulty?

Mrs. Swanwick: Well, women are people, aren't they?

Mr. Asquith (doubtfully): I suppose so. At least it is another very ingenious suggestion, and deserves consideration.

Kathleen Courtney pointed out with some acerbity that these suggestions would have been made when the bill was being drawn up, had he not refused to meet with them at that time.[53]

Millicent Fawcett later reported, with characteristic low-key wit, that "We noted ... in his attitude and language a notable improvement; we felt that his education in the principles of representative government was progressing."[54] The *Nation*'s leader writer also thought it clear "from the temper of his remarks that the Prime Minister was himself considerably impressed by the force of the exhibition [the pilgrimage]."[55] The NU officers were pleased with the deputation. They had had no unrealistic expectations, but, while Asquith had again revealed himself as being susceptible to no arguments as to the rightness of the cause, he had shown a decided interest in what they could tell him of the state of public opinion, and particularly working-class opinion. With no certainty of any agreement with the Labour party for the next election, Asquith had reason to take seriously the unfavourable image of the government which the NU was reporting.

The NU deputation, which received good press coverage, was unquestionably at least as significant a hint of possible movement on Asquith's part as his meeting with a deputation from Sylvia Pankhurst's East London Federation (ELF) nearly a year later (20 June 1914), which some historians have viewed as the first sign that he might see the writing on the wall.[56] The NU's reserved optimism received confirmation when Catherine had "a most cheering letter from Lord Lytton," who had talked with Asquith shortly after the deputation;[57] Margaret Robertson commented, "It's a real satisfaction to know that one's feeling that Asquith was moving was not a delusion," and made plans to reinforce the impression that had been made.[58]

If the NU leaders got more from Asquith than they had dared to hope for, they did much less well than they expected with their supposed allies, the suffragist ministers, with whom they met on the same day. Indeed, this meeting came off the rails badly, and Catherine and the whole NU deputation came away furious at the treatment they had received. Catherine had prepared carefully for the meeting, though perhaps in less detail than for the meeting with Asquith; after all, it was expected to have some of the character of a meeting with fellow women's suffragists. C.P. Scott, believing the chancellor to be "in a very friendly disposition towards the women," had encouraged her to ask Lloyd George both for his good offices in arranging for the deputation, and for an informal meeting with him first;[59] in fact Lloyd George invited her to breakfast on 30 July, and Margaret Robertson and Catherine had also met him over tea on 6 August.

The first of these two preliminary occasions seems to have been an amicable one, although Catherine tackled Lloyd George on what he was saying publicly about militancy, particularly in a recent article in *Nash's* magazine, in which he enlarged on the "organized lunacy" of the militants and failed to mention the constitutionalists; worse still, he had concluded that there would be no enfranchisement for women as long as militancy continued.[60] Catherine once more pointed out that this line of argument was "a tacit admission that force counts for more than reason (the very proposition of the militants themselves)";[61] she followed up by sending him quotations from Lord Morley's speech on introducing Indian Reform proposals in the House of Lords, and Morley's comment, in his *Life of Gladstone*, that "No reformer is fit for his task who suffers himself to be frightened off by the excesses of an extreme wing."[62] She also sent a longer extract from Lord Macaulay's speech in the House of Commons during the debate on the 1832 Reform Bill, which neatly described the attitude the NU found so frustrating: "If the people are turbulent, they are unfit for liberty – if they are quiet they do not want liberty. ... Reformers are compelled to legislate in times of excitement, because bigots will not legislate in times of tranquillity," or, in Catherine's words, "Them as asks shan't have. Them as don't ask don't want."[63]

The second preparatory occasion had gone less smoothly; over tea Margaret Robertson and Catherine "waxed rather pugnacious," as Catherine admitted. What Catherine hoped for was an acknowledgment that the facilities offered to the Dickinson bill did not constitute any fulfilment of Asquith's pledge, and that plans must be made for a next step. But when Lloyd George coolly claimed that indeed "Mr. Asquith had discharged his debt," the women's temperature rose.[64] Catherine wrote a reasonably conciliatory letter the same evening, once more reviewing the series of events of the past three years, and spelling out what she would most like to see emerge from the formal deputation, that is, "some definite limit to the time we shall have to wait."[65]

Unlike the meeting with the prime minister, the deputation to the chancellor of the Exchequer and the other suffragist ministers (as also the meeting of Millicent Fawcett and Eleanor Rathbone with Bonar Law) was private, and no report was published. However, a transcript of the encounter with the ministers, purportedly verbatim, was made and preserved among Lloyd George's papers.[66] This "official" transcript does not convey the heat that was generated, but it does show that from the outset the meeting got off on the wrong foot. In the first place, several of the ministers who had been expected to be present, including Sir Edward Grey, were not there (the ministers present, in addition to Lloyd George, Sir John Simon, and Acland, were Augustine Birrell, Thomas McKinnon Wood, and Thomas MacNamara, secretaries for Ireland, for Scotland, and to the Admiralty). Worse, within a few minutes Mrs Fawcett and Lloyd George were trading quotations and misquotations from various speeches and statements made by Asquith, an exchange that put the ministers on the defensive on the prime minister's behalf, and was productive of nothing but bad feeling.

Moving to the NU's other major concern, Mrs Fawcett tried to address the question of the response to militancy, but was subjected to a number of interruptions from Lloyd George and Birrell, who were smarting from experiences at the hands of the WSPU. Some impression comes through the transcript that Fawcett, imperturbable in almost all situations (including dead rats thrown at her during the pilgrimage) but used to commanding the courtesy of politicians, did indeed become somewhat rattled, and hectored the ministers on how they should learn to deal with hecklers, even suggesting that they could take a lesson from some of the Labour politicians "who have most magnificent voices, and ... go on roaring and drown all these little shrill cries that arise."

Mrs Fawcett was followed by Maude Royden, whose theme was the success of the pilgrimage in firmly establishing in the minds of the public the difference between militants and constitutionalists, and the strength of support for the latter. Margaret Robertson spoke much as she had spoken to the prime minister earlier in the day, and Mrs Rackham reminded the ministers of the continuing hope among Liberal women that the cause would be taken up by the Liberal party. Then it was the turn of the cabinet members to have their say. Birrell went first, giving a long rambling speech, full of contradictions, doubt concerning the evidence brought by the deputation, and complaints about militancy, and the hardships attendant on defending women's suffrage. Simon made two points, both very welcome to his NU hearers: he spoke of the need for suffragist ministers to stand up and be counted during the coming campaign; and he admitted that, no matter how good intentions had been, the result of the failure of the Reform Bill had been that "expectations have not been realised."

The burden of Dr Macnamara's remarks, which he (and to a lesser extent McKinnon Wood) reiterated in further discussion, was that he simply did not believe what Margaret Robertson had said about the extent of support among working men, that he did not find women's suffrage well received by his constituents, and that his advice to the NU was to get busy and do more. The nastiest blow was dealt by Lloyd George himself, who fully endorsed Macnamara's view, belittled Robertson's work, putting the support she received down to skilled speaking, "but that is not what I call public opinion," and took the opportunity, quite inconsistently, to boost his own achievement in carrying the Insurance Act against public opinion because of his deep belief in it. He did, however, consider, like Simon, that there had as yet been no equivalent for what the Reform Bill would have given. Both Birrell and Lloyd George spoke of their prior commitment to other pressing issues – Birrell to Irish Home Rule, and Lloyd George to Welsh Church Disestablishment[67] – but when Catherine asked if, when these were settled, women's suffrage would have the next claim on them, Lloyd George said it would not, only that the position would be different then.

Catherine, who had listened in silence throughout the meeting until the very last, finally pressed a point now increasingly central to her work, suggesting that "apart from making Women's Suffrage speeches ... what would be more valuable still ... would be if you would help us to make people realise it as part of the democratic reform." She also asked the ministers, "who by your own confession are not very successful in creating enthusiasm for Women's Suffrage," to consider inviting women to speak on their platforms "because certainly our speakers are much more successful," and gained Lloyd George's assurance that he at least would do so. But the meeting did not end without one last little interchange in which the women suggested Lloyd George did little to show public commitment to suffrage, even in his own constituency, and he again threw the actions of the militants in their faces.[68] If Lloyd George's considered judgment – given some weeks later – was that "the suffragist Pilgrimage was one of the cleverest political moves of recent times,"[69] he was far from giving the deputation the satisfaction of hearing that opinion, or believing it had affected him favourably.

When she wrote to Francis Acland a couple of weeks later, from the peace of the Lake District, Catherine's frustration and anger at the way the meeting had gone were still with her; fortunately Acland was not their target. She told him how glad she had been to get the letter he had written within a few days of the meeting: "It had," she said, "made me feel on better terms with the world than I had done since that hateful Friday afternoon." She went on, "I said to the other members of our deputation that I was quite sure you must be feeling as sick as we were. Yes, it *was* a sorry show. With regard to the letter we sent to you all afterwards, we ought to have added a definitions clause, explaining that 'for the purposes of this Act' the expression 'Gentlemen' applies to Sir J. Simon and Mr. Acland, and the rest of the letter applies to the other ministers present. For heavens sake don't repeat that. ... Seriously, I am *very* glad you feel as you do about that interview, because I hope Sir Edward Grey will hear your version of it as well as Mr. Ll. George's."[70] The "quite diff[erent] att[itude] from [the] previous week"[71] shown by Lloyd George on this occasion had been a particular shock to Catherine.

She wrote to thank Sir John Simon for his part in arranging the deputation, and was quite open with him also, saying: "We came away from the interview very sick at heart. I think we all felt that we preferred Mr. Asquith's attitude, and even Mr. McKenna's, to that of any one of you except yourself and Mr. Acland. They at any rate met us quite fairly and frankly according to their lights. I wonder whether, listening to Mr. Birrell's and Dr. Macnamara's speeches, you realised how militants are made?"[72]

Catherine's letter is worth quoting further for the light it sheds on the process of alienation from the Liberal party being experienced by Catherine and a number of other Liberal women. After bitterly comparing the dedication and sacrifice of the women in their work for suffrage with the indifference and minimal effort invested by the Liberal suffragists in the House of Commons "who profess to believe in the cause quite as much as we do, are prepared to 'mention it in their speeches on suitable occasions' – and that is all," she commented on the greater zeal shown by the antis in the House, citing a donation of £1,000 made "to the Anti-Suffrage funds" by Lewis Harcourt. "That," she wrote, "is what fosters the 'Anti-man' spirit which is such a regrettable feature of the mil[itant] mov[emen]t. It would not exist if men took their share of the work." She went on:

The failure of a Liberal Government to recognise the biggest movement for political liberty of its day is very bitter to those of us who are Liberals. I grew up burning with zeal for the great principles of Liberalism, and as soon as

I left school I started working for the Liberal Party almost as hard as I am working for w.s. now. It has been the greatest disillusionment of my life to find how little these principles really count with the majority of Liberal men. They seem to regard them as catchwords to pad a leaflet or adorn a peroration, not as vital principles to be applied in their dealings with other human beings. ... so long as you feel that the Prime Minister's attitude makes it impossible for you to bring any pressure to bear on your party from within. ... a great deal of our work fails to bear all the fruit it might, so far as the Liberal party is concerned.[73]

Catherine also wrote to Lloyd George, thanking him for what she felt she could, but adding, "I won't say anything about the rest of our interview on Friday, except that I came to the conclusion that I preferred not only Oliver Cromwell, but Mr. Asquith, and even Mr. McKenna, to any one of you, except Sir John Simon and Mr. Acland."[74] After she received a reply she described as "pained,"[75] in which Lloyd George had called her "cantankerous,"[76] she wrote again, conceding that unlike the other cabinet ministers, he at least had at times put himself on the line for suffrage, and had been attacked by the militants for his pains. But she was determined to get through to him:

When you are working night and day for a cause, giving up all the things you care about most in life for the sake of it (as hundreds of women are doing for Women's suffrage today), it *is* disappointing when those who alone have the power to make your work bear fruit in an Act of Parliament say, in effect: 'Yes, you are good little girls; we quite approve of the way in which you are working and the object you are working for, and our advice to you is to go on pegging away. Don't get tired, and don't get cross. Some day, when we have settled all our own business, we will bring in a Bill to give you what you want – only of course we can't do anything so long as some of you are naughty and throw stones'. When we know that it is just that attitude which makes the naughty ones throw stones we feel that you are asking us to work in a vicious circle.

I often wish you were an unenfranchised woman instead of being Chancellor of the Exchequer! With what fire you would lead the woman's movement, and insist that no legislation was more important than the right of those whom it concerned to have a say in it.[77]

Lloyd George again replied promptly to this, her second letter in as many days; unfortunately, and inexplicably, none of his letters remain among her papers, though some of the content can be inferred from her replies. She wrote again on 29 August. Once more, her letter contains a great deal of interest, and reveals something of the extent of Catherine's political activities at the time:

I have left your letter of August 14th unanswered, not out of rudeness, but because I did not want to disturb the peace of your first fortnight's holiday. There are 50 things I want to say in answer to it, but I will only say one – no, I won't even say that, lest you should think me cantankerouser than ever, and I do not want to lose what I value very much – your permission to come and see you again next time that there is an important matter in which I want to ask for your help or advice. Believe me, I am really grateful for that. Since I took over the Parliamentary work of the N.U.W.S.S. last year I have felt it a very great drawback that we have not been more closely in touch with the friends of our cause in the Government. With the exception of Mr. Acland they have shown no desire to know how the movement was progressing in the country, what new developments we were planning, or what results had already been achieved. This has been a great disappointment to me, because it was from the Liberal Suffragists that I expected to get most help, being a Liberal myself, by nature and upbringing and tradition. ...

Instead of finding help where I had most hopefully looked for it, in the Liberal party, it was the Suffragists in the Conservative and Labour parties who held out friendly hands. I see the chief of them constantly, sometimes two or three times a week when there are any important plans on hand. Their advice is often very helpful, and I think they find it useful to keep the work they are doing in the House of Commons in close touch with the work we are doing in the constituencies.

Doubtless Catherine was here playing one party off against another, and not artlessly, but she did it with good reason; she went on to describe what must have been one of the NU's most bitter frustrations with the attitude of the so-called suffragists among the ministers, and one which she rightly felt called into question the extent of their commitment:

Sir Edward Grey said a short time ago: "Why does not the National Union hold meetings and get Miss Royden to speak at them?"; and you suggested that we should set other people to do the same kind of work that Miss Robertson is doing among the working classes. Both these suggestions showed how completely out of touch you were with what is actually happening, because for the last 3 years Miss Royden has been addressing large meetings all over the country on an average 5 days a week, and 14 of our best organizers and speakers are specialised for the kind of work Miss Robertson is doing, concentrating on the industrial districts, with very striking results.[78]

Of course I know it is much more difficult for members of the Government to spare time to consider any question which is not on the Government programme, and it is unfortunate for us that our two best friends in the Cabinet – you and Sir Edward Grey – are even busier than most of your colleagues. I never expected that you yourselves would be directly accessible, and I do think it was very good of you to let me come and see you before our deputation the other day. Next year, when the Home Rule and Welsh Disestablishment Bills are safely through – when the situation will, as you said, be "different" – I will ask if I may come again. Till then I understand that I am "not to ask such direct questions", so I had better keep away! But do persuade some of your less busy colleagues that if they mean business about Women's Suffrage they really ought to keep in touch with the work that is being done by the N.U.W.S.S.

Catherine referred supportively (and diplomatically) to Lloyd George's current "Land Campaign," saying that it had been the land question and free trade which had first interested her in politics, and asking him if he would send her "on a post-card the names of any specially good recent books on the Land question." At the end of her letter, she reverted to the suffrage issue and to the frustration of being told to go back "and do all the work of these last few years over again – and I suppose raise another £60,000 in 2 years – until the Government is ready to give us another chance, which will not be before the next election, and perhaps not then – unless you are going to do what I have always hoped you meant to do, start a really effective demand for Adult Suffrage (which there has never been yet) at the same time as your Land campaign. It would be a grand programme on which to go to the country."[79]

Was Catherine's suggestion totally implausible? Lloyd George was above all else politically ambitious and an opportunist. In the existing situation, it was in his interest to downplay the differences between himself and Asquith; should it ever come to the point where these differences could be turned to his advantage (as was to happen, in an unpredicted context, during the war) Lloyd George could be counted on to make the most of them. The extension of the franchise, raised by Asquith, and now dropped, was a useful card to have up his sleeve. The speaker's ruling, right or wrong, had rendered it virtually impossible to introduce a measure significantly widening the male franchise without including the vote for some women. Lloyd George believed in a wider male representation, and even (other things being equal) in votes for women. At present it was convenient to use the militants as an excuse to do nothing; when the time came to open up the question, as come it must, it would become useful to acknowledge and give a higher profile to the work of the nonmilitants. And so Lloyd George was as willing to be cultivated by Catherine as she was to cultivate him. There is some evidence that he also enjoyed her frankness,[80] even as he tried to keep her questioning under control. Catherine, I think, was free of flirtatiousness in the ordinary sense;[81] but she had a gift for spontaneously varying her approach to suit the person she was dealing with, and her approach to Lloyd George was *sui generis*; she did not deal with anyone else in quite this way. She was to enjoy a measure of his confidence for many years.

Underlying all talk of adult (or of manhood) suffrage, but seldom openly discussed (as it had been in the case of the Conciliation Bills), was the question of which party would gain most were it enacted. After the initiation in the 1870s of a conscious Liberal policy of encouraging and enabling labour representation, which had had some success in the mining areas, from which had come a number of "Lib-Lab" MPs, the Liberal party had come to view the working class as a potential source of greatly increased support, but had not perhaps nursed this support with the care needed. The emergence of Labour as a separate party had changed the configuration, and had tied the question of the wider franchise into the complex issue of relations between the Liberal and Labour parties. As we have seen, those who recognized that the Labour party was moving towards standing on its own feet had reason to be leery of introducing a vast mass of new voters, mainly from the working class. When the Lib-Lab miners' representatives moved over on to the Labour benches in 1909, as a result of the affiliation of the Miners' Federation, alarm bells must surely have rung in some heads. The Liberal whips and agents had assessed "the likely effects of adult suffrage" in 1911, concluding that Labour would benefit in Yorkshire, North England, and West Scotland;[82] this was a plus in terms of a combined radical front against the Unionists, but had a different aspect if Labour were to emerge as a rival to the Liberal party.

This was not the kind of threat that could be talked about; publicly, the attitude of the Liberal party had to be that it was the party for the working man (if not for the working woman), which was truly the view of those Liberals who confidently hoped for a continuance of cordial relations between the two parties, or indeed hoped for a merger between the two; these believed that the wider franchise could only benefit them. In a letter to Catherine immediately after the defeat of the Dickinson bill in May 1913, Eleanor Acland had strongly criticized the new "anti-government" policy, and had given an interesting analysis of the Liberal party as she saw it: "As to your policy – I can only beg you to reconsider it. Surely with 78 Liberal antis there is room for your Election Fighting Fund without attacking the faithful 160. We *must* have a party Bill. Well then we must have a Bill of a party *strong* enough to carry it. That party will be a Radical-Labour one. So are you wise to set the Radicals (and the suffragist Liberals are the Radical-est of the Libs) and Labour people by the ears? The cleavage in the Liberal party is becoming clearer and in the main it's a double cleavage, running on same lines – Whig-antis versus Radical-suffragists."[83]

Francis Acland had also shown concern about the nature of the developing relationship between the NU and the Labour party. As a minister, he was not in a position to be as frank about divisions among the Liberals as his wife was, but at a meeting with Catherine, "he talked a great deal about ... our relations with the Lab. Party," and "[t]ried to draw me as to extent of help we were giving them. [He m]ade wild assumptions, which I neither agreed to nor contradicted." The issue of working-class support came up; Catherine reported that "He was impressed when I told him of the keenness among the [illegible] Lab. men, the Scotch miners, Blackburn etc. (He had begun by saying no working men came to his meetings. I assured him they came to ours!)."[84]

The refusal of the women's suffragists to throw in their lot with the Liberal party has at times been criticized, usually with the aim of exonerating the Liberal leadership for their failure to adopt this so-liberal cause.[85] But all the evidence is that the NU was and remained ready and waiting at least until late summer of 1913; and even the opposition to Liberal candidates was directed towards bringing the Liberal party to a better frame of mind as much as towards getting it out of office. However, we have seen that there was a growing group in the NU executive whose own political allegiance was to the Labour party, and who therefore viewed the EFF alliance as a satisfying way to go as well as strategically convenient. Catherine, it seems, despite her dedication to the EFF policy, clung as long as she could to a hope that the Liberal party would indeed come through, and that the Radicals, together with their Labour allies, would triumph in the way suggested by Eleanor Acland, and she worked to have this reflected in NU policy. But such a hope must depend on real commitment on the part of those ministers who had identified themselves as suffragist, and the disastrous delegation of 8 August amply demonstrated that, in Eleanor Acland's category of "Radical-suffragist," even if "Radical" were writ large, "suffragist" was still written extremely small. Eleanor had, of course, omitted to say how the "Whig-antis" were to be removed from positions of power within the

Liberal party. Nor does her analysis contain any mention of the ideological and practical problem of reconciling Liberal capitalism with the socialism of the more radical elements of the Labour party.

Catherine told Sir Edward Grey that the NU had "ceased to hope for anything from [the] Liberal Party." She herself, she said, had "always believed [the] Liberals did mean to do something," and now she was discredited. In the coming general election the NU was committed to supporting the Labour party, " – but how? To damage Liberals or avoid damaging them? I cannot obstruct [in the NU council] any longer."[86] Disillusion with the Liberal party, together with the discovery of more and more that was congenial in the Labour party, was preparing Catherine to move left, taking much of her liberal idealism with her.

The corner of Barton Street, Westminster. In the background is the Victoria Tower, where ballot papers are stored for a year and a day following a general election.

12 Life in London and an Interlude in Keswick: Summer 1913

Late in August 1913, as soon as the deputations which followed the pilgrimage were over, and the immediate follow-up completed, Catherine packed up her goods (characteristically leaving boxes and parcels to be sent on after her)[1] and retreated to Keswick for the extended break she had promised herself and her parents she would take. She did not go back to London until January, except for a brief visit in December.[2] In this chapter we shall take a look at some of the more personal factors affecting the life of a political woman in that period, and follow with an exploration of Catherine's general analysis of the political situation at this crucial time. Her correspondence during these months with leading figures in the Liberal and Unionist parties, and her continuing involvement in the politics of labour, merit separate treatment.

Alice Clark, who had been coopted on to the NU executive in June (proposed by Catherine and Kathleen Courtney), and who was also on the EFF committee,[3] took Catherine's place in the London political work while she was away. Catherine knew Alice well, having lived at 1 Barton Street with her throughout the summer. When Mary Sheepshanks left for her European speaking tour in March 1913, she planned to take a year's leave of absence from the principalship of Morley College, and had let the house to Alice Clark;[4] Catherine and at least one other woman were there as tenants of Alice's.

Mary Sheepshanks's new position, however, brought her back to London earlier than she had originally expected, to open the IWSA headquarters in London. Perhaps unwisely, she moved back into

1 Barton Street, where she did not find things at all to her liking. Mary had had a harder life than the other women; her independence had been dearly bought. The difference was not one of age. Kathryn Oliver was a young student from Morley College, and we do not know the age of Miss Upton, who seems also to have had a room at some time, and who proved quite uncongenial to Mary Sheepshanks.[5] But Alice was almost forty (just two years younger than Mary herself), and Catherine was thirty-three; yet the nature of the tensions suggests that there was still an element of excitement among these women in living away from home, as well as a sense of absolute precedence to be given to the cause for which they worked. They were caught up in a world where they were living the kind of busy, irregular life outside the home that some middle-class political men lived, but they did not have the same financial resources, and they were expected to show a domestic responsibility not generally required of bachelors or shown by married men. For emotional and to some extent material support they relied on other women as busy as themselves, not on any "Angel in the House."

As for Catherine, she was unpunctual for meals in a way she never would have been for appointments with politicians; she was also a lifetime "night owl." In addition, she was a vegetarian by inclination, and only agreed to eat meat at this period in order "to save trouble," and she complained that not enough fruit was provided.[6] More significantly, she surely found it convenient for her work – as well as temperamentally congenial – to live by a parliamentary clock; the House of Commons sat from 2:45 p.m. to 11:30 p.m. These were hard hours for servants to work around, and equally so for a household head who, like Mary Sheepshanks, worked herself, but to quite a different clock.

Alice Clark was in charge of the housekeeping, and, in Mary Sheepshanks's view, was primarily responsible for the problems that arose. This may have been the first time that she had undertaken to run a household, but she certainly had abundant ability and unusual business experience. Of well-to-do Liberal Quaker parentage, she is (ironically) on record as having taken a short course in housewifery before apprenticing in her family's famous shoemaking business in Somerset, where she had continued in management, despite recurrent ill health. Interrupting her successful and serious career with Clark's, she enrolled as a student at the London School of Economics in 1912, where she was much influenced by Fabian socialism. In 1913 she won a scholarship donated by Charlotte Shaw (wife of George Bernard Shaw), and began the research which would lead to a groundbreaking work in women's history, *Working Life of Women in the Seventeenth Century.*[7] She must have had her hands full, with her initiation into the NU's political work, her studies, and the running of the household. The last evidently came in a poor third, but it is tempting to suggest that there may also have been some ideological bases for what was perceived by Mary Sheepshanks as mere discomfort and disorder. A great admirer of the preindustrial household economy in which women of various economic levels worked productively together in home and business, Alice Clark did not disapprove of domestic servants, but may have been inclined to strive for an attitudinal equality that disturbed the social order at 1 Barton Street without making the servants' tasks any lighter. Other members of the household may also have been experimenting with domestic democracy. Remembering the formality with which Catherine and her colleagues had earlier approached the use of each other's first names, it is startling to find Kathryn Oliver and the maid on a mutual first-name basis, though this may have resulted from Kathryn's youth as much as from her declared aversion to "slave souls" – that is to servants who supported the Tories.[8] We may admire these attempts of the Barton Street dwellers to practise what they preached, if that is what they were trying to do; Mary Sheepshanks should not necessarily be condemned for finding them merely disruptive, and we may wonder what was the considered judgment of the maid, "Rose," who lost her job.

Poor Mary Sheepshanks! She prided herself on her well-run and restful household, and on the provision of good meals; at the same time, she needed tenants and she liked the idea of making a home for those who were working in the same cause. But in the summer of 1913 she found the situation so intolerable that she in fact moved out from Barton Street again, taking a house in Rutland Gardens with Kathryn Oliver for a short time, and then renting an attractive house on Cheyne Walk in Chelsea until Alice Clark's lease was up, where she prepared a peaceful, well-ordered haven for an extended visit from Rosika Schwimmer, the Hungarian feminist, whom she had known and liked for a number of years. Alice, on holiday in August, wrote to Catherine after Mary's departure: "Isn't it a curious sort of tangle? I wish Mary had been willing to talk things over, but it is possible that no arrangement would have been really comfortable for us."[9]

By the time Catherine asked for rooms again the following year, Mary was ready to write frankly about her own needs in her own house, and about the problems of the previous two summers. Her letter sheds light on the difficulties of the situation, and we can also read between the lines of a vibrant group of women with changing lifestyles and priorities:

I must ... make an *absolute condition* about punctuality at dinner, and if you really are willing to arrange your evening work accordingly all will be well. After two previous attempts I had come to the conclusion that it was impossible. ... I am definitely unwilling to have the trouble of housekeeping and have the acute discomfort of the last year at Barton Street.

There is one other difficulty, or perhaps two. I have done no entertaining at all since I took up this work, I have no time for the housekeeping involved, and I am too tired at night; what little I do, I do at the Club. You spoke of lunch parties and I feel I couldn't manage them often! and similarly about the evening. Now that I get up at 7 and breakfast at 8 I must go to bed early, and it would be disturbing if there were people in the rooms above till a late hour. This is my personal weakness and idiosyncracy not a principle like punctuality, which I think essential to a decent orderly household, and I am genuinely apologetic for wanting the house quiet, but I know that I do!

I don't know whether that would bother you, you spoke of having visitors late? would it be often, how late would they stay, and would the dining room do? I don't of course want to make a hard and fast bargain about that, but to tell you how things stand and leave it to you. If you find it too restricting and old maidish, as you would be justified in doing, I shall understand. But I have lived so quietly and comfortably this winter and I don't feel I could face the old rackety irregular hours nor constant coming and going. My hours are now just the reverse of yours and of what mine used to be, and early hours are indispensable. I thought over carefully what you told me about the general discomfort and bad food last summer, but it really seems to me *entirely* Alice's fault. It is silly for servants to give better food than is ordered or required; they satisfied their mistress and that is all one can expect. They both told me that meals had been quite hopelessly irregular, and that there was a very great deal of entertaining, and from all I heard and the utter indifference and neglect by Alice as regards all the amenities of a home, I am only surprised it was no worse, but it seems to have become a regular "suffragists' home"! you can't have things both ways!

I will do my share, and make the servants do theirs *only* if the other members of the household do theirs too. Rose is leaving at once, and as she seems to be hopelessly spoiled I am not sorry. I quite agree it will be best for you to have a breakfast tray. This is all very bald and brutal, and if I had more time I would be more suave! but I think it is best to distinguish between a home and a hotel, I don't get the profits of the latter and I want the comfort of the former. I rather suspect you of coveting the advantages of both! and they refuse to be combined at 1 B.St. If you really feel these conditions will suit you, you need not trouble to reply. I go back in April, and after a few weeks' cleaning and tidying, hope all will be comfortable.[10]

We do not know how Catherine replied to Mary's letter, but she decided to try Barton Street again, so she was probably able to read in it the very real and enduring affection the latter felt towards her, and to see that she had some reason on her side; Catherine also found the "rackety" life less than ideal, much as she contributed to it in her own way.

The whole issue of servants is an uncomfortable one to feminists in the late twentieth century. Appropriately, much has been researched and written about the appalling conditions and exploitation to which many domestic workers were subject; yet the context has to be borne in mind. The freedom of some women to engage in political work, or indeed in any public activity, depended directly on the paid domestic labour of others, rather than, as it does now, on appliances and a plentiful supply of hot water, of easily prepared food, of gas and electricity. In every house coals had to be carried for fires in every room; water often had to be heated on a stove or in a copper; cooking was by coal stove; cleaning was done with broom and scrubbing brush, soap and soda, stoveblack and hearthstone; candles and lamps still provided lighting and another source of dirt in many houses. Gas and electricity were bringing better and cleaner lighting and gas fires brought comfort to some bedrooms (at Cheyne Walk but not at Barton Street).[11]

In hindsight we may believe that living could have been simplified, that it was unnecessary to have a cooked breakfast and several courses to other meals, maid service at lunch and dinner, hot water carried to the bedrooms once or twice every day, a well-dressed parlourmaid to open the front door. Early twentieth-century feminists gave thought to these questions; Maude Royden, for instance, as editor of the *Common Cause*, planned to include articles on "labour saving devices," as well as on "good dressing, with economy of time and money spent on achieving that result."[12] But meanwhile many feminist political leaders felt themselves unable to afford relaxation of commonly accepted middle-class standards, if they were to avoid damning (and damaging) criticism. Mary's mention of "a regular 'suffragists' home'!" shows her sensitivity to this; the reference is to antisuffragist propaganda – and probably to a specific postcard illustration[13] – attributing to suffragists a complete lack of homemaking skills.

Catherine was too single-minded in the cause to which she was devoting her own life to have been a wholly considerate employer, either at home or in the office. Her enthusiasm was inspiring, and throughout her life most of those who worked for her trusted her and regarded her with affectionate loyalty; but even that affection could become the unconscious means to further exploitation. Mabel Crookenden ("Crookie"), Kathleen Courtney's secretary, wrote a frank letter to Catherine about her own situation and that of Mary Mackenzie ("Molly"), who was Catherine's secretary for the political work, and who had had several bouts of ill health:[14]

I hoped to write to you yesterday but it was the first free Sunday I'd had for 6 weeks with the result that I was working hard from 10–30 a.m. to 8 p.m. (with short intervals for food!) cleaning up papers, bills and correspondence. I wanted to say Molly did come away just before 3 and arranged to telephone you instead of writing, and on Sat^y evening we had a long talk about her hours in the office, waiting late "lest she could help you in any way," and she did agree that she must be more careful in future. There is no getting over 2 facts, that she did absolutely over do herself in the autumn of 1912, and that her heart got bad last Xmas when she had to be away for a couple of months; and that on both occasions her work suffered. I think she realises that anyone depending on making a living must consider health – as the supreme asset – before anything else; and also that every time one overworks one has less power of resistance and in the end it counts against one, looking at it purely from the professional point of view. She put it to me quite truely [sic] that when I live in town I hate leaving the office before Kathleen – also that I seldom do – of course it *is* true, but I do sometimes succeed in making myself ask K.D.C. if she will want me any more, and we shall have to make a practice of it to both of you.

The work is intensely interesting, and it's so delightful working with such dears as our officers that one wants to not consider hours and so forth, but I'm sure one ought: and it does make a difference being regularly at the office by 9.30 day after day, though I feel too horrid for words when I *know* how awfully hard the officers work – and in one sense it doesn't matter if they get overdone they can take a holiday at will – I'm sure you will see what I mean – and also will forgive a scratchy note I left on Sat^y.[15]

Catherine, as well as Mabel Crookenden herself, is entitled to some credit for the openness of this letter; it is also somehow reassuring to find these four women, working so closely together, comfortable with each other's first names or the almost equally informal initials (though the letter is addressed to "Dearest Miss Marshall").

None of that exonerates Catherine from the charge of a rather reckless disregard for the limits of other people's strength, and even for their rights. But, after all, she never learnt to husband her own resources. Unfortunately, the letter is undated, and we do not know if it bore fruit. For one reason or another, Molly Mackenzie was not working in the office when Catherine went on holiday in August 1913, but she was back at her desk by November, and seemingly in good spirits, writing a humorous account to Catherine of how badly the members of the executive had behaved at a recent meeting.[16]

Before leaving London, Catherine took a look at her wardrobe, putting some effort into repairing the ravages of the past few busy months and bringing it into shape for the coming pleasures of the late summer season in the Lake District. Every now and then, Catherine's papers shed a sidelight on just what a bother clothes were to look after in those days. Most washing was not done on the premises in her London accommodation, but was sent out weekly to the laundry, an arrangement whose convenience and novelty delighted Rosika Schwimmer.[17] Even everyday dresses were heavy and required a good deal of attention to keep them looking good. Middleclass women did not own as many outfits as they do nowadays, but no gown was a small item to be replaced easily, and there were no wash and wear fabrics, no washing machines or laundromats. Wear and tear and dirt were all problems exacerbated by trailing the hems along dusty and muddy streets and country lanes, which, if free of concentrated gasoline fumes, were shared by a great deal of horsedrawn traffic, making its own impression. True, women of Catherine's class seldom had to do their own washing; nevertheless, to keep one's clothes in good repair was time-consuming and could be expensive. Cottons could be laundered, although not always without risk; silks and woollens needed care, and cleaning was not an advanced science. It was also slower than today (unlike the mail); when Catherine left a batch of things at the cleaners on 24 August 1913, before leaving for her holiday in Keswick, she identified some items which she would like to have sent back by 1 September if possible. The list of what she sent is of some interest: one white silk petticoat, one white silk blouse, and no fewer than twenty-five pairs of gloves, long and short, coloured and white. And then the cleaner made an error and kept the package waiting on the shelf for pick-up for another week or two, before responding to an urgent inquiry from Catherine.[18] In preparation for her time in the north, too, Catherine sent an evening gown, a white gown, a black velveteen gown, and a coat to a dressmaker for repair and refurbishing. She was at first somewhat disappointed in the results, but the dressmaker tried again and later was able to report that steaming and pressing had renewed the velveteen gown, while a new collar had done wonders for the coat.[19]

There were also hats. When the fashion was for outrageous large hats, wide-brimmed and covered with a veritable garden of fruit or flowers, or high, and topped with a towering feather, the NU had to give serious thought to how to manage this millinery at conferences; the final decision was to require the removal of hats, since they made it impossible to see except from the front row, but the request had to be accompanied with a reassurance that special provision would be made for adequate storage space meanwhile.[20] Hats were expensive, and although they too were expected to last, even having a hat freshened up for further use cost good money; Catherine's milliner charged 12 shillings and sixpence in May 1913 for "Trimming hat with own ... feather, with green roses, and putting black hat into shape."[21] But these last sound like London hats, suitable for interviews and delegations to ministers; the Keswick holiday, though it probably still demanded hats, may have been better served by something wide-brimmed, floppy, and light – at least in the fine weather that prevailed that September.

Catherine and her parents had arranged that she was to be in Cumberland for about four months, from September to December 1913. First she would take some time off, and later she was to be free to do some suffrage work, but only in the north. So she would attend the council in Newcastle in November, do constituency work in the northwest, renew contact with the NWF, engage in any by-elections that took place in the region, and write numerous letters. From time to time she also had household responsibilities, freeing Caroline. But for the first few weeks after she first left London this time there was a real sense that she was taking a well-deserved and happily anticipated holiday, rather than going into a reluctant exile or snatching a few distracted days of partial rest.

Shortly after arriving in the Lake District, Catherine included a lighthearted account of her relaxations in a letter to Francis Acland: "I am taking the first real holiday I have had since Mr. Asquith's first promise in 1908. ... But now some of us are at the end of our tether, and absolutely *must* take a holiday this autumn, for the sake of the work still to come. I am enjoying every minute of mine, on the hills, and on and in the lake, with tennis and dancing and music, and nice restful household occupations, and I am beginning to feel quite young and human again, instead of a machine working out one idea day and night. I am off tomorrow with a knapsack to Mardale."[22]

Catherine's walk to Mardale will have taken her through well over twenty kilometres of rugged country, up and down hills and over or around the base of Helvellyn; we do not know whether she went alone or with a companion. She loved this kind of vigorous walking, and found healing and refreshment in the mountains. Many of her holiday occupations, however, though equally strenuous, were of a sociable nature, and she put her organizing skill into action in the planning of what she called "Keswick Week," coordinated by several local families, but probably including some activities open to all the neighbourhood. There were children's sports, tennis, handball, a picnic lunch, a dance every night of the week, and a marathon race. Like the Hawse End version of "Manhunt," which too may have been revived that year, the rules for the marathon were carefully thought out – surely by Catherine – to enable women to compete without disadvantage, and allowance was made for age. A number of guests stayed at Hawse End, including Catherine's young cousins, Horace and Tom Marshall. Jermyn Moorsom was back at Fieldside for the occasion, and he and his family played an active part in the festivities, hosting two dances; he was also Catherine's partner at tennis.[23]

The NU office in London felt Catherine's absence. Miss Evans, now working as Catherine's secretary for the political work, wrote several times within the first few weeks, with the good news and the bad. Although she hastened to say that Miss Clark would be fine to work with, she was missing Catherine: "I feel as if my nice safe crutches had been stolen from me and I had to learn to walk, doubtless it is good for me ... I seemed to depend on you for every detail of the work."[24]

Meanwhile, her holiday, exile, or mere change of location provided Catherine with an invaluable opportunity to stand back for an overview of the political scene. Political people of every stamp were trying to peer into the future in Britain in late 1913 and in 1914. Catherine was sharply aware of the different scenarios which might occur, depending on the resolution of, or failure to resolve, the Irish Home Rule question, on whether new or old Liberalism prevailed within the Liberal party, on whether Asquith's leadership would continue, on which of the two major parties should win the general election and (vitally important to the women's suffragists) by what majority, on whether the Parliamentary Labour party would grow or diminish and would become more or less dependent on the Liberal party, more or less socialist in its orientation.

Catherine had already written a clear and sophisticated analysis of all these factors for the *Englishwoman* of August 1913.[25] Eleanor Acland had argued in the July issue that the Liberal party was still the party most likely to bring in women's suffrage, and had called on

Liberal women to use their undoubted power by supporting the newly formed Liberal Women's Suffrage Union (LWSU), whose object was "to *unite* suffrage and party forces, with the object of securing a suffrage measure as part of the next Liberal programme, and thus bringing to an end the miserable situation of a Liberal Party at loggerheads with an essentially Liberal movement."[26]

Eleanor Acland's argument provided Catherine with her point of departure. As we know, she had worked for many years to get the Liberal women's organizations to put effective pressure on the party, and she, as much as Eleanor Acland, believed their role could be vital in securing the adoption of fully committed Liberal candidates. And, "If they succeed still further and obtain for Women's Suffrage a place on the official party programme at the General Election, then the present Anti-Government policy of the non-party Suffrage Societies will have to be reconsidered. ... But, meanwhile," wrote Catherine, "what shall be the work of the non-party Suffrage Societies in preparation for the General Election ... ? And what results are we to hope for?"

The article was presumably written before the NU's deputation to Asquith on 8 August, but despite the slight hint of movement there, it is unlikely that Catherine would have greatly modified what she wrote. Asquith's past record and continuing refusal to entertain the idea of a government women's suffrage measure led her to declare flatly that: "Obviously, ... the worst thing that could happen from the suffrage point of view would be a General Election before the Home Rule Bill has become law, and the return to power of the Liberal Government as at present constituted, with an Anti-Suffragist Leader prepared to resign rather than consent to the introduction of a Government measure enfranchising women, and with the Suffragist Ministers prepared to set aside their suffrage principles and acquiesce in a breach of faith with women rather than risk the resignation of the Prime Minister, which in their view would probably involve the loss of Home Rule, and a consequent breach of faith with the Irish Nationalists." Because of this worst-case possibility, Catherine continued, the NU "is quietly but steadily preparing the ground for effective opposition to Anti-Suffragist Liberals, and effective support of Labour Candidates in three-cornered contests." If, however, the Home Rule Bill became law before the election, what should be the NU's attitude? It must depend on whether Asquith remained as leader, and on whether the Liberal party, with or without his leadership, moved to take up the cause. Inevitably, Catherine had to answer her own question: "We can only 'wait and see'."

She went on to discuss a problem that was to concern her for a long time. If there was no significant change in the Liberal party's official position, could the women "best serve the interests of Women's Suffrage by working for the return of a Conservative Government" or should they "aim merely at such a reduction of the Liberal majority as would make them more amenable to pressure from the Labour party and the suffrage forces in the country than they are at present"? Catherine made an honest assessment of the chances of some measure of enfranchisement at the hands of a Conservative government. She knew well that there were some good suffragists among the Conservatives and Unionists, but she admitted that there were also "some very bitter enemies," and she summed up: "All that can be said is that the return of a Conservative Government would be better than the return of the present Government with a big majority and with Mr. Asquith still Prime Minister."

The conclusions reached in Catherine's article were simple and incontrovertible: "On the whole it looks as if the best result which could come of the General Election, so far as the prospects of Women's Suffrage are concerned, would be the return of a Liberal Government with a small majority,[27] and a strong Labour party demanding the enfranchisement of women." Accordingly, the NU did not have to wait for the answers to all its questions; support for the Labour party must continue. So long as it kept women's suffrage "in the forefront of its programme ... to strengthen the Labour party is to strengthen the position of Women's Suffrage." Even in the event of a Conservative victory, "it will still be desirable to have a strong Labour party in the House of Commons. They would have some voice in shaping the policy of the Opposition and determining the programme of the Liberal Party at the next election; and the time when pressure can be most effectively brought to bear upon any party is when that party has been out of office and hopes that it is on the eve of returning to power."[28] We need to keep in mind that Catherine consciously and meticulously limited her public comments (and no private ones survive) to an evaluation of the situation in terms strictly of the best chance for women's suffrage – leaving it frustratingly difficult to assess how far she had moved towards adopting a socialist ideology, or indeed how she viewed the prospect of a Unionist government in general terms.

Although the article is primarily a justification for energetic support of the Labour party, and a warning to the Liberals, using the EFF policy as a stick and a carrot, Catherine's actual strategy in the uncertain climate was to cover all bases. Whatever happened, nothing could be lost by having leading parliamentarians in every party who took the women's suffragists seriously, and with whom personal contact had been made.

13 An All-Party Campaign: Wooing Liberals, Unionists, and Labour, September to December 1913

The preelection climate became more and more palpable while Catherine was in the north in the autumn of 1913. Parliament was in recess from 15 August 1913 to 10 February 1914, with members back in their constituencies, many of them campaigning in all but name. Close attention was paid by the press, and no less by the NU, to the statements and speeches of party leaders, and indeed of all MPs.[1] Together with the lessons of the unsatisfactory meeting with the Liberal suffragist ministers, and its ironic juxtaposition with the cautious encouragement the NU women had felt in their meeting with Asquith, the covert preelection tension made up the background to Catherine's political activity while she was at Hawse End.

Keeping in close touch with the NU executive, Catherine made use of the change of pace and the enforced distancing from the day-by-day pressure of her political work in London to do what she could to influence the situation by a more leisured correspondence. She continued to believe – probably rightly – that the cause would take a great step forward if any political leader of distinction took it up with devotion, allowing his name to be associated with women's suffrage, inviting speakers to join him at public meetings and in his constituency, and giving it prominence in his public speaking. The meeting with the so-called suffragist ministers had shown how far down the agenda of most politicians was the question of women's suffrage, but the women were determined to change that, and the election was going to be crucial. Catherine continued to build her one-to-one bridges, and meanwhile the local NU organizations were encouraged to make sure that the nonmilitant women's suffragists were visible wherever the leading politicians went.

Determined to keep the momentum resulting from the pilgrimage going, Catherine selected the targets she would address by correspondence. Besides Lloyd George and the faithful Francis Acland, the Liberals of most promise were Sir Edward Grey and Sir John Simon. Lord Haldane was also supportive, but was in the United States during the autumn of 1913 – where, the NU was pleased to learn, he spoke out for women's suffrage.[2] Among Conservatives and Unionists, she worked principally on Lord Robert Cecil, Lord Lytton, and Lady Selborne. As for the Labour party, Ramsay MacDonald remained the least satisfactory as well as the most important of the leaders; but the major work still needed in that party was to consolidate support among trade unionists, especially the miners, and to keep the issue alive and sweet-smelling for Labour supporters at all levels. Catherine laid or cemented the groundwork for this multidirectional strategy while she was "on sabbatical" at Hawse End.

Johanna Alberti describes Catherine's all-party negotiations on behalf of the NU as having taken "an enormous toll of her ... political integrity."[3] I believe the more detailed analysis given here enables me to dispute this; Catherine's public commitment at this time was to the gaining of the vote for women; she could not separate this from her private hope for a revived Liberalism, and as this hope began to fade, she personally moved to the left as the NU did. If there is any appearance of deviousness it is attributable to the evasiveness of all parties on the women's suffrage issue, which made it essential for the women's suffragists to hedge their bets. And indeed, Catherine made no secret of the surely legitimate strategy of playing one party off against the others.

LIBERALS: LLOYD GEORGE, SIR JOHN SIMON, SIR EDWARD GREY

Among Liberals, Lloyd George was clearly a fish worth angling for. The tone of Catherine's letters to him shows that she had accurately summed him up as an opportunist, not necessarily without principle, but one who would pursue those causes also likely to redound to his political advantage, and she continued to tempt him to come out as the White Knight of the women's cause, a role that she held out to him as one that would suit his personality, enhance his public image, and mesh with his other objectives. There were others in the NU who found him positively repugnant,[4] but Catherine at least would do her best to keep him up to his recurrent promises. When he was about to make a major speech at Bedford in October – launching his new land reform policy – she cabled him a reminder of a point worth making, following her telegram up with a letter: "With so many other things to occupy your mind before your great meeting at Bedford yesterday," she told him, "I was afraid you might have forgotten a most excellent point in connection with your Land policy which you made in a conversation I had with you at your own breakfast table – that it is impossible to talk about Land reform without considering the housing problem, and that housing is a question which pre-eminently concerns women, and is a good example of their need for representation, and of the sort of question in which the women's vote would strengthen the hands of those who are working for reform." Mentioning also his promise to refer to women's suffrage in his autumn speeches, she told him that she "would not want the first reminder to come in the form of a militant interruption!", and added, "... I hope your meeting was a great success – as indeed it was bound to be. I am looking forward with the greatest interest (like thousands of other people) to reading the report of it tomorrow. ... Land reform and Free Trade were the two questions which first interested me in politics, and I have just been re-reading Henry George's "Progress and Poverty."[5]

Land reform had amply proved its popular appeal when some elements had been included in the famous 1909 budget, and this, combined with a personal antipathy to overprivileged landlords, made it a natural for revival by Lloyd George, and by the Liberal party, as the election drew near. Lloyd George had expected to have cabinet backing for his plans before he gave the Bedford speech, but in fact did not have an opportunity to put them before his colleagues until 17 October, when they readily gained acceptance. So he was now officially promoting the first two parts – land reform and housing reform – of the conjunction which he had discussed with Catherine, providing at least a possible political motive for him to commit himself to the third, the enfranchisement of women.

Peter Rowland has suggested that Lloyd George was prepared to resign at this time on the land question.[6] While it might have been a promising issue around which to build a new party, it met with virtually no opposition within the cabinet, so surely there was no reason to consider resignation. However, if indeed Lloyd George thought the link with the women's vote genuinely important, here was additional fuel for his undoubted ambition, when the moment should come, to supplant or dominate Asquith, so obstructionist on that question. On 22 October Lloyd George announced the government's new land policy at Swindon, and the following day, before leaving the town, he made a very odd speech to a deputation from the local NUWSS. In it he raised the question as to why women's suffrage did not come in despite support within the cabinet (and he named supporting ministers), leading right up to the brink of the obvious answer, "Asquith," before slithering sideways and putting the blame on militancy. After that he went to the hopes for the next general election, at which he said suffragists, if well organized, "will be able to make such an impression at the polls that men who are opposed to the suffrage will find that it will be better for them to reconsider their views and to pledge themselves to support an advanced measure of women's suffrage."[7]

If those words have the ring of a warning to Asquith, there was no such suggestion two weeks later. Speaking to rather unskilled deputations from an NU branch in the northeast and from the WFL on 8 November 1913, Lloyd George once more put all the blame on the militants. Further, needled by the WFL group, who thought the suffragist ministers should resign, he came out categorically for cabinet solidarity, declaring that such resignations would mean "that every great question for the promotion of which we have been working all our lives and which is just as sacred to us as the cause of suffrage is to be wrecked. ... Is it suggested that I should wreck the Liberal party, not for the sake of women's suffrage, because I can assure you that it would not promote women's suffrage, but for the sake of a particular view of tactics taken by a few people whom I do not consider to be any better judges of tactical considerations than we are? ... I have a great horror of splitting great Parties." He named the causes at risk: Welsh Disestablishment, Home Rule, and land reform, saying of the last, "I find a Ministry prepared to take it up and a Party solidly supporting me," and stressed the importance to women of housing reform.[8] The speech does not remotely hint at a breach with the cabinet, and is not that of a man contemplating resignation on any issue, but it could be that of a man anxious to reassure his colleagues and his chief of his loyalty.

The NU, of course, had no wish to see Lloyd George leave the cabinet, though they may privately have hoped that *Asquith* would be more disposable once Irish Home Rule was settled; or, if not more disposable, at least more amenable to suffrage pressure from within or without the cabinet. Lloyd George's acknowledgment of the potential relationship of land and housing reform to the women's vote gave grounds for hope.

Despite his continuing willingness to use militancy as an excuse for delay, and his now reasonable assumption that there would be no women's suffrage measure in the present Parliament – where the failure of the third Conciliation Bill and the Dickinson bill enabled him to claim that there was no majority in favour, a view not shared by the NU – Lloyd George was willing to let himself be identified with the cause when it suited him, swinging from point to point like a weathercock. At Oxford on 28 November 1913, he met a deputation from the NLOWS, who pressed him to insist on a referendum, and claimed that a majority of women were opposed to enfranchisement. He dealt with them courteously but gave short shrift to their arguments, pointing out that the only kind of mandate recognized by Parliament was at the polls, and that the next election would determine whether a majority of MPs, and by implication, of their constituents, favoured giving the vote to women. But meeting with two deputations of male suffragists, he again resorted to "the usual scolding of militants and the allegation that nothing could be done as long as the suffrage agitation was accompanied by disorder."[9]

Catherine continued to do her utmost to keep the chancellor up to the mark, but she felt that she was "becoming rather discredited as a false prophet because [she had] so often predicted better things of Mr. Lloyd George than he has performed."[10] She was not the only one who was tiring of his approach, nominally prosuffrage but always emphasizing the one thing most damaging to the cause. In November, after Lloyd George had received a delegation at Middlesborough, Kathleen Courtney wrote in disgust, "I am really sick of these lectures on militancy. Why he should see fit to deliver them to the N.U. rather than to a militant society when he has the chance is a little difficult to understand."[11]

By now Catherine knew well that Lloyd George would blow hot or cold as it suited him; all the more reason to court other influential Liberals. Apart from Francis Acland, who, blessedly, did not need courting, the other two Liberal leaders worth cultivating were Sir John Simon and Sir Edward Grey; both had solid reputations for integrity and carried weight in Parliament, the party, and the country.

Sir John Simon had emerged as a strong supporter at the meeting following the pilgrimage, and was now chair of the Liberal suffragist group in the House of Commons. When the NU learnt that he was to give two important speeches in Manchester on 12 November 1913, one by invitation of the Free Trade Union (FTU) and the other to the local Liberal party, he was asked to receive a deputation of representative local suffragists, and Catherine wrote on behalf of the NU to support the request. She referred to the "industrial districts of the north [as] the stronghold of the Women's Suffrage movement," and to his prospective candidacy for the northwest Manchester riding.

She made a number of specific suggestions as to how he could introduce at least a brief mention of women's suffrage into his discussion of every issue.[12] In his reply, Simon said he could not possibly introduce the subject in the meeting under the auspices of the FTU ("They are not meetings organised by the Liberal party at all, and one does not speak at them in any capacity except that of a Free Trader"), but that he had already written to Margaret Ashton (chair of the Manchester WSS and of the Manchester and District federation) "to tell her in confidence that I mean to take the opportunity which my first speech in Manchester will give me of saying something in favour of Women's Suffrage."[13]

The Manchester deputation was of particular importance, because it was representative of the range of suffrage opinion in this industrial region. Margaret Ashton was there to introduce the members, and Helena Swanwick on behalf of the NU executive. Also present were representatives of the National Labour party, the Labour Group of the Manchester City Council, and the Manchester LRC, some who spoke as members or officials of the Liberal party, and two male suffragist journalists. In total, twelve of the nineteen-member deputation were men.[14] The notes Catherine prepared for the participants (some of whom, she well knew, had little experience as polemicists for women's suffrage) provide a remarkable window on the care and insight she brought to the task of winning converts, and make visible a part of her political work usually hidden. She began with "The chief things to remember about Sir J. Simon," listing "1) that he is a comparatively recent convert to w.s. and is not alive yet to its *urgency*; 2) that he has a very legal mind – hates any tendency to exaggeration or irrelevance; you will gain more by understating than by overstating your case to him. 3) that he is a scrupulously honest person, and believes that other people are the same. Mr. Asquith has evidently taken special pains to convince him that he (Mr. A) has treated the question of w.s. with absolute fairness. I should guess that he has gone out of his way to ostentatiously refrain from influencing someone against it in Sir J.S's presence."[15]

Catherine laid out the points she would suggest for the deputation, beginning with a penetrating analysis of the issue of priorities, modified by practical advice (the emphasis is hers):

Try to make him realise that w.s. is a *vital* and *urgent* question: When people say to us: "We are in favour of w.s., but we think other measures are more important" we cannot accept that as reason for delay. *The more important those measures are the more important is it that women should have a say in settling them* – if they concern women. *Show how all current questions do affect women v. closely.* ...

N.B. Remember that he was pledged to Home Rule before he was pledged to W.S., and considers himself bound to put that claim first. Personally I think it is as well to admit that position (since it is now obviously to our advantage to get the H.R. question finished off and out of the way ...). I should not dispute his contention that he owes a first duty to H.R., but should point out that this present Parl' will see that question through, and say we want to know what Suff[ragist]s in the Gov' are prepared to do then. We consider no other question has a prior claim to ours then – certainly not the land question.

Reverting to things particular to Simon, Catherine continued:

I should *not* attempt to make him see that Asquith has behaved dishonourably:

(a) because he is hardly ripe for that (Asquith has evidently taken great trouble with him to convince him to the contrary, and he feels Asquith has behaved extremely well to him personally in this matter – not reproaching him for "the difficult position in which I put him, first by my speech at the Opera House and secondly by drafting the Bill so as to incur the Speaker's ruling").

He is, in my opinion, more worth making friends with than any of the other Ministers except Grey and Haldane, and any aspersions on Asquith's personal honour would put him on the defensive and in a very unapproachable mood[.]

(b) Because even if you could persuade him that Asquith had not acted honourably it would take you all the time at your disposal to do it, and there are other things more worth doing.

Avoiding a focus on Asquith did not mean letting the government off. Catherine went on: "I should try to make him see that we *do* consider the Gov' responsible for the impasse which the W.S. question has reached. I should review our case against the Gov', calmly and dispassionately. A quite colourless statement of the facts will be enough to impress him, I think – will probably impress him more than an emotional indictment would."

Five pages of notes on the salient points in the history of women's suffrage during the previous three years followed, from the refusal of time to proceed with the well-supported first and second Conciliation Bills, through the "torpedoing" of the 1912 Conciliation Bill, the failure of the government to do anything to counteract rumours of Asquith's possible resignation on the issue, the lack of positive support from the suffragist ministers for the amendments to the Reform Bill, the way in which the introduction of the Reform Bill had been left so late in the session that there was no time "to reintroduce the Bill, re-drafted in a way which *would* allow the fulfilment of Asquith's pledges." Here Catherine broke off, to put in a caveat: "*N.B.* Remember that Sir J. Simon drafted the Bill himself, and is very much distressed about it. It is certain that he took every precaution about it, and that *the Speaker's ruling was wrong* according to all the authorities. I think it would be well at the outset to say that we do not attribute any blame to Sir J.S. in the matter."

Catherine concluded her historical survey with a note on the Plural Voting Bill, again showing sensitivity to the need to balance the forcefulness of argument against the effect it may have on the particular ear to which it is directed. Pointing out that the wreck of the Franchise Bill had left the women "in the lurch," she stressed that it would "*not* be honourable to save from the shipwreck just the particular bit which most closely affected [the government's] own interests – viz. plural voting," and continued, "I think it *would* be worthwhile to develop our argument about the P.V. Bill to Sir J.S. I think he might see it. (It is rather a legal and subtle point likely to appeal to him.) It w[oul]d be a very great gain if he did. You will see when you begin what chance there is of convincing him. I think it would be wiser not to press any point to the extent of hardening and antagonising him. *If we can get him friendly disposed now, we can bring him along and say much more later.* The great thing is to leave him convinced that we are reasonable people to deal with."

Experience had taught Catherine that there were some things – at this time, the Dickinson bill, and, at this and any other time, militancy – almost certain to be brought up by a government politician in such a meeting, and for these, too, she prepared the deputation. "*If Sir J.S. attempts any defence of the Dick[inson] Bill,*' she wrote, "I think it is important to rub it in to Members of the Gov[ernmen]t not only that the promise of facilities for the Dick[inson] Bill gave nothing approaching an equivalent to the former promise of *Government support after a single favourable vote in the Commons,* but that the *Gov[ernmen]t support* promised in connection with the *Fran[chise] Bill* would have been of *a life-and-death kind,* because the w.s. clause would have been part of a Bill on which the Gov[ernmen]t's existence would have depended, as much as it depends on H[ome] Rule and Welsh Disest[ablishment]."

On militancy there was little new to say, except for the all-important evidence of country-wide recognition of the nonmilitants revealed by the pilgrimage, and the blame that must attach to the government itself for the frustrations which fuelled militancy. "The only people," said Catherine, "who have the power to stop militancy are the Suffragist Ministers."

Finally, Catherine advised the deputation to return the ball to Simon's court by some direct questions: what advice did he have for the NU's work at the next general election? and what was he himself prepared to do to ensure that women's suffrage would be an issue at that election? On the first of these, she anticipated that he might say, as Lloyd George had, "'make an impression at the polls' ... secure the return of a majority of suffragist M.P.s." But, as Catherine pointed out, there had been a majority of suffragists in the Commons since 1886, and over four hundred of those returned in 1910 were in favour ("N.B.", added the meticulous Catherine, "Be careful not to say *over 400* were *pledged*.") In what way did Simon suggest such a majority could be made more effective in the next Parliament?

As for the question of what he could do, Simon would "be sure to say ... nothing more can be done during this Parl[iamen]t." "But," concluded Catherine, "a great deal can be done *in the country* between now and the General Election. What is most needed is wholehearted advocacy by the Party leaders who believe in w.s. – by the men to whom the electors are accustomed to look for guidance. We have done our part – we have carried out every task that has been set us. What has been lacking is evidence to the elector that the *leaders of the Suff[rage] movement in the H. of C. really mean business*, and *think this question is important*. So far we have had very little help from them – they do not even subscribe towards the cost of all the work which this long delay makes necessary."

Realizing that twelve pages of notes might prove a little daunting, Catherine drew up a one-page summary of her suggestions, a model of clarity, and the kind of thing members of the deputation may easily have kept before them during the meeting; a glance would remind them of the points to be covered.[16]

These notes shed a brilliant light on Catherine's way of working, her sophistication of approach, and a kind of seamlessness in the NU's historical view, where the pattern of government procrastinations (for which the ministry had a different excuse every time) was seen as one consistent and damning whole.

The deputation to Sir John Simon went well. Despite the presence of the journalists, it was informal and largely confidential, a shorthand record being made only at the request of Margaret Ashton. Not all of Catherine's points were developed, but, in a cordial atmosphere, the deputation brought home the extent of support, the need for a government measure, and the necessity for open commitment on the part of the suffrage ministers. Although Simon found it impossible to stay off the subject of what he called "militantism," and reiterated the view (now tacitly accepted within the NU, though not formally conceded, and not recognized in the other women's suffrage groups) that there was no hope of a government measure in the present Parliament, he went on to make a strong statement on the need for leading suffragist politicians to be prepared to stand up and be counted, saying that "the real hope for the movement was that everybody in any sort of position should take every opportunity of saying that this was his view, and of putting it forward as part of his fundamental principles." His advice to the delegation was "Make the most of your Suffrage Ministers, and tell them as you have told me to-day, not to talk about Women's Suffrage as a fad, but a faith."[17] If nothing else, he was admitting that politicans had to share the blame for the long delay, that the fault could not always be laid at the door of the voteless women themselves, and that some active responsibility must henceforth be taken by those ministers who were declared suffragists – very close to Catherine's concluding points.

After the event, Catherine received a rather irritating note from C.P. Scott, the generally sympathetic editor of the *Manchester Guardian*, who explained that he had not felt able to go to the deputation (Catherine, it seems, had written urging him to attend), "because I felt quite doubtful whether I could take the same line as they might with him. What they would like, of course, is that suffragist ministers should refuse to serve in a Cabinet which did not make women's suffrage part of its elective programme ... I could not ask a man like Sir John Simon to give a promise of this sort in advance."[18] Scott underestimated the sophistication of the NU, and its ability to control its followers. Catherine and her associates may have seen such a stand on the part of suffragist ministers as a desirable future strategy in so far as it could be used to influence party policy at the next general election or after, but were too wise to expect to bring it about by attempting to force an extreme public statement out of any individual before he was ready, especially a new convert. Furthermore, they believed the suffragist ministers could be far more useful in the cabinet than on the sidelines. No one at the deputation as much as raised the issue.

The WFL, however, as we have seen, *was* demanding immediate resignations from any ministers claiming to be suffragists. Worse, the WSPU backed the same demand by focusing attacks specifically on those ministers, more even than on out-and-out antisuffragists; besides attacks on property and person, they did their best to make it almost impossible for them to speak anywhere on the suffrage issue. Two weeks later at Walthamstow, when his speech was drowned out by interruptions,[19] Simon may have had to remind himself of his own declaration to the deputation that "any Liberal who believes in Women's Suffrage and qualifies his support of it because of militantism is a very illogical person."[20] To his credit, he showed himself able to separate the sheep from the goats, writing to Molly Mackenzie that he would still do whatever he could, adding, "I do not think we ought to be too much disturbed by the antics of a very small section, though they certainly make it rather difficult for Cabinet Ministers to do all that they might wish."[21]

Catherine's management of Sir John Simon was not flawless. In her anxiety to make the most of his commitment, she failed to follow her own advice on moderating the pressure that could be put on a new convert, and by February 1914, he was reacting with some irritation and defensiveness to Catherine's wish to have him mention women's suffrage even on occasions when he thought it irrelevant and inappropriate.[22] For her, of course, there were no such occasions; every political question affected women, and accordingly whatever the subject under discussion, there was an opportunity to point out the need for women's influence at the ballot box.

The deeper significance of the prolonged failure of the Liberal government to move on the issue of the women's vote can be even better seen in Catherine's approach to Sir Edward Grey, where she spoke as a woman who had been a lifelong convinced Liberal. Catherine had a good deal in common with Grey; he was a northerner and a countryman, and generally perceived as a man of principle, in politics for duty not ambition. In some ways he appeared as a Liberal of the same school as Catherine's father.

Grey had long put himself firmly on the side of women's suffrage within the cabinet, though his position as foreign secretary kept him busier than he had any taste for. The NU saw it as vital to strengthen the tenuous liaison, since Grey was by far the most distinguished and credible government supporter of women's suffrage, on whose attitude much would depend at the next election. His absence when the NU deputation met the suffrage ministers after the pilgrimage had been a major disappointment, and Catherine had tried to get a private meeting with him shortly afterwards. Although she did not succeed, he let her know cordially that he intended "to express his views on the subject when [he] address[ed] his constituents" in the autumn. In October she tried again, suggesting a meeting at his home in Northumberland "some time between now and January, – if possible before Nov.6 when our half-yearly Council meets at Newcastle, and our future policy will be under consideration."[23]

Catherine also enlisted the help of Francis Acland. In October 1913 Eleanor Acland's mind was temporarily distracted from politics by the birth of a daughter; Catherine wrote to Francis, sending her good wishes, and her hopes "that you are glad it is a daughter" and that she "will grow up to make a good use of the vote which her parents will have had so large a share in winning." She told Francis how much she thought depended on Grey, explaining, "I am personally very anxious to ask his advice as to the most fruitful way of spending our time and energies between now and the General Election – and to find out whether he can give us any more hope than Mr. Ll. George has done that when Home Rule and Welsh Disest[ablishment] are out of the way the Suffragist members of the Gov[ernmen]t will turn their attention seriously to the question of W[omen's] Suffrage." To both Grey and Acland she reiterated the importance of the coming NU council to be held in Newcastle in early November, when policies would be set. "It would be of the greatest possible use," she wrote, "if I could see Sir Edward Grey before that, even if he could not say anything which I might repeat. I feel that everything really depends on his attitude, and if we decide our policy without knowing what that attitude is we are likely to make mistakes." With a rare reference to foreign policy, she went on, "I have always felt this, because I have always had the most complete confidence in him, whether it was a Balkan crisis, or Persia, or Women's Suff[rage]. But as you know it has generally been very difficult for us to obtain access to him. I should be so grateful if you could persuade him to give me an interview some time this autumn, if possible before our Council meeting, and before he makes any public statement about the situation as regards W[omen's] S[uffrage]. ... Tell him I won't waste his time or be obnoxious (if your conscience will allow you to say as much!)"[24]

But Acland too was unsuccessful. Clearly, Grey did not yet see any complexities over suffrage which made an immediate meeting necessary. However, Acland promised that he and Dickinson would "have a good go at him soon," and described a recent meeting he had addressed in Lincoln, where he had had "a fine time with 2000 people," using a technique now becoming common with committed Liberal suffrage supporters: "I had got them very keen," he explained, "on land and other questions and finished up with ten minutes on suffrage as hot as I could pile it in. There was great disgust expressed by some of the high and mighty ones but they were so keen on the rest of my speech that they couldn't say much, and I had the audience completely with me in the main."[25] The message here, of course, was mixed; while rank-and-file Liberals might favour women's suffrage, much of the leadership was unwilling to have it made an issue. All the more reason, Catherine may have reflected, to get a man such as Grey to identify positively with the cause.

Since Grey would not meet with her in the north, Catherine had to give up her hope of seeing him before the council meeting. We are left with the impression that she had made an absolute commitment to her parents that, although she was free to do some travelling in the north, she would not be drawn south during these months, no matter how pressing the occasion.

Meanwhile, Grey showed his sincerity, but also, alas (as Catherine had feared), a lack of familiarity with the details of what was going on, when he met with a deputation from the Northern Men's Federation for Women's Suffrage in his Berwick constituency on 27 October 1913. Catherine took the risk of letting him know how she had reacted to the newspaper report, telling him, "Your speech is very similar to the one in which you told us not to hope for anything further in 1910, but to 'concentrate on 1911'. The similarity, in the light of the events of 1911 and 1912 and 1913, is not very encouraging. You said yesterday that the essential condition for success is 'a majority in the House of Commons which is really in earnest about Women's Suffrage', and that 'everything depends on the next election and how the candidates for the House of Commons who are elected Members pledge themselves with regard to it'."

Catherine recognized this as the standard argument for putting the responsibility back on the voteless women themselves to see to the election of suffrage candidates, rather than on the party leaders. She spelled out the effect of the continuing lack of a party direction:

I am afraid we have got to face the fact that we can never again hope to have a majority in the House of Commons pledged to Women's Suffrage until one or other of the 2 great parties adopts Women's Suffrage as part of its programme. Candidates, and especially Liberal candidates, are refusing now to give any pledges on this question on the ground that their doing so might embarrass their party at some future date. The fact that you said what you did yesterday is evidence, of course, that you cannot be aware of this fact (it is one of the things we were anxious to tell you before you made any public pronouncements on the present situation); but to many Suffragists throughout the country who do not realize that a Cabinet Minister does not necessarily know of all the influences that are at work in the rank and file of his party, I am afraid your advice will seem rather cynical – especially when they remember how little good the present suffragist majority in the House of Commons has been to us. Over 400 of the members returned to Parliament in 1910 had declared themselves in favour of Women's Suffrage; but when reminded of their pledges last autumn, in connection with the Women's Suffrage amendments to the Franchise Bill, a number of Liberal members told us quite frankly that they could only keep those pledges *provided that when the time came their doing so would not embarrass the Government or the Prime Minister.* The idea was very prevalent amongst Liberals, and especially amongst Liberal Agents, and was a profound conviction with all the [Irish] Nationalist members, that the passage of any kind of Women's Suffrage measure *would* embarrass the Government.

I am not making any suggestion as to the origin of this belief; but until our friends in the Government realize that it exists, and is growing, it seems to me impossible (to use your own phrase) that any progress should be made. Unless some change can be brought about from within the Liberal party I am afraid it is useless to hope that we shall get many Liberal candidates to pledge themselves to support W[omen's] S[uffrage] at the next election.

Please believe that we are very grateful for all that the cause of W[omen's] S[uffrage] owes to you personally. I should not venture to write to you so frankly and at such length if I did not believe that we have as good reason to put our faith in you for the future as we have had to be grateful to you in the past.[26]

Catherine had touched on a problem increasingly evident to the NU as they worked towards the election. As long as the Liberal party remained deadlocked on the suffrage question – or even if it was merely avoiding consideration of the divisive issue – election work was conducted largely in the dark. As Catherine told Grey, aspiring Liberal candidates shared the problem. Molly Mackenzie had just sent Catherine some scraps of evidence she had collected. For example, in August a prospective candidate had been reported as refusing to take the chair at a suffrage meeting on the grounds that he was planning to stand as a Liberal candidate at the next election and "We're not allowed by Headquarters to take sides on this question until its [sic] settled!"[27] Later in the year, rumour focused on bias one way or the other, rather than enforced neutrality. On the one hand the antisuffragist members of the cabinet were said to have sent out a circular successfully discouraging the selection of suffrage candidates; and on the other the whips were accused of "making it an essential to official recommendation that an aspiring candidate should pledge himself to support votes for women." This last, of course, was pleasing to the NU, and they did their best to make it a reality; Catherine made sure, for instance, that copies of all prosuffrage resolutions passed at meetings were sent to the whips.[28]

Since Grey's speech had been unsatisfactory, it was little comfort to have Lord Haldane, back from the USA, refusing to meet with a deputation on the grounds that, while he was still a supporter, he had nothing to add to what Grey had said.[29] In other words, uncertainty reigned, and no matter how Eleanor Acland might urge the women's suffragists to put their faith in the Liberals, no solid foundation for that faith had yet been laid.

Meanwhile, the Newcastle council meeting had to be faced on 6 and 7 November 1913. No difficulty (other than a sprained wrist, incurred in the previous week) surrounded Catherine's attendance, which had probably been built into her plans from the start – and Newcastle was, conveniently, in the north. The anxiety she had expressed about the meeting was real. She had no wish to see the NU back down on its commitment to support of the Labour party, but neither did she want the NU to move into a strategy that would inevitably alienate many of the faithful among the suffragist Liberals. Realistically, it was hard to foresee a time when they would not have an essential role to play in getting women's enfranchisement through parliament.

To Francis Acland, in a letter marked "Absolutely confidential," Catherine described the issue confronting the council:

One of the reasons why I was so anxious to see Sir Edward Grey before then is that there is a move – strongly supported, I believe – to extend the scope of our Election Fighting Fund work in preparation for the General Election. At present our funds and workers are concentrated on constituencies of

1) *specially bad* Liberals (from the Suff[rage] point of view)
2) *specially good* Labour men
   The proposed new development of the policy would aim at
1) securing the defeat of the *largest number* possible of unsatisfactory Liberals
2) securing the return of the *largest number* possible of Labour members;
   i.e. *quantity* would be our aim rather than quality, – we should take into consideration not so much the attitude of the individuals concerned, as the strength of the local Labour vote and the smallness of the Liberal majority.

I am all for this policy as the most effective *if* when the General Election comes, the attitude of the Liberal party remains unchanged; and in order to be able to carry it out effectively we must, of course, be *preparing* on those lines now; but I am all against *committing* ourselves now to a policy which would, if successful, do the maximum amount of damage to the Liberal party. And to adopt the resolution which will be moved at Newcastle would be to commit ourselves, because of course we could not leave the Labour party in the lurch in cases where we had definitely led them to count on our support.

Hitherto we have limited the number of constituencies in which we have committed ourselves for the *General* Election to those in which we have some special reason for intervening. But of course there are a good many others

in which we could help the Lab[our] party. In the N.E. Fed[eration] for instance, where there is a strong Labour vote in most places, our people have
been working in close co-operation with the Labour organizations, often
with a joint Lab[our]-Suff[rage] Com[mit]tee.[30]

Francis Acland was away from home when Catherine's letter arrived, so she went to the council meeting without any light he could
have shed (and it would only have been faint) on Grey's views and
possible future Liberal policy. The challenge to harden the EFF policy, based on a resolution from the Newcastle-on-Tyne WSS, was exactly as she had described it. A number of factors contributed to
support for the move, which was a further step in a trend which had
antedated and led up to the very formation of the EFF. Women's suffragists had much to congratulate themselves on in November 1913.
Over £25,000 had been received in donations at the head office during the year (as well as what had been collected and used in the
branches), including £4,000 for the EFF. About 10,000 new members
had joined the NU, and 28,000 had expressed their support as
Friends of Women's Suffrage.[31] And the international scene was encouraging, especially in Scandinavia. But there was every reason to
feel frustrated with the indifference or hostility of the prime minister, the government, and the Liberal party, and this frustration was
reflected (not for the first time) in a number of the resolutions before the council, for example calling for a government measure,
condemning the introduction of the Plural Voting Bill, mandating
the executive to consider asking MPs to move women's suffrage
amendments to the address in reply to the King's speech at the next
opening of Parliament. More significant than mere frustration, however, is the message in the crucial resolution on EFF policy, and in the
closeness of the vote on it, that the centre of balance was continuing
its shift from south to north and from Liberal to Labour. But this
was not to be a smooth or ultimately a successful progression. In the
outcome, the resolution was lost by a narrow majority.[32]
Catherine's relief was surely based on her realistic assessment of
what was best for the suffrage cause, no longer, as it might have
been a scant three years earlier, on a starry-eyed faith in the Liberal
party. Yet she must have felt some justification for her stand when
she got Acland's delayed answer to the letter she had sent him just
before the council, providing substance for her belief that it was too
soon to give up all hope of the Liberals. On Grey's attitude Acland
came directly to the point: "The answer," he wrote, "... wholly depends on the circumstances of the next election: Grey is quite certain that if we have to have a G[eneral] E[lection] on Ulster i.e. to

finish Home Rule, he could do nothing, but if we'd got the two big bills out of the way and it was a question of fighting on a new programme (viz land etc.) he could do a good deal. I feel just the same." There was nothing new here, nothing that Catherine had not already deduced, but to hear it, if not from the horse's mouth, at least from that of the groom, was a great deal better than deduction. And Francis Acland gave a charming and encouraging description of how he saw his own role. "My part," he wrote, "I have ... discovered to be to go on just a little in front of Grey and to show him what pleasant country it is there. I did it with great success when Dickinson and I met him ten days ago." He described a promising new initiative: "We want to start – as I think I've told you – a men's Liberal society working on much the lines of the new Women's society and concentrating on making the party a suff[rage] party after the G[eneral] E[lection]. He was very silent about the scheme for an hour, but Dickinson and I played battledore and shuttlecock with it in front of him so attractively that at last he wholly accepted the idea and said he would lead – if he could get George and Runciman and Simon to agree. He promised to see them and try to get them to help – and I have not heard the result."[33]

Acland was also the first minister really to lay himself on the line for women's suffrage, going as far as to tell a meeting of the League of Young Liberals (not always the most sympathetic of audiences): "I say for myself – and I hope there are others of far more importance than I – that I shall be unable permanently to adhere to a Liberalism which refuses to treat women as citizens."[34]

While the NU's leaders worked so assiduously towards a concrete preelection commitment from those who counted in the cabinet, one more scheme was hatched which, in their view, could have set back indefinitely the whole process of obtaining a government measure. It was proposed to Eleanor Acland by P.W. Wilson, a Liberal journalist from Kendal and a former MP – but in Kathleen Courtney's opinion it had "been devised by Lloyd George who has quite taken in the simple P.W.W."[35] Briefly, the proposal, which Wilson also sent to Courtney, was for Asquith to receive a delegation now and pledge the Liberal party to confer the vote of women in the next Parliament if the House of Commons then passed a resolution in favour. Kathleen and Catherine saw at once that it was subject to all the same objections as the so-called "free vote" on a private member's bill, and Mrs Fawcett thought it "a device to satisfy the Liberal women; apparently large numbers are joining Mrs. Acland's society [the LWSU] and the matter is creating some stir." Courtney was also fearful lest the scheme should be used to sidetrack Sir Edward Grey, whom,

rather surprisingly, she regarded as "stupid enough for anything."
But the NU had underestimated Eleanor Acland, who saw at once
– even before Catherine did as Kathleen urged her and tried to
"pour iron into her [Eleanor's] veins"[36] – that "It won't wash."[37] She
refused her support, and after a few days of alarmed exchanges the
scheme died a natural death, providing only yet another example of
the sophisticated political understanding of the NU's leaders, and of
the speed and effectiveness of their networking.

A kind of 'flu seems to have gone around at the council, and a
number of members were ill after it, including Catherine, who had
already been somewhat unwell for several weeks.[38] In December she
was sent by her parents to holiday in Switzerland as a final preparation for her return to full-time work in London. Her illness had not
been severe enough to prevent her from keeping a long-standing
engagement to speak in a week-long suffrage campaign in the Cumberland mining district around Whitehaven in mid-November;[39]
and in early December she fitted in a trip to Edinburgh to shop and
enjoy a visit with her old suffrage friend Alice Low, who was anxious
to talk with her about the implications of the Scottish Home Rule
Bill.[40]

Sir Edward Grey had said that he could talk with Catherine in
London in December, and she was enabled to fit the meeting in on
her way through to catch her boat – but only just, since 15 December
was the last day on which he could see her, and the first on which she
could get away from Cumberland. She saw Grey alone, as Kathleen
Courtney had strongly advised, saying that she was sure that in that
way she would get more out of him.[41] Even Francis Acland was not
present. Catherine saw the meeting as of quite exceptional importance, and had been jotting down notes of what she wanted to say
ever since she had first tried to arrange it.[42] Now it was too late to
have a word from him to influence the Newcastle council meeting,
too late to improve his well-meant speech at Berwick. But the central
issue remained the same, all the more urgent because of the passage
of time: how might the women's suffragists best use the remaining
months until the general election? Catherine had originally put this
in the form of a question on which she wanted Grey's advice, knowing that reflection on it must bring Grey up against the unknown
factor of Liberal policy, or lack of it – as it constantly did the suffragists of the NU. Catherine hoped Grey would give her, and those who
thought like her, something concrete to strengthen the case against
the adoption of the proposed new EFF policy. Although she did not
want to sound as if she was making a threat, she pointed out that the
change to a harder line was bound to come up again at the next

council meeting in February, and, said Catherine, "We shall *have* to settle our policy then for [the] G[eneral] E[lection] so as to be preparing. Once committed to Labour [we] can't leave them in the lurch *whatever happens*." She let Grey know that she herself had reached a decision, telling him, "Personally, if [the] sit[uation] is unchanged, I should not be prepared to take [the] resp[onsibility] of opposing again – even if I could do so successfully."

Catherine's intent had always been to talk to Grey as one believer in Liberal principles to another, and she also hoped she could make him see the question as far from irrelevant to his position as foreign secretary. In her meeting with him, as with no other, she put the women's suffrage campaign in a global context. The wider implications had long been present for her, and increasingly, as she worked with socialists and with grassroots labour, she had drawn the parallel between the movements to break down "class-barriers and sex-barriers"; in an article she had written for the *Labour Leader* in late August this theme was central.[43] But by December the concept had fallen into place with particular clarity, and had gained a third dimension, that of race, possibly as a result of reading a remarkable article by Beatrice Webb, in which Webb, just back from the Orient, commented on common factors in "these three simultaneous movements all over the world, ... woman's emancipation ..., the International Movement of Labour ..., unrest among subject peoples struggling for freedom."[44]

Catherine drew Grey's attention to support within the Liberal party for women's suffrage – the recent formation of the Liberal Men's Suffrage Association in Manchester, the strong line taken by the LWSU.[45] But she told Grey that whatever action the NU took would have wider consequences than its effect on the Liberal party or on the progress of the suffrage movement. She believed that it would be the first step in a direction which would profoundly affect the whole future of the women's movement (of which suffrage was only a part), not only in Britain but throughout the world, and would affect not only the course of the women's movement but also of the coming great struggle between capitalism and labour. The women's suffragists ("our people") were building close relations with the labour movement, and felt, too, a close kinship with the "struggles of [the] subject races." This, she told Grey, was her reason for talking to him, because when the showdown came, he would have an important part to play in it, both in Britain and in Europe.

The immediate results, were the NU to embark on a "policy of blind hostility" to the Liberals, could indeed, Catherine assured Grey, be the loss of a good many seats. She told him something of how the EFF policy operated, describing the effective work already done in some constituencies, and emphasizing that a change in policy would lead to its extension to many more three-cornered contests. She warned him that if NU "Headquarters won't fight" – that is, even if the anti-Liberal policy was not formally adopted – "there are plenty who will. *And that is ... where [the] danger comes in.* "Not only was there strong feeling against the Liberal government, but there was dissatisfaction with the NU leaders; "wholesome to [a] certain extent" as that might be, it could get out of hand and lead to an anarchical situation. A wish to get the Liberals out could turn into a wish to wipe them out. Catherine later reported that Grey "had seemed impressed, and evidently thought that the situation was a serious one, realising that there are about 40 constituencies where the labour vote is large and the Liberal majority small."[46]

Catherine was not expressing an aversion to a leftward drift of which she was surely in many ways a leader. Nor was she concerned only to frighten Grey with the political danger. At a deeper level, what she wanted to do was to interest him in what she saw as the common ground of principle behind the contemporary movements. Put another way, she was raising with him the whole vexed question of the future direction of Liberalism. And Catherine believed that women must be involved in the process by which the problems would be resolved. "It matters enormously to [the] whole of future civilisation," she told him, "whether these 3 great movements run on sound and healthy lines, or are driven into revolution. [The] W[omen's] M[ovement] ought to be a steadying factor, but if it runs off the rails ... [illegible]. ... It is going to matter all over Europe *how* we win the vote here." Catherine may be presumed to have had in mind militant suffragism, the syndicalist substitution of direct action for parliamentary procedure, and the danger of armed revolt over Irish Home Rule.

Concluding, Catherine came back to the immediate situation. They were, she told Grey, at the "parting of [the] ways." She understood that Home Rule currently "fills [the] horizon," but after that women's suffrage was the most urgent issue to be settled. What she wanted from Grey was for him and the other suffrage ministers "to come to some conclusion what they will do *after* H[ome] R[ule] and let us know before the coming Council meeting."[47] Grey was sufficiently impressed with what Catherine had told him of the import of the possible harder policy to twice ask the date of the council meeting, leading Catherine to believe that he might indeed "communicate with the N.U. again before then."[48]

Catherine asked Grey not to repeat what she had told him about the controversy in the NU council, or the details of the cooperation with Labour, but indicated that she hoped he would share the gist of what she had said (without actually quoting her), with Haldane, Simon, and Asquith. Interestingly, she classed Lloyd George with Winston Churchill, the most outspoken antisuffragist in the cabinet, as one of those to whom little should be disclosed. One of the variables affecting Lloyd George's behaviour was thought to be the degree of closeness between him and Churchill, who poured scorn on women's suffragists.[49]

During Catherine's few days in London, she stayed with Alice Clark at 1 Barton Street (bringing some of her "belongings" with her from Cumberland), and spent some time with Kathleen Courtney, besides fitting in as much suffrage work as she could.[50] She was able to catch up with any happenings that had not been fully reported to her by mail or at the recent council, but thanks to Molly Mackenzie, who wrote frequently and fully, formally and informally, these may have been few. Before leaving for Switzerland, Catherine made her report to the NU executive on 18 December on the extent – and the limits – of her success with Grey. He had been remarkably frank with her, admitting "that at the present moment the Cabinet were face to face with the prospect of civil war," which (hardly surprisingly) "outweighed other considerations." It is in fact worth comment that Grey had spared the time to meet with her at a juncture when serious difficulty beset the administration, acute in the case of Ireland and endemic in his own sphere of foreign affairs, and may lend force to what he felt able to say about the suffrage question. What he said about Ireland was no exaggeration – although he would have been unlikely to say it in public. On 28 November 1913, Bonar Law, the leader of the Unionist opposition, had made an inflammatory speech in Dublin, encouraging the army (whose officers, largely recruited from the Anglo-Irish gentry, were predominantly Unionist in sympathy), to disobey orders if the time came to enforce Home Rule, and desperate secret negotiations were even then going on between Asquith and Edward Carson, the Ulster leader.[51]

In response to Catherine's urging that as soon as Home Rule was settled "Women's Suffrage should take its place as the most important political question of the day, and the one to which the Government was devoting its attention," Grey "had said he was not prepared to go on indefinitely as a Member of the Government which would not take up the question of Women's Suffrage," a remarkable statement, as strong as anything the NU could hope for in defining Grey's own position, and very similar to Francis Acland's recent declaration. To the realists of the NU, its sincerity was only reinforced by his caveat that "on the other hand, he would do nothing which would imperil the Government until Home Rule was settled." They knew this well enough, and Catherine herself "thought that he would also take into consideration the position the country might then be in with regard to Foreign affairs." Further, Grey warned Catherine that "the N.U. must recognise that if Women's Suffrage were taken up as a government measure, it would inevitably result in a split in the Cabinet." This statement is puzzling in that, according to Catherine's report, "he thought that the difficulties with Mr. Asquith were not insuperable," although he had said "there are others," by which she believed he meant Churchill.[52]

Here is further confirmation that Asquith would in the end yield to the inevitable. His characteristic tendency to wait in the face of disunity (considered variously by his biographers as weakness or consummate political skill) continued to cause difficulties for the women's suffrage movement, but it seems likely that the necessary appearance of consensus would eventually have been achieved, even if, in this instance, it had been Asquith himself who had to find a face-saving formula for capitulation, without benefit of the rationalization which was to be provided by the war. The ambitious Churchill was highly unlikely to resign on the issue. Lewis Harcourt, secretary for the colonies, might have been in a more embarrassing position than Churchill, since it was well known that he had put a great deal of money where only Churchill's mouth was, and had allowed his name to go out as a vice-president of the NLOWS, despite an understanding that ministers would not join such organizations, whether for or against suffrage.[53] But it is improbable that he would have split the cabinet.

Catherine had every reason to feel pleased with the interview. She summed up her impressions of Sir Edward Grey, saying that he "had seemed anxious to face, and not evade difficulties."[54] Certainly, it was short of the wishful thinking Kathleen Courtney had indulged in a few weeks earlier, when she had written to Catherine: "[Grey] really ought to give a definite lead soon otherwise it will be too late. Why can't he and Simon and Buckmaster come out together. Lloyd George would follow at once."[55] Nevertheless, the interview marked an advance, and at the very least did something to remove the nasty taste left in the NU's mouth by the deputation to the suffragist ministers in July. As for grassroots Liberalism, an article in the *Common Cause* of 19 December 1913 claimed hopefully, and with some justice, that there was division in the Liberal party, and increasing resentment of the illiberality of the leaders, pointing out that the leading Liberal press – the *Manchester Guardian*, the *Daily News*, and the *Nation* – all favoured women's suffrage. But the Liberal party was still far from being a safe basket for suffrage eggs.

UNIONISTS: LADY SELBORNE, LORD ROBERT CECIL

Catherine's anxiety to keep the NU from adopting a policy of out-and-out hostility to the Liberal party was undoubtedly based in large part on her realization that such a policy could be expected to contribute at least as much to the success of the Conservatives at three-cornered elections (as it had already done at the Crewe by-election of July 1912) as it would to that of the Labour party. A Conservative majority in the next general election would not, on the face of it, be good news for women's suffragists, as Catherine had admitted in her article in the August *Englishwoman*.[56] But if that should come about, as it very well might, the women's suffragists had no intention of throwing up their hands in despair. They knew well that there is a bandwagon effect in franchise reform (well illustrated by the 1867 Reform Act); once an extension of the electorate becomes inevitable, there comes a point at which parties cease to resist and suddenly vie with each other to make sure that the new measure favours them as far as possible, hoping to claim the gratitude of the new voters and to exercise damage control.

Accordingly, in 1913 and 1914 the NU cultivated Unionist supporters almost as assiduously, though less openly, than they did the leading Liberal suffragists. At the constituency level, Alice Clark, following Catherine's instructions, sought detailed information from secretaries of local NU branches about the attitudes of Unionist party agents towards the suffrage question. Careful secrecy surrounded the use to which these lists were to be put; they had in fact been requested by Lord Robert Cecil for some purpose in connection with a Unionist party conference to be held at Norwich in September, and Catherine collected all the material to forward to him, without disclosing its destination to any one at the office.[57]

Meanwhile she sounded out those Unionists whose support could be counted on as to what was the best that could be hoped for from the party. Throughout the autumn of 1913, Catherine corresponded at length with Lady Selborne. Born Maud Cecil, a daughter of the former Conservative prime minister Lord Salisbury, sister of Lord Robert Cecil, and a cousin of A.J. Balfour, Lady Selborne was as passionately interested in politics as her male relatives, and was exceptional in her insistence on her right to her own political views, which indeed remained those of the family she was born into but differed from those of her husband and his family at the time of her marriage in 1883. By 1886 she and William Palmer (who became Lord Selborne in 1895) were, after all, on the same side, but because of movement on his part, not on hers; he left the Liberal party over Home Rule, becoming a Liberal Unionist in coalition with the Conservatives. Lady Selborne had been president of the Conservative and Unionist Women's Franchise Association (CUWFA) since 1907, though she remained more active behind the scenes than in public.

Catherine opened the exchange, asking Lady Selborne about several matters, and bringing her up to date on NU affairs. Probably knowing of her long-standing interest in housing conditions, she sent details of an education campaign being conducted at that time by the NU, focused on "The State and the Child."[58] She told her that the NU was disappointed that Lord Selborne had not spoken in the House of Lords on the Plural Voting Bill, but that she understood that he had been instrumental in framing an amendment which had at least opened up the debate. She told her (perhaps somewhat disingenuously, since Lady Selborne did not favour universal suffrage), of the growth of support among trade unionists; and, in commenting on the success of the pilgrimage, she asked her whether there was any foundation to the rumour that something in connection with the pilgrimage had caused offence to some members of CUWFA. She asked Lady Selborne whether she could "get Lord Sydenham [a new member of the House of Lords] talked to before he got caught by [Lord] Curzon and [Lord] Cromer," the leading antisuffragist peers. Most important, she asked Lady Selborne whether plans were on foot to introduce a suffrage bill in the House of Lords in the coming session.[59]

Lady Selborne responded promptly and at length. She scotched the rumour of problems surrounding the pilgrimage; it had, she said, been welcomed by the CUWFA, which had organized welcoming meetings in various parts of the country. What she had to say about the possibility of a bill in the Lords was of great interest (note also Lady Selborne's use of the first person plural): "We do intend to bring in a W.S. *Bill in the Lords* next spring if the parliament is not dissolved first, which is possible. However, we are keeping very quiet about it, as Lord Curzon could do us a lot of harm if he started canvassing now. So please do not talk about it." She went on to say that when the time came, she thought "the best way to impress the peers ... would be to get as many women's associations as possible – National Women Workers [sic], – Women's Cooperative Guild – Headmistresses, Nurses etc. to pass resolutions asking for the Bill;" the CUWFA had a list of those lords who attended, and would send the resolutions "round to each individual peer." She went on to make a rather remarkable generalization about the peers, who, she said, "are really quite well disposed to women, but their own wives and sisters are mostly 'anti' and they don't realize that there are a great number of respectable women who feel that the vote would be a great safeguard."[60]

Both women surely understood, as Catherine said in her reply, that there was not "the remotest chance of the Bill reaching the H[ouse] of C[ommons]," but it could provide a valuable opening for propaganda (and, Catherine doubtless reflected, a promising stick to beat the Liberals with). So she welcomed the scheme, carefully quizzing Lady Selborne on the nature of the proposed measure and on how the NU could best help. "[I]t is very useful to me," she explained, "to know of likely events beforehand, *even if I cannot tell my Com[ittee]*. We might, through ignorance, unwittingly hinder instead of help your scheme. I imagine the Bill will be on the 'equal terms' basis – simply removing the sex-disability?" The Liberals would obviously be unreservedly opposed; however, it was not impossible that, "in their present mood," Labour "might be worked up to support an 'equal terms' Bill," probably now preferring it to the old conciliation formula, and given that the bill would not reach the Commons, and so would have to be supported only at meetings and in the press. Catherine asked Lady Selborne "whether you think their support, supposing it could be obtained, would have a good or bad effect on your plan."[61]

Lady Selborne, continuing this remarkably open exchange, confirmed that the bill would probably be on "equal terms" lines, although she added acidly that "Lord Newton thinks we should have a better chance with Conciliation, which seems incredible if one did not know how extraordinarily stupid the Conservative party are." She did not think the Labour people could be of much assistance – "in fact, the quieter they keep the better."[62] Catherine, not surprisingly, was "rather relieved" to hear that this kind of support would not be sought; she may have had second thoughts about her rather rash claim that Labour could be brought on side, despite her professed faith in the NU's propaganda arm among Labour organizations. She did not share Lady Selborne's view that the Conciliation formula was altogether inappropriate, since it should be already well understood, and "anyhow it will strengthen the case for the Bill if it can be shown to be framed in [a] conciliatory spirit." But she added that, at the same time, "the more we can rub it into [the] Lib[eral]s that [the] natural bill for [the] Con[servative]s to bring in would be on the equal terms basis," the better; "they need not expect Con[servative]s to be prepared to compromise as far as the C[onciliation B[ill] again."[63]

What was important here was again, to a great extent, promotion of the bandwagon effect. Without telling Francis Acland of the proposed House of Lords bill, Catherine let him know that the Conservative suffragists were inclining to the "same terms" formula. His response delighted her. "I am glad," he wrote, "the Tories are back on to 'the same terms' formula – of course if they carried it it would keep us out of office for a generation – and as our people realise that they are quite capable of putting it through it'll wake them up with a jerk and do them good ... the chance of a one-sided Tory bill makes my Cornishmen fairly jump" (although he added, less satisfactorily, "it'll take 20 years to make them really want the women they live among to vote!").[64] When Catherine met with Sir Edward Grey the following month, she made a point of drawing his attention, too, "to the line that the Conservative suffragists were taking in going back to the original demand for the enfranchisement of women on equal terms with men."[65]

Lady Selborne's reputation with the NU for stateswomanship was somewhat tarnished when she wrote in November, raising, as if it were a novel plan, the well-tried and wholly discredited idea of getting "*written undertakings* from Members to vote for *any Suffrage Bills* that come before the House of Commons." She was, she said, trying to organize a campaign among individual constituents to write to Conservative members asking for such a commitment. Some one (probably Molly Mackenzie), put two exclamation marks in the margin beside Lady Selborne's comment that she believed that a member "could hardly go back on such a specific engagement as that" and three beside her query, "I do not know whether you could organise something of the kind in the case of Liberal members." Mackenzie, forwarding or returning the letter to Catherine, said "Lady Selborne's innocence is pathetic."[66]

Such naivety did not make Lady Selborne's help less valuable – and, naive or not, she was intelligent, politically knowledgeable, and potentially influential. Catherine did not bother to give her the history of all the suffrage pledges that had been forsworn, but sent her instead an analysis of the current political situation. Francis Acland may not have realized what a gift he had given Catherine, who began her letter to Lady Selborne with the good news of his key comment (which lost nothing in the retelling, with Catherine making Acland spokesman for all Liberals), saying, "I have just learned, on good authority, that our attempts to frighten the Liberals with the argument that a Conservative Government might bring in an 'equal terms' measure of Women's Suffrage are being surprisingly successful. They believe that such a measure would 'keep them out of office for a generation'." Extrapolating from Acland's view that the threat might do the Liberals good, Catherine went on: "They are afraid that the Conservatives may possibly arrive at that conclusion also, and believe, apparently, that no further argument would be needed to persuade a Conservative ministry to bring in a Government Bill on those lines."

Catherine gave Lady Selborne some details of the growth of Labour interest in the franchise question, which "naturally takes the form of a demand for full adult suff[rage] for men and women." This, she explained, was also perceived as something of a threat by many Liberals: "Though many Lib[eral]s are prepared to concede this demand to *men* they are v[ery] much afraid of it if women are to be included. Even Mr Ll[oyd] George is afraid of a measure wh[ich] w[oul]d put women electors (an unknown quantity) in the majority." The result of these pressures from both sides, Catherine believed, might make it "just possible that we might get a Gov[ernment]t Bill on Dick[inson] lines even now."[67]

Lady Selborne's brother, Lord Robert Cecil, had long been one of the NU's most stalwart supporters among the Unionists, where women's suffrage was an exceedingly unpopular cause. In the autumn of 1913, he spoke out on a number of public occasions, and Catherine kept closely in touch with him. The possible importance of this contact was multiplied when it was rumoured that he would be the next leader of the Unionist party[68] (although in fact this was never a likely development, in view of his support for free trade). In September the Ulster Unionist Council, headed by Edward Carson, issued draft articles for the provisional government of Ulster (to be implemented in the event of an attempt to enforce Home Rule) which included recognition of the principle of women's suffrage, on the basis of the municipal register.[69] Catherine, who never missed an opportunity to reinforce an impulse towards the women's cause, no matter what the context, wrote to thank Lord Robert for any part he might have played in bringing about the inclusion. He disclaimed any credit, although he said Carson had told him of his intention; credit must go to the Irish women themselves.

Lord Robert, however, was feeling more than a little irritated with "ungracious" comments made in the *Common Cause*, or possibly was rendered crotchety by his own struggle to reconcile his rather moderate conservatism with the slide of the Unionist party towards outright rebellion over Home Rule. He treated Catherine to a lecture on militancy and the attitude of the NU – members of which, indeed, made comparisons from time to time between the rhetoric of those who advocated concessions as a means of defusing the Ulster situation, and those – often the same people – who argued that the continuation of militancy made it impossible to consider conceding the women's franchise. "It is merely folly," he wrote, "to confuse militancy with rebellion. Both may be equally objectionable, but they are entirely different things. The object of rebellion is to substitute one Government for another. The object of militancy is to destroy or impede government altogether and the methods employed are as different as the objects aimed at. The truth is that there is too much Liberal prejudice in the National Union. Not party prejudice, but old Whig feeling, which has made them on more than one occasion exceedingly difficult for Unionists to work with." He added, in a more conciliatory spirit, "Please do not think that in these observations I am including yourself or any other individual members of the National Union. I am merely speaking of their action as a body."[70]

The distinction made in the first part of Cecil's diatribe between militancy (or the terrorism so familiar to the late twentieth century) and rebellion, or the threat of rebellion, is a valid one, and one better understood by the nonmilitants than it was by the WSPU, which sometimes claimed an analogy between its tactics and the kind of mass popular disturbance that had been brought to bear during the Reform Bill agitation of the early 1830s. The second part of his comments also contained some justice; Liberals had always vastly outnumbered Unionists in the support for women's suffrage, and in the NU. Catherine, however, was anxious to cultivate the Unionists, who might well form the next government, and from whom any visible support for a limited measure of women's suffrage, in this preelection period, might prove an invaluable spur for the Liberals. For her, any current difficulties between Unionist suffragists and the NU had little to do with "old Whig feeling," and were rather caused by practical difficulties. In November 1913, after the Unionist party conference at Norwich in which Lord Robert had courageously brought forward a well-prepared but unsuccessful motion favouring women's suffrage (and afterwards had been castigated by a member of the WSPU for his pains), he wrote to Catherine that if a Unionist government did get in at the general election, it would have to do something towards women's suffrage. But he pointed out that any Unionist cabinet would surely contain a large antisuffrage majority, so that the route to go might be through a provision "for the reference of Women's Suffrage to the Electorate."[71]

For Catherine, Lord Robert's letter was good news and bad news. In her reply she congratulated him warmly on his suffrage speech at Norwich, which she had heard "made an effect much greater than was represented by the voting" and by which he had "added one more item to the large debt of gratitude that all suffragists owe to you," and went on: "It is cheering to know that you think that the next Unionist Government will have to do something in the way of legislation on the Women's suffrage question," but had to add, "though I wish that 'something' were anything rather than a Referendum."[72] The proposal to tie the women's suffrage issue to a referendum, an idea as beloved of antisuffragists as it was of fence-sitters, had long haunted the NU, especially in its attempts to build support in the Unionist party. Since it was no part of the normal constitutional procedure, and would involve only the existing male electorate, it was an infuriating and humiliating proposal, and more threatening, with its veneer of democracy, than any narrowness of the measure itself. At the very best, it would be an effective delaying tactic. But to put it bluntly, the women believed they would lose; and once lost, the setback could be for a generation.

Catherine explained to Cecil: "If only the apathetic and indifferent both could be eliminated from the Referendum I should not fear it. The *active* Suffragists undoubtedly outnumber the *active* Anti-suffragists, except in a few benighted corners of the country. But the people who have not thought much about a proposed change, or whose interests or imaginations are not touched by it, will always vote for leaving things as they are. You might get a majority on a referendum in favour of *repealing* some grossly unjust or oppressive measure, the evil of which had been proved by experience; but I don't believe you would ever get a majority for *enacting* something new and untried. Perhaps," she added with some asperity, "that is why the Referendum appeals so strongly to Conservative politicians?"[73] In the same letter, Catherine gave Cecil good news of the progress of the women's suffrage cause among miners and in the cabinet — in other words, she gave him news of what was being done in the other parties for him to measure the Unionist party against.

The NU continued to be troubled by the referendum possibility, the more so now that they had a clear picture of the use that could be made of even a hint of a commitment by Unionist leaders to the introduction of a women's suffrage measure. Besides her interview with Grey, Catherine fitted in a meeting with Lord Robert Cecil on her way to Switzerland, this time going with Kathleen Courtney and Alice Clark. Lord Robert repeated much of what he had said in his letter, emphasizing that he thought there was little chance of a government bill from a Conservative government unless it should be on the basis of a referendum. He himself "was not prepared to admit that a Referendum would be so dangerous as the N.U. thinks" – unless, as he admitted, Lloyd George were to work for the defeat of the proposed measure on the referendum. The NU officers pointed out that that would surely be the case, "as it was improbable that a Women's suffrage bill put to the Referendum by a Conservative Government would be on lines broad enough to satisfy Mr. Lloyd George." At this rather unsatisfactory point, the matter had to rest for the time being, although the executive, receiving Catherine's report, may have garnered a crumb of comfort from hearing that, outside the Selborne family, the referendum scheme "was not warmly supported by the rest of the Conservative Party."[74]

Catherine's exchanges, whether by mail or face to face, with politicians who showed an interest in the suffrage question were disarmingly frank and friendly, carefully calculated, and yet, in another sense, without guile. She wrote and spoke as a suffragist, as near to the NU's official nonparty stance as could be managed, but not denying the Liberal indoctrination of her youth, and indeed making use of it when she was among Liberals. If a statesman declared himself a suffragist, she took him at his word, expecting him to stand up and be counted and, more than that, to work actively within his party for the cause; her assumption that he and she had the same cause at heart, and that he was honest, may have made it hard to deny her, at times even pushing a politician a little further into active prosuffrage intervention than he had first intended to go.

In a sense, Catherine had every reason to feel at home among Liberal and Unionist politicians, who were, almost without exception, from her own class. But we should not lose sight of the fact that one of the strongest barriers to women's enfranchisement lay in the indoctrination of that class of man with a view which was far from a good environment for the notion of women's equality to grow in.

One of Catherine's most striking qualities, and one that may at times have cost her internally a good deal, although it contributed hugely to her success, was her assumption of equality in her dealings with men; she neither begged nor attempted to demand; she neither cringed nor dominated; she never apologized for being where she was or who she was. It has become almost a truism to write about the socialization of women to see themselves as inferior. A useful and fascinating new book by Pat Jalland[75] develops this point well in relation to a number of the principal political families in Britain in the late nineteenth and early twentieth centuries. Many of the

women in her study, in fact, scraped a good education for themselves from the rather casual opportunities available to them: a
succession of good, bad, or indifferent governesses and tutors;
exposure somewhat haphazardly to the conversation of distinguished visitors; their fathers' libraries; their brothers' schoolbooks;
sometimes even the condescending generosity of those same brothers in sharing some part of their superior scholarship during vacations from public school and university. Very few indeed, from these
families, were among the young women now newly breaking into the
university world, from which much of the suffrage leadership came.
What most of them were taught consciously and deliberately was to
prepare themselves to be good wives, mothers, and hostesses; in
other words, to train for invaluable (and sometimes interesting) but
subordinate political support roles.

What is much less frequently the subject of comment is the obverse side of this picture.[76] While the girls learnt to see themselves as
subordinate, the boys were immersed in a view of themselves as in-
nately superior and dominant, by sex as by class, and – perhaps still
more important – in a view of women as creatures of lesser strength
and ability. Stephen Koss has commented on the youthful Asquith's
condescending and unpleasant attitude towards his sister, by no
means moderated by his own initial position on the very fringe of
the political and social society he was determined to make his way
in.[77] But women had a good deal of potential usefulness of various
kinds in accessory roles. What this political culture did directly to the
women in it may be of much less significance, in the long view, than
what it did to the men. Some of the women within the inner political
circle, it is true, were a drag on the suffrage movement, others did
what they could to help it along; with a few exceptions (of which
Lady Selborne is the most notable), girls grew up to mirror the position of those men to whom they were ancillary. Their independent
power was slight and circumscribed, although they were known in
political circles and often knowledgeable in political matters. But the
boys grew up to rule the country.

The Conservative and Liberal political leaders with whom Catherine wrestled had come to adulthood with this ingrained certainty of
their own superiority, and an understanding of what that meant
goes far to explaining the attitudes she encountered. It can be heard
in Asquith's amused contempt at the idea that he might resign on
women's suffrage, and in Churchill's uncomprehending disparage-
ment of the "mawkish frenzy" of colleagues who supported it.[78] It
can be seen as much in the halfhearted approach of the Liberal suffragist ministers as it can in the out-and-out opposition of antisuf-

fragists in both parties. At best, those boys who had brought home some crumbs of their education to share with their importunate sisters – when they could spare the time – grew up into men who might agree that it was acceptable to give women the vote – when they could spare the time, and as long as it did not too much threaten their own comfort and effectiveness. A politician needed a wife (and if, like A.J. Balfour, he never married, there had to be a handy sister to fill in),[79] and it was unimaginable that these convenient auxiliaries might one day themselves go into politics. Greatly to Catherine's credit, she found an effective approach to many of these privileged men; and she would have been the first to share the credit with the very few who were able to meet her with some degree of openness.

LABOUR: MINERS, VOTERS, AND BY-ELECTIONS

The progress and setbacks occurring in Catherine's and the NU's relations with the Labour party in 1913 to 1914 took place in a context very different from that we have been describing with leading members of the two old parties. Among the Liberals and the Unionists, a relatively small coterie of leaders was all-important; with the Labour party, grassroots activity made up the bulk of the work, and groups and bodies of people were courted collectively rather than individually.

The NU had decided on three targets for its autumn campaign in 1913. One, which need not concern us, was to raise the circulation of the *Common Cause*. A second was to carry out an education campaign to focus "public attention on one particular aspect of the case for Women's Suffrage." "The State and the Child" was chosen, as a topic of concern to working women and men, and to provide a vehicle for outreach to the working class, a purpose dovetailing neatly with the NU's third and major focus, the organization of work among the trade unions and trade councils, aimed at getting strong resolutions passed at local and national gatherings.[80]

Despite the amount of effort Catherine gave to wooing Liberals and Conservatives, her belief in the importance of the Labour connection was unshaken. She cannot but have had a clearer view by this time of the Labour party's feet of clay – that is, of imperfections in its organization, and some lack of openness, let alone agreement, between centre and periphery. At the same time, her theoretical thinking was moving away from liberal economics and closer to democratic socialism. Shortly after her article in the August 1913 *Englishwoman*, which we may suppose was addressed primarily to

Liberals, she wrote another, entitled "The Labour and Woman Suffrage Entente," published in the *Labour Leader* of 28 August. In the *Englishwoman* article, the advantages for women's suffragists of supporting Labour in any other event than the adoption of women's suffrage by the Liberal party are argued for solely strategic reasons. For the *Labour Leader*, Catherine went further, speaking of "the dawn of a new spirit of understanding and sympathy between the two most vital movements of the day – the Labour movement and the Women's movement." Although – of course – she lauded the concrete benefits of cooperation, her main emphasis was on the common philosophical ground shared by the two movements. While socialism, she said, had always "made sex-equality one of the planks in its platform," it was only now that trade unions were taking up the cause: "Now, however, the Labour movement, all along the line, is waking up to a recognition of the claims of women, not so much as a sex question, but rather as an inseparable part of the democratic ideal. On the other hand, the women who are working for the political emancipation of their sex are coming more and more to realise that the fight they are waging is in its essence the same fight as that which the Labour movement is waging for the economic emancipation of the working classes."

Catherine identified a common enemy of labour and women's suffrage: "the old enemy which has always barred the way to progress – the spirit of monopoly and privilege, the opposition of those who possess power to those who demand liberty, the reluctance of those who have to share with those who have not," and went on to claim that "class-barriers" and "sex-barriers" were "in reality part of the same fence erected round different sides of the same field – the field of equal opportunity, wherein all human beings may have scope for the full development of every power they possess. ... Those who are at present excluded from this field by class, and those who are excluded by sex, are beginning to realise that their efforts have the same immediate object, and to wonder whether the fence might not give way sooner if they combined their forces of attack. ... [W]hat we are attacking is the whole theory of fences, the spirit that puts up fences to keep some people out of what should be the heritage of all." Catherine praised the equal treatment accorded women in the Labour party, "which admits women members on the same terms as men, welcoming them as comrades, not using them (as the other parties do) merely as unpaid drudges," and to expound on the democratic structures of the NU, adding that "the Women's Suffrage movement has done more than any other movement of the day to break down class-barriers and class prejudice."

The two movements, Catherine wrote, should maintain their independence; their relationship must be "a free co-operation ...
based on the recognition that one of the principles they stand for
(equality of opportunity for all) is the same and can be served in
many cases by joint action." But both should beware of attempts to
break up the *entente*, being made at that very time, by "[t]hose who
fear the growing strength of the Labour movement; those to whose
interest it is to keep women unenfranchised and women's labour
cheap; those who, for reasons of party convenience, wish to delay
still further the settlement of the Women's Suffrage question." The
subscription list of the NLOWS, "with its £1,000 contributions, and
the significant sources from which they come," bore witness to "the
kind of person who is opposed to Women's Suffrage." (Catherine
does not name names here, but a recent list had apparently included
the Rothschild name, as well as that of the cabinet minister Lewis
Harcourt.) Pointing out that whispered warnings about each other
emanated from enemies, not from friends, Catherine wound up to
a conclusion that is unexpected only in its rather radical terminology: "The fact that the Capitalist and the party wire-puller are so
much alarmed by the policy of co-operation between the Labour and
Women's Suffrage movements is the best possible testimony to the
effectiveness of such a policy."[81] But the terminology *was* radical,
and the whole article shows how far Catherine had moved towards
an acceptance of an ethical socialism close to that held by the more
idealistic ILP members, and even closer to early Owenite utopianism,
summed up by a recent writer as a "call for a multi-faceted offensive
against all forms of social hierarchy, including sexual hierarchy."[82]
Margaret Robertson, who had had trouble walking the fine non-
party line between support for Labour candidates on suffrage, and
overt support for the Labour party in its own right, wrote: "I liked
your article in the Labour Leader – but *I* daren't say as much in print
– nor would you let me! Why you say the very things which, in a
much milder form, loosed a tempest on my devoted head after
Houghton! I shall quote you next time I'm in disgrace!!"[83]

Inevitably, Catherine's article oversimplified the issues, and there
must have been real doubt in her mind, too, whether its optimistic
conclusion was justified. The nearer the inevitable election drew,
without the Liberal party being prepared to make a statement on
women's suffrage, with the Home Rule question still unresolved,
and with electoral negotiations between Liberal and Labour a real if
unacknowledged possibility, the harder it became to keep up the
juggling act between the parties. Many Labour party members, and
particularly members of the ILP, whose loyalty to women's suffrage

was matched by their determination to be entirely independent of the Liberal party, had an understandable wish for a firmer electoral commitment from the NU. Equally, as we shall see, those trade unionists still on the fence were watching the NU with some suspicion, and were extremely sensitive to anything that could be seen as evidence of incomplete support from the NU. Perhaps most difficult of all was the impossibility of finding out what was going on in the minds of the National Executive Committee of the Labour party (NEC) and the PLP.

The NU may not have deserved the lion's share of the blame for any inability to close the distance between themselves and Labour. Certainly some among the Labour party leaders – most notably, as we have seen, Ramsay MacDonald himself – may still have been keeping the door open for the possibility that the Liberal party would be willing to jump into bed with the Labour party when the election came, and, in the absence of any Liberal commitment to women's suffrage, did not wish to have to deal with complications caused by the presence of the NU already cosily established in that bed; and so did little actively to further the women's suffrage entente. On this issue, MacDonald was a pragmatist, and those who argue that his heart and soul were in the development of a separate independent labour party do not nevertheless prove that he was yet convinced that the time had come to drop the pact – on which, it will be remembered, his own seat at Leicester had depended.[84]

Catherine wrote to MacDonald from Hawse End in October 1913, seemingly challenging him to take a stronger stand as chair of the PLP. His reply came from the ss *Arabia* off Port Said, written on his second trip of 1913 to India as a member of the royal commission on India's public services, and contained little but non sequiturs, self-justification, self-pity, and a sententious attempt to put all the responsibility on the NU. He claimed that in "a little campaign" he had finished before leaving Britain, "at four out of the five meetings I pinned my faith to you. I cannot possibly do more," and went on, "As regards the newspapers and the critics … if I cooed at you like a sucking dove they would find a selfish harshness in my note. Of course you can see that for the time being I am the object of an attack planned to divide the cooperating sections of the whole movement from each other. Until the day I go down to my grave you will be troubled about me. … The defence of our position is in our own hands. You must come back just to this (how often in life we *have* to come back to it!): Do you or do you not trust us? You are 'tired of having so often to explain', you say. But explanation is your lot and you had better just take up the yoke. I wish you had my job … ."[85]

Catherine can hardly have felt that MacDonald had given her any concrete help with her "lot," or that he was doing all he could to open the possibility that a woman might indeed one day have his job.

MacDonald's attitude can be summed up as willing to pay lip service to women's suffrage, but unwilling to make any inconvenient commitment to a means for bringing it about. He blotted his copybook with the NU even more completely in February 1914, when, in reply to a circular letter sent out by Catherine urging support for a proposed women's suffrage amendment to the address in reply to the throne speech, he wrote that he was "in favour of the N.U. working for a Private Member's Bill."[86]

Alice Clark told Catherine in December 1913 that Philip Snowden (himself a strong suffragist, but perhaps with more inside knowledge of the pact than he was comfortable with) had told her and Kathleen Courtney that he was "sure that the labour party wont [sic] do anything for us against the liberals either before or after the election," although he thought the EFF useful in "causing the liberals uneasiness in the country."[87] Snowden said, in the *Englishwoman* of December 1913, that the only hope of getting women's suffrage "in this generation" was from a Liberal government, with a strong suffrage majority in Parliament, and urged Lloyd George and Sir Edward Grey to come out as the "political leaders of this cause." Interestingly, he dismissed the value for this purpose of the likely situation in which the Labour party might hold the balance of power, saying, "unless there is a large majority of Liberals who are pledged to a Government measure of woman suffrage, that will be of little use to the cause."[88] In other words, Philip Snowden did not expect that his fellow-Labour MPs, even if they were in a position of power, would use that power effectively for the women's cause. Ethel Snowden also "spoke [at an EFF committee meeting] in a most depressing way of the general situation in the Labour party. She said there were practically only about six men in the Labour party, who could be depended on, the rest were practically Liberals, this was her husband's opinion too."[89]

Philip Snowden was on the Labour party's national executive committee as a representative of the ILP, and the ILP was the section of the Labour party seen by some in the NU as "our friends to a man, through thick and thin."[90] As we have seen, the EFF's constituency network tended to lean heavily on ILP connections, and to run into fewer problems where there was a good ILP presence. Generally speaking – and setting aside the easily forgotten fact that MacDonald was also a member of the ILP – the ILP was ideologically more committed to women's suffrage, and because of the ILP's wish to see the Labour party cut free from Liberal party strings, they relished the EFF policy of tackling important antisuffrage Liberals in three-cornered elections.[91] The good relationship could not be taken for granted, and we shall see it threatened at times by events or even by personal animosities.

With the exception of Philip Snowden, who may have been trying to warn the NU, senior Labour party officials were generally hard to reach and noncommittal, probably for the simple reason that they had not made up their own minds, much less reached any consensus. Subordinate officials were encountered from time to time in the constituencies, usually when a by-election was in progress. Indeed, the NU executive and the EFF committee were clear that the best way to keep Labour on side might be to keep up the pressure at the grassroots, converting the unconverted and making sure that the converted stayed that way. The two routes to this were through constituency work – at by-elections or in preparation for the general election – and through the trade unions. Catherine's autumnal exile in the north did not prevent her from taking a keen and active interest in the special campaign planned for the autumn of 1913.

There was good reason to focus on the miners. Of the constituent bodies of the Labour party, the trade unions had been seen at the start of the EFF policy as likely to be the section most in need of coaxing along. By 1913, little anxiety remained as to most of the unions. An unpublished EFF report dated 27 December 1912 comments, "most of the Trades Unions will stand by the women," but adds, "The real anxiety is the vote of the miners, who have been joining the Labour party in large numbers lately. ... Let us hope that the miners will not be a drag on the wheel of progress."[92] The miners' unions had in fact affiliated to the Labour party in 1909, but remained in many areas at best Lib-Lab; the miners in the PLP also often showed signs of their old Liberal allegiance, and at times took a somewhat independent attitude to party policy. Robert Cooper, a staunch suffragist and the husband of Selina Cooper, one of the NU's best organizers and speakers, wrote in early 1913 that he did not think the miners' MPs could be counted on for support of women's suffrage. George Barnes, for instance, favoured supporting a government male suffrage bill, and Cooper was not reassured by his saying that he would go with whatever the party decided, since Cooper thought this might mean Barnes would try to sway the party to reverse its decision not to vote for any bill that did not include women.[93]

Margaret Robertson devoted a great deal of her time in 1913 and 1914 to what was virtually a special mission to the miners. She kept in close touch with Catherine, and worked with the aid of several able helpers among the trained organizers. Particularly "bad places" were targeted, and "good individuals there" identified; Robertson reported that "Mrs. Townley w[oul]d be good for *bad* miners," and Mrs Oldham also particularly liked working with this group, while Selina Cooper too was regarded as very successful with miners.[94] Eleanor Rathbone (one of the few independently wealthy members of the NU) contributed substantially to the salary of a special worker for the propaganda campaign among the miners.[95] The concrete objective was to get a strong resolution passed at the Trade Union Congress in September 1913. Catherine consulted with Arthur Peters about finding a good man to move the resolution – all were agreed that it must be moved by a man to have its best chance of success, and that "a miner would be best." Robertson saw herself as working almost from the inside, and warned Catherine to be careful whom she approached, and how. The NU must keep a low profile, as the TUC was not, she pointed out, like the Labour party conference, where the ILP, the Fabians, the Women's Labour League (WLL), and so on were all represented: "This is *pure Trade Union*, and *very* jealous of outside interference." Robertson was working closely with Margaret Bondfield, of the ILP and the WLL, who had no official connection with the NU.[96] In June a further imaginative step was taken; the NU organizers formed a union and took steps to affiliate with the TUC, becoming entitled to send a delegate to the congress.[97]

Catherine had just left for Hawse End when the Trade Union Congress met in Manchester (1 to 6 September 1913). For some reason, and greatly to the NU's dismay, there was initially no women's suffrage resolution on the agenda, but the women's friends managed to get the issue before the congress in the form of an addendum to a resolution on electoral reform, brought forward annually by the parliamentary committee.[98] A much stronger resolution condemning the government's treatment of the franchise issue was also introduced by several unions. Although Peters sounded confident of the outcome when he wrote to Catherine on the second day of the congress, the issue turned into a cliffhanger. The miners' caucus met that day and decided not to give their support to the women's suffrage resolution. Margaret Robertson described what happened, writing to Catherine, "Did I tell you of the agonies at the Trades Union Congress? How the miners actually decided to vote *against* and I had to chase all round and see them individually and get them to meet again and reverse it (deadly secret of course that I had anything to do with it). That sort of thing makes the grey hairs sprout!" Robertson's powers of persuasion were astounding, and the outcome of the second miners' caucus, on the Thursday, was all that could have been hoped for. Annie Townley, one of the EFF's labour organizers, worked with Robertson in bringing the miners on side, and Ben Turner of the textile union is described as "Miss Robertson's most valuable ally." Turner had long been a friend of Isabella Ford, cooperating with her on the organization of women workers in Leeds, and the incident provides a good example of how the groundwork for suffrage work in industrial areas had been laid by the earlier work of such women as Ford.[99] When the question came to the floor on Friday, the congress was markedly impatient with the one brave soul (not a miner) who attempted to speak against women's suffrage, and passed the resolutions with only six dissentients. The resolution was sent out at once, together with Robertson's report from the *Common Cause*, to the prime minister, other ministers, and MPs in industrial and mining districts.[100]

The triumph at the TUC was part of a long and carefully orchestrated campaign among the miners. The ground had been skilfully prepared not only by the work of Margaret Robertson and other organizers, but by leaflets and articles in the *Common Cause* on mining conditions, dangers, and the needs of miners' wives; and an extensive follow-up had been planned even before the outcome of the congress was known. The annual meeting of the Miners' Federation of Great Britain (MFGB) took place in Scarborough on 8 October, and Robertson, working with the local suffrage society, planned a women's suffrage demonstration for the same evening, booking a large theatre for the occasion. She herself went on holiday immediately after the TUC, and had to miss the Scarborough meeting, but she wrote to Catherine from Italy, "I am wildly excited about that. I *do* hope its [sic] a success. I wish I could be there." [101] It was a precedent-setting occasion; "for the first time in history, one of the largest and most influential trade unions in the country sent speakers officially to represent it at a Suffrage demonstration."[102] Two of the miners' MPs (W. Brace and Albert Stanley) spoke "really well"[103] on behalf of the MFGB, Robert Smillie said a few strongly supportive words, Isabella Ford chaired the meeting and one of the NU's liveliest speakers, Muriel Matters (a recent convert from the WSPU), also spoke. Selina Cooper had spent the previous month in the North and East Ridings of Yorkshire "more or less working the meeting up." Even before the meeting, Margaret Robertson told Catherine, "I have great hopes of its political effect, and of its effect in binding the miners to us."[104] Miss Evans, the NU secretary, sent Catherine a vivid account of the trimmings of the occasion, taken care of, apparently, by a local suffrage leader: "They had a reception to the speakers and delegates on the platform first which seems to have been a complete success, all the speakers and delegates were given button holes in our colours and all the women sprays of flowers in our colours. Besides the miners they had representatives of the Trades Council, the Shop Assistants Union, Plumbers Union, Railway Men's, Women's Cooperative Guild, Women's Railway Union. They seem to have thoroughly well organised the meeting."[105]

The political effect Robertson referred to was directed not only at the Labour party, but at the Liberal party, which had always had so much support in the mining areas. Asquith, too, might well be pushed farther along the road to women's suffrage by the demonstration of massive grassroots support – and that from what had been regarded as the most recalcitrant group – for a truly democratic franchise, rather than for adult male suffrage. The politically minded leaders of the NU knew what they were doing. The *Common Cause* reported: "The question of the vote is no longer a question of sex; Cabinet Ministers who delude themselves with this belief – if any exist – are lamentably out of touch with public feeling, and particularly with the labour movement. In the Scarborough speeches, the note continually struck was: 'This [is] a question of democracy,' and the audience responded with an enthusiasm and a unanimity which indicated that the hour of women's triumph is not so far off as many politicians think."[106]

Talking women's suffrage to miners was nothing new to Catherine, who had spoken to mining audiences in Cumberland from almost her earliest suffrage days. By 1913, and in this new, major campaign, Margaret Robertson took most of the responsibility for planning, coordination, and making the best use of the EFF's labour organizers, although always in consultation with Catherine (or Alice Clark), and ultimately subject to their direction as officers of the NU. But it was not to be expected that Catherine would resist any opportunity that presented itself for hands-on involvement, and she managed to spend a week in her old stamping ground in the largely mining community of Whitehaven and the Egremont division. This time she did not have to do all the work alone, but had the help of several EFF organizers, including some who paid attention to the area on a regular basis.[107] Writing to Lord Robert Cecil just after her return to Hawse End, she described the experience at some length, such length in fact that she cut the story down drastically before sending it. Once more, her description leaves an impression of hard work, yet also of keen enjoyment:

I have just got home from a week's campaign in the Cumberland mining district. I should have no fear of a referendum there! We had 3 or 4 meetings a day ... and carried our resolution demanding the fulfilment of the Government's pledges every time, in most cases unanimously. At one village we held a very successful meeting, catching two shifts of the miners. They insisted that we must go again some morning to catch the other shift, so I and a labour man (a really fine speaker) tramped out there at 11 o'clock one day, and talked to a keenly interested audience in the village billiard room – in an atmosphere so thick with smoke you couldn't see to the far end of it. At twelve o'clock I was going to stop, as I knew the men went down the pit at one, and had to get their dinner first; but an old man at the back stood up and said: "We can have our dinners every day. We can't have this every day. You go on, Miss – unless you're wanting *your* dinner." Every single man then signed a "Friends'" card, and filled his pockets with more to get his neighbours to sign.

At another meeting in the Egremont Division, where we filled the largest hall in the place – after carrying our usual resolution I asked if any supporter[s] of Mr. Grant's [Conservative MP] in the audience would move and second a resolution asking him to reconsider his attitude towards w.s., or to refrain from opposing w.s. measures even if he could not support them. Two men responded at once, and when they gave me their names afterwards I found they were both members of Mr. Grant's Executive Com[mit-]tee. One of them said he should go on strike till Mr. Grant *did* change his mind. I am afraid he will have to stay on strike as long as Mr. Grant remains Member for the Division – he is one of the most ingrained anti-Suffragists I have ever come across. But a sheaf of resolutions from his constituency ought to make him uncomfortable – though of course our real object in attacking that district was the pressure which can be brought to bear by the Cumberland Miners' Federation on the Lab. Party and the Trades Union Congress, and support of Richardson [the Labour candidate for the division].[108]

Catherine's Cumberland campaign was, as she pointed out, directed towards long-term aims, both in relation to the miners' constituency within the Labour party and in relation to the coming general election. The more immediate EFF work of by-elections also continued, and two important elections took place while she was in the north. The first was at Keighley, in circumstances which threatened the NU's delicate balancing act between parties and within its own organization, and it sheds some light on the Labour party's internal difficulties, and serves as a case study of some of the problems that could arise.[109]

In October, Sir John Simon had become attorney-general, and Stanley Buckmaster, MP for Keighley, was knighted and took Simon's place as solicitor-general, a cabinet appointment, necessitating his resigning his seat and standing for reelection. Buckmaster was a declared suffragist, and might in fact be a welcome addition to the lacklustre band of suffrage ministers. In his election address he named three issues: Home Rule, Welsh Disestablishment, and Women's Suffrage, although his affirmative answers to the NU's test questions were hedged with conditions. In any event, the NU's policy no longer permitted them to give him active support, so the decision was made to do propaganda only. Buckmaster was expected to have an easy ride, as the Unionist, Lord Lascelles – initially his only opponent – was not a strong candidate.[110]

However, late in the day – two weeks after this decision had been made, and barely two weeks before the polling date – the local ILP nominated William Bland. The wish to enter the contest proved to be so strong in the local Labour party, including among the trade union representatives, that the party executive gave in and endorsed the candidature four days later. Evans told Catherine that "[t]he Central [Labour party] has been forced practically by the local to fight, they did not want to. Henderson, Anderson and Peters all against it, so Mr. Middleton told me this morning." Bland and his supporters believed he should receive EFF backing, but local NU reports indicated that Labour was too late in the field, and very poorly organized (a view shared by the Labour party's own NEC), and the EFF committee, meeting again, "decided not to take any part in the contest because it is impossible to get an effective fight."[111] Since W.C. Anderson had made a very respectable showing at a Keighley by-election in 1911, it was feared that if Bland did less well now, "the result must appear as a disastrous failure for the National Union Policy."[112] The NU by-elections committee in turn passed responsibility for further action to the executive. Meeting on 3 November, they had before them letters from Isabella Ford, Margaret Ashton, and Eleanor Rathbone, all northern members of the executive but unable to be present, and all recommending that only propaganda work be done; interestingly, of the three, only Rathbone was a Liberal, the other two being Labour in their sympathies.

The executive decided (by eight votes to two, Edith Dimock and Chrystal Macmillan opposing), "owing to the special circumstances of this Election," to do propaganda only, "in spite of the fact that strict adherence to the policy of the National Union would require it to support the Labour Candidate"[113] – presumably because Bland was Labour and the only one of the candidates to answer all the NU's questions unconditionally in the affirmative. On the other hand, Buckmaster might be considered to come under the clause expressly allowing the NU to opt out of opposing "tried and true" friends of women's suffrage in any party. The discussion is not recorded in any detail, so we have no way of knowing whether the "special circumstances" were solely Bland's late entry and a belief that he could not make a fight of it, or whether, as seems probable, they included also the desirability of having Buckmaster in the cabinet – and not subjected to a head-on collision with the NU on his way there.

As it turned out, Bland made Keighley a real contest, and keenly felt the lack of the extra push he might have gained from the EFF. In a letter to the *Labour Leader*, Egerton Wake, chair of the Lancashire divisional council of the ILP, suggested that the NU had backed away from the contest because a Liberal minister was involved, because "the Keighley society is dominated by women who are Liberals first and suffragists a long way after," and because "these women [are] heavy contributors to the funds."[114] The NU responded at once; Alice Clark told Catherine that Isabella Ford spoke to Wake "and convinced him ... of his mistake, and he was quite apologetic," though a different source reports that Ford "did not quite trust" Wake.[115] Clark herself, consulting with Courtney, got a response off to the *Labour Leader*; someone also made sure that the next issue contained a description of the work being done by the NU in the South Lanark by-election.[116] But the damage had been done, and not only by Wake's letter. A factor in the escalation of natural disappointment into a bitter resentment widely felt in and beyond the local Labour party was the perception that the local NU conducted their propaganda campaign in a far from neutral spirit, and in effect, gave active support to Buckmaster. The perception doubtless had some foundation; the Liberal women in the local society (probably a majority of its members) would understandably be delighted that their MP, whom they knew as a devoted suffragist, was going on to a position of greater influence. And the *Common Cause* of 14 November welcomed Buckmaster's election in "Notes and Comments," and gave a laundered account in its reports on by-elections, speaking of the "extreme friendliness" of the atmosphere and saying nothing of Labour's resentment.[117]

Besides seriously souring relations with the Labour party, the Keighley election threatened to make unpleasantly visible disagreements which were just below the surface within the NU. Ethel Williams wrote: "My belief is that the good Liberal women under the guise of propaganda did support Stanley Buckmaster. Our Labour friends are hurt and bitter to an extent hardly explained by the facts as we know them. I think the said ladies should be told what very serious harm they have done the cause."[118] Margaret Robertson and Clementina Gordon, closely in touch with Labour sentiment all over the north, were also angry at the attitude taken by the local suffrage society, but still more at the EFF and the NU committees, which they thought should have stayed out altogether if they could not support the Labour candidate.

Some others, like Kathleen Courtney and Alice Clark, were beginning to lose faith in the Labour party, because of its passivity, its refusal "to embarrass the Government in Parliament,"[119] and its reluctance to contest elections. "I don't understand them a bit," wrote Courtney; a sentiment that would have been echoed by many Labour party adherents at the periphery. But consequently, she and Clark both thought that the risk of seeming too Labour to the Liberals was more serious than the risk of seeming too Liberal to Labour. Courtney was in fact again beginning to pin her hopes on the Liberal party, and specifically on Sir Edward Grey; she wrote that she did not regret "the Keighley business" (although she admitted it had been a nuisance), "as it will have opened the eyes of quite a number of people. I include my own which are open to the fact that C. Gordon is more Labour than suffrage, and that M. Robertson inclines that way. This is serious and may in the future be calamitous. What are we to do about it?"[120] At the very least, she and Alice Clark thought it would be wise to bring Robertson into closer and more regular contact with the EFF committee, if for no other reason than "a little [to] detach her from the other organizers," whose work she had to oversee and criticize.[121]

Certainly the sympathies of Robertson and Gordon remained engaged with Labour – after all, it was these sympathies, garbed in a correct but rather transparent nonparty cloak, which had made them such valuable workers for the EFF. They wrote a joint letter to Catherine, in which among other things they said that Keighley had been "a mistake which must lower the Labour party's opinion of our political acumen, in thus proving that the Liberals can still buy off our opposition with fair promises."[122]

Catherine took the threat to the EFF work very seriously, as did a number of others. Margaret Ashton wrote, "We can't afford to be thrown by the Labour party – we have only them to rely on (and a broken reed at that) for the next general election."[123] Catherine's initial thought was that the Labour people had misunderstood the NU position – indeed, had "not realised that N.U. ... is still *non-party*" – and she blamed herself and the EFF organizers "for not discovering that such serious misunderstanding of our policy existed, and taking steps to remove it."[124] Although this may seem to be in conflict with the executive's admission that it was *not* acting in strict accordance with policy, Catherine was technically right, in that the bottom line for by-election decisions, as for all other matters, rested with the NU executive, and the NU had to keep the final say as to which candidates it supported. But it was a fine distinction, and the organizers can be excused for refusing to take the blame.

Rather than escalating the divisive discussion, Catherine, as usual, turned to the future and to damage control. She firmed up her plans to go to the by-election then just beginning in South Lanark, where the EFF was fully engaged under the direction of Robertson and Gordon,[125] and where, she correctly assumed, the full impact of Labour anger at the Keighley contretemps would be felt. She hoped to be able to mollify both organizers and Labour party.

The NU was conscious that a strong element in their difficulties was the result of divisions and distrust within the Labour party, and indeed the whole Keighley episode sheds as much light on the party's problems as it does on those of the NU; and the latter had the benefit of a great deal more openness of process than prevailed in the Labour party – though there were limits to this, too. Two versions of the NU executive minutes for 20 November 1913 exist; what is presumably the second has a repressive five lines on Keighley, while the other gives a frank account six times as long.[126] Alice Clark told the NU executive on 4 December that "misunderstanding and frictions caused by our decision not to support the Labour candidate at Keighley are still causing difficulty in our relations with the Labour party, partly because the leaders of the Labour party did not always take the same view as the rank and file."[127] McKibbin's account of the Keighley by-election, although he does not mention the EFF, the NU, or women's suffrage, helps give substance to the impression that the NU may have been the whipping-boy for the real and suspected sins of the Labour party's own national executive. When Catherine went to South Lanark, she found that a "report, probably fostered by the Liberals, had been spread among the Labour party that their own leaders and our Union had been bought by the Liberal party."[128]

However much of the responsibility for the emergency lay with the Labour party, Catherine's report leaves little doubt that Keighley caused a real crisis, which might have undone much of what had been achieved by the EFF policy in the past eighteen months. She found Labour people in Lanark "very angry," and she acknowledged that the propaganda work done at Keighley, and "the action of members of the local society," had contributed largely to the bad feeling. "The Rank and File," she said, "had begun to distrust the N.U., and to think that we might leave them in the lurch at the General Election, and that it would be better to make the rupture now."

She urged them to talk things over openly in future, and discussed Wake's letter to the *Labour Leader* with them, and had, she reported, "succeeded in winning back their confidence." John Robertson, vice-president of the Scottish Miners Federation, and one of the miners' representatives who had taken part in the NU's Scarborough demonstration, had been particularly enraged, and "had intended to do his best to defeat the Women's Suffrage Resolution at the Glasgow Conference [the next annual Labour party conference, to be held in January 1914], with a view of ending all relations between the two parties, but he will instead continue to work in its support as heretofore."[129]

So far, so good. Catherine's efforts had gone far towards saving the entente. But even after this, the South Lanark election was not entirely a happy experience. This time, it was Margaret Robertson and Clementina Gordon who lost patience with the Labour party, whose organization they found so poor that they pulled out before polling day. Robertson's letter to Catherine is worth quoting for the light it sheds on the state of Labour party organization, and indirectly on what the experienced EFF organizers would have been in a position to contribute in those constituencies which they were already working up on a long-term basis for the general election:

It is true that we are all going off on polling-day because we have found that there is really nothing we can do to help, especially in Scotland. They do not, you see, have any systematic canvas here, and with regard to what casual canvassing has been done we have taken no part in it at all, so we have no personal acquaintance with the voters. We all stayed at Midlothian [at another recent by-election], and kicked our heels all day – the same at Houghton and the same at Crewe. As to their organisation of vehicles we have been able to get them no motor-cars at all and I don't think they have any of their own: and as to carts etc. it is vain for us to make any suggestions with a man like Duncan Graham in charge. He will listen to nothing and is absolutely incapable of organising. ... I am afraid there is nothing we can do now. We are *very* angry with Graham. He asked Mrs. Robinson to speak at 3 meetings yesterday and never advertised them, and *Keir Hardie* was only advertised at 5.0 to speak at 7.0 that night!! and they had fixed it up for a week. It is heart-breaking. [130]

The Labour candidate, Tom Gibb, came in a poor third, but may have contributed to the defeat of the Liberal, George Morton, a result on which the *Common Cause* congratulated the EFF, though the unfortunate Morton was himself a suffragist, while the Unionist candidate was variously described as antisuffragist or as in favour of a limited suffrage measure. However, an EFF objective was to send a message to the Liberal party "so long as it refuses to put into practice its own Liberal principles," so congratulations were not really out of order.[131] At about the same time, the interview which Catherine, together with Kathleen Courtney and Alice Clark, had with Lord Robert Cecil led to a discussion in the NU executive "as to the present attitude of the N.U. towards the Liberal party," and Catherine expressed herself strongly enough to suggest that she at least had no qualms about the South Lanark result, giving her "opinion that Liberals should be made to understand that unless they were prepared to do more for Women's Suffrage in the next Parliament than they had done in the present one, the N.U. would just as soon see a Conservative Government returned to power, as if the Liberals were in opposition much more might be expected of them."[132] But it was not the kind of election result that helped make a good case for the EFF to those within the NU who already had reservations.

Catherine's four months at home at Hawse End at the end of 1913 were certainly no holiday, after the brief break she took in September. In addition to her extensive correspondence with leading parliamentarians, her attendance at the NU council in Newcastle, her close attention to if not oversight of EFF work, her personal involvement in the South Lanark by-election, and her Whitehaven campaign, she apparently organized a great deal of invaluable reference material, some of which had presumably already been collected with the assistance of NU branch secretaries and the office staff. Immensely detailed information on TUs came to her for the compilation of lists of trade unions, their addresses, names of secretaries, whether and when they had considered women's suffrage resolutions and if so with what result, and what NU speakers had addressed them. Dating from about this time, too, there is a list of "Labour M.P.s whom the N.U. wishes to help in preparation for the General Election" (including columns indicating whether they need help, and whether they deserve help), and another list of "Labour M.P.s whom the National Union does *not* wish to help in preparation for the General Election", with a column for "Remarks" – which range from "Safe" (referring to the candidate's election prospects), or "Retiring," to "'Hates rich women' Not friendly to N.U.," usually with the source of the information (most often Peters or Snowden) included in brackets. There is also a twenty-eight-page typed list of "Liberal M.P.s, December 1913," complete with exhaustive notes of their voting records on suffrage, brief quotations from speeches, and reports from suffrage workers, all duly referenced and dated; and another twelve-page one of "Liberal Candidates: January, 1914."[133] This kind of list was not of course the product of a few weeks' work, but was the result of effective record-keeping over several years; for example, the NU office kept a card index of the suffrage records of MPs. But it was Catherine who saw to it that it was kept up to date, and made sure that the information was checked and augmented by the federation secretaries.[134] The dates suggest that she may have at least overseen the polished version, while at Hawse End.

Catherine may have been absent in body from NU headquarters for the final months of 1913, but she was undoubtedly present in spirit.

14 Pre-election Strains on the NU's Nonparty Stance, January to March 1914

Catherine's return to London in January 1914 was eagerly awaited and warmly welcomed by her closest co-workers. She quickly plunged in and was soon involved in a number of issues. As ever, her main job was the political work, and she began again to report to the NU executive as parliamentary secretary, although Alice Clark continued for a while to report on the EFF work.[1]

There was tension among London NU suffragists at the beginning of 1914. A letter from Philippa Strachey, from about this time, suggests that Mrs Fawcett had confided that she was distressed by differences arising among supporters. Philippa's reply was in general and personal terms, warmly reassuring (it was fortunate that she could not see to the end of the year): "Internecine feuds are more hateful than can be said," she wrote, "and it is a great addition to their horror to think that you are being worried about them. I do not think though, that you need ever be afraid of any really grave scandals because we are all of us too deeply attached to the National Union in the abstract and to the President in the concrete."[2]

The inevitable stress of entering yet another year in the long-drawn-out struggle, with the need to keep the pressure still escalating in a very uncertain climate, is in itself enough to explain and excuse some fraying at the seams of the would-be nonparty garment of the NU, stitched together as it was from diverse materials. The two particularly divisive issues of the time were the internal one of whether, and if so how, the London Society for Women's Suffrage should undergo reorganization, and the familiar external one of the direction of EFF policy. Both showed up political, class, and even temperamental differences within the NU.

Catherine, it will be remembered, had played a role in the 1910 reorganization leading to the formation of the regional federations, which had proved itself as an important and successful step in the democratization of the NU.[3] Almost all regions had quite rapidly (and often enthusiastically) formed themselves into federations, but London had resisted. No active steps were taken to persuade it to come into line, nor was there, as far as we know, any extensive grass-roots pressure in London for federation, though Catherine was certainly among those who had hoped that this would happen.

A plan for reorganization was brought to the LSWS annual meeting on 24 November 1913 by Ray Strachey (formerly Costelloe and now honorary secretary of the Hampstead branch and a candidate for the LSWS executive). Sponsored by Hampstead, the plan had the blessing of most incoming and outgoing LSWS executive members, and was seconded by Maude Royden. But Helena Swanwick moved an amendment negating the plan and substituting nothing less than complete conformity to the NU's normal federation rules,[4] and a stormy and confused gathering ensued, with proposals and counter proposals from every quarter. Most seriously, the attack on Strachey's scheme came mainly from women connected with NU headquarters. Indeed, much of the tension derived from the fact that many members of the NU executive and staff – perhaps as many as fifteen,[5] including Catherine – were also members of the LSWS, some as born and bred Londoners, others as London residents only because of their suffrage work, and they formed the core of the resistance to Strachey's plan, which they saw as subverting the purposes of the overall federation structure. No resolution was reached by the time the hall had to be vacated, so an adjourned meeting was called for 15 December.[6]

On one level, the issue of LSWS reorganization was a complicated constitutional one, and its details need not concern us. On another level it can be seen as an important phase of the struggle of the democratic suffragists, many of them northerners, against the traditional leadership and direction of the NU. The issue was the extent to which the LSWS was prepared to become truly democratic by building in provision for an equal voice and equal control over funding to be given to the suffragists from the East End and South London, rather than continuing the hegemony of the upper- and middle-class members from the city's West End and northern suburbs. On the one hand, the LSWS executive, which had already lost its former control over the wider NU, was anxious not to see disappear its class cohesiveness or its ascendancy over the London region. On the other hand, to the more radical of the democratic suffragists, who now dominated the NU office, Strachey's scheme seemed merely an attempt to protect the special status of the LSWS and the control of its middle-class leaders, rather than being, as its proponents considered it, "a well thought out and drastic measure of reform calculated to unite all sections in some degree, and having the official support of the newly elected committee."[7]

The financial arrangements were the focus of the dispute. Strachey euphemistically described as "financial independence" (a phrase marked with an exclamation mark in the margin of Catherine's copy) a clause under which branches would receive from the executive "an annual income proportionate to their annual subscriptions." Although this may well have been an improvement on the previous arrangement, under which all subscriptions were absorbed by the London society headquarters, it still left the poorer areas disadvantaged and the LSWS in control.

The structure for the appointment of the executive was equally significant, although apparently less discussed. Since the LSWS had always operated as a single unit, its twenty-member executive had no built-in regional (and hence class) representation, and this was to be maintained. In Strachey's words, this made it "possible to choose the 20 most competent people, no matter where they live"; in practice the executive could be, and always had been, drawn predominantly if not exclusively from middle- and upper-class west, central, and north London. Under NU federation rules, in contrast, each local society was affiliated directly to the NU, and each federation committee was composed of representatives from every member society in its area.[8]

A great deal of the persistent mythology of the NU as an ineffective genteel kind of drawing-room suffragism for middle- and upper-class women with nothing better to do derives from too much attention having been paid to the London area, to the exclusion of the provincial scene and even of the London-based but radicalized NU headquarters. But it is not altogether fair to perpetuate this stereotype even of London, without at least taking into account the special conditions there, as well as remembering the honourable history of the suffrage women who had kept the cause alive for fifty years before the final push began. Not all Strachey's proposals were directed to maintaining the status quo, and the probability is that she and Maude Royden had gone as far as they thought would prove acceptable towards democratizing the LSWS, at the same time keeping it as an effective functioning unit.[9]

Furthermore, there was some justification for the irritation felt that opposition to Strachey's scheme seemed to emanate from NU headquarters, even though the NU executive properly avoided taking an official position. Between the two meetings Catherine received a nine-page letter from Helen Ward, a member of the LSWS executive (though she wrote as a private individual), which makes it clear that some of those supporting the new scheme perceived the NU executive, individually and collectively, as having taken little interest in the question of London's constitution until Strachey's scheme was before the membership, at which point they came out strongly in favour of federation, throwing into the scale against the alternative reform proposal "the personal and official prestige, and great eloquence of N.U. leaders."[10]

Helen Ward's long letter provides a vivid and salutary picture of the exceptional difficulties under which the LSWS operated, and makes a much better case than Ray Strachey herself had done for a modest reform rather than the full-blown federation scheme. Five years earlier, the LSWS had fought off an attempted takeover by the militants,[11] but the threat remained, and Helen Ward clearly believed that decentralization might lead to a loss of discipline that could have a centrifugal effect as the same danger surfaced in one local society after another. The militants were ever present as they were in no other part of the country.

Ward's own particular interest was not a selfishly middle-class one, but lay with the political and trade union work, which was also exceptionally difficult in London, "owing to the absence of a good Labour organisation and of strong local feeling." What Ward was describing was a situation peculiar to London, where every kind of territory from middle- and upper-class drawing-rooms to working-class areas was the subject of the erratic but incessant attentions of a bewildering variety of suffrage organizations.[12]

The complaint that the issue had not been well considered in advance of the November meeting finds some justification in the amount of lobbying and changing of position that went on between the two meetings, with Maude Royden, for instance, withdrawing her support for the very scheme she had seconded, and appearing among the signatories of a modified federation scheme drawn up by Helena Swanwick, an action which may have reinforced fears that the NU executive was ganging up on the majority of the LSWS executive.[13] Other difficulties arose because of comments that had been made about the position taken by members of the NU staff at the annual meeting, comments to which the staff in turn had "taken exception." The NU executive reiterated that its staff and executive members did indeed retain the right to act in their private capacity as LSWS members, but sent a reasonably conciliatory letter to the LSWS, repeating that the NU as such "had taken no official action in the affairs of the [London] Society," and expressing regret "that any misunderstanding should have arisen."[14]

Helen Ward ended her letter on a rather despairing note, saying she did not expect her long explanation to do any good, that matters had gone too far already, and that it was too late to prevent a grave struggle which could only result in lasting harm.[15] In the final outcome, things were not as bad as she feared; we cannot know whether her letter contributed to the resolution of the issue. In any event, tempers cooled and a compromise was reached. Indeed, the manifestos issued between the two meetings, rather than indicating a hardening of positions, opened the door to a middle solution, with Ray Strachey's scheme being adopted in the main and Helena Swanwick (on behalf of the Richmond branch) withdrawing her total opposition, and resting content to introduce important amendments to the financial arrangements and to insist on the use of the term "federation."[16] The revised constitution was presented and adopted at the February 1914 council of the NU. In effect, the London society was admitted to "the status of a Federation, with all its rights and responsibilities, though, owing to the special character of its work and organisation, the Society does not adopt the ordinary federation rules."[17]

While the heat surrounding the LSWS reorganization showed up the differences in political principle within the NU, and some personal animosities, it showed also the intensity of the will to maintain unity and the focus on the goal of obtaining the vote. The compromise solution may have fully satisfied no one. But it enabled the NU and the LSWS to continue together the work for which both existed.

The NU's now annual demonstration at the Albert Hall was held on 14 February 1914. Some friction (again involving the LSWS as well as some other branches) had arisen over the way in which funds raised there would be allocated, and even over the location for the meeting, but by the time it took place all were pulling together for its success. On this occasion, in particular, it was a meeting for men, and there was an impressive representation from nearly 350 men's organizations. Although two of the advertised speakers were unable to come (Robert Smillie because of a mine disaster, Lord Lytton because of the illness of one of his children), there was still a good variety in the speeches, which were enthusiastically received.

Millicent Fawcett's speech was given in moving the resolution, which roundly condemned Asquith for refusing to receive any deputation from the many men present who had come to London for the occasion,[18] and it was seconded by William Barton, the Liberal MP for Oldham. The NU had not found it easy to obtain a speaker from the Liberal party (the faithful Francis Acland held that his cabinet position made it impossible for him to accept), but this function was performed courageously by Barton, who described himself as a supporter of Mr Asquith, and said that he refused to regard the prime minister as "a hopeless case." Maude Royden spoke on "Our Common Humanity," with her usual blend of wit and deeply serious intent.[19]

The only speaker subjected to continuous disruption, by militants acting in accordance with their policy of focusing their hostility now on the Labour party, was Arthur Henderson, and he enhanced his reputation with the NU considerably by refusing to be moved. According to the *Common Cause*, he "simply set to work, pitched his voice at its loudest, and gave us his speech, unshortened, clear, to the point, without losing the thread or taking the slightest notice of the riot. How many people heard him, one cannot know, but there was not a person in the hall who did not know that they were witnessing one of the pluckiest things they ever saw." When he finished, he was given a standing ovation, and treated to a round of "For he's a jolly good fellow." Molly Mackenzie commented, "For once in a way we can feel grateful to the Militants for giving us the opportunity to give him such an ovation. It ought to have a marked effect on his attitude to w.s. ... And *what* a meeting it was! Albert Hall meetings are always stirring, but this one was epoch-making."[20]

Despite the clear orientation of the Albert Hall meeting towards fostering labour support, and indirectly the development of the EFF policy, such an upbeat occasion was generally heartening to all NU members. Nevertheless, friction about the EFF policy had been endemic in the NU since the inception of the EFF, and was harder to deal with than the LSWS issue, because the NU officers were caught between the demands and criticisms of the Labour party on the one hand, and the at times contradictory demands and criticisms of their own organization on the other. A serious incident occurred in mid-January 1914, when the reconciliation between the NU and the ILP patched up by Catherine at Lanark threatened to come apart. Egerton Wake still harboured resentment over the NU's stance at Keighley, and was easily influenced by a Mr Wallhead, another ILP official, with a personal grudge against the EFF. Whatever their motives, Wallhead and Wake were able to do considerable damage by again raising and playing on fears that the NU was toeing the Liberal party line and could not be trusted.

A Miss Wallhead had been taken on late in 1913, on a three-month probationary basis, as were all NU organizers and other employees, and was sent to the South Lanark by-election to gain some experience. Miss Evans, the NU secretary, told Catherine that Miss Wallhead did not do well as a speaker, and yet was unwilling to do the routine tasks. By December she had proved unsuitable, and Alice Clark wrote to Catherine, " I am much perplexed [as] to how we can get rid of Miss Wall[head] without annoying her father."[21] Unfortunately, Clark did not solve the problem; Miss Wallhead's father was indeed very much annoyed when she was not hired at the end of her probationary term. Whether rightly or not, the NU executive believed that it was his personal pique at his daughter's rejection that led Wallhead, together with Wake, to initiate a serious attack on the NU at a conference of the northwestern division of the ILP on 17 January 1914.[22]

The press had not been admitted to the conference, so the reports which appeared in the *Manchester Guardian*, the *Northern Daily Citizen*, and the *Labour Leader* "must have been officially communicated." The conference had discussed the situation in Rossendale, the seat of Lewis Harcourt, the noted cabinet antisuffragist, and so one of the EFF's targeted constituencies. The ILP had earlier agreed to appoint an organizer there, with financial help from the EFF, but the ILP divisional council now went back on this decision, giving as the reason that "more light had been thrown on the policy of the N.U.W.S.S." Challenged by dedicated suffragists who were present, Wallhead claimed "that the N.A.C. [national administration council of the ILP] had twice thrashed the matter out, and each time rejected the N.U.W.S.S. proposals. No alien or outside organisation should use finance so as to bias the judgment of the I.L.P." Annot Robinson objected to the term "alien," and Wallhead became even more hostile, retorting "that the I.L.P. was Socialist and the Union was not. The Union's policy was to sit on the fence and see which way the cat jumped. There were Conservatives and Anti-socialists in the Union, and on Socialist matters some of them were talking from the teeth outwards."[23]

A heated discussion followed, with Fenner Brockway coming to the defence of the NU, and another supporter pointing out that the trade unions were also not "socialistic." But another Labour candidate, Hudson, concurred with Wallhead's view, and Wake, who was in the chair, came out strongly in favour of the reversal of policy, claiming that, "[I]n an interview with himself, Miss Catherine Marshall, Parliamentary Secretary, had admitted that if the Liberals made ever so small a contribution towards Women's Suffrage in their programme, the Union would desire the Party's return, and only support Labour candidates who were fighting Anti-Suffrage Tories, or where Labour stood the best chance in three-cornered fights. 'Of course,' said Miss Marshall, 'we should desire a strong Labour party to keep the Liberal party to their programme'." Even this rather distorted version of Wake's meeting with Catherine in Lanark says nothing about *working against* Labour candidates, much less those to whom a commitment had been made, and does not justify his further alleging flatly that the NU "would be opposing both Mr. Hudson and Mr. Wallhead in favour of Liberals who were not nearly so sound on the question of the suffrage." In the ensuing vote, the divisional council's action was confirmed "by a large majority."[24]

The NU officers were sufficiently alarmed to call a special executive meeting for Saturday, 24 January, and by the time it met letters had already been sent to the *Manchester Guardian* and the *Daily Citizen*, with the approval of the national officers, but signed by northern NU officials, and there was also a report in the *Common Cause*. The damage done by Wallhead was evidently not confined to the conference; Alice Clark reported that he had said in North-West Durham (where there was a by-election in progress) "that he had documentary evidence that it had been said by Miss Marshall that if Liberals put Women's Suffrage in their programme for the next election, the N.U. would oppose Labour up and down the country."[25]

The NU's defence was once again patiently to explain its election policy: "It is true that the general policy of the Union at the next election will have to be determined by a Special Council called when the occasion arises; but whatever that Council may decide, it will certainly not decide on any policy which would involve a breach of promises already made, or opposition to a party which places Women's Suffrage in the forefront of its programme, and has resolved to oppose any Franchise Bill which does not include women."[26] The statement was as strong as the executive could make it in the circumstances, and was clear to those who fully understood the position, but it is not hard to see why it did not perfectly satisfy those whose inclination was to doubt.

The members of the NU executive most closely engaged with Labour evidently felt a particular sense of urgency because of the possible damage Wallhead and Wake, and the conference report, might do at the coming meeting of the ILP national administrative council [NAC], which was scheduled for Monday, 26 January, just two days away, at the beginning of the even more important annual Labour party conference in Glasgow. Catherine, together with Kathleen Courtney and Alice Clark, had already met with Margaret Bondfield, now one of the few women members of the ILP executive, who "had promised to do all in her power at the Labour Conference to put things right."

Fortunately, an interview with W.C. Anderson, the chair of the ILP (and the husband of Mary Macarthur, noted women's TU organizer and close friend of Bondfield), was helpful if not reassuring. Alice Clark reported that "he understood the N.U. position, and was evidently anxious to avoid rupture. He thought it important that the mischief should be stopped at once, and suggested that a deputation should be sent to the N.A.C. Meeting in Glasgow" on the coming Monday. Since the NU had already asked the NAC to receive a deputation some time soon to discuss finance, the officers had written off at once to ask for time at the coming meeting, and the executive agreed that Catherine, Kathleen Courtney, Alice Clark, and Margaret Robertson should go to lay before the NAC "a simple and explicit statement of the position of the N.U.," which they accordingly did.[27]

As we have seen, the vulnerability of the NU to innuendo and attack such as had been whipped up in the northwestern division resulted largely from uncertainties as to election policy within the Liberal and Labour parties, and as to suffrage within the Liberal party. Once more, the women's suffragists were caught in the squeeze between a central Labour party and the constituencies, neither of which knew what the relation between Liberal and Labour parties would be at the next election, but who were meanwhile acting on different knowledge and different assumptions. And while the NU was constantly being put on the defensive, the Labour party's NEC was still coy about its own strategy; an attempt to get a firm statement as to the determination of the party to be independent of any electoral pact at the general election was still unsuccessful as late as April 1914.[28]

Nevertheless, Catherine saw a need to do whatever could be done to reassure Labour of the good faith of the NU, and asked the executive for three things to this end. First, the statement (already included in the recent responses to the press), that no Labour candidate would be opposed by the NU, should be endorsed. This was agreed, but only after considerable discussion and the addition of a proviso "that the personal attitude of the Labour Candidate on Women's Suffrage be satisfactory." Catherine's second and third requests were laid over for discussion at the next regular executive; they were that an emergency resolution to the same effect should be put on the agenda for the coming NU council; and that the executive should support a resolution which had been put on the council agenda by Edinburgh, "That where the Labour candidate is satisfactory, the National Union shall either support him on EFF lines, or take no part in the election," clearly directed at the avoidance of the kind of difficulty that had arisen at Keighley.[29]

Of significance, too, was the statement about financial arrangements that Catherine took to the NAC, which she had also had authorized by the special executive. The ability of the EFF to provide direct funding to Labour party candidates had undoubtedly been of considerable importance in cementing relations between the NU and the Labour party, particularly at the grassroots; indeed, any of the party officials who disliked the entente may have had reason to regret that they had insisted that funds must be offered locally and not channelled through the head office. Finding the ILP the most sympathetic and the easiest to work with of the bodies making up the Labour party, the NU suggested that EFF funds might be given directly to the ILP for the salary of an organizer in certain key constituencies. But the ILP had a policy banning the acceptance of money given for any special purpose, "and ... the N.U., as a non-party organisation, could not give money to any party except for a special purpose." Discussions on whether any form of financial cooperation could be agreed on had bogged down on several previous occasions (probably the basis for Wallhead's pejorative comments on NAC's refusal of the NU's suggestions). The deputation now advised NAC that "the question of financial co-operation had better be dropped."[30] Direct financial contribution of course was not involved in what was perhaps the more valuable part of the NU's work, the provision of a team of trained organizers paid by the EFF, and the work of local NU volunteers at the time of elections. This side of the work, "which was in the opinion of the N.U. much more important, depended upon the possibility of maintaining full understanding and confidence between the two Societies, and this appeared to be in danger owing to the recent difficulties in Lancashire."[31]

The deputation also made it clear that "the freedom of the N.U. to abstain from taking an active part in any given contest must be recognised by the I.L.P., otherwise no co-operation is possible," and handed each NAC member a written statement of the NU's policy and objectives.[32] The deputation met with an extremely cordial reception and complete agreement, and the NAC promised to draw up a statement "setting forth from their point of view the basis on which co-operation could be undertaken, and the extent to which it could be carried"; once this had been agreed by the NU as well, it could be sent out to ILP branches.[33]

An interesting footnote was provided by Catherine's report that she had later "had an interview with Mr. Wake and Mr. Wallhead at their request, and ... they appeared anxious to explain away the statements which they were said to have made."[34] We can assume that they had not found their views popular with their fellow ILPers. Nevertheless, Wallhead continued to work against the EFF policy.[35]

Little of the fallout reached the floor of the Labour party annual conference, where there were only three dissentients to "a resolution asking the [Parliamentary] Labour party (a) to oppose any franchise reform which does not recognise women's claim to citizenship, and (b) to raise the question at the earliest possible moment in the House of Commons." Brockway's report in the *Labour Leader* described this as "an extraordinary advance in Labour opinion," as the previous year there had been "a heated debate when the I.L.P. had suggested that the extension of the franchise to all men should be opposed if women were not also enfranchised."[36]

Necessary and successful as the swift action of the officers and the special executive may well have been, it did not readily meet with the approval of the full executive when that met again on 5 February. At that time, Kathleen Courtney introduced a resolution, to go forward to the council, which read: "That so long as the Labour party puts Women's Suffrage in the forefront of its programme and opposes any extension of the franchise which does not include women, the N.U. will not support candidates of other parties in constituencies where Labour candidates are standing (it being understood, of course, that in every case the personal attitude of the Labour candidate is in accord with the attitude of his party)." Helena Swanwick, who had been in the chair at the special executive on 24 January, defended both the action taken and the proposed resolution, saying that no change in policy was being made, only a clarification and interpretation.

But objections came from some of those who had not been at the emergency meeting. Eleanor Rathbone thought a real change was proposed, and that therefore the special executive had exceeded its powers, and was proposing to tie the NU too firmly to support of Labour candidates. Margery Corbett Ashby, too, "considered that the Labour party was practically valueless, that the Liberals or Unionists were more valuable, and that the N.U. ought to be free to take a line of its own in as many constituencies as possible."

Catherine's patience may have been wearing thin by this time. The proposed resolution has the hallmarks of something which has been hammered out not easily, but with care; and to make the matter more critical, it represented the interpretation of the election policy which had in fact been taken to the ILP national council. She explained once more that it "would not commit the N.U. to *supporting* any Labour candidate, but only to *not opposing* him. She objected to making the Labour party a tool of the N.U., and urged that the N.U. was in honour bound not to *oppose* Labour candidates, and said that this was what Mrs. Fawcett herself had said." Trying to find a middle ground, Margaret Ashton moved an amended resolution: "That while the N.U. reserves to itself the right to reconsider its policy at any subsequent Council Meeting, it states that as long as the Labour party takes a line on Women's Suffrage, which in the opinion of the N.U. is in the best interests of Women's Suffrage, the N.U. cannot support candidates of other parties in constituencies where Labour candidates are standing (it being understood, of course, that in every case the personal attitude of the Labour candidate is satisfactory to the N.U.)."

As sometimes happens when a compromise is offered, the executive picked this up, probably with relief, and sent it forward to stand on the council agenda in the name of the executive. Catherine's was the only dissenting vote, "on the ground that the resolution as amended was a withdrawal from the position the N.U. had already adopted with regard to the Labour party."[37] As one in the front line of negotiations with the Labour party, and charged, as she saw it, with keeping the Labour party sweet, we can hardly wonder at her reluctance to be saddled with explaining away such a conglomerate of ifs, ans, and buts as the amended resolution presented. The argument as to whether the release to the press sanctioned by the officers, and the statement to the NAC approved by the special executive, had in fact modified NU policy and were therefore ultra vires, continued to rumble away, characteristically troubling Chrystal Macmillan, in her valuable if irritating role of constitutional watchdog, more than it did anyone else.[38] But the attention of the executive was soon engaged by a more serious threat now surfacing.

Within the NU, the discomfort over the actions of the special executive was only the tip of an iceberg of trouble, the product of the approach of the election. If the political climate surrounding women's suffrage had not been so uncertain – in other words, if it had been possible to know what attitude would be taken by the major parties – the NU could and probably would have made its own decisions, as it had before, on a rational estimate of the best chance for the cause, more or less regardless of personal party preferences. But while the Liberals remained uncommitted for or against, while Unionist suffragists toyed with the idea of introducing a limited franchise (although still inclined to see a referendum as a desirable precondition), while the Labour rank and file continued to mistrust its own leaders, some members of the NU executive understandably tended to make their guesses on the basis of their individual loyalties and wishes, a divisive process.

The most serious issue was a revolt against the firm pursuit of the EFF policy, led by Eleanor Rathbone, who, as we have seen, had never been convinced of its value, and now believed it might be an actual source of danger and damage to the cause. Her home branch, Liverpool, had submitted a resolution for the coming council, to prevent the EFF embarking on work "in any constituency where the effect would be to put in a Unionist candidate." On 15 January Rathbone asked the executive to give the resolution its official support, giving her reasons in full. Rathbone thought it suicidal for the NU to adopt a policy which could contribute to a Liberal defeat and the return of the Unionists, who at best would only bring in a narrow bill unacceptable to Liberal supporters in parliament and subject to a referendum, which she believed would be lost, if only because of militancy. Such a defeat "would prejudice Women's Suffrage for future Parliaments; when the Liberals were returned to power, it would be impossible for them to overlook the fact of such defeat." But if the Liberals won, she said, "it was conceivable that Mr. Asquith would not be at the head of the Government, or that in any case with a large majority pledged to Women's Suffrage, supporters might take the line of refusing to belong to a Cabinet which would not bring in a Women's Suffrage Bill. This had been hinted already by Sir Edward Grey."

None of these arguments was fresh to Catherine. Rather than answering them directly at this time, she addressed the strategy issue, speaking strongly against committing the NU "now to the policy it would adopt at the General Election ... as there was some fear in the Labour circles of the National Union leaving them in the lurch in particular constituencies where the National Union was already committed to support Labour." The executive refused to support the resolution.[39]

On 5 February, immediately following Eleanor Rathbone's success in tempering the support given by the executive to the action of the special executive, and therefore in an already loaded atmosphere, she again asked the executive to endorse the Liverpool resolution. Catherine took the opportunity to reply more fully to Rathbone's arguments, admitting that indeed "the N.U. would have to decide when the General Election came between (1) the desirability of the return of a Unionist Government which would probably introduce the Referendum and (2) the return of a Liberal Government with Mr. Asquith probably still at its head," but stating plainly that in her judgment, though "the Referendum was a great danger ... the return of the Liberals, still lead by Mr. Asquith, and feeling that they could continue to ignore the w.s. demand with impunity, might be more dangerous still." The NU manifestly was putting a great deal of hope on the role of Grey, but Catherine, who shared the hope, was realistic. Despite the fact that just then, in the first few months of 1914, the European scene was relatively quiet and crisis-free, the underlying problems of relations between the major powers remained, and Catherine told the executive that "Sir Edward Grey would probably not feel free to resign on Women's Suffrage so long as he was Foreign Secretary, and the European situation 'remained critical'; but that when out of office, he would feel free to take a stronger line on Women's Suffrage than he had hitherto done. If the Liberal Government, having promised nothing definite, were returned to power, it would be exceedingly bad for Women's Suffrage." Rathbone repeated in brief the arguments she had made in January, and after some further discussion the executive "decided by 11 votes to 2 not to support the resolution standing in the name of Liverpool."[40]

Catherine and those who, with her, saw the coming general election as the testing-ground for the EFF policy had reason to heave a sigh of relief. The Liverpool resolution – apart from the difficulty of implementing a policy which called for a prediction as to the result of every three-cornered election – would have gutted the EFF strategy, the main effectiveness of which lay in its power to threaten the Liberal party with loss of seats, regardless of the beneficiary. Catherine had seen enough straws in the wind to be convinced that the threat was taken seriously by at least some Liberals. Although she herself was clearly more and more attracted by socialism, the EFF was not simply an anti-Liberal move, but could be seen as a strategy towards purging the Liberal party of its more illiberal elements and empowering the progressives within the party.

A month later, in her report on the political situation to the executive of 5 March, Catherine further expounded on the way to get (and not to get) the suffrage message across in the run-up to the election. She urged NU members, "in speaking of the outlook at the General Election ... not [to] emphasize their fears of a Referendum as the greatest danger when they were talking to Liberals, nor their fears of the continuance in office of the present Government when they were talking to Conservatives. It was a mistake to let either party think that we should prefer their return to power, however unsatisfactory they might be, rather than the return of the other party." Liberals, it seemed, "were hearing a good deal about the National Union's fears of a Conservative Referendum," but she had been told by two Liberal MPs that even an unfavourable "Conservative referendum on Women's Suffrage would act as an incentive to the Liberal party to take up the matter, and would not necessarily delay a settlement."[41]

Catherine also drew attention to two speakers, quoted in the current *Common Cause*, who had affirmed the effectiveness of the EFF policy. The Liberal MP A.F. Whyte, whose questioner had expected him to condemn the policy, was found instead prepared to admit "that it was unquestionably the right policy in the long run," and ready to acknowledge that the EFF had significantly contributed to the defeat of Liberals in by-elections, which he clearly accepted as a necessary part of suffrage pressure. The other quoted speaker was Lord Robert Cecil, who had challenged the CUWFA to press for the adoption by the Unionist party of some measure of enfranchisement for women. He admitted that the strategic wisdom of the EFF policy was "unassailable," and gave a rather curious reason for demanding that the CUWFA provide a rallying point for more conservatively-minded women; he feared the influence on the active women's suffragists of the working association with Labour – in other words, he was aware of (and naturally deplored) the drift to the left within the NU. Although he did not spell it out, he made it plain that he was also considering the direction of women's votes once the reform he saw as inevitable should come to pass.[42] In a letter to Catherine he had articulated his fears more explicitly, writing, "I am very much afraid that you will find it impossible to avoid the operation of the almost universal law, that when you co-operate with a political party for any purpose you tend to adopt all their political opinions ... all this means that I expect the National Union will become the women's wing of the Labour party, and very possibly they are right to do so."[43] Despite the rather resigned tone of this letter, however, we shall see that Cecil was not prepared to leave the field to Labour without a struggle.

The discussion reflects the uncertainties of the political scene as much as it shows up the potential divisions in the NU executive, and again we are in the curious situation, so unusual for historians, of not having the benefit of hindsight, since no general election remotely resembling the one the NU had every reason to anticipate was ever to take place, the ordinary course of events being completely derailed by the advent of war.

Meanwhile, the potential for division within the NU was raised to crisis level by the actions of four members of the executive, led by

Eleanor Rathbone, who were increasingly anxious about what they saw as the "anti-government policy" of the union. Rathbone sent out a circular on 7 February (immediately following the rejection by the executive of the Liverpool resolution), saying that it had been suggested "that it might be a good plan if delegates to the Council from Societies which dislike the Anti-Government policy of the N.U., or at least do not think it suitable to be extended to the General Election, could meet to discuss the situation informally, and possibly to appoint a Corresponding Secretary or to take any method of facilitating common action that might be desirable."[44]

The letter was apparently addressed exclusively to those societies that Rathbone thought shared her discontent, and invited delegates to a meeting at the Horticultural Hall, at which a committee was elected, which in turn held its first meeting on the morning of 5 March, before the regular meeting of the NU executive – at which time Rathbone announced the formation of the committee. The NU officers were appalled at Rathbone's action, which indeed seems uncharacteristic in its lack of openness and of consideration for procedure. There is a distinct line between making use of opportunities for informal discussion of a dissident view, and moving to set up a structure for opposition; and any argument that Rathbone failed only in not seeing just where this line lay falls before the element of near secrecy attending her first moves.[45] The second big issue, of course, was loyalty to majority executive decisions; although not spelled out, the expectation was that the executive, like the cabinet, would present a united front, except that when a council was imminent, executive members were not prevented from letting the membership at large know where they stood on current issues (as Rathbone had done in February 1913 with her circular on "The Gentle Art of Making Enemies"). Full discussion as to what response the executive should make was laid over until the following meeting, on 19 March. Eleanor Rathbone was unable to attend, and explanation was left mostly to the unfortunate Margery Corbett Ashby, another member of the dissident committee, although she did have the supportive presence of the other two rebels, Mrs Cross and Mrs Haverfield, both of whom were new members of the executive.

The officers had been busy since the last executive meeting and came to that of 19 March well prepared. Millicent Fawcett had already written to Eleanor Rathbone, expressing her serious perturbation at a kind of action which, if followed by "various groups of the Executive," must lead to "the necessary break up of the Union," and asking for more information. The officers had prepared a series of five resolutions to focus the discussion. The first merely established the object of Rathbone's committee as "to organise opinion in the National Union with a view to eliminating a particular course of action at the General Election," and passed unanimously, approved by the dissidents as well as by the majority. In the discussion, Helena Auerbach admitted that there might indeed be nothing "illegal" in what the new committee was doing, but that it could only lead to fragmentation of policy, and now that the situation had arisen it was essential to get a council ruling on how the union wanted its executive to operate.

Other resolutions also were statements of position. The second affirmed that the effectiveness of the NU's policy depended on its ability to shape policy according to circumstances, "and on the knowledge of politicians that the course it adopts at the General Election will depend on the action of the political parties in the meantime." In moving this resolution, Mrs Fawcett drew attention to what was undoubtedly an important reason for the degree of concern felt by the officers, and for their perception of a need for prompt action, when she "pointed out that the actual effect of the action taken by [Rathbone's] Committee had been to set abroad the rumour that the N.U. policy was reversed at the last Council Meeting." The resolution was such a "motherhood" statement – not one that the rebels could go on record as opposing – that it was carried nem. con., from which we can infer that there were abstentions.

The third resolution more directly addressed the action of the dissidents, reading: "That any attempt on the part of members of the Executive Committee to organise support or opposition for any course of action at the General Election before a Special Council has been called to consider all the circumstances must inevitably damage the present effectiveness of the Union's policy, and thus stultify the decisions of the Council." This was carried by twelve votes to four;[46] the remaining two resolutions are noted as carried, with no record of the division. The fourth read: "That no policy can be effectively carried out unless the Executive Committee are united in acting upon the expressed will of the majority at a Council," and the discussion brought to light several disturbing features of the buildup to the formation of Rathbone's committee. Margery Corbett Ashby had written to a member of the London society, speaking of "wide spread dissatisfaction of the existing election policy" and asking for "the names of any such dissatisfied members in order that she might communicate with them," although her purpose was not to attack the by-election policy as much as to identify those "most likely to be opposed to its extension to the General Election." Mrs Haverfield thought the resolution unjustly implied "that the Committee had acted against the express will of the majority of the Council." That it fell to the usually conciliatory Isabella Ford to sum up the damning evidence testifies to the depth of shock the executive was experiencing. She listed, "that the four members of the Executive had acted without consulting their colleagues; there was the letter of Miss Rathbone to certain Societies; the formation of a Committee; the letter from Mrs. Corbett Ashby ... and although the Committee did not intend to prevent the present policy from being effectively carried out this was being the actual result of their action."

The final resolution moved from statement to action, calling for a special meeting of the council to be summoned "in view of the gravity of the situation created by the part taken by four members of the Executive Committee." Mrs Fawcett moved the resolution, as she had all the others, and this one was seconded by Kathleen Courtney, "who urged that the Officers and the Executive must know on what terms they were elected." After some discussion it was decided to move the half-yearly council meeting (due in July) to an earlier date and to devote a session to the issue.[47]

A striking feature of the Rathbone rebellion is the lack of support it received within the NU executive, apart from the three who joined Rathbone's committee. The executive, of whom a number of members must have been Liberal in their long-term sympathies, maintained a high degree of solidarity and a sophisticated understanding of what was at stake, not only in condemning Rathbone's unorthodox methods, but in the continuing adherence to the EFF policy. In the self-same traumatic meeting described above, when the executive moved on to its other business, it was confronted with more than one rather delicate decision directly bearing on the implications of the EFF policy. Alice Clark, reporting for the EFF, described the situation that had arisen in Bishop Auckland, which had been adopted as an EFF constituency in 1912, because the incumbent Liberal, Sir Havelock Allen, was a noted antisuffragist. Ben Spoor, "a particularly keen supporter of our movement has been adopted as prospective Labour candidate with the expectation of receiving N.U. help at the General Election." But Allen had now announced his intention of retiring, and a Dr Rutherford, reported to be a strong suffragist, was the prospective Liberal candidate. However, the EFF "considered that such help could not now honourably be withdrawn," and the executive accepted its recommendation that the adoption of Bishop Auckland as an EFF constituency be renewed.

The other important issue raised by Catherine in her customary political report concerned a bill being introduced by the Labour party, to give "both the vote and eligibility for Parliament to men and women on equal terms, on an Adult Suffrage basis with a short residential qualification." The NU must decide what attitude to take both to the bill and to the associated campaign for adult suffrage which the Labour party would probably launch in the summer or autumn. Catherine introduced the discussion with an explicit exposition of the relationship between women's suffrage and adult suffrage, a relationship (although she did not say so) which she and the EFF had done a great deal to bring about. As she explained, at present, "the Government knew they could not proceed with Franchise Reform because the Labour party would not have any Franchise Bill which did not include women." However, the government would be content to wait for further franchise reform, as long as they carried their Plural Voting Bill, "unless driving power of some kind could be applied. The only quarter from which such driving power was likely to come was the Labour party, but the Labour party would not of course organise a campaign for Women's Suffrage alone; they would treat Women's Suffrage as part of their demand for Franchise Reform as a whole. The reason for the Labour Party Bill and for their proposed campaign was to bring pressure to bear on the Government to put franchise reform including Women's Suffrage, on their programme at the General Election."[48] Later in the discussion, she added "another reason for desiring the passage of the [second reading of the] Bill, because it would provide Mr. Asquith with an excellent excuse for giving way on the Suffrage question; if it passed its second reading he might yield to pressure from the Labour party and take it up as a Government measure."

In the main the discussion turned on a number of rather technical questions – for instance, the NU's policy of not supporting any further private member's bills (which this was, strictly speaking), and the awkward circumstance that the bill included clauses outside the NU's mandate. Strikingly absent is any questioning of the principle of adult suffrage, although the executive correctly worded its response in terms of support for sex equality, in accordance with long-established NU policy. The only sour note was struck by Chrystal Macmillan, who "asked whether the N.U. had any assurance that the Labour party would drop their Bill if Women's Suffrage were cut out of it in Committee stage," to which Catherine replied that she "thought that the resolutions passed by the Labour Party Conference were a guarantee that this could not happen." Overall, however, the executive took a cautious approach, clearly anxious to offer what support it could, but not to exceed its mandate, deciding that the bill, as a private member's bill, could not be officially supported, but that it would support any demand for a government bill. The question of cooperation in the adult suffrage campaign was laid over for a council decision. In passing, we should note a brief but interesting exchange, when Margery Corbett Ashby "suggested that it was not good tactics to ask that women should be eligible for Parliament," the first and perhaps the last time, as far as I am aware, that this obvious issue was discussed by the NU executive. Most of the executive agreed with Corbett Ashby, and the caveat was incorporated into what should be passed on to the Labour party, despite Chrystal Macmillan's dry comment (well justified, we may think) that she "thought it was undesirable for the N.U. to say that it did not want women to be eligible for Parliament."[49]

Although the Labour party's franchise bill came to nothing, the proposal suggests that suffrage had become a policy area – thanks in part to the government's own ill-fated 1913 Reform Bill, and in large part to the efforts of the NU – in which the Labour party was preparing to show an independent attitude and to put effective pressure on the present and possible future Liberal government.

The officers had made every effort to separate the issue of election policy from the matter of the limitations on what was permissible to members of the executive, and to keep the latter as impersonal as possible. Eleanor Rathbone, however, did not think they had succeeded, and said as much at the next executive meeting on 2 April 1914; she held indeed that the resolutions passed, together with a decision now made to send out relevant executive minutes as preparatory documents for the coming council, "would inevitably suggest that the four members of the Executive Committee had been disloyal, and were undermining the existing policy of the Union," and that "if this were intended it would be better definitely to move a vote of censure on these members of the Committee." Chrystal Macmillan alone concurred with Rathbone, and most of the ensuing discussion reads, as might be expected, as a highly uncomfortable attempt on the part of several members to allay some of the hurt being felt by valued colleagues, and particularly by Eleanor Rathbone, without backing down. Catherine's was the most germane attempt at clarification; she "pointed out that, as she understood it, the Resolution was intended not as a comment on past action, but as a ruling for the future. It would be improper," she added, "for one section of the Executive Committee to move a vote of censure on any of its members on a difference of opinion as to the will of the Council." Catherine took another conciliatory step when she seconded Eleanor Rathbone's request to have a statement from herself sent out to the societies from the executive. Despite all this, Rathbone, seconded by Mrs Haverfield, moved to have "the action of the four members of the Executive in joining the Committee ... submitted to an Arbitrator, and his [sic] opinion reported to the council." Maude Royden suggested that bringing in an outside opinion could only prejudice her case with the council, which "would wish to decide all such matters themselves," and the motion was lost.[50]

The council was held in the Chelsea Town Hall on 28 and 29 April 1914. The questions at issue had roused a great deal of interest in the societies, and the meeting was as expected a strenuous occasion, with every seat full, even in the galleries.[51] All shades of opinion as to the action of Rathbone's committee had been sent in as amendments to the executive's resolutions; and even more relating to the NU's by-election and general election policies. However, the executive majority had prepared carefully and came through well, while for Catherine herself the meeting – which happened to take place on the weekend of her birthday, and was attended by both her parents – proved to be something of a personal triumph.

First of all, despite opposition from Chrystal Macmillan, the council reassuringly endorsed the statement made to the ILP's NAC at the Glasgow meeting in January. Then, after many amendments had been rejected, the resolution concerning the behaviour of executive members was passed in a form which was clear but less repressive than the original version: "That this Council while expressing its confidence in the Executive Committee, lays it down as a principle for future guidance that except at Council meetings and during the interval after Council has been summoned, Members of the Executive Committee are not free outside the Executive Committee to take or advocate a course which in the opinion of the majority of the Executive must prejudice the effectiveness of the existing policy of the Union." Later a further admonitory resolution passed, specifically relating to the need not to attempt to limit the courses which could be taken at a general election before policy was determined by the special council.

Coming to by-election and general election policies, we find Catherine, Kathleen Courtney, and Alice Clark advocating an increase in flexibility. Catherine and Alice spoke against an executive resolution moved by Helena Swanwick that laid it down categorically that "the policy of the National Union at a General Election shall not be further determined until a Special Council has been called to consider all possible courses," specifically holding the NU to the support of Labour candidates in given circumstances, and not leaving room for much encouragement to suffragists in other parties. Catherine lost on this one, the resolution being carried. Some light as to her thinking comes from a further resolution, moved by Kathleen Courtney and seconded by Catherine, "That while approving of the e.f.f. policy in those constituencies where it is at present in operation, this Council suggests to its Societies that in other than three-cornered and Labour constituencies the National Union should consider the advisability of helping tried friends at the General Election." An earlier version shows that the intent of this was conciliatory, directed at "avoiding bad feeling" with suffragist Liberals, "minimising local difficulties in the Branches of the n.u.," and "allowing the n.u.w.s.s. to offer something in exchange for pledges demanded from a candidate." Curiously, Alice Clark spoke against this, as did Mrs Fawcett, but it was carried, and may have had a significant effect in mollifying those branches which felt that they received little understanding from the executive.

Eleanor Rathbone's policy proposals for the next general election were on the agenda, but were withdrawn after discussion. Her suggested modifications to policy were not, on the face of it, immoderate. Her belief was reiterated that the only hope of a government measure of women's suffrage (free of a referendum) lay with a Liberal government, and that the "anti-Liberal" by-election policy would not advance this. She therefore advocated that the nu executive inform the leaders of the Labour party that "except in constituencies to which they are already committed, they may not be able at the General Election to support the Labour candidate in three-cornered contests when the result is likely to be merely the return of the Unionist candidate at the expense of the Liberal." In other circumstances, "the Labour party shall have preferential treatment."

Catherine, who spoke against the proposals before they were withdrawn, left no notes of the points that she made, but may be presumed to have made a clear and passionate defence of the need to maintain room to manoeuvre, of the essential importance of having the flexibility, as long as neither major party committed itself to a government measure, to play the parties off against each other – as she was indeed doing to such good effect – to make the utmost use of the eff as a threat to the Liberal party, to keep a finger in even with the Conservatives, and above all, to do nothing which might lose the support of the Labour party, in which lay the only hope of a Liberal party sufficiently radicalized to take up women's suffrage. Whatever it was that she said, it made so profound an impression on the delegates that, in a very rare move, an urgency resolution was brought forward and carried: "That this Council accords its hearty thanks to the Hon. Parliamentary Secretary for her excellent statement, and the exhaustive and lucid replies she has given to the questions that have been addressed to her."

Immediately following the passage of the resolution of thanks to Catherine, the chair announced the resignation from the executive of the four dissidents, Eleanor Rathbone, Margery Corbett Ashby, and the lesser-known Mrs Cross and Mrs Haverfield.[52] Fortunately, and probably at least in part thanks to Catherine's clarity and patience, no other resignations followed, although a number of branches, especially those which had always been uneasy with the EFF policy, had found the council meeting an opportunity to air the problems. To some extent, an ongoing dispute with the Scottish federation, for instance, had temporarily been subsumed into the larger controversy, with Dr Elsie Inglis giving considerable support to Rathbone. Sadly, a vote of thanks to Eleanor Rathbone was also moved, but was not reported in the proceedings, "in deference to a personal request from Miss Rathbone."[53]

Millicent Fawcett wrote to Caroline Marshall on 1 May. The letter reads, in full:

So many thanks for your kind letter about the recent Council. I thought the whole tone of it was excellent and the result most satisfactory. I feel with you that it was much better to bring the whole difference of point of view between us and the 4 into the open, and have it out. The only one of the 4 that I really regret is Miss Rathbone. The other three I part with, without a sigh. I believe Miss Rathbone has been seriously overstrained of late (she has had much illness in her home); and that she would not have acted as she did if she had been in her normal condition. Very often at the Council she could really hardly get her words out. Her last speech was really generous and large minded. I think we must try to get her back some day.

I was delighted also by the unanimous and spontaneous tribute to Catherine. It was most thoroughly deserved. I am more and more impressed by her great capacity for political work, combined with absolute openness and candour – the two things don't often go together in this wicked world. Part of my joy in the tribute to her was in knowing what pleasure it must be giving to you and Mr. Marshall.

I am hoping to get away for a holiday almost directly after our next Executive.[54]

Pleasure in Millicent Fawcett's understanding of and charity towards Eleanor Rathbone may be tempered by her cold and ruthless attitude to the other three, who included the feisty and later distinguished Margery Corbett Ashby – surely a loss to be regretted, quite apart from any empathy with what they might all be feeling. The tribute to Catherine is significant and sincere, and Caroline valued it so highly that she put the letter away with a small group of very special papers which remained with her until her death. But it too was soured for Caroline and is soured for us by the knowledge that next time around – about a year later – it would be Catherine herself who was allowed to go "without a sigh," indeed, with such anger and bitterness that Millicent Fawcett was prepared to contribute to the erasure from history of all Catherine's striking political work.[55]

15 All Parties Consider Boarding the Bandwagon, and the Election That Never Came, April to August 1914

However much encouragement Catherine felt at the affirmation she had been given by the NU council at the end of April 1914, she was overwhelmed by the work confronting her after the council. Millicent Fawcett, Alice Clark, Maude Royden, and Kathleen Courtney were all going abroad for a month. Catherine was desperate enough to send H.N. Brailsford "a piteous cry for help," as she called it.

I shall be left to cope single-handed with any crises that may arise and to take partial responsibility for the running of the Common Cause. My courage fails me at the prospect. It was quite bad enough when they were all away at B[uda] P[est] last year for only a fortnight. I do not want any of the four to know how much I dread them all going out of reach, because 3 of them at any rate need a holiday *very* badly. But I have been casting round in my mind to think whom I can turn to for help if things go wrong, or if any very important decisions have to be made; and I can think of no one who could in any sense replace the absentees except yourself. May I appeal to you at need to come and discuss things? ... it would be an immense relief to my mind if I knew you could and would help with advice in an emergency.[1]

Specifically, Catherine mentioned "a legacy of trouble from the events which necessitated the calling of our Special Council," a possible serious quarrel with the Scottish federation, "federal schemes" (referring to Scottish, Welsh, and Irish Home Rule) which were developing apace, and a "very interesting, but very difficult, question" put to the NU by Lord Lytton. She might have mentioned at least a dozen other issues which would cross her desk and occupy her time during the coming weeks – speaking engagements, requests to lecture, letters to answer on every subject from local branch problems to discontent with the NU policy, by-elections to be watched, EFF organizers to be kept on track, continuing problems with the militants, a plan to divide the NWF, an important effort being made by W.H. Dickinson to amend a new British nationality bill to make it less discriminatory against women, correspondence with suffrage leaders in every party, a women's suffrage bill just then being debated in the House of Lords, and preparations which had to be made for the coming visit of the IWSA executive in July 1914.

Despite the pressure, Catherine wrote to Kathleen Courtney on 7 June, urging her (and Maude Royden) not to hurry back, but to stay away long enough to get themselves fit to face the work of the general election, advice she certainly was not following herself. She had slipped off for a brief visit to Hawse End at the end of May, "combining home with work, always the most wearing of all," she said. From there she went to visit the West Riding EFF committee at Leeds, and spent a weekend with Isabella Ford at Adel, her home on the outskirts of Leeds, spending much of the time still catching up with letter-writing, before going on to see what was being done in the other Yorkshire constituencies selected for EFF attention.[2] Catherine was showing signs of serious overwork throughout this summer of 1914. Characteristically (and in a syndrome some of us can recognize), as she fell farther behind in her work, her files reflect repeated attempts to get some kind of control over the paperwork, and we find file after file marked with such categories as "Unanswered," "To answer," "To do," "Unanswered letters," "Urgent." But on the whole she seems to have held things together, with a great deal of help from Molly Mackenzie, and although some letters were never dealt with (or were met only by a response from Mackenzie promising later attention), she accomplished much of importance.

An issue which absorbed a great deal of Catherine's attention in the early summer of 1914 was the Channing Arnold affair, an unsavoury and complicated case, which had begun in Burma in 1911, and involved the alleged abduction, forcible detention, and rape of a Malayan girl, aged about ten or eleven years, by a man called McCormick, who was subsequently charged with kidnapping and rape, but was discharged. Channing Arnold, the editor of a Rangoon newspaper, took up the case, claiming that the reason for the acquittal had been the accused's friendship with the magistrate, one G.P. Andrew, who colluded with Captain Finnie, the district superintendent of police. Andrew initiated proceedings for defamation against Arnold, who was convicted and sentenced to a year in prison, of which he served four months. He appealed from the Burmese courts to the judicial committee of the Privy Council; the case was heard in February 1914, and judgment given in April. He lost his appeal, but the official report was not available when the NU first took up the issue. When a further civil action was launched against him in Rangoon in about April 1914, this time for libel against Finnie, a hot controversy erupted in the British press.[3] The cause was taken up by a David Alec Wilson, who had corresponded extensively with Arnold, and who set out to gain public attention for his plight. Arnold's case appealed to liberal journalists (he was, after all, one of their own kind) and to those critical of colonial administration. Wilson's letters appeared in a number of papers, including the *Spectator* and the *Nation*, and later he wrote an article for the *English Review*. A number of editorials appeared, some of which did raise issues of racism and discrimination.[4]

Millicent Fawcett and Maude Royden got in touch with Wilson, suggesting other influential people who might be approached to take up the case, which they followed throughout with a great deal of interest and indignation. The feminist perspective was not that of either side in the mainstream press controversy; the more important question was not whether Arnold had been justly treated, but whether the abuse and perhaps sale of a child could be condoned under British colonial rule. In other words, questions and future action should centre not on Channing Arnold but on what had happened to the little girl, Aina, whose fate, and its implications, had almost completely disappeared from the polemics. On the evidence, there is little doubt that the child had been abused – it should not be of much relevance whether her parents did or did not connive, whether she was bought or abducted, or even whether she had or had not already been a prostitute and infected. However, the medical evidence in fact indicated that she had been raped, and had never been a prostitute, while McCormick's defence seems to have been based largely on his view that he had acquired Aina by the payment of thirty rupees, and that there had been a proper agreement to this effect.[5]

Mrs Fawcett confessed herself "stirred" by the press accounts,[6] and she pressed Catherine to pursue it, and to get questions asked in Parliament. Catherine conducted full and careful research to get at the facts, and consulted extensively with her political contacts, including Lord Robert Cecil, Lord Haldane, Philip Snowden, the Aclands, and a number of others not within her usual orbit – for example, Lady Selborne was asked to approach the notorious antisuffragist Lord Curzon, former viceroy of India, and Catherine prepared information to lay before Charles Roberts, the undersecretary of state for India. Through Maude Royden, she obtained an interview with the Bishop of London. Ramsay MacDonald and Keir Hardie she ruled out, because she thought that "anything either [of them] said about India would be discounted to some extent in the House of Commons."[7]

It was Catherine's misfortune that the major crisis in the Arnold case occurred while Fawcett, Courtney, and Royden were all out of town. On Helena Swanwick's advice, Catherine consulted Lord Lytton, "on account of his known interest in the welfare of children, his family connection with India, and the respect which he personally always commands."[8] Lytton, indeed, was extremely helpful, responding fully to Catherine's questions and making time to fit in a visit to her in her office in between two out-of-town trips.[9]

The extent of documentation of the Arnold case remaining in Catherine's papers indicates the thoroughness with which she went into the issue, and the extraordinary amount it must have added to her work-load. Yet it is impossible to avoid a feeling that she was not completely at home in handling it. Her letters frequently refer to it as something Mrs Fawcett has asked her to do, rather than as her own concern, and have a less confident tone than when she is working in her own area of expertise, the political field. She told Lord Lytton, "It is a great responsiblity having to decide important questions like that in the absence of Mrs. Fawcett and Miss Courtney and the Editor of the Common Cause."[10] The issue was, of course, highly emotive, and Catherine found herself at odds with Wilson, whom she considered "a sentimental good-hearted *muddler*,"[11] and who, she thought, was "acting very unwisely, even from the point of view of Mr. Arnold's interests."[12] She was also troubled by Mrs Fawcett's emotionally charged impatience. All Catherine's instincts were towards obtaining full documentation, including a report of the Privy Council appeal, and doing or initiating a complete study before leaping in with action of any kind based on information which would be at best incomplete, and might at worst prove to be inaccurate – something which was not only anathema to Catherine, but could be politically disastrous.

The connection that could be made with women's suffrage, of course, was clear, if indirect; the case was seen as further proof that a political system in which women were not represented must necessarily have laws and administration which inadequately protected women and children. But Catherine may well have felt that Mrs Fawcett was in danger of taking the NU beyond its mandate. While articles and correspondence on every kind of women's interest, and on the Arnold case,[13] appeared in the *Common Cause*, the NU purposefully steered clear of action or the expression of official opinion on anything except the suffrage, and Wilson at least was anxious to draw them into a deputation, and possibly other active intervention.[14]

Further, Wilson's objective, which was to stop the civil action against Arnold from proceeding, did not seem to Catherine the right route to take: "It seems to me," she told the Bishop of London, "that the objects for which Mr Arnold has already sacrificed so much – namely the protecting of the child, and the securing of justice for the native people – would be best secured by going through with the case, securing the utmost publicity for the facts, and stirring up public opinion to demand that all the available evidence shall be fully examined (as was not done in the original trial in Burmah [sic])."[15] Lord Lytton, Lord Haldane, and Philip Snowden all gave some support to her view, and to her sense that the matter should not be rushed, as did Helena Swanwick and Helen Ward. Haldane, in fact, said "the man [Arnold?] had lost his case, and instead of keeping to the *undoubted evils*, had wildly accused people who would have helped him, and had muddled his own case."[16]

Nevertheless, Wilson's wishes prevailed, but fortunately, it seems, without any active intervention by the NU beyond supportive articles in the *Common Cause*, and the alerting of what might be called the NU's political constituency. It was announced in the House of Commons on 14 July 1914 that Finnie had withdrawn his case "as he 'considers his character to be vindicated by the criminal conviction'." Interestingly, the *Common Cause* report says that "Mr. Arnold, as becomes an honourable man, has himself consistently stated his desire to face the Rangoon Court and there to prove his case, but Mr. Alec Wilson, who has put up so chivalrous a fight on his behalf, has stated ... that he would regard [the dropping of the case] to be in effect a moral victory for Mr. Arnold." Whether or not Arnold was vindicated, one may think that Catherine's caution was, and that the kind of support she would have chosen to offer him would have been more to his liking than Wilson's determined interference on his own terms. On the other hand, to do him justice, Wilson may have been right in believing that only the agitation he had promoted had saved Arnold from bankruptcy and a further spell in jail; Arnold had indeed cabled him for financial help in some panic when the date for the civil case had been set.[17] And later in July, Wilson told Fawcett he was "exerting himself now with Editors in India to get the necessity for further safeguarding children raised."[18]

The Channing Arnold case had added an unexpected burden to Catherine's commitments, if only because of the thoroughness with which she approached it. Whether Mrs Fawcett was satisfied we do not know, but it is doubtful whether Catherine felt that the small amount of publicity given to the exploitation of children in a colonial situation – and no clear answers had come through on this aspect – warranted the amount of time and effort that she had put into it.

Of the questions Catherine had listed in her letter to Brailsford, the most pressing, and undoubtedly one of the most interesting to her, was the proposal brought by Lord Lytton. The matter, which had come to the executive the previous week, was so momentous that it is almost surprising that the other NU officers had felt free to continue with their vacation plans; but they had named Brailsford as a suitable person to be brought into the discussion, and it was, after all, not something that had to be decided instantly.

Lord Lytton had shown himself genuinely devoted to the cause of women's suffrage, and prepared, as few politicians were, to put the issue before personal ambition, and – perhaps even more remarkably – to submit his ideas to the judgment of the NU. The March 1914 *Englishwoman* carried an article by him, in which he insisted on the need for a government bill, and more significantly urged that "a situation has been created as to the treatment of which no Government can any longer afford to be divided," and that before the next election the leaders would need "to inform the electors what remedy they propose to adopt."[19] Now he came to the NU executive, on 7 May, fresh from a two-day debate in the House of Lords on the women's suffrage bill introduced there by Lord Selborne (as Lady Selborne had promised Catherine in confidence six months earlier). The terms of the bill were narrow, as might be expected; it would have given the vote to those women who had the municipal vote, that is, to property holders, but it provided the first opportunity to have the subject aired in the House of Lords. Behind the scenes, the NU had been busy whipping up speakers and providing material for speeches. Lytton's speech, the final one of the debate, had "undoubtedly moved his audience deeply," and the Bishops of London and Oxford had been among the eleven who spoke on the suffrage side.[20] Women were agreed that the overall tone had been good; the issue had not been trivialized. An article in the *Englishwoman* commented that "the discussion was conducted wholly without the gibes, jeers, and sneering allusions with which utterances upon this subject in 'another place' have made us only too wearisomely familiar."[21] The bill had been defeated by 104 votes to 60; the suffragists were quick to point out that "that was a better vote than the Government could get in the Upper House for their 1910 Budget, or for the Irish Home Rule Bill,"[22] and Lord Lytton, at least, was dedicated enough to see it as part of an overall strategy to push all parties a little nearer to acceptance of the inevitable.

What Lytton brought to the executive was neither completely new nor completely formulated. It was, in fact, "something between an Initiative and a Referendum,"[23] a modification of the referendum scheme that had proved such a stumbling-block in the proposals of Unionist suffragists. Rather than a referendum attached directly to a suffrage bill, he suggested "a sort of Initiatory Referendum, not on any particular form of Women's Suffrage, but on the general principle whether the country desired legislation to admit women to the electorate." The executive discussed the proposal with a great deal of frankness, suggested possible variations (Catherine wondered whether the question could be put on the ballot paper at the general election), and found Lytton very open and ready to answer questions on the attitude of his party, the strength of the antisuffragists, and the chances of getting the enabling legislation passed for the referendum procedure. The risk of failure, and the extent of the damage this would do were also talked about; Lytton said cogently that "The question to consider at the moment was whether the risk was worth running on the chance of winning; an adverse vote would certainly be a set-back to the Movement; but what other hope was there of obtaining anything? The alternative was probably a Conservative[24] Anti-Suffragist Government in power opposed by the National Union, with further militancy and coercion; and then in all probability a Liberal Suffragist Government which would bring in a Women's Suffrage measure." The ensuing discussion showed that some of the executive had lost their earlier dread of a referendum, particularly in the suggested circumstances, where it would not be attached to a particular bill which could be voted down on its specific content by some suffragists as well as on principle by antisuffragists. Some doubts persisted, and Lytton was sensitive and sensible enough not to press for an immediate answer.[25]

The most important part of Lytton's approach to the executive lay outside the substance of his proposal. He had told Kathleen Courtney that "the time had now come when no Government could be neutral on Women Suffrage." As soon as he came into the meeting on 7 May, he said "that he wished to consult ... [them] as to how he could be of any use to the cause of Women Suffrage, with the Lead-ers of the Conservative Party. He was prepared to discuss with them what action they proposed to take should they be returned to power, and he would tell them he would not support a Government which did not adopt Woman's Suffrage." Although he expected resistance from the party leaders, his view was that "it was quite clear that every Government would be anxious to avoid the necessity of dealing with the prevailing discontent and that the Conservatives would be glad to avail themselves of any opportunity for doing this which was con-sistent with Conservative principles."[26] In effect, Lytton had come to work out with the NU, if possible, a formula that would both be as near as possible to meeting their wishes and would stand the best chance of adoption by his party.

Few women's suffragists could regard Lytton's proposal as an ideal one, yet the idea challenged and invigorated the NU executive. The most politically astute saw it at once as the beginning of what might be a real breakthrough. Catherine recognized in it a promis-ing counter in her game of playing one party off against another, valid even if the suffragists did not win the referendum. Before Lyt-ton came in, she had said that she "had asked a Member of the Gov-ernment what effect an unfavourable Referendum taken by the Conservatives would have on the action of the Liberal party. He had replied that it would undoubtedly hasten the Liberals in taking action in the matter, since they would regard it, not as a decision against the principle of Woman Suffrage, but against a Conservative form of Woman Suffrage, a decision which might go the other way next time and establish a franchise very detrimental to Liberal interests."[27]

Lord Lytton was not the only Unionist looking for a solution. The notes that Catherine sent to Brailsford after the 7 May executive meeting referred to the opinions of Lady Selborne and Lord Robert Cecil as well as to Lytton, the big difference between Lytton and Cecil being that the latter favoured making a referendum procedure part of the constitution in principle, while the former disliked it, but saw it as a way out of the present impasse. Catherine had quickly ob-tained Lytton's permission to follow up his overture with an invita-tion to Brailsford to a meeting at 1 Barton Street, which took place on 20 May (over tea), with Lord Lytton, Lord Robert Cecil, Helena Auerbach, as the only other available NU officer, Catherine, and Brailsford.[28] By this time, Lytton had also discussed the matter with Arthur Balfour and Gerald Balfour.

Catherine reported the discussion at the next meeting of the exec-utive. No firm proposal had emerged, and the various suggestions

need not concern us in detail. What is of significance is the seriousness of the consideration being given to the issue, although Lytton
and Cecil did not agree as to the viability of different suggested
courses of action. Cecil had obviously been impressed by the debate
and the division on the recent House of Lords bill, commenting that
it "pointed to the fact that w.s. would have the support of the
Church," and adding the interesting observation that "he did not believe that Anti-Suffrage feeling was nearly so strong among working
class Conservatives as among the middle and upper classes."

In the discussion following Catherine's report, the members
clearly felt encouraged by the approach that had been made to
them. The committee passed a resolution declaring "that it would be
an advantage if [Lord Lytton and Lord Robert Cecil] would approach their party Leaders and discuss with them what a Conservative Government would be prepared to do if returned to power."
The NU, it was emphasized, was not to be seen to be directly involved
with the deputation. The executive, indeed, was appreciative of the
fact that Lytton had made it plain from the start that, while he would
only act in accordance with what the executive saw to be good, the
NU would be free to take whatever public position seemed to them
most advantageous. The executive did not plan to make any proposals of its own, but authorized Catherine to tell Lytton and Cecil "that
the N.U. would consider a Government Bill with a Referendum pref-
erable to inaction on the part of a conservative Government, but that
a private Member's Bill with a Referendum clause attached would be
worse than the present situation."[29] And they were aware of the salutary effect on the Liberal party that could be expected from any
hint that the Unionists might take up suffrage. Knowing well that
leaders need followers, immediately after Lord Lytton's approach to
the executive, Catherine set in train grassroots support for suffrage
leadership in the Conservative party, writing to secretaries of the societies and federations for the names of local Unionist supporters of
suffrage, and asking them to urge these individuals to put pressure
on the party leaders.[30]

The talks with Unionist suffragist leaders also touched on "Federalism," a reference to the possibility that what might emerge from the
ongoing discussions of measures of Home Rule not only for Ireland
but also for Scotland and Wales would be some kind of federal Britain. As we have seen, the NU had been watching all the Home Rule
developments with care. The possible inclusion of women in the
franchise for regional legislatures was more acceptable to Conservatives, and to many antisuffragists, including Asquith (according to

hints Catherine had received), than was a women's franchise for the traditional parliament. Other important antis who might at least not oppose were said to be Lord Loreburn, Lewis Harcourt, and Mrs Humphry Ward, the leading antisuffragist woman, who (they may have remembered) had declared as early as 1908 that "if there were any practical possibility of dividing up the work of Parliament so that women should vote only on those matters where they were equally concerned with men, there would be a great deal to be said for a special franchise of the kind."[31] Sir West Ridgeway, an avowed "Anti-Suffragist as far as Imperial affairs were concerned," had told Mrs Fawcett in late 1913 of his support for votes for women in the federal parliaments, "which will deal with domestic as contra-distinguished from Imperial affairs," and she had replied encouragingly.[32]

But this attractive coin had danger on the obverse. Significantly, Mrs Humphry Ward refused to cooperate with the NU on the issue of women's federal franchise unless the NU would agree to renounce all claim to the imperial franchise. Rather than proving to be the first step to a complete enfranchisement, the federal franchise might be used to restrict women to concerns seen as "domestic," in the same way as municipal government had come to be regarded as a mere extension of women's appropriate role. However, the danger was for now outweighed by the setback and bad precedent that would be created by the passage of any constitutional act excluding women, and Catherine had long lost no opportunity for urging on the key figures on every side the need to include women as voters in any new constitution, whether it was part of a unified federal scheme or the piecemeal Home Rule bills now under consideration.[33]

The women's suffrage lobby had been so far successful that the Welsh Home Rule Bill introduced on 11 March, and the Scottish Home Rule Bill, which reached second reading on 15 May 1914, both included women as electors for the proposed regional parliaments. Catherine and Scottish NU members were very busy in the first week of May lobbying Scottish Liberal MPs and office holders, as well as English Liberal and Labour MPs, to make sure that women were included from the start in the Scottish bill, rather than having their status left to future amendment, and they were indeed only included at almost the last minute "at a specially convened meeting of the Scottish Liberal Members [the sponsors of the private bill], by a majority of 16 to 12, some of them not voting." Once the clause was in, "all the Scottish M.P.s [claimed] the credit for it," according to Chrystal Macmillan.[34] Catherine continued to put pressure on, writing three different form letters to Scottish Liberals, Liberal and Nationalist suffragists, and Unionist suffragists.[35] Although the bill did not come to a division, much less stand any chance of passing, its importance lay in the promise of the government to introduce a Scottish bill, for which it was hoped this would in some measure serve as a model, and in once more keeping the women's suffrage issue up front. Balfour's speech had had an additional value: "although opposing the main principle of the Bill, he made a special point of expressing his approval of the Clause enfranchising women," and this added fuel to the "Marked feeling of anxiety amongst Liberals lest the Conservative Party should begin to take action, with regard to Women's Suffrage, and bring in a Bill, in Conservative interests," which was also reflected in an article by H.W. Massingham in the *Daily News* of 15 June.[36]

While the NU was unable to take any position on the merits of devolution itself, Catherine, on behalf of the NU, argued that, if it were to take place, the enfranchisement of women for the federal parliaments "offers the possibility of a peaceful solution of a large part of the Women's Suffrage controversy."[37] Inevitably, in pressing the case for inclusion in Home Rule bills, the NU stressed the less controversial aspect, and made use of "motherhood" arguments, to the extent that some of the wording sounds a little strange over Catherine's signature, who was so soon to be outstanding in her recognition of the need to have women involved in all kinds of major decision making, even at the international level.[38] But, by the middle of June, Catherine "had heard from Mr. Snowden that Mr. Churchill was entirely in favour of the inclusion of women in the electorate for the Scottish Parliament," and that "Mr. Asquith had also said that he was prepared to support the Bill with women in it."[39]

Catherine made sure that she kept the lines of communication with the Unionist suffragists open, now that they seemed so willing to have it so. Increasingly, she found that "the Conservatives appeared to be as much agitated as the Liberals lest the other Party should take up the Women's Suffrage queston."[40] On 16 June, she had another interview with Lord Robert Cecil; her notes indicate that she covered a great deal of ground. The headings cover everything from Irish Home Rule, federalism, Scottish Home Rule, and Unionist policy to the coming visit to London of the leaders of the IWSA, although they tell us little about the substance of the discussion. But Cecil had told her "that he was being approached by influential Conservatives, both in the House and in the country, who were anxious that steps should be taken by the Party towards a settlement of the question."[41]

Irish Home Rule was at this time the subject of intense anxiety and the most complicated machinations on every side. Catherine was probably considerably better informed than the average citizen,

making it her business to find out all she could about any major political issue, particularly one in which the bearing on women's enfranchisement was so clear. She kept in touch with opinion in every
party, corresponded with her Irish cousins, the Monteagles, and
consulted frequently with the leading members of the Irishwomen's
Franchise League (IWF) and of the Irishwomen's Suffrage Federation (ISF). But the complexity and even deliberate obfuscation surrounding the question has not been dispelled by seventy-five years
of historical research, and no one at the time was in a position to
know where all sides stood, or what the outcome was most likely
to be.[42]

The Irish Home Rule issue bore on women's suffrage in two ways.
The first and major way was that its dominance of the political scene
in 1913 and 1914 was the worst piece of bad luck that the suffrage
cause could have encountered. As we have seen, all the efforts of the
NU did not avail to get adequate attention paid to women's suffrage
by the nominally suffragist members of the Liberal cabinet as long as
the Irish question hung over the nation. At one level this was understandable, but at another it was clear that, like militancy, it was a welcome excuse to avoid dealing with an inconvenient issue, one on
which the cabinet was divided, and one whose importance they were
bent on minimizing.

The more immediate interest for the women's suffragists in the
Irish question was the same in principle as it was for Scottish and
Welsh Home Rule, the need to ensure inclusion of women in any
new constitution that might be promulgated. With the bewildering
variety of possibilities being canvassed, from separation to federalism, from Home Rule for all Ireland to exclusion of from four to
seven of the northeast counties, from imposition of a constitution by
force to something described as "Home Rule within Home Rule"
with a proviso for a referendum, Catherine struggled to get a handle
on some simple principles that could be made the objective no matter what course events followed. She succeeded remarkably well. In
June 1914 it was announced that the Irish Home Rule Amending
Bill would be introduced in the House of Lords instead of in the
Commons. Catherine told the NU executive on 18 June that this
would probably be advantageous for the suffragists. "There were
two points on which Suffragists must concentrate," she went on, "(a)
The inclusion of women in any Referendum taken in Ulster, (b) the
inclusion of women in the electorate for the Irish Parliament."
Kathleen Courtney and Catherine had met with Lord Lytton and
Dora Mellone, the secretary of the ISF, to discuss "the best means of
procedure." After a discussion in which the contribution of each one
had been important, representing a different perspective, they

agreed on deceptively simple recommendations: to cancel a planned demonstration, to keep the issue of women and the referendum before the public, and to work towards the inclusion of a women's suffrage clause before the bill left the House of Lords.[43]

Lord Lytton had played a part in almost every major suffrage development from the Conciliation Committee on. But now, although still acting as an individual, he had taken on the role of broker between the NU and his party, a very significant development, and it was evident that he could command at least some attention among Unionists. Catherine was not one to ignore an open door, even if the gap was not wide, and she kept in close touch with Lytton and other Unionists throughout the rest of the summer[44] — until the door was slammed shut, like so many others, by the outbreak of war.

The problems Catherine had told Brailsford she feared might arise with the Scottish federation and following the decisions made at the NU half-yearly council in April both concerned the resistance of some NU branches to the EFF policy. Direct repercussions from the firm stand taken at the NU half-yearly council at which the EFF policy had been reaffirmed were not as great as Catherine had feared they might be. Letters of protest at the handling of the issue came in from several societies, but so did letters of approval.[45]

The quarrel between the NU and the Scottish federation was a tedious though important dispute concerning whether the Scottish federation or the Edinburgh society should be responsible for EFF policy in the area, and the degree of control which the national EFF committee should exercise. The Edinburgh society, reporting directly to the EFF committee, had hitherto been actively promoting the EFF work, particularly, in difficult circumstances, in Leith Burghs, an EFF constituency; Edinburgh wanted the present arrangement to continue. However, the Scottish federation had decided to take over the EFF work, and wanted to have it done throughout the region in a different way, "building up Suffrage societies which could be used to support a Labour candidate in an election but not cooperating with the Labour party in the meantime." The federation had correctly submitted its proposed constitution and list of members to the EFF committee, but had taken extreme offence when changes had been made, and in particular when the EFF committee had objected to one of the proposed names, that of a Mr Ballantyne, who was admittedly opposed to the whole EFF policy.[46]

Reading between the lines, we see that one of the issues here was again surely that of where the party sympathies of the NU members lay. Chrystal Macmillan shared the indignation of the Scottish feder-

ation, claiming that Ballantyne's appointment appropriately ensured the representation of minority opinion. The matter had been
discussed at length at the executive meeting of 7 May (which must
have been a horrendous meeting, in view of the amount of difficult
business that came up), and the executive had taken a firm line, reviewing the EFF rules, and reaffirming the absolute need to have EFF
policy controlled from the centre.[47] The Scottish federation was not
content, but no serious trouble erupted. Dissatisfaction with the EFF
policy was endemic, a substantial number of individual members
may have left the NU on this account, and even a few strongly Liberal
branches seceded, but the officers of the NU remained confident that
they could hold together, and even win more support.

To its supporters, it seemed the EFF work was going well. There
had only been one other EFF election, at North-West Durham, since
the difficulties at Keighley and the partial recovery of credibility at
South Lanark, and it had provided a useful chance for the NU to re-
habilitate itself. In a mirror image of events at Keighley, the Labour
candidate, Mr Stuart, had been adopted before the Liberal came,
late, into the field. The latter was Aneurin Williams, an old friend of
suffrage and of Millicent Fawcett, who said "if the party which he
represents were even half as good as he about Suffrage" the difficulty would never have arisen.[48] But the EFF was clear on its obligations in these circumstances, and stood by their support of the
Labour candidate. Williams was hurt, but the stock of the EFF rose
with the Labour party, and those in the NU who understood the
value of the EFF work may well have felt that no more useful situation could have occurred.[49]

On the other hand, some NU members were indignant. The
Haslemere WSS, for example, was extremely upset, and by a majority
vote sent a resolution of protest to the NU executive, an action causing great embarrassment to the three minority members, who described their committee in letters to Catherine as having "lost its
senses," "gone stark staring mad," or as being "unbalanced ... hyster-
ical," and themselves as "dreadfully ashamed and very angry" at an
action which they saw as being completely inappropriate.[50] To allay
the unease and anxiety felt in some areas about general election policy, the executive planned, at Catherine's suggestion, to hold meetings in each federation, in the autumn, at which there could be
discussion of alternative general election policies.[51]

Now, in these same hectic weeks of May, a critical EFF by-election
occurred in North-East Derbyshire, at very short notice. After meeting with the EFF and by-elections committees, Catherine spent fren-
zied days writing and cabling to round up and send the best EFF

organizers to Clementina Gordon, who would be in charge, together with some who could help and would benefit from the experience. Previous engagements had to be cancelled, holidays postponed, federations asked for the loan of organizers in their employment, all and sundry begged for the loan of motors, hospitality sought, coverage in the *Common Cause* arranged, extra funds raised, and the payment of expenses set up.[52] Encouraging word came in from Miss Dring, one of the organizers, that the EFF had quickly got quite a lot of notice, and had been welcomed by the candidate, while Arthur Peters had "said he never liked to go into a fight now without the backing of the nonmilitant women – they were also the finest platform assett [sic] he knew!" Miss Dring went on to beg, "Will you *please, please* get us all the money you can: we groaned at the bills on our survey yesterday and wondered however we were going to pick up our family [of organizers] at night with only one car. If you see *Coun[cillor] M. Ashton will you please ask for hers!*"[53] Cars were always in great demand at elections, so much so that at North-West Durham the organizers had got carried away and had actually bought one, which had been sold at a loss when the election was over.[54]

Catherine had, as usual, quickly grasped the importance of the election in North-East Derbyshire, which was not merely to do with the acceptance of the EFF by Labour. The election had been occasioned by the death of W.E. Harvey, a Lib-Lab MP who had held the seat since before the miners' unions had thrown in their lot with the Labour party. With almost indecent haste, the Derbyshire Miners nominated James Martin to run as Labour candidate. The nomination can be seen as exactly reflecting the stage at which the miners found themselves, for Martin was himself a Liberal of long standing. But he was also president of the Derbyshire Miners' Association, and declared himself bound to support of the Labour principles of the MFGB, to which the Derbyshire Miners were affiliated. He was clear that this committed him to independence of the Liberal party, and if necessary to opposition to it. The local Liberal party accordingly nominated their own candidate, J.P. Houfton, managing director of the Stavely colliery, manifestly representative of middle-class interests. Houfton did not receive much support from London, but the fact that he stood at all underlined the separation of Liberal and Labour interests.[55]

The North-East Derbyshire by-election then became a test case, in different but related ways, both for the left wing of Labour and for the EFF. The miners were faced with a choice between the kind of candidate they had previously elected and one who, although not alarmingly socialist, was identified with an independent Labour stand. The EFF was in the kind of situation it relished, where a new and direct challenge to the Liberal party was mounted, with more than local ramifications, and where they could play an important role. Because of the Lib-Lab history of the constituency, Labour party organization was almost nonexistent. However, the NU organizers found that in this case, the weak state of organization made them all the more welcome – a different state of affairs from what they had experienced at Lanark, where Labour organization had been inefficient rather than nonexistent, and had constantly got in their way. The EFF set to work with a will, setting up their office in Stavely, at the centre of the scattered constituency, and holding at least forty meetings in the brief ten-day campaign, indoors and out, some of them joint meetings with the Labour party. In the outcome, the Unionist candidate won the three-cornered contest, but Martin scored a more than respectable 3,000 votes against the Liberal Houfton's 6,155, after a campaign described by McKibbin (*without mentioning the EFF*), as "truly astonishing," a campaign in which the Labour party had started from nothing.[56] There was some backlash within the NU; Agnes Gill, the honorary secretary of the Sheffield branch, wrote to Helena Renton of the extremely hostile feeling among the Liberal men in her area, who were saying, "if you have turned your Society into a Tory organisation you must fight your own battles", a reference to the splitting of the vote between Liberal and Labour, which had enabled the Unionist to win. Even her own husband, the secretary of the local Liberal party, had, she wrote, lost interest in trying to ensure the adoption of a suffragist candidate.[57] However, Renton was equally sure that Martin had been, in any event, the only reliable suffragist among the candidates.

Catherine's sense was that the miners had been won for Labour – and also for women's suffrage. At the end of June 1914, quite a remarkable exchange took place between Catherine and Samuel Hall, a local party official, providing a rare window on constituency opinion, and on how close the NU was to Labour grassroots decisions in some places, even though the story, like so many from 1914, is incomplete. Catherine had had a chat with Hall at a recent meeting of the Leeds EFF committee, and he had promised to keep her in touch with the Rotherham situation, where the incumbent was J.A. Pease, an antisuffragist minister and director of several colliery companies. Hall wrote to Catherine concerning the general election. The prospective Labour candidate had dropped out, and Hall suggested approaching Robert Smillie, as a distinguished mining man, though from outside the constituency. He wanted Catherine to sound Smillie out. Catherine replied, "As you know, there is no Labour

candidate whom we should support more gladly than Mr. Smillie,"
but asked Hall for his candid opinion as to what Smillie's chances
were in Rotherham, since "we should like to support him in a constituency which he could *win*." Hall thought "seriously and strenuously"
before giving his reply in a long and thoughtful letter. He gave a
breakdown of the membership of the principal trade unions in the
riding, and as far as he could, of the state of opinion: he thought
there were over seven thousand miners on the register, and although he knew some would go with Liberal, he believed "the great
majority would vote Labour." The Steel Smelters and Railway Workers, a powerful factor in the division, would, he thought, "strongly
support the Labour candidate," and there were "14 or 15 other
crafts of well organized men" making up another four thousand
voters. The previous prospective candidate had been hopeful that
he could win, and indeed, much would depend on who the candidate was; in conclusion, he said, "I know of no man more likely to
command a greater measure of support than Mr. Smillie."[58] In fact,
Smillie did not stand, and Hall's estimates of support may have been
greatly overoptimistic, since a few weeks later the local Labour party,
although it had found a candidate, was having trouble finding the
money to pay his agent on an ongoing basis. However, the will was
there, and finally a candidate from the Steel Smelters was chosen,
and funding guaranteed locally.[59]

Relations between the NU and the Labour party at the centre were
also stabilizing again in the summer of 1914, after the rather rough
patch of the previous fall. Although the NU had been troubled in
early April by rumours of an electoral pact between the Labour and
Liberal parties, and had failed to get a denial from Henderson,[60] the
North-East Derbyshire election had seen MacDonald speaking out
angrily – if, as McKibbin suggests, somewhat ambiguously – against
the Liberal party.[61] By mid-June, Catherine "had received most encouraging assurances" from Henderson in reference to the general
election. He had suggested that, if the NU requested it, the party
would be almost certain to agree to make women's suffrage "a test
question for securing the Labour Vote in the constituencies in the
same way as was done with regard to the Taff Vale judgment in the
Election of 1906."[62]

   That the two major parties might be more or less reluctantly moving towards the adoption of some form of suffrage platform did not
make the NU's relationship with the Labour party less valuable. No
one can now be sure whether there would have been a renewal of
the electoral alliance between Liberal and Labour; on balance, I be-

lieve the indications are that grassroots pressure would have prevented it, or made its success questionable. Nonrenewal of the pact
might have led to the loss of a number both of Liberal and of Labour
seats, and so favoured a Unionist victory. By the same token, it
would have added to the value of EFF support for Labour candidates. But however the dice had fallen, Labour pressure for adult
suffrage would have been a factor to be reckoned with, in and out of
parliament, to be taken seriously as a counter to place in the scale
against potential disillusionment with the parliamentary system and
a resort to syndicalism and direct action.

Catherine believed the common ground that the voteless women
had found with grassroots Labour would have far-reaching effects,
and that there were dangers. She wrote to Francis Acland: "The
present state of things is creating a revolutionary spirit in the Wom-
en's Movement (quite apart from Militancy) which will inevitably
help to stimulate, and join hands with, the revolutionary element in
the Labour Movement. If that happens on a large scale the women,
instead of having a steadying influence in the social upheaval that is
coming, will have the opposite effect, reinforcing all that is most violent and uncontrolled and bitter. ... I think the prospect is rapidly
becoming very serious. It affects not only this country, but the whole
of Europe, because the Women's Movement, like the Socialist Movement, tends to develop strongly on International lines."[63]

Catherine was not deploring or resisting social change. The article
she had published in the *Labour Leader*, and everything that we know
of her thinking in 1913–14, shows that by this time she saw major
political and social movement towards socialism essential as well as
inevitable, and was excited by the prospect of women playing a role
in bringing it about. But she greatly wished to see it accomplished by
peaceful political means, and she feared the drift towards direct revolutionary action, the rejection rather than the modification of the
political system, that was characterized by the syndicalist movement
and – for the women – by Sylvia Pankhurst's East London Federation of Suffragettes (ELFS).

Catherine was not alone in her thinking. Beatrice Webb had described the movement of which Catherine formed part, in an article
in the *New Statesman* in February 1914, pointing out that some early
resistance to women's suffrage had been based on the perception of
women (especially those who would qualify under a limited franchise) as essentially conservative. Now, women even of the professional classes were becoming radicalized, and the interest of masses
of women of all classes and occupations was engaged in the struggle.
"But this increase in both the membership and the income of suf-

frage organisations is by no means the most significant feature of the present situation. Owing to the refusal of the two great political parties to take up the women's cause the whole of the women's movement finds itself side-slipping, almost unintentionally, into Labour and Socialist politics." Admitting that once the vote was won, many women would revert to their previous party affiliations, Webb went on, "But the longer women are excluded from citizenship the smaller will be the number of reversions to the creed of *laissez-faire* in social and economic questions, even among women of the upper and middle classes. But this is not all. Among the ... salaried and wage-earning women ... the growing intensity of sex-consciousness is being fused, by close comradeship with Socialists, into the 'class consciousness' of the proletariat eager not merely for political but for economic 'enfranchisement'."[64]

Others shared Catherine's fear that unless satisfaction through legitimate means came soon, the change would be a violent one. Among her papers there is a typed copy of selected passages from an article by P.W. Wilson which appeared in the *Englishwoman* of April 1914. Wilson's main theme is the incalculable harm he saw coming to the Liberal party from its obstinate rejection of the women's cause, and some of the more striking passages concern themselves with what he saw happening to the energy refused a reasonable channel. One that Catherine excerpted reads, "Thousands of women who, a year or two ago, belonged, as it seemed irrevocably to the upper and middle classes are now devoting themselves to the social revolt. With the main body of them, the manner of the revolt is peaceful and constitutional, resulting only in a long succession of seats lost to the Government. But the extreme wings of both parties, the Larkins and the Lansburys and the Pankhursts, are also in touch, nor should we underestimate the folly in these unrestful times of an interpretation of the older political creeds, and especially of Liberalism, which forces the women's movement ... into the arms of Labour-Socialism and Syndicalism."[65]

As a prediction, this view of the direction of the women's movement has failed the test of subsequent history. But war, whatever barriers it may appear to break down in the short term, is fundamentally a reactionary force. Further, no prediction made in the year 1914 was destined to be fulfilled, because no one was predicting the long, devastating war that came out of the summer skies.

Despite the Irish situation, and the political uncertainties which were consequent upon it, the women's suffragists had good reason in the summer of 1914 to feel hopeful that the next election would see a breakthrough. The enfranchisement of women had crossed some kind of watershed and was now no longer seen as a fad that could be laughed off or waited out. Instead, it had become inevitable, only the timing being uncertain, and the hints that Catherine had picked up of anxiety in each of the major parties that the other might introduce the women's franchise in a form advantageous to itself were extremely significant.

The role of militancy in these developments needs examining. During the summer of 1914, the activity of the WSPU continued, escalating in the violence of the incidents, although in fact, the WSPU's human resources were nearly exhausted. It has to be conceded that fear of having to deal with continuing militancy, should they come to power, was one of the factors being used by Unionist suffragists to motivate their reluctant party to look for a compromise, and the topic came up often in talks with Lord Lytton. However, frequent mention is made of a militant outbreak at the time of any referendum as the one circumstance most likely to damn the outcome.[66] More pertinently, it was of course the NU with whom most parliamentary suffragists had chosen to talk, the NU which had undoubtedly kept the realities of the issue alive, and the NU which had managed to put in the thin end of the wedge to make it a respectable cause. Had there been no nonmilitant visibility, who can doubt that the Unionist party anticipating power would have been contemplating firmer repression of the agitation rather than any solution involving compromise? And on the other hand, had there been no militant wing by 1913, what excuse could have been offered by the Liberal party for not making women's suffrage part of its platform for the coming election?

Even despite the excuses of militancy and the Irish situation, the Liberal party too was moving. In July 1914, Bertrand Russell wrote privately to a friend that one of Asquith's sons had been to tea with him, and had "started the subject of suffrage and said his father's opposition was very much weakened. He also said (presumably repeating his father's opinion) that, whichever party is in power, suffrage seems sure to come in a few years." [67] Here is another straw indicating that Asquith would not have stood in the way much longer.

The most public evidence of change, and the one which has most often found its way into history, came with Asquith's reception of the East London Federation of Suffragettes on 20 June 1914.[68] Catherine and her fellow constitutionalists were disgusted. Asquith may well have picked his audience for its working-class base, but more probably, as Holton suggests, a major factor was that he and

Lloyd George believed there was a real possibility of detaching the ELFS still further from the WSPU, and also of persuading them to declare a truce which would immensely improve the climate for the adoption of a broad franchise.[69] If hope of a renewal of the electoral pact with the Labour party were fading, as is suggested by the increased cordiality of Labour party headquarters towards the NU, the Liberal party may have also felt an urgent need to try to salvage some labour votes.

But meanwhile Catherine knew nothing of Asquith's motivation, and when she went two days later to hear a lecture by Annie Besant, who was now supporting militant methods, she wrote to Francis Acland the following day, "I came away feeling sick at heart. It was a pitiful exhibition of great gifts degraded – high ideals cheapened and dragged in the dust. I used to have a great admiration and affection for her when I was a child,[70] which made the experience all the more saddening. ... Mr Asquith's consent to receive the 'East End Suffragettes' was hailed, of course, as a triumph for militancy. 'Mr Asquith has at last proved his claim to be called a great man. It was a great act to say 'yes' after he had said 'No', *in order to save a woman's life.*'"[71] The underlined reference is to Sylvia Pankhurst's threat to starve herself to death outside the House of Commons, made just before Asquith's acceptance of the delegation.[72] Acland reproved Catherine, writing, "I think if you are so anxious that the grant of the suffrage should not seem to be yielding to militancy you might perhaps refrain from treating Asquith's action as an encouragement to militancy!"[73]

Asquith agreed to Lloyd George's following up on the ELFS deputation, and July saw active and promising negotiations opened with Sylvia Pankhurst and George Lansbury. This development was not known to the NU, and Catherine might have found it hard to accept when the time had come to bring the NU into the negotiations, as it surely would have. However, her reflections on the revolutionary danger pointed to the urgent need of effective action to relieve the frustration of the unenfranchised, and had she come to be persuaded of Sylvia Pankhurst's sincerity, there can be little doubt that she would have welcomed the enabling truce.

Liberal anxiety about the effect of the EFF policy manifested itself in a variety of ways. On 27 July Catherine and the other NU officers attended a conference between the LWSU and the NU, called at the request of the LWSU, whose members, many of them long-standing members of the NU – including Eleanor Acland – felt that the NU election policy was pushing them out of the NU and debilitating their own policy. They thought that the result of the NU policy, especially if applied at the general election, would undermine the LWSU's present function, which was to encourage their party to pull out antisuffrage candidates in favour of suffragists – who, they realized, might nevertheless lose the seat because the EFF policy encouraged a Labour man to come in and split the vote. They came in fact to beg the NU not to oppose Liberal candidates who were good suffragists, and who had LWSU endorsement. The report of the meeting suggests that the NU officers got more information from their visitors than the other way round. In particular, it became clear that the Liberal women had little hope that their party would adopt women's suffrage in its general election platform. Accordingly, the most they could hope for was to obtain what Eleanor Acland called "a very strong suffrage party within the Liberal party." The NU expressed difficulty seeing any great difference between this and the discredited strategy of putting faith in a body of pledged suffragists, who later, as Catherine said, "considered it as a matter of course that their pledges were only binding if it did not embarrass the Government." The pessimism of the LWSU is puzzling in light of the evidence we have cited of movement in high places. The two organizations parted, agreeing rather sadly to differ; Catherine and her old friend Eleanor Acland were now poles apart.[74]

A major international suffrage occasion occurred in July 1914, when the board of officers of the IWSA met in London to plan the program for the next congress, scheduled to take place in Berlin in 1915.[75] The board included representatives from around the world, and many would stay on in England for an extended visit after the business meetings of 8 to 10 July. As soon as Catherine returned from Yorkshire, she was involved, on top of all her other work, in organizing the political side of the visit. She saw in it a great opportunity to raise the profile of women's suffrage, and she knew, too, that the visitors would like to see as much as they could of British political institutions. Francis Acland readily agreed to arrange for their entertainment at the House of Commons, by the various parliamentary women's suffrage committees; Arthur Henderson and Lord Robert Cecil (from the other two parties) would help set this up. "Apart from politeness," said Catherine, "I think it will be really useful to the movement both abroad and here to make rather a fuss over their visit."[76]

In the midst of all her work, Catherine took time out to give some thought to suitable clothes to wear to the many social and formal functions which would be occasioned by the IWSA visit. As always in times of great busyness, Catherine had already allowed unpaid bills to accumulate, and this additional pressure on her wardrobe added substantially to her debts. However, much of the expense was for the refurbishing of clothes which she already owned, and in particular the all-important hats. A single bill for £4–12–9, dated 11 July, included a new hat (grey, with velvet flowers), two velvet flowers to match those on the grey hat, and a new "Champagne Ninon Blouse with embroidered collar," together with new tulle on a white hat, a "new crown and top brim to blue Hat with posies," and "New Foliage and Rose on Garden Hat."[77]

With an eye to press coverage, as well as to the enjoyment of the guests, Catherine tried to arrange meetings with leading politicians. She wrote to Lady Betty Balfour, sister-in-law of A.J. Balfour, asking her to try to persuade him to invite the visitors to his house and to make a short speech emphasizing the nonmilitant character of the IWSA. Catherine wanted "someone so important that his words would be reported in all the foreign papers."[78] She and Millicent Fawcett wrote to Balfour himself, but he was out of town and the letter was passed to Alice Balfour (sister and housekeeper to A.J. Balfour), who invited the suffragists to tea with her (to "see the Burne Jones Pictures [sic]") and allowed Catherine to manage the guest list, but held out little hope that Balfour would be there, and was very annoyed when a notice of the occasion appeared in the *Times*. However, on Catherine's apology, the tea party went ahead, although Catherine's hope of having it a rather public event must have been modified. Catherine may have acted with less than her usual tact when she had assumed that Lady Betty, herself a suffragist, would be able to help arrange hospitality at the Balfour house; Pat Jalland has shown that there was no love lost between the dutiful unmarried sister and her sisters-in-law.[79] However, Catherine's letter resulted in a lunch meeting with Lady Betty, who joined the ranks of those Unionist suffragists scrambling to find a suggestion which, by softening the referendum requirement, would make for a Unionist women's suffrage initiative that would be at least marginally acceptable to the NU.

Once the IWSA board members were in town, the pace of Catherine's activities undoubtedly increased to a still more furious rate, but at least she had now for some weeks had the support of the other NU officers. The Balfour tea party, even though private, turned into a real suffrage occasion, and Balfour did more than put in an appearance. The Unionists were represented not only by Balfour and the stalwart suffragists, Lord Lytton and Lord Robert Cecil, but by Arthur Steel Maitland, the chair of the Unionist party, who was moving rapidly towards conversion to women's suffrage, and all, according to Catherine, "talked of nothing but Women's Suffrage for an hour and a half."[80]

There were still arrangements to be made. The IWSA was entertained at the House of Commons on 14 July, and as many as Catherine could obtain tickets for attended a debate in the House of Lords on the previous day. Catherine made use of all her contacts, and some of her contacts' contacts, to try to raise enough tickets, since only two were allowed to each peer, but even then some of the visitors had to be disappointed. Lord Lytton also had to reassure Black Rod, the steward of the House, that the "distinguished foreign visitors" could surely not have been those responsible for writing "Votes for Women" across a notice board in the lobby.[81] Other activities included a luncheon given by the NU offices and executive for the guests, and a number of other formal and informal events.[82]

During the same busy week, Catherine met up again with Lloyd George over breakfast, introducing him to Rosika Schwimmer. Teasingly, Catherine struck a bet with him about the probability of the Liberal party adopting adult suffrage. She followed up the conversation with a letter, enclosing the NU's new pamphlet on the achievements of the EFF,[83] making sure that he knew of the willingness of the Unionists to discuss suffrage, and adding a postscript, "About that bet – I should not consider a vague declaration in favour of Adult Suffrage as a fulfilment of the conditions on the Liberal side. What I had in mind was a definite promise of legislation. Do you accept it in that sense? – and what is the wager to be?"[84] A day or two later, Catherine had a daring idea, and wrote to ask Lloyd George to spare her a few minutes – she was, she said, "at the House almost every evening."[85] She had intrigued him, and he saw her the same day. What she proposed was that he should attend a big Miners' Gala being held in Durham on 25 July, where he could see for himself how much enthusiasm there was for the suffrage cause; by permission of the Miners, the NU was to have a platform, at which Margaret Robertson and Muriel Matters would speak. Since there were difficulties in the way of his going openly, she proposed that he go in disguise (she even suggested at one point that he might bring Mr Asquith with him),[86] and not getting his agreement (but perhaps aware that he was tempted), she wrote yet again, enclosing a railway timetable and exact directions as to what trains he should take, arriving eventually at "Ferryhill Junction, where I could meet you and take you, begoggled, to the scene of action. Our meeting," she told him,

will probably begin about 1 o'clock, but it will be necessary to be there early to secure a place near the lorry. If you do go I will arrange for Robert

Smillie (President of the Miners' Federation of Great Britain) and Mrs. Chapman Catt (President of the International Women's Suffrage Alliance) to speak in addition to Miss Robertson and Miss Matters. There's a programme for you! I shall be sorely tempted to mount the lorry myself and invite you to heckle!

It will really be an excellent opportunity for you to test for yourself how much the Suffrage question counts today with the working classes. ... And it would surely be a refreshing distraction to forget Home Rule and Budget worries for a few hours, and turn from the cares of the present to the hopes of the future.

I cannot believe that it is past the wit of man and Cabinet minister to devise some means of getting to King's X unobserved and without the loss of dignity when the wit of woman is prepared to do all the rest.[87]

Asking him to give her his final answer early the following week, she concluded, "I have at present cancelled a very attractive weekend engagement to have the honour – (and the fun!) – of escorting you to this meeting." The picture conjured up by Catherine brings into the forefront a quality of enjoyment, adventure, and high spirits which does not easily filter through the correspondence, minutes, and working documents through which we so largely know her. We do not have Lloyd George's replies to her letters, but she received a definitive refusal from him on 21 or 22 July, when the extremely serious situation on the Irish Home Rule Bill had led to the calling of the Buckingham Palace conference (21–24 July 1914), in which Lloyd George took part. There is even some evidence that he had allowed himself to be persuaded and did indeed briefly plan to come; Catherine told him she had spent the previous weekend "devising an effective and eminently dignified disguise for you." Hoping that he would manage to come to a later demonstration (perhaps the Trades Union Congress in September), she rejected his offer of sending a secretary to report for him, saying, "We want you to see for yourself, first-hand, because there is no one so good as you are at judging the temper of a crowd, and gauging with what force the tide is running."[88]

Despite her lightheartedness, which had justification in the way the women's suffrage tide was running in all parties, Catherine knew well how serious the Irish situation was; apart from her own natural interest in all things political, the attempts to make sure of a women's suffrage clause had kept her involved at every stage with whatever part of the negotiations was in the public domain. In common with almost all the British public, she was much less aware of the consequences that were following inexorably after the shot fired in Sarajevo on 28 June 1914.

A recent writer has said, "Total absorption in suffrage work meant that the outbreak of war came to Marshall, as it did to so many suffragists, as a sudden and almost incomprehensible shock."[89] Catherine was indeed intensely busy during the days that led up to the declaration of war; but she was at the House of Commons almost every day. She was no more ignorant than any other citizen and indeed than most members of Parliament of what was going on behind the closed doors of Number 10, Downing Street at the end of July, and probably more knowledgeable of the context than many. The divided cabinet had the effect of imposing a complete blackout on news as to what position Britain was going to take in the European conflict, with the result that the public was held in a false sense of security until the very last minute.[90] There is an eerie feeling in reading correspondence between usually well informed people for the last week of July 1914, or indeed in reading the newspapers. There is plenty about the Irish crisis, and there may be mention of the danger of war in Europe. But one finds scarcely a mention of the possibility of Britain becoming implicated in the war. Catherine received a large batch of mail on 31 July; Caroline Marshall's was the only letter in which the possibility of war was mentioned.[91]

If any generalization can be made about those to whom the war was a total shock and those to whom it was not entirely unexpected, the difference is probably one of political philosophy. The conservative press, which had long looked forward to a showdown with Germany, was marginally ahead in predicting British intervention. The liberal newspapers discussed the European crisis with increasing anxiety, but assumed that Britain would remain neutral. Not until 28 July was this being called into question, and only just before the weekend (31 July was a Friday) did fear of British intervention become palpable, and a great campaign for British neutrality begin, especially supported by liberal and left-wing people. Many had grown up, like Catherine, believing that humanity was reaching an era when major wars were outmoded as a means of settling international disputes.

Many women, and women's organizations, joined the several neutrality leagues and committees which were hastily formed. Others were anxious that women's distinctive voice should be heard.[92] Late on 31 July, Catherine was approached by a number of women's organizations, including the women's Trade Union League, the Women's Cooperative Guild, the National Labour League, and the Women's Labour League, to ask whether the NU would take the lead, as a nonparty body, in a cooperative meeting to be held as soon as possible, "with the object of strengthening the hands of those who were working to limit the area of the European War, and to provide a platform from which the Women's Organisations could express their point of view." All the NU officers except Catherine and Mrs Fawcett were out of town, but they decided to cooperate in the preparations for the meeting, and to call a special executive for the morning of Monday, 3 August, the bank holiday. Meanwhile the date was fixed for Tuesday, 4 August, and arrangements for the meeting went on. There were still a number of the board of the IWSA in Britain, and when they made the decision to take part, the LSWS asked that the NU step back and act only as the auxiliary of the IWSA until the executive had had time to meet.[93]

When the special executive gathered on 3 August, the day of Grey's momentous speech in the Commons, ten members had managed to get back into town for the meeting, and Catherine reported on the state of arrangements, and on the list of those who had agreed to speak. Most represented organizations, and Rosika Schwimmer would speak as a Hungarian woman. Later, IWSA members from Germany, Switzerland, and Finland also agreed to speak. Millicent Fawcett's name headed the list. The committee felt itself to be in a difficult position, making decisions which would normally not have been within their competence but would have required the calling of a council; however, the emergency left them little choice, and they decided to take part, as long as the other participants would agree that the resolution to be put to the meeting should not involve "support of any particular policy in relation to the war," and that it should be made clear that "each speaker speaks only for herself or for the organisation she represents." Helena Swanwick would speak for the NU, and a resolution was drafted.[94]

Next day, when Catherine made her way to the meeting in the Kingsway Hall at 8 pm, Britain was within three hours of declaring war, following the expiry of the ultimatum given to Germany. Whether or not Millicent Fawcett by now found her situation uncomfortable, she did not back out, but chaired the gathering. The audience was made up of all classes, with the majority working-class women. They showed an unequivocal horror of the war and a realistic recognition of its probable effects. The main resolution stressed in the preamble that the coming of war depended "on decisions which women have no direct power to shape," and went on to call on "all Governments not yet involved to work unceasingly towards a settlement, not by force, but by reason." A second resolution encouraged the women's societies to make use of their organization to alleviate the distress caused by the economic and industrial dislocation of the war.[95]

Leaving the crowded hall at the end of the long meeting, Catherine, and all the others with her, stepped into a world irreparably changed from the social and political world in which they had lived their lives to that day.

16   Conclusions

Britain's declaration of war on 4 August 1914 brings to an end our account of prewar women's suffrage politics, and of Catherine Marshall's life in prewar Liberal England. The effects of the war on the women's suffrage movement, on feminist theory, and on Catherine Marshall and her closest colleagues in particular has been discussed elsewhere and will be told in detail in a later work, which will also form the second part of Catherine's biography, giving the story of the remainder of her life.

Historical mythology likes to attribute the granting of the vote to the splendid work done by women for the war effort.[1] In fact, women's war work merely provided a face-saving cover for what the women's suffrage movement had brought to the point of inevitability. The examination of Catherine's life has shown how overwhelmingly important had been the role of the NUWSS; and within the NUWSS, perhaps only Millicent Fawcett, with her fifty years of service to the cause, had played a more significant role than had Catherine, although the latter was on the suffrage scene for less than a decade.

The NUWSS has been shown as far more closely entwined with the history of mainstream British politics than has previously been established. Much of this book has concerned itself with various shades of opinion within each of the three major political parties, and with Catherine's attempts to reach the individual holders of those opinions with appeals to principle, conscience, or party interest on behalf of some one or other of the many possible variants of women's suffrage. By the end of 1913, she was of all lobbyists probably the best informed, and possessed of an extremely rare degree of access to leading politicians in all three parties.

Speculation on a "What if ... ?" basis is a dangerous pastime for an historian, yet it can hardly be avoided in evaluating the contribution of the women's suffrage movement before the First World War, deprived as it was of the legitimate testing ground of the expected general election.

The year 1914 had been in some ways another intensely frustrating one for the NU, with everything held in abeyance pending the settlement of the Irish Home Rule question, and a multitude of different scenarios possible for the imminent election. Every party was divided, and by and large the divisions on the women's suffrage issue, visible or latent, followed the lines of preexistent cracks that were deep and potentially threatening.

The Labour party, as the only party to have women's suffrage as a plank in its platform, might seem, and perhaps was, the least divided. But if it was not seriously divided on women's suffrage, it was in danger of debilitation as a result of other strains. The by-elections in which the EFF or the NU had been involved had demonstrated serious mistrust between the centre and the periphery, and some fragmentation among the different components in the local LRCs as in the National Executive Committee. While the summer of 1914 at last brought signs indicating that the Labour party would probably go for electoral independence in the general election, perceptions at Westminster and in the party headquarters differed so greatly from the view in the constituencies that there can be no certainty. Further, electoral independence might have diminished the Labour presence in the House of Commons, while a continued pact might have led to a large but docile PLP. The major ideological division in the party was to be shown up sharply by the war, when the socialist ILP stayed in opposition, splintering off from the main body of the Labour party, which agreed to support the war initiative. The consensus of support for women's suffrage within the party, and particularly among the hard-won trade union converts, might also have proved contingent on other factors and on the service of other interests.

However, all that said, the task of education, conversion, and cooperation which the NU had accomplished in its relationship with the Labour party between 1912 and 1914 was phenomenal, and its results too solid to melt away completely. The effects can be characterized in three ways. In the first place, the NU's impressive constituency work had put a growing number of candidates and local branches considerably in debt to the women, and better still, had led them to build on hopes of a relationship continuing into the general election.

Despite a rosy view taken by some historians,[2] the party's own constituency organization was at best limping along towards improvement, and the substantial contribution of the EFF in funds, experience, and organizers could be a godsend. Secondly, many individuals, both among the leadership and in the rank and file of Labour, not least in the trade unions, had had personal exposure to the women's suffrage question and had been convinced of the justice and inevitability of the cause; it may also be fair to say that it was a contributing factor to growing grassroots labour distrust of the ruling Liberals. Thirdly, and closely related, is the momentous success that the new wave of more radical suffragists within the NU had had in linking women's suffrage with the cause of adult suffrage, and in identifying both as part of an essential move towards full democracy. A demand was beginning to be heard, and the danger that it would be a demand for manhood suffrage rather than adult suffrage was fading.

In the Liberal party the problems and the possible solutions were not the same as in the Labour party. The control exercised by the central party over constituencies was less subject to question. Indeed, the impression is left that many rank and file Liberals, and Liberal women supporters, were inclined to sit on the fence on controversial issues and "wait and see"[3] which way the leaders would jump before following. This is most strikingly evidenced by the extreme difficulty of getting the WLF to make any kind of stand for suffrage, the tendency both locally and nationally to take an attitude which could almost be characterized as "Father knows best." On women's suffrage very little leadership was forthcoming, and it was her perception of the acuteness of the need for leadership which made Catherine pursue so assiduously the suffragists within the cabinet, and especially those who, like Grey, seemed to have a principled commitment.

Much as they tried to turn the Irish question to their own advantage through campaigns for women's representation in regional parliaments, the Home Rule issue stood between the women's suffragists and their every attempt to get a concrete commitment from the Liberal party. But eventually that had to come to a resolution, and meanwhile we have seen that distinct opposition was steadily being eroded, with even Asquith coming reluctantly to recognize the inevitability of the enfranchisement of women. The erosion of indifference was equally important, and here again Catherine's contribution was major one, though perhaps not entirely conscious. One of the deep roots of indifference was the kind of trivialization of women to which most leading politicians had been conditioned since birth, the attitude that had made Asquith laugh spontaneously at the preposterous idea that women's suffrage could be an issue on which he might resign. But women such as Catherine Marshall, Kathleen Courtney, Margaret Robertson, Helena Swanwick, Maude Royden, Eleanor Rathbone, and Millicent Fawcett were hard to trivialize, and they were constantly visible in one context or another from 1912 on. The NU had helped ensure that these women were harder to dismiss than the ever-present militant suffragettes.

It is still not clear how genuine was the desire within the Liberal party, often expressed particularly by Lloyd George, for manhood or universal suffrage. Those Liberals who whole-heartedly supported this view presumably saw Labour as the firm ally of Liberalism; any who saw the Labour party as a possible rival or indeed successor to the Liberal party may well have had secret fears of so broad an extension of the franchise – secret, because it was manifestly "illiberal" to oppose (male) democracy. But whatever uneasiness there might be about too broad a franchise, too narrow a new franchise was certain to favour the Conservatives. Hence, the signs we have related of Asquith's gradual change of attitude indicate that the suffragists' prolonged attempts to convince him that there was a popular working-class demand for the vote were bearing fruit in 1913 and 1914. He was surely preparing to accept the inevitable; as he eventually did with the convenient excuse provided by the war.

Until the end of July 1914, the Liberal party had room in it for an almost uncomfortably wide range of opinion and ideological underpinning. No issue better demonstrates this than women's suffrage. The distribution of support in the party for women's enfranchisement was not random. With some exceptions, one could surely demonstrate that the more progressive "New Liberals" and those whose liberalism was strongly idealistic were the supporters of the cause. Those in the middle ground would at least have been prepared to concede the granting of the vote to women, however much they might have hedged their adherence with considerations of supposed party interest and with other matters which they could represent as being of greater urgency. The hardliners, already uneasy at progressive social policies, were also those most firmly opposed to women's suffrage.

Early in 1913, Mary Sheepshanks had written to Bertrand Russell that she feared "it is true that women have nothing to hope from any party's sense of justice, only from its interest."[4] Probably this is the bottom line, and despite all her appeals to the better nature of the politicians with whom she dealt, Catherine had never neglected any opportunity of pushing arguments of their own enlightened party self-interest, and had also been aware of the extent to which the personal ambition of such men as Lloyd George might be a stumbling-block (unless it could, on the other hand, be turned to advantage). Catherine had done a fine job of playing one party off against another, a task again greatly complicated by the lack of clarity in the relationship between the Liberal and Labour parties.

Overall, the most significant achievement of the women's suffragists by 1914 was to make women's suffrage an issue that would not go away. They had not yet succeeded in making it a part of the platform of any party except Labour, and, with Home Rule still dominating the scene, most politicians were keeping it out of their speeches as far as they could. But if it was not in their speeches, the seed had been planted in their minds, and, kept well watered by the NU, it would inescapably grow. We have seen distinct signs of the bandwagon effect which comes into play in franchise reform at the point at which politicians perceive some measure of reform as inevitable; all parties conclude, however reluctantly, that they had better be the ones to sponsor the reform, so that they may shape it to their advantage and reap the gratitude of the new electorate. By 1913, even the leading suffragists in the Unionist party, themselves acting out of conviction, were beginning to have hopes of carrying a modest measure of suffrage reform as a plank in the party platform in the coming general election. For Catherine, a Unionist victory at the polls, with a narrow Unionist suffrage measure, was the least promising option; but it would have been better than nothing, and if a future Liberal government had then widened the franchise for men, women would surely have benefited again. Meanwhile, it was a good bogey to scare Liberals with, and seems to have begun to have its effect.

In her role as honorary parliamentary secretary, Catherine had moved the NU from a nonparty position hopelessly dedicated to bringing together suffragists from all parties in support of a private member's bill to a position – still nonparty – in which they were heard in the inner counsels of every party. There they could play the parties off against each other, and there they would be able to take advantage of events as they occurred. Those who have argued that the winning of the suffrage was dependent on political events beyond the issue itself are only repeating a lesson that the NU were the first to learn. They are wrong when they imply that the role of the women's suffragists was therefore of little significance.[5] In general terms, it is unreasonable to ignore the fact that women's enfranchisement would never have been a political issue had the women not made it so, and would not have remained one if the women had not kept it before the politicians constantly throughout the prewar years. Even more important, by 1914, the women were watching developments with an intimate and highly sophisticated knowledge in the certainty that sooner or later the opening they needed would appear, and that they and their friends in high places would be ready to exploit the breakthrough.

Catherine's intense involvement in the suffrage struggle lasted from 1908 to 1914, though it was with her both before and after those dates. The NU had entered the period as a mainly middle-class, Liberal-dominated, southern-based body working for the extension of the franchise to a privileged group of women. By the end it was a highly structured democratic organization, with a strong northern and working-class component in its constituency, working towards the most democratic franchise that could be obtained. The leadership at the centre, if still predominantly middle class, was now representative of all regions, on average decidedly farther to the left, and much more involved and knowledgeable about working-class concerns. Further, provincial councils and local branches provided a forum for leaders who were not drawn from the traditional ruling classes, and the work of the EFF provided both need and opportunity to acquire knowledge and experience of working-class political ideals and aspirations.

Catherine had been at the centre of all these developments, a number of which she had initiated. In the course of these changes she too had been profoundly changed. She still clung to some liberal ideals, but her disillusionment with Liberalism as a political vehicle was only waiting for the outbreak of war to complete it. Meanwhile, she was increasingly attracted to a diffuse ethical socialism, which she did not see as sharply opposed to the kind of ethical liberalism she had grown up with; again, the war would complete the transition. She looked to a socialism which she hoped could change political, economic, and social structures by peaceful means. And she and those who thought with her were developing a powerful feminist ideology which would attempt to modify socialism and ultimately internationalism as it had modified suffragism.

Catherine still continued to respect politicians and to seek the best from them, but she knew their frailties. She must surely have seen that she and her closest colleagues could generally at least match the average politician in wits and often outmatch him in commitment to principle. No wonder that she began to see that women's need for the vote was no greater than the need of the nation to have them in positions of political influence. Until quite shortly before the war, she had couched this argument mostly in what can be seen as maternalist terms, pointing out the absurdity of having women excluded from decision-making in the ever-expanding areas of social legislation. By the end of 1913, however, we have found her advocating a new approach to the questions of colonialism and industrial unrest, and making it plain that she believed women should be heard on all major issues. In this lay the seed of an important development in feminist thought. Elsewhere, I shall elaborate on what I see as the core and the significance of the new kind of feminism which Catherine and her closest colleagues had pulled from their experiences in prewar England, found themselves inevitably committed to when war showed the same picture in much sharper definition, and took into the postwar world.

Biographical Notes

The purpose is to make identifying information available to readers. Short biographies of men have been included, although information on many of these is readily available; this is in the hope that the book will interest a wide range of readers, not necessarily familiar with British malestream political history, who may wish to place the men with whom Catherine Marshall dealt. Wherever available, more extensive information on lesser-known women is given, as well as on the better known, as this is still hard to come by. I have not included people who are only casually mentioned, or those of whom I know very little more than is in the text or notes. I greatly appreciate the help given to me in preparing this appendix by Eleanor Segel. Unless otherwise indicated, sources used are the following (in addition to information gleaned from archival collections cited in the bibliography): *Concise Dictionary of National Biography: 1901–1950; Dictionary of National Biography: 1951–1960*; A.J.R., ed., *Suffrage Annual and Women's Who's Who, 1913*; Olive Banks, *Biographical Dictionary of British Feminists*, vol. 1; M. Stenton and S. Lees, eds., *Who's Who of British Members of Parliament*; Jennifer S. Uglow, ed., *International Dictionary of Women's Biography*.

ACLAND, Eleanor, née Cropper (c. 1880?–1933): from Kendal in the Lake District; had been at St Leonard's School with Catherine; devoted Liberal, m. Francis Acland; tried hard to rouse Liberal women in support of suffrage; founded LWSU in 1913.

ACLAND, Francis (1874–1939): Liberal MP for Richmond, Yorks, 1906–10, North-West Cornwall, 1910–22, Tiverton, 1923–24, North Cornwall, 1932–39; various junior ministerial posts, 1908–15; fourteenth Bart, 1926; husband of Eleanor.

ANDERSON, Mary Reid: see Macarthur.

ANDERSON, W.C. (1877–1919): Labour; apprenticed to a manufacturing chemist, 1893; organizer of Shop Assistants' Union, 1903–7; chair of ILP, 1911–13; chair of Labour party, 1913–15; unsuccessful candidate in Cheshire, Jan. 1910, in Keighley, 1911; MP, Sheffield, 1914–18; defeated 1918; died in flu epidemic, 1919.

ANNAKIN, Ethel: see Snowden.

ASHBY, Margery Corbett, née Corbett (1882–1981): lifelong Liberal; Newnham College, 1901–3, where she was much involved in college politics; Training College Cambridge, 1905; active in social concerns, esp. living conditions; head of Hull Vacation School 1906–7; NUWSS, 1908–9; NUWSS executive, 1910–12; active in NUSEC in 1920s; pres. IWSA, 1923–26,, and went to Geneva every year for League of Nations Assembly; fluent in French and German; substitute delegate for Britain at disarmament conference, 1931; repeatedly stood unsuccessfully for Parliament as Liberal; later created Dame; active in feminist causes into her nineties, refusing to allow physical frailty to interfere with her independence and mobility; told me when she was ninety-six that failing balance sometimes caused her to "crash to the ground" when she was alone in London but added cheerfully that "*three* splendid people always rush to pick me up." [*Sources*: B. Harrison, *Prudent Revolutionaries*, Johanna Alberti, *Beyond Suffrage*, and my own recollections of lunching with her in Cambridge]

ASHTON, Margaret (1856– ?): chair, Manchester WSS and Manchester federation; Labour; formerly a strong Liberal worker; resigned from the Liberal party in 1906 on the refusal of the Liberal premier to introduce or forward any measure of WS; on Manchester and Salford Women's Trade Union Council.

ASQUITH, Herbert Henry, first Earl of Oxford and Asquith (1852–1928): Liberal PM, 1908–16, the culmination of a career in law and politics; was created Earl of Oxford and Asquith in 1925; published *Memories and Reflections, 1852–1927* (1928).

AUERBACH, Helena (1871– ?): lived at Reigate, Surrey; for many years honorary treasurer of the NU; personal friend of Mrs Fawcett.

AUGSPURG, Dr Anita (1857–1943): German feminist; close friend of Lida Gustava Heymann, q.v., studied law in Zürich; active in German feminism from 1890s, campaigning against very restrictive German civil code, and for the vote; a founder and vice-pres. IWSA; took a pacifist stand in First World War; attended conference of the International Committee of Women for Permanent Peace (later the Women's International League for Peace and Freedom) at the Hague in April 1915; with Heymann went into exile in Switzerland when Hitler attained power.

BALFOUR, Alice (c. 1855– ?): the *CDNB* entry for A.J. Balfour remarks on his "enormous social prestige" and on the "wide hospitality" he extended at his home at Whittingehame; Alice, his unmarried sister, who "disliked household management," kept house for him, without pay, with little appreciation, and sometimes as the butt of his verbal contempt; her other brothers and her sisters-in-law (and their eight children, of whom she was fond) often lived there, tending to usurp what little status she had, and her brother Eustace's wife, Lady Frances (a suffragist), quarrelled constantly with her (although in this A.J. gave her some protection); A.J. never married; she was obsessively devoted to him; what spare time she had was given to social concerns; she never fully developed her considerable talent as an artist, although she exhibited at the Royal Academy. [*Source*: P. Jalland, *Women, Marriage and Politics*]

BALFOUR, Arthur James (A.J.) (1848–1930): philosopher; scholar; held many positions in cabinet and in foreign affairs; Conservative PM, 1902–5; leader of Unionist party in the Commons, 1891–1911; member of Peace Conference, 1919; MP for Hertford, 1874–85; for Manchester 1885–1906; for City of London 1906–22, when was created Earl of Balfour; declared supporter of a limited women's suffrage measure; author of many philosophical works.

BALFOUR, Lady Betty, née Lytton (dates unknown): Conservative suffragist; m. Gerald Balfour, brother of Alice, q.v., and A.J., q.v.; sister of Lady Constance Lytton, militant suffragette, and of Lord Lytton, q.v.; suffragist; supportive of her sister when latter was jailed.

BARNES, George (1859–1940): general sec. to the Amalgamated Society of Engineers, 1896–1908; Labour MP, Glasgow Gorbals division, 1906–22; served in war cabinet; resigned from Labour party 1918; minister plenipotentiary at peace conference, helping to establish the International Labour Organization; delegate to League of Nations, 1920; author of *From Workshop to War Cabinet*.

BATESON, M.: see M. Heitland.

BELLOC, Hilaire (1870–1953): Liberal; a prolific poet, author, and historian, Catholic, of both French and British citizenship, son of Bessie Rayner Parkes, a noted member of the feminist Langham Place group of the 1860s; MP for South Salford, 1906–10.

BENTHAM, Ethel (1861–1931): joined Labour party, 1902; medical doctor, educated London, Dublin, Paris, Brussels; Fabian; leading member of WLL; active in Newcastle WSS; had been pressing since 1907 for mutual support between Labour and the suffragists; MP for East Islington, 1929–31; member of national executive of Labour party, 1918–20, 1921–26, 1928–31; became Quaker, 1920. [*Additional source*: S. Holton, *Feminism and Democracy*]

BESANT, Annie, née Wood (1847–1933): socialist; religious enthusiast; birth control advocate; separated from her husband in 1873; published, with Charles Bradlaugh, a birth-control treatise called *The Friends of Philosophy* (1875); was prosecuted and convicted; sentence was reversed on appeal; lost custody of her daughter for this and her public avowal of atheism; became a Fabian socialist and played a major role in organizing the Match Girls' Strike in the East End of London, 1888; later became a theosophist and spent years in India studying and teaching, and promoting Indian self-government; elected president of the Indian National Congress, 1917–23; advocacy of Commonwealth status for India won British Labour support; became a believer in the messianic claims of Krishnamurti; died in India.

BIRRELL, Augustine (1850–1933): author, politician; Liberal MP for West Fife, 1899–1900; for North Bristol 1906–18; chief sec. for Ireland 1907–16.

BODICHON, Barbara, née Leigh-Smith (1827–91): a member of the Langham Place Group of the 1860s; a close friend of Emily Davies with whom she cofounded Girton College; a leader in feminist law reform and women's education; women's suffragist.

BONDFIELD, Margaret (1873–1953): TU leader; first British woman cabinet minister; daughter of a Somerset Methodist minister and also a laceworker; left school at thirteen; shop assistant in Brighton, 1887, and London, 1892; active in National Union of Shop Assistants; joined ILP; soon a speaker and leader; worked towards larger federated unions; active in WLL and WCG; adult suffragist; worked with Mary Macarthur; during the war worked for better conditions for women workers; delegate to important postwar socialist and TU conferences; went with British Labour delegation to Russia, 1920; Labour MP, 1923–24, 1926–35; minister of labour, 1929; refused to join MacDonald's "national" government.

BRAILSFORD, Henry Noel (1873–1958): socialist (ILP); journalist and foreign correspondent; student of history, economics, philosophy, and classics; fought in Greek war of independence, 1897, learning to hate war; m. Jane Malloch, 1898, who later became a militant, and Eva Jarvis, 1944; with Nevinson, q.v., resigned his position as leader-writer for the *Daily News* in 1909, because the paper refused to condemn forced feeding of the suffragette prisoners; turned from support of militancy to the NUWSS, c. 1910; helped form the Conciliation Committee, 1910; founded MLWS, 1910; actively promoted the EFF policy, 1912–13; founding member of the Union of Democratic Control, 1914; his pacifism gave way to antifascism in the 1930s; with Rathbone, q.v., supported family allowances; in addition to a huge output as a journalist, writings include *Shelley, Godwin and Their Circle* (1913); *The War of Steel and Gold* (1914); *The Levellers and the English Revolution* (pub. posthumously).

BROCKWAY, A. Fenner, later Lord Brockway (1888–1988): journalist, politician; of middle-class parents; had made the transition from Liberalism to Socialism by 1907, joining the ILP; a man of deep convictions, active throughout his life in political and social causes; pacifist; with his wife, Lilla, founded No-Conscription Fellowship in First World War; imprisoned as conscientious objector; refused to support MacDonald's National Coalition Government of 1931; campaigned for imperial devolution; and for end to Vietnam war; Labour MP for East Leyton, 1929–31; for Eton and Slough, 1950–64; writings include *Inside the Left* (1942).

BUCKMASTER, Sir Stanley (1861–1934): Liberal; solicitor-general, 1913–15; MP, Cambridge, 1906–Jan. 1910; for Keighley, 1911–15; lord chancellor, 1915–16; viscount, 1933.

BURNS, John (1858–1943): labour leader and politician; for many years active trade unionist; MP for Battersea, 1892–1918; moved from socialism towards liberalism; pres. of the Local Government Board, 1905–14; resigned from cabinet and from politics on outbreak of First World War.

BUTLER, Henry Montagu (1833–1918): headmaster of Harrow School 1860–85; Dean of Gloucester 1885–86; Master of Trinity 1886–1918; publications include volumes of school and university sermons.

BUXTON, Noel Edward (1869–1948): Liberal MP for Whitby, 1905–6; for North Norfolk, Jan. 1910–1918; Labour MP for North Norfolk, 1922–30; one of the radical Liberals who moved left during and following the war; socially concerned; causes included antislavery; child welfare; miners' welfare; created baron, 1930.

CAMPBELL-BANNERMAN, Sir Henry (1836–1908): Liberal; favoured Home Rule; after serving in a number of cabinet positions, and as leader of the opposition, became PM, 1905; resigned 3 Apr. 1908 because of illness, dying three weeks later; MP for Stirling, 1868–1908.

CARLISLE, Rosalind née Howard (Lady Carlisle, Countess of Carlisle) (1845–1921): interests included Women's Liberal Federation (pres. 1894), Temperance, Women's Suffrage, administration of estates, Home Rule; was pro–Boer War, pro–First World War; her sister was Lady Amberley (Kate Stanley), mother of Bertrand Russell.

CARSON, Sir Edward (1854–1935): Irish lawyer; politician; leader of Irish Unionist party 1910–21; unsuccessfully moved exclusion of Ulster from Irish Home Rule Bill, Jan. 1913; Unionist MP for Dublin University, 1892–1918; for Belfast, 1918–21.

CATT, Carrie Chapman (1859–1947): US women's suffragist; educator; journalist; gifted administrator; a leader of NAWSA from 1895; pres. NAWSA, 1900–1903; pres. IWSA, 1904; organized the major campaigns which led to the winning of the vote, by the ratification of the Nineteenth Amendment to the US constitution in 1920; supported US entry into First World War, despite her later involvement in the peace movement.

CECIL, Maud: see Selborne.

CECIL, Lord Robert (1864–1958): Independent Conservative and Free Trader; son of the Marquess of Salisbury (a Conservative PM); MP for East Marylebone, 1906–10; Hertfordshire, 1911–23, when was created Viscount Cecil of Chelwood; career in foreign affairs; particularly noted for his contribution to the work of the young League of Nations after the First World War.

CHADWICK, Marion (1848– ?): member of CUWFA, Kensington branch; interested in local government; on managing committee New Hospital for Women; member of executive committee, National Society for Epileptics, and Kensington Local Government Association; vice-pres. Amalgamated Women's Unionist and Tariff Reform Association.

CHEW, Ada Nield (1870–1945): left school at age eleven; a factory tailoress at Crewe, she exposed conditions in a series of anonymous newspaper articles, 1894; owned authorship when the manager retaliated against all the women workers, and was fired; travelled as socialist speaker, 1894–98; women's trade union organizer, 1900–1908; NUWSS speaker, writer, and organizer, active at a number of by-elections, 1911–14; businesswoman, 1915–30. [*Sources*: Doris N. Chew, *Ada Nield Chew: The Life and Writings of a Working Woman*; J. Liddington, *One Hand Tied behind Us*]

CHURCHILL, Sir Winston Spencer (1874–1965): journalist, author, politician; Conservative 1899–1904; Liberal 1904–23; Constitutionalist, 1924; Conservative, 1923–65; followed a military and journalistic career off and on when young; increasingly important cabinet positions in Liberal and Conservative governments, 1905 on; PM 1940–45 and 1951–55.

CLARK, Alice (1874–1934); author; feminist; Quaker; after finishing *Working Life* in 1918, gave herself to Quaker relief work, at first with her sister Hilda in Vienna, then taking charge of the London office of Quaker relief; returned to her career in the Clark shoe factory (Street, Somerset), in 1922; served there as personnel manager; a director of Clark's, 1903–34. [*Source*: intro to *Working Life*]

COOPER, Robert (dates unknown): post office worker; later a weaver; supportive husband of Selina Cooper, q.v.

COOPER, Selina (1868–1946): half-timer in cotton mill, became trade unionist, 1878–90; m. Robert Cooper, q.v., 1898; active in ILP, Social Democratic Federation, and Women's Cooperative Guild; went on textile workers' suffrage deputations to Westminster, 1901, 1902; NUWSS organizer, 1906–14, travelling widely and working many by-elections; worked against war and fascism, 1918–39; went to visit Nazi Germany, 1934; many other concerns and activities. [*Sources*: J. Liddington, *One Hand Tied behind Us* and *The Life of a Respectable Rebel*]

CORBETT, Margery: see Ashby.

COSTELLOE, Rachel: see Ray Strachey.

COURTNEY, Kathleen D'Olier (1878–1974): educated Lady Margaret Hall, Oxford; close friend of Maude Royden, q.v.; hon. sec. NUWSS; resigned, 1915; one of only three British women able to get to the women's international conference at the Hague, Apr. 1915; founding member of WILPF; relief work during and after the war; chair of WIL (British section of WILPF); later active in British League of Nations Union; later still, in United Nations Association; Dame, 1952.

CRIPPS, Rev. J. Ivory (dates unknown): Baptist minister; active in the MLWS; one of the principal speakers at the MLWS demonstration on 20 Feb. 1911; was said to have been active in the cause for sixteen years (but looks quite young in a photograph published at about this time); later appears as pres. of Swindon WSS. [*Sources*: program of MLWS demonstration, Queen's Hall, 20 Feb. 1911, CEMP, *MG*, 24 Oct. 1913]

CROPPER, Eleanor: see Eleanor Acland.

CUNLIFFE, Helen (1853– ?): NUWSS; pres. NWF; vice-pres. Ambleside society.

CURZON, George Nathaniel, Marquess Curzon of Kedleston (1859–1925): traveller, with particular interest in the East; supported colonial rule; held appointments in Conservative governments; viceroy of India, 1898–1905; increasing controversy ended in his resignation; leading antisuffragist, and raised huge sums in this cause; helped found National League for Opposing Women's Suffrage, 1910, which gave male antis control of what had previously been a largely women-led organization; during the war pressed for conscription; main interest continued to be foreign and colonial affairs. [*Additional source*: B. Harrison, *Separate Spheres*]

DAVIES, Emily (1830–1921): feminist; educational reformer; distinguished pioneer suffragist and proponent of equal employment opportunities; became editor of feminist *Englishwoman's Journal*, 1861; founder of Girton College, dedicated to gaining for women the same opportunites in higher education given to men; helped organize suffrage petition presented by John Stuart Mill in 1866; was still a member of the NU executive until 1913, but she was eighty-two years old at this time and seldom attended meetings, although she had been on a delegation to Asquith in 1910; withdrew her name from the NU executive in 1913, perhaps as a result of the EFF policy; aunt to Margaret Llewelyn Davies, q.v.

DAVIES, Margaret Llewelyn (1861–1944): educated Queen's College, London, and Girton College, Cambridge; became general sec. of the WCG, 1889; with Lillian Harris ran the guild until 1921, developing it into a pressure group supporting adult suffrage, minimum wage, and especially the rights of working women, wives, and mothers; played leading role in founding PSF, 1909; her demands for such measures as equal laws and easier divorce in 1910 and her pacifism in 1914 met with opposition from male cooperators; helped found the International Women's Cooperative Guild (1921); publications include the *Women's Cooperative Guild* (1883–1904) and the anthologies *Maternity: Letters from Working Women* (1915) and *Life As We Have Known It* (1930).

DENMAN, Richard Douglas (1876–1957): sat as Liberal for Carlisle, Jan. 1910–1918; joined Labour party, 1924; Labour MP for Leeds, 1929–31, and National Labour, 1931–45; held various minor positions as parliamentary private sec. etc.; chair of National Labour Organization, 1943.

DESPARD, Charlotte, née French (1844–1939): broke with WSPU because of despotic methods of Pankhursts; pres. and founder of the WFL, which practised nonviolent civil disobedience; Irish patriot, working with rebels even while her brother, Sir John French, was lord lieutenant of Ireland (1918–21); social worker; tax resister; theosophist; antifascist activist.

DICKINSON, W.H. (1859–1943): women's suffragist; lawyer; member of Speaker's Conference on Electoral Reform, 1916–17; London County Council, 1889–1907; interests included mental health, education; Liberal MP for North St Pancras, 1906–18; joined Labour party, 1930, National Labour, 1931; substitute delegate, League of Nations, 1923.

DIMOCK, Edith (dates unknown): NUWSS executive, LSWS executive; worked for Metropolitan Association for Befriending Young Servants and the Travellers' Aid Society; taught at College for Men and Women in Queen's Square; for a short time hon. sec. NUWSS.

DOEG, Gladys: see Duffield.

DRUMMOND, Flora (c. 1879–1949): leading militant; WSPU; disqualified from becoming a postmistress after training because of a regulation excluding people under 5ft. 2in.; early member of ILP and Fabian Society; drawn into suffrage movement after Christabel Pankhurst's arrest, 1905; WSPU organizer; known as General Drummond because she wore a uniform, rode a horse, and led a fife and drum band on London marches; exhilarating speaker; imprisoned nine times; always able to make her audience laugh at her jokes and stories; became more conservative, and opposed strikes in 1920s.

DUFFIELD, Gladys, née Doeg (1882–1973): NUWSS; born into well-to-do Manchester family but left without means at eighteen years old; teacher; m. Albert Duffield, 1906; when Albert went out to India, Gladys and her five-year-old daughter went to stay temporarily with her mother-in-law near Keswick; saw the KWSA group setting off on the 1913 pilgrimage and joined on the spur of the moment, leaving child with her mother-in-law; walked whole way to London; a pianist, became a well-known accompanist; had a radical mastectomy at age sixty-five; on receiving a small windfall at age seventy, took a trip to visit two brothers and their families who were living in Canada and USA, having many amazing adventures; eventually returned to her patient husband; continued to travel within Britain, lecture, and play the piano until her death. [*Sources*: James Duffield, "The Amazing Life Story of Gladys Duffield," CRO; Gladys Duffield, "On the March," typescripts, CRO]

EGERTON, Lady Beatrice: see Kemp.

FARMER, John (1835–1901): musician, studied music at Leipzig and Coburg; worked in father's lace business, 1853–57; ran away to Zurich and taught music there; on staff of Harrow School, 1864–85; composed numerous Harrow school songs; possessed a capacity for inspiring enthusiasm; interested in bringing music to people who were not privileged with wealth or special gifts; left Harrow, 1885; at Balliol College, Oxford, until 1901. Farmer was an early champion in England of Bach and Brahms; published works include oratorios and fairy opera; in 1890 edited *Gaudeamus* and other song collections.

FAWCETT, Millicent Garrett (1847–1929): a women's suffragist even before hearing John Stuart Mill speak in 1865; influenced also by her sister Elizabeth Garrett Anderson, who was engaged in a struggle to obtain a medical education, and by the Langham Place group of the 1860s; m. (1867) Henry Fawcett, a blind radical Liberal MP, and Cambridge professor, who died 1884; soon became a leader of the women's suffrage movement; stayed out of the attack on the Contagious Diseases Acts, for fear of damage to the suffrage cause, but had a lifelong interest in combating the sexual exploitation of women; became for a short time a Liberal Unionist because of her opposition to Home Rule; but, despite her outspoken criticism of the Liberal party (and specifically W.E. Gladstone and Asquith) for its refusal to take up women's suffrage, remained ideologically Liberal or Liberal Imperialist; refused to allow the NUWSS to turn its attention to peace education, 1915, and carried her way despite the opposition of a majority of the executive; committed to a liberal concept of equality, she resigned from the National

Union of Societies for Equal Citizenship (the renamed NUWSS) because she could not support the family allowance policy promoted by Rathbone, q.v.; created Dame, 1925; author of numerous pamphlets, several books on women's suffrage and other topics, and an autobiography, *What I Remember* (1924).

FORD, Isabella Ormston (1850–1924): socialist; feminist; Quaker; in *Women and Socialism* (1904, reissued 1907), argued that the emancipation of women and the emancipation of labour were aspects of the same great force; from a well-known Radical Quaker family, she and her sister Bessie (long-time friends of the Marshall family) lived near Leeds and made their home a meeting place for socialists, trade unionists, and Radicals. Isabella supported mill girls on strike in 1890s; joined ILP, 1903; spoke frequently for socialism and feminism and advocated suffrage cause to all wings of Labour; writings include novels and books about women's working conditions. [*Source*: June Hannam, *Isabella Ford*]

FRENCH, Charlotte: see Despard.

FRENCH, Katherine (Kate): see Katherine Mary Harley.

GILL, Helga (1885– ?): NUWSS organizer and speaker; born and educated in Norway; graduate of Christiana University; gold medal for lifesaving from drowning; correspondent to several Norwegian newspapers; published historical essays.

GILMAN, Charlotte Perkins (Stetson) (1860–1935): US feminist; writer; economist; teacher; commercial artist; deprived of affection in childhood; m. Charles Stetson, 1884; deeply depressed after birth of child; divorced 1894; m. George Gilman, her cousin, 1902; examined issues of women's dependent status, advocating cooperative housekeeping; committed suicide after a diagnosis of cancer; writings include *Women and Economics* (1898); *The Yellow Wallpaper* (1892, based on her own breakdown); *Herland* (1915), a feminist utopia.

GLADSTONE, Herbert John (1854–1930): Liberal; son of William Ewart Gladstone, PM; held various government positions in Liberal governments; chief Liberal whip, 1899–1905; home sec., 1905–10; interested in problem of young offenders; governor-general, South Africa, 1910–14; MP for Leeds, 1880–85; for West Leeds, 1885–1910.

GORDON, Clementina (dates unknown): NUWSS organizer; Newcastle society; took part in many by-elections and constituency campaigns; strong Labour supporter.

GOULDEN, Emmeline: see Pankhurst.

GRANT, James Augustus (1867–1932): Conservative, Unionist; JP for Cumberland; MP for Egremont, Jan. 1910–18; for Whitehaven, 1918–22; for South Derbyshire, 1924–29.

GRANT, Julia (dates unknown): one of the first pupils of St Leonards under the headship of Louisa Lumsden; went on to Girton; returned to St Leonards as an assistant mistress; became a house mistress; succeeded Miss Dove as headmistress in 1896 when the latter left to found Wycombe Abbey.

GREY, Sir Edward (1862–1933): Liberal; parliamentary sec. for foreign affairs, 1892–95; sec. of state for foreign affairs, 1906–16; MP for Berwick-on-Tweed, 1885–1916, when created Viscount Grey of Fallodon; leader of Liberal party in Lords, 1916, 1921–24.

HALDANE, Rt. Hon. Richard Burdon (Viscount Haldane) (1856–1928): educated Edinburgh and Gottingen; barrister; sec. of state for war, 1905–12; a Liberal in favour of Home Rule; one of the few influential peers who supported women's suffrage; MP for East Lothian from 1885 until created first Viscount Haldane in 1911; lord high chancellor 1912–15 and 1924; became progressively estranged from Liberal administration; helped form official Labour opposition in House of Lords, 1925–28; wrote on philosophy and education.

HARCOURT, Sir Lewis ("Loulou") (1863–1922): Liberal MP, Rossendale, 1904–16; like his father, Sir William Harcourt, a lifelong antifeminist; first commissioner of works, 1905–10; colonial sec., 1910–15; created first Viscount, 1917; described by C. Hobhouse as "subtle, secretive, adroit, and not very reliable" (*Inside Asquith's Cabinet.* 229); the WSPU tried to set fire to his house in July 1912; he later committed suicide.

HARDIE, James Keir (1856–1915): socialist and labour leader; miner; journalist; ILP chair, 1893–1900, 1913–15; MP, 1900–15; friend of Pankhursts and a devoted women's suffragist; pacifist.

HARLEY, Katherine (Kate) Mary, née French (1855–1917): the youngest sister of Charlotte Despard, q.v., noted WFL leader (and of General French); NUWSS executive; killed by Bulgarian shellfire, Serbia, March 1917, while with the Scottish Women's Hospital.

HARVEY, William Edwin (1852–1914): left school at age ten; worked in mines, 1862–81; miners' agent; general sec. Derbyshire Miners' Association; JP Chesterfield and Derbyshire; vice-pres. Miners' Federation of Great Britain; Liberal MP for North-East Derbyshire, 1907–9, joined Labour with other miners' MPs in 1909, sat till 1914.

HEITLAND, Margaret, née Bateson (1860– ?): active in women's suffrage since the 1880s; pres. Cambridge WSA; particularly interested in women's employment and labour questions generally; of academic family (her father was Master of St John's College, Cambridge, her brother a distinguished biologist, her sister an early Newnham graduate and well-known medieval historian, and her husband a classicist), but herself not a graduate; journalist.

HENDERSON, Arthur (1863–1935): labour leader and politician; trade unionist; MP, 1903–31, 1933–35; chair of PLP, 1908–10, 1914–17; sec. of the Labour party, 1911–34; member of war cabinet, 1916–Aug. 1917, when he resigned; sec. of state for foreign affairs, 1924, 1929–31; leader of Labour party, Aug.–Oct. 1931; chair of Disarmament Conference, Geneva, 1931; Nobel Peace Prize, 1934.

HEWART, Gordon, first Viscount Hewart (1870–1943): educated Bury and Manchester grammar schools and Oxford; barrister; Liberal MP, Leicester, 1913–22; solicitor-general, 1916–19; attorney-general, 1919–22; lord chief justice, 1922–40.

HEYMANN, Lida Gustava (1867–1943): German feminist; wealthy; active in social concerns; worked with Dr Anita Augspurg, q.v., for women's civil liberties and the vote; active in IWSA; pacifist in First World War; attended conference of the International Committee of Women for Permanent Peace (later the WILPF) at the Hague in April 1915; became vice-pres. WILPF, 1919; went into exile, 1933; Augspurg and Heymann's memoirs were published, 1972.

HIGHTON, Rose Elspeth (dates unknown): NUWSS; hon. treasurer to Keswick branch.

HIRST, Margaret E. (1882–1954): a friend and school companion of Catherine Marshall at St Leonards; went on to study classics at Newnham College, Cambridge, 1902; later studied in Germany; her best-known publication is *Quakers in Peace and War* (1923); lecturer in Greek and Latin at University of Birmingham, 1920–47; attracted by the peace testimony, she became a Quaker in her twenties. [*Source*: Edwin Bronner, introduction to *Quakers in Peace and War*. Garland ed. 1972]

HOBHOUSE, Sir Charles (1862–1941): Liberal politician; from a traditional Liberal family; held ministerial posts from 1907; entered cabinet as chancellor of the Duchy of Lancaster, 1911; postmaster-general, 1914–15; never a noteworthy politician, but kept diaries of great interest, commenting on politicians and political affairs, which were discovered and published after his death. The diaries confirm his reputation as an adamant opponent of women's suffrage. When there was a rumour that he was to be appointed governor-general of Australia in Feb. 1914, the NUWSS received a cable from the Women's Political Association of Australia describing the suggestion as "an affront to the women of Australia."

HOUSMAN, Lawrence (1865–1959): MLWS executive committee; a convincing speaker on women's suffrage; brother of the poet A.E. Housman; a writer whose varied works reflect the opinions and feelings of this era.

HOWARD, Geoffrey W.A. (1877–1935): Liberal; a Liberal whip, 1911–18; MP for Eskdale division of Cumberland, 1906–10; for Westbury, Wiltshire, 1911–18; for Luton, 1923–24.

HOW MARTYN, Edith (1875–?): WSPU, 1906–7; helped found WFL; active in demonstrations, 1906–13; imprisoned on one occasion.

INGLIS, Elsie (Maude) (1864–1917): active in Scottish federation of the NUWSS; MD (Edinburgh); born in India; studied in Edinburgh and Glasgow; founded a maternity centre; travelled widely to other clinics; on outbreak of war, 1914, raised money and founded Scottish Women's Hospitals, all female, to serve soldiers; British War Office refused the offer; French accepted and two units went to France; her own unit was sent to Serbia; remained there, 1915–16, 1916–17; she died the day after returning to England, Nov. 1917.

JACOBS, Aletta (1851–1929): pioneer woman doctor and birth control campaigner; after qualifying (the first Dutch woman to do so), worked in her father's practice and then on her own; many other feminist causes, including suffrage, from 1880s on; helped found IWSA, 1904; toured world with Carrie Chapman Catt, q.v., 1911; helped convene International Conference of Women at the Hague, Apr. 1915; after war, worked for International Alliance of Women.

JEX-BLAKE, Sophia (1840–1912): a leader in opening the medical profession to women in Britain; the focus of notable struggles at Edinburgh University; the beneficiary of financial independence which came ironically at the death of her father in 1868; graduate in medicine at Berne and Dublin; a tireless fighter, finally successful, for medical education and registration for women in Britain.

KEMP, Lady Beatrice, née Egerton (1871– ?): NUWSS; daughter of the Earl of Ellesmere; pres. Rochdale WSS; member, Keswick WSA; m. Sir George Kemp, q.v., 1896; spoke, helped at suffrage stalls, etc.; took part in processions; author of children's books.

KEMP, Sir George (1866–1945): army officer, served in South Africa, 1900–1902; Unionist until 1904, when joined Liberal party over free trade issue; MP for Heywood, Lancashire, 1895–1906; for North-West Manchester, Jan. 1910–12; created Baron Rochdale, 1913.

KENNEY, Annie (1879–1953); WSPU; millworker from age of ten; trade unionist; attracted to women's suffrage by Christabel Pankhurst, q.v.; became her devoted follower and companion in militant activities; frequently imprisoned; remained in charge of WSPU London office when Christabel fled to Paris, 1912, travelling to and from Paris weekly for orders; was saddened by split with Pethick-Lawrences, q.v.; hunger-struck, 1913; after the war, broke with Christabel; became a theosophist.

KNIGHT, Sidney (dates unknown): NUWSS; hon. sec. Keswick WSA; speaker, NWF.

LAGERLÖF, Selma (1858–1940): Swedish feminist, educator, and prolific writer; winner of Nobel Prize for literature 1909 (the first woman so honoured); teacher at a girls' high school. [*Source: Who's Who of Nobel Prize Winners*]

LANSBURY, George (1859–1940): labour leader and politician; active in municipal and national politics; a founder and later (1919–23) editor of the *Daily Herald*; a socialist and pacifist whose convictions had a deep spiritual base; his pacifism does not seem to have been troubled by the escalating violence of the WSPU, perhaps because the violence was still directed against property; MP, Bow and Bromley, 1910–12, 1922–40.

LAW, Andrew Bonar (1858–1923): leader, Unionist party in Commons, 1911–21, 1922–23; various cabinet positions in Conservative ministries; member of Lloyd George's war cabinet, 1916–18; chancellor of the Exchequer; plenipotentiary, Peace Conference, 1919; PM, 1922–23; MP for Glasgow Blackfriars, 1900–1906; for Dulwich, 1906–10; for Bootle, 1911–18; for Glasgow Central, 1918–23.

LAWSON, Sir Wilfrid (1862–1937): Liberal; unsuccessfully contested Penrith, 1886 and Cockermouth, Jan 1910; MP for Cockermouth, Dec. 1910–16.

LEAF, Emily (dates unknown): hon. press sec., NUWSS, from 1911; educated Newnham College, Cambridge; social, educational work in Bermondsey; sec. to Women's Liberal Association in St George's, Hanover Square; gave up this work for full-time suffrage work.

LEIGH-SMITH: see Bodichon.

LLOYD GEORGE, David (1863–1945): Liberal; pres. of Board of Trade, 1905–8; chancellor of the Exchequer, 1908–15; minister of munitions, 1915–16; sec. of state for war, 1916; PM, 1916–22; MP for Caernarvon, 1890–1945, when was created Earl Lloyd George of Dwyfor; leader of Liberal party, 1926–31; of Independent Liberal Group, 1931–35.

LOW, Alice Mary (dates unknown): daughter of Lord Low, senator of the College of Justice, Scotland; on international hockey team, Scotland v England, 1903; executive committee, Edinburgh society and Scottish federation of WSS; a speaker, Edinburgh society, and its organizing sec. from 1909.

LOW, Josie (dates unknown): daughter of Lord Low, senator of College of Justice, Scotland, sister of Alice Low, q.v.; little is known of her outside of her intriguing surviving correspondence in CEMP.

LOWTHER, James William (1855–1949): Conservative MP for Rutland, 1883–85; Unionist MP for Penrith, 1886–1918; for Penrith and Cockermouth, 1918–21; Speaker of House of Commons from 1905 to 1921, when was created first Viscount Ullswater; chair of "Speaker's Conference" on electoral reform, 1916–17; author of *A Speaker's Commentaries*.

LYTTLETON, Rt. Hon. Alfred (1857–1913); sec. of state for the colonies, 1903–5; a member of the Council of the Bar; Privy Councillor, 1903; a Unionist; MP for Warwick and Leamington, May 1895–Jan. 1906, and for St George's, Hanover Square, June 1906 until his death.

LYTTON, Lady Constance (1869–1923): WSPU; a shy and private woman of exceptional courage; becoming convinced that militancy was only way to win the vote, she took part in a deputation to the House of Commons, was arrested, but was treated well and soon released on grounds of ill health (her heart was affected by childhood rheumatic fever), 1909; believing the real reason was her social position, disguished herself as plain and unattractive "Jane Wharton," was again arrested, forcibly fed eight times before release, 1910; continued militant activity; suffered stroke, 1912; remained partly paralysed for rest of her life; sister of Lord Lytton, q.v., a leading suffrage advocate in the Lords.

LYTTON, Lord (1876–1947); pres. MLWS; idealist; proponent of free trade; Conservative Unionist; held junior appointments, 1916–22; governor of Bengal, 1922–27; chair, League of Nations mission to Manchuria, 1932; chair, Council of Aliens, 1939–41.

MacARTHUR, Mary Reid (1880–1921): women's labour organizer; general sec. Women's Trade Union League, 1903; formed National Federation of Women Workers and helped to create National Anti-Sweating League, 1906; m. W.C. Anderson, 1911; member of reconstruction and other committees, protecting women's rights, 1914–18; British representative, labour conference in America, 1920.

MacDONALD, James Ramsay (1866–1937): labour leader and politician, sec. Labour Representative committee (later the Labour party), 1900–12; active in ILP; later first labour PM, 1924, 1929–31; coalition PM, 1931–35.

McKENNA, Reginald (1863–1943): politician, banker; barrister; Liberal MP, North Monmouthshire, 1895–1918; first lord of the Admiralty, 1908–11;

home sec., 1911–15; responsible for forced feeding of hunger-striking suffragettes and for "Cat and Mouse" Act, 1913; chancellor of the Exchequer, 1915–16; opposed conscription; resigned when Asquith left office, 1916; director and then chair, Midland Bank, 1917–43.

MACKENZIE, Mary Lilias (Molly) (1888– ?): NU staff parliamentary sec.; a Cambridge Modern Languages graduate, former pres. of Newnham College WSS.

MCLAREN, Walter (1853–1912): independent Liberal; from Edinburgh; strong women's suffragist; also in favour of Free Trade, Disestablishment; MP for Crewe, 1886–95, Apr. 1910–1912.

MACMILLAN, Chrystal (1872–1937): a leading Edinburgh suffragist; like Catherine Marshall, an alumna of St Leonards School; B.Sc. (first class hons. Mathematics and Natural Philosophy) and MA in Mental and Moral Philosophy, both from Edinburgh University; also attended Berlin University; particularly noted in suffrage circles for her major role in the case brought by Scottish women graduates in 1908, which based their claim to the vote on their degrees; pleaded the final (unsuccessful) appeal of this case before the bar of the House of Lords in 1908; also active in IWSA; later a founding member of the WILPF; attended International Women's Conference at the Hague, 1915; went as delegate from this to Russia, etc.; called to the bar 1923; helped found Open Door Council; president of Open Door International; active in many concerns of working women.

MACNAMARA, Thomas (1861–1931): Liberal; journalist, educator; pres. National Union of Teachers, 1896; Hon. Ll. D., St Andrews, 1898; parliamentary sec. to the Local Government Board, 1907–8; sec. to the Admiralty, 1908–20; minister of labour, 1920–22; MP for North Camberwell, 1900–1918 and North-West Camberwell, 1918–24; serious and humorous publications on education.

MASSINGHAM, Henry W. (1860–1924): journalist, editor; resigned as editor of *Daily Chronicle*, 1899, because of his opposition to the South African war; editor of the *Nation* (liberal weekly journal), 1907–23; joined Labour party and transferred his "Wayfarer's Diary" to the *New Statesman*, 1923.

MELLONE, Dora (1872–?): sec. Northern Committee Irish Women's Suffrage Federation; local sec. Irish Women's Suffrage Federation; member of temperance society.

MORRELL, Philip Edward (1870–1943): Liberal MP for Henley, 1906 to Jan. 1910: for Burnley, Dec. 1910–1918; husband of Lady Ottoline Morrell, the noted patron and hostess of the Bloomsbury group, and of conscientious objectors during the war; opposed British intervention in the war; founding member, Union of Democratic Control, 1914.

NEVINSON, Henry Woodd (1856–1941): journalist, war correspondent, essayist, philanthropist; organized relief for Macedonians, 1903; for Albanians, 1911; columnist for the *Nation*; founded MLWS with Brailsford and both resigned from the *Daily News* when the editor refused to condemn forcible feeding; crusaded against slavery in Angola, 1906; against "Black and Tan" outrages in postwar Ireland; publications include a collection of his *Nation* articles.

O'MALLEY, Ida (dates unknown): Honours History graduate, Oxford; active in suffrage at Oxford, then in LSWS; member and vice-pres. Oxford Old Students' Women's Suffrage Society; NUWSS executive; hon. sec. for both the literature subcommittee and friends of women's suffrage subcommittees.

PALLISER, Edith (1859– ?): sec. LSWS, 1895; then chair LSWS; co-sec. NUWSS, 1899–1913; fulltime women's suffragist, 1895–1914.

PALMER, W.W. (became Earl of Selborne, 1895) (1859–1942): began life as a Liberal, but changed over on the Home Rule issue, 1886; Unionist suffragist; husband of Lady Selborne, q.v.; committed to a narrow women's suffrage bill; MP for West Edinburgh, 1892–95; under-sec. for the colonies, 1895–1900; first lord of the Admiralty, 1900–1905; with Admiral Fisher, furthered naval education and weapons development and approved Dreadnought battleship design; governor of the Transvaal, 1905–10; instrumental in South African Union of 1910; pres., Board of Agriculture, 1915–16; active as layman in Anglican church government, 1924–42.

PANKHURST, Christabel (1880–1958): WSPU; Ll. B., Victoria University, Manchester; executive, North of England SWS, 1901; cofounder with her mother, Emmeline, of WSPU, 1903; left ILP; initiator of militant action, with Annie Kenney, q.v., 1905; editor, *The Suffragette*, 1912–14; several times imprisoned; charged with conspiracy, 1912; fled to France and directed the WSPU from there; inspired devoted followers, but, with Emmeline, became increasingly autocratic; wrote *The Great Scourge and How to End It*, on the prevalence of venereal disease; on outbreak of war, returned from Paris and gave full support to the war; with Emmeline, founded Women's Party, 1917, which failed, 1919; became a Second Adventist, and lectured in USA on the Second Coming; writings include *Unshackled: The Story of How We Won the Vote* (1959).

PANKHURST, Emmeline, née Goulden (1858–1928): founder, WSPU; m. Richard Pankhurst, 1879; left Liberal party, moved left, joining ILP in 1894; Richard d. 1898; for founding of WSPU, etc., see under Christabel Pankhurst; imprisoned many times, 1908–14; like Christabel, became very patriotic on outbreak of war; by 1917 was working against trade union activity; continued to move right; joined Conservative party and stood unsuccessfully for Parliament; had broken with her daughter Sylvia in 1913, and finally in 1914; writings include *My Own Story* (1914).

PANKHURST, E. Sylvia (1882–1960): militant; artist; prolific writer; reluctantly left her promising art studies, although continuing some art work, to join her mother and sister in WSPU, 1906; close friend of Keir Hardie, q.v.; imprisoned several times; while Emmeline and Christabel moved right, she moved left; working in East End of London, founded the East London Federation of Suffragettes; during the war, became fiercely pacifist, and was vilified by her mother; changed name of her paper from *Women's Dreadnought* to *Workers' Dreadnought*; developed a communist analysis; welcomed Russian Revolution (as did most peace advocates); had long-term relationship with Silvio Corio, but refused marriage on principle; had one son, born 1927; antifascist activist; took up cause of Ethiopia, 1936; moved there after Corio's death in 1954; writings include *The Life of Emmeline Pankhurst* (1935); *Suffragette: The History of the Women's Militant Suffrage Movement 1905–1910* (1911); *The Suffragette Movement* (1931).

PEARSALL-SMITH, Alys: see Russell.

PEASE, Joseph Albert (1860–1943): Liberal; director of a number of colliery companies; JP; local government positions, 1882–1903; mayor, Darlington, 1889–90; various government posts, 1892–1911; pres. of Board of Education, 1911–15; postmaster-general, 1916; MP for Tyneside, 1892–1900; for Saffron Walden, 1901–10; for Rotherham, Mar. 1910–1917; created Baron Gainford, 1917; chair of BBC, 1922–26; vice-chair, 1926–32; pres. Federation of British Industries, 1927–28.

PETHICK-LAWRENCE, Emmeline, née Pethick (1867–1954): after an unhappy childhood and a period of social work, m. Frederick, q.v. 1901; socialist; joined WSPU, 1906; imprisoned a number of times; with Frederick, shared leadership with Pankhursts and edited *Votes for Women*; they disagreed with Pankhursts over escalating militancy, 1912, and were expelled from the WSPU, retaining *Votes for Women*: during the war Emmeline campaigned for peace; a founding member of WILPF; between the wars, continued feminist activity, promoting birth-control information; pres., WFL; vice-pres., Six Points Group; executive, Open Door Council; assisted refugees and struggled with tension between pacifism and antifascism.

PETHICK-LAWRENCE, Frederick (1871–1961): well-to-do; a brilliant scholar; worked in East End university settlement; met Emmeline, q.v.; moved left in response to Emmeline's influence; added her name to his; served as treasurer and donated generously to WSPU; imprisoned for nine months, 1912; for suffrage career, see also Emmeline Pethick-Lawrence, above; during war supported Union of Democratic Control; pacifist; Labour MP, 1923–31, 1935–45; increasingly involved in financial aspect of politics; received a peerage, 1945; sec. of state for India, 1945–47, assisting in negotiations leading to Indian independence.

PHILLIPS, Marion (1881–1932): born in Australia; active in municipal government; in the Fabian Society; in the Fabian Women's Group; in the NUWSS; became general sec. WLL, 1913, replacing Margaret Bondfield, q.v., in that position; later (1918) chief woman officer of the Labour party; Labour MP for Sunderland, 1929–31; writings include *Woman and the Labour Party* (1918).

PIGOU, Arthur Cecil (1877–1959): economist; in Frank Marshall's house at Harrow; read history and moral sciences at Cambridge; pres. of the Cambridge Union; taught economics, King's College, Cambridge, 1901–43; pupil of Alfred Marshall, and succeeded him in the chair of political economy, 1908; a much clearer and more systematic lecturer than Marshall, passed Marshall's work on to a generation of students; a conscientious objector to military service, he was enabled to remain in Cambridge during the war, but drove for the Friends' Ambulance Unit at the front during his vacations; climbed in the Alps when young; had a cottage at Buttermere; was in poor health in later years and became a rather eccentric recluse; a prolific writer; his major work was *The Economics of Welfare*.

POTTER, Beatrice: see Webb.

RANDLES, Sir John (1857–1945): Unionist; ironmaster; director of several Cumberland railway companies; member of Cumberland County Council; JP for Cumberland; knighted, 1905; MP for Cockermouth, 1900–1916, Aug. 1906–1910; for North-West Manchester, 1918–22; member, executive of National Trust.

RATHBONE, Eleanor Florence (1878–1946): NUWSS executive until resigned in 1914, and again after the 1915 disagreements; from a wealthy Liverpool family; humanitarian; educated Somerville, Oxford, and Liverpool University; active in Liverpool WSS, 1897 on; first woman elected to Liverpool Council, 1909–35; pres. of National Union of Societies for Equal Citizenship; among many social concerns, chief were family allowances and refugees; philosophically liberal; sat as Independent MP for Combined English Universities, 1929–46.

REDMOND, John (1856–1918): leader of Parnellite Nationalists, 1891–1900, and of the reunited Nationalist party, 1900–1918; Irish political leader, generally regarded as a conciliatory nationalist who would have agreed to a federal type of Home Rule and would have made concessions (short of exclusion) to Ulster to obtain this, had the Unionists not taken such a hard line; on outbreak of European war (1914) did utmost to promote recruiting in Ireland, but opposed Ireland's inclusion in first national service bill, 1916;

lost confidence of Ireland, which passed into control of nationalists under Eamon de Valera.

REID, Mary: see Mary Reid MacArthur.

ROBERTSON, Margaret (dates unknown): a Newnham graduate; socialist; by 1914, had unique experience of political organizing, and showed outstanding ability in this field; however, she married a Dr Hills, c. 1914, and little is heard of her after that, except for an occasional mention in CEMP; she joined the Union of Democratic Control.

ROYDEN, A. Maude (1876–1956): NUWSS executive; edited *Common Cause* 1913–14; tireless speaker for suffrage; daughter of a Conservative MP; educated Cheltenham and Lady Margaret Hall, Oxford, where she formed friendship with Kathleen Courtney, q.v.; deeply religious, but never narrow, she did parish work with the Rev. Hudson Shaw, whom she eventually married, after the death of his wife; although a staunch Anglican, she preached at the nonconformist City Temple, because there the pulpit was open to her as a woman; campaigned for the ordination of women; pacifist; founding member of WILPF; resigned from NUWSS executive over issue of peace education, 1915; supported Six Point group, 1920s. [*Additional source*: S. Fletcher, *Maude Royden*]

RUNCIMAN, Walter (1870–1949): Liberal to 1931, then National Liberal; extensive interests in shipping; government positions, 1905 on; pres. of Board of Education, 1908–11; of Board of Agriculture, 1911–14; of Board of Trade, 1914–16, 1931–37; MP for Oldham, 1899–1900; for Dewsbury, 1902–18; for Swansea, 1924–29; for St Ives, 1931–37; created viscount, 1937; succeeded as baron, 1937.

RUSSELL, Alys, née Pearsall-Smith (1867–1951); women's suffragist; speaker; member of a family of very strong women, herself strong but of relatively gentle nature; first wife of Bertrand Russell, q.v.; stayed with NUWSS as active speaker when he left to join the PSF; their marriage had long been in trouble and broke up finally in 1911.

RUSSELL, Bertrand (1872–1970): philosopher; mathematician; peace activist, but not absolute pacifist; women's suffragist; stood as women's suffrage candidate for Wimbledon with NUWSS backing, 1907; joined PSF, 1909, and thereafter was little visible in women's suffrage campaign; horrified by outbreak of First World War; founding member and speaker for Union of Democratic Control, 1914–15; active associate, later acting chair, No-Conscription Fellowship, 1916–1918, where worked closely with Catherine Marshall; imprisoned, 1918; welcomed Russian Revolution, but believed opportunity for complete change of Western world was subsequently missed; for a short time regarded fear of nuclear war a legitimate route to peace; later a leading anti–nuclear weapon activist, and served his second jail term in 1961; FRS, 1908; Nobel Prize for literature, 1950.

SCHWIMMER, Rosika (1877–1938): journalist; lecturer; pacifist; had been a leader in the Hungarian feminist suffragist movement from the turn of the century; active in the IWSA from its inception; made annual lecture tours, including frequent visits to Britain; after outbreak of war, campaigned in Europe and the USA for a mediated peace; attended the Hague Congress of Women, 1915; helped organize International Committee for Immediate Mediation, 1916; Hungarian minister to Switzerland, 1918; fled Hungary after Béla Kún's advent; emigrated to USA, 1921, but was denied citizenship because of refusal to promise "to bear arms in defence of the Constitution"; with Lola Maverick Lloyd, established Campaign for World Government, 1937. [*Source*: article by E. Wynner in H. Josephson et al., eds., *Biographical Dictionary of Modern Peace Leaders*]

SCOTT, Charles Prestwich (1846–1932): journalist; editor, *Manchester Guardian* 1872–1929; owner of the paper from 1905; raised standing of paper in every aspect, esp. political; supported Home Rule; opposed South African war; supported women's suffrage; intelligent critic of foreign policy; supported Lloyd George during the war, but moved towards a more critical stance after 1917; largely represented radical liberal opinion; Liberal MP for Leigh, 1895–1905.

SEELY, J.E.B., first Baron Mottistone (1868–1947): politician and soldier; entered Parliament as Conservative but became Liberal in 1904 in protest against Joseph Chamberlain's advocacy of tariff reform; best known for his action in March 1914 of allowing the resignation of Ulster army officers, which led to the impression that the English army was about to precipitate civil war by forcing Home Rule on Ulster; this was followed by his resignation.

SELBORNE, Lady, née Maud Cecil (1858– ?): daughter of the former Conservative PM Lord Salisbury, sister of Lord Robert Cecil, cousin of A.J. Balfour; remained a lifelong Conservative; married William Palmer, q.v., 1883; pres. CUWFA since 1907, though she remained more active behind the scenes than in public, practising feminine political influence subtly and traditionally, educating her son as a politician, and giving well-informed and intelligent help to her family and friends in election campaigns; lifelong interest in social reforms, esp. those affecting women's lives; promoted a narrow women's suffrage bill, and was opposed to universal suffrage, but later became more open to it. [*Source*: P. Jalland, *Women, Marriage and Politics: 1860–1914*]

SHACKLETON, David James (1863–1938): Labour; Lancashire weaver; trade unionist, active in weavers' unions; JP; favoured Home Rule, free trade, universal suffrage, but prepared to promote more limited women's bill as a step; MP for Clitheroe, 1902–10, when appointed senior labour adviser to the Home Office; permanent sec. to minister of labour, 1916–21; chief labour adviser, 1921–25.

SHAW, Dr Anna Howard (1847–1919): US orator, suffrage leader; studied theology at Boston University, where, deprived of the meal privileges given to the men, she nearly starved; gained a medical degree, 1886; worked in Boston slums; became a leading speaker for women's suffrage; pres. NAWSA, 1904–15; not a good administrator, and the suffrage campaign became disorganized and stagnant until her retirement in 1916 opened way for Carrie Chapman Catt, q.v.; accepted with grace that her best contribution was in her inspiring speaking. [*Source*: E. Flexner, *Century of Struggle*]

SHEEPSHANKS, Mary (1872–1958): suffragist, pacifist, educator; NUWSS; IWSA; the oldest of the seventeen able but quarrelsome children (four of whom died in infancy) of a clergyman; all her life, felt herself unlovable, but toughed it out and made a good if not a happy life; educated at Newnham; social work in London; vice-principal, Morley College, London, 1897; edited *Jus Suffragii* for IWSA throughout the war; worked with Fight the Famine Council and WILPF after the war; kept in touch with Catherine Marshall until the end of her life [*Source*: S. Oldfield, *Spinsters of this Parish*]

SICKERT, Helena M.: see Swanwick.

SIMON, Sir John (1873–1954): barrister; Liberal MP, 1906–18, 1922–40; solicitor-general, 1910; attorney-general, 1913; nearly resigned on Britain's going to war, 1914; home sec., 1915–16; resigned on conscription issue, 1916, but regretted decision; served in Royal Flying Corps; chaired commission on Indian constitutional reform, 1927–29; supported coalition government, 1931; formed Liberal National party (antisocialist); foreign sec., 1931–35; home sec., 1935; chancellor of the Exchequer, 1937.

SMILLIE, Robert (1857–1940): labour leader; politician; miner; pres. Scottish Miner's Federation, 1894–1918, 1921–40; helped found Miners' Federation of Great Britain; pres. MFGB, 1912–21; founder-member of ILP; pacifist; labour MP for Morpeth, 1923–29; chair of PLP, 1924.

SNOWDEN, Ethel Annakin (1880–1951): teacher, suffragist; trained at Edge Hill College; converted to socialism; preached teetotalism in Liverpool; lectured for ILP; m. Philip Snowden, 1905; invited to USA, 1907; invited back nine times; active speaker for NUWSS; pacifist; supported Women's Peace Crusade; elected to women's section of the Labour party; travelled in Europe to reestablish United Socialist International; member of Board of Governors of BBC (1926); took leading part in revival of Covent Garden Opera; Philip died 1937; Ethel continued to write and speak chiefly about temperance.

SNOWDEN, Philip (1864–1937): ILP MP for Blackburn; chair, ILP, 1904–7 and 1917–20; resigned from ILP, 1927; chancellor of the Exchequer, 1924 and 1929–31; created Viscount Snowden, 1931; vice-pres. MLWS; champion of women's suffrage and later of conscientious objectors in the House of Commons; husband of Ethel Snowden.

SPOOR, Benjamin (1878–1928): Labour; MP for Bishop Auckland, 1918–28; held office in Labour government of 1924; suffragist; Wesleyan lay preacher.

STANGER, Henry Yorke (1849–1929): Liberal; lawyer; women's suffragist; MP for North Kensington, 1906–19; County Court judge, 1910–22.

STEEL-MAITLAND, Sir Arthur H.D. Ramsay (1876–1935): politician, economist; Conservative Unionist; Conservative MP for East Birmingham, 1910–29; for Tamworth, 1929–35; head of the Central Conservative Organization, 1911–16; chair, Unionist party, 1911; held various appointments in colonial and foreign affairs, 1915–19; minister of labour, 1914–29; responsible for Unemployment Insurance Act, 1927; baronet, 1917; Maitland was his wife's surname and Ramsay part of her father's name, which he adopted legally at the time of his marriage in 1901.

STERLING, Frances Mary (1869– ?): NUWSS executive, 1909 on; joined NUWSS c. 1881; painter, exhibiting at Royal Academy until 1902; gave all time to women's suffrage, 1902–14; executive, LSWS, 1903–8; hon. sec. NUWSS, 1903–9; speaker; pres. Falmouth WSS; executive, Surrey, Sussex, and Hants.

STRACHEY, Marjorie (1882–1964): one of the ten remarkable children of General Sir Richard Strachey; described as a "wild creature and no beauty, possessed of a quite extraordinary bawdy wit"; through Marjorie, Ray got to know the Stephen family and other members of what came to be called "Bloomsbury"; a sister of Philippa and of Lytton Strachey, the author. [*Source*: Barbara Strachey, *Remarkable Relations*]

STRACHEY, Philippa (1872–1968): member of NUWSS parliamentary sub-committee; long time hon. sec. to the LSWS; suffragist; Ray Strachey's closest friend and colleague; sister of Oliver (Ray's husband) and of Marjorie Strachey.

STRACHEY, Ray, née Costelloe (1887–1940): NUWSS; writer and political activist; educated at Newnham College, Cambridge and then at Bryn Mawr in the US; m. Oliver Strachey, 1911; active suffragist from her Cambridge days; supported Fawcett's pro-war stand; replaced Catherine Marshall as parliamentary sec. on the latter's resignation, 1915; chair, Women's Service Bureau; upheld rights of working women during and after the war; attended informal conference of Inter-Allied Suffragists attempting to influence the peace conference in Paris in favour of women's rights, 1919; stood unsuccessfully for Parliament several times; unpaid part-time sec. to Nancy Astor (first woman MP); writings include *The Cause* (1928), and *Millicent Garrett Fawcett* (1931).

SWANWICK, Helena M., née Sickert (1864–1939): NUWSS executive; born in Munich; moved to England, 1868; her feminism dated from childhood experiences of her five brothers' privileged position; graduated from Girton College, Cambridge, 1885; m. Frederick Swanwick, 1888, moved to Manchester and later Knutsford; occupied in housekeeping, and, more happily, in gardening; began to write suffrage articles, 1905; editor, *Common Cause*, 1909–12; moved to London, 1911; resigned as editor, 1912, but remained on executive; strongly pacifist; when war came, active in Union of Democratic Control, 1914–15; resigned from NUWSS executive on pacifist issue; founding member WILPF; chair, WIL (British section of WILPF), 1915–22; between the wars, worked for a more soundly based peace; socialist, internationalist; member of British Empire delegation to League of Nations, 1924, 1929; writings include *The Future of the Women's Movement* (1913); *I Have Been Young* (1935).

TREVELYAN, Robert (1872–1951): author, esp. poet, playwright; educated Harrow and Trinity College; brother of historian George M. Trevelyan and politician Charles Trevelyan.

TURNER, Sir Ben (1863–1942): Labour; trade unionist; experienced in local government; JP; chair of National Executive Committee of Labour party, 1911–12; Labour MP for Batley and Morley, 1922–24; 1929–31; chair of TUC, 1928; sec. for mines, 1929–30.

WALTON, Sir Joseph (1849–1923): Liberal; colliery owner; widely travelled, JP; supported Home Rule, and the general radical program; MP for Barnsley, 1897–1922.

WARD, A. Helen (dates unknown): from Beaconsfield; had also a central London address; she held a LL.A. from St Andrews University; had served as treasurer for a number of charitable organizations; now gave all her time to suffrage work and had worked for the NUWSS in numerous elections; applied successfully for reelection to the LSWS executive in November 1913, and nominated Maude Royden, q.v., for reelection at the same time.

WARD, Mary Augusta (Mrs Humphry Ward), née Arnold (1851–1920): novelist; leading woman antisuffragist; speaker; first pres. Anti-Suffrage League; active in the NLOWS; educated in private boarding schools, and on her own in Oxford, where her parents lived; supported higher education for women; believed women should be involved in lower (local) levels of government, as this was where "domestic" legislation was dealt with; founded a social settlement, and encouraged women's involvement; prolific writer;

her novels reveal a brilliant mind and a strong tendency to sublimate her own abilities in her male characters, the female characters remaining on the whole conventional "good" or "bad" women – even the most intelligent of them are outclassed by the male heroes.

WEBB, Beatrice, née Potter (1858–1943): writer and student of economics, public affairs, and cooperation; worked closely with her husband, Sidney Webb, in writing and public service (all the following activities were joint with Sidney, except that she alone served on the Poor Law commission); launched London School of Economics and Political Science; served on and drafted minority report of commission on poor laws, 1905–9; founded Fabian Society; influenced many important political figures; drafted *Labour and the New Social Order*, the policy statement of the Labour party, 1918; published works on trade unionism, Soviet Communism, local government.

WILLIAMS, Dr Ethel (dates unknown): NUWSS; leader, with Ethel Bentham, q.v., in Newcastle WSS; pres. Newcastle Women's Liberal Federation, but committed to working with Labour, and to adult suffrage. [*Additional source*: S. Holton, *Feminism and Democracy*]

WILSON, Philip Whitwell (1875–1956): from Kendal, in the Lake District; MP for St Pancras South, 1906 to January 1910, when he was defeated; contested Appleby unsuccessfully in December 1910; journalist and author; parliamentary correspondent and later USA correspondent for the *Daily News*.

WOOD, Thomas McKinnon (1855–1927): sat on London County Council as progressive, 1892–1907; Liberal MP for Glasgow Rollox, 1906–18; various positions under Liberal government, 1908–11; Sec. of state of Scotland, 1912–16.

"Questions for Organizers"

The following document, found in CEMP, is undated, but was probably used in 1913 to test the growing number of organizers undergoing training. It has been amended in a few very small particulars by Catherine Marshall, and her alterations are included in the text given here. The document is reproduced here in full, except for a few notes which precede the questions. Candidates were allowed to use books, and there was no time limit.

1. Give a brief account mentioning dates, of the history of the N.U.W.S.S.
2. Describe the Election Policy of the N.U.W.S.S. shewing
   (a.) How it has been developed.
   (b.) Exactly what it is now.
3. How would you deal with the following questions or remarks? (It is supposed that the questions are asked at a meeting so the answers must be brief and to the point.)
   (a.) I'm quite in favour of giving votes to women as pays rates and taxes, but you are asking for votes for all women, and I don't hold with that.
   (b.) You will never get it till you work for Adult Suffrage; why don't you ask for votes for all women, Miss, instead of only women of property?
   (c.) Would my Missus get a Vote?
   (d.) Why do you call yourselves Non-Party if you support the Labour Party?

(e.) Are you asking for women to sit in Parliament?

(f.) If women want the Parliamentary vote why don't more of them vote at Municipal Elections?

(g.) You can get all the reforms you want through the Municipal vote; why aren't you satisfied with that?

(h.) What is the National Union going to do at the general election?

(i.) What will women do when they have got the vote? What reforms are you going to support?

4. How would you show that the vote affects wages? Do you consider that women could secure higher wages by forming Trades Unions even if they have no political power?

5. In what respects is the law unfair to women?

6. In what countries and States are women now enfranchised? Mention some reforms which you think may be attributed to the women's vote.

7. Mention the principal Anti-suffragist arguments or objections, and state briefly how you would answer them.

8. Write a letter to a newspaper explaining the attitude of the N.U.W.S.S. towards "militancy".

THE SUPPORTER.

Postcard produced by the Artists' Suffrage League, c. 1910 (Catherine E. Marshall collection, Cumbria Record Office, Carlisle)

"You want to know why I am going to vote for the 'Woman's Suffrage Man'? My mother worked for me when father died, and was taxed like the rest of us, and never asked for a stick of Charity—that's why!"

CONFIDENTIAL

Questions for Divisional Secretaries.

1   Name of Constituency.
2   Name of present Member, his party and his views.
3   Names of Candidates.
    Remarks: public utterances, etc.
4   Names and addresses of Party Agents and their views.
5   Names and addresses of Members of Executive Committee and Secretaries of Party Organisations likely to be concerned in the selection of Candidates.
6   Names and addresses of Secretaries of Organisations in the constituency such as Primrose League, W.L.A., B.W.T.A. and Co-operative Guild, I.L.P.
7   Chief towns and villages, population, voters and party feeling.
8   General character of the division, agricultural, industrial or residential.
9   Industries (if any).
10 The head quarters of the constituency, *i.e.*, where Candidates are selected and the result of an election announced.
11 Places suitable for Committee Rooms in order of importance.
12 Halls in the division: seating capacity, price, to whom application for hiring should be made, character of neighbourhood.
13 Schools, Theatres and Lecture Rooms with similar details.
14 Names of local newspapers, editors and their views.
15 Open Air Meetings: suitable sites, from whom should permission be asked? Notes of any police regulations in regard to these.

16   Factories. Number of men or women employed. Dinner hour. Do workers come out to dinner? Would owner allow meeting inside?

17   Names and addresses of possible chairmen.

18   Names and addresses of possible helpers.

19   Names and addresses of possible friends to lend motor cars.

20   Names and addresses of persons willing to give hospitality.

21   Means of communication between different parts of the division.

22   Notes concerning local events useful to speakers.

23   Stations.

24   List of Restaurants, Cafés and Lodgings.

25   Name and address of printer and furniture shop, also charwoman, livery stables and bill poster.

N.B.—Secretaries are requested to enter their names, titles and addresses and the date on which the information is supplied. Secretaries are further requested to answer each question on a separate page.

Issue by the N.U.W.S.S., 25, Victoria Street, London, S.W.

Notes

1 The collection at Hawse End also contained a vast documentation of the No-Conscription Fellowship of the First World War (see my *Bertrand Russell and the Pacifists*), and a good deal on the early years of the Women's International League for Peace and Freedom, and peace movements were as much out of fashion as women as subjects of historical inquiry: but since these parts of Catherine's life will form part of my next book on her, and not of this one, I have chosen to focus my fantasy on the suffrage papers.

2 See bibliography for the works referred to.

3 I believe, and may yet find evidence to support my belief, that Catherine had sounded out some archival collections to see whether there was any interest in taking her papers. But the date was 1956: she was fifteen years too early. Even in the late 1960s, Elise Boulding, then president of the Women's International League for Peace and Freedom, faced with closing the Maison Internationale in Geneva and moving the organization into much smaller premises, looked in vain for a British or European library which would accept the archive documenting fifty years of women's international work, and finally persuaded her own university (the University of Colorado at Boulder) to make space for them. Even later still, when the Fawcett Society's lease on its old premises in Westminster expired, they too had difficulty in finding anyone in London willing to take them and keep them together; ultimately, a more than happy solution was offered by the

London Polytechnic. Ironically, any history student in the 1950s and 1960s who expressed a wish to write a thesis or dissertation on some aspect of women's past would be likely to be told that it was a nice idea but no materials existed to form the basis of research.

4 This part of the story is based on information given to me by Bruce Jones in 1969. With the reorganization of British counties, the Cumberland Record Office is now the Cumbria RO; the Marshall papers are still at the Carlisle branch.

5 For an elaboration of this analogy see my "Double Tunnel Vision."

CHAPTER ONE

1 CM to CEM, 28 Apr. 1916, CEMP. CEM's birthday was 29 April.

2 "F.E.M.," obituary recollections by several authors, some identified and some not, in the *Harrovian* 35, no. 6, 21 Oct. 1922. Hereafter, "Obit." (author's name added when known). The whole obituary is warm and informal.

3 *The Suffrage Annual and Women's Who's Who 1913*, ed. A.J.R., s.v. Mrs C. Marshall.

4 From letters, papers in the possession of Frank Marshall (FMP).

5 J.H. Colbeck to "Carrie," 4 July 1880. FMP.

6 *Women's Who's Who 1913*.

7 "Obit." Mark Greenstock, the present housemaster, and his wife kindly showed me over Newlands House, drawing attention to the excellence of its design, the work of Frank Marshall's architect brother, William Cecil Marshall, 1849–1921, which has stood up well to needs throughout the one hundred years of its existence.

8 Ibid., W.N. Bruce. J.A.G. Marshall, a cousin, was killed climbing on Mont Blanc in 1873.

9 Ibid., A.C. Pigou. See also FEM to CEM 26 June 1896 for a reference to what is probably the same drowning death, CEMP.

10 Several letters from CM and FEM, Jan. 1884, Sept. 1884, CEMP.

11 P/20 July 1889, FMP.

12 Draft ms "Humility and Self-Respect," n.d., CEMP.

13 For more on the remarkable John Farmer, see biog. appendix, below, and for his importance to FEM, see "Obit.," Bruce.

14 "Obit.," Bruce.

15 "Harrow Music School Register," May 1893 to Nov. 1894, CEMP.

16 Rimmer, *Marshalls of Leeds, Flaxspinners*, gives an account of the family history and contains a most useful family tree.

17 Prof. T.H. Marshall, Horace Marshall, and Rachel Marshall, Cambridge. Personal communication and interviews, also notes of an interview with T.H. Marshall by Brian Harrison, 25 July 1978, seen by

courtesy of Prof. Harrison. See also Rachel (Tom's sister) to CEM, 3 Sept. 1896, CEMP.

18 "Aunt Rosa Turquard" to CEM, 16 Mar. 1893, CEMP. Aunt Rosa died later that year, in Oct. 1893, aged seventy, FMP.

19 [Signature illegible] to CEM, 26 Feb. 1893, CEMP.

20 HGM to CM, P/10 Mar. 1896; FEM to CEM, 28 Feb. 1896, CEMP. Even in 1900, when CEM had German measles, her father wrote, "and do not dare to tell me that you have *grown*." Tom Marshall also recalled her as "Very large and in a way rather masculine." Harrison, interview.

21 Ibid.

22 "Humility and Self-Respect," CEMP.

23 "Jenkins" to CEM, 14 Feb. 1896; CM to CEM, 14 Feb. 1896, 18 Feb. [1896]; Norah F. Luck to CEM, 2 Mar. 1896, CEMP.

24 F. Colbeck to CEM, 26 April 1896; FEM to CEM, 26 June 1896; FEM, 2 Apr. 1897, CEMP. CEM had begun a lifelong habit of keeping correspondence and preserved all these letters. Her replies are not extant, although a few useful letters are present which she began to write and for some reason did not finish.

25 CM to CEM, 21 Feb. 1896, CEMP.

26 CM to CEM, 22 Feb. 1898, CEMP.

27 CM to CEM, 20 May 1897, CEMP.

28 FEM to CEM, 15 Oct. 1897, CEMP.

29 FEM to CEM, 1 Feb. 1896, CEMP.

30 For St Leonards School, see Macaulay, ed., *St. Leonards School, 1877–1977,* and Bowerman, *Stands There a School.* Also information from Aylwin Clark, history teacher at St Leonards, and Catriona Stewart, who carried out research for me there. For an analysis of traditional and progressive values in girls' expanding educational opportunities, see Dyhouse, *Girls Growing Up in Late Victorian and Edwardian England*; for an interesting discussion of "gender education" see F. Hunt, *Lessons for Life*, introduction. For sports, see also McCrone, *Playing the Game.*

31 *St Leonards School*, 1.

32 FEM to CEM, 30 Sept. 1898, CEMP.

33 CM to CEM, 9 July 1896, CEMP.

34 FEM to CEM, 2 Nov. 1898, CEMP.

35 CM to CEM, Sept. 1897, CEMP.

36 CEM to CM, 24 Jan. 1897, FMP.

37 CM to CEM, 25 Jan. 1897, FMP.

38 FEM to CEM, 27 Jan. 1897, FMP.

39 CEM to FEM, 3 Feb. 1897; FEM to CEM, 6 Feb. 1897, FMP. I do not know if she sought confirmation the following year, but think it unlikely.

40 FEM to CEM, 13 Mar. [1896], CEMP.

41 FEM to CEM, P/19 Mar. 1897, CEMP.

42 FEM to CEM, 9 Oct. 1897, CEMP.

43 CM to CEM, P/10 Mar. 1896, CEMP.

44 CM to CEM, 20 May 1897, CEMP.

45 CM to CEM, 20 June 1897, CEMP.

46 CM to CEM, 22 Feb. 1898, CEMP; date of cricket injury uncertain.

47 Shortly after Catherine entered school, Hal wrote, "I suppose Catherine is pretty high up in the school. I think I am 27th." HGM to CM, 2 Feb. 1896, CEMP. However, he came top of his class a few weeks later (marks were probably computed weekly). HGM to CM, 10 Mar. 1896, CEMP. But in June 1898, his parents were again disappointed (and Leonard Colbeck was again doing very well). He wrote to his sister, "I really am trying hard. Daddy gave me a talking [to] on my birthday; it was so nice, so quiet, so gentle, but I felt as if I could never do any wrong again." HGM to CEM, June 1898, CEMP. Though he wrote about a month later that he was "trying hard at work, but not doing very well" (and that Leonard had won a scholarship), he in fact maintained a high place in class, as well as excelling in sports.

48 *St Leonards School*, 6.

49 Bowles to CEM, 17 Jan. 1904, CEMP. (Were these early trams quieter or was Emily Bowles deaf?)

50 Material in CEMP. Members of the Scribblers' Club used pen-names and circulated their work for comment by other members. For "Humility and Self-Respect," CEM used the pen-name "C.R. Maxwell"; she also wrote under the pen-name "Theta." The period covered is about 1901–05.

51 CEM to "Hirstlet," not sent, CEMP.

52 Account book, CEMP.

53 Order for stockings, and reply from "Dr. Lahmann's Cottonwool Underclothing Agency," 20 Sept. 1901, CEMP.

54 "Hirstlet" to "Kitten" (another of CEM's nicknames), 6 Oct. 1901; CEM to Hirstlet, 14 Oct. n.d. [probably 1900] to "Hirstlet," unfinished, not sent, CEMP. No name is given to CEM's illness in extant correspondence; some of the symptoms suggest hyperthyroidism.

55 Ibid.

56 To "Paul," 22 Feb. n.d., unfinished, not sent, CEMP.

57 Information in FMP.

58 Interview with Agnes Fyfe, Basel, Switzerland, 1978, and roughly borne out by the family tree in Rimmer.

59 Interview with Lord Rochdale, Lingholm, Keswick, August 1978.

60 FEM supported the concept and work of the secular and locally controlled school boards, established by the 1870 act and abolished in 1902.

A bill of similar effect to the 1902 one had been brought in in 1896, but had been dropped, to his great delight, FEM to CEM, 26 June 1896, CEMP. Now in Cumberland he worked with the County Education Authority.

61 "Obit.," Bruce.

62 Harrison, interview; "Obit."

63 Hawse End Guest Book (hereafter HEGB), FMP.

64 Information from Tom Faber, Cambridge.

65 Maps, rules, etc. in CEMP.

66 Josie Low to CEM, P/1 June 1908; 12 Aug. 1908, CEMP.

67 J. Low to CEM, n.d., CEMP. It is not clear whether "the Platonist" was the unnamed fourth friend or whether this was for a while a nickname given to Malcolm. I am also not able to be certain when the "Malcolm" referred to was Malcolm Robertson, and when it was Malcolm Darling, another friend of Josie's.

68 J. Low to CEM, n.d. [Aug. 1908], CEMP. James Lowther, Speaker of the House of Commons, later described James Moorsom as "subject to fits of eccentricity," and related how "on one occasion, dispossessing a fly-driver from his seat on the box, [he] took his place and galloped the fly up and down the streets of Keswick, cracking his whip and vociferating, 'I am the mad flyman of Fieldside!'", Lowther, *A Speaker's Commentaries*, 122.

69 J. Low to CEM, 12 Aug. 1909, CEMP.

70 Jermyn Moorsom to CEM, 11 May 1909, CEMP.

71 CEM to Miss Grant, 17 Feb. 1903, unfinished, not sent, CEMP. I admit to wondering whether the cost of this month's holiday might not have been better employed in paying higher wages; though it is unlikely the Marshalls paid less than the going rate.

72 Harrison, interview.

73 CM to CEM, n.d., CEMP. For some discussion of servants and of middle-class housekeeping, see Lewis, *Women in England, 1970–1950*, 112–16.

74 Ms titled "Jemima" [1905], CEMP.

75 To "Alice" [Low?], 1 July 1907, unfinished, not sent, CEMP.

76 Monteagle to CEM, 27 Jan. [1907], CEMP.

77 "Obit.," Pigou.

78 Pigou, *Principles and Methods of Industrial Peace*.

79 Keynes, "Alfred Marshall, 1842–1924," 55, and Edgeworth, "Reminiscences," 72. Edgeworth explains that "Concern for the practice of family duties was the ground of Marshall's opposition" and that "He regarded the family as a cathedral, something more sacred than the component parts." Keynes, more sympathetic to the women's cause, suggests that "a congenital bias, which by a man's fifty-fourth year of

life has gathered secret strength, may have played a bigger part ... than the obedient intellect." For a feminist the connections to Alfred Marshall's own life jump out from between the lines. Marshall's wife, Mary Paley, was a lecturer in economics at Newnham before he married her, but after marriage she lived always in his shadow, gaining a reputation for devotion, but losing what had promised to be a distinguished career in her own field. Keynes has a full account of the fate of her writing; see also Perry Williams, "Pioneer Women Students at Cambridge," in F. Hunt, ed., *Lessons for Life,* 188.

80 Pigou's major contribution to economics was *Wealth and Welfare,* 1912. Later editions were titled *The Economics of Welfare.*

81 CEM to Miss Grant, 17 Feb. 1903, CEMP, not sent.

82 HGM to CEM, 20 Oct. [P/1906?], CEMP.

83 Ms notes on back of Amy M. Smith to CEM, 11 Jan. 1906, CEMP; interview with Tom Graves of Skelgill (1978), who had been a member of the choir.

84 FM to HGM, 31 Oct. 1906, CEMP.

85 Julius (Frankfurt) to CEM, 11 Nov. 1899, CEMP.

86 "Tatton" to CEM, 12 Jan. 1906, CEMP.

87 CM to CEM, 18 Jan. 1906, CEMP.

88 E.F. Gerrard to CEM, 11 Aug. 1907, CEMP.

CHAPTER TWO

1 CM to CEM, 18 Jan. 1906, CEMP.

2 "Bow-wow" [Margaret McKerrow] to CEM, 22 Jan. 1906, CEMP.

3 There was a lingering prejudice against women of well-off families accepting pay. The women themselves sometimes felt guilty about taking jobs needed by less well-off sisters; males in the family, however, were often articulating pure paternalism.

4 For an important discussion of the emphasis on traditional motherhood within the feminism of this time, see S. Holton, *Feminism and Democracy,* ch. 1. Garner, *Stepping Stones to Women's Liberty,*, ch. 1, also refers.

5 *DNB,* 1951–60, s.v. Pigou.

6 Hobson, *Imperialism..* There is an extensive recent literature of controversy on the New Liberalism of the early twentieth century: see, *inter alia,* Bernstein, *Liberalism and Liberal Politics in Edwardian England;* Clarke, *Lancashire and the New Liberalism; Liberals and Social Democrats;* Emy, *Liberals, Radicals and Social Politics;* Freeden, *The New Liberalism;* Laybourn and Reynolds, *Liberalism and the Rise of Labour;* Meacham, *A Life Apart;* Searle, *Corruption in British Politics, 1900–1935;* Weiler, *The New Liberalism..*

7 Ms notes for speech, Keswick Liberal Club, 18 Nov. 1909, CEMP.

8 CEM to Lady Carlisle, 15 Oct. 1910, ms copy of letter, CEMP. The passage quoted has been interpolated by CEM in the copy and is marked "N.B. (*Not* mentioned in letter)."

9 Liddington and Norris, *One Hand Tied behind Us*, passim.

10 Hume, *The National Union of Women's Suffrage Societies 1897–1914*, 22.

11 "Hirstlet" to CEM, 28 Jan. 1906, CEMP.

12 "Bow-wow" [Margaret McKerrow] to CEM, 22 Jan. 1906, CEMP.

13 HEGB. Lovers of the Lake District may like to have the itinerary, as follows: leaving Hawse End, 24 July; to Patterdale via Penrith; 25 July, Skelwith via Kirkstone and Troutbeck; 26 July, Coniston via Burn Gates; 28 July, Grasmere via Oxenfell and Ambleside; 29 July back to Hawse End via Thirlmere. Even now, in the 1990s, road gradients of 25 per cent are not unknown.

14 Information from Jill Liddington. For the deputation, see Hume, *National Union*, 26.

15 "Suffragettes" is used only for the militants.

16 Marion Hartley to CEM, 12 Dec.[1906?], CEMP. Note that the date is not quite certain. For the role of women in local government, where many had the right to vote and to stand, see Hollis, *Ladies Elect*.

17 Various material in CEMP. For details of Dickinson's bill and other WS measures see invaluable table in Rover, *Women's Suffrage and Party Politics in Britain 1866–1914*, 211–17.

18 CEMP.

19 *W'sF*, 6 Feb. 1908, where there is a full account. For a brief mention, see HMS, Diary, 30 Jan.,1908, SCPC. Swanwick interpreted Asquith as saying that "he had an open mind."

20 HMS, Diary, 13 April 1908, SCPC.

21 For mention of Liberal fears of a propertied women's vote, see e.g. Harrison, *Separate Spheres*, 47–50; Rover, *Women's Suffrage*, 124–5; Rosen, *Rise Up, Women!*, 150–2; Pugh, *Electoral Reform in War and Peace*, ch. 3.

22 NUWSS, Annual Report, 1908, 12. For a somewhat fuller report, see Manchester NUWSS, *Women's Suffrage: A Survey, 1908–1912* (pamphlet) and District Federation, [1912].

23 HMS to B. Russell, 25 May 1908, BRA.

24 *W'sF*, 28 May 1908.

25 *W'sF*, 4 June 1908 (actual date of Fawcett's letter, 29 May 1908). For the parliamentary exchange, see *H.C. Deb.*, 4th series, vol. 189 (19 May–2 June 1908), 962–3.

26 *W'sF*, 28 May 1908.

27 *W'sF*, 4 June 1908 (under the imprint of the MLWS).

28 B. Russell to M.L. Davies, 5 June 1908, BRA. See also Hume, *Na-*

tional Union, 45–7, and B. Russell to MGF, 21 May 1908 (quoted by Hume, 46); Russell to MGF, 26 May 1908, Fawcett Lib.. Russell still held this view in August 1908, Russell to M.L. Davies, 8 Aug. 1908, BRA.

29 Russell's correspondence throughout this period with Margaret Llewelyn Davies, hon. sec. of the Women's Cooperative Guild and a convinced adultist, led to his transferring his allegiance from the NU to the People's Suffrage Federation, which she founded in October 1909. Both sides of this correspondence, which sheds a great deal of light on the adult suffrage position, are in BRA.

30 Less constructively, the Pankhursts were also impatient with their fellow-suffragists, and sometimes failed to take account of careful work that had been done. See, e.g. Liddington and Norris, *One Hand*, 171, 178–9.

31 Hume, *National Union*, 29–32, ; S. Holton, *Feminism and Democracy*, 37–8.

32 NUWSS, *Annual Report*, Jan. 1909, CEMP. Exceptionally, this report covers a period of fifteen months, Oct. 1907 to Jan. 1909.

33 S. Holton, *Feminism and Democracy*, ch. 2.

34 Ibid., 31.

35 Hume, *National Union*, 33.

36 How, and by whom, this paper was put together remains unclear. The top-of-the-page imprints of the contributing organizations might suggest that each body sent its own copy in, edited in its own office, but possibly the unknown editor was responsible for receiving copy direct from contributing individuals. This is suggested, e.g., by Fawcett's response – a week later – to B. Russell's letter of 28 May 1908, in which she was at pains to correct any impression that he was speaking for the NU executive. The paper also always contained a few pages of general interest and information, unsigned. M. Llewelyn Davies described it as a "a terrible rag" after "they cut out all the parts ... bearing on 'democratic lines'." M.L. Davies to B. Russell, n.d. [June 1908, misdated "[1907]"], BRA.

37 Accounts of this contretemps vary substantively.

38 Ms, KWSA, "Report on 1st Quarter's Work" (hereafter KWSA, "1st Quarter"), CEMP. The report is in CEM's handwriting, and is almost certainly of her authorship, but was clearly to be read out by someone else, (perhaps CM as president) since it concludes by calling on CEM to give a report on the quarterly council meeting of the NU. For founding and principles see also ms "KWSA" [18 May 1908], CEMP, outlining object and rules.

39 Report of CEM's speech at Grange on 22 Sept. 1909, *West Cumberland Herald*, clipping in CEMP.

40 The speech which follows has been reconstructed from ms notes, n.d., in CEM's handwriting. The particular occasion can be dated approximately as probably between Feb. and June 1908, because of the reference to Stanger's bill. Other more scrappy notes indicate that the speech was similar to others that she gave throughout 1908. The material was familiar to her and much is in note form; I have felt able to take some minor liberties with the text in confidence that I was not departing from her meaning. The direct quotations are from passages which she wrote out in full, usually, I think, because they had a good ring to them which she did not want to lose. In the original they are often in quotation marks, which I have omitted from my quotations to avoid confusion. For the sake of comfortable reading and where the meaning is clear, abbreviations have been expanded without the conventional use of square brackets.

41 CEM noted only a short title for the story she would use; in this case the story is found in full in a leaflet, *Some Objections to Women's Suffrage Considered* (CSWS [Central Society for Women's Suffrage]: March 1907), CEMP.

42 Draft, probably for a leaflet, n.d. [c. 1908], CEMP.

43 Much has been written on politics and suffrage; little of it takes the electors into account as people, though there is much anxious counting and recounting of heads to be enfranchised, as there was on all sides at the time.

44 LSWS (formerly CSWS), report of the executive committee to the AGM, 10 Nov. 1908. See also *W'sF*, 28 May 1908; M.L. Davies to B. Russell, [19?] June 1908, BRA; Rover, *Women's Suffrage and Party Politics in Britain 1866–1914*, 65, 114.

45 J. Low to CEM, 2 July 1908, CEMP.

46 Typescript of parts of Ray Costelloe's letters home during her caravan tour (hereafter Costelloe, "Caravan") 7 July, 9 July 1908, Barbara Strachey Papers, seen by courtesy of Barbara Strachey Halpern. Ray Costelloe was later Ray Strachey, and active in the LSWS. See also *W'sF*, 2 July, 23 July 1908.

47 Costelloe said there were about two hundred, CEM claimed "over 300."

48 Costelloe, "Caravan." For another participant's account, see E. Rendel, "Caravan Tour," *W'sF*, 23 July 1908.

49 KWSA, "1st Quarter," CEMP.

50 Ibid. A small part of the ms is damaged and illegible.

51 Ibid.

52 Ibid.

53 J. Low to CEM, n.d. [c. June 1908], CEMP.

54 J. Low to CEM, [12 Aug. 1908], CEMP.
55 HEGB; KWSA "1st Quarter"; and various in CEMP.
56 KWSA, *Annual Report*, 1908–9 (hereafter KWSA, *AR* '09), CEMP.
57 Ibid.
58 KWSA, "1st Quarter," CEMP.
59 KWSA, *AR* '09.
60 Ibid.
61 *HEGB*; for Isabella Ford, see Hannam; *Isabella Ford*. Theodosia
   Marshall, a sister of Catherine's father, had been a close friend of the
   Ford sisters from the 1860s, and they had often spent holidays on
   Derwent Island, Hannam, 20.
62 NUWSS, *Annual Report*. 1908, (27 January 1909) (hereafter NU, *AR*
   '08); ms, KWSA, "Report of first nine month's work" [30 Jan. 1909],
   CEMP. On the literature stall, see also a letter from Mary Cudworth,
   hon. sec. of York WSS, asking for advice on how to start one, 25 Oct.
   1908, CEMP.

CHAPTER THREE

1 Harrison, *Separate Spheres*, 118–19, a good source for the political
   aspects of antisuffragism.
2 For Mrs Somervell's views, see Somervell, *Speech Delivered at Queen's
   Hall Demonstration, March 29th, 1909*.
3 *Mid-Cumberland Herald*, 16 Jan. 1909. Clipping in CEMP.
4 Ward, *Speech by Mrs. Humphry Ward*, pamphlet. For Ward, see also Janet
   Trevelyan, *The Life of Mrs. Humphry Ward*. For a discussion of the
   relation between gender "roles" and "spheres," see my "Historical Reflections on Votes, Brooms and Guns," 36–9.
5 The Canadian suffragist Nellie McClung also dealt neatly with this argument: "'Who will mind the baby?' cried one of our public men,
   in great agony of spirit, 'when the mother goes to vote?' One woman
   replied that she thought she could get the person that minded it
   when she went to pay her taxes – which seemed to be a fairly reasonable
   proposition." McClung, *In Times Like These*, 51.
6 *Mid-Cumberland Herald*, 6 Feb. 1909, clipping in CEMP.
7 Black, *Social Feminism*, is useful for clarifying the relationship between equity feminism and social feminism. See also S. Holton, *Feminism
   and Democracy*, ch. 1; Garner, *Stepping Stones to Women's Liberty*,
   ch. 1, ch. 2.; see Liddington, *The Long Road to Greenham*, 64 and passim
   for the blending of equal rights and maternalist arguments in the
   women's peace as in the women's suffrage movement; Vellacott,
   "A Place for Pacifism," also refers.

8 Printed circular, 18 Jan. 1909; advance notice, *W'sF*, 31 Dec. 1908, CEMP.

9 CEM's desk diary (hereafter Diary), 26 Jan., CEMP.

10 Various material in CEMP, esp. Diary. The lectures I have listed are those she seems to have attended.

11 HEGB.

12 Diary, 29–31 Jan. 1909.

13 LSWS, report of executive committee at AGM, 10 Nov 1908; subscriptions include CEM and CM; Mrs John Marshall of Derwent was a vice-president, Lady Frances Balfour was president.

14 [Jermyn Moorsom] to CEM, ms letter, unsigned or incomplete, 21 March 1909, CEMP.

15 Harrison, *Separate Spheres*, 119.

16 Quoted, ibid., 113.

17 KWSA, *AR* '09.

18 Diary, 3 Apr. 1909. A pamphlet copy of Chapman Catt's address (stenographic report) to the IWSA Congress in St James Hall, 26 April 1909, published by the NU, July 1909, is in CEMP.

19 Hirst's book was on the life and writings of Friedrich List, a nineteenth-century German proponent of tariffs. For Hirst, see Edwin B. Bronner, introduction, Garland edition of Hirst, *The Quakers in Peace and War*, where, however, List is described as an advocate of free trade.

20 Diary, 4, 5 April 1909, CEMP.

21 Ibid., 9 April, CEMP.

22 Ibid., 12 April, CEMP.

23 Jermyn needed considerable urging; on 21 March he wrote to CEM, "Thank you very much for asking me again to your Tuesday [lectures]. I'm sure I don't know. I always feel dreadfully out of it listening to people talking in London," CEMP.

24 Jermyn Moorsom to CEM, 11 Aug., 19 Aug. 1908, CEMP. Gissing, *The Odd Women*, originally published in 1893, was reprinted in the popular Nelson's Library series in 1907. The novel concerns the lives and difficulties of middle-class women having to survive without the financial support of men.

25 Jermyn Moorsom to CEM, 4 Aug., 11 May 1909, CEMP.

26 Ibid.

27 Diary, 13 Apr., CEMP.

28 In October 1908, Jermyn wrote warmly to CEM saying "what a very good friend you've been to me and Josie." 4 Oct. 1908, CEMP.

29 Jermyn Moorsom to CEM, n.d. [probably March/April 1909], CEMP.

30 Josie at least seems always to have held to this, and also had decided, for (in her words) "serious insurmountable reasons" not known to

us but apparently connected with his health, that the unfortunate Jermyn "ought never to marry" though she "love[d] him more than most people or things in the world." The Marshalls also doubted the wisdom of Jermyn's marrying. With characteristic openness, Josie and Jermyn had, she said, "spoken of this matter more than once." Josie Low to CEM, [12 Aug. 1908], and to Mrs Marshall, n.d., CEMP.

31 Jermyn Moorsom to CEM, 11 July 1909, CEMP.

32 Diary, 15 Apr. 1909, CEMP.

33 Ibid., 16–29 April, CEMP.

34 Jermyn Moorsom to CEM, 11 July 1909, CEMP. No further details are known to me. As far as I know the marriage went ahead. Despite her close friendship with Jermyn, Catherine's role was that of mentor; she was clearly not one of the "quartet."

35 Guests at Hawse End in May included Emily Leaf and Mary Sheepshanks (from London), and Rosamund Spedding and Minnie Broatch, both active in the KWSA, and both, like Catherine, becoming experienced open-air speakers, HEGB.

36 Ms "Hon. Organizing Sec's Report" [24 June 1909], CEMP.

37 Ms notes, "Carlisle, June 2nd, 1909," CEMP; CC, 10 June 1909.

38 CC, 24 June 1909.

39 Ms "Hon. Organizing Sec's Report," CEMP.

40 CC, 15 July, 29 July 1909; Diary, 19–23, CEMP.

41 Costelloe to CEM, 13 July 1909, CEMP. Costelloe's aunt, Carey Thomas, was president of Bryn Mawr. For more about Ray, see Remarkable Relations, Barbara Strachey's fascinating history of the Pearsall Smith family. The World at Eighteen had been published in 1907.

42 I. Ford to CEM, 13 July 1909, CEMP.

43 Hannam, Isabella Ford, ch. 3; Rowbotham, Hidden from History, 62; Hannam, "In the Comradeship of the Sexes," 214–38.

44 Catharine Pattinson to CEM, 26 June 1909, CEMP. Clearly, her brother was also not sufficiently worked up about his sister's liberation to offer or be asked to look after his mother for a few hours to allow Miss Pattinson to attend one of the July meetings; this may never have occurred to anyone in the family.

45 CC, 29 July 1909.

46 Ibid.

47 Ms draft letter, CEM to "Dear Sir" [13 July], CEMP. CEM reported that all the local papers published the notices and her letter.

48 J. Braithwaite, Mayor of Whitehaven, to CEM, 19 July 1909, CEMP.

49 H. Walker to CEM, 19 July 1909, CEMP.

50 CC 29 July 1909; for another account of the tour, see Hannam, Isabella Ford, 133–4.

51 Walker to CEM, 11 Aug. 1909, CEMP.

52 See, among many examples, report of the LSWS executive to AGM, 10 Nov 1908, where reference is made several times to activities as a response to Asquith's "request for evidence that there is a strong and widespread demand for this reform,"CEMP.

53 *CC*, series beginning 20 May 1909. The first article is signed by Margaret Robertson, the NU's leading professional political organizer. Most of the others are unsigned. "Questions for Divisional Secretaries," together with notebook, Whitehaven copy in CEMP; see also *CC*, 22 April 1909. See Appendix C.

54 S. Holton, *Feminism and Democracy*, esp. ch. 3.

55 The controversy over the width of the franchise to be demanded was aired in the *CC* extensively, May–June 1909; see also "The National Union and Adult Suffrage," *CC*, 11 Nov. 1909; HMS to B. Russell, 25 May 1908, BRA. See also Holton, *Feminism and Democracy*, 53. Most NU members (with the exception of some Conservative and Unionist suffragists) seem to have been pragmatic, prepared to advocate the widest possible suffrage *that they thought there was any chance of getting*.

56 B. Russell to M.L. Davies, 2 Apr. 1907; Russell to Miss Phillips, 25 November 1909, BRA.

57 See p. 38 above.

58 S. Holton, *Feminism and Democracy*, 65–8.

59 In a speech given in Glasgow on 22 Nov. 1909, MGF was still firmly re-iterating her opinion that "adult suffrage is both undesirable and unnecessary at the present time." Speech reprinted as a pamphlet, *Wanted, a Statesman*. But by 1911, KDC and HMS were able to declare that her principle was "the more suffrage for women the better," S. Holton, *Feminism and Democracy*, 73.

60 For controversies surrounding Liberal dominance in the NU, see S. Holton, *Feminism and Democracy*, 49–50.

61 Liddington and Norris; *One Hand*, 203–6, 209–10; Hume; *National Union*, 31 n. 13.

62 HNB in *CC*, 15 Sept. 1910, also quoted in S. Holton; *Feminism and Democracy*, 51.

63 *Bye-Election Policies Compared*; Rover, *Women's Suffrage and Party Politics*, 79.

64 S. Holton, *Feminism and Democracy*, 41–2. Relative autonomy of local WSPU bodies – and a lack of consistency and predictability in their policies – was surely the *result* of the WSPU's lack of a constitution, not in spite of it, as Holton's wording suggests.

65 HMS, Diary, 20 March 1908, SCPC.

66 *Bye-Election Policies Compared*. The statement of WSPU policy was very properly sent to Christabel Pankhurst, and the changes made by her incorporated verbatim.

67 M.L. Davies to B. Russell, "Friday," n.d. [probably summer 1908], BRA.

68 Ms "Nottingham Quarterly Council, July 1909: Keswick Resolution," (hereafter Notts ms), CEMP. The speaker was probably Ethel Snowden, the societies Ambleside, Penrith, and Keswick.

69 Ms, mimeo, with additional notes, "KWSA Quarterly General Committee Meeting, Agenda," 24 June 1909, CEMP. 24 June, the date of the KWSA meeting, would have been too late for the resolution to be accepted by the NU central office, and it could only go on to the council meeting in the name of a society, not of an individual, so CEM apparently circulated it ahead of time, asking any who were unwilling to have it go forward to notify her without delay. Since it did go forward, there were presumably no objections, and there is some evidence that it was then discussed and ratified when the KWSA meeting was held. The document is one of many that appear from about this time on, reproduced by CEM on some type of mimeographing device, similar to the more recent "Ditto" process.

70 Notts ms, CEMP.

71 Minutes, NU quarterly council, Nottingham, 6 July 1909, Fawcett Lib.; CC, 17 July 1909.

72 Marion Phillips to "Dear Madam," 29 Oct 1909, re the proceeding for voting for this committee, CEMP.

73 Emily Chubb to CEM, 1 Sep. 1909, CEMP. Emily Chubb came with her sister, and described herself as an Independent Socialist "of a *very* mild type," and aware of the need to avoid party politics. Mrs Harrison Bell was the defaulting speaker; as was her habit, CEM had made careful inquiries as to her strengths; I.O. Ford n.d.; Mary Fielden to CEM, 29 July 1909, CEMP. Harrison Bell shortly left the NU executive for the PSF, M.L. Davies to B. Russell [Nov. 1909], BRA.

74 *CC*, 5 Aug. 1909. Catherine had made the opportunity known through the correspondence columns of the *Common Cause*.

75 Chubb to CEM [16 Sept. 1909], CEMP, with a report on a meeting at Threlkeld on 15 Sept.; report on meeting at Grange, 22 Sept, *West Cumberland Herald*; "Village Meetings in Cumberland," clipping, CEMP; report by CEM, *CC*, 30 Sept. 1909. Other speakers and chairpersons included Minna Rathbone (cousin of Eleanor Rathbone); a Mr J.R. Brooke, from London; Mrs Wynn-Williams; Lady Beatrice Kemp, next-door neighbour (at Lingholm) of the Marshalls; Caroline and Frank Marshall; Mr H.M. Jenkins; and Anthony Wilson, managing director of the Thornthwaite Mines, near Keswick, and a leading local Liberal. All except Brooke were KWSA members, *CC* 30 Sept. 1909 and other material in CEMP.

76 *CC*, 30 Sept 1909.

77 Diary, Oct. 1909, CEMP.

78 CEM to Miss [Philippa] Strachey, 2 Nov. 1909, Fawcett Lib.
79 Ibid.
80 Diary, 25 Aug. 1909, CEMP.
81 Ibid., 8–13 Nov. 1909.

CHAPTER FOUR

1 Hume, *National Union*, 215.
2 CEM referred to this as her earlier state of mind in a letter to Sir John Simon, draft copy, 10 Aug. 1913, CEMP; Hume, 215.
3 *CC*, 10 June 1909.
4 *CC*, 3 July 1909.
5 The following speech is reconstructed from ms notes "Keswick Liberal Club, Nov. 18, 1909." Two ms versions exist, both in CEMP, one fuller (but unfortunately harder to read) and the other in note form. Similar manuscripts suggest that CEM wrote her more formal speeches (such as this one) more or less in full, practised them and reduced them to short note form for delivery. Because the fuller version, though very rough, is available, I have had to do less "filling in" on this one than for the speech reported in ch. 2.
6 *CC* 25 Nov. 1909. *CC* has "Moorsum," a misprint.
7 See, e.g., "Is the Demand for the Enfranchisement of Women on the same terms as Men a Demand for a Property Vote? Statistics prove that it is not," leaflet, n.d. [1909], copy in CEMP.
8 *CC*, 25 Nov. 1909.
9 "Cumberland and Westmoreland Organisation," *CC*, 16 Dec. 1909; Diary, 27 Nov. 1909, CEMP.
10 Diary, 4 Dec. 1909, CEMP.
11 NUWSS, "Report of Council Meeting," 6 Dec. 1909, Fawcett Lib.
12 FEM to MGF, faint carbon copy of ms, 18 Dec. 1909, FMP.
13 MGF to FEM, 20 December 1909, FMP. Fawcett addressed her reply to "Dear Friends," and owned herself "greatly puzzled" by Frank Marshall's objections. Wisely, she explained at length the process by which the manifesto had been arrived at – that it had arisen from a suggestion by Walter McLaren (an MP, and a leading Liberal member of the NU executive); that she had written it and sent a copy to every member of the executive; that the executive had approved it with only textual changes; that no single objection, other than the one from the Marshalls, had reached her. She reviewed the background to the council decisions, and stressed that "It will be quite possible, as we are a nonparty society, to sort out our workers so that no one shall be required to support a candidate with whom he or she is in disagreement on general politics," adding, "I do not think that in practice

the difference between us is more than infinitesmal." This interesting
exchange has just come to light and I am grateful to Frank Marshall
for bringing it to my attention.

14 Diary, 7 Dec., CEMP; *CC*, 25 Nov. 1909.

15 Jermyn Moorsom to CEM, 27 Nov. 1909, CEMP.

16 Diary, 10–13 Dec. 1909, CEMP.

17 NUWSS, "Election Campaign in Cumberland: Carlisle, Whitehaven and
Cockermouth Divisions" (printed in Keswick), CEMP.

18 Diary, 15 Dec. 1909, CEMP; *CC*, 23 Dec. 1909.

19 Copy in CEMP.

20 Copy of leaflet in CEMP.

21 Report, anon., in *CC*, 20 Jan. 1910.

22 *CC*, 10 Feb. 1910, also draft in CEM's handwriting in CEMP. The two
versions differ only slightly. "Miss Rathbone" here is probably
Minna, rather than her more famous cousin Eleanor.

23 This comment is on a separate sheet, part of a draft for an appreciative paragraph by CEM, giving high praise to Gugenheim's contribution, published in MLWS, *Monthly Paper*, no. 5, Feb. 1910.

24 Ms speech notes, n.d., untitled [dated by content], CEMP.

25 See n. 22 above.

26 Marion Phillips, "The Executive Committee," *CC*, 17 Feb. 1910; for an
account of the difficulties faced by suffragists collecting signatures,
see "The Story of a Petition," *CC*, 10 Feb 1910.

27 *CC*, 20 Jan. 1910.

28 Louis Walker to CEM, 3 Feb. 1910, CEMP. A Carlisle suffragist, Miss Fell,
saw the Carlisle campaign in a less jaundiced light (N.L. Fell to CEM,
[2 Mar 1910], CEMP), although she herself was described by Louis
Walker as "very nice but very undependable," the latter for reasons
worthy of record: "Her brother evidently rules at home and is very
selfish about the motor wh: belongs to *both* – and she is 4 miles out
of Carlisle – so she could not do much." This shared motor came up
again in the election of Dec. 1910, when Louis speculated that it
had helped the antisuffragist candidate: "her brother would be sure
to lend *his* half and I don't see how she could stop *her* half going
too!!" Walker to CEM, 8 Dec. 1910, CEMP.

29 B. Russell to Lucy Donnelly, 2 Jan. 1910, BRA; see also *CC*, 10
March 1910. Alys Russell (née Pearsall Smith) was B. Russell's wife, and
a very active NU worker; she appears constantly as a speaker in notices in the *CC*. She stayed with women's suffrage when he left it for
the PSF. For more on Alys Russell, see Strachey, *Remarkable Relations*.
R. Irwin (Cockermouth) to CEM, 14 Feb. 1910, CEMP, also comments
on the extent of the interest shown by women at this election, and
mentions another instance of a friendly reception, experienced by a

sister-in-law collecting signatures near Manchester. Copies of the petition are in CEMP, and *CC*, 23 Dec. 1909, has a reproduction on the front cover of a poster which includes the petition.

30 The WSPU claimed credit for the defeat of many Liberals, but "Even the Union's best friends were dubious." Rosen, *Rise Up, Women!*, 150.

31 B. Russell to Donnelly, 2 Jan. 1910, BRA. Russell rated the land tax question also among the major election issues. See also P. Morrell to B. Russell, 3 Dec. 1909, BRA, where he says he favours WS on the lines advocated by the PSF and is prepared to mention it in his election address, but will not dwell on it, since, as Russell will agree, the Lords and the budget are the principal issues.

32 Ibid.; B. Russell to Miss [Marion] Phillips, 25 Nov. 1909, copy, BRA.

33 See, e.g., B. Russell to M.L. Davies, 27 May 1908; M.L. Davies to B. Russell "Friday," n.d., marked [Nov.'09]; B. Russell to Donnelly, 18 Oct 1909. BRA. Ironically, Russell left the NU just as it was on the eve of taking a giant stride forward, although, since his disillusion with the Liberal party did not come until the war, possibly not in the direction he would have approved. Possibly his move to the PSF (where he was never very active) was in part unconsciously motivated by a wish to distance himself from Alys, with whom the final break came in 1911.

34 HMS to B. Russell, 27 Nov., 3 Dec. 1909, BRA.

35 Rosen, *Rise Up, Women!*, 150; Ensor, *England, 1870–1914*, 418.

36 Annie Dover to CEM, 23 Feb. 1910, CEMP.

37 Cheque for eight shillings and 8 pence, Margaret Bennett Brown to CEM, 28 Feb. 1910, CEMP.

38 *CC*, 17 Mar. 1910.

39 S. Holton, *Feminism and Democracy*, 40. Hume, *National Union*, describes the reorganization in a footnote (95 n. 126), where only its administrative utility is mentioned.

40 E.g. Mrs Harrison Bell, like B. Russell, joined the executive of the PSF.

41 Gerda Robertson to "My dear Jankie" [CEM], 28 Oct. 1910, CEMP.

42 B. Russell saw the width of proposed franchise reform as being the major issue, but also specifically the behaviour of Fawcett and those close to her: he wrote that the PSF "is having a very great success, but is regarded with grave suspicion by most ardent suffragists, and I am having a difficult time with Mrs. Fawcett and Co. However, Mrs. Fawcett is having a much more difficult time with me: she misbehaved again the other day by going directly contrary to the decision of the committee, and several of us banded together to tell her what we thought of her conduct ... I was myself denounced on three several counts by different people, among them Margery Strachey, who

reproached me sadly and fiercely for talking against Mrs F." Russell to Donnelly, 18 Oct. 1909, BRA.

43 In Bentham's view, Bertha Mason would be useless as parliamentary secretary, Edith Dimock not much better as honorary secretary; it was a serious mistake not to allow an overlap with the outgoing secretary (Marion Phillips; MGF's comment was that this was considered best); and no provision had been made for a new treasurer, now that Mason had resigned from that position. Bentham to McLaren, 8 Mar 1910, MPL 50/2/1/294. Fawcett made notes on the letter, 13 Mar 1910, but commented to McLaren that she thought his fears of trouble groundless. McLaren to Fawcett, 14 Mar 1910, MPL 50/2/1/297,298. Bentham was no better pleased by the "New Organisation," and re-signed from the NU executive early in 1911 because (amongst other things) she thought the formation of federations had lessened the NU influence. E. Bentham to A.G. Whitehead [NU secretary], 13 Feb. 1911, CEMP. The issue of whether criticism of Fawcett could be tol-erated arose again in June, when the *CC* (16 June 1910) published a letter from Phillips commenting unfavourably on a letter to the *Morning Post* from Fawcett, which she felt could be read as endorsing militancy; Swanwick, as editor, was sharply attacked for printing it, and the LSWS executive held a special meeting to pass a resolution of deep regret. Not until 4 July was the issue laid to rest by a request from Fawcett that no notice be taken of the incident. Various material in Fawcett Lib. (box 294) refers. The LSWS never became reconciled to the federation scheme, and never implemented it in full; see below, pp. 311–15.

44 NUWSS, "Report of Annual Council Meeting," 19 Mar. 1910, Fawcett Lib.; leaflet (printed in Keswick), "New Organisation of the N.U.W.S.S.: as adopted by the General Council, March, 1910"; mimeo leaflet, in CEM's handwriting, "Organization of the National Union of Women's Suffrage Societies: as adopted by the General Council, March 1910 (and slightly modified in 1911)," CEMP.

45 Ms, n.d., untitled, probably notes for a speech given by CEM at the NWF conference, Penrith, 28 May 1910, CEMP.

46 Report of proceedings, NU annual council, London, 19 Mar. 1910, Fawcett Lib.; report, *CC*, 24 Mar. 1910.

47 Royden to CEM, 23 Mar. 1910, CEMP.

48 Ms notes for a speech ... 28 May 1910 (n. 45 above), CEMP.

49 E. Gardner to CEM, 22 Mar. [1910], CEMP.

50 Copy of leaflet, "New Organisation of the N.U.W.S.S.," CEMP.

51 "The Work of Federation," *CC*, 21 Apr. 1910.

52 See, e.g., "TGW p.p. Edith Dimock" to CEM, 25 May 1910, CEMP.

53 Ms notes for a speech ... 28 May 1910 (n. 45 above), CEMP.

54 Ms notes on printed agenda of NWF "Conference at Penrith,"
  28 May 1910; extensive material relating to this meeting and to the con-
  stititution of the NWF, CEMP.

CHAPTER FIVE

1 Hume, *National Union*, 63.
2 HNB *The "Conciliation" Bill, an Explanation and Defence* (pamphlet), n.d.
  [c. Sept./Oct. 1910: HNB sent CEM a copy of "my new pamphlet"
  on 18 Oct.] CEMP; Holton, *Feminism and Democracy*, 69–75; Hume, *National Union*, ch. 3; Rosen, *Rise Up, Women!*, 130–56; Rover, *Women's
  Suffrage*, 95–8, 129–34 and passim; Leventhal; *The Last Dissenter*,
  ch. 5; Pugh, *Electoral Reform*, 34–6.
3 HNB to MGF, 18 Jan., 25 Jan. [1910], MPL M/50/2/1/291, 292. For a recent life of HNB, see Leventhal, *Last Dissenter*.
4 HNB to MGF, 28 Feb. [1910] MPL M50/2/1/293.
5 For text of Conciliation Bill, see Rover, *Women's Suffrage*, 215.
6 HNB to MGF, 21 Mar. [1910], MPL M/50/2/1/300.
7 MGF notes on reply to HNB, 21 Mar. 1910, MPL M50/2/1/301.
8 HNB to MGF, 27 Mar. [1910], MPL M/50/2/1/303; Edith Dimock to HNB,
  9 Apr. 1910, MPL M50/2/1/305.
9 See, e.g., HNB to MGF 27 May [1910], MPL M50/2/1/306; 1st leader *MG*,
  30 May; *CC*, 2 June, 9 June 1910.
10 If a bill, on passing second reading, was sent to a Grand Committee,
  this committee was able to sit at the same time as the House went
  on with other work; however, a Committee of the Whole House, as its
  name implies, took up the time of the House of Commons, and was
  therefore dependent on the government to find time and grant facilities
  for further progress. Hume, *National Union*, 84 n. 80.
11 *CC*, 21 July 1910; *H.C. Deb.*, 5th series, vol. 19 (11 July-13 August 1910),
  307. *CC* ran long articles on the attitudes of LG and Churchill, char-
  acterizing the former as "The Wrecker" and the latter as "The Con-
  tortionist," *CC*, 28 July, 4 Aug 1910. Hobhouse overheard LG,
  18 June, telling the press that WS "if raised now, would completely dish
  H of L. question," Hobhouse, *Inside Asquith's Cabinet*, 93.
12 Clipping, CEMP.
13 Various material, CEMP.
14 Ms "Copy of letter sent to C and W MPs," 6 June 1910, CEMP.
15 Ms copies of letters sent to party leaders, 8 June 1910, CEMP.
16 Correspondence, CEMP.
17 NU executive, 5 May 1910, copy in CEMP; HNB to MGF, 27 May
  [1910], MPL M50/2/1/306; HNB to MGF, 30 June [1910], MPL
  M50/2/1/315; HMS to MGF, 3 July 1910, MPL M50/2/1/316; mimeo

"circular," report and summary of negotiations with WSPU, MPL
M50/2/1/314; *CC*, 28 July 1910; material, CEMP, 19 May 1910;
Hume, *National Union*, 76–80.

18 S. Holton, *Feminism and Democracy*, ch. 2, offers an analysis of the
militant and constitutional movements. See also Garner, *Stepping Stones*,
passim. Harrison, "The Act of Militancy," is based *inter alia* on much
little-used material, including Harrison's own interviews with surviving
suffragettes, and is valuable for an understanding of their perspective. The NU had a prolonged struggle over militancy. For a while, the
NU in general had suspended judgment, disagreeing with militant
method but sharing the frustration that underlay it, and condemning
the government's harsh response. Meanwhile, there were some defections to the militant camp, and some attempts by militants to take
over NU branches. Increasingly, NU members and leaders were hampered in their own work by militant activity and the reaction to it, and
accordingly attitudes hardened. Joint membership in the NU and
WSPU was disallowed for executive members and in most branches in
1909, and condemnation became more and more outspoken. See
also below, ch 7, n. 62. correspondence in MPL M50/2/1/279–81; NU,
proceedings of annual council, 27 Jan 1909; NU, proceedings, quarterly council, 7 Oct. 1909, Fawcett Lib.; MGF to Helena Auerbach,
1 Oct. 1909, IAV; *CC*, 14 Oct. 1909; MGF to Mrs Dowson, 15 Oct.
1909, MPL M50/2/1/286; MGF, Wanted; a Statesman. For individual responses and comments, see, e.g., W.J. Dalzall Burnyeat, MP, to CEM,
13 July 1909; H[?] Martyn Jenkins to CEM, n.d.; FEM ms notes, Sept.
1909; Eleanor Acland to KDC, n.d.; B.N. Sewell to CEM, 3 Jan. 1910;
Mrs Kitchin to CEM, 16 Jan. 1910; FEM to CEM, 26 June 1910, CEMP;
CM to editor, *CC*, 8 Dec. 1910. For controversy in branches see, e.g.
Girton Review, no. 27, Michaelmas term, 1909; Agnes Garrett (LSWS)
to CEM, 6 Nov. 1908, CEMP. Militancy was discussed frequently in
CC, e.g. a defence of constitutional policy, 12 Aug, 1909; "Violence and
Reaction," 16 Sept. 1909. While the press generally indulged in sensational reporting of militant incidents, there was also serious coverage
in some papers (mostly the more liberal) of the reasons behind militancy, and the share of reponsibility which rested with the government:
e.g. letter, (Mrs) J.E.M. Brailsford, "The Suffragettes at Bye-
Elections," *Nation*, 24 July 1909, and correspondence following; "The
Women's War," *Nation*, 7 Aug. 1909, and correspondence following; "The Tactics of Violence," *Nation*, 25 Sept. 1909, and correspondence following; article (on ladies' page) by Filomena, *Illustrated
London News*, 23 July 1910. Particular thanks to Margaret Kamester for
this research.

19 HGM to CEM, 22 June [1910]; FEM to CEM, 24 June 1910, CEMP. Cath-

erine's parents continued to play an active part in local suffrage work, and FEM also wrote supportive letters to the press and to influential acquaintances from time to time. My remark about shopping is based on scant evidence as concerns this particular London trip (an advertising flier for a "SPECIAL SALE OF FRENCH MILLINERY ... MODEL COSTUMES, MANTLES AND BLOUSES ... ALSO LADIES BAGS ... at greatly reduced prices" remains among her papers) but on ample evidence from other periods of her life.

20 " Annotated agenda, CEMP.

21 "Anti-Suffragist" is underlined, probably indicating a perceived danger that MPs might merely pair with an adultist. CEM ms note, attached to her ms copies of the NWF correspondence of 6–8 June, CEMP.

22 CC, 21 July 1910; notes on payment of expenses for KWSA members (including HGM) attending demo of 9 July, 1 Sept. 1910, CEMP.

23 "Conciliation Committee for Women's Suffrage," n.d. [c. March 1910], MPL M/50/50/2/1; see also The Times, 14 June 1910.

24 Harrison, "Women's Suffrage at Westminster, 1866–1928," 105. Harrison, although wishing to be fair to the suffragists, takes (eighty years later) a position difficult to distinguish from that of the all-male parliamentarian Liberal lukewarm suffragists of the time, who thought the women should be glad to subordinate their cause to recognized Liberal ideals and party directives in the hope of some future reward when the really important issues should have been dealt with. S. Holton's more profound and convincing analysis of the adult suffrage issue (Feminism and Democracy, ch. 3) disposes of many of Harrison's arguments, though his article was probably not available to her at the time of going to press. In any case, negotiation always has to be based on discovery of the highest denominator common to the parties – except where it is based merely on threats of force. The accusation of "attracting support on contradictory grounds" was more true of the 1832 Reform Act, for which some had voted because they hoped it would stave off more radical reform or revolution, others because it was the best they could get at the time. The Conciliation Committee planned only to effect agreement between those who believed in the principle of WS.

25 Clipping from an unidentified Cumberland weekly paper; also ms draft, CEMP.

26 The quotation is from a speech by Philip Snowden on 29 July 1910, H.C. Deb., 5th series, vol. 19 (1910), 2588.

27 Ms notes, "arguments to Liberals: F.E.M.'s reply to Eighty Club Soc.," CEMP; see also The Times, 14 June 1910. For the Constitutional Conference, see below p. 103.

28 Hume, National Union, 86.

29 Ms notes, marked "O.A.Sp." [open-air speech], n.d., CEMP. Catherine had developed the analogy as soon as the rejection of the budget had caused the cry of "Monopoly!" to be raised.

30 CC, 25 Aug., 1 Sept. 1910; HEGB shows Helga Gill as a guest from 5–30 Aug. 1910, FMP.

31 CC, 17 Nov. 1910; for Selina Cooper (1864–1946), see Liddington, *The Life and Times of a Respectable Rebel*. S. Cooper to CEM, n.d., CEMP, is a succinct autobiography of Cooper's impressive TU and suffrage work, presumably sent to CEM when Cooper was applying for paid work as NU organizer, or when she came as a visiting speaker.

32 Maude Royden spoke at a number of meetings, and other speakers included Chrystal Macmillan, Isabella Ford, Lady Betty Balfour, Alice Low (Josie's more serious-minded sister), Helena Swanwick, Millicent Fawcett, and Bertha Mason (who had developed a lantern lecture on the history of the suffrage movement, which was later expanded into an excellent little book, *The Story of the Women's Suffrage Movement*, 1912). Copies of CEM's speech were sent to the party leaders, to HNB, and to the Cumberland and Westmoreland MPs, CC, 4 Aug., 17 Nov. 1910. Ms "Speech on Bill," n.d., CEMP, may refer. See also ms "Expenses of Organization Work 1910–1911" (most dates in this are given erroneously as 1911 instead of 1910), CEMP.

33 In a letter to Miss [Philippa] Strachey, 4 Oct. 1910, CEM asked, "Why is not London sending anyone to the Council? Are you not going to have a London Federation?", Fawcett Lib. The LSWS continued to resist the move to federation; see below pp. 311–15.

34 "Programme," Fawcett Lib.; various ms notes, CEMP; CC, 13 Oct. 1910; see also CC, 11 Aug. 1910.

35 HMS to MGF, 3 July 1910, MPL M50/2/1/316.

36 CC, 13 Oct. 1910.

37 CC, 20 Oct. 1910.

38 [Inspector], signature illegible, to CEM, 9 Sept. 1910, CEMP.

39 HNB to CEM, 12 Aug. [1910], CEM. Geoffrey Howard, the son of the Countess of Carlisle, had introduced an adult suffrage measure in March 1909, which had received less support in the House of Commons than the more limited bills, and was regarded by the NU as poor strategy. Rover, *Women's Suffrage*, 71, 222; Hume, *National Union*, 48, n. 72.

40 CEM's letter to HNB is not extant; its general contents can be deduced from his reply.

41 Opponents claimed that the bill's basis in property or occupancy left it open to exploitation by wealthy men who might set their female relatives up each with minimal requirements and so acquire influence over "faggot" votes. The Conciliation Committee had already tried

to meet this objection, and would do more if necessary. S. Holton, *Feminism and Democracy*, 70.

42 HNB to CEM, 20 Aug. [1910], CEMP. See also Hume, *National Union*, 68–9, for more on the reasoning behind the limited Conciliation Bill. M. Llewelyn Davies, on the other hand, wrote to CEM, n.d. (1910?) strongly advocating the adoption by the NU of "womanhood" suffrage, CEMP.

43 Above, p. 31; Pugh, *The Making of Modern British Politics, 1867–1939*, 11, 47.

44 Rover, *Women's Suffrage*, 140–1; Walker, "Party Political Women," 170. Rover says the NWLA was formed by a dissenting *majority*; Walker has it that the secessionists were in a *minority*. It is often impossible to sort local groups out, as they seem often to have called themselves "Associations" regardless of which national body they affiliated to. See also n. 58 below.

45 Russell said of her, "She puts Temperance first, the Liberal Party second, and Suffrage a bad third"; Russell to M.L. Davies, 11 Sept 1908. Lady Carlisle was B. Russell's aunt. For another negative view, see [Cunliffe] to CEM, 9 Mar. [1913], CEMP; for Lady Carlisle, see Roberts, *Radical Countess*; Pugh, *The Making of Modern British Politics, 1867–1939*, esp. ch. 14.

46 M.L. Davies wrote that "the Liberal women ... follow and ask advice, instead of thinking for themselves and being a little ingenious." To B. Russell, n.d., BRA.

47 CEM, ms "Draft of letter to Carlisle" [Miss Matravers], n.d. [c. 14 Nov. 1910], CEMP.

48 CEM, "Notes of letter to L.W.," 14 Nov. refers, CEMP.

49 Ms copy, CEM to Lady Carlisle, 15 Oct. 1910, CEMP.

50 "Draft ... Carlisle," CEMP.

51 M.A. Armstrong to Miss Walker, 24 Oct 1910; 24 to 27 Oct. 1910, various letters addressed to "Madam" or "Miss Walker," CEMP.

52 "Draft ... Carlisle," CEMP.

53 CEM, ms notes for speech, "Conference of Liberal Women Suffragists," 29 Oct. 1910, CEMP.

54 Draft and printed agenda; various ms notes, CEMP.

55 L. Walker to CEM, 26 Oct. 1910, CEMP.

56 CEM, ms "Notes of letter to L.W.," 14 Nov. [1910], CEMP.

57 "Draft ... Carlisle," CEMP.

58 B. Morton to CEM, 6 Nov. [1910], CEMP. The picture here is very different from Walker's view of the WLF as showing a "conviction that women should shape their own political destiny," Walker, "Party Political Women," 190; also Rendall's introduction to the volume in which Walker's essay appears, *Equal or Different*, 22. If it had earlier

been true that "The Liberal women ... campaigned only for candidates whose policies they supported," it was not so by 1912. While providing useful detail on the early days of the WLF, Walker appears to be ignorant of its failure to show effective commitment to women's suffrage in the crucial period of 1910–14. Her thesis, that Liberal women were more independent and more prepared to stand up for suffrage than were Conservative women, is based on inadequate data. It needs reexamination in a study which would include not only the WLF (with more detail on 1908–14) and the Primrose League but also the LWSU (pp. 229, 260–1) and the CUWFA.

59 B. Morton to CEM, 10 Nov. [1910], CEMP.

60 Ms draft or copy, "Letter to Mrs Morton," 14 Nov. [1910], CEMP.

61 Denman to CEM, 7 Nov. 1910. For some justification for Denman's plaintiveness see Denman to CEM, 9, 14 July, 28 Aug., 9, 15 Nov.; Denman to FEM, 15 Nov.; CEM to Denman, rough ms draft or copy, 8 Nov., ms draft, incomplete, 16 Nov., all 1910, CEMP.

62 For the impact of the King's death and the Constitutional Conference, see Gilbert, *David Lloyd George*, 411; Jenkins, *Asquith*, 236–47.

63 "An Instalment of Justice," first leader, *CC*, 2 June 1910.

64 *H.C. Deb.*, 5th series, vol. 20 (22 Nov. 1910), cc 272–3; Hume, *National Union*, 91.

65 Hume, *National Union*, 91, citing Nevinson Journals, e616, 29 Nov. 1910 (Bodleian Library); Rosen, *Rise Up*, 139–42; Rover, *Women's Suffrage*, 81.

66 For the militant movement as a profound spiritual movement, see, e.g., Vicinus, *Independent Women*, 247–80; also "Male Space and Women's Bodies." I am more convinced, as well as personally more attracted, by the view that the appeal of militancy lies in its sheer ability to liberate women from conventionality and free them to be brave and outrageous. Eleanor Acland wrote to KDC, "I hate the militants' methods but I do admire the way they put [all] ladylike scruples aside," ms letter, badly damaged by damp, n.d. [1910?], CEMP.

67 H. Gill to CEM, n.d. [August 1910], CEMP. I believe "respectable people" here to refer to the working class, not to the middle class.

68 Ms, L. Walker's handwriting, draft/copy of letter to editors from CEM and Walker, headed "Outbreak of the Suffragettes," n.d., CEMP; for an appreciative response to the NU attitude see E. Atter (Whitehaven) to CEM, 24 Nov. 1910, CEMP.

69 Hume, *National Union*, 90–1. See also NU, report of proceedings: special council, 26 Nov. 1910, Fawcett Lib.

70 "A Compromise on Suffrage," *Nation*, 28 May 1910; "Woman as Politician," *Nation*, 16 July 1910; HNB, "The Tactics of Woman Suffrage," *Nation*, 23 July 1910; correspondence in *Nation*, e.g., 9, 16, 23 July 1910.

71 In East St Pancras H. Jacobs polled 22 votes, in Camlachie William
Mirlees polled 35 votes; Hume, *National Union*, 93; S. Holton, *Feminism and Democracy*, 50; *CC*, 8 Dec. 1910.

72 CEM, ms, "Women's Suffrage Triumph in South Salford," n.d.,
damaged and illegible in part; copy of Charles Russell's letter to electors,
affirming support of Women's Suffrage, CEMP; HMS, *I Have Been
Young*, 209–210; MLWS *Monthly Paper*, no. 15, Dec. 1910; Hume, *National Union*, 93. I have not been able to find a precise reference for
Belloc's use of the phrase "immoral and unsavoury," but see Fulford,
Votes for Women, 218–19; Blewett, *The Peers, the Parties, and the People*, 334.

73 *CC*, 1 Dec. 1910; see also *CC*, 24 Nov. 1910; CEM's annotated
agenda, NU special council, 26 Nov. 1910, has a long note of Bertha
Mason's report to council on the South Salford contest (possibly CEM
wrote the report for Mason, as parliamentary secretary, to give; CEM
has tried to write legibly, and it does not look like notes on someone
else's speech).

74 Ms, "Women's Suffrage Triumph," CEMP.

75 *CC*, 1 Dec. 1910.

76 Ibid.; HMS, *I Have Been Young*, 210; both Speaight, *Hilaire Belloc*,
292–3, and *DNB*, s.v. Belloc (which does not mention women's suffrage), suggest that the expense of a second election (in which he
might not have had official party support) was the major factor in
Belloc's withdrawal, though the timing suggests otherwise. Blewett,
Peers, Parties, People, ascribes Belloc's withdrawal to his committee having
broken with him because of his obsession with the evils of the party
system and his contempt for teetotalism, 223, but then says of Brailsford
that he "devoted his talents to ousting the Liberal Belloc, a vocal
anti-suffragist," 338; see also McCarthy, *Hilaire Belloc*, 162.

77 CEM described her draft letter, "Women's Suffrage Triumph," as
"a brief summary of events from one on the spot," and she had told
Denman that she was off to South Salford, CEM to Denman, rough
ms draft/copy, 8 Nov. 1910. Lord Lytton, chairman of the Conciliation
Committee, wrote to Margaret Robertson on 27 Nov. explaining
why he had been unable to support HNB against a Conservative, much
as he would have liked to see HNB in Parliament, MPL M/50/1/2/87.

78 CEM's annotated agenda, NU special council, 26 Nov. 1910, CEMP; *CC*,
1 Dec. 1910. Private members' bills brought before Parliament were
limited in number, and were chosen by lottery from among those submitted; if several MPs would ballot for a women's suffrage bill,
chances were increased.

79 CEM ms comment on printed circular letter from Annie T.
Brunyate, hon. sec. NU Dover, 22 Nov. 1910, CEMP.

80 CEM's annotated agenda, CEMP. The NWF went ahead and used its

proposed questions, ms "Questions put to Candidates," together with the MPs' responses, [Dec 1910], CEMP.

81 Polling dates were 2–19 Dec. 1910.

82 CEM ms agenda and various notes, KWSA executive meeting 20 Oct. 1910, CEMP.

83 *CC*, 22 Dec. 1910; handbill "Women's Suffrage Meetings" (CEM as speaker), and other material, CEMP.

84 Despatch notice, A & N Co-operative Society, Books and Music Department, [19th? not clear] Dec. 1910, CEMP. Included – unexpectedly – is a gift of A.E. Housman's *A Shropshire Lad* for Philip Snowden.

85. Gerda C. Robertson to "My dear Jankie" [CEM], 28 Oct. 1910, CEMP.

CHAPTER SIX

1 Documentation of Catherine's life is sometimes less complete for periods which she spent away from Hawse End, and this is true for the first few months of 1911, by comparison with the earlier wealth of material on the local and regional suffrage campaign.

2 The election of Jan. 1910 returned 275 Libs., 273 Cons., 82 Irish Nationalists, and 40 Labour; in Dec. 1910 the figures were 272 Libs., 272 Cons., 84 Irish Nationalists, 42 Labour.

3 NU executive, 19 Jan. 1911, Fawcett Lib.; Hume, *National Union*, 94, n. 125.

4 This was the reason for NU and Conciliation Committee opposition to the bill introduced in April 1911 by W.H. Dickinson, with the backing of a group of Liberal suffragist MPs. The bill would have given the vote to married women as joint occupiers with their husbands, and the NU had good reason to believe that it was too broad to pass but might draw some Liberal and Labour support away from the Conciliation Bill, Hume, *National Union*, 99.

5 Ibid., 101; Rover, *Women's Suffrage*, 133. In what now seems an extreme attempt to get round the fear of faggot votes, the new bill prohibited a husband and wife from registering in the same constituency in case he might set her up as a qualified "occupier" and influence her vote, the secret ballot notwithstanding.

6 Hume, *National Union*, 100–1.

7 NU, results of ballot, annual council meeting, 26–8 Jan. 1911, copies in Fawcett Lib. and in CEMP.

8 NU executive, 16 Feb, 1911; T.G. Whitehead (NU secretary) to Mason, 17 Feb. 1911; Mason to Whitehead, 28 Feb. 1911, CEMP. Mason wrote to Bertrand Russell, referring rather oddly to his "*forced* retirement" from the executive, and saying "and during the last fortnight

I have been *sent* to join you in the wilderness! – After *rejecting* me at the poll the Council sat down to pass a vote of thanks to me for my past services – in which I was described as *heavensent*!", Mason to Russell 13 February 1911, BRA. Russell in fact had probably seen Mason as an impediment to progress in the NU, sharing M. L. Davies' view that she was likely to be content with a very limited women's franchise, M.L. Davies to Russell, n.d. [c. August 1908], BRA.

9 Above, pp. 82–3; 417n.42; Bentham to Whitehead, 13 Feb. 1911, printed copy, CEMP; Bentham to Whitehead, 21 Feb. 1911, CEMP. The following February, Broadley-Reid, active in the WLF, was reported as "v. hostile" to the NU, CEM ms notes, "W. Lib. Fed. Campaign: Mrs. Acland," 29 Feb 1912, CEMP.

10 CEM, ms notes, London Suffrage Conference, 27 Feb. 1911, CEMP.

11 NU executive, 16 Mar. 1911, copy in CEMP.

12 KDC to CEM, 10 Jan. 1911, CEMP. For the friendship of Maude Royden and Kathleen Courtney, see Fletcher, *Maude Royden*. For Fawcett, see Rubinstein, *A Different World for Women*.

13 NU, results of ballot, annual council meeting, 26–8 Jan. 1911.

14 NU executive, 2 Mar. 1911, CEMP.

15 Circulation lists, with only the Marshalls' names checked, are present with the results of the ballot taken at the annual council and with executive minutes, 27 Feb., 4 Apr. 1911; for decision to make them available to societies, see NU executive, 16 March 1911. Printing was done by the "Women's Printing Society."

16 NU, resolutions, annual council, 26–8 Jan., 1911; copy of flier, n.d.; NWF, "General Election Policy," n.d. [1910], CEMP. For the 1910 exchange see *CC*, 24 Nov. 1910; CEM to ed., *CC*, 22 Dec. 1910; Emily Davies to ed., *CC* (supporting CEM's suggestion), 29 Dec. 1910; CEM to ed., *CC*, 29 Dec. 1910. The idea may have originated with Mrs Fawcett's earlier letter to FEM (above, pp. 75–6; 415–16n.13), in which she had said, "It will be quite possible ... to sort out our workers so that no one shall be required to support a candidate with whom he or she is in disagreement on general politics," MGF to FEM, 20 December 1909, FMP.

17 CEM to ed., *CC*, 26 Jan. 1911.

18 CEM, "The Suffrage Exchange Scheme," *CC*, 16 Feb., 1911, and correction 23 Feb. The scheme continued to be debated extensively in the *CC*, see 5 Jan., 12 Jan., 19 Jan., 9 Feb. 1911.

19 NU executive, 2 Feb. 1911, Fawcett Lib.

20 CEM, "Women's Suffrage and the Press," *CC*, 16 March 1911; CEM notes for report to KWSA annual meeting, [17 May 1911], CEMP.

21 CEM, "Women's Suffrage and the Press," *CC*, 6 Apr.; CEM, "Press Department," *CC*, 13 Apr. 1911.

22 Ibid.; see also report marked "Great Britain. Feb. 1911-Feb. 1913" in IWSA file, M/50/2/22/15, MPL.

23 Report on provincial council, 7 Apr., *CC*, 13 Apr. 1911. For a review of the truly remarkable operation of this department during its first eight months, see E.M. Leaf, "Work of the Press Department," *CC*, 14 December 1911.

24 The following account is taken from CEM, ms notes, CEMP, and from *CC*, 23 February 1912; see also MLWS, *Monthly Paper*, March 1911.

25 Lord Selborne (Unionist, formerly a Liberal Unionist) had been billed as the main speaker, but seems to have cancelled for the curious reason that he had mistakenly thought he was being invited to speak at an all-Conservative meeting.

26 The words of the songs are given in full on the program.

27 See e.g. NU executive, 16 Feb. 1911, and n.d. material in CEMP. Few details are known; representation on the board was intended to be open not only to WSS, but to other interested groups.

28 MLWS, *Monthly Paper*, March 1911; "Charges against the Police" (which includes substantial quotations from HNB's memorandum), *CC*, 2 March 1911; HNB to ed., *Nation*, on "The Home Office and the Suffragists," 4 March 1911; Leventhal, *Last Dissenter*, 80–1; Rosen, *Rise Up, Women!*, 139–45.

29 NU executive, 16 March 1911, CEMP.

30 LSWS resolution, 27 Apr. 1911, Fawcett Lib.

31 HMS to CEM, 22 March 1911, CEMP.

32 Memorial and draft letter, n.d., CEMP.

33 Hume, *National Union*, 104.

34 CEM, ms notes headed "Dissolution – Breakup of Cabinet," 14[?] or 17[?] March [1911?], CEMP.

35 CEM, ms notes on the opening of the IWFC, 23 Feb. 1911, CEMP; *CC*, 9 March 1911.

36 Ibid.; Hume, *National Union*, 103; for an account of the referendum issue, see Harrison, *Separate Spheres*, 158–60. On the one hand, the suffragists were told that their cause did not merit a week or two of parliamentary time; on the other it was made out to be of such major import that it must be tested by a completely new procedure, time-consuming and expensive. To be fair, there were some who saw the referendum as a useful and democratic device, applicable to a number of issues; Balfour of Burleigh introduced a bill to establish an ongoing referendum procedure in the House of Lords later in the year, while the Lords were struggling with their own reform. The bill was shelved after two days.

37 Hume, *National Union*, 104–5; Rover, *Women's Suffrage*, 117; HNB to MGF, May 7 [1911], M50/2/1/339, MPL. The tone of a letter from

Alfred Lyttleton to MGF, 1 May 1911, suggests that he was glad to be relieved of having to speak – he wrote that he *would* have spoken in favour but for the agreement, but that he would rather not have had the question opened again for a year, M50/2/1/338, MPL.

38 NU executive, 4 May 1911, CEMP.

39 HMS to Margaret Ashton, 25 June 1911, M50/1/2/88, MPL.

40 Augener Music Publishers to CEM, 10 May 1911, CEMP.

41 Although it was not introduced in the House of Commons until May 1911, Lloyd George had opened up the topic for public discussion in January, and it was mentioned in the King's speech in early February. See Gilbert, *The Evolution of National Insurance in Great Britain*; Rowland, *David Lloyd George*, 201–3, 243–7; Ensor, *England 1870–1914*, 445–6, 519–20; Jenkins, *Asquith*, 262.

42 Various notes in a red notebook, n.d., CEMP. The act became law in December 1911. According to Miller, the scheme was an example of the evils of socialism, which "tends to discourage the best and to encourage the mediocre." Already the old age pension scheme could be seen "as a long step ... towards Socialism," but was not enough to satisfy the Socialists. Forcible redistribution schemes went "against [the] command not to covet [one's] neighbour's goods." People must be taught not to gratify their minor immediate wants and then expect others to look after them later. The *duty* to work was more important than the *right* to a pension, and then again "we should hear less of [the] *right* to be provided with work when work is scarce." Finally, the compulsory scheme would damage the Friendly (Insurance) Societies, and therefore the railways would suffer, since the Friendly Societies were large railway investors.

43 CEM, ms "Notes for Miss Knight and Miss Highton" [for 1 April 1911], CEMP; *CC*, 11 May 1911. The notes are quite brief, probably a short version of what she sent to Knight and Highton.

44 Catherine had attended its formal inauguration as a branch of the KWSA on 18 January, before she left for London, CEM ms minutes of Whitehaven meeting, 18 Jan. 1911, CEMP; *CC*, "Federation Notes," 26 Jan. 1911.

45 CEM, ms notes on a copy of the typewritten petition to Whitehaven Borough Council, CEMP. Emphasis in the original. Omission dots in this quotation indicate single words or very short passages which are illegible.

46 CEM, ms draft or copy of letter to the *Whitehaven News*, n.d. [May 1911], CEMP; other material in CEMP also relates.

47 CEM, mimeo ms, text of letter, "For use in local Press," n.d. (damaged), CEMP.

48 CEM, ms notes on KWSA annual meeting, 17 May 1911, including notes for her report; extensive other material, CEMP.

49 "Some Cogent Remarks on Women's Suffrage," *Kendal Mercury*, 26 1911, a report on a speech by Royden, clipping in CEMP; *CC*, 8 June 1911.

50 CEM, ms notes, "Conciliatory Spirit," 20 May 1911, CEMP.

51 CEM, ms report (damaged) [20 May 1911]; newspaper clipping of same report (unsigned, n.d.), from the *Kendal Mercury*; other material, CEMP; *CC*, 1 June 1911. Tax resistance was widely discussed at this time as an appropriate and logical strategy for suffragists, and a Women's Tax Resistance League, open to militants and constitutionalists, had been formed in 1910. For an individual experience, see Montefiore, *From a Victorian to a Modern*. The topic is outside our provenance, but might reward further study.

52 Denman to CEM, 1 June 1911, CEMP.

53 Kemp to CEM, 23 May 1911; Lawson to CEM [incomplete], n.d.; ibid., 18 May 1911, CEMP.

54 Mimeo ms, text of letter, "For the Local Press," n.d., CEMP; for cabinet discussion see Hume, *National Union*, 106–7.

55 Hume, *National Union*, 107–9.

56 CEM, ms "To the Editor of the Common Cause," [incomplete], 6 June 1911.

57 Louis Walker reported on this impressive occasion in articles entitled "Seven Miles of Suffragists" and "Women's Suffrage Procession: Westmoreland and Cumberland Suffragists in London," mss, CEMP.

58 Carrie Chapman Catt to MGF, 15 May 1911, M/50/2/22/7, MPL; NU executive, 4 May 1911, CEMP.

59 Stamps, in CEMP.

60 Catt to CEM, 25 May 1911, CEMP.

61 Carrie Chapman Catt, *The World Movement for Woman Suffrage, 1904–1911*, presidential address 13 June 1911 (pamphlet); IWSA, *Report of Sixth Congress, Stockholm, Sweden, June 12–17, 1977*, hereafter Stockholm *Report* 1911, CEMP.

62 CEM, ms notes for speech, 13 June 1911, several drafts, CEMP; Stockholm *Report* 1911; *MG*, 14 June 1911, clipping, CEMP; *CC*, 29 June 1911.

63 My account is drawn from the Stockholm *Report*, and from CEM ms notes (mainly in English but sometimes in French or German) and others on sessions, speeches, and the work of the resolutions committee; also preliminary agenda, final agenda, IWSA rules of order, photographs, CEMP.

64 The later part of Catherine's life, 1914–61, will be dealt with in a forthcoming book.

65 For an interesting discussion of this tension in the context of the British Labour movement, see Hannam, "'In the Comradeship of the Sexes.'" See also Vellacott, "'Transnationalism' in the Early Women's

International League for Peace and Freedom"; Vellacott, "A Place for Pacifism."

66 CM to CEM, [P/10 July 1911], CEMP.

67 Proceedings, NU council, Edinburgh, 7, 8 July 1911, Fawcett Lib.; CEM, ms, "To the Editor of the Common Cause," 6 June 1911, incomplete, CEMP.

68 Ensor, *England 1870–1914*, 442.

69 Payment of MPs was introduced on 10 August 1911, by financial resolution; an embarrassing emergency had arisen for Labour members when a court case (the Osborne judgment) forbade the use of trade union funds for political purposes, ibid., 444.

70 CEM, ms notes "Mrs. Pankhurst's Keswick Meeting, Aug. 15, 1911," CEMP.

71 S. Holton, *Feminism and Democracy*, 28, and ch. 2, 29–52.

72 CEM notes, including two sentences at the top of a page which look like a note of advice to a companion, CEMP.

CHAPTER SEVEN

1 KDC and Edith Palliser, NU circular letter to secretaries of federations and societies, 13 Oct. 1911, M50/2/9/3, MPL; correspondence between Asquith and Lytton *MG*, 24 Aug. 1911.

2 Conciliation Committee circular, to members of the committee, signed by Lytton, 10 Aug. 1911, M50/2/9/4, MPL.

3 HEGB, 5 to 14 Sept. 1911. Younger than Catherine, Ida had enjoyed the friendship shown her by Caroline and Frank Marshall on one of their visits to London, was grateful for Catherine's support and encouragement during her early days of involvement with the NU headquarters, and continued to consult her about the needs of the literature department of the NU, which she now headed, I. O'Malley to CEM, 3 June 1911.

4 Letters in CEMP.

5 Royden, ms untitled report, with letter to CEM, 28 Sept. 1911, CEMP. Royden explains, with distress, that she has a long-standing commitment to go to America during the winter.

6 Ibid.

7 Material on both meetings, CEMP. At Keswick, the WLA speaker (Alison Garland) made fierce noises about withdrawing support from Liberals if they did not do more for women, but failed even to mention the Conciliation Bill. CEM was invited to address a conference of WLAs at Workington on 12 October, on Lloyd George's Insurance Bill, but it is not known whether she did so, Margaret Irwin to CEM, 13 Aug. 1911, CEMP.

8 Hume, *National Union*, 115–16; HMS, *I Have Been Young*, 215.

9 CEM, ms notes for speech, 2 Oct. 1911; also notes on a copy of HNB's pamphlet, *Woman Suffrage: The Conciliation Bill – an Explanation and Defence*, marked in CEM's writing "Annotated for Lib. meeting," CEMP.

10 CEM to Denman, ms draft or copy, 3 Oct. 1911; Denman to CEM, 4 Oct. 1911, CEMP; "Carlisle Liberals and Women's Suffrage," *CC*, 19 Oct. 1911.

11 CEM, ms notes, "Speech to Carlisle Municipal Women," 3 Oct. 1911; CEM to editor, clipping marked "Cumb. News Oct 13?", CEMP. CEM undertook a canvass of women municipal voters in Keswick and seven rural parishes early in the summer; the position changed with the so-called latch-key amendment, and some new surveys were undertaken. After Asquith announceed the Reform Bill, further surveys were abandoned. Material in CEMP; NU executive, 14, 28 Sept., 19 Oct., 2, 16 Nov. 1911, Fawcett Lib; Leventhal, *Last Dissenter*, 81–2 n. 54.

12 "Proceedings of Provincial Council," 6 Oct. 1911; ms notes, "Meeting of Federation Press Secretaries"; related material, 6 Oct. 1911, CEMP; for CEM's press work, see also *CC*, 9 Nov. 1911.

13 CEM, "North-West Federation," *CC*, 12 Oct. 1911.

14 Ibid.; extensive materal relating to the campaign, agenda, speech notes, drafts of the resolution, etc., 23–8 Oct. 1911; clipping *Mid-Cumberland Herald*, 4 Nov. 1911, CEMP; *CC*, 2 Nov. 1911.

15 Ms "Division of Federation work," n.d. [c. 22 November 1911] unidentified handwriting, apparently copied from notes made by CEM, and sent to Louis Walker, since there is a note in CEM's writing at the end, "The above notes are really for my own benefit, to clear my head," and requesting return, CEMP.

16 *Whitehaven News*, 26 October 1911, clipping, CEMP. Another clipping in CEMP, almost certainly from the same issue, carries a long, rather curious report of the same meeting, clearly taken verbatim from a shorthand report. It gives prominence to a rambling and irrelevant speech by the chair, a local alderman named Musgrave, who had been called upon by Catherine at the last moment, and drops to a minuscule typeface on reaching the report of Norma-Smith's speech. Foster, editor, *Whitehaven News*, to CEM, 1 Nov. 1911, refers to complaints she has made of inaccuracies in the paper's report, and regrets that he cannot publish her long letter "in tomorrow's paper," because of its late arrival (this letter presumably came out on 9 Nov).

17 Clipping, *Whitehaven News*, 26 Oct. 1911, CEMP.

18 Ibid.; there is also a ms draft of CEM's letter, dated 13 Nov. 1911, differing slightly, CEMP.

19 Bill from *Whitehaven News*, 31 Mar. 1913, CEMP.

20 The fullest account of these extremely complicated developments is that of Hume, *National Union*, 112–24; see also MGF, *Women's Suffrage*, 69–83; *The Women's Victory – and After*, 7–29; *What I Remember*, 201–10;

Hammond, *C.P. Scott of the "Manchester Guardian"*, 105–18; S. Holton, *Feminism and Democracy*, 70–5; Leventhal, *Last Dissenter*, 82–7; David Morgan, *Suffragists and Liberals*, 79–101; Pugh, *Electoral Reform in War and Peace*, 36–42; Rosen, *Rise Up, Women!*, 150–3; Rover, *Women's Suffrage*, 95.

21 CEM, ms, untitled, incomplete, n.d., [c. 21 Nov. 1911], evidently part of hastily written notes for a speech, CEMP. The occasion and the audience are unknown.

22 NU special executive, 9 Nov. 1911, Fawcett Lib.

23 Ibid.; copy of the manifesto, *CC*, 16 Nov. 1911; MGF, *Women's Suffrage*, 79; Hume, *National Union*, 117.

24 "Questions put to Mr. Asquith by the National Union 1912" [actually 17 November 1911], HMS Papers, SCPC. This appears to be the original carried by HMS to the deputation; questions are typed, answers in pencil, and the title (as given above) is in ink and was probably added years later, possibly at the time of deposit of the papers; also HMS, *I Have Been Young*, 213. See also Hume, *National Union*, 116–17; MGF, *Women's Suffrage*, 81; *The Women's Victory – and After*, 9; the version of the questions given in MGF's later and better-known *What I Remember*, 202, is less exact, omitting the proviso in no. 2 about amendments allowing for *different* qualifications for women than those for men, important because the NU was only too well aware that womanhood suffrage would not pass. By the time CEM made her notes (n. 21 above), she knew about the deputation, and summarized the questions in a few words, knowing them well enough to be able to expand them for her audience.

25 *CC*, 23 Nov. 1911.

26 HNB to KDC, 12 Nov. 1911; CEM, ms [c. 21 Nov. 1911], CEMP.

27 Hume, *National Union*, 122; HMS, *I Have Been Young*, 216–17; KDC,"Mr. Lloyd George at Bath," *CC*, 30 Nov. 1911.

28 HNB to MGF, 26 Nov. 1911, M50/2/1/341, MPL.

29 HNB to Scott, telegram, 25 Nov. 1911, enclosed with Scott to KDC, 29 Nov. 1911, Fawcett Lib.

30 Scott to KDC, 29 Nov. 1911; HNB to Scott, telegrams, 25, 26, 27 (two) Nov., and carbon of telegram, Scott to HNB [n.d., probably 26 Nov.] 1911, Fawcett. When I saw these they were in a bundle marked "Very old letters" in a suitcase of KDC's papers deposited at the Fawcett Library.

31 *CC*, 23 Nov 1911.

32 LG to MGF, 30 Nov., Fawcett Lib; for the NU manifesto, see Hume, *National Union*, 123; *The Times*, 1 December 1911; for the effects of militancy at this time, see *inter alia* Hume, 121–4; Leventhal, *Last Dissenter*, 83–5.

33 Postscript in an unidentified handwriting to a letter not present,
n.d. [possibly Mar. 1912, but may be earlier], CEMP. The MP was identified as Haddock [Unionist member for North Lonsdale]. A cartoon in *Common Cause*, 21 July 1910, shows a woman rolling a large rock
uphill towards the crest of Parliament, but the rock is identified as
"Women's Suffrage," not specifically as MPs; see also cartoon in *Punch
or the London Charivari*, 13 July 1910; Read, *Edwardian England*, 37.

34 CEM, ms "Militant Tactics," 17 Dec. 1911, marked "Letter to Women's
Platform" [the *Standard*'s women's section], CEMP.

35 Her grasp of the situation, and her detailed knowledge of the response
made by the NU executive, shown in rough speech notes which can
be dated as after 17 Nov. and probably before the end of the month
(n. 21 above), suggest that she had been in London by this time.

36 L. Walker to CEM, 17 Nov. 1911; and see n. 21 above (a passage about
the proposed statement has been crossed out, and CEM has added
the information about reprints of the *MG* articles); also ms letter, CEM
to Walker, incomplete, 22 Nov. 1911, CEMP. Catherine also took
time to help the honorary secretary of the West Midland federation
with an explanation of the structure and purpose of the federation
system, [Miss] Noël Herbert Wright to CEM, 29 Nov. 1911, CEMP.
Wright's letter is appreciative of CEM's help, but unpleasantly con-
temptuous of her fellow-Midlanders, whom she clearly despises.

37 I have been unable to locate full proceedings of this council; the
resolutions are in Fawcett Lib., and it is well reported in *CC*, 14 Dec.
1911.

38 *CC*, 14 Dec. 1911; for HNB's analysis see also his "Women and the Reform Bill," *Englishwoman*, Dec. 1911, 241–50.

39 CEM, ms mimeo sheet, headed "National Union of Women's Suffrage
Societies," n.d. [c. Dec. 1911], CEMP.

40 Rover, *Women's Suffrage*, 97.

41 Hume, *National Union*, 129; Morgan, *Suffragists and Liberals*, 87–90;
Harrison, *Separate Spheres*, 158–60.

42 NU account for 6 blotting pads and 3 writing pads, marked "CEM
Xmas," CEMP.

43 CEM, ms, "Notes for Appleby," 10 Jan. 1912; also present are FEM's
notes for his speech; other material relating to the NWF campaign, CEMP.

44 *CC*, 8 Feb. 1912; NU executive, 18 Jan. 1912; for deputations see
also minute of CEM's report to the NU executive, 15 Feb. 1912, Fawcett
Lib.

45 NU executive, 18 Jan., Fawcett Lib.

46 NU council, proceedings, 24 Feb. 1912, Fawcett Lib.

47 For FEM's letter and extensive other material on the referendum, *CC*,
18 Jan. 1912; for the referendum crisis, KDC to MGF, 22 Jan. 1912,
M50/2/1/349; HNB to MGF, 22 Jan. [1912], M50/2/1/348, MPL; Scott to

KDC, 31 Jan. 1912, KDC suitcase, Fawcett Lib.; "Circular to Unionist M.Ps" (from KDC's files) nd; "Lord Robert Cecil on the Referendum," typed extract from article in *Sussex Daily News*, 27 Jan. 1912, CEMP. Lady Constance Lytton, one of the few WSPU leading members who were prepared to talk to NU members on the subject at all, continued, perhaps understandably, to believe LG might still veer over to the referendum idea, C. Lytton to MGF, 6, 22 Feb. 1912, M50/2/1/350, 353, MPL.

48 See, e.g., HNB to MGF, 7 Jan. [1912], M50/2/1/347, MPL.

49 *CC*, 18 Jan. 1912.

50 Among CEM's papers are some dated early 1912 which are marked "From K.D.C.'s files."

51 NU executive, 15 Feb. 1912, Fawcett Lib; ms copy, CEM to "Dear ——", 6 Feb. 1912, CEMP.

52 For HNB's attempt to open discussion with Emmeline Pankhurst, see HNB to MGF, and KDC to MGF, both 22 Jan. 1912, M50/2/1/348, 349, MPL; for the joint board see A. Neilans (WFL) to KDC, 18 Jan.; MLWS to CEM, 13 Feb.; CUWFA to CEM, 7 Feb.; Scottish WLF, 16 March; ILP to CEM, 14 Mar.; Fabian Women's Group (suffrage committee) to CEM, 12 Mar. 1912; WLF to CEM, 1, 5, 13 Mar.; CEM, ms, copy of letter to WLF, 14 Mar.; CEM, notes "Joint Board to organize dealings with M.P.s," n.d.; copy of CEM's letter to organizations, n.d., CEMP; NU executive minutes, 7 Mar. 1912, Fawcett Lib.

53 West Essex Women's Franchise Society to "Madam," 28 Feb. 1912; CEM, ms note headed "Party Agents," n.d.; several undated letters [1912] from E. Acland to CEM; CEM, ms notes, "W. Lib. Fed. Campaign ... Feb. 29th, *Mrs. Acland*"; NU executive minutes, 21 Mar. 1912, CEMP.

54 Liddington, *The Life and Times of a Respectable Rebel*, 211–12.

55 KDC to Arthur Henderson, 23 Apr. 1912; ILP campaign leaflets, n.d., CEMP; *Labour Leader* (*LL*), 12 Jan. 1912.

56 Pelling, *Popular Politics and Society in Late Victorian Britain*, 119.

57 Even the CUWFA included among its objects "to oppose *Manhood suffrage in any form*" (their underlining), Rover, *Women's Suffrage*, 23–4.

58 MacDonald to MGF, 29 Jan. 1912 (from KDC's files), CEMP; C. Lytton to MGF, 6 Feb., 1912, M50/2/1/351, MPL.

59 At CEM's prompting, ILP branches were asked to send deputations to their MPs, Mylles to CEM, 8 Feb.; Mylles to "Dear Comrade," 9 Feb. 1912, CEMP.

60 CEM, rough draft of letter to LG, 22 Feb. 1912; HNB, copy of letter to Mrs Metge,[15 Mar. 1912]; NU executive, 21 Mar. 1912, CEMP.

61 *CC*, 8, 29 Feb. 1912.

62 Norma-Smith to CEM, P/3[?]Mar. 1912; for effect of militancy and NU attitude see also (*inter alia*) Theo Taylor to MGF, 9 Mar. 1912, CEMP; "Notes and Comments: Our Handicap," *CC*, 7 Mar. 1912; KDC, "The

NU and Methods of Violence," *CC*, 14 Mar. 1912. Some protests at
the harshness of the attitude to the WSPU shown by the NU, or sometimes
the *CC*, came in from individuals and branches, e.g. NU executive,
21 Mar. 1921, CEMP. But HMS thought the NU should have been far
more outspoken in its condemnation of militancy, and resigned the
editorship of *CC* in July 1912 mainly because she found herself restricted from expressing her views as strongly as she thought right,
and in particular because of a letter from Ramsay MacDonald in which
he accused the NU of trying "to run with the hare and hunt with
the hounds," *I Have Been Young*, 223.

63 MGF to Lyttleton, ts copy, 12 March 1912, CEMP, where MGF points
out that convictions for militant offences show the same names again
and again, and that while it is hard to get accurate figures for WSPU
membership or finances, the growth of the NU (for which she gives the
figures) probably far exceeds that of the WSPU. She also reiterated
that NU opposition to violent militancy had never wavered.

64 Evidence on CEM's role in initiating the dinner parties is inconclusive; she reported on the plan at the executive on 7 Mar., Fawcett Lib.;
list of [proposed] hostesses, and material relating to one given on
Friday 8 Mar. [some items are misdated Friday 7 Mar.] by Lady Farrer;
G. MacLean to CEM, 7 Mar. 1912; Beatrice Kemp to CEM, 9 Mar.
1912; E. Rathbone to CEM, 9 Mar. 1912, CEMP. The list of proposed
parties and a letter from Margaret Robertson discussing future
dates at which she might be available to speak (21 Feb. 1912, CEMP)
suggest that the plan was to continue on, following a successful second reading of the Conciliation Bill, to oil the wheels towards its final
passage. At-homes were nothing new to the NU in London and even
elsewhere (Caroline Marshall had hosted a number, including a very
large one at a Keswick hotel in autumn 1911), but the context of
these parties makes them of special interest.

65 Catalogue; also sample leaflets, CEMP.

66 E.g., Lady Maud Selborne to MGF, [c. 2 Mar. 1912]; HNB to MGF, 1,
2 Mar., M50/2/1/354.355,356, MPL.

67 CEM form letters to federation secretaries, 2 Mar. 1912; a few responses,
including some addressed to KDC, Mar. 1912, CEMP.

68 Amy Sharp to CEM, 21 Mar.; Cecilia Mathews to CEM, 26 Mar.; H. Chapman to CEM, [26 Mar. 1912]; Florence Walker to CEM, 26 Mar.
1912; NU executive, 21 Mar., CEMP.

69 Wright to *The Times*, reprinted as a pamphlet, *Suffrage Fallacies: Sir
Almroth Wright on Militant Hysteria*. Copy in CEMP has a printed
message:"With the compliments of the National League for Opposing Woman Suffrage, Caxton House, Westminster, SW," with a plain
sticker affixed over the message. For Ward's response, and a similar

one from Violet Markham, an antisuffrage public servant, see correspondence in *The Times* for several weeks following; *CC*, 11 Apr.
1912; Harrison, *Separate Spheres*, 194. See also Wright, *The Unexpurgated
Case against Woman Suffrage*, published the following year. For a
long and rather patronizing (to women) review of the latter and comments, see Sir Ronald Ross, "Man and Woman," *Nation*, 11 Oct.
1913; correspondence, *Nation*, 18 Oct. 1913; Beatrice Webb, introduction to *New Statesman*: Special Supplement on the Awakening of
Women, 1 Nov. 1913. Wright was ingenious and productive as a bac-
teriologist, introducing antityphoid inoculation and some vaccines.
He shows such virulent misogyny that it would be interesting to know
more about his own life and relationships. Alas, he was only expressing in extreme terms views held by an influential school of physicians
around the turn of the century, see e.g. Lewis, *Women in England,
1870–1950*, 83–92; Ehrenreich and English, *For Her Own Good*, 109–15.

70 NU executive, 21 Mar. 1912, CEMP; "From Headquarters," and a
notice of the gathering, *CC*, 28 Mar. 1912.

CHAPTER EIGHT

1 NU executive, 29 Mar. 1912, CEMP.
2 NU executive, ts, damaged, untitled, n.d., CEMP, *CC*, 4 Apr. 1912;
Hume, *National Union*, 135–9.
3 Catherine had won many Cumberland miners to the cause, and had
a pledge from their representatives, but Cumberland miners were a
small part of the mining unions, which accounted for the largest
part of the TU vote against support for women's suffrage.
4 Lord Robert Cecil, "The Suffrage Crisis," *Englishwoman*, no. 40,
Apr. 1912, 1–5. While the NU executive agreed with Cecil's analysis,
they had been at pains to deny that suffrage was unpopular, though
militancy was.
5 Ts; see n. 2 above.
6 NU executive, 29 Mar. 1912, CEMP.
7 CEM, ms "Political Situation: Report for Manchester Council," [9,
10 Oct. 1912], CEMP.
8 Macmillan, like CEM, was an alumna of St Leonard's School.
9 NU executive, 21 Mar. 1912, CEMP; NU executive, 1 Feb. 1912; ibid.
24 Feb. 1912, Fawcett Lib.
10 AMR to CEM, 8 Apr. 1912, CEMP.
11 Amy Sharp (Ambleside society) to CEM, 10, 11 Apr. 1912, CEMP.
12 MGF to CEM, 15 Apr. 1912, CEMP.
13 Arthur Hirst to CEM, 18 Apr. 1912; J. Moorsom to CEM, 14 May 1912,
CEMP.

14 AMR to CEM, 8 April 1912, CEMP. For discussion of friendship in the suffrage movement see Alberti, *Beyond Suffrage*, passim.

15 NU, printed "List of Speakers," issued periodically, e.g. June 1911, CEMP. Over a hundred names and addresses are listed, with a brief note for each, indicating the geographical location and limits, special area of interest (e.g."economic and moral," "political and historical," "the educational side of the question"), fee (if any), occasionally the preferred audience ("prefers working class audience," "prefers educated audience"), and any limitations (a number of women would not speak in the open air, or alone). Some fees were estimated in shillings, some in the more classy guineas, the denomination always used by professionals.

16 "M[argaret] R[obertson]" to CEM, 13 Apr. 1912, CEMP. Robertson was organizing secretary of the Manchester federation, a noted speaker, and later the chief organizer of the EFF.

17 Mabel Barton to CEM, 2 July 1912, CEMP.

18 For Sophia Jex-Blake see Josephine Kamm, *Rapiers and Battleaxes*, 74; also Dyhouse, "Miss Buss and Miss Beale," 26–7, where there is an interesting brief discussion of dependence; see also Burns, "Education," in Gollancz, ed., *The Making of Women*, 1917. For Bodichon see Matthews, "Barbara Bodichon," 91. For a discussion of parental authority, and an extreme example, see Jalland, *Women, Marriage and Politics*, 276–9.

19 Frank's support is regularly reflected in his correspondence; see, eg, FEM to CEM, 30 June 1912, CEMP.

20 The financial material of CEMP is now gathered together under the heading "Vouchers," including an impressive collection of unpaid bills and dunning letters.

21 NU executive, 19 Dec. 1912, 2 Jan. 1913. CEM's EFF expenses may have been paid, but I have not come across any minute to that effect, whereas when Robertson was appointed to a paid position, it was carefully minuted that her expenses would be paid, in addition to her salary.

22 Bakewell, printer, 17 Dec. 1912, re bills of 3 May 1912 and 26 Apr. 1910; J. Bendelack to CEM, 14 Jan. 1912, CEMP.

23 CEM to Auerbach, with cheque, not sent, 1 Oct. 1912; literature secretary to CEM, 2 Oct. 1912, CEMP. The literature committee had difficulty with other outstanding accounts besides CEM's, and brought the matter to the executive at just this time, NU executive, 3 Oct. 1912, Fawcett Lib.

24 "Vouchers," CEMP.

25 Cheques, dated 26 Feb. 1913, CEMP. I found these cheques in 1969, in a sealed, unstamped envelope addressed to CEM at 1 Barton Street, her London address.

26 Correspondence in CEMP refers, esp. letters from L. Walker; also CEM to members of NWF committee, 9 May 1912, summarizing work plans agreed on at meeting of 4 May; agenda, NWF meeting 4 May 1912 (marked "Sample" and annotated by CEM with explanations of why items were taken in a particular order and so on, apparently for use by others planning similar meetings), CEMP.

27 E. Acland to CEM, 1 Apr. 1912, CEMP.

28 KDC to MGF, 8 Apr. 1912, M50/2/1/357, MPL.

29 Ibid. Brailsford hoped to make use of the Conciliation Committee, the Irish suffrage societies, and the cabinet suffragists to introduce a women's suffrage amendment to the Irish Home Rule Bill, which "might bring the Irish to their senses." Initially, Courtney described it as something Brailsford was going to organize, not as any part of NU policy, but it was in fact picked up by the executive. Hume sees this as having developed into a rather unscrupulous policy by which the Irishwomen's franchise amendment to Home Rule was to be made a sort of bargaining chip in the campaign, to be given up in exchange for a commitment from Redmond of Irish Nationalist support for the Reform Bill amendment, but I have not found evidence for so negative a view, though undoubtedly it was hoped to use it to bring pressure to bear on the Irish party. Snowden, with the support of the NU, did indeed introduce such an amendment, and the NU were not troubled about any inconvenience it might prove to be to Redmond's Home Rule cause, in light of the damage the Irish nationalists had done to the suffrage cause. However, there is no reason to believe that Fawcett was insincere in saying that the NU could not see a representative body created without making an attempt to have women included among the electors. The NU maintained to the last that the amendment would be abandoned only in return for a guarantee from Redmond that his party would vote for a particular amendment to the Reform Bill, so virtually ensuring its passage; and if that occurred and women were admitted to "the Imperial vote," they could hardly be denied the franchise for their own home government. Hume, *National Union*, 168; "Mr. Snowden's Amendment to the Home Rule Bill," *CC*, 1 August 1912; for CEM's views see her unsigned report under "Election Fighting Fund," in *CC*, 25 July (authorship confirmed by HMS to CEM, 24 July 1912); I have found no references in NU executive minutes which tend to bear out the more cynical view.

30 KDC to MGF, 8 April 1912, MPL. While the role of HNB was undeniably significant, Leventhal, *Last Dissenter*, 87–8, writes as if he were single-handedly responsible for the EFF, which I shall show to have been far from being the case. Hume, *National Union*, 144–9, gives a more balanced account, though she also underplays the role of new leaders within the NU.

31 "A Message from Mrs. Fawcett," *CC*, 4 Apr. 1912.

32 KDC to MGF, 8 Apr., MPL.

33 S. Holton, *Feminism and Democracy*, 66–7.

34 Proceedings, NU council, 6 Dec. 1909, Fawcett Lib.

35 KDC to MGF, 8 Apr. 1912, MPL.

36 An undated document in CEMP (two pages typescript), headed "Proposed Cooperation with the Labour Party," appears to be resolutions, with supporting material, brought or sent to this executive meeting by the Newcastle society. Newcastle seems to have feared more resistance to its ideas than it encountered; the document begins with a firm statement that if the executive does not call a special council, Newcastle will proceed to use a constitutional provision forcing the calling of a council on the demand of a certain number of societies; reference is also made to similar proposals coming from the Manchester and District federation. Especially when it is read with KDC's letter to MGF of 8 Apr., I do not think this document warrants Holton's claim (*Feminism and Suffrage*, 76) that the special council was actually *called* by the Manchester and Newcastle societies. The document concludes with three [proposed] resolutions; numbers 1 and 3 refer to the calling of the special council and of a special executive to follow it, number 2 is the one empowering the officers "to interview officials of the Labour Party." A ms addendum inserts the word "confidentially" after the words "Labour Party," and it seems this confidentiality had to be extended to the executive minutes themselves: the minutes refer to the decision to hold a special council, but do not mention the authorization of the officers to open conversations with the Labour party, although later correspondence refers to this as having been resolved on at this meeting; see, e.g., letter to "Dear ——" [probably other members of the executive], signed by Fawcett, Auerbach, Courtney, and Palliser, n.d. [c. 1 May 1912], CEMP; see also NU executive minutes, 18 Apr. 1912, CEMP; KDC to Henderson 19 Apr. 1912, LP/WOM/12/1, MPL.

37 KDC to Henderson, 19 Apr. 1912; Henderson to KDC, 20 Apr. LP/WOM/12/1, 2, also CEMP; KDC to Henderson, 22 Apr. (copy); Henderson to KDC, 22 Apr., both in CEMP; KDC to Henderson, 23 Apr., and enclosure, a letter from NU executive; Henderson to KDC, 25 Apr.; KDC to Henderson, 26 Apr.; Henderson to KDC, 27 Apr., LP/WOM/12/3, 4, 5, 6, also in CEMP. Both sides kept a careful file of the correspondence; KDC's is among those passed to CEM.

38 "List of suggested questions ... for Tuesday's meeting"; letter to "Dear ——", n.d. [c. 1 May 1912], CEMP.

39 Letter to "Dear ——", n.d. [c. 1 May 1912], CEMP.

40 Henderson to Palliser, 3 May 1912, CEMP and copy, n.s., in LP/WOM/12/11.

41 KDC and Palliser to Henderson, 6 May 1912, LP/WOM/12/15, and copy in CEMP. The NU had accepted the need to offer support for Labour candidates rather than to the party as such, in recognition of the party's fear of being seen as "having been bought by the suffragists"; the officers also saw this as a help in preserving the NU's own nonparty stance, letter to "Dear — —", n.d. [c. 1 May 1912], CEMP.

42 HNB to Henderson, 6 May 1912, LP/WOM/12/14; Hume, *National Union*, 155–6.

43 Ts report, "Interview of Mrs. Fawcett and Miss Courtney with Mr. Ramsay Macdonald, M.P. May 13th 1912," CEMP.

44 While the press had been given only the most general announcement that the meeting would be held, and would be in private, the notice that went out to secretaries of the societies on 2 May was accompanied by a copy of the executive's proposed resolutions and a confidential explanation written by Courtney, press release, 3 May 1912; KDC to "Dear Madam," 2 May 1912; CEM, ms notes for and of KWSA 6 May 1912; attention was also drawn to the following articles: MGF, "The Record of the Labour Party on Women's Suffrage," *CC*, 2 May; HNB, "The Reform Bill and the Labour Party," *Englishwoman*, 41 (May 1912), 121–30; "Mr. Brailsford on a Practical Policy," *CC*, 9 May 1912.

45 Cardiff and District WSS, 7 May 1912, Fawcett Lib.; NU response, signed by MGF, KDC, Palliser, and Auerbach, 10 May 1912, CEMP.

46 Rathbone to MGF, cc to KDC, 10 May 1912, CEMP.

47 Proceedings, NU special council, 14 May 1912, Fawcett Lib.; Hume, *National Union*, 155. The "E. Davies" referred to in the proceedings was Emily Davies (1830–1921), the founder of Girton College and a distinguished pioneer suffragist.

48 *Englishwoman*, June 1912, 243; see also press release 16 May 1912; "Resolutions," sent out with KDC to "Dear Madam," 2 May 1912, CEMP; NU special council, 14 May 1912, Fawcett Lib.

49 Rathbone to Auerbach, 17 May 1912, IAV; MGF in *Englishwoman*, June 1912, 244.

50 Rathbone to Auerbach, 17 May 1912, IAV.

51 Cf., e.g., Hume, *National Union*, 141.

52 Liddington and Norris, *One Hand*, passim. HNB was conscious of the significant change within the NU, writing later that he had known the NU before CEM and KDC came to London "and it really did not exist as an effective national organisation at all," HNB to CEM, 9 Mar. 1915, CEMP.

53 For the ability of the NU to offer a choice of skilled workers to branches wanting an organizer, see assistant secretary, for KDC, to Howell (Cardiff WSS), 15 July 1912, CEMP.

54 Rathbone to Auerbach, 17 May 1912, IAV.

55 NU executive, 20 June 1912, Fawcett Lib.

56 Mabel E. Howell, Cardiff wss, with copy of Cardiff resolutions, to
   KDC, 27 June 1912; KDC to Howell, 11 July 1912, copy; Howell to KDC,
   13 July, CEMP.

57 Rathbone to CEM, 23 May 1912; leaflet "To Liberal Women: the Provisional Strike Policy," with tear-off pledge sheet, CEMP.

58 Royden to CEM, 8 Apr. 1912, CEMP; Royden, "An effective plan of campaign" (correspondence) CC, 11 Apr. 1912; correspondence and
   editorial note, CC, 18 April 1912; KDC, "A Business-Like Policy," ibid.

59 FEM, ms text of speech, n.d. [July 1912], FMP; executive, 2 May
   1912, Fawcett Lib., and agenda in CEMP; proceedings, special council,
   14 May 1912, Fawcett Lib.; CEM, ms notes for and on KWSA general
   committee 6 May 1912, CEMP. Another purpose in bringing this forward
   in the wake of the Conciliation Bill defeat was to suggest, as Royden
   did, that there were more constructive ways of reacting than the WSPU
   was demonstrating in its latest wave of window-smashing. A further
   useful function was to remind women – especially the Liberal women
   – of the extent to which the parties counted on their canvassing
   work before elections, and of the power this placed in their hands.

60 NU executive, 1 August 1912, Fawcett Lib.

61 Later in the meeting, Courtney reported that Catherine was preparing
   a leaflet to explain the new policy, at which point "Miss Macmillan
   handed in one which she had prepared in order that it might be compared with Miss Marshall's," a curious minute hinting at further tension between Macmillan and CEM, NU executive, 16 May 1912, CEMP.

62 CC, 6 June 1912.

63 CM to CEM, 12 June [1912], CEMP.

64 Rosen, Rise Up, Women!, 166. Common criminals served their time
   in Second or Third Division; political prisoners (and the favoured)
   served in the First Division, where conditions were substantially better. See, e.g., Vellacott, Bertrand Russell, ch. 15. A good source for prison
   conditions before and during the First World War is Hobhouse and
   Brockway, eds., English Prisons Today.

65 HMS, I Have Been Young, 221–3, 231; NU executive, 6 June 1912,
   and note amendments to these minutes in those of 20 June 1912, both
   in Fawcett Lib.; for the whole episode, see Rosen, Rise Up, Women!,
   166–7. CM approved of the supportive gesture, CM to CEM, 12 June
   [1912].

CHAPTER NINE

1 EFF, 14 June 1912; NU executive, 20 June 1912, Fawcett Lib.; "The
   Fighting Fund and the New Policy," CC, 20 June 1912. KDC's files containing the correspondence leading up to the agreement with the

Labour party are in CEMP, and may have been handed to CEM at the time of her appointment.

2 The causes, development, and consequences of the EFF campaign have never been fully explored, although Hume, *National Union*, and S. Holton, *Feminism and Democracy* are valuable. Extensive documentation exists, making possible a far more detailed study than I can include here, even though it was central to CEM during that period. My choice has been to give something of an analytical outline, illustrated by example rather than described in every detail, bringing out the nature and extent of Catherine's contribution, interwoven with the other public and private matters which helped to make up the fabric of her life, and showing the significance of the EFF policy in the political context.

3 NU executive, 6 June 1912; special executive 8 and 10 June, Fawcett Lib.; CEM, ms notes on the two special meetings; CEM, ms notes "Interview with Henderson," 8 June, CEMP.

4 EFF report in proceedings, NU council, 11 July 1912, CEMP; "The Fighting Fund and the New Policy," *CC*, 20 June 1912; EFF, 14 June 1912, Fawcett Lib. Selina Cooper, whose experience with miners and textile workers had made her particularly valuable, apparently felt that there was still much work to do to make the policy effective, Liddington, *Life and Times of a Respectable Rebel*, 231–2.

5 CEM to EFF committee, 18 June 1912; FEM to CEM, 19 June 1912, deploring bad feeling likely to be caused by such a breach of the Labour party's understanding with the Liberal government, and enclosing clipping from *Westminster* [sic], CEMP; CEM, ms to Henderson, 20 June 1912; Henderson to CEM, 20 June 1912, both in LP/WOM/12/24–5; J. Thomas White to Mrs C.E. Cowmeadow, 21 June 1912; Cowmeadow to CEM 23 June 1912; Cowmeadow to Voiceless, London [the NU's telegraphic address], telegram, and copy of reply from Voiceless to Cowmeadow, 24 June 1912; CEM to Henderson, 25 June 1912; NU press release [25 June 1912], CEMP; NU executive, 20 June 1912; EFF urgency committee, 24 June 1912, Fawcett Lib. See also Hume, *National Union*, 165; S. Holton, *Feminism and Democracy*, 84. Leventhal is mistaken in stating that it was the report of the £500 contribution that "proved so incriminating that the party felt obliged to refrain from contesting" this by-election, *Last Dissenter*, 88 and n. 78, though the party was certainly leery of being accused of having been bought. He also overestimates the role of Brailsford in the EFF, although he does not follow its story in any detail, ibid. 88–9. The substantial nature of the sum offered can be gauged by reference to Belloc's estimate of his possible election expenses at £600, Speaight, *Hilaire Belloc*, 293.

6   Hume, *National Union*, 165.

7   Henderson to CEM, 26 June 1912, CEMP; copy in LP/WOM/12/26.

8   CEM, "The Election Fighting Fund," *CC*, 26 Sept. 1912.

9   Ts "EFF report to Council," 11 July 1912, CEMP. The passage quoted is toned down in the council proceedings.

10 NU executive, 1 Aug 1912, Fawcett Lib.; CEM, ms and ts of organization chart of Labour party national executive, n.d.; CEM, notes on relationship of Labour party to socialist societies and to the TUs, n.d., CEMP.

11 S. Holton, *Feminism and Democracy*, 83.

12 Marquand, *Ramsay MacDonald*, 78–81. For an incident bearing on this agreement, see Brockway, *Inside the Left*, 36–8.

13 Marquand, *Ramsay MacDonald*, 142–51; for a rumour (Oct. 1912) that there was to be a new electoral alliance see S. Holton, *Feminism and Democracy*, 85.

14 Marquand, *Ramsay MacDonald*, 125.

15 NU, annual report, 26, 27 Feb. 1913, CEMP. The Hanley by-election was necessitated by the death of a Lib-Lab MP, and no Labour party organization or campaign had been developed ahead of time; for more detail see Gregory, *The Miners and British Politics*, 48–9.

16 CEM, "The Election Fighting Fund," *CC*, 26 Sept. 1912.

17 EFF urgency committee, 6 July 1912, Fawcett Lib.

18 NU executive, 6 June 1912, Fawcett Lib.; see also NU executive, 18 Apr. 1912, CEMP; NU executive, 16 May 1912, CEMP, Fawcett Lib.; KDC to Mrs Robinson, 22 May 1912, CEMP; P. Snowden, "The ILP Conference and Women's Suffrage," *CC*, 6 June 1912.

19 Letterhead, 6 July 1912, on a letter from Edward McGegan (sec. to WSC) to KDC; Roper to MGF 16 May; MGF brief covering note for Roper's letter, [to KDC], CEMP; NU executive, 20 June 1912, Fawcett Lib.; S. Holton, *Feminism and Democracy*, 89–90. In addition to "Members of Parliament" (whose names are not listed on the letterhead), the WSC represented the Fabian Society, the MLWS, the National Industrial and Professional Women's Suffrage Society, the National Women's Labour League, the Women's Cooperative Guild, the WLF, the Scottish WLF, the NUWSS, and the PSF. Marginally, as can be seen, it was still an interparty body; the chair was Henderson, the honorary secretary the prominent Liberal Walter Rea. For the earlier joint board, the forerunner of the joint campaign committee, see pp. 147–8 above.

20 KDC received the replies from WSS only, now in CEMP. I have not seen others (i.e. from labour organizations), though a favourable response is sometimes reported in the existing correspondence. Opposition from WSS came mainly from regions where Liberals

dominated in the membership, see, e.g., E.M. Inglis, Scottish federation, to KDC, 13 June 1912, reporting that Dundee will "be quite ready to help, Greenock will find it a good deal more difficult as the Society is more Liberal there"; extensive correspondence between KDC and WSS and NU federations, and with McGegan, in KDC's original file marked "J.C. Cmttee," now in CEMP; see also NU executive, 18 Apr. 1912, 1 Aug. 1912, Fawcett Lib.

21 See Philip Snowden, "The By-Elections and Woman Suffrage," *Englishwoman*, Oct. 1912.

22 CEM to Henderson, 2 July 1912, LP/WOM/12/27; 5 July 1912, LP/WOM/12/31; 30 Aug. 1912, LP/WOM/12/34; 14 Oct. 1912, copy in CEMP; 5 Oct. 1912, LP/WOM/12/39.

23 [CEM] "The Crewe Result," *CC*, 1 Aug. 1912.

24 Kent, *Sex and Suffrage*, 29. Kent's understanding of the women's suffrage campaign is superficial and based on very limited sources, although her analysis of some feminist writings on sexuality might have stood on its own merits.

25 Neal Blewett, "The Franchise in the United Kingdom, 1885–1918", 27–56.

26 [CEM] "The Crewe Result," *CC*, 1 Aug. 1912.

27 CEM to Henderson, 3 July 1912, LP/WOM/12/30.

28 CEM, ms notes, "To bring before Executive, July 4 191", CEMP.

29 Palliser to Henderson, 21 May 1912, LP/WOM/12/20; Henderson to Palliser, 21 May 1912, copy, LP/WOM/12/21; CEM to Henderson, 2 July 1912, LP/WOM/12/28 (this is a typed letter on EFF letterhead; LP/WOM/12/27, of the same date, see n. 22 above, is an informal ms letter).

30 E.g. CEM to Henderson, 14 Oct. 1912, copy, CEMP.

31 MacDonald to MGF, 29 Jan. 1912, CEMP. Above, p. 149.

32 The letter, originally appearing on 28 June, was reprinted in *CC*, 4 July 1912; see also Hume, *National Union*, 150.

33 EFF urgency committee, 6 July 1912, Fawcett Lib.; see also CEM to Henderson, 5 July 1912, LP/WOM/12/31:i.

34 EFF urgency committee, 10 July 1912, Fawcett Lib.

35 [CEM], "The Crewe Result," *CC*, 1 August 1912. Other misunderstandings with MacDonald occurred from time to time; CEM was always ready to go to see him and clear things up, see e.g. EFF, 2 August 1912, Fawcett Lib.

36 Holmes, the candidate in the Crewe election, wrote on 31 July 1912 to ask Margaret Robertson about the chances of further support, saying "we have been tied up by the Osborne judgment, and we have three railwaymen in Parliament and we are £700 in debt in their division, so its hopeless looking there," CEMP. For a discussion of Labour

party financing, and the way in which dependence on local sources favoured TU candidates over ILP candidates, see Blewett, *Peers, Parties, and People*, 294–8. The EFF's financial contribution could be significant, especially together with their contribution of skilled, paid womanhours; see n. 5 above.

37 NU executive, 1 Aug. 1912, Fawcett Lib.

38 Ibid.

39 EFF, 2 Aug. 1912, Fawcett Lib.

40 Henderson to CEM, 6 Aug. 1912, CEMP.

41 EFF, 2 Aug. 1912, Fawcett Lib.

42 NU executive, 19 Sept. 1912; EFF urgency committee, 9 Aug. 1912, Fawcett Lib.; [CEM] to Anderson, 14 Aug. 1912; various ms notes Aug. 1912; CEM to Miss Price, 1 Aug. (ms copy) 3 Aug., cc; KDC to Price, 2 Aug.; Price to CEM 2, 4 Aug., Waring to CEM, [4 Aug.]; CEM and McKenzie, extensive ms notes, "E. Carmarthen," CEMP; report in *CC*, 8 Aug. 1912. Waring was the NU organizer, Janet Price the organizing secretary of the Cardiff and District WSS and hon. sec. of the S. Wales and Monmouthshire federation.

43 MGF to Auerbach, 26 Aug. 1912; also MGF to Auerbach, 29 Aug. [1912], IAV.

44 NU executive, 4 July, 1 Aug. 1912, Fawcett Lib.

45 McGegan to KDC, 6 July 1912; KDC to CEM, 21 Aug. 1912, CEMP.

46 HNB to CEM, 5 Aug. 1912, FMP.

47 MGF to CM, 13 Aug. 1912, FMP; for another reference to the possibility of Catherine's leaving the EFF, see M.L. Mackenzie to CEM, n.d. [Aug. 1912], CEMP.

48 CEM to M. Robertson, 3 Aug. 1912, CEMP.

49 Mackenzie to CEM, n.d. [Aug. 1912], CEMP.

50 See e.g., CEM's attempts to influence the wording of a resolution coming before the TUC, CEM to Henderson, 29 Aug. [1912], LP/WOM/12/34; n.s., assistant secretary, to CEM, 30 Aug. 1912, copy, LP/WOM/12/35; EFF 20 Sept. 1912, Fawcett Lib; CEM also sent a report to this EFF meeting, and the minutes contain other references to her activities; she wrote a long article on the recent by-elections for the *CC*, 26 Sept. 1912, and may have paid a visit to Midlothian while the election was in process.

51 FEM, ms text of a speech, n.d. [mid–1912], FMP.

52 CEM, ms "Notes on Parliamentary work," n.d., CEMP.

53 HNB to CEM, 5 Aug. [1912]; Palliser to CEM, 13 June 1912, CEMP, where Palliser says she will adopt some of CEM's suggestions for her work.

54 This is probably Philippa Strachey, a member of the parliamentary sub-

committee, and long honorary secretary to the LSWS, but may have
been her younger sister Marjorie.

55 *CC*, 31 October 1912.
56 *H.C. Deb.*, 5th series, vol. 40 (1912), 2268; see also MGF, *What I Remember*, 204.
57 NU executive, 20 June; special executive, 2 July; executive, 4 July 1912, Fawcett Lib.
58 NU executive, 3 Oct., 17 Oct., Fawcett Lib.
59 NU executive, 4 July 1912, Fawcett Lib.
60 Lytton to KDC, 4 May 1912, CEMP.
61 MGF to H. Auerbach, 25 August [1912], IAV. For another Conservative suffragist who praised the policy, though she was unable to contribute to the fund herself, see V.N. Courtauld to [CEM], 18 July 1912, CEMP.
62 Above, pp. 143–4.
63 "Points for Parliamentary Interviews," July 1912, CEMP; see also CEM, "ABC of Women's Suffrage: Women's Suffrage Amendments to the Reform Bill," *CC*, 27 June 1912; numerous articles in *CC*, June 1912 to Jan. 1913; Rover, *Women's Suffrage*, 201–2. Surprisingly, even the writer of the *Manchester Guardian*'s "Political Notes" on 26 Nov. assumed that the removal of "male" from section I, subsection 1 meant adult suffrage, and defended his position on 28 Nov. in the face of letters from Swanwick and Robert Cecil. It was not a completely clear issue, but the most convincing exposition was given in Swanwick's letter. She concludes: "The deletion of the word "male" makes it possible to confer the vote on women by subsequent provision, but it does not actually confer it. This is a point of paramount importance, and if it is not understood the amendment will be wrecked from sheer misunderstanding." "Political Notes," *MG*, 26 Nov. 1912; HMS to the editor, *MG*, 27 Nov.; R. Cecil to the editor, 28 Nov.; reply from "Our Parliamentary Correspondent," *MG*, 28 Nov. 1912. See also NU executive, 4 July 1912, where Cecil "gave advice as to the best method of introducing Women's Suffrage Amendments to the Reform Bill." For an interesting account of the history of the words "man" and "male person" in English law, see Ethel Snowden, *The Feminist Movement* (1913), 142–4.
64 "Points for Parliamentary Interviews," July 1912, CEMP.
65 EFF minutes, 4, 18 Oct. 1912, Fawcett Lib.
66 EFF and NU by-election committees, joint meeting, 20 Aug. 1912, Fawcett Lib.
67 Letter from Robertson, quoted in NU executive minutes, 19 Sept. 1912, Fawcett Lib.

68 NU executive, 19 Sept. 1912, Fawcett Lib.

69 CEM, ms notes "Political situation: Report for Manchester Council" [9, 10 Oct. 1912], CEMP; see also NU executive, 3 Oct. 1912, Fawcett Lib.; HMS, "Women's Suffrage and Lobby Rumours" (letter), *MG*, 29 Nov. 1912.

70 CEM, ms notes "Political situation" [9, 10 Oct. 1912], CEMP; NU executive, 17 Oct. 1912, Fawcett Lib.

71 CEM, ms notes, "Organizers' Meeting," [9, 10 Oct. 1912], CEMP.

72 NU, annual report, 26, 27 Feb. 1913, CEMP; proceedings, NU council, Manchester, 9 Oct. 1912, Fawcett Lib.

73 NU executive, 19 Sept. 1912; EFF, 20 Sept. 1912, Fawcett Lib.; CEM to Henderson, 5 Oct. 1912, LP/WOM/12/39; CEM to Henderson, 14 Oct. 1912, CEMP. E. Rathbone had dissented from the last of these resolutions at the executive.

74 Proceedings, NU council, Manchester, 9 Oct. 1912, Fawcett Lib.; *CC*, 17 Oct. 1912; S. Holton, *Feminism and Democracy*, 83.

75 NU executive, 17 Oct. 1912, Fawcett Lib.

76 NU executive, 5, 19 Dec.; EFF, 6 Dec. 1912, Fawcett Lib. S. Holton, *Feminism and Suffrage*, 97, points out that the first burst of contributions tailed off at this time, but that the flow was renewed in early 1913 (after the Reform Bill fiasco). To me, this suggests that people did not see a need to give money when the cause might already be won, rather than lack of support.

77 EFF, 6 Dec. 1912, Fawcett Lib.

78 "Parliament and the Franchise: Effects of Militancy," *Standard*, 8 Oct. 1912, clipping, LP/WOM/12/40. The *Standard* was generally one of the most supportive papers. Even the Labour papers, the *Labour Leader* and the new *Daily Citizen*, not infrequently published articles which caused anxiety to the NU. On the harm being done by this kind of press report and by "the reported speeches of some Labour Members of Parliament in their constituencies" see also CEM to Henderson, 14 Oct. 1912, copy, CEMP; NU executive, 21 Nov. 1912; EFF, 22 Nov., 6 Dec. 1912, Fawcett Lib.

79 The matter of Lansbury's stand was complicated by an unfortunate press report which confused the PLP's refusal to back Lansbury's proposed policy with a refusal to stand by MacDonald's pledge, given at the Albert Hall the previous December, to reject the third reading of the Reform Bill if women were not included (a pledge which he had in any event later claimed bound only himself); Henderson wrote a strong letter to the *Daily Herald* to clear up the misunderstanding, but some damage had already been done, [Henderson] to the editor, *Daily Herald*, 17 Oct. 1912, copy, LP/WOM/12/43.i. See also EFF, 18 Oct. 1912, Fawcett Lib.; *Votes for Women*, 4 Oct. 1912. Lansbury

had earlier tried to have his policy adopted by the ILP, but his resolution had received only one vote in the National Administrative Council of the body, ILP, NAC minutes, 26 May 1912, BLPES/Misc/464 (M890)/1/6.

80 See Rosen, *Rise Up, Women!*, 180–3.

81 NU special executive, agenda, 14 Nov. 1912, CEMP; ibid., minutes; EFF, 14 Nov., Fawcett Lib.; CEM, ms lists of arrangements "For Com^tee Room," "For Miss Ward," and notes e.g., on people who will lend cars [14 to 26 Nov.],CEMP. The WSPU also had cars, but according to Rosen, spent the morning of the very rainy polling day arguing with Lansbury's campaign manager about the extent to which they could be put at his disposal.

82 "Bow and Bromley By-Election," *CC*, 22, 29 Nov. 1912. We do not know for certain the sex of the cadets, but they are extremely unlikely to have been girls.

83 *CC*, 6 Dec. 1912.

84 NU executive, 21 Nov., Fawcett Lib.

85 EFF, 6 Dec. 1912, Fawcett Lib.

86 EFF, 20 Dec. 1912, Fawcett Lib.

87 CEM, ms notes, "To bring before Executive, July 4 1912," CEMP.

88 See e.g. EFF, 19 July, 2 Aug., 18 Oct. 1912, Fawcett Lib.

89 NU executive, 17 Oct. 1912, Fawcett Lib.

90 [CEM], ts, "Notes of Interview with Birrell," 1 Nov. 1912, CEMP; see also HMS, "Women's Suffrage and Lobby Rumours," letter, *MG*, 29 Nov. 1912; NU executive, 5 Dec. 1912, Fawcett Lib.

91 [CEM], tss, "Notes of Interview with Birrell," "Notes of Interview with Mr. Redmond," 1 Nov. 1912, CEMP; NU executive, 7 Nov. 1912, Fawcett Lib.

92 NU executive, 5 Dec. 1912, Fawcett Lib.

93 NU executive, 7, 21 Nov. 1912, Fawcett Lib.; see also HMS, "The Debate on Mr. Snowden's Amendment," *CC*, 14 Nov. 1912.

94 NU executive, 7 Nov. 1912, Fawcett Lib..

95 NU executive, 5 Dec. 1912, Fawcett Lib.

96 Asquith to C.P. Scott, 9 Dec. 1912, in reply to an anxious inquiry from Scott, in Hammond, *C.P. Scott of the "Manchester Guardian"*, 114; see also D. Morgan, *Suffragists and Liberals*, 110–11; NU executive, 19 Dec. 1912, Fawcett Lib.

97 NU executive, 5 Dec. 1912, Fawcett Lib.

98 CEM, "Unfounded Rumours," *CC*, 6 Dec. 1912; for less confident views and for other rumours, see, inter alia, L. Housman, "A Hidden Danger," *CC*, 22 Nov., and C. Macmillan, *CC*, 29 Nov. 1912.

99 MGF, "The Joint Campaign," *CC*, 13 Dec. 1912. Catherine felt that this meeting had been unduly expensive, and was very angry when she

found that an agreement not to plant plainclothes police in the audience
had been broken, and entered "a very strong protest on behalf of
the N.U. executive at the next meeting of the Joint Campaign Committee," NU executive, 5 Dec. 1912, Fawcett Lib.

100 NU executive, 17 Oct. 1912, Fawcett Lib.

101 NU executive, 19 Dec. 1912; EFF, 20 Dec. 1912; NU executive,
5 Dec. 1912, Fawcett Lib. For CEM's later work with him, see Vellacott,
Bertrand Russell and the Pacifists, passim.

102 NU executive, 2, 17 Jan. 1913, Fawcett Lib..

103 Mackenzie to secretaries of WSS, enclosing schedules for entering
answers given by MPs to deputations regarding how they would vote
on the amendments, 11 Oct. 1912, CEMP; CEM, parliamentary report, *CC*, 20 Dec. 1912, 3, 10, 24 Jan. 1913; frequent references in
CEM's reports to the NU executive.

104 Letter to MPs, enclosing "Statement of Evidence of Support for Wom-
en's Suffrage," 2 Dec. 1912, CEMP; "Public Support for Women's
Suffrage," *CC*, 13 Dec. 1912, 10, 17 Jan. 1913; frequent references
in CEM's reports to the NU executive.

105 [M. Mackenzie] to Middleton, 9 Dec. 1912, asking for names of Labour
people CEM should meet, LP/WOM/12/46, and list typed from tele-
phoned reply, LP/WOM/12/47; NU executive, 19 Dec. 1912, Fawcett
Lib.

106 Extensive material in CEMP.

107 NU executive, 17 Jan. 1913, Fawcett Lib.

108 Ibid. The WSPU took a deputation of working women to meet with
Lloyd George on 23 Jan., "Women's Suffrage Deputation from
Working Women Suffragists," transcription from shorthand notes,
Lloyd George Papers, C/17/3/23.

CHAPTER TEN

1 Special executive, 24 Jan. 1913, Fawcett Lib.

2 Ibid.

3 Special executive, noon, 27 Jan. 1913, Fawcett Lib.

4 Ibid.

5 Hobhouse, *Inside Asquith's Cabinet*, 131. However, Burns (president
of the Local Government Board) noted in his diary that the Radicals
were "not pleased with the dropping of the Franchise Bill," quoted
D. Morgan, *Suffragists and Liberals*, 117. Hobhouse was never a noteworthy politician, but kept diaries of great interest, commenting on
politicians and political affairs, which were discovered and published
after his death. The diaries confirm his reputation as an adamant
opponent of women's suffrage, see 92–5, 128–33.

6 Special executive, noon, 27 Jan. 1913, Fawcett Lib.

7 MGF to Miss Leigh Browne, 30 Jan. 1913, copy, CEMP.

8 Special executive, 6 p.m., 27 Jan. 1913, Fawcett Lib.

9 Special executive, 6 p.m., 27 Jan.; noon, 28 Jan. 1913, Fawcett Lib.

10 NU executive, 6 Feb. 1913, Fawcett Lib. Catherine also reported to the executive that a Liberal suffrage committee had been formed in the House, and discussed the complications arising from Conservative objections to supporting any private member's bill which required the application of the 1911 Parliament Act to secure its passage through the House of Lords.

11 "Political Situation," statement by the executive, *CC*, 7 Feb. 1913; HMS, "The NU and a Private Bill," *CC*, 14 Feb. 1913; Lytton,"Woman Suffrage: The Only Way," *Englishwoman*, March 1914, CEMP.

12 D. Morgan, *Suffragists and Liberals*, 117–18.

13 S. Holton, *Feminism and Democracy*, 92.

14 Lowther, *Speaker's Commentaries*, 136–7; D. Morgan, *Suffragists and Liberals*, 117–18.

15 M.L. Davies to B. Russell, "Friday," n.d. [1908]; Russell to M.L. Davies, 11 Sept. 1908, BRA. Some fears had arisen in late 1912 as to whether the WS amendments might not be ruled out of order as too close to the Conciliation Bill already rejected in the same parliamentary session; see Laurence Housman, "A Hidden Danger," *CC*, 22 Nov. 1912; C. Macmillan, *CC*, 29 Nov. 1912.

16 CEM, ms "Notes for Dep^n to Sir John Simon, Manchester, Nov. 12 1913," CEMP. There is no mention of the women's suffrage campaign in Simon's memoirs (*Retrospect*), but there is one passing reference to "the violence of the Suffragettes," 94.

17 CEM, ms "Notes for Dep^n to Sir John Simon, Manchester, Nov. 12 1913," CEMP (emphasis in the original).

18 P. Snowden, "The Position of Woman Suffrage," *Englishwoman*, Feb. 1913.

19 Jenkins, *Asquith*, 278; see also Rover, *Women's Suffrage*, 195–6; Hume, *National Union*, 186–7. Even in the midst of the supposed embarrassment caused by the anticipated speaker's ruling, Asquith showed little contrition and no sympathy for the women's suffragists. According to the antisuffragist Hobhouse, Asquith declared "very emphatically" to the cabinet on 24 January "that he considered that he had done his best to give the suffragists a fair opportunity and that he held [himself] absolutely absolved from his pledge after this year," Hobhouse, *Inside Asquith's Cabinet*, 131. In later writings, Asquith continued to maintain mendaciously that the ruling had been "not only unpalatable but unexpected," Oxford and Asquith, *Memories and Reflections*, 1: 221.

20 Letter to CEM, initialled "FKU"[?, probably a "Miss Upton"], n.d. [assumed to be roughly of this time], CEMP. Catherine may have sug-

gested sharing accommodation, but "FKU" moved into her studio instead, though she lived at 1 Barton Street at some time.

21 CEM, ms brief notes under headings "Parl. work in future" and "Parl^y work: plans," n.d., found with material of 13 Dec. 1912, CEMP. The phrase "without an Honorary" meant that Robertson would have been paid for the job (but it would also have put her in a different relationship with the committee from that enjoyed by Catherine).

22 FEM to CEM, 9 Jan. 1913, CEMP.

23 Samples of letterhead, n.d.; carpenter's bill, Mar. 1913, CEMP.

24 See e.g., articles and comments by HMS and MGF and others (some of the unsigned ones are probably by CEM), CC, 31 Jan., 7 Feb. 1913; NU leaflet, "The Position of the N.U.W.S.S.: February, 1913", copy in CEMP.

25 MGF to "My dear Friend," 11 Feb. 1913, IAV. The TU bill referred to, passed in 1913, restored the right of TUs to levy contributions for political purposes, which had been taken away by the 1909 Osborne judgment.

26 NU executive, 19 Dec. 1912; EFF, 20 Dec. 1912, Fawcett Lib.

27 "The Labour Conference," and "Notes and Comments," CC, 7 Feb. 1913; NU special executive, 28 Jan. 1913; NU executive, 2 Jan.; 6 Feb. 1913, Fawcett Lib.; MGF, What I Remember, 212.

28 NU executive, 6 Feb. 1913, Fawcett Lib.

29 NU executive, 2 Jan. 1913, Fawcett Lib.

30 Cable, NU to Roberts, 30 Jan. 1913, LP/WOM/12/48.

31 M. Phillips (general secretary of WLL) to Henderson, 3 Feb. 1913, LP/WOM/12/49. The WLL had tended to follow rather than to try to push the Labour party until this time.

32 NU executive, 6, 20 Feb. 1913, Fawcett Lib. CEM coordinated speakers for this deputation, which included inter alia Fawcett, Royden, and Courtney.

33 NU executive, 6 Feb. 1913, Fawcett Lib.

34 Ibid.

35 NU executive, 7 Nov., 5 Dec. 1912, Fawcett Lib.

36 "Notes and Comments," CC, 7 Mar. 1913.

37 "Notes and Comments," "NU Annual Council: Proceedings," and "The New Campaign," CC, 7 Mar. 1913.

38 E. Rathbone, "The Gentle Art of Making Enemies: A Criticism of the proposed Anti-Government Policy of the National Union," n.d., Fawcett Lib., italics in the original.

39 Royden, under "Correspondence," emphasis in original, CC, 14 Mar. 1913.

40 In July 1912, Catherine had said of the EFF policy, "We have at last got a real sword in our hands instead of a foil with a guarded tip," NU provincial council, 11 July 1912; and see CEM's report as hon. parl.

sec. to the provincial council, Exeter, 23 May 1913 for a particularly
elaborately developed military metaphor, Fawcett Lib.

41 List of nominations prepared for the council meeting, 27, 28 Feb. 1913;
NU executive, 6 Feb. 1913, Fawcett Lib. A breakdown was made
available of attendance of members at the various committees on which
they served. Catherine had been at fifteen of about twenty regular
executives (it is a tribute to the dedication of these women that this was
only an average attendance record), and at eleven of the twelve
"special" or emergency meetings. Her increasing concentration on direct
political work is marked by a poor attendance at the press committee. The EFF was not strictly an NU subcommittee, so is not listed; Catherine had probably been at every EFF meeting except during her
September absence in Cumberland.

42 "Chrystal Macmillan Memorial," leaflet, [1937], in my possession.

43 Adela [Stanton] Coit to MGF, 3 Sept. 1915, M/50/2/22/44; see also Emily
Hobhouse to "Friend" [probably Aletta Jacobs], Easter Day 1916,
where she says Macmillan is known to be hard to work with, IAV. Too
much should not be made of the letter, which is unspecific and the
kind of thing few of us escape having said of us at some time or other;
Coit's remarks, however, are more significant because they confirm
what can be read into various minutes. An obituary says that "she was
utterly without the spirit of enmity, even towards those who opposed her most bitterly." While I question the accuracy of this for our
period, I believe her attitude is partly illuminated by the next comment, "Her dislikes were for policies, not for persons ... If there was
enmity towards herself she did not even perceive it [because] ... she
was thinking ... only and always of the work to be done," *Chrystal Macmillan Memorial*.

44 "An interesting 'At Home,'" *CC*, 7 Mar. 1913.

45 Robert and Bessie kept open house at the Shiffolds for London
friends. Bertrand Russell was a frequent visitor there from at least 1902;
during the First World War, leading members of the No-
Conscription Fellowship often spent a weekend walking on Leith Hill
and visiting the Trevelyans.

46 Handwritten bill "To Mrs. Enticknap" for use of rooms, and for trap
to Dorking and Gomshall, 3 Mar. 1913, CEMP; interview (1988) by
Isobel McCallum Clark with May Johnson, daughter of the Enticknaps,
at whose farm (Sewhurst Farm) Catherine stayed. Catherine probably stayed there for weekends quite frequently when she was working
in London; see e.g. MacKenzie to CEM, 20 Apr. [1913], CEMP, and
much later would have a cottage there.

47 NU executive, 6 Mar. 1913, Fawcett Lib. Much time was spent at
this meeting on a novel idea put forward in the *Nation* by the editor,
H.W. Massingham: he proposed that the government should bring

forward a moderate measure for women's suffrage, which, when passed, would be permissive, and would go into effect in each constituency only when approved by a local referendum. Catherine was asked to talk to Lord Robert Cecil, Francis Acland, and Arthur Henderson to find out their views of the scheme; but the majority of the committee was not prepared to wait, and passed a resolution expressing strong disapproval. Rathbone and Corbett Ashby voted against the resolution, and Catherine abstained, probably thinking a heated reaction unwise. The tortuous solution found little support, and faded into oblivion. NU executive, 6, 13 Mar. 1913, Fawcett Lib.; CEM to Rathbone, copy, 14 Apr. 1913; R. Cecil to CEM, 22 Apr. 1913, CEMP. Had it gone into effect, it could have resulted in a situation like that of the Swiss cantons, where women in one locality were kept waiting for full federal political rights until the 1970s, and in one half canton waited until 1990 for the cantonal (regional) and communal (local) vote.

48 CEM to Rathbone, 14 Apr. 1913, CEMP.

49 "The New Policy declared," *CC*, 14 Mar. 1913. For the WSPU attitude see, e.g., "The Labour Members' betrayal of women," *Suffragette*, 7 Feb. 1913.

50 CEM to F. Acland, 28 Aug 1913, ms copy, CEMP.

51 KDC to "Dear Madam," marked "Private and Confidential" [probably to branch secretaries], 2 May 1912, CEMP.

52 CEM, report of the hon. parl. sec., provincial council, 23 May 1916, Fawcett Lib.

53 According to Hobhouse, the cabinet decision to salvage this part of the Reform Bill, which was expected to benefit their party (though this might not in fact have been the case), had been taken as early as 27 Jan. as soon as it was clear the Reform Bill would have to be withdrawn, Hobhouse, *Inside*, 132.

54 For text of ILP resolution, see NU executive, 17 Apr. 1913, Fawcett Lib.

55 CEM, "Labour and the Women: Case of Plural Voting Bill," to the editor, *Daily Citizen*, 4 April 1913, clipping in CEMP. Catherine's address is given as St Jean de Luz. See also *CC*, 25 Apr. 1913; P. Snowden, "The Labour Party and the Plural Voting Bill," *Englishwoman*, May 1913.

56 CEM, *Daily Citizen*, 4 Apr. 1913.

57 CEM, ms notes on meeting with Acland, 14 Apr. 1913, CEMP.

58 *CC*, 9 May 1913; for the history of the Plural Voting Bill, see Pugh, *Electoral Reform in War and Peace, 1906–18*, 43, 58–60; for its significance, which may have been less than the Liberals believed, see Blewett, "The Franchise," 43–51.

59 CEM to MacDonald, 19 Oct. 1912, J.R. MacDonald Papers in the PRO, quoted by Holton, 85.

60 CEM, ts "The Best we can get," n.d., CEMP; *CC*, 2 May 1913.

61 For an outspoken criticism of Asquith's attitude to the bill by an officer of the newly created Liberal Women's Suffrage Union, see Lady Aberconway, *The Prime Minister and Women's Suffrage*, pamphlet, copy in CEMP; Rover, *Women's Suffrage*, 197; for the debate, see *CC*, 9 May 1913.

62 HMS, ms draft, "To the Rt. Hon. H.H. Asquith, M.P.," n.d., CEMP; see also ms "The Whitewashing of Mr. Asquith," n.d., unsigned (titled in CEM's handwriting, and written either by HMS or CEM, whose handwritings are sometimes indistinguishable from one another, HMS's writing closely resembling CEM's at the latter's neatest), CEMP; for CEM's comments after the bill, see ms, "Dick. Bill [sic]," n.d., CEMP. CEM had also corresponded with Lord Robert Cecil about the possibility of a narrowing amendment which would make it easier for Conservatives to vote for the bill, CEM notes headed "Lord R. Cecil"; R. Cecil to CEM, 22 Apr. 1913; Maud Selborne to CEM, 22 Apr. 1913, CEMP.

63 See ts (damaged) "... dishonour of victory," n.d., CEMP.

64 CEM, meeting with Acland, 14 Apr. 1913.

65 CEM to W.H. Dickinson, 14 Apr. 1913, copy, CEMP. Dickinson was annoyed by the NU's indifference to the bill, which he believed seriously affected its hope of success at second reading, but he bore no grudge, and agreed to take part in the suffrage pilgrimage demonstration on 27 July, Dickinson to CEM, 24 Apr. 1913, 15 July, 1913, CEMP.

66 E. Acland to CEM, [7 May 1913], CEMP.

67 "The Dickinson Bill: Analysis of Division List" [almost certainly by CEM], proof copy in CEMP, *CC*, 16 May 1913.

68 Lyell to [Alice] Low, 8 May 1913. Lyell, however, found another excuse for not supporting the inclusion of the women's vote in the Scottish Home Rule Bill; it would be proper to wait until the Scottish Parliament was established and then put it in if Scottish men and women wanted it. For Scottish Home Rule, see also Holden to CEM, n.d.; Price to Low, 12 May 1913; Low to Mackenzie, 22 May, 30 May 1913; Denman to Campbell, 30 May 1913; Lawson to Holden, 16 June 1913; Campbell to CEM, 2 Nov. 1913, Mackenzie to CEM, 25 Nov. 1913; exchange with Alexander Ure (became Lord Strathclyde, Oct. 1913), 18 Oct. to Nov. 29, 1913, CEMP; NU executive 15 May, 5 June 1913, Fawcett Lib.; Hume, *National Union*, 200. For Welsh Home Rule see, *inter alia* CEM, ms notes, n.d., CEMP; *CC*, 20 Mar. 1914.

69 NU executive, 20 Feb., 13 March, 17 Apr., 1 May, 15 May 1913, Fawcett Lib.

70 NU, "Particulars of E.F.F. Bye-Elections," n.d., MPL/M50/2/10/34; Hume, *National Union*, 205–7; S. Holton, *Feminism and Democracy*, 82–3.

71 E.g., McKibbin, *The Evolution of the Labour Party, 1910–1924*, 20–87,

passim. I have found this work valuable for an understanding of the complexities not only in Labour party structure but also besetting the path of every activity it undertook; but it remains fascinating how selectively blind a good mainstream historical researcher can be. The same may be said of Marquand's *Ramsay MacDonald*, although this does not in any case contain as much detailed work on by-elections. One would expect the sources used by McKibbin and Marquand to include enough mention of the suffragists' involvement to have sparked further inquiry.

72 Hume, *National Union*, 208–9.

73 CEM to E. Acland, 25 Apr. 1913, copy, CEMP; see also Brockway in *CC*, 7 Mar. 1913.

74 Marquand, *MacDonald*, 151; for a full discussion of the problems that this election caused MacDonald and the Labour party, see McKibbin, *Evolution*, 62–6.

75 Ibid., 65 n. 69. Some women's suffragists also felt that it was important that the Liberal party should be opposed at Leicester to demonstrate outrage at the recent "Cat and Mouse" Bill, "L.H." to "Sarah," 21 June 1913, CEMP.

76 "Liberal M.P.'s, December 1913", a full list of the voting records of all Liberal MPs on all recent women's suffrage measures, with quotations on the issue where available, evidently supplied by CEM to Lloyd George, together with a list of Liberal candidates, Jan. 1914, with their stance where known, LG/C/17/3/26 and 27. S. Holton, *Feminism and Democracy*, 121 says "it is most likely [these lists] originated from National Union sources," and this is confirmed by the notation on them "Private and Confidential" which is in CEM's handwriting.

77 McKibbin, *Evolution*, 66–9.

78 CEM to MacDonald, [c. 2 July 1913], ms draft; ts "[Extract from] Mrs Cowmeadow: report after Leicester By-election," 1 July 1913, CEMP; Cowmeadow, "Leicester By-Election," *CC*, 4 July 1913.

79 NU experience with the Labour party bears out McKibbin's assessment of the difficulties in Labour's situation, *Evolution*, esp. 72–87.

80 NU executive, 17 Oct. 1912, Fawcett Lib.

81 NU executive, 5 June 1913, Fawcett Lib.; Hilston to CEM, 21 June 1913; Peters to CEM, 22 June 1913, CEMP; S. Holton, *Feminism and Democracy*, 102–3.

82 Chew to Robertson, 28 May 1913; CEM to Anderson, 28 June 1912; Evans to CEM, 8 Sept. 1913; Peters to Alice Clark, 15 Sept. 1913, CEMP; S. Holton, *Feminism and Democracy*, 103.

83 Ibid.; McKibbin, *Evolution*, 73–5.

84 NU executive, 19 Dec. 1912, Fawcett Lib. The transferable fund had

been set up to enable a reserve fund of donations to the NU to be used for EFF work, unless the donor specifically stated otherwise, S. Holton, *Feminism and Democracy*, 88. For those interested in the theory of negotiation, this incident may be seen as a nice example of a principle spelled out by Fisher and Ury, *Getting to Yes*, esp. 41–7; what Catherine had achieved, in their terminology, was to separate *positions* from *interests*. The *position* of the executive was that it decided which constituencies would be worked by the EFF; the *position* of the Bristol and South Wales Federation was that it opposed the EFF policy. On these points there could be no successful negotiation. By identifying the underlying *interests*, which for both sides turned out to be to oppose antisuffragists without alienating Liberal supporters (although the two parties to the negotiation would have put these in opposite order of priority), Catherine was able to come up with a negotiated agreement in which neither side had been overruled.

85   S. Holton, *Feminism and Democracy*, 100–1, 105–9.

86   Gordon to Evans, 12 June 1913; to CEM, 3 June; to KDC, 3 June, CEMP; NU executive, 15 May 1913, Fawcett Lib.; for a full discussion of the operation of the EFF in the North-East Federation, see S. Holton, *Feminism and Democracy*, 103–5.

87   See extensive correspondence in CEMP, esp. during summer 1913, e.g., Matravers to CEM, 29 May [1913], 3 June 1913; Oldham to Mackenzie, 28 May 1913; Renton to CEM, 27 May [1913].

88   See e.g. NU executive, 17 Oct. 1912, Fawcett Lib.; CEM, ms note of advice marked "MR," n.d., CEMP.

89   Robertson to CEM, 29 May 1913, CEMP; S. Holton, *Feminism and Democracy*, 99.

90   NU provincial council, 23 May 1913, Fawcett Lib.; see also CEM, "Help our Friends in the Labour Party," *CC*, 13 June 1913.

91   CEM, ms notes, "Exeter Council," CEMP.

92   CEM, ms and draft ts notes, "Exeter Council," and related material, [23 May 1913], CEMP; NU provincial council, 23 May 1913, Fawcett Lib.; CEM, "Help our Friends," *CC*, 13 June 1913; "Report," *CC*, 30 May 1913.

93   CEM to E. Acland, draft or copy, 25 Apr. 1913, marked "Destroy this," CEMP.

94   CEM to LG, 29 August 1913, LG/C/9/5/20.

95   Organizers were actively recruited among workers and university graduates; e.g. in March 1913, a Mrs Robertson Garrett told a Girton audience that NU organizing work was especially suitable for graduates; the requirements were tact, physical fitness, neatness, and social knowledge; the training was usually a month's probation with an

organizer (learning to conduct meetings, take minutes, write reports, and deal with the press), followed by a month in the NU offices; after this a full-time salary would be paid ("depending upon the worth of the individual"), of c. £100 p.a., plus expenses, *Girton Review*, Lent, 1913, 5–6. On 2 Oct. 1913, "It was reported [to the executive] that 16 students are attending the School for Organizers in the Office," and that the London society was kindly giving them practical experience; see also "Questions for Organizers" (appendix B, below) and answers by Florence L. Dixon, marginal comment in an unrecognized hand; CEM ms headed "Miss Courtney's report of Miss Dixon," 20 Oct. 1913. The unfortunate Dixon did not do very well, and despite allowance made for her having been suffering from sleeplessness and toothache during the training period in London, KDC hoped that secretarial work would be found for her in her own federation, as "she would do much better in that capacity than as organizer," CEMP. There are many references in the NU executive minutes and in CEMP to the hiring and evaluation of organizers. See also "Information and Instructions for Organisers" (proposed alterations to an existing leaflet), n.d. [Dec. 1913], CEMP.

96 Blewett, *Peers, Parties, and People*, 284–6.
97 See below p. 308; also Robertson to CEM, 10 Dec. 1913; Clementina Gordon to CEM, 10 Dec. 1913, CEMP; S. Holton, *Feminism and Democracy*, 110; for deficiencies of Labour party organization, see McKibbin, *Evolution*, 4–11.
98 Chew to M. Robertson, 28 May 1913, CEMP.
99 Peters to A. Clark, 15 Sept. 1913, CEMP.
100 S. Holton, *Feminism and Democracy*, 103.
101 Peters to CEM, 22 June 1913; Hilston to CEM, 21 June 1913, CEMP. For other accounts of the NU's voter registration work see "Parliamentary," *CC*, 4 July 1913; EFF report, *CC*, 29 Aug. 1913; *CC*, 21 Nov. 1913.

CHAPTER ELEVEN

1 NU executive, 6 Feb. 1913, Fawcett Lib.
2 Sheepshanks to B. Russell, 26 Apr. 1913, also n.d. [1913], BRA; see Oldfield, *Spinsters*, 153–9 for a fascinating description of Sheepshanks's travels.
3 NU executive, 1 May 1913, Fawcett Lib.; *CC*, 16 May 1913.
4 CEM to Ashton, ts copy, 9 June 1913; CEM to Lowndes, 9 June 1913; CEM to Corbett Fisher, 11 June 1913, CEMP; NU executive 17 April, 5 June 1913, Fawcett Lib.

5   CEM had already cleared with Sheepshanks that she would take the secretaryship if offered, CEM to Sheepshanks, 8 May, copy; Sheepshanks to CEM (from Galicia), 18 May 1913, CEMP; Oldfield, *Spinsters*, 159–61; *CC*, 12 Sept. 1913.

6   CEM, ms, "International press Bureau, Mrs. Chapman Catt's suggestions," n.d., "Scheme for an International press Bureau," printed, in English, French, and German; various notes and drafts relating to this scheme, CEMP; NU executive, 1, 15 May 1913, Fawcett Lib.; report on the congress, NU executive, 3 July 1913, Fawcett Lib.; *CC*, 20, 27 June, 4, 25 July 1913. Preliminary activities of the NU international subcommittee were reported regularly to the executive, minutes, July 1912 on, Fawcett Lib.

7   CEM, ts "The Prospects of enfranchisement for British women in the near future," n.d., CEMP.

8   CEM, ms and ts "What relation should Suffrage organisations bear towards political parties?", several drafts; CEM to Catt, 5 June 1913, copy, CEMP.

9   Ibid.

10 E. Acland to CEM, 7 May 1913, CEMP; see also FEM's letter on the LWSU in the *Nation*, 23 Aug. 1913. Walker, "Party Political Women," mentions neither the Tonbridge resolution nor the LWSU. See above, pp. 423–4n.58.

11 CEM, "What relation."

12 Rosen, *Rise Up, Women!*, 189–202. Although the WSPU refrained from attacks on human life, arson and bombing could not be carried out without risk of an unforeseen death or serious injury, especially when the crusade was conducted in so haphazard a fashion, with some followers acting on their own initiative (see, e.g., Rosen, 189, for Emily Wilding Davison's bombing of Lloyd George's property at Walton Heath on 18 Feb. 1913) and others taking a pride in blind quasi-military obedience (e.g., Richardson, *Laugh a Defiance*, passim); see Vicinus, *Independent Women*, ch. 7.

13 Rosen, *Rise Up, Women!*, 195; *CC*, 11 Apr. 1913.

14 See, *inter alia*, several articles in *CC*, 28 Mar. 1913.

15 CEM to *Daily Citizen*, 18 Apr. 1913, clipping; see also CEM, ms notes on militancy, n.d. [probably notes for the former], CEMP.

16 B Russell to M.L. Davies, 16 Apr. 1913, BRA. He went on: "I think some wild member of the W.S.P.U. will murder a Minister, and then they will collapse." In fairness, it should be said that he continued to praise and encourage Davies' work with the WCG and PSF.

17 NU executive, 1, 15 May; 5 June 1913, Fawcett Lib.; *CC*, 2 May 1913. The press report concerned specifically the Nottingham Town

Council's refusal of police protection at suffrage meetings. Catherine had already discussed the issue with Lord Robert Cecil, with a view to having it raised in the Commons, and had ascertained that the *Manchester Guardian* would pursue the matter. The Hyde Park meetings were later continued till the end of September, NU executive, 3 July 1913.

18 *CC*, 23 May, 13 June 1913. On 25 May Catherine planned to speak, but for some reason did not do so, CEM, ms "Notes for speech, Hyde Park," 25 May [1913], marked "not made"; she did speak two weeks later.

19 Organization subcommittee, 18 Apr. 1913, in ms minute book, labelled "Women's Interests," Fawcett Lib.; *CC*, 2 May 1913; Rover, *Women's Suffrage*, 66; MGF, *Women's Victory*, 58–9.

20 *CC*, 9 May 1913.

21 See, e.g., NU executive, 15 May, 3 July 1913. General references for the planning and execution of the pilgrimage are: minutes, under various titles (Organisation, March and Demonstration, Pilgrimage, Demonstration and Decorations) May/July 1913, Fawcett Lib.; reports (also under varying headings), in NU executive throughout the same period, and in the *CC*; Hume, *National Union*, 198–9; MGF, *Women's Victory*, 55–64.

22 Duffield, "On the March," 6–7, used by courtesy of James Duffield. This account is as stirring as the much-publicized exploits of the militants.

23 Swan and Edgar advertisement, *CC*, 20 June 1913; NU executive, 31 July 1913, Fawcett Lib.

24 "Pilgrims from the North-West," signed C.M., *CC*, 4 July 1913; the tone is rather more self-congratulatory than the Marshalls usually permitted themselves.

25 Duffield, "On the March," v, 4–6.

26 "Pilgrims from the N-W," *CC*, 4 July 1913. For the vicar's text, see Hebrews 11: 13, 14, 16.

27 E. Snowden, "The Women's Pilgrimage," *Nation*, 2 Aug. 1913.

28 A. Watson to Holden, 3 June 1913, CEMP.

29 Snowden, "The Women's Pilgrimage."

30 "C.M.G.," "Pilgrims from the North-East," *CC*, 4 July 1913.

31 Ida S. Beaver, "The Pilgrimage: I. – Its Effect in the North," *Englishwoman* 57 (Sept. 1913).

32 Ibid.

33 Snowden, "The Women's Pilgrimage."

34 Information from Bruce Jones, previously Cumbria archivist, and pellets and banner seen in CRO. The date at which the pellets were fired is unknown, but the pilgrimage was possibly the last occasion on which

the banner was carried. An "airgun" is a weapon which expels a small pellet by the use of compressed air, known in North America as a "beebee gun." While not normally lethal to humans, and possessed by many youths, these weapons are capable of killing a bird, severely damaging a human eye, or at best causing considerable pain.

35 NU executive, 31 July 1913, Fawcett Lib.; MGF, *Women's Victory*, 60.

36 "Hooliganism at Suffrage Meetings," *CC*, 22 Aug. 1913; H. Renton to CEM, 6 Aug. 1913, CEMP.

37 For a good analysis of the difference between MacDonald's intellectual understanding of the suffrage issue and his emotional response to militancy, see Marquand, *MacDonald*, 148–9. For an example of the kind of thinking which has made women cynical about "chivalry," see C.F. Keary's comprehensively chauvinistic comment on Sir Ronald Ross's review of Sir Almroth Wright's *Unexpurgated Case* (see above, p. 153), correspondence, *Nation*, 18 Oct. 1913. Keary agrees with Ross's view that "a highly complex structure of civilization has now been built upon the original barbaric basis of force," but argues: "But the most important element in all this new structure is the sentiment of chivalry which has in reality pervaded the whole of society. Even the wife-beater, in his sober moments and in the case of *another man*, feels a scorn for the man, 'as 'its a woman.' I am told by those who know the working class well that anything of the nature of wife-beating is, on the whole, considered such 'bad form,' that female drunkenness has of late increased through its disuse." He believes (correctly) that chivalry depends on a separation of function between men and women, and is particularly affronted by the unfair and "unsportsmanlike" advantage being taken by the militants, who trade on being treated more gently than men would be.

38 CEM to MacDonald, n.d. [c. 1 July 1913], ms copy, CEMP.

39 CEM, rough ms notes, "Oxford, July 19 1913," CEMP; Duffield, "On the March," 76.

40 Ibid., 106.

41 E. Snowden, "The Women's Pilgrimage." The event was on the whole well treated in the press. In addition to sources already cited, sympathetic coverage included an excellent article in the issue of the *New Statesman* which came out the day of the Hyde Park demonstration; and the *Illustrated London News*, 2 Aug. 1913, published photographs of the Hyde Park meeting under the heading "Better is Wisdom than the Weapons of War: Non-Militant Suffragists in Hyde Park." At the same time, the extraordinary difficulty and frustration of trying to get a wilful press to distinguish between militants and nonmilitants is well illustrated by a London report in the Toronto *Globe*, which threw a reference to the pilgrimage being organized

by what it called a "Suffragette Society," and even a reference to Fawcett's manifesto, into the middle of an account dilating on the activities of the militants, the closing of Blenheim Palace to the public because of threats, and so on, "May 9 1913 London," clipping from *Globe*, n.d., in TPL/WS, 5-C-14. However, possibly even the *Globe*'s London correspondent received some education from the pilgrimage, since the report of 28 July refers respectfully to the conclusion of the nonmilitants' crusade, TPL/WS, 5-E-4. Special thanks to Margaret Kamester for this research.

42 CEM, ms note responding to request for report from platform Chairs, M. Crookenden to "Dear Madam," 29 July 1913, CEMP.

43 C.P. Scott commented favourably on the Hyde Park demonstration, adding, " I didn't know there had been so many ugly incidents on the march," Scott to CEM, 28 July 1913, CEMP.

44 Harley, "The Pilgrimage: II: A London Impression," *Englishwoman*, no. 57, Sept. 1913.

45 NU provincial council, Exeter, 23 May 1913, Fawcett Lib.

46 *New Statesman*, 26 July 1913.

47 CEM, ms notes, n.d.; ts "Suggestions for Political Side of Pigrimage," n.d., CEMP.

48 CEM to Redmond, 25 July 1913, copy; T.J. Hanna (for Redmond) to CEM, 28 July; Cecil to Voiceless, telegram, 9 Aug.; Marcus Dawkins [for Lansdowne] to CEM, 9 Aug.; CEM to Lansdowne, 9, 11 Aug.; Lansdowne to CEM, 11 Aug. 1913, CEMP.

49 NU executive, 31 July, Fawcett Lib.

50 Robertson to CEM, 3 Aug. 1913, CEMP.

51 Transcript of deputation, 8 Aug. 1913, proof copy, CEMP. The proof copy differs in some respects from the report in *CC*; CEM's ms notes indicate that she did not think the transcript, probably from the PM's office, accurate in every detail, especially as regards Asquith's own words, CEM ms notes, made on the back of a leaflet, CEMP. A pamphlet, "Deputation to the Prime Minister (August 1913)," was on the NU publications list by November 1913, but I have not seen a copy. See also D. Morgan, *Suffragists and Liberals*, 125–6, who uses a document in the Asquith Papers (box 89, F. 47–85), "Mr. Asquith's reply to the suffrage delegation," which again appears to differ substantially from both the versions I have seen, and shows Asquith as even more conciliatory; see also S. Holton, *Feminism and Democracy*, 117–18, who uses Morgan's version.

52 Elizabeth Tapper, ts note on correspondence copies prepared for Gertrude Bussey, n.d., WILPF, microfilm R42/11/124.

53 "After the Pilgrimage," *CC*, 8 Aug. 1913. Asquith's doubtful "I suppose so" does not appear in the transcript. He had also professed respect

for the NU's methods, and had conceded that "the militant faction ... is a very small minority," saying that it was most regrettable that so much prominence was given to the activities of the latter, admissions which are ironic in view of his later writings, which make no mention of the nonmilitants, while enlarging on the difficulties caused by the militants, Oxford and Asquith, *Fifty Years of British Parliament*, 2: 140–1; *Memories and Reflections, 1852–1927*, 1: 259–63.

54 MGF, *The Women's Victory*, 61.

55 "Mr. Asquith and Woman Suffrage," *Nation*, 16 Aug. 1913.

56 For an important new view of the ELF deputation see S. Holton, *Feminism and Democracy*, 124–6, and below, pp. 354–5.

57 CEM to F. Acland, 28 Aug. 1913, ms copy, CEMP.

58 Robertson to "Cruel woman!" [CEM], 18 Sept. 1913, CEMP. The soubriquet refers to Catherine's having disturbed Robertson's holiday in Italy by writing for advice on aspects of NU work.

59 Scott to CEM, 28 July 1913, CEMP.

60 "Trying to Remember," *CC*, 27 June 1913; see also press report, *CC*, 3 Oct. 1913. I have not seen LG's article.

61 CEM to LG, 26 July 1913, LG/C/9/4/85; MGF, "Votes for Women: a Reply to Mr. Lloyd George," *Review of Reviews*, Sept. 1913, clipping enclosed with CEM to LG, 12 Oct. 1913, LG/C/10/1/20.

62 Ts, n.d., headed in CEM's writing "Militancy," CEMP. MGF used the same material in her article for the *Review of Reviews*.

63 CEM to LG, ms draft 5 Aug. 1913, CEMP.

64 CEM to LG, ms draft 6 Aug. 1913, CEMP.

65 Ibid.

66 *CC*, 15 Aug. 1913; "Deputation from the National Union of Women's Suffrage Societies," transcript, 8 Aug. 1913, LG/C/17/3/24. The transcript was made from "from the shorthand notes of F[rances] Primrose Stevenson," formerly governess to LG's daughter Megan, since December 1912 his private secretary and his lover, and finally (1943) his wife. There is one blank space of almost a page, suggesting that something may have been taken out when LG saw the typescript. On the last few pages the typist (Stevenson?) has repeatedly typed "The Prime Minister" in error for "The Chancellor of the Exchequer" (in most cases the error has been corrected in handwriting). No comment.

67 Disestablishment of the Anglican church within Wales was a leading Welsh nationalist cause, where the majority of the native population were Nonconformists and resented the privileged and authoritarian position held by the state Church of England. Disestablishment had been adopted by Gladstone in 1891 as a plank of Liberal policy, part of his "Newcastle programme."

68 "Deputation," 8 Aug. 1913, LG/C/17/3/24; S. Holton, *Feminism and Democracy*, 118.

69 "Lloyd George and Women's Suffrage," *MG*, 24 Oct. 1913, typed transcript in LG/C/36/1/18.

70 CEM to F. Acland, 28 Aug. 1913, copy, CEMP.

71 CEM, ms notes, n.d., headed "To Sir E. Grey," CEMP.

72 CEM to J. Simon, ms draft, 10 Aug. [1913], CEMP.

73 Ibid.

74 CEM to LG, 10 Aug. 1913, LG/C/9/5/11.

75 CEM to F. Acland, 28 Aug., CEMP.

76 CEM to LG, 11 Aug. 1913, LG/C/9/5/13; see also Stevenson, *Lloyd George*, 18. LG's letters to CEM have not survived.

77 CEM to LG, 11 Aug. 1913, LG/C/9/5/13.

78 For an earlier and even less excusable failure of LG to get his facts right, see his remarks on the Conciliation Committee, above, p. 87. LG was notoriously no student of the papers or even of facts; Hobhouse describes his refusal "to read any office files or papers" and "his absolute contempt for details and ignorance of common facts of life," but also his "extraordinary power of picking up the essential details of a question by conversation," Hobhouse, *Inside Asquith's Cabinet*, 73.

79 CEM to LG, 29 Aug. 1913, LG/C/9/5/20; for land reform, see below, pp. 264–5, 467–8n.5.

80 Stevenson, *Lloyd George*, 18.

81 Hume, *National Union*, 217, seems to suggest that CEM was being deliberately flirtatious with LG, as part of a plan consciously adopted by the NU; although the objectives were those of the NU, I believe the style was CEM's own.

82 Pelling, *Popular Politics*, 119.

83 E. Acland to CEM, 7 May 1913, CEMP.

84 CEM, ms notes, interview with F. Acland, 14 Apr. 1913, CEMP. For another interesting Liberal prosuffrage analysis of the prospects, see P.W. Wilson, "The Future of Women's Suffrage," *Englishwoman*, June 1913, which, despite avowing loyalty to Asquith, describes the PM as the only important anti in the cabinet, and explains his antisuffrage views as "an accident." The women's vote, Wilson predicts, will inevitably come because it is now inseparable from other important and inevitable Liberal democratic reforms, such as general franchise reform and Home Rule for Wales and Scotland.

85 Harrison,"Women's Suffrage at Westminster, 1866–1928", 98–105, seems to hold that all the women suffragists had to do to get the Liberal party in unity with them was to declare for an adult suffrage measure, and that Asquith himself would then have gladly come on side. Although Harrison mentions the NU, he does a poor job of distin-

guishing their policies from those of the WSPU, and seems ignorant of the support the NU readily accorded to the adult suffrage amendment proposed for the abortive government Reform Bill; see above, pp. 143–4, 179–80, 190–2, 242–3, 260. See also Harrison's more recent *Prudent Revolutionaries*, 23, for a similar argument.

86 CEM, faint ms notes, n.d., headed "Sir E. Grey," CEMP. These notes, which may be for a letter, but are probably for an interview, can confidently be assigned to the second half of 1913, in part because of a crossed-out marginal note reading, "I think if we have a Pil[grimage] next year we shall have to ask you to come and take part in it."

CHAPTER TWELVE

1 R[ose] C. to CEM, 12 Sept. 1913; Kathryn Oliver to CEM, 4, 13 Sept. 1913, CEMP.

2 CEM made a list of events and concerts that would be on in London, Oct.-Dec. 1913, list n.d., CEMP, suggesting that she originally planned to return sooner; but CEM, ms draft of letter to Grey, 16 Oct. 1913, CEMP, says definitely that she will not be in the south again before January; see also CEM to Reynolds, 10 Oct. 1913, CEMP.

3 NU executive, 5 June 1913, Fawcett Lib.

4 Sheepshanks to B. Russell, n.d. [end March 1913], BRA.

5 Sheepshanks to CEM, n.d. [c. Dec. 1913], CEMP.

6 CEM, ms draft letter to Sheepshanks, n.d., CEMP.

7 M. Chaytor and J. Lewis, introduction to Clark, *Working Life of Women in the Seventeenth Century*, which also contains an interesting analysis in the light of recent feminist scholarship; Davis, "'Women's History' in Transition"; S. Holton, *Feminism and Democracy*, 81, 171 n. 30.

8 Oliver to CEM, 13 September 1913, CEMP. Oliver seems to have moved temporarily with Sheepshanks into a large house in Rutland Gardens. The passage is worth quoting as a naive (and offensive) attempt by a young socialist feminist to address the servant issue; she told Catherine, "personally I don't much like it – I prefer humbler houses. Fortunately all the servants are away except one very elderly housemaid. Poor old thing! She is rather a politician – a tory – I asked why. 'Because all the gentry are conservative'!! 'But you are not the gentry' I said playfully 'how dare you ape the manners of the great?' She didn't understand me – and she is too old to attempt to educate. I can quite understand the employing and the parasitic class being conservative; it is very natural but I simply can't understand Labour [sic] backing and supporting its exploiters – its [sic] pitiful because it demonstrates the slave soul."

9 Clark to CEM, 3 Aug. 1913, CEMP.

10 Sheepshanks to CEM, n.d. [c. Dec. 1913], CEMP. Sheepshanks's apologetic attitude to her request for quiet at night seems curious in juxtaposition to her treatment of punctuality not as an important courtesy but as an absolute principle.

11 Schwimmer to her mother, Feb., Mar. 1914, Schwimmer-Lloyd Collection, Schwimmer Papers, NYPL, research and translation by Edith Wynner. We owe a great deal of information about domestic life at 1 Barton Street to Schwimmer, who wrote to her mother describing in detail the daily routine, the food, and the accommodation when she stayed with Sheepshanks first at Cheyne Walk and then in Barton Street.

12 NU executive, 23 May 1913, Fawcett Lib. Royden's plan met with some opposition; the Surrey, Sussex and Hants federation stated its disapproval in a resolution (the grounds are not on record), NU executive, 2 Oct. 1913, Fawcett Lib., also in CEMP.

13 For the "suffragists' home" postcard, see illustration.

14 Mackenzie had also had the strain of caring for a sick mother earlier in 1913, Mackenzie to CEM, 7 May 1913, CEMP.

15 Crookenden to CEM, "Monday," CEMP. The letter is signed "Yours affec^{ly}, Crookie."

16 Mackenzie to CEM, 20 Nov. 1913, CEMP. Before the end of the year Mackenzie was again on sick leave, having her tonsils out, Mackenzie to CEM, 28 Nov. 1913, CEMP.

17 Schwimmer to her mother, Mar. 1914, SLC.

18 "To clean at Eastman's," 24 Aug. 1913; Eastman and Son Ltd., Dyers and Cleaners, to CEM, 24 Sept. 1913, CEMP.

19 Whitaker Meredith, court dressmaker, to CEM, 29 Aug., 20 Oct. 1913, CEMP.

20 See e.g. NU executive, n.d. [16 Oct. 1913], referring to arrangements for the coming council in Newcastle, CEMP.

21 Bill from Madame Etel, 3 May 1913, CEMP. Advertisements in CC suggest that a smart but unexceptional new hat could easily cost between 6 and 7 guineas (£6 " 6 to £7 " 7, more than Margaret Robertson earned in two weeks, and about ten times what Catherine paid to have her hat made over). It is hard to estimate comparative prices without a battery of technology, which still might leave us with little feel for the reality. A rough and ready indication may be based on our knowledge of pay. The NU paid its beginning organizers £1 (20 shillings) or 30/- (30 shillings) a week, rising to £100 p.a. when training was complete; Robertson, as chief organizer, received an annual salary of about £150 (150 pounds). One pound (written £1 or 20/-) = 20 shillings; 12 pence (now officially called "old pence" to distin-

guish them from the new decimal coinage) = one shilling. Sixpence was written 6d, one shilling and sixpence was generally written 1/6, but a larger sum would be written thus: £2 " 3 " 9 (two pounds, three shillings and ninepence); readers may not want to be further confused by a lesson on farthings and halfpence. A useful book for getting a feel (by immersion) for the purchasing power of money for necessities is Meacham, *A Life Apart;* see also Reeves, *Round about a Pound a Week.*

22 CEM to F. Acland, 28 Aug. 1913, copy in CEMP.

23 CEM, ms notes, "Keswick Week," 1 to 6 Sept., and "Marathon Race," 3 Sept., CEMP.

24 J. Walbrand Evans to CEM, 3 Sept. 1913, CEMP.

25 CEM, "Women's Suffrage and the Next General Election," *Englishwoman*, Aug. 1913.

26 E. Acland, "Prospects of a Government Suffrage Measure," *Englishwoman*, July 1913.

27 Catherine meant what we should now describe as a Liberal "minority government."

28 CEM, "Women's Suffrage," *Englishwoman*, Aug. 1913.

CHAPTER THIRTEEN

1 Alice Clark to "Dear Madam" (secretaries of societies and federations, and to organisers, with copies to the executive), headed "*M.P.'s in the country*", 7 Oct. 1913, CEMP.

2 *CC*, 5 Sept. 1913.

3 Alberti, *Beyond Suffrage*, 11. Alberti also cites CEM to Charles Trevelyan, 26 Sept. 1913, responding to a letter in which he had described her activities as "parliamentary intrigue and badgering MPs and Ministers." I have not seen the original, which is in Trevelyan papers, Newcastle University Library.

4 HMS wrote privately in Nov. 1912, "I don't trust him. I get horribly depressed at having to use such a man. I can't get over the nausea at having to treat him more or less as a friend"; quoted in *I Have Been Young*, 215, and see 211–20, passim.

5 CEM to LG, 12 Oct. 1913, LG/C/10/1/20. Henry George's *Progress and Poverty*, 1880, advocating a yearly land value tax, has been called "one of the dozen most influential books written in the nineteenth century," Douglas, "'God Gave the Land to the People'" (a useful short article on the land question), 149. Land reform had been the subject of serious study ever since the 1880s. As CEM's correspondence indicates, the new land policy had two prongs. One involved the setting up of a Ministry of Land, with extensive powers to register land and

regulate many areas of ownership, tenancy, and employment on landed estates. The second dealt with agricultural housing, and with ways of assisting and putting pressure on landlords to increase the supply of acceptable cottages. The proposals dealt only with rural landholding, to be followed by a second stage which would tackle urban issues, Douglas, "'God Gave,'" 158–9; Hobhouse, *Inside*, 147–8.

6   Rowland, *David Lloyd George*, 269. Unfortunately Rowland does not give his source for this suggestion.

7   Ts "Mr. Lloyd George and Women's Suffrage. Chances in the Next Parliament: *Manchester Guardian*, Oct. 24th, 1913," LG/C/36/1/18.

8   Ts "Mr. Lloyd George and Women's Suffrage: North-Eastern Daily News, 8th Nov. 1913", LG/C/36/1/20.

9   *Jus Suffragii*, 1 Dec. 1913.

10   CEM, rough ms draft for letter to F. Acland, 4 Nov. 1913, CEMP.

11   KDC to CEM, 9 Nov. 1913, CEMP.

12   CEM to Simon, 8 Oct. 1913, copy, CEMP. She made the legible ms copy preserved here from rough notes which she had kept.

13   Simon to CEM, 11 Oct. 1913, CEMP.

14   "Deputation to Sir John Simon held at the Manchester Liberal Federation Offices. November 12th, 1913," transcript, CEMP. The journalists were George Armstrong, of the northern edition of the *Daily News and Leader*, who was emerging at this time as a committed supporter of women's suffrage, and Brockway of the *Labour Leader*. See an exchange of letters between Armstrong and CEM, 9–12 Oct. 1913, about a suffrage speech he made to a Young Liberals' meeting; he agreed reluctantly, and only because the Young Liberals would not accept a woman speaker, CEMP.

15   CEM, ms "Notes for Dep. to Sir John Simon, Manchester, Nov. 12 1913," CEMP. Although Simon was generally liked, not all his colleagues would have agreed with every detail of Catherine's flattering description. Hobhouse, e.g., thought Simon "a most attractive personality," but saw him as possessed of "boundless ambition ... and though he will not advocate principles in which he does not believe, he will certainly push aside those in which he was trained, if they happen to stand in the way of political advancement," *Inside*, 229–30. Simon was to risk his career in 1916 by resigning on the conscription issue; but he later thought his decision had been the wrong one, Simon, *Retrospect*, 106–8.

16   CEM, ms "Notes for Dep[utation] to Sir John Simon, Manchester, Nov. 12 1913," CEMP, all emphases are in the original. The probability is that this is a copy, and that the notes were sent to the deputation; however, we have no hard evidence that they were put to the intended use.

17 "Deputation to Sir John Simon ... November 12th, 1913," CEMP; NU executive, 4 Dec. 1913, Fawcett Lib.

18 C.P. Scott to CEM, 13 Nov. 1913, CEMP.

19 Mackenzie to CEM, 28 Nov. 1913, CEMP.

20 "Deputation to Sir John Simon ... November 12th, 1913," CEMP.

21 Simon to Mackenzie, copy, n.d., enclosed with Mackenzie to CEM, 28 Nov. 1913, CEMP.

22 CEM to Simon, 5 Feb. 1914, copy; Simon to CEM, 6 Feb. 1914, CEMP.

23 CEM (from Hawse End) to Sir E. Grey, 16 Oct. 1913, ms copy, referring to a letter from Grey dated 16 Aug.; CEM, rough ms notes "To Sir E. Grey," n.d., probably c. 10 Aug. 1913, CEMP.

24 CEM to F. Acland, 17 Oct. 1913, ms copy, CEMP. The suffragists have been accused (see, e.g., Alberti, *Beyond Suffrage*, 11) of being so much absorbed by the cause that they were oblivious of major public events, and Catherine has been unfavourably compared in this respect to Beatrice Webb and Kate, Lady Courtney, whose comments, however, were preserved in private diaries. Catherine did not leave a diary, and little of her private correspondence has survived; and she generally kept her public political comments focused narrowly on suffrage, a necessary precaution to avoid controversy within the NU, let alone obloquy outside it. It would have been completely out of character for Catherine to be ignorant of or uninterested in foreign affairs at so critical a period (nor would she ever have gone to see Grey without showing herself familiar with his likely current interests, as she did with land reform when writing to Lloyd George). But, like Bertrand Russell, she had grown up in an optimistic liberal climate, and believed progress towards a rational governance of international affairs was in fact much more advanced than it proved to be.

25 F. Acland to CEM, 29 Oct. [1913]; see also F. Acland to CEM, 18 Oct. 1913; for Catherine's attempts to meet with Grey see also Grey to CEM, 22 Oct. 1913; "Extract from letter to Mr. Acland" from Grey, 21 Oct. 1913; CEM to Grey, 27 Oct. 1913, ms marked "Copy. (2nd.)" (another draft or copy is also present), CEMP.

26 CEM to Grey, 27 Oct. 1913, ms marked "Copy. (2nd.)," CEMP. Grey's Berwick speech was reported in the *Scotsman*, 28 Oct. 1913, with the stress laid on Grey's comment on the impossibility of initiating a government measure in a divided cabinet.

27 Copy of part of letter, Mrs Mott (Stafford) to Mackenzie, 18 Aug. 1913, sent to CEM; CEM, ms notes "For Sir J. Simon," [Feb. 1914?] CEMP.

28 Extract (typed) from *MG*, 28 Nov. 1913; *MG*, 10 Dec. 1913, clipping; CEM, ms note, n.d., CEMP.

29 Copy of letter, Lord Haldane to Northern Men's Federation for WS, 6 Nov. 1913, CEMP.

30 CEM to F. Acland, 4 Nov. 1913, ms copy, incomplete, CEMP.

31 Fawcett gave these figures in her opening address to the council, Report, *CC*, 14 Nov. 1913.

32 Newcastle council, "Agenda," annotated by CEM, CEMP; "Proceedings," Fawcett Lib.; Report, *CC*, 14 Nov. 1913.

33 F. Acland to CEM, 9 Nov. 1913, CEMP.

34 NU executive, 4 Dec. 1913, Fawcett Lib.

35 KDC to CEM, 17 Nov. 1913, CEMP.

36 Ibid. In their view, the proposal did nothing to commit the government, left Liberal candidates free to take whatever line they liked (or none) in the coming election, would leave the PM or those who wanted something from him as free as ever to manipulate the situation, and was not at all the way other important measures were treated ("What would you think of such a method of procedure for Home Rule, Land Reform or any other Liberal measure?" Courtney asked Wilson), KDC to Wilson, ts partial draft/copy, 17 Nov., with KDC to CEM, 17 Nov. 1913, CEMP.

37 E. Acland to KDC, 21 Nov. 1913; see also E. Acland to CEM, 20 Nov.; CEM notes of a letter to E. Acland [illeg.] Nov. 1913, CEMP.

38 KDC to CEM, 17 Nov. 1913, CEMP. CEM's illness after Newcastle evidently hung on for long enough for news of it to reach friends and relatives; see KDC to CEM, 9, 17, 23 Nov.; A. Clark to CEM, 20 Nov.; Mackenzie to CEM, 11, 20 Nov.; Leaf to CEM 28[?] Nov.; "Sheila" [a cousin] to "Tartie," 7 Dec. 1913, CEMP. Even before the Newcastle meeting she had been prescribed a tonic, and had been trying to get an appointment with a travelling "bonesetter" from Aspatria (Cumberland), perhaps because of the sprained wrist, Mary Wilson to CEM, 17, 20 Oct. 1913; "Tonic prescribed by Dr. Burnett," 29 Oct. 1913, CEMP.

39 CEM to R. Cecil, 24 Nov. 1913, draft, CEMP; *CC*, 5, 12 Dec. 1913; and see below, pp. 302–3.

40 Alice Low to CEM, 25 Nov. 1913.

41 Grey to CEM, 31 Oct. 1913; correspondence between Grey's secretary and CEM, 28 Nov.–4 Dec., 14 Dec. 1913; KDC to CEM, 23 Nov. 1913, CEMP.

42 There are a number of scribbled notes in CEM's handwriting, marked "Sir E. Grey," n.d., but clearly of this period, CEMP. Except where otherwise noted, my account of what she had to say to Grey is derived (sometimes extrapolated) from a five-page series (to which one or two other scraps are attached), headed "Notes of private interview with Sir E. Grey, Dec. 15, '13," which form something of a coherent sequence, although there is some repetition, probably resulting from Catherine's habit of summarizing the points she wished to make, so that she could have them up front. Her notes are even more than

usually full of abbreviations, although familiarity with Catherine's style (and handwriting) makes it possible to gain a clear sense of what she said; accordingly, I have given only a few short passages in direct speech, but have kept close to the text in my report.

43 CEM, "The Labour and Woman Suffrage Entente," *LL*, 28 Aug. 1913, and ms drafts in CEMP; for further reference to this article, see below, pp. 294–6.

44 Beatrice ("Mrs. Sidney") Webb, Introduction, *New Statesman*, "Special Supplement on The Awakening of Women," ed. Mrs Sidney Webb, 1 Nov. 1913. In a striking passage, Webb comments on the race and class prejudice, as well as the obvious sex prejudice, shown in Sir Almroth Wright's *Unexpurgated Case against Women's Suffrage*, and reproduces a section of Wright's text, inserting "only the words necessary to show how easy it is to use all the arguments in favour of the dominance of the male sex as reasons for a similar dominance of a class of property owners or a white race." Particular thanks to Margaret Kamester for bringing this article to my attention.

45 NU executive, 18 Dec. 1913, Fawcett Lib.

46 Ibid.

47 CEM, "Notes of private interview with Sir E. Grey," CEMP.

48 NU executive, 18 Dec. 1913, Fawcett Lib.

49 CEM, "Notes of private interview with Sir E. Grey." A few months previously, CEM had told the NU executive that "the Marconi affair had had one bad effect on the prospects of Women's Suffrage. It had apparently brought about a renewal of the alliance between Mr. Lloyd George and Mr. Churchill." NU executive, 3 July 1913, Fawcett Lib.

50 Clark to CEM, n.d. [Dec. 1913], CEMP.

51 See, *inter alia*, Ensor, *England*, 474–5.

52 NU executive, 18 Dec. 1913, Fawcett Lib.

53 For Harcourt's antisuffragism, see Harrison, *Separate Spheres*, 165, 167; CEM, ms notes, "To ask Mr. Acland," n.d., CEMP.

54 NU executive, 18 Dec. 1913, Fawcett Lib.

55 KDC to CEM, 23 Nov. 1913, CEMP. "Come out" here meant "come out in the open," not "resign from the cabinet."

56 CEM., "Women's Suffrage and the Next General Election."

57 See, *inter alia*, CEM to R. Cecil, 24 Nov., ms draft; Clark to federation secretaries, 20 Oct.; Harrison to CEM, 23 Oct.; Dixon to CEM, 23 Oct.; Walford to Knight, 3 Nov.; P. Strachey to Clark, 8, 11 Nov.; Samuels to CEM, 19 Nov. 1913, CEMP.

58 For Lady Selborne, see Jalland, *Women, Marriage and Politics*, 237–41; for education campaign, see below, pp. 298, 473n.80.

59 CEM, ms notes of letter to Lady Selborne, 11 Oct. 1913.

60 M. Selborne to CEM, 15 Oct. [1913], CEMP.

61 CEM to Lady Selborne, 15 Oct. 1913, ms copy, CEMP.

62 M. Selborne to CEM, 18 Oct. 1913, CEMP.

63 CEM, ms notes of letter to Lady Selborne, 20 Oct. 1913, CEMP.

64 F. Acland to CEM, 9 Nov. [1913], CEMP.

65 NU executive, 18 Dec. 1913, Fawcett Lib.

66 M. Selborne to CEM, 18 Nov. 1913; Mackenzie to CEM, 8 Dec. 1913. Catherine's mail was opened in the NU office before it was forwarded, in case there was something urgent, and in order to channel the work to Alice Clark; but in this case Mackenzie was probably returning a batch of correspondence which Catherine had sent for Courtney to see. Other evidence exists that a high degree of confidentiality existed among the officers and included the secretaries, and that things might at times be shared among this inner circle that could not be brought yet to the executive or committees.

67 CEM to Lady Selborne, ms draft or copy, 13 Nov. 1913, CEMP; S. Holton, *Feminism and Democracy*, 122.

68 *Nation*, 22 Nov. 1913, clipping enclosed in Mackenzie to CEM, 25 Nov. 1913.

69 See Dora Mellone, hon. sec., Northern Committee of the Irishwomen's Suffrage Federation, in *CC*, 19 Sept. 1913.

70 R. Cecil to CEM, 25 Sept. 1913, CEMP. CEM's letter to Cecil is not present, but its content can be inferred from his to her.

71 R. Cecil to CEM, 19 Nov. 1913, CEMP.

72 CEM to R. Cecil, 24 Nov. 1913, ms draft, CEMP.

73 Ibid.

74 NU executive, 18 Dec. 1913, Fawcett Lib. For comments by Alice Clark on the complicated general election outlook, see NU executive, 4 Dec. 1913, Fawcett Lib.

75 Jalland, *Women, Marriage and Politics*, passim; for the socialization of girls, Lewis, *Women in England*, 75–141; Dyhouse, *Girls Growing Up in Late Victorian and Edwardian England*, passim; F. Hunt, ed., *Lessons for Life*, passim; Vicinus, *Independent Women*, ch. 5.

76 Jalland, *Women*, provides a great deal of material which illuminates this point, but does not herself develop it.

77 Koss, *Asquith*, 5. For the male sense of superiority, see also Thompson, *The Edwardians*, 253–5; for reinforcement by the Anglican church, Fletcher, *Maude Royden*, esp. ch. 7, 132–55.

78 D. Morgan, *Suffragists and Liberals*, 117, 87–90; Blewett, "The Franchise in the U.K.," 54; for a useful statistical analysis of the economic and social character of the House of Commons, see Thomas, *The House of Commons 1906–1911*. Churchill was still declaring himself a "friend" to the "ladies" in late 1913, notes, M. Mackenzie, n.d. [c. Nov. 1913], CEMP.

79 Jalland, *Women*, 268–72.

80 The campaign aimed at facilitating public lectures, making appropriate readings available, and generally encouraging discussion. No one political or legislative program was to be promoted, but it was hoped to raise the level of awareness and knowledge of all aspects of the question, and, as Catherine said "Show that *something wants doing*, and by women. ... We can't pretend to speak for all classes of women; they must all have power to voice their own experience and needs, so that these may be taken into account in framing legislation." NU, Exeter council, 23 May 1913, various notes, including "Resolution," CEMP; NU executive, 3, 31 July 1913, Fawcett Lib.; "Suggestions for carrying out education campaign," n.d.; other material, 1913–14, CEMP. In 1915, Catherine and others tried to get the NU to initiate a similar education campaign on the subject of peace.

81 CEM, "The Labour and Women Suffrage Entente," *LL* 28 Aug. 1913; ms drafts, n.d., CEMP. Quite concrete evidence of the truth of Catherine's accusations of a deliberate attempt to sow doubt remains in clippings from papers hostile to WS, which suggest difficulties between suffragists and labour: the wording is almost identical in all of them, CEMP.

82 B. Taylor, *Eve and the New Jerusalem*, xv, and passim.

83 Robertson to CEM, 1 Sept. 1913, CEMP.

84 See, e.g., A. Morgan, *J. Ramsay MacDonald*, 56–7.

85 MacDonald to CEM, n.d. [dated by CEM, 21 Oct. 1913], CEMP. MacDonald's agent in Leicester had made an attempt, just before MacDonald left, to meet with Robertson (away on holiday) or Catherine (unable to travel south) on some unspecified matter "that I have his [Macdonald's] permission to consult you about," but seems to have declined to meet with Clark, copies of A.H. Reynolds to Robertson, 4 Oct.; A. Clark to Reynolds, 6 Oct.; Reynolds to Clark, 7 Oct. 1913, CEMP.

86 NU executive, 19 Feb. 1914, Fawcett Lib. Macmillan, however, argued that a private bill brought forward by a party would not be the same as the discredited private member's bill.

87 A.C[lark] to CEM, n.d. [c. Dec. 1913], badly damaged, CEMP.

88 Philip Snowden, "The Present Position of Woman Suffrage," *Englishwoman*, Dec. 1913.

89 Evans to CEM, 4 Oct. 1913, CEMP.

90 "The Election Fighting Fund," uncorrected proof copy, ns, "for December 27" [1912], marked "not printed," CEMP.

91 For the relationship between the NU and the ILP, see, *inter alia*, NU executive, 17 Oct. 1912, 19 Dec. 1912; EFF, 20 Dec. 1912, Fawcett Lib.; CEM, ms notes, apparently on a conversation with Clementina Gor-

don, organizer for the North-East Federation, 26 May [1913], CEMP. The machinery for giving financial support to ILP candidates at by-elections differed from that of the Labour party; while the latter insisted on funding going direct to the candidate (in order, it seems, to distance itself from the process), the ILP did not allow donations direct to the candidate, so that support had to go through the head office.

92 "The Election Fighting Fund,"[1912], CEMP.

93 Clementina Black, editing the *CC* at the time, sent the first letter to CEM, asking her to reply, Black to CEM 10 Mar. 1913; R. Cooper, n.d.; R. Cooper 4 Apr. 1913, CEMP.

94 CEM, ms notes, headed "T.U. Congress," n.d. [c. 30 Apr. 1913], CEMP; Hilda Oldham to Mackenzie, 28 May 1913, CEMP; *CC*, 5 Sept. 1913.

95 NU executive, 15 May; 31 July 1913, Fawcett Lib.

96 CEM, ms notes, headed "T.U. Congress," n.d. [c. 30 Apr. 1913]; Robertson to CEM. 29 May 1913, CEMP; see also S. Holton, *Feminism and Democracy*, 99.

97 NU executive, 5 June 1913. References to the special campaign among the miners abound in NU executive minutes, in *CC*, and in leaflets issued by the NU throughout 1913 and 1914, and in correspondence in CEMP.

98 Peters to CEM, 2 Sept. 1913, CEMP.

99 Robertson to CEM, 18 Sept. 1913; Evans to CEM, 8 Sept. 1913, CEMP; NU executive, 18 Sept. 1913, Fawcett Lib.; Hannam, *Isabella Ford*, esp. chs. 3–5.

100 M. Robertson, "Democracy and Women's Suffrage Again," *CC*, 12 Sept. 1913; NU executive, 18 Sept. 1913, Fawcett Lib.; Evans to CEM, 9 Sept. 1913; n.d. [c. 16 Sept. 1913], CEMP.

101 Robertson to "Cruel woman!" [CEM], 18 Sept. 1913; Evans to CEM, 8 Sept. 1913, CEMP.

102 *CC*, 17 October 1913.

103 Evans to CEM, 10 Oct. 1913, CEMP. Of Smillie, Evans (NU secretary) said, "Mr. Smillie [was] the strongest, hasn't he come on? Miss Robertson again I suspect, is there anyone like her on that special field of work? I have a tremendous admiration for her." Unfortunately the admiration was not reciprocated; Robertson had a low opinion of Evans's work, an opinion not shared by Clark or Courtney, or in all probablility by Catherine. I have found Evans's accounts of events, meetings, and so on clear and succinct.

104 Robertson to CEM, 1 Sept. 1913, CEMP.

105 Evans to CEM, 10 Oct. 1913, CEMP.

106 *CC*, 17 Oct. 1913.

107 Evans to CEM, n.d. [c. Oct. 1913]; Robertson to CEM, 29 May 1913; [Holden] to CEM, 3 June 1913, CEMP.

108 CEM, draft letter to Lord Robert Cecil, 24 Nov. 1913, these pages marked "much abbreviated," CEMP.

109 For brief accounts of this election, see S. Holton, *Feminism and Democracy*, 110–11; McKibbin, *Evolution*, 68–71.

110 *Jus Suffragii*, 1 Dec. 1913; Evans to CEM, 30 Oct. 1913, CEMP; NU special executive, 3 Nov. 1913, Fawcett Lib.

111 Evans to CEM, 30 Oct. 1913, CEMP; McKibbin, *Evolution*, 69.

112 Unidentified typescript apparently part of NU executive, 20 Nov. 1913, Fawcett Lib.

113 NU special executive, 3 Nov. 1913, Fawcett Lib.; NU council, Newcastle, 6 Nov. 1913, EFF urgency resolution, Fawcett Lib.

114 *LL*, 13 Nov. 1913.

115 Clark to CEM, 18 Nov. 1913; KDC to CEM, 9 Nov. 1913, CEMP; NU executive, 20 Nov. 1913, first version, Fawcett Lib.

116 Clark, letter, *LL*, 20 Nov. 1913; Robertson, "Women Help Labour," *LL*, 20 Nov.; Clark to CEM, 18 Nov.; KDC to CEM, 17 Nov.; CEM, ms notes "Reply to Wake: Lab Leader, Nov. 13," CEMP.

117 *CC*, 14 Nov. 1913.

118 Williams to CEM, 26 Nov. 1913, CEMP; S. Holton, *Feminism and Democracy*, 111.

119 KDC to CEM, 23 Nov. 1913; Clark to CEM, 28 Nov. 1913, CEMP.

120 KDC to CEM, 23 Nov. 1913, CEMP.

121 Clark to CEM, 28 Nov. 1913, CEMP. Of incidental interest is Clark's view, radical in its time, and still a focus of difficult discussion in feminist organizations, that "I don't think we ought to make a difference between paid and unpaid office. I don't see that I am any less the servant of the committee than M.R. – and we don't want to make that distinction – it is far better for M.R. to bring us her ideas as she has them and hear the discussion on them and either convince us or be convinced."

122 M. Robertson and C. Gordon to CEM, 25 Nov. 1913, CEMP.

123 Ashton to CEM, 26 Nov. 1913, CEMP; see also S. Holton, *Feminism and Democracy*, 110–11.

124 CEM note on her reply to an earlier letter from Robertson and Gordon (not extant), written on the bottom of Robertson and Gordon to CEM, 25 Nov. 1913, CEMP.

125 Robertson and Gordon welcomed her visit; see their letter to CEM, 25 Nov. 1913.

126 NU executive, 20 Nov. 1913, Fawcett Lib.

127 NU executive, 4 Dec. 1913, Fawcett Lib.

128 NU executive, 18 Dec. 1913, Fawcett Lib.

129 Ibid.

130 Robertson to CEM, 10 Dec. 1913; Gordon to CEM, 10 Dec. 1913, CEMP; S. Holton, *Feminism and Democracy*, 110.

131 *CC*, 19 Dec. 1913; "Particulars of E.F.F. Bye-Elections" n.d. [c. Mar. 1914], MPL/M50/2/10/34.

132 NU executive, 18 Dec. 1913, Fawcett Lib.

133 The Labour lists are in CEMP (handwritten addenda are not in CEM's writing and seem to have been written by a secretary); a number of references to the TU lists can be found in CEMP and in executive minutes; the Liberal lists have "Private and Confidential" written on them in CEM's hand, and were probably sent by Catherine to Lloyd George in the course of correspondence she had with him in the summer of 1914, LG/C/17/26–27.

134 See, e.g., NU executive, 20 Feb. 1913, Fawcett Lib.

CHAPTER FOURTEEN

1 M. Mackenzie to CEM, 20 Nov. 1913; KDC to CEM, 9 Nov. 1913, CEMP; NU executive, 15 Jan.; special executive, 24 Jan.; executive 5 Feb. 1914, Fawcett Lib.

2 Philippa Strachey to MGF, dated 1 Jan. 1913, but probably 1 Jan. 1914, Fawcett Lib.

3 Above, pp. 81–5, 94, 422n.33. London, it will be remembered, had shown little interest, and had sent no representatives to the first federal council in Keswick.

4 "Present Position of the London Society and its Branches," printed with covering letter from Ray Strachey, n.d.; LSWS, list of candidates for election to LSWS executive, for 14 Nov. 1913 annual meeting; LSWS, "Annual Meeting: Adjourned Business," together with "Mode of Procedure at the Meeting," for 15 Dec. 1913; KDC to CEM, 23 Nov. 1913, CEMP; *CC*, 21, 28 Nov. 1913.

5 [A. Helen Ward] to CEM, 7 Dec. 1913, CEMP. The letter is badly damaged and the signature missing; the correspondent has been identified from the address, which appears on a list of NU speakers.

6 LSWS, "Adjourned Business," CEMP.

7 [Ward] to CEM, 7 Dec. 1913, CEMP.

8 "Present Position" and covering letter, CEMP.

9 Ibid. There was to be a quarterly London council composed of elected members from all branches – although its role would only be advisory to the executive; and local branches were to have the freedom to affiliate directly to the NU if they thought that would better suit their needs.

10 [Ward] to CEM, 7 Dec. 1913, CEMP. Ward admitted, "I have reason to believe that some whose general opinions and character I deeply respect, as well as a section of irresponsible 'malcontents' hold that the London Society's system is effete, and that it is a positive obstacle

... in the path of the N.U. ... I know often we must appear reactionary and obstinate. ... But the work grows and flourishes amazingly."
Ray Strachey and others in "the young set of University and N.U.
women they represent," she claimed, had all previously been among
the critics and those who thought the solution lay in federation, "but
... a year or two's hard work in London as local secretaries and suchlike
has changed their view." Ray (married to Oliver Strachey, thirteen
years her senior) does seem somewhat different by this time from the
unconventional, adventurous young Ray Costelloe who came to
Keswick with the suffrage caravan in 1908.

11 Resolutions and preliminary material relating to LSWS AGM, 10 Nov.
1908, CEMP.

12 "No one," wrote Ward, "who does not face organisation problems
in London has any conception of the embarrassments of the Militants
and Pseudo Militants, the Actresses F[ranchise] L[eague], the
Church League, the Men's Political Union, Miss [?] Broadhurst, the Tax
Resisters, the Freedom League, the New Constitutional. These
flood the 'social' suffrage life of London, the Clubs, the At Homes and
suchlike, and they all, or nearly all, misunderstand and misrepre-
sent the London Society." [Ward] to CEM, 7 Dec. 1913, CEMP.

13 Ibid.; M.I. Corbett Ashby et al. [ten signatories, including Courtney, Swanwick and Royden] to "Dear Madam," December 1913 [op-
posing the proposal]; twenty-eight local committees of the LSWS to
"Dear Sir or Madam," 9 Dec. 1913 [supporting the LSWS executive];
LSWS executive to "Dear Sir or Madam," 3 Dec. 1913. Signed by
seventeen members of the committee; this purports to come from "the
Executive Committee elected on November 24th.," but makes no
mention of the minority view of Royden and H.F.A. Fyffe, another dissenting member, whose signatures are absent, but are on the Corbett Ashby letter, CEMP. Bad feeling ran so high at one point that the
LSWS executive wrote a letter complaining about "a private conversation which had taken place in Miss Clark's house on the subject of
the reorganization," which Kathleen Courtney read at the NU executive of 18 Dec. The NU executive, appropriately enough, brought
protocol to its defence, minuting coldly that it "felt that a private
conversation of this nature was not a matter which could be discussed
by the Executive Committee of the National Union."

14 NU executive, 18 Dec. 1913, Fawcett Lib.

15 [Ward] to CEM, 7 Dec. 1913, CEMP.

16 M.I. Corbett Ashby et al. to "Dear Madam," Dec. 1913, CEMP.

17 CC, 19 Dec. 1913, 20 Feb. 1914.

18 The NU made as much capital as possible of this refusal, which is doc-
umented in an exchange between MGF and Asquith, enclosed with

a letter to "Dear Sir" [to go to MPs?], 14 Feb. 1914; and in correspondence between Elsie Inglis and Asquith, 24–8 Jan. 1914, CEMP; see
also NU executive 15 Jan., 5 Feb. 1914. Inglis specifically asked that
Asquith receive a deputation of men's groups, not of women's suffrage groups, but Asquith merely claimed that his views were known.

19 Fletcher, *Maude Royden*, 100; Royden, *Our Common Humanity*, NU
pamphlet; Louise Creighton, *Women's Suffrage*, NU pamphlet; *CC*,
20 Feb. 1914. Louise Creighton also spoke; the widow of a former
Bishop of London, she was a supporter of the feminist movement within
the church (although, unlike Royden, she did not go as far as advocating the priesthood of women).

20 *CC*, 20 Feb. 1914; Mackenzie to CEM, 2 Apr. 1914, CEMP.

21 Evans to CEM, 27 Nov. 1913; A.C[lark] to CEM, n.d. [c. Dec. 1913], damaged, CEMP.

22 NU special executive, 24 Jan. 1914, Fawcett Lib.

23 *LL*, 22 Jan.; NU special executive, 24 Jan. 1914, Fawcett Lib.

24 Ibid.

25 NU special executive, 24 Jan. 1914, Fawcett Lib.

26 *CC*, 23 Jan. 1914, quoted in NU special executive, 24 Jan. 1914, Fawcett
Lib.

27 NU special executive, 24 Jan. 1914, Fawcett Lib.

28 Ibid.

29 Ibid.

30 NU special executive, 24 Jan. 1914; NU executive, 5 Feb. 1914,
Fawcett Lib.

31 NU executive, 5 Feb. 1914, Fawcett Lib.

32 NU special executive, 24 Jan. 1914; NU executive, 5 Feb. 1914, Fawcett
Lib.; *CC*, 30 Jan. 1914; *LL*, 5 Feb. 1914.

33 NU executive, 5 Feb. 1914; ILP NAC minutes, 26 Jan. 1914, BLP/MISC/
464/1/7/ILP. This last is the first substantial mention of the EFF that
I found in the NAC minutes. It is interesting to find the EFF described
in a recent work as "the Socialist wing of the suffrage movement"
– not a description that would have appealed to Fawcett or a good many
of her colleagues, however much some others might have secretly
relished it, A. Morgan, *J. Ramsay MacDonald*, 56.

34 NU executive, 5 Feb. 1914, Fawcett Lib.

35 CEM to W.C. Anderson, 8 June 1914, copy, CEMP.

36 *LL*, 5 Feb. 1914.

37 NU executive, 5 Feb. 1914, Fawcett Lib.

38 CEM to Macmillan, 6 Apr.; Macmillan to CEM, 8 Apr.; CEM to Macmillan, 20 Apr. 1914, CEMP.

39 NU executive, 5 Feb. 1914, Fawcett Lib.

40 NU executive, 5 Feb. 1914, amended 19 Feb. 1914.

41 NU executive, 5 Mar. 1914.

42 *CC* 6 Mar. 1914.

43 Cecil to CEM, 18 Feb. 1914, CEMP.

44 Quoted, NU executive, 19 Mar. 1914.

45 Except for this one major exception, I have seen Rathbone as acting appropriately on the several occasions when she was at odds with the majority of the executive; and she does not appear to have used her relative wealth manipulatively.

46 Since Eleanor Rathbone was absent, we are left to speculate as to who joined the known Rathbone committee members; it may well have been Macmillan, who stood with them on most points at the subsequent council meeting, "Proceedings of the Half-Yearly Council" 28 and 29 Apr. 1914, Fawcett Lib.

47 NU executive, 19 Mar. 1914, and corrections, NU executive, 2 Apr. 1914, Fawcett Lib.

48 NU executive, 19 Mar. 1914, Fawcett Lib.; see also *LL*, 20 Feb. 1914. For Plural Voting Bill, see above, pp. 216–18.

49 NU executive, 19 Mar. 1914, Fawcett Lib.

50 NU executive, 2 Apr. 1914, Fawcett Lib.

51 *CC*, 1 May 1914. *CC* limited its description of the event to one short paragraph, and said *nothing* about the content, except "The business was, of course, confidential."

52 NU, "Proceedings of the Half-Yearly Council held at Chelsea Town Hall," 28, 29 Apr. 1914, Fawcett Lib. Neither Cross nor Haverfield appears in the *Women's Suffrage Annual* (1913); Cross is not on the NU speakers' list (Oct. 1913); Haverfield is there shown as being from Chester. Corbett Ashby came from Surrey, but presented an amendment on this occasion "on behalf of Liverpool," while Rathbone proposed one "on behalf of Bangor."

53 NU executive, 21 May 1914.

54 Fawcett to Caroline Marshall, 1 May 1914, FMP.

55 In later writings neither Fawcett nor Ray Strachey paid any tribute to Catherine's work, and there is an almost complete absence of correspondence from that prolific letter-writer remaining in the Fawcett collection.

CHAPTER FIFTEEN

1 CEM, ms draft or copy of letter to HNB, 10 May 1914, CEMP.

2 CEM to KDC, 7 June 1914; [Crookenden?] to CEM, incomplete, 2 June 1914; the Hawse End "Manhunt" may have been played for the last time this weekend.

3 Lord R. Cecil to CEM, 26 May 1914; CEM to Lord R. Cecil, 27 May

1914; C. Macmillan, "The Empire's Need for Women's vote," *CC*, 10 July 1914; *In the Privy Council: On Appeal from the Chief Court of Lower Burma: No. 26 of 1913: Case for the Appellant*, CEMP. The case was covered in *The Times* from February on, see, e.g., 17, 19, 20, 26, 27, 28 Feb.; 8 Apr.; 15 May 1914. An unusual if not unprecedented feature was that the expenses of the civil suit were being paid by the government of Burma, which also allowed Finnie the services of the government advocate. Special thanks to Susan Shea for research on this case.

4   *Spectator*, 11 Apr.; *Nation*, 18 Apr.; *English Review*, June 1914.

5   Typed "Extract from Privy Council Record: Appeal 26 of 1913," the report of the doctor who examined Aina shortly after the incident (July 1911); CEMP. The *Case for the Appellant*, CEMP, is detailed and convincing. I have not seen the reasons given by the Privy Council for dismissing the appeal, but Catherine had the full record before her at some time, and there are typed extracts in CEMP; the appeal, and its dismissal, seem to have been on a legal technicality.

6   MGF to Wilson, 13 May 1914, ms copy; Wilson to MGF, 15 May 1914; typed "Extracts from letters from Mrs. Fawcett to Miss Marshall bearing on [the Channing Arnold case]," 10, 21, 24, 26 May, with ms notations by CEM, CEMP. Fawcett had gone along with the move in the 1870s to keep the ws movement separate from the agitation for repeal of the Contagious Diseases Acts, but she was always deeply concerned with the issue of sexual exploitation, and in 1885 had publicly supported W.T. Stead in his exposure of the traffic in young girls. In 1927 she published (with E.M. Turner) a biography of Josephine Butler. For more on Fawcett's role in the Arnold case, see Rubinstein, *A Different World for Women*, 206–7, which has only been available to me as this book goes to press. Rubenstein makes use of India Office papers which I have not consulted, and shows MGF to have been very actively involved in lobbying the India Office. See Rubinstein also for MGF's lifelong concern for the protection of children and young women.

7   CEM to MGF, 27 May 1914, copy; see also CEM to MGF, 19 May 1914; CEM to Wilson, 26 May 1914; R. Cecil to CEM, 26 May 1914; CEM to Cecil, 27 May 1914; Royden to CEM, postcard, partially in French (clearly because of the delicate nature of the topic), n.d. [June 1914]; various typed and ms notes, CEMP.

8   CEM to MGF, copy, 27 May 1913, CEMP.

9   CEM to Lytton, 26 May 1913; Lytton to CEM, 27 May 1913, CEMP.

10   Partial copy of CEM to Lytton, 28 May 1914, CEMP. See also CEM to MGF 27 May 1914, CEMP.

11   CEM to Royden, 7 June [1914], CEMP.

12   CEM to Lytton, 16 June 1914, CEMP.

13 *CC*, 8, 29 May; 5, 12 June; 10, 17 July 1914.

14 Wilson to Bramall, 29 May 1914, CEMP. The significant mention of a deputation in this letter, and a passage describing MGF as "anxious to help us get justice done in the Arnold case" (note that Wilson did not mention Fawcett's concern about what had happened to Aina, and what could be done to prevent recurrence of such abuses), were also typed up separately, presumably at Catherine's orders, suggesting to me that these were the aspects of Wilson's approach that Catherine saw as inappropriate or politically risky, and which she wanted to draw to the attention of those she consulted.

15 CEM to the Lord Bishop of London, 26 June 1914, CEMP.

16 "Reported private conversation with Lord Haldane," n.d. [18 June, 1914]; CEM to Lytton, 26 May, copy; CEM to MGF, 27 May 1914.

17 Cable, Arnold to Wilson, 30 June, copy; *CC*, 17 July; Wilson to H. Ward, 17 July 1914, CEMP.

18 MGF to CEM, 31 July [1914].

19 Lord Lytton, "Woman Suffrage: The Only Way," *Englishwoman*, Mar. 1914.

20 NU executive [7 May], CEMP; *CC*, 27 Mar.; *CC*, 8, 15 May 1914.

21 M. Lowndes, "Women's Suffrage in the House of Lords," *Englishwoman*, June 1914.

22 Hon. parl. sec.'s report to NU provincial council, 12 Nov. 1914, MPL and CEMP.

23 "Lord Lytton's Proposal for an Initiative on Women's Suffrage," marked "ABSOLUTELY CONFIDENTIAL" [7 May 1914], CEMP. See S. Holton, *Feminism and Suffrage*, 122 for a brief discussion. None of these reports was sent out to the wider circle of recipients of the executive minutes, but only to executive members.

24 Note that "Conservative" is the term frequently used in the primary documents, although "Unionist" might be more accurate.

25 "Lord Lytton's Proposal" [7 May 1914], CEMP.

26 Ibid.

27 Ibid.

28 CEM to Lytton, 10 May, copy; CEM to Brailsford, 11 May 1914, copy; "Political Situation: Lord Lytton's Proposal" [NU executive, 21 May 1914], marked "ABSOLUTELY CONFIDENTIAL: DESTROY WHEN READ," CEMP.

29 "Political Situation: Lord Lytton's Proposal" [21 May 1914], CEMP.

30 CEM to secretaries of societies and federations, n.d., and replies, 9–31 July 1914, CEMP.

31 "Speech by Mrs Humphry Ward," pamphlet, copy in CEMP. See also above, pp. 48–9. Supporters of the federal movement with whom Catherine had been in touch included Lord Henry Bentinck, Lady

Selborne, C.P. Scott, P.W. Wilson, and McKinnon Wood (secretary for Scotland).

32 NU executive [incomplete, 7 May 1914], CEMP. The term "federal" was applied to the proposed regional assemblies, not, as in Canada and the USA, to the national parliament/congress.

33 NU executive, [7 May 1914], CEMP, includes lengthy discussion both of federalism and of the Irish and Scottish Home Rule bills.

34 NU executive, "Political Situation," 18 June 1914.

35 NU executive, incomplete, 21 May, marked "Political Situation (cont), TO BE DESTROYED WHEN SUBMITTED," CEMP; CC, 15 May. Arthur Ponsonby, usually a suffragist, opposed the women's suffrage clause, explaining to Catherine that it had been divisive and had taken time from the issue of Scottish Home Rule, CEM to Ponsonby, 29 May; Ponsonby to CEM, 2 June; CEM to Ponsonby, 4 June, CEMP. The Scottish WSS were appreciative of Catherine's help, NU executive, "Political Situation," 18 June 1914, CEMP.

36 NU executive, "Political Situation," 18 June 1914, Fawcett Lib.

37 CEM to "Dear Sir," 14 May 1914, LG/C/11/144. For an interesting reflection on devolution and federalism, see H. Auerbach to CEM, 16 May 1914, CEMP.

38 See, e.g., NU, "Women's Suffrage and Federal Devolution," n.d., signed by MGF, Helena Auerbach, KDC, and CEM, enclosed with CEM to "Dear Sir," 14 May, LG/C/11/1/44. Helen Ward, currently editing the CC, reacted with horror to this statement, both on grounds of its apparent favouring of federalism, and of the way in which it might possibly weaken the wider suffrage argument, Ward to CEM, 17 May; also "Summary of Miss Ward's letter," ms, 17 May 1914, CEMP. For CEM's later position, see Vellacott, "Feminist Consciousness and the First World War" and "Women, Peace and Internationalism." My work on Catherine's later life will have as an important focus the refusal of some women to accept the limitation of their political influence to "women's issues"; see also Vellacott, "'Transnationalism' in the Early Women's International League for Peace and Freedom." However, she (and her parents) saw admission to the franchise for regional parliaments as an important step forward, CM to CEM, 8 July; FEM to CEM, 9 July 1914, CEMP.

39 NU executive, 18 June 1914, Fawcett Lib.

40 Ibid.

41 Ibid.

42 See, e.g., Jalland, The Liberals and Ireland.

43 NU executive, 18 June 1914, Fawcett Lib. Catherine had kept closely in touch with Mellone for months, correspondence, Feb. to July 1914, CEMP.

44 See correspondence between CEM, Lytton, Cecil, and Lady Selborne, Feb. to July 1914, analysing every possibility and detail of changes in the Home Rule Bill, CEMP.

45 E.g., Oxford, Glasgow, NU executive, 18 June 1914, Fawcett Lib.

46 NU executive, [7 May 1914], CEMP.

47 Ibid.

48 Circular, signed by MGF, n.d. [January 1914], MPL M50/2/9/7; S. Holton, *Feminism and Democracy*, 111.

49 For North-West Durham by-election, see inter alia *CC*, 16, 23 Jan. 1914; NU executive, 5 Feb. 1914, Fawcett Lib.

50 LHC [Lilian Hay Cooper] to Mrs Marshall [M.A. Marshall], 6 June 1914, enclosed with "M.A.M." to CEM; Hay Cooper to CEM, 8 June 1914, CEMP.

51 NU executive, 2 July, CEMP; Anne Watkins to CEM, 22 June 1914, CEMP. Despite the fact that Catherine was supposed to be going home for an autumn holiday "under vow not to do any suffrage work," the executive was hoping that she would make herself available for these meetings, CEM to H. Renton, 17 July 1914, CEMP.

52 Letters and telegrams, 9–11 May 1914, CEMP.

53 Dring to CEM, [10 May 1914], CEMP; *CC*, 15, 22 May 1914.

54 NU executive, 5 Feb. 1914, Fawcett Lib.

55 McKibbin, *Evolution*, 60–2; Gregory, *The Miners and British Politics*, ch. 7.

56 McKibbin, *Evolution*, 61; *CC*, 29 May 1914.

57 Agnes Gill to H. Renton, 11 June, enclosed with Renton to CEM, 12 June 1914, CEMP.

58 Samuel Hall to CEM, 29 June; see also CEM to Hall, 25 June, 1 July; Hall to CEM, 24 June 1914; H. Renton to CEM, enclosing clipping from a Rotherham paper, which indicates that the Steel Smelters' Union was declaring strong Labour support, but suggests that they might run their own candidate, CEMP.

59 H. Oldham to CEM, 24 June, 13, 15 July, 31 July, and cable 16 July, 1914; CEM to Oldham, 14 July 1914, and cable 16 July, CEMP.

60 [Henderson] to CEM, 2 Apr. 1914, copy, LP/WOM/12/52; NU executive, 2 Apr. 1914, Fawcett Lib.

61 McKibbin, *Evolution*, 61; NU executive, 2 Apr. 1914, Fawcett Lib.; for a view of Henderson and MacDonald as straight forwardly "committed [by 1914] to fighting the election as a genuinely independent party," see Leventhal, *Arthur Henderson*, 47.

62 NU executive, 18 June 1914, Fawcett Lib.

63 CEM to F. Acland, 23 June 1914, copy, CEMP. There is also the interesting possibility, suggested (rather indirectly) by Jane Lewis, that Asquith may personally have been more comfortable contemplating

working-class women voters than he was in visualizing women of his own class – where spheres were more rigidly separated, and where any breakdown of the separation would have been personally threatening – as political animals, Lewis, *Women in England*, 97. This is consistent with Jalland's view of Asquith, *Women, Marriage and Politics*, passim.

64 B. Webb, "Voteless Women and Social Revolution."

65 P.W. Wilson, "Women's Suffrage and Party Policies"; Harrison, *Separate Spheres*, 192, suggests that by 1914 the ELFS constituted a real threat of mass revolutionary violence; for an interesting analysis of the ELFS's class-based stand, see Garner, *Stepping Stones*, 80–93.

66 "Political Situation: Lord Lytton's Proposal" [21 May 1914]; "Lord Lytton's Proposal" [7 May 1914], CEMP.

67 Russell to Lucy Donnelly, 24 July 1914, BRA. Russell added, "I don't quite take this view myself, but I was glad to hear it taken."

68 D. Morgan, *Suffragists and Liberals*, 153–4; Dangerfield, *Strange Death*, 382–4; for a different view, see Rosen, *Rise Up, Women!*, 236–7; Hume, *National Union*, 220.

69 S. Holton, *Feminism and Democracy*, 124–7.

70 Annie Besant had visited at Hawse End in 1900, HEGB.

71 CEM to Acland, 23 June 1914, copy, CEMP.

72 Mitchell, *Queen Christabel*, 244–5; S. Holton, *Feminism and Democracy*, 124.

73 F. Acland to CEM, 24 June 1914, CEMP.

74 "Conference between LWSU and NUWSS," 27 July 1914, ts, 23 pp, inexpertly done, with omissions and inaccuracies; E. Acland to CEM, 28 July [1914], CEMP.

75 NU executive, 5 Feb. 1914, Fawcett Lib.

76 CEM to Acland, 19 June 1914, copy, CEMP.

77 "Vouchers," CEMP.

78 CEM to Lady Betty Balfour, 22 June 1914, copy, CEMP.

79 Correspondence between CEM, MGF, and Lady Betty and Miss Alice Balfour, 22 June to 7 July 1914; CEM to Lord Robert Cecil, 22 June 1914, CEMP. Alice's relations with Lady Betty were better than with Lady Frances, but it is evident that both patronized the unmarried Alice, whose personal potential as an artist had been suppressed in favour of the needs of her distinguished brother, who took it all completely for granted, showing neither affection nor appreciation. Jalland, *Women, Marriage and Politics*, ch. 9.

80 CEM to LG, 11 July 1914, LG/C/11/1/68; CEM to Sir E. Grey, 14 July 1914, copy, CEMP. Alice Balfour insisted on seeing the report of the occasion which would go in the *CC* and removed from it a reference to Balfour having discussed the women's suffrage movement; her letter

reached the *CC* office after the paper had gone to the printer and caused a furor, A. Balfour to the editor, *CC*, 15 July 1914; H. Ward to Mackenzie, 16 July 1914, CEMP.

81 Lytton to CEM, 14 July 1914; extensive correspondence, July 7–13, CEMP.

82 *CC*, 10, 17, 24 July.

83 NU, "What the Election Fighting Fund has achieved," [July 1914].

84 CEM to LG, 11 July 1914, LG/C/11/1/68.

85 CEM to LG, 14 July 1914, LG/C/11/1/70.

86 CEM to LG, 15 July 1914, LG/C/11/1/71.

87 CEM to LG, 17 July 1914, LG/C/11/1/72.

88 CEM to LG, 22 July 1914, LG/C/11/1/75.

89 Alberti, *Beyond Suffrage*, 11, which does a remarkable job of synthesis from the papers and writings of fourteen feminist activists. Harrison, curiously, pillories the weekly militant journals for their lateness in mentioning the "impending catastrophe," a lateness shared by every journal known to me, and even by the daily papers, "Women's Suffrage at Westminster," 112.

90 See, e.g., Hazlehurst, *Politicians at War*, 25–103; Vellacott, *Bertrand Russell and the Pacifists in the First World War*, ch. 2.

91 CM to CEM, 31 July 1914, CEMP.

92 For a striking analysis of the British press at the outbreak of war, see Willis, *England's Holy War*, 16–85.

93 NU special executive, 3 Aug. 1914, MPL/M50/2/7/6.

94 Ibid.

95 *CC*, 7 Aug. 1914; Vellacott (Newberry), "Anti-War Suffragists"; NU special executive, 3 Aug. 1914, MPL/M50/2/7/6; Wiltsher, *Most Dangerous Women*, 22–5.

CHAPTER SIXTEEN

1 For a recent repetition of this attribution and of the myth that suffrage activity "was dead for the duration of the war," see Kent, *Sex and Suffrage*, 220

2 E.g., Leventhal, *Arthur Henderson*.

3 "Wait and see" was a nickname often applied to Asquith.

4 Sheepshanks to Russell, 26 Apr. 1913, BRA.

5 Harrison, "Women's Suffrage at Westminster," 121.

Bibliography

ARCHIVAL MATERIALS

Collections

British Library of Political and Economic Science. (BLPES)
Fawcett Library, City of London Polytechnic. London, England.
Girton College Archives.
Barbara Strachey Papers. In private possession.
International Archives for the Women's Movement. Amsterdam (IAV)
Labour Party Archives. Transport House, London, England. (LPA)
Lloyd George, David. Papers. House of Lords. (LG)
Manchester Public Library. Suffrage papers. (MPL)
Marshall, Catherine E. Papers. Cumbria Record Office, Carlisle, England. (CEMP)
Marshall, Frank. Papers. In private possession. (FMP)
Russell, Bertrand. Archives. McMaster University, Hamilton, Ontario, Canada. (BRA)
Schwimmer-Lloyd Collection. New York Public Library.
St Leonards School Archives.
Swanwick, Helena M. Papers. Swarthmore College Peace Collection. (SCPC/HMS)
Swarthmore College Peace Collection. Swarthmore, Pennsylvania, USA (SCPC)
Toronto Public Library. Women's suffrage files. Microfiche. (TPL/WS)

Newspapers and periodicals

Common Cause
Englishwoman
Illustrated London News
Jus Suffragii
Labour Leader
Manchester Guardian
Men's League for Women's Suffrage, *Monthly Paper*
Nation
New Statesman
Punch
Suffragette
The Times
Votes for Women
Women's Franchise
Also clippings from various papers, in CEMP and other collections, esp. *Daily Herald; Whitehaven News; West Cumberland Herald; Mid-Cumberland Herald.*

Miscellaneous

Hawse End Guest Book. In possession of Frank Marshall. (HEGB)
United Kingdom. *Parliamentary Debates* (Commons), 5th series (1909–) (*H.C. Deb.*)
Duffield, Gladys. "On the March." Cumbria Record Office, Carlisle. n.d. Typescript.
Duffield, James. "The Amazing Life-Story of Gladys Duffield." Cumbria Record Office, Carlisle, n.d. Typescript.

PUBLISHED SOURCES

Aberconway, Lady. *The Prime Minister and Women's Suffrage.* London: Grosvenor Press 1913.
Acland, Eleanor. "Prospects of a Government Suffrage Measure." *Englishwoman*, July 1913.
Alberti, Johanna. *Beyond Suffrage: Feminists in War and Peace, 1914–1928.* London: Macmillan 1989.
Asquith, H.H. *See* Oxford and Asquith, Earl of.
Bacchi, Carol Lee. *Liberation Deferred? The Ideas of the English-Canadian Suffragists, 1877–1918.* Toronto: Univ. of Toronto Press 1983
Banks, Olive. *Faces of Feminism.* Oxford: Martin Robertson 1981
– *Biographical Dictionary of British Feminists*, vol. 1: 1800–1930. New York: NYUP 1985

– *Becoming a Feminist: The Social Origins of First Wave Feminism.* Brighton: Wheatsheaf 1986.

Barker, Rodney. "Socialism and Progressivism in the Political Thought of Ramsay Macdonald." In *Edwardian Radicalism 1900–1914*, ed. A.J.A. Morris. London: Routledge and Kegan Paul 1974.

Barnes, George. *From Workshop to War Cabinet.* London: Herbert Jenkins 1924.

Bealey, Frank. *Labour and Politics 1900–6: A History of the Labour Representation Committee.* London: Macmillan 1958.

Bean, J.M.W., ed. *The Political Culture of Modern Britain: Studies in Memory of Stephen Koss.* London: Hamish Hamilton 1987.

Bennett, Daphne. *Emily Davies and the Liberation of Women, 1830–1921.* London: Andre Deutsch 1990.

Bentley, Michael, and John Stephenson, eds. *High and Low Politics in Modern Britain.* Oxford: Clarendon Press 1983.

Bernstein, George L. *Liberalism and Liberal Politics in Edwardian England.* London: Allen and Unwin 1986.

Billington-Greig, Teresa. *The Militant Suffrage Movement; Emancipation in a Hurry.* London: Frank Palmer [1911].

– *Suffragist Tactics, Past & Present.* London: Women's Freedom League [1913].

– *Towards Woman's Liberty.* Letchworth, Herts.: Garden City Press n.d.

Black, Naomi. *Social Feminism.* Ithaca and London: Cornell UP 1989.

Blewett, Neal. "The Franchise in the United Kingdom, 1885–1918." *Past and Present* 32 (1965): 27–56.

– *The Peers, the Parties, and the People: The British General Elections of 1910.* Toronto: Univ. of Toronto Press 1972.

Bosch, Mineke. "On the Meaning of Gossip: Letters from the International Woman Suffrage Alliance." Paper presented at the Berkshire Conference on Women's History 1977.

Bowerman, Elsie E. *Stands There a School.* High Wycombe, Bucks.: Wycombe Abbey School 1966.

Brailsford, H.N. "Women and the Reform Bill." *Englishwoman*, December 1911.

– "The Reform Bill and the Labour Party." *Englishwoman*, May 1912.

– *The Conciliation Bill: An Explanation and Defence.* London: Women's Press n.d.

Brailsford, J.E.M. "The Suffragettes at Bye-Elections." *Nation*, 24 July 1909.

Brand, Carl F. *The British Labour Party: A Short History.* Rev. ed. Stanford: Hoover Institution Press 1974.

Brittain, Vera. *Pethick-Lawrence: A Portrait.* London: Allen and Unwin 1963.

Brockway, Fenner. *Inside the Left: Thirty Years of Platform, Press, Prison and Parliament.* London: Allen and Unwin 1942.

Bronner, Edwin B. Introduction to *The Quakers in Peace and War*, by Margaret E. Hirst. New York: Garland 1972.

Butler, David, and Jennie Freeman. *British Political Facts, 1900–1968.* 3rd ed. New York: St Martin's Press; London: Macmillan 1969.

Caine, Barbara. "John Stuart Mill and the English Women's Movement." *Historical Studies* 18 (1978): 52–67.

– *Destined to Be Wives: The Sisters of Beatrice Webb.* Oxford: Clarendon Press 1986.

Cameron, Barbara. "Three Liberal Models of the Political Role of Women." Paper presented at the York/Univ. of Toronto Women's Research Colloquium, Toronto, Ontario, 5 March 1982.

Catt, Carrie Chapman. *Presidential Address to the IWSA Congress in St. James Hall, 26 April, 1909.* London: NUWSS 1909.

– *The World Movement for Woman Suffrage, 1904–1911.* Presidential Address to the IWSA Congress, Stockholm, 13 June 1911. London: NUWSS 1911.

Cecil, Sir Robert. "The Suffrage Crisis." *Englishwoman*, April 1912.

Central Society for Women's Suffrage. *Some Objections to Women's Suffrage Considered.* London: CSWS 1907.

Chatfield, Charles, and Peter van den Dungen, eds. *Peace Movements and Political Cultures.* Knoxville: Univ. of Tennessee Press 1988.

Chaytor, Miranda, and Jane Lewis. Introduction to *Working Life of Women in the Seventeenth Century*, by Alice Clark. 1919. Reprint London: Routledge and Kegan Paul 1982.

Chew, Doris Nield. *Ada Nield Chew: The Life and Writings of a Working Woman.* London: Virago Press 1982.

Churchill, Randolph S. *Winston S. Churchill.* Vol. 2, *The Young Statesman, 1901–1914.* Boston: Houghton Mifflin; London: Heinemann 1966.

Churchill, Winston. *Liberalism and the Social Problem.* London: Hodder and Stoughton 1909.

Clark, Alice. *Working Life of Women in the Seventeenth Century.* London: Routledge 1919. Reprint London: Routledge and Kegan Paul 1982.

Clarke, Peter F. *Lancashire and the New Liberalism.* Cambridge: CUP 1971.

– "Bertrand Russell and the Dimensions of Edwardian Liberalism." In *Intellect and Social Conscience: Essays on Bertrand Russell's Early Work*, ed. Margaret Moran and Carl Spadoni. Hamilton, Ont.: McMaster Univ. Library Press 1974.

– *Liberals and Social Democrats.* Cambridge: CUP 1978.

Close, David. "The Collapse of Resistance to Democracy: Conservatives, Adult Suffrage, and Second Chamber Reform, 1911–1928." *Historical Journal* 20 (1977): 893–918.

Cole, Margaret. *The Story of Fabian Socialism.* Stanford: Stanford UP 1961.

Concise Dictionary of National Biography, vol. 2: 1901–1950. Oxford: OUP 1961.

Cook, Chris. *A Short History of the Liberal Party 1900–1976*. London: Macmillan 1976.

Costelloe, Rachel (see also Strachey, Rachel) *The World at Eighteen: A Novel*. London: T. Fisher Unwin 1907.

Craig, F.W.S., ed. and comp. *British Electoral Facts 1885–1975*. 3rd ed. London: Macmillan 1976.

Cregier, Don M. *Chiefs without Indians*. Washington: Univ. Press of America 1982.

Creighton, Louise: *Women's Suffrage*. London: NUWSS n.d.

Cross, Colin. *The Liberals in Power (1905–1914)*. London: Barrie and Rockliff with Pall Mall Press 1963.

– *Philip Snowden*. London: Barrie and Rockliff 1966.

Dangerfield, George. *The Strange Death of Liberal England, 1910–1914*. New York: Capricorn 1935.

David, E. See Hobhouse.

Davies, Emily. *Thoughts on Some Questions Relating to Women, 1860–1908*. Cambridge: Bowes and Bowes, 1910. Reprint New York: Kraus 1971.

Davin, Anna. "Imperialism and Motherhood." *History Workshop* 5 (1978): 9–65.

Davis, Natalie Zemon. "'Women's History' in Transition: The European Case." *Feminist Studies* 3 (Spring-Summer 1976).

Douglas, Roy. "God Gave the Land to the People." In *Edwardian Radicalism*, ed. A.J.A. Morris. London: Routledge and Kegan Paul 1974.

Dowse, Robert E. *Left in the Centre: The Independent Labour Party 1893–1940*. London: Longmans; Evanston, Ill.: Northwestern Univ. Press 1966.

DuBois, Ellen Carol. "The Radicalism of the Woman Suffrage Movement: Notes Toward the Reconstruction of Nineteenth-Century Feminism." *FS: Feminist Studies* 3 (1975–76): 63–71.

– *Feminism and Suffrage: The Emergence of an Independent Women's Movement in America, 1848–1869*. Ithaca, NY: Cornell Univ. Press 1978.

Dyhouse, Carol. *Girls Growing Up in Late Victorian and Edwardian England*, London: Routledge and Keagan Paul, 1981.

– "Miss Buss and Miss Beale." In *Lessons for Life: The Schooling of Girls and Women*, ed. Felicity Hunt. Oxford: Blackwell 1987.

Edgeworth, F.Y. "Reminiscences." In *Memorials of Alfred Marshall*, ed. A.C. Pigou. New York: Kelley and Millman 1956.

Edmondson, Linda. "Sylvia Pankhurst." In *European Women on the Left: Socialism, Feminism, and the Problems Faced by Political Women, 1880 to the Present*, ed. Jane Slaughter and Robert Kern. Westport, Conn.: Greenwood Press 1981.

Ehrenreich, Barbara, and Deirdre English. *For Her Own Good: One Hundred and Fifty Years of the Experts' Advice to Women*. New York: Anchor Press/Doubleday 1979.

Emy, H.V. *Liberals, Radicals and Social Politics: 1892–1914.* Cambridge: CUP 1973.

Ensor, R.C.K. *England 1870–1914.* London: OUP 1936.

Evans, Richard J. *The Feminists: Women's Emancipation Movements in Europe, America and Australasia, 1840–1920.* London: Croom Helm; New York: Barnes and Noble Books 1977.

"F.E.M." [obituary recollections of Frank E. Marshall]. *Harrovian* 35, no. 6, 21 October 1922.

Fair, John D. "The Political Aspects of Women's Suffrage during the First World War." *Albion* 8, no. 3 (Fall 1976): 274–93.

Fawcett, Millicent Garrett. "Men Are Men and Women Are Women." *Englishwoman*, February 1909.

– *Wanted, a Statesman.* Address given at the Athenaeum Hall, Glasgow, 22 November 1909. London: NUWSS 1909.

– *Women's Suffrage: A Short History of a Great Movement.* London: T.C. and E.C. Jack 1911.

– "The Election Policy of the National Union." *Englishwoman*, June 1912.

– Introduction to *On Liberty; Representative Government; The Subjection of Women: Three Essays*, by John Stuart Mill. London: OUP 1912.

– "Votes for Women: A Reply to Mr. Lloyd George." *Review of Reviews*, September 1913.

– *The Women's Victory – and After: Personal Reminiscences, 1911–1918.* London: Sidgwick and Jackson 1920.

– *What I Remember.* London: T. Fisher Unwin 1921. Reprint Westport, Conn.: Hyperion Press 1976.

Fisher, Roger, and William Ury. *Getting to Yes.* Harmondsworth, Middlesex: Penguin 1983.

Fletcher, Sheila. *Maude Royden.* Oxford: Blackwell 1989.

Ford, Isabella O. *Women and Socialism.* London: ILP 1904.

Fraser, Helen. [A Reply to "An Interrogatory Note on the Franchise of Women," by J. Lionel Taylor.] *Westminster Review* 167 (Jan.–June 1907): 670–2.

Freeden, Michael. *The New Liberalism: An Ideology of Social Reform.* Oxford: Clarendon Press 1978.

Friedl, Bettina, ed. *On to Victory: Propaganda Plays on the Woman Suffrage Movement.* Boston: Northeastern Univ. Press 1987.

Friedlander, Judith, Blanche Wiesen Cook, Alice Kessler-Harris and Carroll Smith Rosenberg, eds. *Women in Culture and Politics: A Century of Change.* Bloomington: Indiana Univ. Press 1986.

Fulford, Roger. *Votes for Women: The Story of a Struggle.* London: Faber and Faber 1957.

Garner, Les. *Stepping Stones to Women's Liberty: Feminist Ideas in the Women's Suffrage Movement, 1900–1918.* Rutherford, NJ: Fairleigh Dickinson Univ. Press 1984.

Gaskell, Ellen S. "Women's Sphere of Work." *Westminster Review*, March 1907.

George, Henry. *Progress and Poverty: An Inquiry into the Cause of Industrial Depressions and of Increase of Want with Increase of Wealth: The Remedy*. New York: D. Appleton 1880.

Gilbert, Bentley B. *The Evolution of National Insurance in Great Britain: The Origins of the Welfare State*. London: Michael Joseph 1966.

– *David Lloyd George: A Political Life. The Architect of Change, 1863–1912*. Columbus: Ohio State Univ. Press 1987.

Gissing, George. *The Odd Women*. London: Lawrence and Bullen 1893. Reprint New York: Norton Library 1971.

Gollancz, Victor, ed. *The Making of Women*. London: Allen and Unwin 1917.

Gregory, Roy. *The Miners and British Politics, 1906–1914*. London: OUP 1968.

Grey of Fallodon, Viscount. *Twenty-five Years: 1892–1916*. 2 vols. New York: Frederick A. Stokes 1925.

Guardian, Manchester, 3–5 May 1978. Articles on Women's Suffrage.

Halevy, Elie. *The Rule of Democracy, 1905–1914*. Vol. 6 of *A History of the English People in the Nineteenth Century*. London: Ernest Benn 1961.

Hamilton, Mary Agnes. *Beware! A Warning to Suffragettes*. With sketches by M. Lowndes, D. Messon Coates, and C. Hedley Charlton.

– *Remembering My Good Friends*. London: Cape 1944.

Hammond, J.L. *C.P. Scott of the "Manchester Guardian."* New York: Harcourt, Brace 1934.

Hannam, June. "'In the Comradeship of the Sexes Lies the Hope of Progress and Social Regeneration': Women in the West Riding ILP, c. 1890–1914." In *Equal or Different*, ed. Jane Rendall. Oxford: Blackwell 1987.

– *Isabella Ford*. Oxford: Blackwell 1989.

Harley, K.M. "The Pilgrimage: II: A London Impression." *Englishwoman*, no. 57, September 1913.

Harrison, Brian. "State Intervention and Moral Reform." In *Pressure From Without in Early Victorian England*, ed. Patricia Hollis. New York: St. Martin's Press 1974.

– *Separate Spheres: The Opposition to Women's Suffrage in Britain*. London: Croom Helm 1978.

– "The Act of Militancy: Violence and the Suffragettes, 1909–1914." In *Peaceable Kingdom: Stability and Change in Modern Britain*, ed. Harrison. Oxford: Clarendon 1982.

– "Women's Suffrage at Westminster, 1866–1928." In *High and Low Politics in Modern Britain: Ten Studies*, ed. Michael Bentley and John Stevenson. Oxford: Clarendon Press 1983.

– "Bertrand Russell: The False Consciousness of a Feminist." In *Intellect and Social Conscience: Essays on Bertrand Russell's Early Work*, ed. Margaret

Moran and Carl Spadoni. Hamilton, Ont.: McMaster Univ. Library Press 1984.

– *Prudent Revolutionaries: Portraits of British Feminists between the Wars.* Oxford: Clarendon Press 1987.

Harrison, Brian, and James McMillan. "Some Feminist Betrayals of Women's History." *Historical Journal* 26, no. 2 (1983): 375–89.

Hart, Michael. "The Liberals, the War, and the Franchise." *English Historical Review* 97 (October, 1982): 820–32.

Hazlehurst, Cameron. *Politicians at War, July 1914 to May 1915: A Prologue to the Triumphs of Lloyd George.* London: Jonathan Cape 1971.

Hirst, Margaret E. *The Quakers in Peace and War: An Account of Their Peace Principles and Practice.* 1923. Reprint New York: Garland 1972.

Hobhouse, Charles Edward Henry. *Inside Asquith's Cabinet; From the Diaries of Charles Hobhouse,* ed. Edward David. London: John Murray 1976.

Hobhouse, Stephen, and Fenner Brockway, eds. *English Prisons Today: Being the Report of the Prison Enquiry Committee.* London: Longmans, Green 1922.

Hobson, J.A. *Imperialism: A Study.* London: Allen and Unwin 1988.

Hollis, Patricia. *Ladies Elect: Women in English Local Government 1865–1914.* New York: Clarendon Press of OUP 1987.

Holton, R.J. "*Daily Herald* v. *Daily Citizen,* 1912–1915: The Struggle for a Labour Daily in Relation to 'the Labour Unrest.'" *International Review of Social History* 1974, part 1: 347–76.

– *British Syndicalism 1900–1914: Myths and Realities.* London: Pluto Press 1976.

Holton, Sandra. "Women's Worlds, Women's Consciousness and Feminism." 1984. Typescript.

– *Feminism and Democracy: Women's Suffrage and Reform Politics in Britain, 1900–1918.* Cambridge: CUP 1986.

Hume, Leslie Parker. *The National Union of Women's Suffrage Societies 1897–1914.* New York: Garland 1982.

Hunt, E.H. *British Labour History 1815–1914.* Atlantic Highlands, NJ: Humanities Press 1981.

Hunt, Felicity, ed. *Lessons for Life: The Schooling of Girls and Women, 1850–1950.* Oxford: Blackwell 1987.

Ignota [pseud.] "The Case for the Immediate Enfranchisement of the Women of the United Kingdom." *Westminster Review,* November 1906.

International Women's Suffrage Association. *Report of Sixth Congress, Stockholm, Sweden, June 12–17, 1911.* London: Women's Printing Soc. for NUWSS 1911.

Jaggar, Alison M. *Feminist Politics and Human Nature.* Totowa, NJ: Rowman and Allanheld 1983.

Jalland, Pat. *The Liberals and Ireland: the Ulster Question in British Politics to 1914.* New York: St Martins 1980.

– *Women, Marriage and Politics, 1860–1914*. Oxford: Clarendon Press 1986.

Jeffreys, Sheila. *The Spinster and Her Enemies: Feminism and Sexuality, 1880–1930*. London: Pandora 1985.

Jenkins, Roy. *Asquith*. London: Collins, Fontana Books 1967.

Johnston, Sir Harry Hamilton. *Mrs Warren's Daughter: A Story of the Women's Movement*. London: Chatto and Windus; New York: Macmillan 1920.

Kamester, Margaret. "The Secondary Feminist Interests of the Women's Social and Political Union and the National Union of Women's Suffrage Societies." Simone de Beauvoir Institute, Concordia University, Montreal, 1982. Manuscript.

Kamm, Josephine. *Rapiers and Battleaxes: The Women's Movement and Its Aftermath*. London: Allen and Unwin 1966.

Kent, Susan Kingsley. *Sex and Suffrage in Britain 1860–1914*. Princeton: Princeton Univ. Press 1987.

Key, Ellen. *The Woman Movement*. New York: Putnam 1912.

Keynes, J.M. "Alfred Marshall, 1842–1924." In *Memorials of Alfred Marshall*, ed. A.C. Pigou. New York: Kelley and Millman 1956.

Koss, Stephen. *Asquith*. London: A. Lane 1976.

Kraditor, Aileen. *The Ideas of the Women Suffrage Movement 1890–1920*. New York: Doubleday, Anchor Books 1971.

Lance, Keith Curry. "Strategy Choices of the British Women's Social and Political Union, 1903–18." *Social Science Quarterly* 60, no. 1 (June 1979): 51–61.

Laybourn, Keith, and Jack Reynolds. *Liberalism and the Rise of Labour: 1890–1918*. London: Croom Helm; New York: St Martin's 1984.

Leventhal, F.M. *The Last Dissenter: H.N. Brailsford and His World*. Oxford: Clarendon Press; New York: OUP 1985.

– *Arthur Henderson*. Manchester: Manchester Univ. Press 1989.

Lewis, Jane. *Women in England, 1870–1950: Sexual Divisions and Social Change*. Brighton: Wheatsheaf Books 1984.

Lewis, Jane, ed. *Labour and Love: Women's Experience of Home and Family, 1850–1940*. Oxford: Blackwell 1986.

Liddington, Jill. "Rediscovering Suffrage History." *History Workshop Journal* 4 (1977): 192–201.

– *The Life and Times of a Respectable Rebel: Selina Cooper (1864–1946)*. London: Virago Press 1984.

– *The Long Road to Greenham*. London: Virago Press 1989.

Liddington, Jill, and Jill Norris. *One Hand Tied behind Us: The Rise of the Women's Suffrage Movement*. London: Virago Press 1978.

Lindsay, James E. "The Failure of Liberal Opposition to British Entry into World War I." PhD dissertation, Columbia University 1969.

Linklater, Andro. *An Unhusbanded Life: Charlotte Despard, Suffragette, Socialist and Sinn Feiner*. London: Hutchinson 1980.

Lowndes, M. "Woman's Suffrage in the House of Lords." *Englishwoman*, June 1914.

Lowther, James William (Viscount Ullswater). *A Speaker's Commentaries.* Vol. 2. London: E. Arnold and Co. 1925.

Lytton, Lord. "Woman Suffrage: The Only Way." *Englishwoman*, March 1914.

Macaulay, J.S.A., ed. *St. Leonard's School, 1877–1977.* Glasgow: Blackie 1977 (privately printed).

McBriar, A.M. *Fabian Socialism and English Politics, 1884–1918.* Cambridge: CUP 1962.

McCarthy, John Patrick. *Hilaire Belloc: Edwardian Radical.* Indianopolis: Liberty Press 1978.

McClung, Nellie. *In Times Like These.* New York: D. Appleton 1915. Reprint, ed. Veronica Strong-Boag. Toronto: Univ. of Toronto Press 1972.

McCrone, Kathleen E. *Playing the Game: Sport and the Physical Emancipation of English Women 1870–1914.* Lexington: Univ. of Kentucky Press 1988.

Mackenzie, Midge, ed. *Shoulder to Shoulder.* Harmondsworth: Penguin 1975.

McKibbin, Ross. *The Evolution of the Labour Party 1910–1924.* Oxford: OUP 1974.

Macmillan, Chrystal. Memorial. [1937].

Manchester and District Federation, NUWSS. *Women's Suffrage: A Survey, 1908–1912.* Manchester: Manchester and District Federation, NUWSS 1912.

Marcus, Jane. "Transatlantic Sisterhood: Labor and Suffrage Links in the Letters of Elizabeth Robins and Emmeline Pankhurst." *Signs* 3 (1978): 744–55.

Marquand, David. *Ramsay MacDonald.* London: Cape 1977.

Marshall, Alfred, and Mary Paley Marshall. *The Economics of Industry.* London: Macmillan 1874.

Marshall, Caroline. "Debatable Ground: A Domestic Problem." *Englishwoman*, 1912.

Marshall, Catherine E. "The Suffrage Exchange Scheme." *Common Cause*, 16 February 1911.

– "Women's Suffrage and the Press." *Common Cause*, 16 March, 6 April 1911.

– "The Election Fighting Fund." *Common Cause*, 16 September 1912.

– "Women's Suffrage and the Next General Election." *Englishwoman*, August 1913.

– "The Labour and Woman Suffrage Entente." *Labour Leader*, 28 August 1913.

Mason, Bertha. *The Story of the Women's Suffrage Movement.* Manchester: Sherraton and Hughes 1912.

Massingham, H.W. Introduction to *Liberalism and the Social Problem*, by Winston Churchill. London: Hodder and Stoughton 1909.

Matthews, Jacquie. "Barbara Bodichon: Integrity in Diversity." In *Feminist Theorists: Three Centuries of Women's Intellectual Traditions*, ed. Dale Spender. London: Women's Press 1983.

Meacham, Standish. "'The Sense of an Impending Clash': English Working-Class Unrest before the First World War." *American Historical Review* 77, pt. 2 (1972): 1343–64.

– *A Life Apart: The English Working Class 1890–1914*. London: Thames and Hudson 1977.

Middleton, Lucy, ed. *Women in the Labour Movement: The British Experience*. London: Croom Helm 1977.

Miliband, Ralph. *Parliamentary Socialism: A Study in the Politics of Labour*. London: Allen and Unwin 1961.

Mill, John Stuart. *On Liberty; Representative Government; The Subjection of Women: Three Essays*. London: OUP 1912.

Mitchell, David. *The Fighting Pankhursts*. London: Jonathan Cape 1967.

– *Queen Christabel*. London: Macdonald and Jane's 1977.

Mitchell, Hannah. *The Hard Way Up: The Autobiography of Hannah Mitchell, Suffragette and Rebel*, ed. Geoffrey Mitchell. London: Virago Press 1977.

Montefiore, Dora. *From a Victorian to a Modern*. London: Archer 1927.

Moran, Margaret, and Carl Spadoni, eds. *Intellect and Social Conscience: Essays on Bertrand Russell's Early Work*. Hamilton, Ont.: McMaster Univ. Library Press 1984.

Morgan, Austen. *J. Ramsay MacDonald*. Manchester: Manchester Univ. Press 1987.

Morgan, David. *Suffragists and Liberals: The Politics of Woman Suffrage in Britain*. Oxford: Blackwell 1975.

Morgan, Kenneth O. *Wales in British Politics 1868–1922*. Cardiff: Univ. of Wales Press 1963.

Morley, Ann, and Liz Stanley. *The Life and Death of Emily Wilding Davison*, with Gertude Colmore's *The Life of Emily Davison*. London: Women's Press 1988.

Morris, A.J.A., ed. *Edwardian Radicalism, 1900–1914: Some Aspects of British Radicalism*. London: Routledge and Kegan Paul 1974.

Murray, Bruce K. *The People's Budget 1909/10: Lloyd George and Liberal Politics*. Oxford: Clarendon Press 1980.

National Union of Women's Suffrage Societies. *The Argument from Physical Force*. London: NUWSS 1909.

– *Extracts from Articles and Speeches*. London: NUWSS 1909.

– *Is Woman's Only Sphere the Home?* London: NUWSS 1909.

– *Memorial of Head Mistresses*. London: NUWSS 1909.

– *Some Reasons Why Working Women Want the Vote*. London: NUWSS n.d.

Neale, R.S. *Class and Ideology in the Nineteenth Century*. London: Routledge and Kegan Paul 1972.

Nevinson, Margaret Wynne. *Five Years' Struggle for Freedom: A History of the Suffrage Movement from 1908 to 1912*. London: Women's Freedom League n.d.

O'Brien, Jo. *Women's Liberation in Labour History: A Case Study from Nottingham*. Nottingham: Bertrand Russell Peace Foundation for *The Spokesman* n.d.

Oldfield, Sybil. *Spinsters of This Parish: The Life and Times of F.M. Mayor and Mary Sheepshanks*. London: Virago Press 1984.

O'Neill, William L., ed. *The Woman Movement: Feminism in the United States and England*. Chicago: Quadrangle Books 1969.

Owen, Harold. *Women Adrift: The Menace of Suffragism*. London: Stanley Paul 1912.

Oxford and Asquith, Earl of. *Fifty Years of British Parliament*. Vol. 2. Boston: Little, Brown; London: Cassell 1926.

– *Memories and Reflections, 1852–1927*. Boston: Little, Brown 1928.

– *Letters to Venetia Stanley*, sel. and ed. Michael and Eleanor Brock. Oxford: OUP 1982.

Packer, Harriet. *The Story of the Franchise in England*. London: Conservative and Unionist Women's Franchise Association n.d.

Pankhurst, Christabel. *Unshackled: The Story of How We Won the Vote*. London: Hutchinson 1959.

Pankhurst, E. Sylvia. *Suffragette: The History of the Women's Militant Suffrage Movement 1905–1910*. New York: Sturgis and Walton 1911.

– *The Suffragette Movement: An Intimate Account of Persons and Ideals*. London: Longmans 1931. Reprint London: Virago Press 1977.

– *The Life of Emmeline Pankhurst*. London: T. Werner Laurie 1935. Reprint New York: Kraus Reprint 1969.

Pankhurst, Emmeline. *My Own Story*. London: Eveleigh Nash 1914.

Pankhurst, Richard. *Sylvia Pankhurst: Artist and Crusader*. New York: Paddington Press 1979.

Pelling, Henry. *A Short History of the Labour Party*. London: Macmillan 1962.

– *Social Geography of British Elections, 1885–1910*. London: Macmillan; New York: St Martin's Press 1967.

– *Popular Politics and Society in Late Victorian Britain*. London: Macmillan 1968.

Pethick-Lawrence, Emmeline. *My Part in a Changing World*. London: Gollancz 1938.

Petter, Martin. "The Progressive Alliance." *History* 58 (1973): 45–59.

Pierson, Stanley. *British Socialists: The Journey from Fantasy to Politics*. Cambridge, Mass. and London: Harvard UP 1979.

Phillips, Marion. "The Executive Committee." *Common Cause*, 17 February 1910.

Phillips, Marion, ed. *Women and the Labour Party*. London: Headley Bros. 1918; New York: B.W. Heubsch 1920.

Pigou, Arthur Cecil. *Principles and Methods of Industrial Peace*. London: Macmillan 1905.
– *Wealth and Welfare*. London: Macmillan 1912. (Later titled *The Economics of Welfare*.)
Pigou, Arthur Cecil, ed. *Memorials of Alfred Marshall*. New York: Kelley and Millman 1956.
Postgate, Raymond. *Life of George Lansbury*. London: Longmans, Green 1951.
Pugh, Martin. "Politicians and the Women's Vote 1914–1918." *History* 59 (1974): 358–74.
– *Electoral Reform in War and Peace, 1906–18*. London: Routledge and Kegan Paul 1978.
– *Women's Suffrage in Britain, 1867–1928*. London: Historical Association 1980.
– *The Making of Modern British Politics, 1867–1939*. Oxford: Blackwell 1982.
Ramelson, Marian. *The Petticoat Rebellion: A Century of Struggle for Women's Rights*. London: Lawrence and Wishart 1972.
Read, Donald. *Edwardian England, 1901–15*. London: Harrap 1972.
Reeves, Maud Pember. *Round about a Pound a Week*. London: Virago 1979.
Rendall, Jane. *The Origins of Modern Feminism: Women in Britain, France and the United States 1780–1860*. London: Macmillan 1985.
Rendall, Jane, ed. *Equal or Different: Women's Politics 1800–1914*. Oxford: Blackwell 1987.
Rendel, E. "Caravan Tour." *Women's Franchise*, 23 July 1908.
Richardson, Mary R. *Laugh a Defiance*. London: Weidenfeld and Nicolson 1953.
Rimmer, W.G. *Marshalls of Leeds, Flaxspinners*. Cambridge: CUP 1960.
Robbins, Keith. *Sir Edward Grey*. London: Cassell 1971.
Roberts, Charles. *The Radical Countess: The History of the Life of Rosalind Countess of Carlisle*. Carlisle: Steel Brothers 1962.
Robson, A.P.W. "The Founding of the National Society for Women's Suffrage 1866–1867." *Canadian Journal of History* 8 (1973): 1–22.
Romero, Patricia W. *E. Sylvia Pankhurst: Portrait of a Radical*. New Haven: Yale Univ. Press 1987.
Ross, Ronald. "Man and Woman." *Nation*, 11 October 1913.
Rosen, Andrew. *Rise Up, Women! The Militant Campaign of the Women's Social and Political Union, 1903–1914*. London: Routledge and Kegan Paul 1974.
Rover, Constance. *Women's Suffrage and Party Politics in Britain 1866–1914*. London: Routledge and Kegan Paul; Toronto: Univ. of Toronto Press 1967.
Rowland, Peter. *The Last Liberal Government: The Promised Land, 1905–1910*. London: Barrie and Rockliff, Cresset Press 1968.
– *David Lloyd George*. London: Barrie and Jenkins 1975; New York: Macmillan 1976.

Royden, Maude. *Our Common Humanity*. London: NUWSS

Rubinstein, David. *Before the Suffragettes*. Brighton: Harvester 1986.

– *A Different World for Women: The Life of Millicent Garrett Fawcett*. London: Harvester Wheatsheaf 1991.

Russell, Bertrand. *Anti-Suffragist Anxieties*. London: People's Suffrage Federation n.d.

Sarah, Elizabeth, ed. *Reassessments of "First Wave" Feminism*. Oxford: Pergamon 1982.

Schreiner, Olive. *Woman and Labour*. London: Virago 1978.

Searle, G.R. *Corruption in British Politics, 1900–1935*. Oxford: Clarendon Press 1987.

Simon, Brian. *Education and the Labour Movement, 1870–1920*. London: Lawrence and Wishart 1965.

Simon, The Right Hon. Viscount. *Retrospect: The Memoirs of the Rt. Hon. Viscount Simon*. London: Hutchinson 1952.

Slaughter, Jane, and Robert Kern, eds. *European Women on the Left: Socialism, Feminism, and the Problems Faced by Political Women, 1880 to the Present*. Westport, Conn.: Greenwood Press 1981.

Smith, Harold, ed. *British Feminism in the Twentieth Century*. Amherst: Univ of Massachusetts Press 1990.

Snowden, Ethel. *The Feminist Movement*. London: Collins 1913.

– "The Women's Pilgrimage." *Nation*, August 1913.

Snowden, Philip. "The By-Elections and Woman Suffrage." *Englishwoman*, October 1912.

– "The Labour Party and the Plural Voting Bill." *Englishwoman*, May 1913.

Somervell, E.L. *Speech Delivered at Queen's Hall Demonstration, March 29th, 1909*. London: Women's National Anti-Suffrage League 1909.

Speaight, Robert. *Hilaire Belloc*. New York: Farrar, Straus and Cudahy 1957.

Spender Dale, ed. *Feminist Theorists: Three Centuries of Women's Intellectual Traditions*. London: Women's Press 1983.

Spender, Dale, and Carole Hayman, comps. *How the Vote Was Won and Other Suffragette Plays*. London: Methuen 1985.

Stenton, Michael, and Stephen Lees, eds. *Who's Who of British Members of Parliament, 1886–1979*. Atlantic Highlands NJ: Humanities Press; Hassocks, Sussex: Harvester 1978–81.

Stevenson, Frances. *Lloyd George: A Diary*, ed. A.J.P. Taylor. London: Hutchinson; New York: Harper and Row 1971.

Stocks, Mary D. *Eleanor T. Rathbone: A Biography*. London: Gollancz 1949.

Strachey, Barbara. *Remarkable Relations: The Story of the Pearsall Smith Family*. London: Gollancz 1980.

Strachey, Rachel (see also Colstelloe, Rachel). – *Women's Suffrage and Women's Service: The History of the London and National Society for Women's Service*. London: The Society 1927.

– *Millicent Garrett Fawcett.* London: John Murray 1931.

The Suffrage Annual and Women's Who's Who 1913, ed. A.J.R. London: Stanley Paul 1913.

Swanwick, Helena M. *The Future of the Women's Movement.* London: G. Bell and Sons 1913.

– *I Have Been Young.* London: Gollancz 1935.

Tanner, Duncan. *Political Change and the Labour Party, 1900–1918.* Cambridge: CUP 1990.

Taylor, A.J.P., ed. *My Darling Pussy: The Letters of Lloyd George and Frances Stevenson, 1913–1941.* London: Weidenfeld and Nicholson 1975.

Taylor, Barbara. *Eve and the New Jerusalem: Socialism and Feminism in the Nineteenth Century.* London: Virago 1984.

Thomas, John Alun. *The House of Commons 1906–1911: An Analysis of Its Economic and Social Character.* Cardiff: Univ. of Wales Press 1958.

Thompson, Paul. *Socialists, Liberals and Labour: The Struggle for London 1885–1914.* London: Routledge and Kegan Paul; Toronto: Univ. of Toronto Press 1967.

– *The Edwardians: The Remaking of British Society.* Bloomington: Indiana Univ. Press 1975.

Thoresby, Frederick. "Woman and Woman's Suffrage." *Westminster Review* 166 (Nov. 1906): 522–30.

Tickner, Lisa. *The Spectacle of Women: Imagery of the Suffrage Campaign 1907–1914.* London: Chatto and Windus 1987.

Trevelyan, G.M. *Grey of Fallodon.* Boston: Houghton Mifflin 1937.

Trevelyan, Janet. *The Life of Mrs Humphry Ward.* London: Constable; New York: Dodd, Mead 1923.

Vellacott, Jo. "Anti-War Suffragists." *History* 62, no. 206 (October 1977): 411–25 [published under the name Jo Vellacott Newberry].

– "The Women's Suffrage Movement in Cambridge." *Lucely Speaking,* Lucy Cavendish College, Cambridge 1977.

– *Bertrand Russell and the Pacifists in the First World War.* Brighton: Harvester; New York: St Martin's Press 1980.

– "Beyond the Interstices of Russell's Life." *Russell* (Winter 1986–87): 184–6.

– "Feminist Consciousness and the First World War." *History Workshop Journal,* no. 23 (Spring 1987): 81–101.

– "Historical Reflections on Votes, Brooms and Guns: Admission to Political Structures – On Whose Terms?" *Atlantis* 12, no. 2 (Spring 1987): 36–9.

– "Women, Peace, and Internationalism, 1914–1920: 'Finding New Words and Creating New Methods.'" In *Peace Movements and Political Cultures,* ed. Charles Chatfield and Peter van den Dungen. Knoxville: Univ. of Tennessee Press 1988.

– "Double Tunnel Vision: Some Thoughts on the Writing of History."

Le Bulletin/Newsletter 10, no. 1. Montreal: Simone de Beauvoir Institute 1990.

– "A Place for Pacifism and Transnationalism in Feminist Theory: The Early Work of the Women's International League for Peace and Freedom." *Women's History Review* (March 1993).

– "'Transnationalism' in the Early Women's International League for Peace and Freedom." Forthcoming in proceedings of conference on "The Pacifist Impulse in Historical Perspective." Toronto, Univ. of Toronto.

Vicinus, Martha. *Independent Women: Work and Community for Single Women, 1850–1920.* Women in Culture and Society. Chicago: Univ. of Chicago Press 1985.

– "Male Space and Women's Bodies: The English Suffragette Movement." In *Women in Culture and Politics: A Century of Change,* ed. Judith Friedlander, Blanche Wiesen Cook, Alice Kessler-Harris, and Carroll Smith-Rosenberg. Bloomington: Indiana Univ. Press 1986.

Villiers, Brougham [F.J. Shaw], ed. *The Case for Women's Suffrage.* London: Fisher and Unwin 1907.

Walker, Jane. "Party Political Women: A Comparative Study of Liberal Women and the Primrose League, 1890–1914." In *Equal or Different: Women's Politics 1800–1914,* ed. Jane Rendall. Oxford: Blackwell 1987.

Ward, Mrs Humphry [Mary]. *Speech by Mrs Humphry Ward* (for WNASL, 21 July 1908) Pamphlet. London: WNASL 1908.

Webb, Beatrice, ed. "The Awakening of Women: Special Supplement." *New Statesman,* November 1913.

– "Voteless Women and the Social Revolution." *New Statesman,* Feb. 1914.

Weiler, Peter. *The New Liberalism: Liberal Social Theory in Great Britain, 1896–1914.* New York: Garland 1982.

Williams, E.T., and Helen M. Palmer, eds. *Dictionary of National Biography: 1951–1960.* Oxford: OUP 1971.

Williams, Perry. "Pioneer Women Students at Cambridge." In *Lessons for Life: The Schooling of Girls and Women, 1850–1950,* ed. Felicity Hunt. Oxford: Blackwell 1987.

Willis, Irene Cooper. *England's Holy War: A Study of English Liberal Idealism during the Great War,* with intro. by Jo Newberry [Vellacott]. New York: Knopf 1928. Reprint New York: Garland 1972.

Wilson, David Alec. [The Channing Arnold Case] *English Review,* June 1914.

Wilson, P.W. "The Future of Women's Suffrage." *Englishwoman,* June 1913.

Wilson, Trevor. *The Downfall of the Liberal Party.* London: Collins, Fontana 1968.

Wiltsher, Anne. *Most Dangerous Women: Feminist Peace Campaigners of the Great War.* London: Pandora 1985.

Women's Who's Who. See *The Suffrage Annual.*

Woolf, Virginia. *Three Guineas.* London: Hogarth Press 1938. Reprint Harmondsworth, Middlesex: Penguin Books 1977.

Wright, Sir Almroth E. *Suffrage Fallacies: Sir Almroth Wright on Militant Hysteria.* Reprint from *The Times,* 27 March 1912.

– *The Unexpurgated Case against Woman Suffrage.* London: Constable 1913.

Entrance to Carlisle Castle. Catherine Marshall's papers are kept here, in the Cumbria Record Office.

Index